THE DOCTRINES OF GENESIS 1-11

The Preservation of Sacred Scripture
and Sacred Tradition

THE DOCTRINES OF GENESIS 1-11

A Compendium and Defense of Traditional
Catholic Theology on Origins

Rev. Victor P. Warkulwiz, M.S.S.

The John Paul II Institute of Christian Spirituality
Caryville, TN

THE DOCTRINES OF GENESIS 1-11
A Compendium and Defense of Traditional Catholic Theology on Origins

Copyright © 2007 by Missionary Priests of the Blessed Sacrament
Second Printing 2009 (With minor corrections, additions and clarifications)

Books may be ordered by contacting:
The John Paul II Institute of Christian Spirituality
PO Box 340
Caryville, TN 37714
1-423-566-5178

Because of the dynamic nature of the Internet, any Web addresses or links contained in this book may have changed since publication and may no longer be valid.

ISBN: 0-9715691-4-2

Printed in the United States of America

The views expressed in this work are solely those of the author and do not necessarily reflect the views of the publisher.

The publication of this work is sponsored by

The Kolbe Center for the Study of Creation
952 Kelly Road
Mount Jackson, VA 22842
www.kolbecenter.org

The Kolbe Center for the Study of Creation is a Catholic lay apostolate dedicated to glorifying the Most Holy Trinity by proclaiming the truth about the origins of man and the universe. The Kolbe Center seeks to educate the public, particularly within the Catholic Church, in the truth of creation as revealed in Sacred Scripture and Sacred Tradition and as confirmed by the findings of natural science.

nces
we
be
we
one
ely,
ut

This work is dedicated to St. Joseph the Worker, on whose feast day it was begun, and to St. John Neumann who interceded with God on behalf of the author.

CONTENTS

Doctrine Seven: God created the world several thousand years ago.

PART II—THE HUMAN SPECIES

Acknowledgements

The author gratefully acknowledges:

Hugh Owen, Director of the Kolbe Center for the Study of Creation, sponsor and editor of this work, for his inspiration and encouragement and for the efforts he has made to produce this book.

Dr. Robert Bennett, Gerry Keane, other members of the Kolbe Center advisory council, and Fr. Brian Harrison, O.S., S.T.D. for their valuable input.

Jo Brower and Rosemary Getty, proofreaders, and Martha Osgood, indexer, for their meticulous work in preparing this book for publication.

Most Rev. Robert Francis Vasa, Rev. Paul Rothermel, Bro. Charles Madden, O.F.M.Conv., Dr. Dean Kenyon, and Mrs. Maria Owen for their reviewing the book and for their helpful comments.

Sponsor's Note

The contents of *The Doctrines of Genesis 1–11* represent the views of the author and do not necessarily represent the official views of the Kolbe Center for the Study of Creation or its advisory council members.

Illustration and Photo Credits

Cover: Reprinted from *TANAKH* © 1985 with permission of the publisher, The Jewish Publication Society.

Frontispiece and illustrations preceding Parts I and II: *My Catholic Faith* by Bishop Louis LaRavoire Morrow (public domain).

Illustration preceding Part III: Courtesy of Dover Publications, Inc., Mineola, NY (*Treasury of Bible Illustrations: Old and New Testaments*, Julius Schnorr von Carolsfeld).

Rock Strata, Berlingame Canyon and Mt. St. Helens: Used with permission of Master Books, P.O. Box 727, Green Forest, AR 72638.

Polystrate Fossil: Used with permission of the Creation Research Society, P.O. Box 8263, St. Joseph, MO 64508.

Folded Mountains: Geological Society of Canada, photograph no. GSC180345. Reproduced with the permission of the Minister of Public Works and Government Services Canada, 2005 and courtesy of National Resources Canada, Geological Survey of Canada.

Hubble Deep Field: Robert Williams and the Hubble Deep Field Team (Space Telescope Science Institute and NASA), Photo No. STScI-PRC1996-01a (public domain).

Abbreviations

Versions of Sacred Scripture

DR   Douay-Rheims Bible

JB   Jerusalem Bible

JPS   Jewish Publication Society Version

KJV   King James Version

NAB   New American Bible, 1970

NB   Navarre Bible (English edition)

NIV   New International Version

RSV   Revised Standard Version, Catholic edition, 1966

Sources for Tradition and Magisterial Teaching

ACC   Oden, Thomas C., general ed., Louth, Andrew, ed., *Ancient Christian Commentary on Sacred Scripture, Old Testament, Vol. I, Genesis 1–11*

BV   Bonaventure, Saint, *Breviloquium*

CCC   *Catechism of the Catholic Church*

CCT   *Catechism of the Council of Trent*

CG   Augustine, Saint, *City of God.*

DV   Vatican Council II, *Dogmatic Constitution on Divine Revelation* (*Dei verbum*)

DZ.	Denzinger, Henry, *Enchiridion Symbolorum*
GS	Vatican Council II, *Pastoral Constitution on the Church in the Modern World* (*Gaudium et spes*)
JR	Jurgens, William A., *The Faith of the Early Fathers*
LG	Vatican Council II, *Dogmatic Constitution on the Church* (*Lumen Gentium*)
OTT	Ott, Ludwig, *Fundamentals of Catholic Dogma*
SCG	Aquinas, St. Thomas, *Summa contra Gentiles*
ST	Aquinas, St. Thomas, *Summa Theologica*
TCF	Neuner, J. and Dupuis, J. eds., *The Christian Faith in the Doctrinal Documents of the Catholic Church*

- See Select Bibliography for bibliographic information.

- Scripture quotations are from the RSV unless otherwise indicated.

- Abbreviations for the books of the Bible are those used by the NAB.

- Quotations are from those editions listed in the Select Bibliography unless otherwise indicated.

Style Notes

Scriptural Citations

Words, phrases, verses, and passages from Sacred Scripture are set off by both italic typeface and quotation marks. Block citations are set off by italics only.

Quotations

Quotations have the same capitalization and punctuation as the source, even if they do not conform to the style used in this book.
Parentheses () are used to enclose a parenthetical statement of the original author.
Braces {} are used to enclose a parenthetical statement of a translator or author of secondary source from which quotation was taken.
Brackets [] enclose the comments of the author of this book.

Endnotes and Footnotes

Documentary information is located in the endnotes. Information that supplements the text is put in footnotes rather than endnotes so that it can be accessed at a glance.

Doctrinal Summaries

Preceding the discussion of each doctrine is a box that contains a summary of the status of the doctrine and of its associated doctrines. The information that follows will be useful for assessing the gravity of a doctrine from its summary.

In its "Commentary on the Concluding Formulas of the '*Professio Fidei*,'" issued June 29, 1998 as an accompaniment to Pope John Paul II's Apostolic letter *Ad Tuendam Fidem*, the Congregation for the Doctrine of the Faith identified three kinds of doctrines.

(1) *de fide credenda* (to be believed as divinely revealed)—Assent to this kind of doctrine is based directly on faith in the authority of the Word of God. These doctrines are contained in the Word of God, written or handed down, and defined with a solemn judgment as divinely revealed truth either by the Roman Pontiff when he speaks *ex cathedra,* or by the College of Bishops gathered in council ("defining act"), or infallibly proposed for belief by the ordinary and universal Magisterium of the bishops dispersed throughout the world who are in communion with the Successor of Peter ("non-defining act"). The commentary gives the following examples of this kind of doctrine:

- The articles of faith of the Creed.

- The various Christological dogmas.

- The Marian dogmas.

- The institution of the sacraments by Christ and their efficacy with regard to grace.

- The real and substantial presence of Christ in the Eucharist.

- The sacrificial nature of the Eucharistic celebration.

- The foundation of the Church by the will of Christ.

- The primacy and infallibility of the Roman Pontiff.

- The existence of original sin.

- The immortality of the human soul.

- The immediate recompense after death.

- The absence of error in the inspired sacred texts.

- The grave immorality of direct and voluntary killing of an innocent human being.

(2) *de fide tenenda* (to be held definitively)—Assent to this kind of doctrine is based on faith in the Holy Spirit's assistance to the Magisterium and on the Catholic doctrine of the infallibility of the Magisterium. These doctrines include all those teachings belonging to the dogmatic or moral area which are necessary for faithfully keeping and expounding the deposit of faith, even if they have not been proposed by the Magisterium of the Church as formally revealed. Such doctrines can be defined solemnly by the Roman Pontiff when he speaks *ex cathedra* or by the College of Bishops gathered in council, or they can be taught infallibly by the ordinary and universal Magisterium of the Church as a *sententia definitive tenenda*. The commentary gives the following examples of this kind of doctrine:

- The doctrine of papal infallibility before its definition by Vatican Council I. (Before Vatican I it was held to be definitive; after Vatican I it was also accepted as divinely revealed.)

- The doctrine that priestly ordination is reserved only to men.

- The doctrine on the illicitness of euthanasia.

- The illicitness of fornication and prostitution.

- The legitimacy of the election of the Supreme Pontiff.

- The legitimacy of the celebration of an ecumenical council.

- The canonization of saints.

- The declaration of the invalidity of Anglican ordinations.

(3) *authoritative non-definitive teaching*—This is a teaching on faith and morals that is presented as true, or at least as sure, even though it has not been

defined with a solemn judgment or proposed as definitive by the ordinary and universal Magisterium. Such a teaching is, however, an authentic expression of the ordinary Magisterium of the Roman Pontiff or of the College of Bishops and therefore requires religious submission of will and intellect. Teachings of this kind are set forth in order to arrive at a deeper understanding of divine revelation, to recall the conformity of a teaching with the truths of faith, and to warn against ideas incompatible with those truths or against dangerous opinions that can lead to error.

✳   ✳   ✳   ✳

Theological Notes and Censures

The authors of some older manuals of theology presented Catholic doctrines in the form of theses and attached to each thesis a *theological note*. A theological note is a well-defined term that expresses a judgment based on the *norms of faith* concerning the gravity of a doctrine. The norms of faith are Sacred Scripture, Sacred Tradition, and the teaching of the Magisterium. Authors cited in this work refer to two theological notes: *divine faith* and *theologically certain*. The first indicates a doctrine that is clearly revealed in Scripture and/or Tradition. The second indicates a doctrine that is a logical conclusion from a revealed doctrine.

A *theological censure* is the negative counterpart of a theological note. It is a judgment by the teaching authority of the Church (authoritative or judicial judgment) or by theological science (private theological judgment) that expresses the degree of error in a theological proposition. Three important censures cited in this work are 1) *heretical proposition*, 2) *error in faith*, and 3) *temerarious proposition*. The first indicates a proposition that is opposed to a formal dogma. The second indicates a proposition that is opposed to a truth that is intrinsically connected with a revealed truth. The third indicates a proposition that deviates without reason from the general teaching.

Foreword

By Most Rev. Robert Francis Vasa, Bishop of Baker

The Doctrines of Genesis 1–11: A Compendium and Defense of Traditional Catholic Theology on Origins, by Reverend Victor P. Warkulwiz, M.S.S., is a wonderfully researched and thoroughly stimulating work. Father Warkulwiz, drawing on his very substantial scientific background, walks us through the early chapters of Genesis showing and giving testimony to the essential compatibility between the literal account of Genesis, the understanding of the Fathers of the Church and the modern day observations of natural science.

He very cogently points out that many of the accepted scientific conclusions which contradict the days of creation and the great flood are based on a variety of unproven premises which are pillars set firmly on sand. Father very adeptly tackles the complex issues of cosmogony, astronomy, astrophysics, mathematics, nuclear science, evolutionary theory, geological uniformitarianism, radiocarbon dating, big bang theory, and others to show that the observed phenomena which they try to explain are just as readily, properly and easily explained by such Genesis factors as direct creation by God and the Genesis Flood. In doing so he opens a clear path for dedicated Christians to read the Book of Genesis with a renewed and, to a certain extent, unencumbered faith.

Saint Peter writing to the dispersed people says: *"No one can hurt you if you are determined to do only what is right; if you do have to suffer for being good, you will count it a blessing. There is no need to be afraid or to worry about them. Simply reverence the Lord Christ in your hearts, and always have your answer ready for people who ask you the reason for the hope that you all have"* (1 Peter 3:13-15). Father Warkulwiz provides ready answers for those who ask for the reasons which underlie a deep Biblical faith, a faith which is too readily branded as fundamental or naive.

The work is not, necessarily, easy reading but it is an important work which needs to be studiously read, prayerfully considered and kept on the shelf with Biblical commentaries for future reference.

Preface

This work began with the preparation of a talk that I delivered at the Kolbe Center's International Catholic Symposium on Creation held in Rome, Italy in October 2002. The symposium was a historic event at which theologians, scientists, and scholars, mostly Catholic, from around the world came to endorse the biblical accounts of Creation and the Flood. At the symposium I delivered a talk on the restoration of traditional Catholic theology on origins, in which I outlined a plan for such a restoration. The plan was to uphold traditional Catholic doctrine on origins by presenting it clearly in the form of theses that are defended on theological, philosophical and scientific grounds. The theory of evolution was to be treated in the form of objections to clearly articulated truths of the biblical record. I argued that this is a much better way of upholding the true account of origins than by running to and fro stamping out brushfires set by evolutionists or by trying to undermine the evolutionists' encampment. This book is an effort to fulfill such a plan. I intend it to be a reference work that can be used as a starting point for the full development of a Catholic theology of creation for the twenty-first century.

I tried to use the approach that St. Francis of Assisi prescribed for those in his new community who would write—to be tranquil, not contentious or belligerent. For the most part I used a heuristic approach, letting the facts speak for themselves. But sometimes, when the gravity of a point demands it, one has to be blunt and somewhat critical. I did not hesitate to do so when I deemed it constructive.

This book is directed to all those Catholics who are perturbed by naturalistic scientists who set themselves up as arbiters of all truth about nature and who insist that Genesis must be interpreted according to their theories in opposition to the commonsense interpretation of the Fathers and Doctors of the Church. I also had in mind its use by seminarians and their professors. Those studying to be priests of Jesus Christ should be inspired with confidence in the Word of God and should be given tools to defend its veracity. Some of them will go on to advanced studies in Sacred Scripture, and so they should be well grounded in philosophical and scientific matters that bear on such studies. Pope Leo XIII warned in *Providentissimus Deus* that false science could prove fatal in destroying the principles of true philosophy in young minds. "Hence, to the professor of sacred Scripture a knowledge of natural science will be of very great assistance in detecting ... attacks on the sacred books, and in refuting them."

Another one of my objectives is to present a story of origins that evokes true and vivid images of the creation of the world and the primal history of the human species. Such images help us to form correct convictions not only about our origins but also about our Catholic faith as a whole. This book gives accurate, thorough and readable answers to many questions about origins that perplex the modern Catholic. I have kept the exposition as nontechnical as possible so that the book will be accessible to everyone. Not everyone will be able to understand everything that is presented, but every reader will find enough to set his thinking straight and to nourish his Catholic faith.

*   *   *   *

In this book I try to draw clearly the line between science and naturalism. True science seeks knowledge about the world from whatever source it comes—either from revelation by God or from the observation of the world. Naturalism, on the other hand, seeks knowledge about the world exclusively from the latter. Naturalists hold to the tenet that the world itself can tell us everything there is to know about it. Naturalistic science, by not allowing itself to be guided by divine revelation, becomes prone to error when it ventures into areas where direct observations cannot be done. This susceptibility to error is most notable when natural science delves into the origin of things.

There are two versions of naturalism. The first is an atheistic version, which rejects divine revelation simply because it rejects the existence of God. It holds dominion in the modern sciences. Militant atheists in the scientific community and in the communications media zealously promote it. But they seldom deny the existence of God outright; they just totally ignore Him.

The second is a theistic version, which admits that God created the universe but will not admit that He has told us something about how He did it. Its adherents do not totally ignore God; they just marginalize Him by silencing Him.

Their slogans are, "The Bible is not a science textbook," and "The Bible tells us how to go to heaven, not how the heavens go." Their manner of seeking knowledge about the world differs little from that of their atheistic counterparts.

Today the Catholic Church has well-developed theologies of redemption and sanctification. However, she has no well-developed theology of creation because so many of her theologians, scholars and scientists have embraced theistic naturalism. They have been either lured or intimidated into naturalism by the stunning successes of scientific methods. They fail to observe that those methods are successful only when dealing with the here and now and not when dealing with the past. Further, theistic naturalists are ignorant of, ignore, or dismiss the sound theology of creation developed by the Fathers and Doctors of the Church over the centuries, a theology based on the conviction that Genesis 1–11 speaks the literal truth. My purpose in this book is to revive traditional Catholic theology on creation and to show that it gives a much more credible and consistent account of the origin of man and the universe than the evolutionistic theory of origins of the naturalists.

Rev. Victor P. Warkulwiz, M.S.S.
April 2007

Introduction

The Need for a Catholic Theology of Origins

There is a crying need for a theology of origins today. Cardinal Joseph Ratzinger (now Pope Benedict XVI) in an address to the presidents of the European doctrinal commissions in Vienna, Austria in May 1989 lamented the "almost total disappearance of the theology of the doctrine of creation."[a] Also, in the preface to his collection of homilies on Creation and the Fall entitled '*In the Beginning...*' Cardinal Ratzinger states: "Paradoxically, however, the creation account is noticeably and completely absent from catechesis, preaching, and even theology. The creation narratives go unmentioned; it is asking too much to expect anyone to speak of them."[1][b]

St. Thomas Aquinas in his *Summa contra Gentiles* highlighted the importance of creation doctrine. He stated: "Accordingly it is clear that the opinion is false of those who asserted that it mattered not to the truth of faith what opinions one holds about creatures, so long as one has right opinion about God ... since error

---

a. The complete quotation is: "I must draw attention to the almost total disappearance of the theology of the doctrine of creation. In this connection, it is symptomatic that in the two Summas of modern theology, teaching of creation as contained in the faith is omitted and replaced by vague considerations of existential philosophy....The decline in metaphysics has accompanied the decline in the doctrine of creation."

b. This reluctance to speak about the creation account in Genesis is noticeable even in the *Dogmatic Constitution on Divine Revelation* of Vatican Council II. Its summary of the history of salvation begins with Abraham and not Adam; Genesis 1–11 is ignored (see DV, nos. 14–16).

concerning creatures by subjecting the human mind to causes other than God amounts to a false opinion about God, and misleads the minds of men from God, to whom faith strives to lead them."[2] [c]

We do not have a theology of the doctrine of creation adequate for the twenty-first century because great confusion has been introduced into the thinking of Catholics by the theory of evolution and its associated doctrines, which are rooted in some false claims of natural scientists. Genuine natural science seeks truth about the natural world. But sometimes what scientists present as truth is simply opinion based on a false philosophy. This is the case with the theory of evolution, which seeks to explain the origin of all things by natural causes.

Today, atheistic evolutionists posit primary "causes other than God" for the origin of all things, and theistic evolutionists posit secondary "causes other than God" that replace His role in the origin of all things. Either version of evolution subjects us to "a false opinion about God" and "misleads the minds of men from God."

Correct knowledge about origins is necessary for a complete and consistent theology, a full Catholic life, effective pastoral practice of priests and fruitful evangelization.

The Basis for a Sound Catholic Theology of Origins

Pope John Paul II, in his 1992 and 1996 addresses to the Pontifical Academy of Sciences, pointed to the importance of "a rigorous hermeneutic for a correct interpretation of the inspired text." A sound theology of creation is based on a rigorous hermeneutic for the correct interpretation of Genesis 1–11. Such is found in principles already laid down by Pope Leo XIII in his encyclical letter *Providentissimus Deus* (1893), principles that were praised and upheld by subsequent popes, especially Benedict XV in his encyclical letter on Sacred Scripture *Spiritus Paraclitus* (1920) and Pius XII in his encyclicals *Divino afflante Spiritu* (1943) and *Humani generis* (1950).

---

c.   Also, St. Irenaeus, in his treatise *Against Heresies*, said: "If man, without being puffed up or boastful, has a right belief regarding created things and their divine Creator, who, having given them being, holds them all in his power, and if man preserves in God's love, and in obedience and gratitude to him, he will receive greater glory from him" (Office of Readings for December 19, *The Liturgy of the Hours,* Vol. 1 (New York: Catholic Book Publishing, 1975), p. 337).

Leo XIII looks to the Fathers of the Church as reliable witnesses to tradition and as the safest guides for the interpretation of Scripture. He allows us to move beyond the Fathers, but very cautiously. He said, "[I]t is not forbidden, when just cause exists, to push inquiry and exposition beyond what the Fathers have done." But, he said, in doing so we always must observe "the rule so wisely laid down by St. Augustine—**not to depart from the literal and obvious sense, except only where reason makes it untenable or necessity requires**; a rule to which it is more necessary to adhere to strictly in these times, when the thirst for novelty and unrestrained freedom of thought make the danger of error most real and proximate."[3]

This hermeneutical principle is the only sensible one. It facilitates a consistent theology. It eliminates ad hoc or arbitrary interpretations—this is literal, that is not; this is historical, that is not. It puts constructive constraints on biblical theorizing, just as the law of conservation of energy and other conservation laws put constructive constraints on the theorizing of physicists. It increases credibility of Scripture in eyes of nonbelievers because it shows that believers have confidence in its words, that they are not ready to compromise its literal and obvious meaning at the slightest provocation. It puts Catholics on common ground with Orthodox Christians, who look to the Fathers, and Evangelical Protestants, who look to the plain meaning of Scripture, and facilitates their return to the Catholic Church.

The great majority of the Fathers interpreted Genesis 1–11 in its plain sense. They believed, for example, that the world was created in six natural days, that the heavenly bodies and living beings were created from nothing in their final forms during Creation Week and not slowly over eons of time, that the world is only several thousand years old, and that the worldwide flood of Noah's time destroyed the earth as it was and all the people on it except those on the ark.

But Catholic scholars retreated from that position, thinking that "necessity" required them to do so. They accepted as facts erroneous opinions put forth in the name of science. Following is a brief introduction to those opinions.

Rejection of Genesis 1–11 by Secular Science: Historical Highlights

The literal and obvious sense of Genesis 1–11 was held by all Christians and Jews until the time of so-called enlightenment in the eighteenth century, when men began to think that their own ideas were superior to the Word of God. Then the idea that the world came into being through natural forces gained prominence among intellectuals.

Already in 1796 Marquis de Pierre-Simon Laplace proposed a kind of cosmic evolution in his "nebular hypothesis," which had the earth and planets spin off the sun. This idea was in conflict with the Genesis account, in which the earth was created before the sun. It was the great granddaddy of the modern big bang theory.

Well into the nineteenth century it was widely held by theologians and scientists that the biblical Great Flood produced the sedimentary rock strata throughout the earth. Then in 1830 Charles Lyell published his *Principles of Geology*, in which he promoted a geological theory (originated by James Hutton in the previous century) that rejected the Genesis account of the Great Flood. Lyell argued that the geological features of the earth could be explained in terms of current geological processes working over immense periods of time. He assumed that the same erosion and sedimentation processes at work today laid down the fossil-bearing strata. This theory came to be known as *uniformitarianism*, and modern geologists find it incapable of explaining many geological facts. It is summed up in the doctrine: The present is the key to the past. After Lyell scientists began to think of the age of the earth as being measured in millions of years, rather than thousands.

In 1859 Charles Darwin introduced a theory of the evolution of all living forms that well suited the temper of the times. In his *Origin of Species* Darwin proposed a thesis that contains the notion that there are no natural species, that is, species with a fixed distinct nature inherited from one of the created kinds of animals. For Darwin, species of living organisms are arbitrarily or conveniently defined and not fixed. New species continually arise while others become extinct. This happens by means of the processes of *natural variation of properties* and *natural selection*. A variation in individuals of a species that is beneficial in the struggle for existence will help those individuals survive, and those individuals will pass the variation on to their progeny. Those that do not have it become extinct. Thus nature "selects" the most apt organisms. This process acting over eons of time, beginning with one or several forms produced by the Creator, accumulates variations producing the diversity of life we witness today.

Darwinism is rapidly falling into disrepute, even among evolutionists. Natural variations in living organisms cannot account for changes in species. Also, according to the theory there should be innumerable intermediate forms. But there are no intermediate forms either in the fossil record or in the world of living organisms.

Modern evolutionists have supplanted Darwinism with *neo-Darwinism*, which looks to mutations as the cause of heritable essential changes in organisms. But the facts revealed by modern biology makes their arguments no more convincing than Darwin's. A few mutations can no more transform the nature of a living organism than changing a few letters in the text can transform the *Encyclopedia Britannica* into *The Catholic Encyclopedia*.

Although Darwin in his *Origin of the Species* held on to the existence of a Creator, his theory adapted well to the elimination of a Creator altogether. The idea of evolution grew from simply organic evolution to an all-encompassing cosmic evolution, which is sometimes called molecules-to-man evolution.

Catholic Retreat from Genesis 1–11: Adoption of Theistic Evolution

Despite its thoroughly materialistic foundations and its contradiction of Genesis, some Christians still thought that they could baptize evolution by injecting God into the process. God was fit in as Creator of the original deposit of matter and energy and as Programmer and Director of the natural processes involved in the alleged evolution of the cosmos and life. They either ignored Genesis or allegorized it, twisting it out of shape to accommodate evolution.

Theistic evolutionists give aid and comfort to atheism by succumbing to its propaganda. Atheism needs evolution to intellectually justify itself. Atheistic evolutionists see no need to inject God into the process. They see it as logically consistent without a Creator. That is why it appeals to them so much. The avid Darwinist, Richard Dawkins, makes this clear in his book *The Blind Watchmaker*. Dawkins states: "I could not imagine being an atheist at any time before 1859 when Darwin's *Origin of Species* was published."[4] And he adds: "Darwin made it possible to be an intellectually fulfilled atheist."[5] Sir Julian Huxley, an avowed atheist, said, "Darwin's real achievement was to remove the whole idea of God as Creator of organisms from the sphere of rational discussion."[6]

The most prominent among Catholic theistic evolutionists was certainly Pierre Teilhard de Chardin. His major works on evolution are *The Phenomenon of Man* (1955), which has an introduction by Julian Huxley, and *Christianity and Evolution* (1969), which was published long after his death. He introduced a new genre of literature—theology fiction. Unfortunately, his seductive merging of the spiritual and the secular mesmerized many Catholics. His unitary view of reality, a joining of God and the world, was attractive to many both inside and outside the Church. He became a kind of a cult figure. He's probably better classified with the Rolling Stones and the Beatles than with theologians or scientists.

Teilhard de Chardin was a Jesuit priest, a paleontologist and a thoroughgoing evolutionist. His vision of reality was founded in a fanciful version of theistic evolution that was defended by many of his fellow Jesuits. His theories have received more prominence than they merit on theological or scientific grounds. His writings create havoc with Catholic notions about creation, redemption, sanctification, original and actual sin, evil and grace. In 1957, the Holy Office ordered his works removed from the libraries of Catholic institutions and forbade their sale in Catholic bookstores. The Holy Office issued a monitum in 1962 warning the faithful about errors and ambiguities in his writings, but that has been ignored and has become a dead letter.

Teilhard's guide to God and the world was not Scripture or Tradition or the Magisterium or even genuine science. It was evolution. Evolution was the mold into which he forced everything, as the following quote reveals: "Is evolution a theory, a system or a hypothesis? It is much more: it is a **general condition** to which all theories, all hypotheses, all systems must bow and **which they must satisfy henceforward if they are to be thinkable and true**. Evolution is a light illuminating all facts, a curve that all lines must follow."[7] In other words, evolution defines truth. Teilhard was a dogmatic evolutionist before all else.

Catholic Retreat from Genesis 1–11: Acceptance of False Science

There was opposition to Darwinism in Catholic circles, but it was ineffective because Catholic apologists accepted the uniformitarian interpretation of the fossil record as fact. Uniformitarian doctrine said that the fossil record in the rocks was produced layer by layer over immensely long periods of time. Fossils of the simpler living forms were alleged to have been produced earlier in the history of the earth and those of more complex forms later. Thus, Darwinists argued, the fossil record demonstrated evolution. This was a real stumbling block to Catholic antievolutionists who accepted that explanation. It presented an obstacle to the interpretation of Genesis 1–11 in the literal and obvious sense.

One such apologist was Cardinal Ernesto Ruffini, who was a member of the Pontifical Biblical Commission. In his book *The Theory of Evolution Judged by Reason and Faith* (1959), he clearly lays out three schools of interpretation of Genesis 1–11. The first, which he calls the "strict historical-literal system," interprets Genesis in the literal and obvious sense. He rejects it mainly because it cannot be reconciled with the long geological periods of uniformitarian geology. He thus rejects the creation of all living creatures within the space of a few days along with the catastrophic geology associated with a worldwide flood. He also rejects what he calls the "broad historical-literal system," also called the *day-age theory*, which interprets the Hebrew word *yom* as used in Genesis 1 as a long indefinite period of time, because he argues that the proper interpretation of *yom* is a natural day. He also rejects allegorical and mythological interpretations because they offend the historical character of Genesis. He finally opts for a figurative interpretation that compromises the historicity of Genesis to preserve its religious and moral truths. He was forced to do so because he attempted to reconcile Genesis with the false science he had unwittingly accepted.

Another Catholic antievolution apologist was Father Patrick O'Connell, author of *Science of Today and the Problems of Genesis* (1959). He was a strong defender of the inerrancy of Scripture and the historicity of Genesis. But he also accepted long geological ages as a scientific fact. He expressly states his belief that the vegetable and animal kingdoms have existed for millions of years. This weakens his argument because it leads him to propose that God intervened continually in the history of the earth to create new creatures. This is not consistent with the Genesis account, which states that God finished His work of creation on the sixth natural day of Creation Week.

It seems that the 1909 decision of the Pontifical Biblical Commission (PBC) allowing the Hebrew word *yom* in Genesis 1 to be interpreted as a "natural day" or as "signifying a certain space of time" was strongly influenced by the widespread acceptance of uniformitarian geology. Considering that the Fathers of the Church who wrote on Genesis nearly unanimously accepted the former interpretation, the PBC would probably not have seen the latter interpretation as a viable alternative if its members knew what we know now about the inadequacy of uniformitarianism.

The Gradual Return to Genesis 1–11

Apologetics for the literal and obvious meaning of Genesis 1–11 was advanced with the publication in 1961 of *The Genesis Flood*.[8] In this now classic work John Whitcomb, a Protestant theologian, and Henry Morris, a hydraulic engineer, showed that a worldwide flood like the one described in Genesis can explain the fossil record and other geological features of the earth much better than uniformitarian geology. Specifically, it gave very credible arguments that the great majority of fossils were produced in a short period of time, not over millions of years.

Evolutionists say that the fossil-bearing sedimentary rock strata were laid down one at a time with great intervals of time in between and thus demonstrate evolution. Whitcomb and Morris refuted their arguments. They pointed out first of all that there are no comparable fossil-bearing rock strata forming anywhere in the world today. Secondly, they showed that the geological data provide strong evidence that the different strata were laid down one after another in quick succession. They certainly were not laid down ages apart.

The Genesis Flood gave the impetus to the modern creationist movement-- which was initially comprised of Bible Christians but now includes Catholics, Orthodox Christians and conservative mainline Protestants.

Creationists' arguments and research are resisted in Catholic intellectual circles. Many Catholic scientists and intellectuals have succumbed to scientism, putting more faith in the reigning paradigms of science than in the words of Sacred Scripture. Many of them fear being labeled "fundamentalist," a term which derives from a certain Protestant movement and is used in a pejorative sense by biblical critics to belittle those who uphold the literal and obvious sense of Genesis 1–11.

Reasons for Rejecting Evolution

Catholic scientists and scholars must reject the theory of evolution because a genuine Catholic theology of creation cannot accommodate it. First of all, it is false. Besides that it's dangerous. It has led many away from their theistic faith. It is atheistic in spirit because it is inspired by the desire to explain the origin of the universe and of man in purely naturalistic terms. It is an attack on the authenticity of divine revelation and an attempt to undermine the argument from design for the existence of God. It is the intellectual foundation of modern atheism.

The theory of evolution has caused confusion in the minds of the young because it differs so much from what is in the Bible. They recognize the contradictions and are not sophisticated enough to rationalize them away. Pope Leo XIII said in *Providentissimus Deus*: "[F]or the young, **if they lose their reverence for the Holy Scripture on one or more points, are easily led to give up believing in it altogether.** It need not be pointed out how the nature of science, just as it is so admirably adapted to show forth the glory of the Great Creator, provided it be taught as it should be, so, if it be perversely imparted to the youthful intelligence, it may prove most fatal in destroying the principles of true philosophy and in the corruption of morality."[9] This conversion testimony is revealing: "It wasn't until I could believe the first page of the Bible that I could believe the rest of it."

The notion of an earth billions of years old, which is espoused by Catholic theistic evolutionists, has had a numbing effect on the faith of youth. It pushes God so far into the background of time that He's barely visible and hardly seems relevant today. But the God of Genesis is up front. He created the world only a few thousand years ago and has lovingly and providentially followed, and intervened in, the history of mankind.

Evolutionism has set up a false wall between Sacred Scripture and natural science, a wall just as false as the wall of separation between Church and State. But Sacred Scripture and science are not really antagonistic. On the contrary, they are complementary; they shed light on each other. On the one hand, natural science provides us with facts from its study of creation that help us better understand the Scriptures. On the other hand Sacred Scripture, when treated with due respect, sheds light on the discoveries of natural science and even suggests new areas of research.

Evolution is an instrument for promoting atheism. Pope Pius XII said in *Humani generis:* "Communists gladly subscribe to this opinion [that the world is in continuous evolution] so that, when the souls of men have been deprived of every idea of a personal God, they may the more efficaciously defend and propagate their dialectical materialism."[10]

Men imbued with evolutionism do not believe in divine providence. Rather, many of them believe that the world is blindly evolving towards social and political perfection. That belief, hardening into atheistic ideologies, spawned many atrocities in the twentieth century. The erroneous notion of universal evolution has also worked itself into the minds of some Catholic theologians, who have come to see the Church herself as being in continual evolution toward perfection.[d]

In recent years nonevolutionary scientists have shown that the actual facts of science are much better explained by the creation and flood accounts in Genesis than by the theory of evolution. But for the secular humanists, who dominate the media and academia, there is no acceptable alternative to evolution. All evidence contrary to evolution and all alternate explanations of the scientific data are

---

d. For a discussion of the influence of the doctrine of universal evolution on the thinking of the Fathers of Vatican Council II see Atila Sinke Guimarães, *In the Murky Waters of Vatican II*, 2nd ed. (Rockford, IL: TAN Books, 1999), pp. 130–136.

ignored, shouted down, or dismissed with flimsy arguments. And if the evidence is too convincing, it is suppressed, in much the same way that the media suppresses the truth about abortion. The theory of evolution is politically correct "science."

The evolutionists have waged an intensive and immensely successful propaganda campaign this past century that has all but silenced the opposition. This campaign has been so successful that the scientific establishment cannot tolerate evolution being questioned. The theory of evolution is the received paradigm of academe. Pius XII in *Humani generis* called for a fair hearing of the issue to be given to both sides. But this is ignored even by Catholics.

Unfortunately, many Catholic intellectuals have been too eager to jump on the evolution bandwagon. They think that by injecting God into the theory they can free it from its atheistic roots. But it cannot be baptized because it is foreign to Christianity. Christianity knew nothing of it for eighteen centuries. The Fathers of the Church were familiar with the Greek atomists' idea of the universe being formed over eons of time by natural forces, and they promptly rejected it.

Some Catholics have been smitten by a fatal attraction to the theory, as if the idea of God using blind physical forces to bring about the universe and life over eons of time is somehow more awesome and beautiful than God creating at once in a magnificent act of love. Others feel that by accepting evolution Catholics will not be thought of as behind the times and opposed to science. And some don't think the issue is important. Contemporary Catholic scientists and scholars have made little effort to deny atheists their theory of evolution by pointing out the weaknesses in their arguments and showing the credibility of the Genesis account of origins. This failure has hampered Catholics in our efforts to evangelize because the secular humanists have led us to play the game according to their rules. Evangelization begins with origins. The first questions asked are: What am I? Why am I here? How did I get here?

The Plan of this Work

This work is an effort to formulate a positive Catholic theology of origins. It is a *positive* theology because it is one that *posits* its own true doctrines rather than one that reacts to the false doctrines of evolutionism and the excesses of biblical criticism. The polemical approach is needed, and much good work has been done in that area. But little work has been done to present a systematic presentation and defense of traditional Catholic doctrines concerning the creation of the universe and the creation and early history of mankind. It is also a *positive* theology because it is confident and enthusiastic. It is confident because it places complete trust in the Word of God as it comes to us in Sacred Scripture, Sacred Tradition and the teachings of the Magisterium. It is enthusiastic because it revels in the truth, the goodness, and the beauty of those doctrines, and in their implications for the advancement of religion, knowledge and human welfare.

This work is directed to all the faithful, theologians and nontheologians alike. Its purpose is to help restore a genuinely Catholic vision on origins and the early history of the human species. It is especially directed to those whose thinking has become muddled by the pervasive propaganda for evolution, and to those who have held on to the Catholic vision and want to know how to defend it. Many will not be won over by the arguments presented here because for many people today devotion to evolutionism is not a matter of the intellect but a matter of the will.

The doctrines are gleaned from the text of Genesis 1–11 and presented in the form of theses. These are defended by citations from Sacred Scripture, the Fathers and Doctors of the Church, and magisterial documents. Supporting evidence from natural science and other intellectual disciplines is presented. The study of creation is pandisciplinary. Since one is dealing with all of creation, it follows that just about every field of study would have contributions to make. The most pertinent at this time seem to be Scriptural exegesis, theology, the philosophy of nature, molecular biology, genetics, geology, sedimentology, paleontology, hydrology, astronomy, archaeology, chemistry and physics. The *facts* offered by the various sciences are distinguished from *inferences* made from the *principles* used to interpret the facts. The principles are sometimes based on false philosophy. Aristotle[11] assures us that one does not have to be an expert in a discipline to evaluate the principles by which it interprets its facts. One has only to be liberally educated and clear thinking. Since this is a theological work, evidence from other disciplines is not treated at great length. The pertinent material is presented in summary form, and the reader is referred to reputable sources for detailed explanations. Finally, objections are answered.

The doctrines are both religious and historical in nature. The historical doctrines are important in themselves because of the picture they give us of man and the universe, a picture into which the religious doctrines are fitted. The historical doctrines plant the religious doctrines firmly in the soil of historical fact. To deny the truth of a historical doctrine weakens the credibility of the religious ones as well because it undermines belief in the trustworthiness of Sacred Scripture.

The hermeneutical principle of Leo XIII will be adhered to in this work. Therefore, the plain meaning of the words of Scripture will be accepted unless reason or necessity dictates otherwise. Scripture, in saying something plainly, may employ idioms and metaphorical and figurative language, just as we do in our everyday speech. It is true that some of the figures of speech it uses may not be familiar to us today, but we have the help of competent and faithful scholars. It is the job of Scripture scholars to translate the text as clearly and accurately as possible and to comment on unfamiliar figures of speech. The gross deviations from the plain sense of the words of Genesis that theistic evolutionists would have us accept are not tolerable. The Word of God cannot be so misleading.[e]

It has become continually clearer in the past forty years that Genesis 1–11 can be interpreted in the "literal and obvious sense" without any contradiction from genuine science. On the contrary, genuine science confirms the plain meaning of Genesis. This is true for astronomy and other sciences as well as geology and paleontology.

The Fathers of the Church are used extensively as witnesses to Tradition and as safe guides for the interpretation of Scripture. For, as Leo XIII states, "they are men of eminent sanctity and ardent zeal for the truth, on whom God has bestowed a more ample measure of His light" and who have received the rules of interpretation in direct line from the Apostles. [12] The liberty granted by Leo XIII to go beyond the Fathers of the Church is not a license to annul their doctrine; rather, it is an invitation to develop it, to build on the foundation that they laid.[f] In this work, the Fathers are not appealed to for the establishment of a doctrine as *de fide* unless the Magisterium has already done so. The Doctors and Saints of the Church, especially St. Thomas Aquinas and St. Bonaventure, are also appealed to as eminent witnesses to Tradition.

The inerrancy of Sacred Scripture in all things, including history and matters concerning natural science, is affirmed. Pope Leo XIII stated in *Providentissimus Deus*: "It follows that those who maintain that an error is possible in any genuine passage of the Sacred Writings either pervert the Catholic notion of inspiration or make God the author of such error."[13] The principle of inerrancy is all-inclusive;

---

e. Pope John Paul II warned Scripture scholars: "Those who devote themselves to the study of Sacred Scripture should always remember that the various hermeneutical approaches have their own philosophical underpinnings, which need to be carefully evaluated before they are applied to the sacred texts" (*Fides et ratio*, no. 55).

f. Vatican Council II made this clear in the statement: "[N]o less attention must be devoted to the content and unity of the whole of Scripture, taking into account the Tradition of the entire Church and the analogy of faith, if we are to derive their true meaning from the sacred texts" (DV, no. 12).

it includes *everything* the Bible says. To deny this and to allow Sacred Scripture to err even in some small matter opens a Pandora's box of skepticism that leads to the total discrediting of God's Word. The doctrine of inerrancy applies only to the original text. It is the task of textual criticism to establish a biblical text as close as possible to the original. The differences that do exist in the manuscripts at hand (*variant readings*) have no significant effect on doctrine. The Church guarantees that the Latin Vulgate is entirely free from error in matters of faith and morals.[14]

Apparent inaccuracies or contradictions in Sacred Scripture are not causes for alarm or discouragement. Difficulties raised by Sacred Scripture have always intrigued believers, long before the advent of historical criticism. They are the problems that St. Augustine struggled with when he said that it was God's wish that the Bible "should have difficulties scattered through it so that we might be spurred on to read and study it with greater diligence and thus realize our own limitations and be exercised in due humility."[15] If one has the faith and courage to hold to the veracity of Sacred Scripture in the face of difficulties, he is rewarded with deeper insights, which come to light in the process of resolving or attempting to resolve the difficulties.

Pope Pius XII in *Humani generis* asserted that the first eleven chapters of Genesis "pertain to history in a true sense" and "both state the principal truths which are fundamental for our salvation, and also give a popular description of the origin of the human race and chosen people."[16] This work presents those "principal truths" and historical facts, defends their credibility, and manifests their goodness and beauty by showing how they fit together harmoniously.

The material in this book is not new, but the manner of its presentation is. The aim of the author was to produce a readable and convincing document that can be used as a reference work. In addition to Catholic sources, Orthodox, Protestant and Jewish sources were also consulted. Orthodox Christians have carefully studied Genesis in the light of the writings of the Fathers of the Church. Evangelical Protestants have done much work in the past forty years to show that the *facts* (if not the *theories*) of natural science are very much in harmony with Genesis. And Jewish tradition provides valuable insights that contribute to our understanding of Genesis.

This study is divided into three parts. The first part is entitled "The Cosmos." It deals mainly with Genesis 1. The second part is entitled "The Human Species" and is concerned with human origins. It deals mainly with Genesis 1:26 to 5:32. The alleged evolution of the human body presents its own particular problems that are handled as an objection to the Genesis account. The third part, entitled

"The Earth," treats the early history of the earth. It is concerned mainly with the Great Flood and its effects and the history of mankind from Noah to Abram. Its doctrines are drawn from Genesis 6–11.

For a more fruitful use of this book, it would help to have the following works at hand:

1. A good English translation of the Bible. The RSV is recommended.

2. A copy of the CCC. Indexes of scriptural and nonscriptural citations and an alphabetic index are provided.

3. A copy of DZ. This is the major source for Catholic dogma. Carefully chosen excerpts from Church documents are identified by number. Scriptural, doctrinal and alphabetical indexes are provided. Fortunately, a high quality bound reprint of an English translation has been published by Loreto Publications, Fitzwilliam, NH.

4. The three volumes of JR. This is a treasure trove of excerpts from the writings of the Church Fathers compiled by a Catholic priest. Each excerpt is identified by a number. Scriptural, doctrinal and alphabetic indexes are provided.

5. A copy of ACC. This is a treasure trove of excerpts from the writings of the Church Fathers compiled by a mixed team of Catholic and non-Catholic researchers. The selections are connected with biblical verses. Scriptural, alphabetic and other indexes are provided.

The earliest English poem on record is *Caedmon's Hymn*, which was composed between 657 and 680. Caedmon was a laborer at a Benedictine monastery who totally lacked natural talent for singing and poetry. He was so ashamed of this deprivation that he would sneak away from a feast when he saw the harp coming toward him. One night, however, God gave him the gift of being able to turn Scripture into verse. A voice in a dream said to him, "Sing me a song about the creation of all things." He immediately began to sing verses in praise of God the Creator that he had never heard before. Venerable Bede tells us that their theme ran thus:

> Praise we the Fashioner now of Heaven's fabric,
> The majesty of His might and His mind's wisdom,
> Work of the world-warden, worker of all wonders,
> How He the Lord of Glory everlasting,
> Wrought first for the race of men Heaven as a rooftree,

Then made He Middle Earth to be their mansion.[17]

The author hopes that this book, like Caedmon's poem, will ring out praise to God the Creator. He hopes that it will help restore to God the recognition due Him. The writers of most books, articles and documentaries on nature fail (or refuse) to credit God for the marvels of creation. Most works on nature do not give even a hint of praise to God. Instead the praise is given to a mindless and fictional entity called evolution. Authors have even gone so far as to call evolution the "goddess of creation." That is abominable. The Bible reminds us that God's works loudly sing His praise: *"Bless the Lord, all you works of the Lord. Praise and exalt Him above all forever."[18]*

[1] Ratzinger, Cardinal Joseph, *'In the Beginning...': A Catholic Understanding of the Story of Creation and the Fall* (Huntington, IN: Our Sunday Visitor, Inc, 1990), p. 7.

[2] SCG, Book 2, Chapter 3.

[3] *Providentissimus Deus*, II, C–1d. Emphasis added.

[4] Dawkins, Richard, *The Blind Watchmaker: Why the Evidence of Evolution Reveals a Universe Without Design* (New York: W. W. Norton and Co., 1987), p. 5.

[5] Ibid., p. 6.

[6] Keynote address, Darwin Centennial, 1959.

[7] Teilhard de Chardin, Pierre, *The Phenomenon of Man* (New York: Harper and Row, 1959, trans. from 1955 French edition), p. 219. Emphasis added.

[8] Whitcomb, John C. and Morris, Henry M., *The Genesis Flood: The Biblical Record and Its Scientific Implications* (Phillipsburg, NJ: P & R Publishing, 1960).

[9] *Providentissimus Deus*, II, D–2b. Emphasis added.

[10] *Humani generis*, no. 5 (DZ no. 2305).

[11] *On the Parts of Animals*, Book 1, Chapter 1.

[12] *Providentissimus Deus*, II, C–1c.

[13] *Providentissimus Deus*, II, D–3b.

[14] See DZ, no. 2292.

[15] Quoted by Augustin Cardinal Bea, S. J. in *The Study of the Synoptic Gospels: New Approaches and Outlooks* (London—Dublin: Geoffrey Chapman, 1965), p. 60.

[16] *Humani generis*, no. 38 (DZ, no. 2329).

[17] *Ecclesiastical History of the English People* (New York: Penguin Books, 1990), pp. 248–249.

[18] Daniel 3:57.

PART I

▼

THE COSMOS

The Creation of the Universe

Doctrine One
A personal Supreme Being exists and has revealed Himself.

God revealed His existence in the events recorded in the Book of Genesis, which was composed by Moses under the inspiration of the Holy Spirit. Moses probably used sources written and passed down by the antediluvian and postdiluvian patriarchs. The Council of Trent affirmed the divine authorship of Genesis, and the Pontifical Biblical Commission in a 1906 decree upheld the Mosaic authorship of Genesis. That God revealed His existence is a *de fide credenda* doctrine. The First Vatican Council decreed that the existence of God can also be known "with certitude by the light of human reason from created things."

God Revealed Himself

The Book of Genesis presumes that the reader already knows about God. The existence of God is a given in the narrative. He is mentioned in the first verse by name, as someone already known. Man knew of God's existence from the very beginning because God revealed Himself. Genesis says that God conversed with Adam and Eve and made known His will to them. Adam and Eve passed down their knowledge of God, their origin, and the origin of the world to their descendants. The antediluvian patriarchs, Seth and his successors, preserved that knowledge and passed it on to Noah. Through Noah and his descendants it passed on to Abraham and his posterity. The truths passed on this way comprise what is called *primeval revelation*. Cain and his successors also knew of the existence of God through primeval revelation. It seems from Genesis that men did not lose knowledge of the one God and embrace polytheism until after the Great Flood. Atheism is unheard of in the early history of man.

Because of the spread of sin, primeval revelation was lost or became corrupted. Information about God and origins along with the early history of mankind passed down to Moses. It may have been somewhat corrupted when he received it, but if it was he was able to correct it through direct revelation given him and seal it with divine authority.

Even those people who lost contact with primeval revelation could still have known about the existence of God "with certitude by the light of human reason from created things."[1] Vatican Council I defined this truth. But history shows that most men when left to themselves do not arrive at knowledge of the one true God. Revelation of the existence of God confirms the natural knowledge of God and enables the existence of God to be known easily and with certainty by all.

God's existence is an object of faith in addition to being an object of natural knowledge. The Church formally defined the existence of God. Vatican Council I decreed: "The holy, Catholic, Apostolic, Roman Church believes and confesses that there is one, true, living God...."[2] The same Council condemns the denial of God's existence as a heresy.[3]

The Names of God

In Genesis a name is not simply a conventional designation. Rather it is an expression of a being's relationship to God, to man or to the created world, just as today a child's name reflects its relationship with its parents, who gave it its name. God names His creations: *"Day," "Night," "Heaven," "Earth," "Seas."* He instructed Adam to name the different kinds of animals, each of which was destined to have a unique relationship with Adam.

Throughout the first chapter of Genesis, Moses identifies God with the name *Elohim* (plural of *El*, which refers to gods in general, but used here in a singular sense), which expresses God's incomparable power and might. Elsewhere in Genesis Moses uses not only the name *Elohim* but also the name God Himself revealed to him, YHWH (I AM WHO AM), which emphasizes His transcendence over all created things and that He alone IS.[4] He uses YHWH *Elohim* when he speaks of the creation of Adam and Eve and of God's intercourse with them. This name expresses the closeness of the relationship between God and the first couple.

For some of the ancients, to say the name of a person was an intimate act, like the touching of his soul or being. Out of respect for the holiness of God, early Jewish rabbis restricted the pronunciation of His revealed name YHWH, which they perceived as manifestation of His divinity. They laid down the rule that the name YHWH could be uttered only in the Sanctuary of the Temple. Elsewhere, another name had to be used. When reading Sacred Scripture they would replace YHWH with the Hebrew word *Adonai,* which is rendered "Lord" in English. In English translations of the Bible, *Elohim* is rendered "God," YHWH is rendered "LORD," and YHWH *Elohim* is rendered "LORD God."

Even though Adam and Eve had an intimate relationship with God, they did not address Him by name. Men only begin to invoke YHWH by name at the time that Enosh, son of Seth, was born (4:26). But Eve did refer to God twice by name, once using YHWH (4:1) and once using *Elohim* (4:25).

A Very Personal God

Genesis 1–11 reveals to us a Supreme Being who is

- *Personal*: God uses the personal pronouns *I* and *me* when referring to Himself. He knows and He knows that He knows, which characterizes only a person.

- *Spiritual*: God created the material world. Since matter does not have the power to produce itself, God must be an immaterial person; that is, He must be a spirit.

- *Self-Existent*: The name YHWH used in Genesis 1–11 means I AM WHO AM. This name has a strong ontological connotation. It implies a being that exists in itself, one whose very nature is to exist.

- *One yet Multipersonal*: The name *Elohim* used in the Genesis 1 is a plural used as a singular. God when referring to Himself usually uses the singular, but in 1:26 He uses plurals to refer to Himself: *"Let* US *make man in* OUR *image, after* OUR *likeness."* In 11:7, God says: *"Behold, the man has become like one of* US...." And in 11:7, He says: *"Come let* US *go down, and there confuse their language...."* These are all hints that there is a plurality of persons in the one God. Indeed, the Fathers of the Church understood 1:26 in light of New Testament revelation to mean that the First Person of the Trinity was addressing the Second Person or the Second and Third Persons.[5] The plural form does not seem to be a plural form of majesty because of the infrequency of its use, and there is no evidence in Scripture itself that the plural form was ever used to indicate majesty.[6] Genesis 1:2 speaks of the *"Spirit of God"* moving over the face of the waters. This is sometimes understood simply as a power that proceeds from God, but in the light of New Testament revelation it can be personalized and seen as an allusion to the Holy Spirit.

- *Creator*: In the Hebrew text of Genesis 1:1 the second word is *bara*, which means "created." This word, in the unqualified sense used here, means the production of something from absolute nothingness and is used only with respect to the activity of God. It is never used in the same way to denote works of human beings, as we sometimes use the English word *create*.[7] The production of something from nothing is an infinite act and so must proceed from an all powerful, infinite being.

- *Transcendent*: God is distinct from His creation. He transcends it and is not identified with it. There is no trace of pantheism or monism in Genesis.

- *The Supreme Good*: Genesis 1:31 states: *"God saw everything that He had made and behold it was very good."* God saw that His creatures were good because He gave them all the perfections corresponding to their natures. He was able to communicate goodness to them because He is supremely good. Vatican Council I taught that God by His goodness created "to manifest His perfection by the blessings which He bestows on creatures."[8]

- *Providential Lawgiver*: God is the giver of both the natural law and the moral law. He commands the living creatures to be fruitful and multiply, and He commands Adam not to eat from the tree of the knowledge of good and evil. He gives commands to Noah and enters into a covenant with him as Noah and his family enter into a brand-new world. He knows and cares about what is going on in His creation. He is not the Deist Supreme Being who creates and then gets bored with his creation and ignores it. Vatican Council I stated: "God protects and governs by His providence all things which He created, *'reaching from end to end mightily and ordering all things sweetly'* (cf. Wis 8:1)."[9]

- *Merciful Judge*: God is *"grieved"* (6:6) by sin and expresses His wrath at the sinfulness of man. But His punishments are sweetened with mercy. He makes garments for Adam and Eve after He casts them out of Paradise (3:21), and He protects Cain after condemning him to wander the earth (4:15).

< Objections > and << Replies >>

< Objection 1 >

It is naive to hold that Moses himself composed Genesis 1–11 from direct revelation and from sources handed down to him. It is common knowledge among Scripture scholars that it was written much later in the history of Israel by a number of inspired authors. It is a complex and careful combining of several historical traditions or sources. In order to make revelations about Himself, God led the chosen people to reflect profoundly on the origin of men and the world. Many of Israel's neighbors had done the same, and, to explain things that were beyond the scope of ordinary language, they devised all sorts of myths about the origins of the world and man and about the earliest times of men. The sacred writers of Genesis sifted through these myths and selected certain literary elements suited to the mentality of their contemporaries in order to convey the message of faith that they wanted to pass on, through their writings, to the people of Israel, and, through Israel's religious experience, to all mankind. In this "account of the origins" we can fairly easily distinguish passages whose literary features can be identified as belonging to the J and P traditions. In addition to the symbolic language typical of the Middle East, we can find in this "account of origins" other little literary elements that derived from ancient local traditions of Mesopotamia and Canaan. We also find genealogical lists designed to show that the human race was populating the entire world. All this material is used to fill in the period of time from the creation of the world to the age of Abraham. Positioned as they now all are, at the start of the Bible, the first eleven chapters of Genesis act as a kind of general introduction bringing us up as far as Abraham; with this man, according to the book, history takes a new turn when God calls and man obeys.[a]

<< Reply to Objection 1 >>

In this reply, the position of the Magisterium on biblical authorship will be discussed first. Following that will be a brief history and description of the *documentary hypothesis*, on which the objection is based. The fatal weakness of that theory will then be discussed, and solid evidence in favor of Mosaic authorship of Genesis and the rest of the Pentateuch will be presented. Finally, the traditional docu-

---

a. Much of the material in this objection is taken verbatim from commentaries in the NAB and NB *Pentateuch*.

mentary structure of Genesis 1–11 will be set forth and its literal-historical truth affirmed.

<< Magisterial Teaching on Biblical Authorship >>

The question of the human authorship of the books of the Bible must be distinguished from the questions of inspiration and inerrancy. The latter have been clearly defined and repeatedly affirmed by the Magisterium of the Church.[10] But the Church has made no definitive pronouncements concerning the authorship of any book in the Bible. The first Pontifical Biblical Commission, however, in a 1906 response[11] upheld the Mosaic authorship of the Pentateuch. The decrees of the first Pontifical Biblical Commission are authoritative and must be regarded as directive norms.[12] Msgr. John Steinmueller, a consultor of the first Pontifical Biblical Commission from 1947 to 1971, said, "[I]t would be temerarious to disregard them, even though research may be carried further."[13] A Catholic Scripture scholar who dismisses a PBC decree is as impertinent as a c-minus high school student who dismisses Shakespeare. Some say that the PBC decrees regarding Mosaic authorship have been revoked. Msgr. Steinmueller in *The Sword of the Spirit* shows that to be false.[b]

The author of this book takes Mosaic authorship of Genesis for granted, following the 1906 response of the PBC. That response is a wise and sensible one. Nothing that biblical criticism has to offer can make him lose confidence in it. That response clearly states that the Pentateuch was written under the direct authority of Moses. He had direct revelation from God; and he may have edited and/or paraphrased, under divine inspiration, existing sources. He may have written with his own hand, dictated to scribes, or authorized the final product produced by others under his direction.[c] The response does allow for some later additions to the text in the form of glosses and explanations by inspired writers.

<< The Documentary Hypothesis >>

The documentary hypothesis (DH) was developed outside the Church beginning in the eighteenth century. It led to the rejection of Mosaic authorship of the Pentateuch, held to up to that time by all Christians and Jews. Its founders claimed to be distinguishing different sources for the text of the Pentateuch. A number of scholars were instrumental in its development, but its chief proponent was Julius Wellhausen (1844–1891), who popularized it in his *Prolegomena to the History of Israel.* Its proponents claim that the composers of the Pentateuch used materials from many different periods, some of them very old, some of them not so old. These materials, with no known origins or history, were rearranged and rewritten by an unknown number of anonymous inspired writers. The edited text consists of the five books as they reached the Jewish people and later the Church.

In this theory, four main sources are assigned to the Pentateuch. They are identified as J (from German for "Yahwist"), E (Elohist), D (Deuteronomist), and P (Priestly Code). The use of divine names was the criterion originally used to identify the sources, and it always played a considerable part in the analysis of the text. J designates those parts of the Pentateuch where the divine name YHWH is used, apart from its use in D and P. E is used for the parts using *Elohim*, the ordinary Hebrew name for God, though not used exclusively for God. The J and E sources are supposed to be the oldest sources, with J as the most ancient. The most well known division into sources is that of the creation

---

b. Following are Msgr. John Steinmueller's words:

"I was a consultor of the first Pontifical Biblical Commission from 1947 (after the publication of *Divino afflante Spiritu*) to 1971; and I never heard any intimation that any decrees of the Commission were ever revoked. At most they were clarified (cf. Letter to Cardinal Suhard of Paris, 1948 [DZ, no. 2302]). Recently some Catholic scholars have asserted that the decrees were implicitly revoked by *Divino afflante Spiritu* (1943) and that this is confirmed by two articles written in 1955 by A. Miller and A. Kleinhans, who seem to restrict the scope of the decrees to matters of faith and morals (cf. *Jerome Biblical Commentary*, Vol. II, p. 629). The articles referred to were *unauthorized* and were condemned by the voting Cardinal members of the Commission. A. Miller and A. Kleinhans were to be brought before the Holy Office because of the articles, but were saved from this ordeal through the personal intervention of Cardinal Tisserant before the Holy Father. It was my friend, Father Miller, O.S.B., who told me the whole story before his return to Germany.

"Decisions of this Pontifical Biblical Commission were sent to the Holy Father, who ratified them or sent them back for further consideration. The official decisions were published only at his command.

"This first Pontifical Commission as an independent commission came to an end by the apostolic letter issued 'Motu Proprio' by Pope Paul VI, June 27, 1971. As a new body the Biblical Commission was to be a dependent subcommission under the Sacred Congregation for the Doctrine of the Faith presided over by its Cardinal Prefect. Its members are appointed by the Supreme Pontiff, on the proposal of the Cardinal president after consultation with the episcopal conferences" (*The Sword of the Spirit: Which is the Word of God* (Fort Worth, TX: Stella Maris Books, 1977), footnote on pp. 7–8).

account in Genesis. Genesis 1:1–2:4a is attributed to E because the word *Elohim* is used for God. Genesis 2:4b and following is attributed to J because the name YWYH is used, sometimes by itself and sometimes in conjunction with *Elohim*. The D source supplies the contents of the Book of Deuteronomy. It expounds the Law of Moses in great discourses but is alleged to have been written during and after the Exile. It is supposed to be the product of a literary revival that was inspired by the religious changes introduced by the reforming kings Hezekiah and Josiah in the seventh century B.C. The P tradition is traced to priestly groups in Babylon during the Exile. It is said to provide the genealogies that construct the framework of Genesis and bind its contents together. It gives to Genesis legal institutions such as the Sabbath rest, circumcision, and the alliances between God and Noah and God and Abraham. The Book of Leviticus is considered to be entirely P.

Multiple sources were also postulated to account for the existence of parallel passages in which the same event is treated twice. In Genesis there are two *supplementary* accounts of Creation (1:1–2:4a and 2:4b–24), which some exegetes interpret as *different* accounts. Also, the account of the Great Flood contains two passages that at first sight seem to differ concerning the numbers and kinds of the animals taken on the ark. The Fathers of the Church were also aware of those apparent differences and the differences in divine names; but they interpreted them in terms of the didactic purpose of the narrator, who is telling a story in two different ways.[14] For the Fathers there is a single narrator, and that is Moses.[15] He filled the story of Creation and the Fall with hints about the coming of Christ and the restoration of the world.[16] The Fathers venerated him as a lawgiver and as a prophet with deep insight into creation.

Scholars today see the four-source analysis as an oversimplification. They find that it is not always possible to distinguish the various sources with certainty. Detailed investigations of the text have led to the conclusion that the composers of the Pentateuch did a lot of cut-and-paste work—a snippet of J here, a snatch of E there. The alleged redactors of the Pentateuch come to look like children keeping a scrapbook. And scholars differ among themselves in the attribution of sources. Some attribute a given snippet to one source, others to another source.[17]

---

c.   Jewish sages believed that God dictated the Torah to Moses letter by letter. Therefore the scribes were extremely careful in reproducing the Hebrew text, and transcribed it with very high letter accuracy. God may have guided Moses' transcriptions of existing sources letter by letter.

The upshot is that the four-source theory has lost its potency, but great weight is still given it by scholars.

The documentary hypothesis would not be objectionable if it were not for the late dates assigned to the D and P sources. The PBC response allowed for the use of written and oral sources by Moses; and the J and E sources can easily be reckoned pre-Mosaic sources, as Jean Astruc did when he invented the theory of multiple sources.[18] Pope John Paul II seems to have accepted the theory in this way in the general audience talks he gave on Genesis. For example, in his talk given on September 12, 1979 he shows acceptance of a 'Yahwist' "text" and of an 'Elohist' "tradition" in the accounts of man's creation.[19] And in the talk he gave on January 2, 1980, he refers to the 'Elohist' and 'Yahwist' "narratives of the creation of man."[20] A search of his writings from 1978 to 1997 showed that whenever he used the terms *Elohist* and *Yahwist* it was always in reference to the two accounts of Creation in Genesis.[21] He gave no indication whatsoever that he believed those accounts are post-Mosaic. Another search of those writings showed not one instance of the use of either of the terms *Deuteronomist* or *Priestly Code*,[22] although a passing reference to a "priestly tradition" is made.[23]

Many Catholic scholars came to accept the full-blown documentary hypothesis with gusto in the late twentieth century, at the time Protestant and Jewish scholars were eschewing it. This has evoked comments by a number of Protestant scholars. For example, David Wells observed in 1972: "Present-day Catholicism, on its progressive side, is teaching many of the ideas which the liberal Protestants espoused in the last century.... Since these ideas have only come into vogue in Catholicism in the last two decades, they appear brilliantly fresh and innovative. To a Protestant, whether he approves or disapproves of them, they are old hat."[24]

<< The Fatal Weakness of the Documentary Hypothesis >>

One might ask what the DH has contributed to our understanding of Genesis. Its proponents would be hard put to give a convincing defense of its fruitfulness. It seems that the only thing that it has added is confusion.

The presuppositions of the method are those of the ideology of the time. The all-embracing idea of evolution, whether consciously or unconsciously, is applied to the books of the Bible. The evolution of the books of the Bible imitates the evolution of living species. The books are not seen as integral entities that were originally composed in much the same form as they have come to us. Rather, they slowly evolved under the torturous action of history's cultural and religious forces. Their development was not a natural, organic development like that of an acorn growing into an oak tree. Rather, it was a sporadic, undirected development, highly influenced by the ideologies and religious prejudices of the redactors. Supernatural influence on the composition of the books is ruled out or ignored. The DH will die with evolutionism, which will pass out of history as other *isms* have.

For Catholic scholars the embracing of the full-blown DH method has been a declaration of independence from the decrees of the PBC. But it is not the declaring of independence from a tyrant. Rather, it is a severing of ties with a competent guide who has good knowledge of the territory. As a result, many Catholic Scripture scholars have lost their way and are wandering in the wilderness.

DH is a theory and that's all it is. It's all imagination and speculation. There is no substantial documentary evidence to support it. Rather, the latest evidence from archaeological finds refutes it and supports Mosaic authorship. The most striking of that evidence comes from discoveries in the ancient buried city Ebla in Syria, which was excavated in 1974–1977. More than seventeen thousand clay tablets were found there, dating to around 2500 B.C., around a thousand years before the birth of Moses and several hundred years before Abraham. Giovanni Pettinato, on examining some of the tablets, claimed that the names El and YHWH were known and used at that time and that he found a creation account at Ebla similar to that of Genesis.[25] Needless to say, his discoveries stirred up quite a controversy.

G. L. Archer[26] says that the most serious false assumption underlying the DH is that the Israelites did not commit anything to writing until many centuries after the formation of their nation. He amasses an impressive array of archaeological evidence that shows that writing was commonplace in the Near East from long before the time of Moses, even among the lowest social strata, and that there is no support whatsoever for the notion that the Hebrews didn't put their religious records into written form until centuries after Moses.

<< Evidence for Mosaic Authorship of the Pentateuch >>

The Pentateuch itself affirms Moses as its author. In Exodus 17:14, the LORD said to Moses: *"Write this as a memorial in a book...."* Mosaic authorship is also affirmed in Exodus 24:4,7; 34:27; Numbers 33:1–2 and Deuteronomy 31:9. In Joshua 1:8 the LORD tells Joshua, Moses' protégé and successor, to recite from the *"book of the law"* and to meditate on it and observe its contents. Also in the

Book of Joshua, we read that Joshua built an altar of unhewn stones as commanded by Moses and *"recorded in the book of the law,"* and *"Joshua inscribed upon the stones a copy of the law written by Moses."*[27] There are also a number of other Old Testament references to Mosaic authorship of the Pentateuch.[28]

The New Testament also gives witness that Moses was the author of the Pentateuch. Jesus Himself affirms Mosaic authorship in John 5:46–47. He said to the Jews, *"If you believed Moses, you would believe me, for he wrote of me. But if you do not believe his writings, how will you believe my words?"* Jesus gives further testimony in favor of Mosaic authorship in Mark 10:5, Mark 12:26, Luke 24:27 and John 7:19.

DH proponents often give suave responses when faced with these citations. For example, we are graciously told: "[We do] not deny the role of Moses in the development of the Pentateuch. It is true we do not concede him as the author of the books in the modern sense. But there is no reason to doubt that, in the events described in these traditions, he had a uniquely important role, especially as lawgiver. Even the later laws that have been added in P and D are presented as a Mosaic heritage. Moses is the lawgiver par excellence, and all later legislation is conceived in his spirit, and therefore attributed to him. Hence, the reader is not held to undeviating literalness in interpreting the words 'The Lord said to Moses.' One must keep in mind that the Pentateuch is the crystallization of Israel's age-old relationship with God."[29] The rhetoric in this passage obscures what is essentially a denial of the truthfulness, or at least the accuracy, of Sacred Scripture.

There are other indicators of Mosaic composition in Sacred Scripture. The text clearly shows that the author of the Pentateuch is familiar with the things he is writing about. He alludes to contemporary events and issues. He displays an intimate knowledge of the climate, geography, and social and political conditions of Egypt and the Sinai Peninsula that a writer living in Babylon centuries after the events depicted would not have. Yet the same author displays little or no first-hand acquaintance with Palestine, which he knew only by oral tradition from his forefathers. G. L. Archer[30] has drawn up a long list of these and other evidences. One of those is that a far greater number of Egyptian names and loan words are found in the Pentateuch than in anywhere else in Sacred Scripture. Another is that Jerusalem is never mentioned by name in the entire Pentateuch. This is astonishing if the authors, as proponents of the DH claim, were preoccupied with extrapolating religious practices of the fifth and sixth centuries B.C. back to the time of Moses. A third is that a favorite name for God between 850 and 450 B.C. is LORD of Hosts. This appellation occurs about sixty-seven times in the Book of

Isaiah, eighty-three times in the Book of Jeremiah, thirteen times in the Book of Haggai and fifty-one times in the Book of Zechariah. Yet it does not appear once in the entire Pentateuch. And a fourth concerns the use of musical instruments in worship. During the time the DH postulates that the Pentateuch was written (9th–5th centuries B.C.) various musical instruments were used in worship—all three kinds, stringed, wind and percussion. But the Pentateuch fails to contain a single reference to musical accompaniment in Tabernacle worship.

Modern linguistics supports the Mosaic authorship of Genesis. A computer analysis of Genesis was done at the Technion Institute in Israel. A thorough linguistic analysis of the Hebrew words, phrases and passages of Genesis was done. The project leader, Yehuda Radday, reached this conclusion: "It is most probable that the Book of Genesis was written by one person."[31]

Msgr. John Steinmueller makes the point that Mosaic authorship of the Pentateuch is not a literary and historical/archaeological issue. Rather, it is a doctrinal issue. He states: "Those passages which are directly attributed to Moses by Sacred Scripture must be believed by *divine faith* to have Moses as their author, and the substance of the other parts of the Pentateuch is *theologically certain* to be of Mosaic origin. Hence, it would be an *error in faith* to deny the Mosaic origin of those passages of the Pentateuch which are directly attributed to him, and it would be at least *temerarious* to deny the Mosaic origin of those parts which constitute the substance of the Pentateuch."[32]

<< The Structure of Genesis 1–11 >>

Genesis 1–11 neatly divides into the following six books, each ending with its own signature: *"These are the generations of...."*

The Book of Creation (1:1–2:4a)
The Book of Adam (2:4b–5:1a)
The Book of Noah (5:1b–6:9a)
The Book of the Sons of Noah (6:9b–10:1a)
The Book of Shem (10:1b–11:10a)
The Book of Terah (11:10b–11:27a)

Each book contains the memoirs of the patriarch (or patriarchs) for whom it is named. They were eyewitnesses to the events recorded in their books. God may have dictated the first book to Adam word for word. The second book is actually identified as a book: *"This is the book of the generations of Adam"* (5:1a). It was probably written down by Adam himself and not simply passed on orally. This holds for the other books as well. Written transmission of the books would have helped to insure that the information they contain would be passed on intact.

The beginning of the Book of Adam (2:4b–2:6) is stitched to the Book of Creation by a brief summary of that book along with additional information. The beginning of each succeeding book is stitched to the previous book by the name of the author of the previous book, which gives continuity to the narrative. For example, the Book of Noah ends and the Book of the Sons of Noah begins as follows: *"These are the generations of Noah. Noah was a righteous man ..."* (6:9).

Moses was probably inspired to use these sources for Genesis 1–11 instead of being given direct revelation of the information they contain. Sacred Scripture never says that Moses wrote Genesis himself. The New Testament refers twenty-five times to things Moses wrote in the other four books of the Pentateuch. But it refers to Genesis more than two hundred times without ever accrediting the words to Moses. However, it appears that Moses did add some editorial comments to the text of Genesis as, for example, where he updates place names.

<< The Literal-Historical Truth of Genesis 1–11 >>

The literary form of a writing is often suggested by the text itself and sometimes made known by the author. There is no evidence whatsoever in Genesis 1–11 that it is anything other than what Moses presented it as, a literal-historical document. That is what the Fathers of the Church unanimously understood it to be. They received that understanding from the Apostles, who received it from Christ. That this is genuine Catholic Tradition is confirmed in the liturgy of the Church and in the overwhelming consensus of the faithful over the centuries, as reflected in the writings of the Doctors of the Church and in other Catholic literature.

The unity and Christocentricy of Sacred Scripture is made manifest by the literal-historical truth revealed in Genesis 1–11. The inspired authors of the New Testament held firmly to the literal truth of the Genesis 1–11 account. They clearly saw that it gives continuity, coherence and completeness to the history of salvation.

In 1909 the Pontifical Biblical Commission rejected arguments that deny the literal-historical nature of Genesis 1–3.[33] It rejected the notion that the accounts in those chapters do not "correspond to objective reality and historical truth" but are "presented under the guise of history to inculcate religious and philosophical truths."[34] The PBC further rejected the notion that the accounts "contain legends, historical in part and fictional in part, composed freely for the instruction and edification of souls."[35] It specifically upheld the "literal and historical sense" for a number of things narrated in Genesis 1–3 that "pertain to the foundations of the Christian religion."[36] Recognizing the example set by the Fathers of the Church, the PBC allowed for prudently applied allegorical and prophetical interpretations, but always "presupposing the literal and historical sense."[37] Pius XII in his encyclical letter *Humani generis* deplored a "certain too free interpretation of the historical books of the Old Testament."[38] He upheld the literal-historical nature of Genesis 1–11, saying that it relates "history in a true sense."[39]

The expression of "literal-historical truth" does not exclude the use of metaphorical and other figurative language, which is often used to clearly and unambiguously express truth. The PBC made allowances for the flexibility of language, saying that Genesis 1–3 need not be "interpreted in a proper literal sense" "when expressions are manifestly used figuratively, that is, metaphorically or anthropomorphically, and when reason forbids us to hold, or necessity impels us to depart from, the proper literal sense."[40] Not all expressions of truth are mechanically literal. Modern English is full of metaphors and other figures of speech that greatly enrich the language. Figurative language stretches the meaning of words to give them a wider range of application. Figures of speech colorfully, succinctly and forcefully convey shades of meaning that would be clumsy to do with strict literalism. They reveal and clarify; they do not conceal. Literal-historical truth is truth that is expressed plainly, in either strictly literal or contextually-clear figurative language, without the use of obscure or occult symbolism that is comprehensible only to experts or the initiated.

Pope Pius XII said that Genesis 1–11 was written in "simple and metaphorical language" "adapted to the mentality of a people but little cultured."[41] Since the language was to convey simple truth to a simple people, it makes sense that the metaphors were simple. The power of a metaphor lies in its ability to convey an idea in a way that is quickly and clearly comprehended. Good metaphors appeal directly to common sense. They do not have to be explained by "science." Although some of the metaphors in Scripture might be obscure to us today because of separation in time and culture, most are them are temporally and culturally universal.

Catholic theistic evolutionists attempt to use the notion of "simple and metaphorical language" as a loophole for making the text of Genesis say what they want it to say. For example, they make the gratuitous assertion that the Hebrew word *yom* ("day") represents an undefined period of millions or even billions of years. Simple people would never come to that understanding from the text of Genesis 1. Such a metaphor would be a very poor one indeed because it would obscure the truth rather than reveal it. It would be very misleading, unworthy of its sacred author. Some theistic evolutionists have gone to the grotesque extreme of saying that Adam and Eve were not individuals but represent a community of people. It seems that such a notion never even occurred to readers of Sacred Scripture until the advent of evolutionism.

Further, "literal-historical truth" is not necessarily conveyed with "scientific exactitude of expression." This was affirmed by the Pontifical Biblical Commission in a decree concerning the first chapter of Genesis.[42] The notion "scientific exactitude of expression" is itself vague because the terminology used to describe a natural phenomenon is not necessarily unique; it depends on the scientific model that is used to represent the phenomenon. There is often more than one way to describe a fact of nature. One's description depends on how he views the world. Lack of scientific exactitude of expression according to a favored scientific paradigm does not diminish the correctness of a biblical assertion about the physical nature of a thing. Such assertions typically describe physical phenomena in simple yet accurate language.

It is often pointed out that the purpose of Sacred Scripture is not to teach natural science. That is true, but it does not mean that biblical assertions about the natural world are subject to reinterpretations that contradict the literal-historical meaning of the words. The task of the exegete is to interpret Scripture with faith in its accuracy, not to reinterpret it to conform to contemporary scientific conventions.

[1] DZ, no. 1785. Vatican I condemned the denial of this truth as a heresy (see DZ, no. 1806). Vatican I cited Rom 1:20; also see Wis 13:1–9.

[2] DZ, no. 1782.

[3] DZ, no. 1801.

[4] See CCC, no. 213.

[5] JR, nos. 31, 235, 361.

[6] Taylor, Charles, The First 100 Words (Evansville, IN: Jubilee Resources, 1996), pp. 3, 80.

[7] Ibid., p. 4.

[8] DZ, no. 1783.

[9] DZ, no. 1784.

[10] See DZ, nos. 494, 570q, 706, 783, 1707, 1787, 1951, 1952, 2009, 2010, 2011, 2012, 2102, 2179, 2180, 2186, 3015; DV, no. 11.

[11] DZ, nos. 1997–2000.

[12] DZ, no. 2113.

[13] Steinmueller, John, The Sword of the Spirit: Which is the Word of God (Fort Worth, TX: Stella Maris Books, 1977), p. 7.

[14] See ACC excerpts on Gn 2:4–6, pp. 48–49 and Gn 7:1–3, pp. 134–135.

[15] See, for example, JR, nos. 123, 127, 190, 342, 495, 681, 748, 764a, 767, 819, 864, 882, 937, 993, 1093, 1176, 1262, 1397, 1419, 1493, 1508, 2135, 2161.

[16] See, for example, JR, no. 361.

[17] See Radday, Yehuda T. and Shore, Haim, Genesis: An Authorship Study in Computer-Assisted Statistical Linguistics (Rome: Biblical Institute Press, 1985), p. 8.

[18] See: The Pontifical Biblical Commission, The Interpretation of the Bible in the Church (Boston: St. Paul's Books and Media, 1993), pp. 35–36. Note that this is not a magisterial document. It has no teaching authority, but it does provide some useful historical information. The credibility of any opinion expressed in the document may be judged solely on its merit.

[19] Pope John Paul II, The Theology of the Body: Human Love in the Divine Plan (Boston: Pauline Books and Media, 1997), pp. 27–28 (General audience of September 12, 1979).

[20] Ibid., p. 58 (General audience of January 2, 1980).

[21] John Paul II, The Teachings of John Paul II on CD-ROM (Salem, OR: Harmony Media, Inc., 1998). Searches for the words Elohist and Yahwist were made.

[22] Ibid. Searches for Deuteronomist and Priestly Code were made.

[23] John Paul II, Pope, op. cit., p. 28 (General audience of September 12, 1979).

[24] Wells, David, *Revolution in Rome* (Downers grove, IL: InterVarsity Press, 1972), p. 8.

[25] Pettinato, Giovanni, *Biblical Archaeologist*, May 1976.

[26] Archer, Gleason L., *Encyclopedia of Bible Difficulties* (Grand Rapids, MI: Zondervan Publishing House), pp. 51–53.

[27] Jos 8:30–32 (NAB).

[28] 1 Kgs 2:3; 2 Kgs 14:6; 21:8; Ezr 6:18; Neh 13:1; Dn 9:11–13; Mal 3:22.

[29] NAB, "The Pentateuch," p. xiii.

[30] Archer, op. cit., pp. 46–51.

[31] *Newsweek*, September 28, 1981, p. 59.

[32] Steinmueller, John E., *A Companion to Scripture Studies: Volume II. Special Introduction to the Old Testament*, Revised edition (New York: Joseph F. Wagner, Inc., 1969), p. 23.

[33] DZ, no. 2121.

[34] DZ, no. 2122.

[35] Ibid.

[36] DZ, no. 2123.

[37] DZ, no. 2126.

[38] *Humani generis*, no. 38 (DZ, no. 2329).

[39] Ibid.

[40] DZ, no. 2125 (alternative translation).

[41] *Humani generis*, no. 38 (DZ, no. 2329).

[42] DZ, no. 2127.

Doctrine Two
God created the world from nothing.

That God created the world from nothing is a *de fide credenda* doctrine. It was formally confirmed by Lateran Council IV in 1215 and again by Vatican Council I in 1870. The Fourth Lateran Council also affirmed that God *alone* created the world. Although Genesis does not give an account of the creation of the angels, Sacred Scripture implies and Sacred Tradition holds that they were created *"in the beginning."* Lateran Council IV and Vatican Council I formally declared that the angels were created from nothing at the beginning of time. In 1329 Pope John XXII condemned the notion that God created an eternal world. Pope Pius XII clearly stated that natural science is unable to give assured answers concerning the origin of the world.

The Cosmogony of Genesis

The first verse of Genesis states: *"In the beginning God created the heavens and the earth."* The Hebrew verb translated "created" is *bara,* which is used in Scripture exclusively for divine activity. It "always has God for its subject."[1] It is never associated with matter out of which God produces something. In Genesis 1:1 and elsewhere in the Hebrew Scriptures[2] it expresses creation out of nothing (creation *ex nihilo*).

"In the beginning" means that creation marks the start of time and the course of history. The history of the world began at the beginning of Creation Week; and the history of man began at the end of Creation Week, when God created man and gave him dominion over the world. Since Genesis is a historical document that tells what happened at the very beginning of time, there is no such thing as "prehistory."

Derek Kidner makes the observation: "[T]he beginning is pregnant with the end."[3] All of history is present to God, who says *"I am the first and I am the last,"*[4] *"declaring the end from the beginning."*[5] And the Book of Revelation tells of that end: *"Then I saw a new heaven and a new earth; for the first heaven and the first earth had passed away, and the sea was no more."*[6]

"The heavens and the earth" means that at the beginning of time God gave existence to everything outside of Himself, both the corporeal and incorporeal worlds. The creation of the angels during Creation Week is not mentioned in Genesis but is implied in Exodus 20:11: *"[F]or in six days the Lord made heaven and earth, the sea, and all that is in them."*

The Jewish people firmly believed that God created the world from nothing. Probably the greatest story of faith and courage in Sacred Scripture is about the faith-filled and brave Jewish mother who encouraged her seven sons to endure torture and martyrdom at the hands of the cruel tyrant Antiochus rather than violate the law of Moses. She herself was martyred last, after having seen all her sons executed, from the oldest first to the youngest last. She encouraged her youngest son saying: *"I beseech you, my child, to look at the heaven and the earth and see everything that is in them, and recognize that God did not make them out of things that existed."*[7]

The Fathers gave long, detailed homilies on the six days of Creation. They are called *hexaemera* from Greek for "six days." The foremost are those of St. Basil the Great and St. Ambrose. St. Ephrem, St. Augustine and St. John Chrysostom also preached and wrote extensively on the Book of Genesis.[8] The Fathers regarded the creation of the world out of nothing as a basic truth of the Catholic faith. They defended it against the pagan doctrine of dualism and against Manichaeism. Dualism asserted that there are two eternal and independent realities, spirit and matter. The Manicheans held that there are two sources of creation, the one good and the other evil. St. Basil in his *Hexaemeron* says that the Manicheans assert that "the form of the world is due to the wisdom of the supreme Artificer; matter came to the Creator from without; and thus the world results from a double origin. It has received from outside its matter and essence and from God its form and figure. They thus come to deny that the mighty God has presided at the formation of the universe and pretend that He has only brought a crowning contribution to a common work, that He has only contributed some small portion to the genesis of beings."[9] Basil opposes them saying that God created both the matter and the form of the heavens and earth.[10] Nemesius of Emesa is more explicit. He says that God "brought all things into being from nothing."[11] William Jurgens cites forty-one passages from his collection where the Fathers affirm that God created all things out of nothing.[12]

*   *   *   *

Scholastic philosophy distinguishes *creatio prima* from *creatio secunda*. The first term refers to creation in the strict sense, namely, creation ex nihilo. St. Thomas Aquinas defined creation in the strict sense as follows: "Creation is the production of a thing in its entire substance, nothing being presupposed either uncreated or created."[13] The creation of the world from nothing is implied in the very name of God, YHWH, I AM WHO AM. This name implies that God's very nature is to exist. It carries with it the connotation of necessary self-existence. All things outside of God are contingent; they need not exist. They are not necessary, and so their existence must be attributed to God. Jews and Christians have always been certain that the creation of the world out of nothing is directly expressed in the first line of Genesis: *"In the beginning, God created the heavens and the earth."* The words *"in the beginning"* have always been taken to mean the absolute beginning, when things other than God began to exist alongside Him.[14]

The second term above refers to creation as the act of giving form to formless matter. This is what God did when He formed the earth. Genesis 1:2 says, *"The earth was formless and empty."*[15] The stage of creation when God gave form to matter is recalled in the Book of Wisdom; *"For thy all-powerful hand, which created the world out of formless matter...."*[16] God created in steps. He could have created the earth and everything in it fully formed instantly, but for His own purpose, He chose not to do it that way. St. Ambrose in his *Hexaemeron* gives a didactical reason: "The good architect lays the foundation first and afterward, when the foundation has been laid, plots the various parts of the building, one after another, and then adds the ornamentation.... Scripture points out that things were first created and afterward put in order lest it be supposed that they were not actually created and that they had no beginning, just as if the nature of things had been, as it were, generated from the beginning and did not appear to be something added afterward."[17] E. Gilson summarizes St. Bonaventure's teaching on this as follows: "[T]he matter of all bodies was created on the first day, although the complete distinction of bodies by means of their forms took place afterwards and by degrees, as Scripture affirms and as tradition teaches."[18]

Verse (1:2) mentions only that the *earth* was *"formless and empty."* It does not mention the heavens. This is significant because it means that at this point the only material entity created was the earth. It goes on to say, in light of the verses that follow, that the earth was covered with water to a great depth. *"Darkness was upon the face of the deep"* because light had not yet been created, and so the earth was *"invisible."* ᵃ The earth was *"empty"* because it was not yet filled with the grand variety of magnificent creatures that God had in His plans for it. St. Thomas Aquinas interprets the words *"and the Spirit of God moved over the face of the waters"* as follows: "[B]y the words *'Spirit of God'* Scripture usually means the Holy Ghost, Who is said to *'move over the waters,'* not, indeed, in bodily shape, but as the craftsman's will may be said to move over the material to which he intends to give a form."[19] The creative work of the Holy Spirit is recalled in Psalms 104:30: *"When thou sendeth forth thy Spirit, they are created; and thou renewest the face of the ground."*

✻   ✻   ✻   ✻

Scholastic philosophy uses the terms *matter* and *form* in two ways, corresponding to two kinds of existence—substantial existence and accidental existence.[20] First, a substance, which exists in the absolute sense, is composed of prime matter and substantial form. Prime matter is the principle of permanence; it perseveres through any change. Substantial form is what gives a substance its nature and makes it what it is. It changes when a substance changes into another substance. Prime matter is pure *potency* to substantial existence. It might be contrasted to God, who is pure *actuality*. Prime matter and substantial form exist separately only in the mind. They cannot exist separately in reality. So the formless matter of Genesis 1 was not prime matter.[21] ᵇ

Second, an object like a statue, as a statue, is said to have an accidental existence because it is composed of preexistent material and an accidental form that inheres in the material. The matter of a statue may be marble and its accidental form the shape of Mary holding the Body of her dead Son in her arms. The matter exists in itself. An unshaped piece of marble is potentially a pieta. The sculptor gives it the form and actualizes the pieta. The formless matter of the primordial earth was matter with substantial and accidental forms. It is called *formless* because it had not yet received its final forms. God, by His acts of *creatio secunda*, transformed not only its accidental forms but its substantial forms as well. God's transformation of forms in *creatio secunda* might be compared with Jesus' changing water into wine at Cana. In that miracle Jesus instantly changed both a substance and its accidents.

---

a.   The Septuagint says that the earth was *"invisible and shapeless."*

b.   Another view of formless matter compares it to a shadow in that it has a borrowed reality. Formless matter is a shadow of what it is to become.

The Church has repeatedly professed in her creeds, conciliar decrees and papal documents that God created (or made) all things. In most of her proclamations *ex nihilo* is not stated, but it is implied.[22] In 1215 the Fourth Lateran Council made the first explicit statement, saying that God created "out of nothing."[23] Lateran IV was responding to the Cathars, who claimed that a good deity created the world of the spirit, and an evil god was the author of the material world. The First Vatican Council in opposing the errors of the nineteenth century again explicitly affirmed that God created the world ex nihilo, emphasizing with an anathema that He created it in its totality.[24]

*   *   *   *

God alone created the world. The Fathers attested to this.[25] The Fourth Lateran Council stated that the Triune God is the "one beginning of all," "a Single Principle of all things."[26] No creature of its own power can create something out of nothing because that is an act of infinite power, which is possessed by God alone.[27] Also, St. Thomas and others hold that creatures cannot cooperate even as an instrumental cause in the production of a thing out of nothing because no finite thing can produce something from nothing as its *proper effect*. (You can't cut wood with a hammer because cutting wood is not the proper effect of a hammer.)[28] This applies only to acts of *creatio prima*. God might have employed secondary causes in His acts of *creatio secunda* because these did not involve production from nothing. He could have used causes He created earlier in Creation Week to form things He made later in the week.

An instrument must be directed by a *principal agent*, which is an intelligent cause with a purpose and a plan. Although cutting wood is the proper effect of a saw, the production of a bench from wood is the proper effect of a principal agent.[29]

The creation of life in matter was, like the creation of matter itself, an act of *creatio prima*. "*To all of them you give life.*"[30] Therefore the first living organisms were created directly by God without the use of instrumental causes.

*   *   *   *

Genesis says nothing explicit about the creation of the angels. St. Thomas Aquinas[31] points out that there is a twofold opinion to be found in the writings of the Fathers about when the angels were created. St. Gregory Nazianzen,[32] St. Athanasius,[33] and St. Ambrose[34] held that the angels were created before the corporeal world. Others, like St. Augustine[35] and St. Epiphanius of Salamis,[36] held that they were created at the same time as the corporeal world. St. Thomas believed that the latter opinion was more probable. He said that *"in the beginning God created the heavens and the earth"* would not be true if anything had been created previously. If the angels were created separately they would constitute a separate universe, but both they and the corporeal world constitute one universe because of the creature-to-creature relationship between angels and the things of the corporeal world. Lateran Council IV declared that the angels were created from nothing at the beginning of time. It states that God "from the beginning of time made at once (*simul*) out of nothing both orders of creatures, that is, the angelic and the earthly...."[37] Vatican Council I reinforced this teaching by quoting the Lateran IV declaration.[38]

✳   ✳   ✳   ✳

The act of creation added nothing to God and subtracted nothing from Him. He continuously holds the world in existence. St. Bonaventure said that God's continuous creative presence in creatures is like a seal leaving its imprint on running water for as long as it is impressed on it.[39]

The Church has condemned the idea that things have "arisen" or "emanated" from the substance of God[40] and the idea that the world was made by a being or beings other than God.[41]

The Cosmography of Genesis

Some Scripture scholars presume that the Hebrews had no cosmography of their own but borrowed from the cosmographies of their neighbors. This notion is not consistent with the fact that the Hebrews possessed primeval revelation that was handed down from Adam through the patriarchs. Moses, under divine inspiration, corrected any errors that may have entered it, so that Genesis gives an accurate cosmography of the universe at its creation.

There is no special word in Hebrew for what we call the *world* or the *universe* or what the Greeks called *cosmos.* Instead, Genesis uses more concrete terms like *heaven, earth, waters, land* and *sea.* The Hebrew word *shamayim*[c], translated "the heavens," can also be translated "heaven." But it does not mean God's special abode except in a metaphorical sense, as St. Thomas Aquinas points out.[42] Rather, it seems that it corresponds to our word "space," the abode of the heavenly bodies. It is sometimes translated "sky." In (1:8) God names the *rakia* that

He called into being *shamayim*. The Hebrew word *rakia* is traditionally translated "firmament,"[43] "dome,"[44] or "vault."[45] This is unfortunate because it misleads modern readers. It gives the impression that the Hebrews believed that the Earth was surrounded by a solid dome. The Hebrew word emphasizes strength and fixity, but it does not imply solidity. The most accurate translation is probably "expanse."[46] The idea of a solid dome surrounding the earth probably comes from exegetes interpreting the beliefs of the Hebrews in terms of the beliefs of the Greeks, who received a corrupted form of primeval revelation. More than one expanse is not excluded by the text. There may be one expanse below the separated waters and another above, the one above being the *"heavens"* mentioned in the first verse.

Genesis locates water in three places in the universe—above the expanse (1:7; 7:11), on the earth (1:7, 9), and under the earth (7:11). Both the waters above the expanse and under the earth contributed to the Great Flood (7:11). The waters above the expanse cannot be reckoned as clouds and vapor such as we have in our atmosphere. Clouds and vapor can hardly account for the huge mass of water that was separated from the deep. The text does not say what configuration the waters above the expanse took; it remains a mystery. We look to natural science to provide plausible models to explain it.[47] It is clear, however, that because of those waters the conditions on earth were quite different in the early world from what they are today. For example, it seems that there was no rain before the Great Flood (2:5). During the Great Flood, those waters rejoined the subterranean waters and completely reshaped the face of the earth and totally altered its climate. St. Peter affirms the cosmography of the antediluvian world and its destruction by water as related by the Book of Genesis. He says: *"[O]f old there were heavens and an earth drawn out of the waters and standing between the waters, all brought into being by the word of God. By water that world was then destroyed; it was overwhelmed by the deluge."*[48]

---

c. *Shamayim* is a general term for heaven. The Bible has seven other designations for heaven: *vilon, rakia, sheckakim, zebul, maon, machon,* and *araboth,* which the Jewish sages saw as seven strata of heaven, or as seven heavens. The seventh heaven, *araboth,* is the abode of God. St. Paul refers to being snatched up to the third heaven (see 2 Cor 12:2). There are also seven different words in the Bible for earth, which the rabbis pictured as seven strata. For the rabbinic distinctions of the seven heavens see Abraham Cohen, *Everyman's Talmud: The Major Teachings of the Rabbinic Sages* (New York: Schocken Books, 1975 reprint of 1949 edition), pp. 32–33, 40.

*   *   *   *

There is no evidence to support the idea that the biblical Hebrews had a mythical cosmography. One author depicts the Israelites as believing that the world "resembled … a saucer surrounded by water and resting on water, or better, resting upon pillars sunk in the waters of the deep."[49] [d] He cites a number of verses purporting to show that that view is expressed in Scripture,[50] but he reads into the verses what they do not say. He also interprets metaphorical language literally. For example, the verses speak of water under the earth and of foundations of the earth; but they do not say that the earth is shaped like a saucer, nor do they say that it sits on water or on pillars sunk into the deep. The saucer and the pillars are embellishments. He goes on to say, "Above the earth and its surrounding sea is the vault of the firmament which rests upon pillars, in this case upon the mountains at the rim of the earth. In Job the firmament is said to be hard as a molten mirror, but other inspired poets compare it to a fine cloth or tent covering."[51] Again he cites a number of verses to support this supposed Hebrew picture of the universe. Again he reads into them what is not there and misinterprets metaphorical language. Job 26:11 is cited to show that the Hebrews believed that the firmament rested on pillars. That verse is from a passage that uses highly figurative language to portray the power of God. The verse declares: *"The pillars of heaven tremble and are astounded at his rebuke."* Obviously, it was not intended by the sacred author to be taken literally. How can pillars be *"astounded"*? Furthermore, nothing is mentioned about the pillars being mountains at the rim of the earth. Again, that's an embellishment. Besides, in Job 26:7, just a few verses earlier, it is written: *"He stretches out the north over the void, and hangs the earth upon nothing."* That doesn't sound like the earth resting on pillars! Next, Job 37:18, which is cited to show that the Hebrews believed the firmament is hard, is taken from a highly rhetorical passage that portrays the power of God. Elihu asks Job: *"Can you, like him, spread out the skies, hard as a molten mirror?"* That hardly supports the idea that the Hebrews believed that the sky was hard. The hard mirror simile probably refers to the stability and reflective power of the sky. The "fine cloth or tent covering" is taken from similes in Psalms 104:2 and Isaiah 40:22 that are intended to convey the greatness of God and not the nature of the world.

---

d.   Later rabbinic scholars held this view, probably through pagan influence. But there is no evidence that their ancestors held it. See Cohen, op. cit., pp. 32–33, 40.

After going on like this, the author concludes: "And every attempt by 'concordists' to harmonize the details of scientific data with the Bible has resulted in lowering esteem for the inspired Word."[52] It seems that exegesis of the kind that the author displays is what really lowers esteem for the inspired Word.

The Creation of Time

Time was created with matter. The principal characteristic of the material world is that it is ever changing. And time and change are inextricably united. Aristotle said: "Not only do we measure the movement [change] by the time, but also the time by the movement, because they define each other."[53] St. Augustine makes the point, "[T]he world was not created *in* time but *with* time."[54] It is meaningless to talk about the time before the beginning of the world.[e] The phrase "before the beginning of the world" refers to eternity and not to a time. This is what Jesus meant when he prayed, *"[A]nd now, Father, glorify thou me in thy own presence with the glory which I had with thee before the world was made."*[55] St. Augustine refuted the idea that time existed before the creation of the world because it makes God live in time and the creation of the world look like a thought that suddenly occurred to Him, thus making Him changeable and not eternal. He said: "[I]t is idle for men to imagine previous ages of God's inactivity, since there is no time before the world began."[56] St. Thomas Aquinas concurs with Augustine saying: "Things are said to be created in the beginning of time, not as if the beginning of time were a measure of creation, but because together with time heaven and earth were created."[57] Lateran Council IV and Vatican Council I both decreed that God *"from the beginning of time* created each creature from nothing...."[58]

Creation Ex Nihilo versus Emanation

In the theory of evolution, in its purely materialistic form, the distinction of creatures is an upward movement from undifferentiated matter/energy towards more organized forms, an ascent to greater perfection. The process is driven by natural causes alone, and the spiritual is just an epiphenomenon of highly organized matter. Contrasting with evolutionism is emanationism. In emanationism, the dis-

---

e. St. Thomas Aquinas also held that space was created in the beginning. He stated: "Whereas we hold that there was no place or space before the world was" (ST, Part I, Q. 46, A. 1, Reply Obj. 4).

tinction of creatures is a downward movement, from the infinitely perfect to the less perfect. It is a descent from God to spiritual beings to material beings.[59]

Emanation is an alleged cosmogonic process proposed as an explanation for the origin of things. It holds that all things proceed from the same divine substance, either immediately or mediately. Although the divine substance loses nothing of its perfection, it does give of its substance. An analogy is an infinite reservoir pouring water into a river. The reservoir shares its substance (water) without losing its perfection of being an infinite reservoir. Also, the process of emanation employs intermediates. Using the above analogy, the river would produce other things by the inherited powers of its water.

Emanationism was widely professed by non-Christian philosophers and theologians in the Middle Ages. It emerged in their grappling with the problem of the One and the Many; and was held in one form or another, clearly or vaguely, by Indian metaphysicians, Jewish Cabalists, and Gnostics. Muslim philosophers such as Avicenna professed it, calling it *fayd*. The most notable advocate of emanationism was the Alexandrian Neoplatonist Plotinus (A.D. 204–270). In his collected works, the *Enneads*, he unites the metaphysical thought of Plato with Eastern mysticism. He taught that the highest reality is God, from whom things descended by various stages or emanations to the human soul and the world of phenomena.

There are pantheistic and nonpantheistic versions of emanationism. Its pantheistic versions assert the substantial identity of all things. In its nonpantheistic version, emanated things are seen as substantially distinct from their source and from each other.

Emanationism conflicts with Catholic doctrine in three ways. First, it holds that God did not produce things ex nihilo but from His own substance. Vatican Council I, in addition to affirming Lateran Council IV teaching that God created from nothing, anathematized those who "say that finite things, both corporeal and spiritual, or at least spiritual, have emanated from the divine substance."[60]

Second, emanationism holds that the emanation of things from God's substance is a necessary process because it proceeds from God's nature. God did not produce the world voluntarily but automatically. Thus emanationism denies that God created freely, a doctrine held in Catholic Tradition and formally defined by the First Vatican Council.[61]

Third, the theory uses intermediate causes in the emanation of creatures, thus denying immediate creation of creatures by God. It was pointed out earlier that God alone created the world and that no creature is able to participate in God's work of creating ex nihilo.[62] It is shown elsewhere in this work that God creating immediately also means that God created things at once, that is, instantly.[63]

Even though the Fathers of the Church and other early Christian writers may have borrowed the terminology of emanationism in their explorations of the Christian mysteries, their creation and Trinitarian theologies did not embrace it. Christian Trinitarian doctrine, which holds that the Three Persons are one substance, clearly distances itself from emanationism.

There is a Christian sense in which the word *emanation* is used. It means to come directly from God as a source without implying that He gives of His own substance. In fact, it is a biblical word. Solomon spoke of Wisdom as emanating from God: *"For she is a breath of the power of God, and a pure emanation of the glory of the Almighty."*[64] St. Albert the Great used it in a Christian sense.[65] His student, St. Thomas Aquinas, used the word *emanation* in a broad sense to include *creation*:

> [W]e must consider not only the emanation of a particular being from a particular agent, but also the emanation of all being from the universal cause, which is God; and this emanation we designate by the name of creation. [66]

A noteworthy name in the history of emanationism is Philo of Alexandria (15 B.C.–A.D. 50). Philo was a Jewish philosopher who tried to reconcile Sacred Scripture with Platonistic philosophy. In his *On the Creation* and *Allegorical Interpretation* he sets forth his cosmogony as a blend of Genesis and Plato's *Timaeus*. Philo held that God does not act on the world immediately. Rather, God, who is spiritual and perfect, acts on the material and imperfect world only through powers that proceed from Him but are not identical with Him. These "emanations" are sometimes conceived as angels. Philo is especially important because of his influence on the thinking of early Christian writers.

Summary of Catholic Tradition on Creation

St. Bonaventure neatly summarizes Catholic Tradition on the creation of the world, pointing out that a vestige of the Creator is found in all creatures:

> We must in general understand the following statements about the production of things, for by them truth is found and error refuted. When we say the world was made in time, we exclude the error of those who posit an eternal world. When we say that the world was made out of nothing, we exclude the error of positing an eternity with regard to the material principle. When we

say the world was made by a single principle, we exclude the error of the Manichaeans who posit a plurality of principles. When we say that the world was made by one unaided and supreme, we exclude the error of positing that God has created lesser creatures through the ministration of intelligences. When we say that the world was made *"in measure and number and weight,"* [Wisdom 11:20] we make it clear that the creature is the result of the Trinity creating in a triple role of causality: in the role of efficient cause from which the creature derives unity, moderation, and measure, in the role of exemplary cause from which the creature derives truth, form and number, and the role of final cause from which the creature derives goodness, order, and weight. All these things are found as a vestige of the Creator in all creatures, either corporeal or spiritual or those composed of both qualities. [67]

< Objections > and << Replies >>

< Objection 1 >

Matter and the world need not have had a beginning. They could have always existed.

<< Reply to Objection 1 >>

There are a number of views consistent with this objection. First, there are those who believe that the world exists eternally, either alongside God but independent of Him or with no God. In either version no need is seen for a Creator. Proponents of the former version are found in ancient paganism, and proponents of the latter version are found in modern atheism. Second, there were those, like Aristotle, who saw the world as eternally coexisting with God and somehow dependent on Him. Some imagined that the world exists spontaneously as the shadow of God's power. God, they said, is an involuntary cause of the world. The Fathers of the Church refuted such beliefs.[68] Third, others said that God created an eternal world, that is, the world was created without a beginning. Proponents of this idea are found among some theists, including Catholics. Pope John XXII condemned Meister Eckhart's ideas on creation, which were along those lines.[69] Origen proposed the idea of a series of worlds without a beginning, the first of which was created by God from all eternity.[70] Fourth, some, like Plato, saw God as fashioning the world out of coexisting components. Fifth, some see the world as being fashioned by blind chance working on preexistent matter. Such is the view proposed by the Greek atomists and popularized by the Latin poet Lucretius. It is the view of modern "big bang" advocates, who have clothed it in contemporary scientific idiom.

<< The Temporality of the World >>

The Fathers taught that the material world could not exist eternally alongside God because that would make it equal to God in some way. For example, Tatian the Syrian said: "Matter is not without a beginning, like God; nor is it of equal power with God, through being without a beginning."[71] Tertullian said: "Matter, however, will be made equal to God, if it be reckoned as eternal."[72] And St. Ambrose wrote: "But if such matter [eternal matter] were disordered, how remarkable it is that matter coeternal with God would not have been able to confer beauty and order upon itself, seeing that it did not receive its substance from a Creator but possessed it timelessly itself."[73] William Jurgens cites fifteen more passages in which the Fathers deny the coeternity of the material world.[74]

St. Bonaventure held the opinion that the notion of an eternally created world involves an intrinsic contradiction. For creation out of nothing means to have being in succession to nonbeing, that is, first not to be and then to be.[75] On this point St. Bonaventure was diametrically opposed to St. Thomas Aquinas, who considered an eternal universe logically possible.

St. Thomas argued that the world does not exist of necessity because it is the result of a free act of God. Therefore the eternity of the world is not susceptible to philosophical demonstration, which applies to necessary truths.[76] He also said that the world having a beginning is an object of faith alone. It can only be known from divine revelation. It cannot be demonstrated on the part of the world itself that the things of the world did not always exist, because what we know about them is abstracted here and now. Therefore, the newness of the world is not an object of natural science. It is not an object of philosophical demonstration for the same reason that the eternity of the world is not.[77] Thomas makes explicit that which St. Basil implied when he wrote in his *Hexaemeron:* "[W]e propose to study the world as a whole, and to consider the universe, not by the light of worldly wisdom, but by that with which God wills to enlighten His servant, when He speaks to him in person and without enigmas."[78]

St. Thomas' argument still holds despite modern advancements in science. Scientific investigation deals with the here and now, so the question of origins is beyond the competence of natural science. Any assertions made by scientists about the origins of the universe, life and the human race are speculations based on unprovable assumptions, some obvious, some subtle. No statement made in the name of natural science about origins can be called a fact of science. Pope Pius XII clearly recognized this. He said:

> It is quite true that the facts established up to the present time are not an absolute proof of creation in time, as are the proofs drawn from metaphysics and Revelation in what concerns simple creation or those founded on Revelation if there be a question of creation in time. The pertinent facts of the natural sciences, to which We have referred, are awaiting still further research and confirmation, and the theories founded on them are in need of further development and proof before they can provide a sure foundation for **arguments which, of themselves, are outside the proper sphere of the natural sciences.**[79]

It is clear from this passage that Pius XII saw that natural science is able to give evidence in support of the doctrine of creation, but its methods are incapable of giving certain answers concerning the origins of things in the material world.

The question of creation *in time* must be distinguished from the question of creation *per se*. That the world was created *in time* can be demonstrated neither by philosophy, which deals with the necessary, nor by natural science, which deals with the contingent. But that the world was created *per se* can be demonstrated by philosophy because it is an ontological question rather than a temporal one. In the passage above, Pius XII was careful to make this distinction. He refers to proofs drawn from metaphysics and divine revelation when referring to "simple creation" and to divine revelation alone when referring to "creation in time." "Simple creation" is not only a truth of revelation but also a truth of reason. St. Thomas demonstrated that "every being in any way existing is from God."[80] The proof inheres in the contingency proof for the existence of God. The gist of his argument is that everything in the material world is dependent or contingent, that is, it need not exist. There is no necessity for anything to come into existence or to continue in existence. Existence is not connatural to the things of the world. Since they don't give existence to themselves, they must receive it from another Being, a Being whose existence is necessary, a Being whose very nature is to exist. That Being is God.

The creation of the world was such a unique and stupendous event that even *miracle* isn't a proper word for it. The word *miracle* implies a violation or suspension of the laws of nature. In the act of creation God created the laws of nature. Creation was the event that gave birth to history. For certainty concerning it we need the clear testimony of an unimpeachable witness. We have such testimony in the Book of Genesis because it is the word of the Creator Himself.

<< Eternal Matter and Eternal World Cosmologies >>

No cosmogony other than that of Genesis, whether of ancient paganism or modern materialism, mentions the absolute origin of the universe. All begin with a world already existing or one that is fashioned from or evolves from preexistent matter. An examination, in the light of the Genesis account, of some cosmologies of historical and heuristic significance follows. They show, among other things, how far from reality cosmology can drift without a tether to Genesis.

<< Babylonian Cosmogony >>

According to the Babylonian myth *Enuma Elish* two principles existed in the beginning, Apsu, the personification of sweet water and Tiamat, the personification of salt water. The former was male, and the latter was female. Apsu and Tiamat begat the gods. When the gods sought to put order into universal chaos, Apsu and Tiamat objected. The conflict resulted in the murder of Apsu, which precipitated a war among the gods. Tiamat and her consort, Kingu, were the leaders on one side, and Marduk led the other. Marduk emerged victorious and became king of the gods. He then formed and ordered each part of the physical universe from the body of the defeated goddess and made humans to serve the gods. The gods built a palace for Marduk in Babylon, where he declared his work done by hanging his weapons—storm, lightning, thunder and wind—in the sky. The gods then gave him power over all things.

The story is fantastic, but it does contain traces of primeval revelation, which became more and more corrupted among the nations as sin increased in the world. The separation of the waters in the Genesis account has its counterpart in the sweet-water and salt-water principles of the Babylonian legend. Tiamot's name echoes the Hebrew word *tehom*, which appears in (1:2); it is translated "the deep" and refers to the waters covering the earth. The Babylonian word *tiamot* and the Hebrew word *tehom* can be traced to the same Semitic root.[81] In *Enuma Elish,* the gods wanted to put things in chaos into order. In Genesis God shapes and fills the formless and empty earth. The first gods begotten by Apsu and Tiamat were Lachmu and Lachamu. Their names mean "Light" and "Mother of Light." The "Mother of Light" is the darkness from which light is born. According to Genesis, God created light on the first day and separated the light from the darkness calling them *"Day"* and *"Night."* Marduk is said to have made humans from clay, as in the Genesis account; but instead of having life *"breathed"* into it, the clay is given life by the blood of Kingu. Marduk declares his work done. In

(2:1) it says that God finished His work. So in both accounts the creation (or making) of the world is not an ongoing process. It had an end.

There are also significant differences in the two accounts. In the Babylonian story primal matter existed at the beginning. It is that from which the gods arose. There is no creation ex nihilo. There is no Creator God. This is true for all Babylonian religious and cosmogonic literature.[82] God made man in His own image and likeness, and He gave man dominion over creation. Marduk made men to be servants of the gods, and he reserved dominion over the world to himself. In *Enuma Elish* the focus is on extolling the prowess of Babylon's municipal god, Marduk, while in Genesis it is on showing the glory of YHWH in His works.

<< The Cosmogony of Plato >>

Plato gives his account of the origin of the universe in his dialogue *Timaeus*. In the dialogue, Plato speaks through the mouth of Timaeus, an eminent astronomer who has made the universe his special study. Timaeus gives a detailed discourse on the generation of the world and of men, the gist of which follows: The Creator (God, Demiurge, Artificer) fashions the universe. He himself is incomprehensible. "[T]he father and maker of all this universe is past finding out, and even if we found him, to tell of him to all men would be impossible."[83] The Creator is good and perfect, and He desired to make all things be as like himself as they could. He finds chaos, and out of irregularity and disorder he brings order. He fashions a universe that is a living being with a body and soul. In the beginning, he makes the universe to consist of fire and earth, so that it may be corporeal. Then he made air and water such that "as fire is to air so is air to water, and as air is to water, so is water to earth"[84] so that everything is "harmonized by proportion."[85] [f] Timaeus said that the Creator made only one universe. "For that which includes all other intelligible creatures cannot have a second or companion; in that case there would be need of another living being which would include both."[86]

The Creator made the world in the form of a sphere, the form most like the Creator because it is the most perfect of figures. He made the surface of the globe smooth. Though living it had no need of eyes or ears because there was nothing

---

f.   Here Plato shows the influence of his predecessor Pythagoras. For Pythagoras the universe was a material imitation of the world of numbers. He explained similarities and differences in the material world in terms of proportions of components.

outside it to see or hear. It had no other organs because there was no air outside it to breathe or food to eat and digest. Its own waste provides its food. The Creator made it self-sufficient. It had no need to take anything or to defend itself, so the Creator did not give it hands. The Creator gave it movement most suited to its spherical form, that is, to revolve in a circle. Since this motion requires no legs or feet, the universe was created without them. At the center of the sphere God placed the soul, which he had made prior to the body to be the ruler of it; and he diffused the soul throughout the body, making it also to be its exterior environment. He made the universe "one and solitary, yet by reason of its excellence able to converse with itself, and needing no other friendship or acquaintance. Having these purposes in view he created the world a blessed god."[87]

The generation of all things from the elements—fire, air, water and earth—takes place in space, which Timaeus refers to as the "mother and receptacle"[88] of all sensible things. This receptacle "while receiving all things, never departs at all from her own nature, and never in any way, or at any time, assumes a form like that of the things which enter into her.... But the forms which enter into and go out of her are the likenesses of eternal realities modeled after their patterns in a wonderful and mysterious manner."[89] Space is something *in which* but not *from which* generation takes place. It is that in which all things appear, grow up and decay. It is eternal and indestructible. Space is a plenum. It is completely full; nowhere is it empty. Timaeaus says: "In the revolution of the universe are comprehended all the four elements, and this being circular and having a tendency to come together, compresses everything and will not allow any place to be left void."[90]

In the chaos that existed before the arrangement of the universe, the elements of fire, air, water and earth each had their distinct places in space, but "they were all without reason and measure."[91] [g] "God now fashioned them by form and number."[92] He "made them as far as possible the fairest and the best, out of things which were not fair and good."[93]

Each of the four elements was composed of invisibly tiny atoms of various sizes. The atoms had the shapes of regular solids. Fire had the shape of the tetrahedron (pyramid) because it was pointed and penetrating. Earth had the shape of a cube because of its stability. Water and air were assigned the shapes of the icosahedron and the octahedron respectively. The fifth regular solid, the dodecahe-

---

g. Here Plato shows the influence of his predecessor Empedocles. Empedocles introduced the four elements: fire, air, earth and water. He taught that the four elements combined and separated under the forces of love and hate.

dron, was the form associated with quintessence, the fifth element of which celestial bodies were composed. God used the dodecahedron "in the delineation of the universe with figures of animals [constellations]."[94] The rationale for the construction of the atoms is that every body possesses volume, and every volume must necessarily be bounded by surfaces. The surfaces of the atoms are rectilinear figures and so can be reduced to triangles. Ultimately the atoms are made from two kinds of right triangles of various sizes. Matter is thus reduced to mathematical forms! The elements can be transformed into one another by separation and recombination of the triangles. Fire, air and water can be transformed into each other because they are made of the same kind of triangles. Earth is stable because it is made from a different kind of triangle from the other three elements.

The Creator wanted to make the universe eternal, like himself, to the extent that it could be. So he created time as a "moving image of eternity." "Now the nature of the ideal being was everlasting, but to bestow this attribute in its fullness upon a creature was impossible. Wherefore he resolved to have a moving image of eternity, and when he set in order the heaven, he made this image eternal but moving according to number, while eternity itself rests in unity, and this image we call time."[95] He made the sun, the moon and the planets "in order to distinguish and preserve the numbers of time."[96]

Timaeus' anthropology is vague. It seems to go as follows: The Creator produced the gods. They were creatures and not altogether immortal and indissoluble, but the Creator promised to preserve them from death. The Creator instructed the gods to make three tribes of mortal beings saying, "without them the universe will be incomplete, for it will not contain every kind of animal which it ought to contain, if it is to be perfect. On the other hand, if they were created by me and received life at my hands, they would be on an equality with the gods."[97] However, God would create the immortal principle of each soul and hand it over to the gods who were to "interweave the immortal with the mortal and make and beget living creatures."[98] The superior race was called man. The gods fashioned man's mortal body around the immortal principle of the soul. They "made it to be the vehicle of the soul, and constructed within the body a soul of another nature which was mortal, subject to terrible and irresistible affections."[99] The immortal soul was set in man's head and the mortal soul was encased in his breast. The structure of man's body was fashioned with due regard for the functions of each part. It too was built of the mathematical triangles that constituted the four elements. The immortal soul was subject to reincarnation after death.

Plato considers his story of creation a "probable tale." He held that one could have knowledge about eternal things but not about changeable things. About changeable things one can only have "opinions" or "beliefs." For, "As being is to becoming, so is truth to belief."[100] So man cannot have knowledge about the material world; he can only speculate about it. Plato summarizes this skeptical outlook in the famous passage where Timaeus says: "A man may sometimes set aside meditations about eternal things, and for recreation turn to consider the truths of generation, which are probable only; he will thus gain a pleasure not to be repented of, and secure for himself, while he lives, a wise and moderate pastime."[101]

For centuries, *Timaeus* exerted a profound influence. It was of great interest to Christians because of its parallels to the Genesis account of creation. Plato's universe, like that of Genesis, has an origin in time. For Plato, the things that God created were good, just as in Genesis. The basic elements were fire, earth, air and water. These are the elements mentioned in Genesis 1, if one equates fire with light. In the Timaeus, God brings order out of chaos. In Genesis, God shapes and fills a formless and empty earth. And in Plato's account man was created capable of death but was preserved from it by God. This is what the Genesis account seems to imply.

There are important differences in the two accounts. For Plato, the stuff of the universe is eternal, not created. The Creator simply fashions it. Although Plato comes close to the concept of creation ex nihilo, he does not quite reach it. His Creator constructs the elements out of triangles. The triangles are pure mathematical entities, which are abstractions that exist in the mind only. So God constructs things out of mathematical ideas. But the Creator created from ideas that can only be abstracted from material bodies because geometrical figures have the property of extension in space, which has meaning only for material bodies. Geometric figures are accidents; that is, they have no existence of their own but must have a subject in which to inhere. Thus there is an ontological loop in Plato's account. The geometric forms that compose objects are abstracted from the objects they compose. St. Augustine perceived that God created from innate ideas. He said that God "did not contemplate something located outside Himself as a model by which he might fashion that which He fashioned."[102] It is by "participation" in divine ideas "that a thing is whatever it is in whatever way it is."[103] Another significant difference is that in Plato's account man is not made in the image and likeness of his Creator, whereas in the Genesis account he is.

St. Augustine was quite struck by the similarities in Plato's philosophy and the theology of the Old Testament. So much so, he wondered whether Plato had been exposed to the Hebrew Scriptures. It is well worth quoting a full passage that contains his opinion on the subject:

> But what impresses me most, and almost brings me to agree that Plato was not ignorant of the Sacred Writings, is the answer that was given to the question elicited from Moses when the angel conveyed the words of God to him. For, when he asked what was the name of Him who was commanding him to go and deliver the Hebrew people out of Egypt, this answer was given: *"I AM WHO AM"; and you will say to the children of Israel, HE WHO IS sent me to you."* (Exodus 3:14) This implies that compared with Him who really is, because He is unchangeable, those things which have been created mutable have no real existence. This truth Plato vigorously maintained and most diligently taught. And I do not know whether this sentiment is to be found anywhere in the works of Plato's predecessors, except in the book where it is said, *"I AM WHO AM; and you will say to the children of Israel, HE WHO IS sent me to you."*[104]

<< The Cosmography and Natural Theology of Aristotle >>

For Aristotle the universe is eternal; as it is now it always was. In his cosmology there is no creation in time and no story of origins. But there is a First Mover, who is the source of motion in the universe and who has things in common with the God of Genesis.

Aristotle sees order in the world. He said, "That which is produced or directed by nature can never be anything disorderly: for nature is everywhere the cause of order."[105] In his *On the Heavens* and *Metaphysics* he describes a universe that is highly ordered. It can be thought of as a system of uniformly rotating concentric spheres that accounts for the circular motions of the heavenly bodies. The earth is spherical in shape and at the center of the spheres. The region below the moon is a plenum, in which each of the four elements—fire, air, earth, water—has its proper place. Each of the elements has its proper motion, either up or down, that is directed towards its proper place. Above the lunar spheres are the spheres of the sun and planets. The outermost sphere is the sphere in which the fixed stars are set. It is called the heaven (or first heaven or outermost heaven).[h] There is no place or void or time outside the first heaven. "For in every place body can be present; and void is said to be that in which the presence of body, though not actual, is possible; and time is the number of movement. But in the absence of natural body, there is no movement, and outside the heaven, as we have shown, body neither exists nor can come to exist."[106] The heavenly bodies are made from a fifth element (quintessence). The natural motion of that element is circular, and it is exempt from alteration and decay.

The first heaven moves with an unceasing constant circular motion. That is an observed fact. Aristotle argues that that motion must be eternal because "it is impossible that movement should either have come into being or cease to be (for it must always have existed), or that time should"[107] and "the world would have proceeded out of night ... and out of non-being."[108] Thus he rejects the possibility of creation ex nihilo. And there must also be something that moves the first heaven because it cannot be the cause of its own motion. That mover must also be eternal or the motion would not be eternal. Since it is eternal it must be without parts and indivisible; therefore it cannot be material. It must be something that moves without being moved because it is the ultimate cause of motion. The way it moves without being moved is by being an object of desire and thought. "The final cause, then, produces motion as being loved, but all other things move by being moved."[109] And its very essence must be actuality because if it wasn't it would have the potency not to act and the motion would not be necessarily eternal. Being pure actuality it cannot move or change in any way; it is "impassive and unalterable."[110] It is infinite because it produces motion through infinite time. Since it is infinite it cannot have magnitude because there is no such thing as infinite magnitude. "The first mover, then, exists of necessity; and so far as it exists by necessity, its mode of being is good, and it is in this sense a first principle," on which "depend the heavens and the world of nature."[111]

The First Mover's actuality is also pleasure. And the most pleasant thing is thinking about thought. Therefore the First Cause enjoys eternal blissful contem-

---

h. Aristotle uses the word *heaven* in several senses, which he explains, "First, however, we must explain what we mean by 'heaven' and in how many senses we use the word, in order to make clearer the object of our inquiry. (a) In one sense, then, we call 'heaven' the substance of the extreme circumference of the whole, or that natural body whose place is at the extreme circumference. We recognize habitually a special right to the name 'heaven' in the extremity or upper region, which we take to be the seat of all that is divine. (b) In another sense, we use this name for the body continuous with the extreme circumference which contains the moon, the sun, and some of the stars; these we say are 'in the heaven'. (c) In yet another sense we give the name to all body included within the extreme circumference, since we habitually call the whole or totality 'the heaven'. The word, then, is used in three senses" (*On the Heavens*, Book I, Chapter 9).

plation in a state of "thinking on thinking,"[112] which is thinking about itself. The First Cause is identified with God. "And life also belongs to God; for the actuality of thought is life and God is that actuality; and God's self-dependent actuality is life most good and eternal. We say therefore that God is a living being, eternal, most good, so that life and duration continuous and eternal belong to God; for this *is* God."[113]

The First Mover moves the fixed stars, the sun, the moon and the planets in an eternal uniform circular motion. But the sun, the moon and the planets have additional motions superimposed on that motion. These additional motions can be resolved into combinations of eternal uniform circular movements. The additional movements are more numerous than the sun, moon and planets together because each of those bodies has more than one additional movement. Following Callippus, Aristotle postulates fifty-five such movements (or forty-seven, depending on the method of reckoning), which are identified by fifty-five spheres.[114] An unmovable eternal being moves each of those spheres. Those beings are the gods of ancient lore. But, despite all these movements, there is only one heaven because there is only one First Mover.

St. Thomas Aquinas sums up Aristotle's view on the population of the heavens saying: "Each of the heavenly bodies is animated by its own soul, and each has its own separate appetible object which is the proper end of its motion.... According to the position of Aristotle, between us and the highest God, there exists only a twofold order of intellectual substances, namely, the separate substances which are the ends of the heavenly motions; and the souls of the spheres, which move through appetite and desire."[115]

Good is present in the universe both in the order of its parts and in its ruler. The First Mover gives unity to and rules over nature. Aristotle says: "And all things are ordered together somehow, but not all alike—both fishes and fowls and plants; and the world is not such that one thing has nothing to do with another, but they are connected. For all are ordered together to one end."[116] They are made one by the First Mover: "'For the rule of many is not good, one ruler let there be.'"[117] i

Aristotle did not even guess at the existence of a personal Creator God like YHWH. But he came so close through observation and pure reason! j

---

i. Aristotle quotes Homer's *Iliad* here.

<< The Cosmogony of Greek Atomism >>

The idea that matter is composed of atoms was first proposed by the Greek philosopher Leucippus and developed by his disciple Democritus. A later Greek philosopher, Epicurus, expanded the idea into a full-blown philosophy. The Greco-Roman poet Titus Lucretius Carus put the atomistic philosophy of Epicurus into 7500 lines of Latin hexameter verse in the poem *On the Nature of Things*. In this didactic poem Lucretius sets out to tell "the way things are"[118] according to atomistic philosophy. He gives an account of the origin of things and gives explanations for various natural phenomena. Some of his explanations are similar to those of modern physics.

For Lucretius nothing exists but atoms and void. His atoms are infinite in number and of various sizes and shapes. The natural motion of the atoms is for them to continually fall downward through infinite space, all at the same speed. But in such a situation nothing new would ever happen because the atoms would never collide. To correct this he introduces an "almost infinitesimal deviation"[119] into the motion. "No one knows when or where—they swerve a little. Not much, but just enough for us to say they change direction."[120] This allows atoms to collide and form aggregates, and thus for things to take shape. The swerving introduces an element of chance into an otherwise deterministic system. Lucretius also notices that deterministic processes cannot explain the freedom in human choices, and so he uses swerving to account for it:

> What keeps the mind from having inside itself
> Some such compulsiveness in all its doings,
> What keeps it from being matter's absolute slave?
> The answer is, that our free-will derives
> From just that ever-so-slight atomic swerve
> At no fixed time, at no place whatever.[121]

Things in motion cause time:

Time also has no separate existence,

---

j.   St. Thomas asserted that Aristotle did understand the First Mover as a cause not only of motion but also of being. See Steven E. Baldner and William E. Carroll in *Aquinas on Creation: Writings on the "Sentences" of Peter Lombard 2.1.1* (Toronto: Pontifical Institute of Mediaeval Studies, 1997), pp. 102, 128–129.

But present, past, and future reach our senses
From what occurs, by-products of by-products.
We must admit that no man's sense of time
Exists apart from things at rest or moving,[122]

The gods neither create nor maintain the universe. They are very subtle and far from the range of our senses. The gods

Must, by their nature take delight in peace,
Forever calm, serene, forever far
From our affairs, beyond all pain, beyond
All danger, in their own resources strong,
Having no need of us at all, above
Wrath or propitiation.[123]

Things come about by the chance combination of atoms:

Especially since this world of ours was made
By natural processes, as the atoms came
Together, willy-nilly, quite by chance,
Quite casually and quite intentionless
Knocking against each other, massed or spaced
So as to colander others through, and cause
Such combinations and conglomerates
As form the origin of mighty things,
Earth, sea and sky, animals and men.[124]

There is no purpose in the construction of things:

From all those things, much older, which supplied
Their function from their form. The limbs, the sense,
Came first, their usage afterward. Never think
They could have been created for the sake
Of being used.[125]

And there is no design. There is an orderly universe because

For centuries, for eons, all those motes
In infinite varieties of ways
Have always moved, since infinite time began,
Are driven by collisions, are borne on

> By their own weight, in every kind of way
> Meet and combine, try every possible,
> Every conceivable pattern, till at length
> Experiment culminates in that array
> Which makes the great things begin: the earth, the sky,
> The ocean, and the race of living creatures.[126]

Our world is not the only world. It is one of many:

> Our heaven is only the minutest part
> Of the whole universe, a fractional speck—
> Less than one individual compared
> To the entirety of the earth.[127]

Modern science fiction writers and cosmologists also speculate about the possibility of other worlds. This is what St. Thomas Aquinas had to say on the subject: "The very order of things created by God shows the unity of the world. For this world is called one by the unity of order, whereby some things are ordered to others. But whatever things come from God, have relation of order to each other and to God Himself.... Hence it must be that all things should belong to one world. Therefore those only can assert that many worlds exist who do not acknowledge any ordaining wisdom, but rather believe in chance, as Democritus, who said that this world, besides an infinite number of other worlds, was made from a casual concourse of atoms."[128] He elaborates further saying, "[T]he world is one because all things must be arranged in order, and to one end. Therefore from unity of order in things ... the unity of God governing all, ... and from the unity of the exemplar, proves the unity of the world, as the thing designed."[129]

Lucretius' poem ends with the great plague of Athens. He describes its horrors in detail. It seems an appropriate ending for an outlook that sees no meaning in anything, an outlook that is diametrically opposed to that of Genesis.

<< Big Bang Cosmogony >>

In the past thirty years or so a relatively new cosmogony has captured the imagination of astronomers and astrophysicists. It is now so widely accepted that astronomers have come to call it the *standard model*, popularly known as the *big bang theory*. Proposed by the Belgian priest Fr. Georges-Henri Lemaitre in 1931, it went through several major revisions before reaching its present form.[k] The standard model is the currently reigning cosmic paradigm. It directs the thinking of physicists as well as astronomers and is completely evolutionistic in spirit.

The three pillars of the standard model are 1) the Hubble law, 2) the cosmological principle, and 3) Einstein's theory of gravity.

Astronomers have long observed that the color of the light coming from distant galaxies is shifted toward the red end of the spectrum, a phenomenon called *red shift*. The red shift was originally interpreted exclusively in terms of a Doppler shift caused by a galaxy receding from us.[l] The American astronomer Edwin Hubble noticed that the dimmer galaxies had greater red shifts, which he assumed means that they are moving away with greater speed. Hubble associated the brightness of a galaxy with its distance, and in 1929 he proposed that the speed of recession of a galaxy is proportional to its distance from us. The constant of proportionality is called the *Hubble constant*. A working estimate of its value is 15 kilometers per second per million light-years.

The *cosmological principle* is an assumption that requires everything to look pretty much the same from wherever you stand in the universe. There is no special or preferred place in the universe; it is perfectly "democratic." This rules out, for example, a rotating universe because then there would be a very privileged place, namely, the center of rotation. Physical observations in a rotating universe would not look the same everywhere; they would depend on how far from the center of rotation the observer is located.

An amusing thing happens if one applies the cosmological principle to the Hubble law, that is, if one assumes that the Hubble law applies in every galaxy in the universe. Projecting the motions of the galaxies back in time, one finds that they all come together at the same instant. They can be moving helter-skelter, but

---

k. There is an earlier version of the theory. In 1849 the American fiction writer Edgar Allen Poe, in his essay *Eureka*, proposed the idea that God created a primordial particle of matter in its simplest state that "diffused" into space to produce the universe.

l. This is the same phenomenon as that which occurs when a train's whistle drops in pitch as it passes by. However, not all astronomers agree that red shifts are Doppler shifts or that they have anything to do with an expansion of the universe. See Steven Weinberg, *The First Three Minutes: A Modern View of the Origin of the Universe* (New York: Basic Books, 1993), pp. 28–29. Also, see Robert V. Gentry, "A New Redshift Interpretation," *Modern Physics Letters A,* Vol. 12, No. 37, pp. 2919–2925 (1997). Furthermore, some galaxies manifest a shift toward the blue end of the spectrum, which would indicate that they are approaching rather than receding.

as long as the Hubble law holds in all of them they will project back together at the same instant of time. A little bit of very simple mathematics shows why. Let D be the distance between any two galaxies; let V be their relative speed; let H be the Hubble constant; and let T be how long ago the galaxies started their journeys away from each other. Then $D = VT = (HD)T$; so $T = 1/H$. Since H is a constant, so is T. Therefore, all the galaxies started their journeys together at the same time. To find how long ago you need only take the reciprocal of the Hubble constant. The time does not depend at all on their current distances. The distances cancel out! Making this simple calculation with the value for the Hubble constant given above gives a value of 20 billion years, the age of the universe according to big bang theory.[m] The initial separation took place when all of the mass of the universe was concentrated together. According to the big bang theory the universe at that point was a superdense concentration of matter. The beginning of this separation ("explosion") was the "big bang," after which the universe evolved to its present state.

Theorists can offer no physical reason for the big bang. This is a serious weakness of the theory. One proponent of the theory admits this saying: "There is an embarrassing vagueness about the very beginning."[130] And an opponent of the theory says this: "The vexing problem of what could have propelled this vast explosion, a hundred times or more than gravity could contain, was quietly swept under the rug. The new Big Bang became the standard model."[131]

In his theory of general relativity, Albert Einstein (1879–1955) proceeded to formulate the laws of physics so that they look the same in all coordinate systems moving relative to each other, both uniformly and nonuniformly. To do this the notions of absolute motion in space and absolute rest in space had to be eliminated. This was made possible by the equivalence of inertial and gravitational mass, which allowed for gravity to eliminate absolute motion. Motion of massive bodies could then be looked at as being determined by the geometry of space-time that was shaped by gravitating masses. The first law to be formulated for all possible coordinate systems had to be that of gravity itself because of its

---

m. This is only an approximation because the analysis assumes that the velocities of separation remain constant. Gravitational attraction between galaxies would tend to slow down their separation. This effect appears to astronomers to be quite weak. But recent research gives the surprising result that the galaxies are receding from us at an increasing rate rather than at a decreasing rate as expected. In either case nonuniform speeds of separation would spoil the effect of all the galaxies coming neatly together at the same time.

central importance. Einstein put a lot of effort into this problem.[n] His work bore fruit resulting in his famous gravitational field equations, a set of ten differential equations for the metric of space-time. These are the equations modern cosmologists use to model the universe.

Einstein was the one of the first to use his theory of gravitation to study the structure of the universe as a whole. His equations told him that the universe had to be expanding or gravity would cause it to collapse. But he did not believe that conclusion because the astronomical data available at that time indicated that the universe is static. So he modified his equations to give a static universe, one that was neither expanding nor contracting. He added a term containing a constant that came to be called the *cosmological constant*. This term was ad hoc and marred the mathematical elegance of the equations. It had little effect on local phenomena such as the motion of the planets but had a great effect at huge distances. He later jettisoned the cosmological constant when astronomical observations gave evidence for an expanding universe. In effect the cosmological constant acted as a repulsive force that counteracted the attractive force of gravity thereby preventing the universe from collapsing. In January 1998 Saul Perlmutter and his team of astronomers at the Lawrence Berkeley National Laboratory announced a startling new discovery. Their analysis of astronomical data, which used the standard model, indicated that the galaxies are receding from us at an increasing rate. This phenomenon, called *inflation*, left astronomers flabbergasted. It is the very opposite of what they expect, and it implies a new unknown force in the universe that opposes gravity, a force with the effect of Einstein's cosmological constant.[132] This finding has the potential to destroy big bang theory by giving a cause other than an explosion for the alleged expansion of the universe.

When it came to be accepted by scientists that the universe is expanding, cosmologists began to ask when the expansion began. Einstein's original equations were solved to yield expanding universes. Some of these solutions had singularities at the beginning of the expansion, with the mass of the universe being concentrated in a point. This was seen as the beginning of the "big bang," a name

---

n. Einstein describes the agony of his pursuit in the following passage: "In the light of knowledge attained, the happy achievement seems almost a matter of course, and any intelligent student can grasp it without too much trouble. But the years of anxious searching in the dark, with their intense longing, their alternations of confidence and exhaustion and the final emergence into light—only those who have experienced it can understand that." From Albert Einstein, "Notes on the Origin of the General Theory of Relativity," *Ideas and Opinions* (New York: Dell, 1954), pp. 282–283.

coined by cosmologist Fred Hoyle. Einstein objected to his equations being pushed to such limits. He said: "One may ... not assume the validity of the equations for very high density of field and matter, and one may not conclude that the 'beginning of expansion' must mean a singularity in the mathematical sense."[133] Here he is giving a lesson learned from the history of physics: Do not extrapolate physical theories beyond the range of experience; they probably won't work there. When physicists tried to apply the Newtonian physics of the everyday world to objects moving close to the speed of light they found that it didn't work; and when they tried to apply it to things the size of an atom it didn't work. Einstein's theory of gravitation has been verified empirically only for weak gravitational fields and low material densities, and the possibility of empirical verification for the densities of field and matter tossed around by big bang cosmologists seems slim indeed. How can the cosmologists be sure that the singularity in their cosmogony is not the gravitational equivalent of the "ultraviolet catastrophe," the singularity that showed the insufficiency of classical electrodynamics?[o]

The expansion of the universe, according to the big bang theory, causes an increase in the wavelength of the electromagnetic radiation confined within it. The wavelength increases in proportion to the size of the universe. The change in wavelength depends only on the *amount* of expansion of the universe and not on the *rate* of expansion. It is therefore different from a Doppler shift. If one thinks of the radiation waves as traveling on a sheet of rubber, then the wavelengths stretch as the sheet of rubber is stretched. This notion is called *expansion red shift* because light quanta are shifted toward the red end of the spectrum, where they have less energy. Expansion red shift is a theoretical construct unsupported by

---

o. Big bang theorist Roger Penrose in *The Large, the Small and the Human Mind* (New York: Cambridge University Press, 1997) points out that this singularity (infinite density) is a serious flaw in the physical theory associated with the big bang hypothesis. Physical singularities are avoided in all physically meaningful theories.

Penrose also points out that big bang theory requires the universe to have started in a highly ordered state of very small entropy. The probability of this coming about by chance is vanishingly small. The initial singularity of the universe had to set up with extremely high precision to result in the universe we have, since ours is one out of 10 to the power 10^{123} possible universes. Penrose hopes that this problem could be solved with a quantum theory of gravity. But there is none in sight, despite the fact that physicists have been working on that problem for many years.

empirical evidence. Nothing in modern experimental physics suggests that radiation quanta change energy when moving through free space. Robert V. Gentry points out that expansion red shifts "involve huge and continuing nonconservation of energy losses."[134] This he calls "one of the best kept secrets of Big Bang cosmology."[135]

In 1965 Arno A. Penzias and Robert W. Wilson discovered that the earth is immersed in a bath of microwave radiation corresponding to that found inside a box kept at a temperature of 2.7 Kelvin. This radiation, called *cosmic microwave radiation* (CMR), is very isotropic, having intensity variations with direction no greater than one part in one hundred thousand.[p] According to big bang theory this radiation is the relic of the high temperature thermal radiation of the early universe, its temperature being reduced by the wavelength expansion mentioned above. Supposedly radiation quanta decoupled from matter in the primeval fireball some three hundred thousand years after the big bang took place, when the fireball had expanded to the point where matter and radiation ceased to interact as they did previously. The temperature of the fireball at that point was about 3000 Kelvin. The decoupled radiation propagated through expanding space unobstructed to eventually become CMR.

The essence of big bang theory lies in the three pillars stated above. Other features of the theory—the interpretation of CMR, the derivation of the relative abundances of the elements, and the postulate of "dark matter"—are by-products of the theory that serve only to increase or decrease its credibility.

The objectionable thing about big bang theory is its proposal that the universe came into being some 15–20 billion years ago in an unformed state. This can in no way be reconciled with Genesis. There is no problem with an expanding universe. The Genesis account is broad enough to allow for either a static or expanding universe. One version of big bang theory proposes that the universe rapidly inflated at the big bang and, in a matter of a few moments, matured. This would be in better agreement with Genesis, but only if it happened several thousand years ago.[136]

---

p. Observations show that the CMR wavelength spectrum is shifted down in one direction of the sky and shifted up by the same amount in the opposite direction. This phenomenon is called *dipole anisotropy*. It is attributed to the Doppler effect caused by a speed of about 260 kilometers per second of the earth relative to the frame in which the CMR is isotropic. See Amitabha Ghosh, *Origin of Inertia: Extended Mach's Principle and Cosmological Consequences* (Montreal: Apeiron, 2000), p. 5 and Andre K. T. Assis, *Relational Mechanics* (Montreal: Apeiron, 1999), p 70.

For Christian theologians to grab on to the uncertainty of the origin of the big bang and point to it gleefully as "proof" or "confirmation" of creation is at best naive. Support of big bang theory does no service to theology. Rather, it does a disservice because it places more confidence in scientific speculation than in divine revelation. It makes theology kowtow to scientific whim and ignores the fact that sound theology has shown that creation in time can only be known by divine revelation and not by natural science or philosophy. We have that revelation in Genesis. To accept the big bang theory is to repudiate Genesis. Besides, atheistic and agnostic proponents of big bang theory have their ways of getting around creation. Cosmologist Stephen Hawking in *A Brief History of Time* tells of a conference on cosmology in the Vatican that he attended in 1981. He spoke there about "the possibility that space-time was finite but had no boundary, which means that it had no beginning, no moment of Creation."[137] Farther on in the book he says: "So long as the universe had a beginning, we could suppose it had a creator. But if the universe is really completely self-contained, having no boundary or edge, it would have neither beginning nor end: it would simply be. What place, then, for a creator?"[138]

Militant atheists espouse the cosmological principle because it removes earth from the center of creation. They see this as a step toward dethroning man as the masterpiece and master of creation, the standpoint of Genesis. Materialists like to see man as just one intelligent product of evolution among many in the universe—thus the fascination with "aliens" from other worlds. However, archevolutionist Richard Dawkins admits how unsuccessful the search for extraterrestrial intelligent life has been.[139]

The centrality of man was expressed geometrically in the Christian medieval cosmos by having the earth at rest with the sun and the heavens moving around it, using a model that came from the Greeks but was in harmony with Genesis. Nicholaus Copernicus upset that worldview by having the earth move. But for modern relativistic physics the question of whether the earth moves and the sun is at rest or vice versa is meaningless. One can choose either one to be at rest and the other to be moving. The choice is strictly a matter of convenience or taste. Albert Einstein and Leopold Infeld in considering the possibility of eliminating the notion of absolute motion say that if it was possible then "the struggle, so violent in the early days of science, between the views of Ptolemy and Copernicus would then be quite meaningless. Either coordinate system [earth at rest or sun at rest] could be used with equal justification. The two sentences 'the sun is at rest and the earth moves' or 'the sun moves and the earth is at rest' would simply mean two different conventions concerning two different coordinate systems."[140] q

Einstein maintained that he succeeded in eliminating the notion of absolute motion in his theory of general relativity, making the notion "at rest in space" open to definition. But God had already made that definition. Scripture informs us that God established the earth as a standard of rest. This is made clear in Psalms 93:1:

For He hath established the world which shall not be moved (DR: Ps 92:1).

The Hebrew word *kun* translated "established" has a variety of applications, including "ordain," "appoint." The Hebrew word *tebel* translated "world" means the earth and not the universe.

The stationary earth standard is confirmed by Psalms 104:5:

Who hast founded the earth upon its own bases; it shall not be moved for ever and ever (DR: Ps 103:5).

When God created the earth as the first material body, He created the three-dimensional space it occupies. Space, like time, is an epiphenomenon of material creation. With the creation of the celestial bodies God created the void, which separates and helps distinguish the heavenly bodies from each other and the earth. Void has no meaning except in reference to the material objects it surrounds. Matter lends its dimensionality to the void. Job 26:7 confirms that the three-dimensionality of the void is extrapolated from three-dimensional matter:

He stretches out the north over the void, and hangs the earth upon nothing.

Before creation there was no infinite three-dimensional void into which God injected matter. The mental image of an empty three-dimensional void existing before creation is abstracted by our minds from a world filled with matter. Before creation there was nothing but God. And "nothing" does not mean "three-dimensional emptiness." It means "no thing."

All celestial kinematic and dynamic phenomena can be adequately described with the earth as the standard of rest. It is true that the mathematical description

---

q. Gerardus D. Bouw describes a geostationary model of the universe that exhibits all observable astronomical kinematic phenomena, including the phases of Venus, stellar aberration and stellar parallax. It is a modified version of that of Tycho Brahe with the planets and the stars moving around the sun, which, in turn, moves around the earth. See *Geocentricity* (Cleveland OH: Association for Biblical Astronomy, 1992).

of some celestial phenomena may be simpler in other defined frames of rest. But that is of no consequence. Scripture assures us that God made a good world, but it does not assure us that He made a simple one, that is, one that can be easily understood by man. For some scientists, simplicity of explanation of natural phenomena is a philosophical requirement. They apply the *law of parsimony*, or *Ockham's razor* (see Glossary), as if it were a natural law, that is, as if nature seeks the way of least complexity. But that is just wishful thinking. There are no theological, metaphysical or observational grounds to justify such a claim. For others, simplicity is an aesthetic principle, but aesthetics concerns beauty and not truth. Beauty is largely subjective; truth is objective. And for others simplicity is a practical objective that is often unattainable. Nineteenth-century physicists and astronomers pictured the universe as a well-oiled machine governed by a few simple laws. Twentieth-century physics and astronomy shattered that illusion.

The earth is at the center of the universe because it is a place in the universe with special properties, just as geometric centers and centers of mass are places with special properties. God created the earth first, built the rest of the universe around it, defined it as the standard of rest, and made it the home of man, who is a unique union of matter and spirit. The centrality of earth in the universe might also be expressed geometrically and/or physically. And there is evidence that it is.[r s] But it need not be so to be in accord with Scripture.

One last comment: Steven Weinberg concludes his popular treatise on the big bang theory, *The First Three Minutes*, with the now famous observation: "The more the universe seems comprehensible, the more it also seems pointless."[141] The universe seems comprehensible because it is the work of an intelligent Creator. It seems pointless only if that fact is not recognized.

---

r. Physicist V. F. Weisskopf made this observation concerning the isotropy of the microwave (3 K) radiation from space discovered by Penzias and Wilson in 1965: "It is remarkable that we are now justified in talking about an absolute motion, and that we can measure it. The great dream of Michelson and Morley is realized. They wanted to measure the absolute motion of the earth by measuring the velocity of light in different directions. According to Einstein, however, this velocity is always the same. But the 3 K radiation represents a fixed system of coordinates. It makes sense to say that an observer is at rest in an absolute sense when the 3 K radiation appears to have the same frequencies in all directions. Nature has provided an absolute frame of reference. The deeper significance of this concept is not yet clear."
Quoted by Robert V. Gentry, *Creation's Tiny Mystery* (Knoxville, TN: Earth Science Associates, 1992), p. 292.

<< Steady State Cosmology >>

In 1948 cosmologists Hermann Bondi and Thomas Gold formulated an alternative to big bang theory, called the *steady state theory*, which was further developed and promoted by Fred Hoyle.[142] It is also called the *continuous creation theory* because it proposes the continuous creation of matter in the universe.[s] In contrast to big bang theory, the steady state theory proposes an extended version of the cosmological principle that applies not only to place but also to time. The universe is assumed to look the same to observers at all places *and all times*. This would require the same density of matter in the universe at all times. To achieve this in a universe that seems to be continuously expanding, new matter would have to be continually injected into the universe. Thus Bondi and Gold hypothesized something totally new, the spontaneous and continuous creation of matter. They proposed the creation of one atom of hydrogen per year in every 10,000 cubic meters of space, a rate much too small to permit observation.

The steady state universe is eternal and infinite in extent. It has no beginning or end, either in space or time. It just continually expands with the influx of matter keeping things the same.

Regarding the question of where the all the new matter comes from, Fred Hoyle said that such a query is "meaningless and unprofitable."[143] He did, how-

---

s. In the early 1970s, William Tifft at the Steward Observatory in Tucson, AZ analyzed red shift data from galaxies in all directions. His analysis showed that the red shifts are quantized. This can be interpreted to mean that the galaxies are arranged on concentric spherical shells. The quantization effect could be clearly observed only if the earth was close to the center of the shells. See Russell Humphreys, "Our galaxy is the centre of the universe, 'quantized' redshifts show," *TJ* 16(2):95–104 (2002).

Gentry (op. cit.) quotes Y. P. Varshni who studied the red shifts of 384 quasars. Varshni concluded that if the quasar red shifts are real and distance related then "the Earth is indeed the center of the Universe. The arrangement of the quasars on certain spherical shells is only with respect to the Earth. These shells would disappear if viewed from another galaxy or a quasar. This means that the cosmological principle will have to go. Also, it implies that a coordinate system fixed to Earth will be a preferred frame of reference in the Universe. Consequently, both the Special and the General Theory of Relativity must be abandoned for cosmological purposes" (p. 291).

t. The idea of continuous creation had been suggested earlier by Oliver Lodge in 1925 and James Jeans in 1928.

ever, try to give the theory some respectability by introducing a "creation field." This required an audacious extension of Einstein's gravitational field equations to include what he called a c-field, which supposedly propagates through space like an electric or gravitational field, but is more effective at larger distances than other fields. The c-field, like other fields, somehow depends on the presence of matter. Effects from several sources are additive and can build up to an intensity where "matter happens." Created matter is capable of generating a c-field of its own, which can participate in the creation of more matter. Matter begets matter ad infinitum, as if it were a kind of immortal biological species.

The c-field carries negative energy, and, by judicious arrangements, the increase of the positive energy with the creation of a particle is compensated for by an equal increase in the negative energy of the field. Thus energy is conserved, but no provision is made for the symmetry between particles and antiparticles. Particles are created without their corresponding antiparticles violating a sacred law of quantum electrodynamics.

Observations with radio telescopes in the 1950s seemed to indicate that there was a higher density of radio wave sources farther out in space than nearby. Since it takes radio waves more time to reach the earth from distant sources than from near ones, the distant sources tell about the state of the universe at an earlier time than the nearer sources do. These observations therefore implied that conditions in the universe did not remain constant in time as assumed. This was a major setback for steady state theory.

The final blow came in 1965 with the discovery that the earth is bathed in microwave radiation exactly as it would be if it were enclosed in a big box kept at a perfectly uniform temperature of about three degrees above absolute zero. That could not be explained easily by steady state theory. Hoyle himself stated: "It has proved difficult, although not strictly impossible, to incorporate the microwave background discovered in 1965 by Penzias and Wilson into the steady state model. For this reason the model is not nowadays considered to be a viable representation of the universe."[144] The standard model explains the radiation discovered by Penzias and Wilson as residual radiation from the big bang. In fact, astronomers consider it a confirmation of big bang theory. However, big bang theory doesn't have the only explanation. Some physicists propose other reasons for this radiation.[145]

Hoyle said that big bang models are unable to describe creation in mathematical terms. Thus with the failure of steady state theory, with which he sought to do so, he saw only two alternatives for creation: either the creation of matter falls outside of laws that can be stated in mathematical form or matter was never created.

Steady state theory is objectionable for two reasons. First it postulates an eternal universe. Second, it postulates a universe that is in a process of continuous creation. This contradicts Genesis which states: *"Thus the heavens and the earth were finished, and all the host of them"* (2:1).

Some find the theory objectionable because it holds that the universe extends infinitely in all directions. They quote Psalms 147:4, *"He determines the number of the stars, he gives to all of them their names."* But, as surprising as it may seem, it is not necessary that the *"number"* is finite. The same psalm proclaims in the next verse: *"His understanding is beyond measure."* St. Augustine taught that God's knowledge embraces things that are infinite. "[T]he infinity of numbers cannot be infinite to the knowledge of God."[146] St. Thomas Aquinas, following Aristotle here rather than Augustine, denied that *actually* infinite magnitudes and multitudes could exist, but *potentially* infinite things could.[147] He gives the following example: "Wood is finite according to its own form, but it is still relatively infinite, inasmuch as it is in potentiality to an infinite number of shapes."[148] But elsewhere he says that "if there are infinite things" God is the cause of them and He knows them.[149]

St. Bonaventure argued that the infinite power of God cannot realize the actually infinite, but He can and did create infinites in potency. His arguments are based on the idea that there is and can be only one actually infinite, and that is God. For God to create another actual infinite would be a contradiction.[150]

Nicholas of Cusa, a fifteenth-century cardinal of the Church, believed that the universe is finite from God's point of view, but appears infinite to man. From our point of view, it is without external limits and incapable of extension. He said that the universe is "privatively infinite."[151]

A little over a century later Giordano Bruno, a rogue cleric, influenced by ideas of Nicholas of Cusa but without the faith of the cardinal, loudly expressed his belief in a Deity who contained contradictions within Himself and who expressed Himself in a spatially, temporally, and materially infinite universe. He was a heretic who advocated a monistic philosophy of substance that identified God with the natural world. He was burned at the stake for heresy. He was not condemned for his belief that the universe is infinitely big, as sometimes alleged, but for specific theological errors that he refused to retract. Among those errors were the following: Christ was not God but merely an unusually skillful magician; the Holy Spirit is the soul of the world; the devil will be saved.

The nineteenth-century mathematician Georg Cantor made a fantastic discovery. He found that there is an infinite hierarchy of unequal actually infinite numbers, with the number of natural numbers at the bottom.[152] These he called "transfinite numbers." Transcending all that is finite and transfinite, incomprehensible to the human understanding, is the Absolute-Infinite, God. One could then conceive an infinitely big universe created by God that would be distinct from Him and would not be coequal with Him, a conception free of pantheism, monism and dualism. Cantor's analysis showed that the production of an infinite number of creatures would not exhaust the power and glory of God. [153]

<< Plasma[u] Cosmology >>

In the late 1950s Oskar Klein began to outline a new alternative to both the big bang and steady state theories that was further developed by Hannes Alfvén.[154] Alfvén starts things off with a very tenuous mixture of matter and antimatter, which he calls "ambiplasma," occupying a very large region of space in our part of the universe. Plasma processes separated regions of matter and antimatter. But gravity gradually caused them to come together. After a long lapse of time the matter and antimatter came close enough to mix, annihilating each other and releasing a tremendous amount of energy, much of it in the form of energetic electrons and positrons. These particles became trapped in magnetic fields and generated electromagnetic forces that sent the plasma flying outward, causing the Hubble expansion. Localized regions of plasma began clumping together to form galaxies. This was not a big bang but an explosion in one part of the universe. Alfvén admitted that this explanation is not the only possible one, and matter/antimatter is produced in such small quantities in the laboratory at this time that empirical tests of his hypothesis are not currently possible

Although there are technical difficulties with Alfrén's model, it contains the essential features of plasma cosmology.[155] The idea that plasma processes played an important role in the formation of the universe is offering a formidable challenge to big bang theory. Plasma cosmologists are proposing an entirely different concept of the universe. According to one of the chief advocates of plasma cosmology, Eric Lerner, more than 99% of the matter in the universe is plasma.[156] Lerner paints the big picture of plasma cosmology as follows: "Extrapolating

---

u. A plasma is a hot electrically conducting gas. A gas becomes a plasma when its temperature becomes so high that the electrons are stripped from their atoms and allowed to flow freely.

from the behavior of such plasma in the laboratory, plasma cosmologists envision a universe crisscrossed by vast electric currents and powerful magnetic fields, ordered by the cosmic counterpoint of electromagnetism and gravity.... Instead of working forward from a theoretically conceived beginning of time, plasma cosmology works backward from the present universe, and outward from the earth. It arrives at a universe without a Big Bang, without any beginning at all, a universe that has always existed, is always evolving, and will always evolve, with no limits of any sort."[157]

As part of his zealous promotion of plasma cosmology, Lerner takes a long critical look at big bang theory and points out difficulties that the big bang theorists tend to set aside and ignore. First, as mentioned in the preceding big bang summary, Lerner points out that the big bang theory has no physical explanation for what causes the big bang. Another major problem is that the big bang theory is totally unable to arrive at the complex, structured universe we observe today. He quotes George Smoot of the University of California at Berkeley: "Using the forces we now know, you can't make the universe we know now."[158] A third criticism concerns dark matter, which theorists postulated when they came to the conclusion that the mass required to keep galaxies gravitationally bound together in a cluster was on the average ten times greater than the mass actually observed in the cluster.[v] Big bang theorists say that no galaxies, stars or planets can form without dark matter. Lerner argues that there is no evidence that dark matter exists, and there is research that indicates that there is no need to postulate it. He says that the results of this research "have been published in leading journals, yet have stirred little discussion and no attempts at refutation."[159] Fourth, the big bang should have produced equal amounts of matter and antimatter, which would have quickly annihilated each other leaving only energy.[160][w] Finally, Lerner looks at the microwave radiation from outer space discovered by Penzias and Wilson, which big bang theorists claim as a great triumph of big bang theory.

---

v.   Dark matter is a hypothetical entity that has mass but isn't observed to radiate energy in any part of the electromagnetic spectrum. It is said to be detectable only by its gravitational effects. The nature of dark matter is unexplained.

w.   Physicist Steven Pollock states: "If we work out how much matter and antimatter should be left over today from the Big Bang, based on the standard model, we cannot account for the amount of matter that exists so it's still something of a puzzle." Quoted from *Particle Physics for Non-Physicists: A Tour of the Microcosmos*, DVD Course Guidebook, Part II (Chantilly, VA: The Teaching Co., 2003), p. 47.

Lerner notes that the smooth isotropy and the perfect blackbody spectrum[x] observed for this radiation are as much problems for big bang theory as they are supports. Bumpiness in intensity and spectrum should be observed because of the clumpiness of the universe and because of the observation that something absorbs microwaves as they travel between galaxies.[y]

Lerner, adopting Alfvén's philosophy, believes that astrophysics should be the extrapolation of laboratory physics rather than deductions from a mathematical theory that cannot be confirmed in the laboratory. The former is the method of plasma cosmology; the latter is the method of big bang cosmology. Also big bang cosmology sees the universe in terms of gravity alone. But plasma cosmology also gives an important role to electric currents and magnetic fields.

Lerner makes a number of claims for plasma cosmology. He says that that the universe seen by the plasma cosmologists behaves differently from that seen by big bang theorists. He quotes Alfvén: "I have never thought that you can get the extremely clumpy, heterogeneous universe we have today from a smooth and homogeneous one dominated by gravitation."[161] Plasma becomes inhomogeneous naturally, making the universe a complex, dynamic, uneven place. He claims that helium abundance in the universe, another big bang prediction, can be explained in plasma cosmology by the same cause as in big bang theory. He produces an explanation for the cause, smoothness and spectral purity of the microwave background radiation by appealing to plasma processes. He believes that plasma processes can explain the Hubble expansion, as in Alfvén's ambi-

---

x. Blackbody radiation is the thermal radiation emitted by a blackbody (a body that absorbs all the radiation incident upon it). The spectrum of this radiation has a distinct shape that depends on the temperature of the blackbody. The radiation spectrum inside an enclosed cavity is that of a blackbody at the temperature of the enclosure.

y. In 1992 the popular media made much ado about slight irregularities in the cosmic microwave radiation spectrum discovered by the Cosmic Background Explorer (COBE) satellite. But those variations lent little support to big bang theory. See Paul Davies, *About Time: Einstein's Unfinished Revolution* (New York: Simon and Schuster, 1996), pp. 152–156 and Walt Brown, *In the Beginning: Compelling Evidence for Creation and the Flood* 7th ed. (Phoenix, AZ: Center for Scientific Creation, 2001), p. 71.

plasma theory. And he describes impressive computer simulations of quasar[z] and galaxy formation by plasma processes.

Plasma cosmology and steady state cosmology are even more offensive than big bang cosmology because they attempt to eliminate the need for a Creator by making the universe eternal. At least big bang theory allows for an initial creation. Plasma cosmogony, like big bang cosmogony, assumes that cosmic structures evolved over eons. Even if the notion that the universe is eternal were eliminated, plasma cosmogony still would not be redeemed because it looks to secondary causes operating over an immense period of time for the formation of the universe. However, the methods of plasma cosmology may prove useful for explaining certain observed features of the universe.

<< Machian Cosmology >>

When Isaac Newton (1642–1727) formulated his famous three laws of motion, he postulated the existence of *absolute space*. He believed that inertial effects, like the resistance of material bodies to a change in their speed and the concave surface of the water in a rotating bucket of water, were the effects of motion relative to absolute space.

G. W. Leibniz (1646–1716) and Bishop G. Berkeley (1685–1753), among others, were critical of Newton's concept of absolute space. Leibniz argued that space and time are not independent entities but depend on matter and material phenomena to give them meaning. Berkeley argued that since absolute space in no way affects the senses, it is useless for distinguishing motions. Critics of Newton also pointed out that while absolute space acts on a material body, the body does not react on absolute space.[162]

The most outstanding critic of Newton's concept of absolute space was Ernst Mach (1838–1916). He said that absolute space and absolute motion are "pure things of thought, pure mental constructs, that cannot be produced in experience."[163] Since there is no absolute motion, the motion of bodies is determined only in reference to other bodies. Thus, since there is only one system of the world, "the motions of the universe are the same whether we adopt the Ptolemaic or the Copernican mode of view. Both views are, indeed, equally *correct*; only the latter is more simple and more *practical*."[164] Mach held that inertial effects are

---

z.   Quasars (quasi-stellar objects) are starlike sources of light whose red shifts are large. They must be very bright to be visible at the great distances that Hubble's law assigns to them. Their nature is unknown.

not the result of the action of absolute space on a body; rather they are the combined effect of all the other material bodies in the universe on the body. Thus, for example, the earth bulges at the equator not because absolute space "pulls" on it; rather, the mass of cosmic bodies rotating around it "pulls" on it. And it does not matter if one thinks of the cosmic bodies as rotating or the earth as rotating. Both views are equivalent. The inertial effects are produced by the *relative* rotation of the earth and the heavens. Mach wrote: "[I]t does not matter if we think of the earth as turning on its axis, or at rest while the fixed stars revolve around it.... The law of inertia must be so conceived that exactly the same thing results from the second supposition as from the first."[165] This idea, which has come to be known as *Mach's principle*, implies that if there were no cosmic bodies there would be no inertial effects on the earth, for example, the earth would not bulge at the equator. It is not possible to test this directly because one cannot simply remove all the heavenly bodies. But, in principle, it can be confirmed indirectly by looking for inertial effects caused by the relative motions of terrestrial bodies. But such effects would be very small and very hard to measure. So far Mach's principle has not been verified experimentally.[166] Mach stated his principle in general terms, but he did not implement it. He said nothing about the nature of the interaction of material bodies with the rest of the universe. His principle is a simple concept, but its implementation required the rethinking of some physical concepts.

Einstein was strongly influenced by the thinking of Mach. He wanted to incorporate Mach's ideas into his theory of general relativity but was not able to do so satisfactorily.[167] For Mach, the concept of space as an independent entity has no place in physics, and Einstein did not succeed in removing it. In his theory of general relativity, Einstein did not eliminate space and time as independent entities even though he combined them into *space-time*. But he still treated space and time as realities that are independent of the matter that determines them. So one could contemplate removing all the matter from the universe and yet have space and time remain. That is metaphysical thinking, not physical thinking. But his space-time differed from absolute space in that it was something that both acted and was acted upon. Masses in their passive inertial role were "guided" by space-time and in their active gravitational role "shaped" space-time. General relativity did not eliminate space, but it did deprive space of its Newtonian absoluteness by giving it a passive quality.

General relativity failed to give a cosmic origin to the inertia of a body. According to Mach's principle, a body in otherwise empty space should possess no inertia. But Einstein was not able to achieve that result. According to general relativity such a body would possess inertia. Also, general relativity predicts that the surface of a rotating pail of water would retain its concave shape if the rest of the matter in the universe disappeared. That too violates Mach's principle.

Andre K. T. Assis (1962–)[168] proposed a new mechanics that implements Mach's principle quantitatively. It is a shift of paradigm away from Einstein's theories of relativity, of which he is quite critical. Assis applies Weber's law for the interaction of electric charges to the interaction of masses and posits the *principle of dynamic equilibrium*. The latter states that the sum of all forces of any nature acting on any body is always zero in all frames of reference.

Assis calls this new mechanics *relational mechanics* because it employs only relative quantities, that is, it employs only the distances between material bodies and the relative velocities and accelerations between material bodies. He uses the word *relational* to distinguish this mechanics from Einstein's relativistic mechanics; but relational mechanics, unlike relativistic mechanics, is completely relativistic because all forces are referred to relative distances, velocities and accelerations of bodies and not to absolute space or inertial frames.[aa] According to relational mechanics, Ptolemaic astronomy is equivalent both kinematically and dynamically to Copernican astronomy. The choice of one or the other is one of pure convenience since there is no such thing as absolute motion, either in the kinematic sense or in the dynamic sense.

Relational mechanics posits a principle similar to Newton's third law of motion, but it replaces Newton's second law with the statement that the total force on any material body is zero in every frame of reference. For example, the static gravitational force acting on a freely falling body by the earth is cancelled by the dynamic gravitational force acting on it by the rest of the bodies in the universe. Since both forces are proportional to the gravitational mass, all bodies will fall to earth at the same rate. Another example: The force of attraction of the sun on the earth is balanced by the centrifugal force exerted on the earth by the rest of the bodies in the universe. Because they depend only on relative distances and motions, these forces are numerically the same in any frame of reference even

---

aa. The term "relational" did not originate with Assis. Albert Einstein clearly and succinctly presented the conflicting notions of space as "positional quality of the world of material objects" and as "container of all material objects" in his much cited foreword to Max Jammer's *Concepts of Space: The History of Theories of Space in Physics*. Philosophers and historians of science use the word "relational" space when referring to the first notion and "absolute" space when referring to the second.

though their mathematical expressions may be different. This contrasts with Einstein's relativity, where the mathematical expressions are required to be identical in different frames of reference, but numerical values for the quantities they represent may differ.

Assis applies the mathematical expression that Wilhelm Weber (1804–1891) used to express the electrodynamic force between two electric charges to the gravitational interaction between two masses.[169] The expression has three terms, each of which is proportional to the product of the two gravitational "charges" (masses). The first term is inversely proportional to the square of the distance between the two masses. This is Newton's static gravitational attraction. The second term is also inversely proportional to the square of the distances between the two masses and proportional to the square of their relative speed along the line connecting them. The third term is inversely proportional to the distance between the two masses and directly proportional to the relative acceleration along the line connecting them. The first term always represents an attractive interaction. The second term always represents a repulsive interaction. The third term represents a repulsive interaction if the relative acceleration of the masses is toward each other. All interactions are along the line connecting the two masses.

Assis includes a factor that decreases the force exponentially with distance between the masses to avoid a paradox created by the concept of a universe infinite in extent.[170] However, that factor is not really needed. The only reason for postulating a universe infinite in extent is to avoid the problem of a universe collapsing in on itself because of gravity. And that is only a problem if one considers the universe as having always existed. If one accepts the fact that the universe was created only several thousand years ago, then one need not postulate a universe infinite in extent.

Assis applies his gravitational theory to a model of the universe that is homogeneous on a large scale, static, and in dynamic equilibrium, using the currently accepted values for the average mass density of the universe, the radius of the universe, and the gravitation constant. He looks at the interaction of a mass nestled deeply within that universe with the rest of the universe. He then shows that Newton's second law of motion holds with respect to "the frame in which the distant matter [in the universe] is at rest, despite the peculiar velocities in this frame."[171] In his recovery of Newton's second law of motion the gravitational mass appears where the inertial mass appears in Newton's law. Thus he demonstrates the equivalence of gravitational and inertial mass. He also recovers Newton's first law of motion, again with the gravitational mass in the role of inertial mass and the above-mentioned frame of reference replacing absolute space. Relational mechanics also predicts quantitatively that the inertia of a body would vanish if the rest of the matter in the universe were to disappear. It further predicts that the curvature of the surface of a pail of rotating water is proportional to the amount of mass in the universe. The theory also yields an expression for the precession of the perihelion of planetary orbits that agrees to the first order with that given by general relativity. General relativity's ability to provide a calculated value equal to the observed value for the precession of the perihelion of Mercury helped vault that theory into prominence.

Assis also explains the null result of the Michelson-Morley experiment in terms of relational mechanics. The Michelson-Morley experiment failed to detect the supposed motion of the earth through the luminiferous ether. Assis says that the most straightforward explanation of that experiment is that there is no ether. He says: "Only the relative motion between the light, the mirrors, the charges in them and the earth are important, no matter what the velocity of these bodies relative to the ether or to absolute space. In this regard the results obtained by Michelson and Morley agree completely with Weber's electrodynamics, as in this theory, the ether plays no role."[172]

Assis further proposes that observed phenomena attributed to relativistic time dilation are better interpreted by relational mechanics. For example, the half-lives of mesons are observed to increase with their speed. It is usually explained that it is because the clocks "riding" on the moving mesons run slower than clocks at rest. Assis thinks that a simpler explanation is that "the half-lives of the mesons depend on their high velocity relative to the distant material universe."[173] This way of explaining such phenomena, he says, is more in agreement with the standard procedures of physics and suggests new avenues of experimental research.

Applying Mach's principle but reasoning along different lines, Amitabha Ghosh arrived at a similar mathematical expression to that of Assis for the interaction of two gravitational masses, one of which he treats as a test body.[174] He focuses in on the second term, the term that contains the square of the relative velocity along the line joining the masses. He adjusts this term so that it represents an interaction that always acts in the opposite direction of the velocity in the manner of a cosmic viscous force. Ghosh calls this interaction *cosmic drag*. Cosmic drag is not easily detectable by experiment because it is a very small effect. But, since it acts on photons of light decreasing their energy, it gives rise to the observed galactic red shift. Thus Ghosh gives an explanation for the red shift and Hubble's law without the big bang and expansion of the universe. The notion of light losing energy as it transverses the cosmos is called *tired light*.

Other mechanisms for tired light have been proposed in addition to cosmic drag, but Ghosh claims that cosmic drag is the only testable mechanism.[175]

Relational mechanics cosmology easily accommodates cosmic microwave radiation. Assis and Ghosh shatter the myth that the big bang advocate George Gamow and his associates were the first to predict the existence of the cosmic microwave radiation prior to its discovery by Penzias and Wilson in 1965 and that CMR supports the big bang hypothesis exclusively.[176] They cite a number of researchers that predicted CMR in a stationary, nonexpanding universe. Such predictions not only predate those of Gamow et al. but also more accurately predicted the temperature of the radiation. The earliest prediction discovered in their literature searches was made in 1896 by C. E. Guillaume, who estimated a temperature between 5 and 6 degrees Kelvin for the radiation.

The major objection physicists have to a mechanics that implements Mach's principle is that it requires instantaneous action at a distance. With the ascendancy of the theory of special relativity, it has become scientific dogma that the effect of any physical disturbance cannot be communicated faster than the speed of light. However, Mach's principle demands that any material body and the rest of the universe must instantly sense any change in their relative distances and motions.

The speed of light as an upper limit for the propagation of any physical phenomenon is a result of Einstein's treating the constancy of the speed of light as a kinematic effect. Assis points out that by doing so Einstein made light an oddity in the physical world.[177] The speed of bullets shot from a gun with respect to a flatcar on which it rides does not depend on the speed of the flatcar, but their speed with respect to any observer depends on the speed of the observer relative to the flatcar. The speed of a wave is constant with respect to the medium in which it travels, as long as the medium is homogeneous. But its speed relative to an observer depends on the speed of the observer relative to the medium. However, in special relativity the speed of light does not depend on the speed of the observer relative to anything. According to Assis, that has never been demonstrated (see remarks about the Michelson-Morley experiment above). In fact, Assis cites evidence to the contrary.[178] In physical experiments light always shows similarities to projectiles or waves. But Einstein made light behave differently than either projectiles or waves, and that is the source of the "paradoxes" and the counterintuitional concepts of space and time generated by special relativity.[ab]

There is solid evidence that gravitational effects are communicated instantly. Mach himself made a point of this.[179] Marquis de Laplace concluded from evidence within the solar system that the propagation of gravity has to be at a speed at least a hundred million times that of light. Further research has driven that factor even higher. One researcher explains why gravitational effects must propagate almost instantly:

> Anyone with a computer and an orbit computation or numerical integration software can verify the consequences of introducing a delay into gravitational interaction. The effect on the computed orbits is usually disastrous because conservation of angular momentum is destroyed. Expressed less technically by Sir Arthur (Eddington), this means: "If the Sun attracts Jupiter toward its present position S, and Jupiter attracts the Sun toward its present position J, the two forces are in the same line and balance. But if the Sun attracts Jupiter to its previous position S' and Jupiter attracts the Sun toward its previous position J', when the force of attraction started out to cross the gulf, then the two forces give a couple. This couple will tend to increase the angular momentum of the system. And, acting cumulatively, will soon cause an appreciable change of period, disagreeing with observations if the speed is at all comparable with that of light."[180]

Mach's principle is anathema to quantum theorists, who give great importance to fields. They point out that the fields of elementary particles, either real or virtual, occupy all of space-time. These fields, which they say cannot be eliminated, possess Lorentz invariance and can be considered a modern ether.[181] In response, it can be said that those fields are not physical entities. They are pure mathematical entities, and they are necessary only insofar as one accepts the abso-

---

ab. Nizar Hamdan arrives at the constancy of the speed of light for all observers by applying the relativity principle (the laws of physics have the same formulation relative to any inertial system) to Maxwell's field equations and to the Lorentz force law. He shows that the constancy of the speed of light is a consequence of the relativity principle and need not be postulated additionally as Einstein did. He argues that the constancy of the speed of light is not a kinematic effect, as it is in the special theory of relativity, but a dynamic effect. That is, it is not an effect of the properties of space-time but an effect of the properties of light itself. The wavelength (which is inversely proportional to the momentum) and frequency (which is proportional to the energy) of a photon of light may vary from observer to observer, but their product (which is the speed of light) remains constant. In Hamdan's analysis the notions of length contraction and time dilation and the contradictions associated with them have no physical significance. See "On the Invariance of Maxwell's Field Equations under Lorentz Transformations," *Galilean Electrodynamics*, Vol. 17, pp. 115–117 (2006).

lute space-time of relativity as a working paradigm.[182] Also, the field concept does not explain the quantum phenomenon of *entanglement,* in which physical effects are communicated instantly without the medium of fields.[183]

Although Assis says that the model for the universe he prefers is an infinitely large, unbounded, eternal universe,[184] the model he worked with was a finite, bounded universe. It does not matter in relational mechanics how old the universe is. The main requirement is that it is in dynamic equilibrium. So it seems that relational mechanics cosmology can be made to harmonize with Genesis. Furthermore, it makes it easy to place earth in its rightful position as the center of rest in the universe.[185] Because of its strong foundation in fundamental physics, relational mechanics cosmology has the potential to supplant cosmologies based on Einstein's general relativity.

<< Cosmologies Constructed to be Consistent with Genesis >>

Following are modern cosmologies that employ general relativity and are constructed to explain astronomical observations in concord with the Genesis account:

<< White Hole Cosmology >>

This is a cosmological concept developed by D. Russell Humphreys[186] to solve the puzzle of distant starlight in a young universe. It is a response to the frequently asked question: If the universe is only several thousand years old, how can we see light from galaxies millions of light-years away? The simplest answer to that question is that God created the light from the stars in transit during Creation Week. These beams would also contain *apparent* histories for far distant stars, which would account for the appearance of supernovae occurring many thousands of years ago. But this explanation is not satisfactory to those who would like to see this and other astronomical phenomena explained in terms of natural processes and *real* histories. Humphreys' model gives such an explanation.

Humphreys defends the reliability of the methods that the astronomers use that give such enormous distances for the galaxies. He says that the methods are based on "very reasonable assumptions."[ac]

Big bang cosmology is the product of the theory of general relativity applied to an expanding universe that obeys the cosmological principle. The cosmological principle implies an *unbounded*[ad] universe because a bounded universe could not look the same to all observers in it. Humphreys instead applies the theory of general relativity to a *bounded* expanding universe. This results in what he calls "white hole cosmology."

Humpreys concludes that if the universe is bounded and expanding then it must have expanded out of a white hole. A *white hole* is a region of space bounded by an *event horizon*. Substance within the event horizon expands outward giving birth to light and matter as it crosses the event horizon. The light and matter proceeding from the event horizon cannot reenter the white hole. The diameter of the event horizon is proportional to the amount of substance inside it. So the event horizon shrinks as light and matter travel away from the white hole. Eventually the white hole shrinks to nothing. There is then no white hole but only light and matter moving away from a central point. Such is the apparent state of the universe today. General relativity puts no limit on the rate at which shrinkage of the event horizon can take place.

The white hole is the converse of a *black hole*, which is also a region of space bounded by an event horizon. Substance within a black hole contracts inward. Once matter and light enter a black hole they are trapped inside it and lose their identity. The event horizon expands as the black hole gobbles up light and matter.

---

ac. This is a generous concession. The stars might not be nearly as far as modern astronomers think them to be (see Appendix A). Also, Australian astronomer Barry Setterfield has carefully studied empirical data and has concluded that the speed of light has decreased since Creation (for summaries of his work see Walt Brown's *In the Beginning* and Paul Ackerman's, *It's a Young World After All*). Shorter stellar distances and/or faster light speeds might explain the "starlight problem."

ad. There are two versions of big bang cosmogony. In the most popular version the universe is finite, unbounded, three-dimensional, and expanding. The expansion is analogous to that of the two-dimensional surface of an inflating balloon into a third dimension. However, cosmologists exclude expansion into a fourth spatial dimension because only three spatial dimensions appear in the equations of general relativity. A fourth spatial dimension implies that something exists outside the universe, and that is unacceptable to them. In the other version, the universe is infinite in all dimensions and in material content. An infinite universe expands into an infinite vista. The expansion manifests itself as a decreasing in the density and temperature of matter and energy.

General relativity allows for the existence of both white holes and black holes. An unbounded universe could not have originated in either. Bounded and unbounded cosmologies are profoundly different. Both are equally rigorous deductions from their starting assumptions.

According to the theory of general relativity, in a bounded universe clocks in different places can register time at greatly different rates. At an event horizon time stands still, and near that location clocks run very slowly. If an observer was standing on earth as the event horizon arrived, distant objects in the universe could age billions of years in a single day of the observer's time. This would give ample time for the light from the objects to reach the observer.

Humphrey's white hole construct employs expansion red shifts and accounts for the Hubble relation and cosmic microwave radiation in the same way as the big bang model.[187] But it can be used to construct cosmological models in harmony with Genesis.

<< New Red Shift Interpretation >>

Robert V. Gentry introduced a new interpretation of the Hubble relation and the 2.7 Kelvin blackbody radiation based on Einstein's static solution of his gravitational field equations.[188] Gentry's *new red shift interpretation* (NRI) presents a physically expanding universe without the standard model's singularity, expansion red shifts and cosmological principle. Both the standard model and NRI interpret nearby galactic red shifts as Doppler shifts. The standard model interprets the red shifts from distant galaxies as primarily expansion red shifts, while the NRI interprets them as Doppler and gravitational red shifts.[ae] The NRI associates the 2.7 Kelvin cosmic microwave background radiation with cavity radiation instead of expansion-shifted big bang relic radiation.

The NRI assumes that the universe is bounded by a thin shell of hot hydrogen stars clustered into closely-spaced galaxies. The shell is centered on our galaxy, has uniform temperature of 5400 Kelvin, and fills the universe with blackbody cavity radiation. Because of the radial variation of gravitational potential within the shell, the radiation temperature measured at any point in the universe depends on the gravitational red shift between that point and the shell. Gentry demonstrates that the 5400 Kelvin radiation emitted by the shell is gravitationally

---

ae. A gravitational red shift occurs when light travels from a region with a stronger gravitation field to a region with a weaker gravitational field.

red-shifted so as to appear as 2.7 Kelvin blackbody cavity radiation in our galaxy for a distance from our galaxy to the shell of about 14 billion light-years.

To achieve the required red shift the NRI introduces a vacuum energy density into the gravitational structure of the cosmos. The idea of the vacuum gravitating was first considered by Albert Einstein in 1917 in his attempt to model a stationary universe. Einstein introduced a cosmic force that opposes the force of gravity and makes the universe stationary. This force is universal and does not depend on the masses or other physical properties of the bodies. It is simply proportional to the distance between the bodies. The constant of proportionality is Einstein's cosmological constant. It is much too small to be measured in laboratory experiments. On earth the deceleration it causes on a falling body is about 31 orders of magnitude smaller than the acceleration due to gravity. Its effects can only be observed by exploring the motions of the most distant galaxies. Since it does not depend on the physical properties of bodies, it is logical to call it the "gravity of a vacuum." Einstein eventually abandoned the cosmological constant calling it the "the biggest blunder" of his life. However, recent astronomical observations seem to indicate that perhaps it was not so much a blunder after all.[189]

If such a repulsive cosmic force exists, what is its physical nature? One theory holds that it is caused by virtual particles, which, according to modern quantum theory, are continually being generated in a vacuum.[190] They cannot be detected because they are immediately annihilated, but the effects of their interaction can be detected and have been measured with a high degree of accuracy. Because of their gravitational attraction they exert a pressure, to which corresponds an energy density. If the pressure is repulsive, the energy density is positive. Since the vacuum gravitational repulsion is very sensitive to the mass of the virtual particles and since there is a wide spectrum of such particles, numerical estimates of the repulsive force can vary over many orders of magnitude.

The theory then shows that the average mass/energy density in the universe is diminished by twice the vacuum energy density. If twice the vacuum energy density is greater than the average mass/energy density, then the universe has a net negative enclosed mass, and a photon of light moving from the shell to our galaxy would experience a red shift. For a net positive enclosed mass, which would be the case without a vacuum energy density, such a photon would experience a blue shift.

Gentry investigates the Hubble relation in the NRI framework. He considers contributions to the red shift from both gravitational and relativistic Doppler effects. First he considers the contribution from the gravitational effect alone. The negative mass causes an outward radial acceleration of the galaxies. He shows that the Hubble relation holds and that the Hubble constant is proportional to the square root of the magnitude of the total enclosed negative mass of the universe. Using currently accepted values for the mass/energy density of the universe and the Hubble constant, he calculates the value of the vacuum energy density, from which he calculates the distance from our galaxy to the shell required to give the 2.7 Kelvin cosmic blackbody radiation in our galaxy. He then calculates the average virtual particle mass to be about eighty-two times the electron mass.

Next he adds in the contribution from the relativistic Doppler effect. He assumes that distant galaxies can have both radial and transverse components of velocity relative to ours. The relativistic Doppler effect has contributions from both the radial and transverse components of the velocity, in contrast to the classical Doppler effect, which has only a radial contribution.[af] He shows that for nearby galaxies, the Hubble relation holds. Gentry has also used the NRI to explain a number of other astronomical observations.[191] NRI explanations of cosmological phenomena are consistent with the Genesis account.

$$*\qquad*\qquad*\qquad*$$

< Objection 2 >

We know from quantum mechanics that there is pure spontaneity in nature. So the universe could have come into existence by a spontaneous quantum mechanical fluctuation.

<< Reply to Objection 2 >>

Quantum mechanics tells us that we cannot observe everything that there is to know about an atomic or subatomic event to an arbitrary precision. It says that

---

af. In relativity there is a Doppler shift even for a purely transverse-moving source. This is due entirely to time dilation. See Wolfgang Rindler, *Essential Relativity: Special, General, and Cosmological*, Revised Second Edition (New York: Springer-Verlag, 1977), p. 56.

J. K. West proposed a finite, nonexpanding model of the universe in which the universe is modeled as rotating galaxy of galaxies and the red shifts are interpreted as transverse Doppler shifts. See J. K. West, "Polytropic Model of the Universe" in *Design and Origins in Astronomy*, vol. 2, Don B. DeYoung and Emmett L. Williams, eds. (St. Joseph, MO: Creation Research Society, 2002), pp. 119–146.

we can only speak of probabilities concerning things that can be observed in such an event. But the interpretation of *probability* merits a careful investigation. Such an investigation will help us see why the objection is not valid.

<< Kinds of Probability >>

Probability concerns a lack of information about something we want to know about. There is a completely subjective probability, which is usually based on experience. One might say that he feels that it is very probable that he will get up tomorrow morning and go to work because this is what he has been doing day after day for the past thirty years. However, since he does not know all the possible things that could happen to him between now and tomorrow morning, he cannot quantify that probability.

Probability becomes more objective when it can be quantified. It can be quantified when one is able to count the number of possible outcomes of an event. For example, when we toss a coin there are only two possible outcomes—heads or tails. If we make the assumption that they are equally probable, that is, that the coin is true and the toss random, we can assign a probability of one-half to both head and tails. Careful study of the coin and careful regulation of the toss would give us a high confidence in this assumption but not complete certainty. A close 50–50 ratio after many tosses would confirm that confidence.

There are three kinds of quantified probability. The first involves incompleteness in knowledge concerning the causes contributing to the outcome of an event. For example when one tosses a coin, there are the magnitude, duration, and location of the force applied to the coin and the air pressure and currents it encounters. These things are not measured and their effects are assumed not to favor one outcome over the other. It is presumed that if these effects could be determined with unlimited precision, the outcome could be predicted.

It would be well to note here that it is very easy to do highly improbable things. For example, shuffle a deck of playing cards and lay it on a table. Draw five cards from the top of the deck. The chance of drawing that particular set of five cards is $1/(52 \times 51 \times 50 \times 49 \times 48)$, a very small probability indeed. If the hand you drew is "meaningless," meaning that it has little value in the game of poker, it was still less probable than drawing a hand with four aces because there are a number of possible hands containing four aces but only one of the "meaningless" hand that you drew. However, there are many many more "meaningless" hands than "meaningful" hands that could have been drawn, so that the chance of drawing a "meaningful" hand is quite small. This is one kind of argument that "intelligent design" proponents use to show that the universe must have been designed by an intelligent being. The chance is much much too small for it to have come together by accident, assuming that all the forces and ingredients necessary to make it possible were there to begin with.

The second kind of probability involves the free will of an intelligent agent. For example, suppose a person secretes a coin in one of his hands and asks another to select the hand that contains the coin. Assuming a perfectly free choice on the part of the profferer, the chooser would then have a 50–50 chance of picking the correct hand. The chooser could not predict the outcome because he could never have sufficient information. But if given a hint by the profferer, the probability could be altered.

The probability of an event is relative to the observer (chooser). It depends on the information possessed by the observer (chooser). The profferer above has a 100% chance of picking the correct hand because he knows what hand the coin is in, having put it there. The chooser has only a 50–50 chance. The relativity of probability is illustrated dramatically in the so-called Monty Hall Dilemma.[192] The name comes from the dilemma that guests on Monty Hall's TV game show *Let's Make a Deal* faced. They were given the choice of three doors. Behind one door was a shiny new car and behind the other two were consolation prizes. A contestant chose one door, say door 1, and the host, who knew where the car was, opened another door, revealing a consolation prize. He then gave the contestant the choice of sticking with door 1 or switching to the other closed door. The contestant was thus faced with the question of what to do. Just about everyone who is presented with this dilemma, including professional mathematicians, feels convinced that the choice is 50–50. But Marilyn vos Savant[193] demonstrated that the wise thing to do would be to switch doors. She showed that the first choice gives a one-third chance of winning and the second gives a two-thirds chance. That seems preposterous at first, and her answer caused quite a stir among mathematicians, but it was tested and gradually came to be accepted. Marilyn, in responding to her critics, pointed out that if a third person appeared on stage who had not known what had gone on before and were offered the choice, then his odds would be 50–50. But the original contestant was given information by the fact that Monty did not open the door the contestant selected but opened another door instead. This additional information is what changed the odds for the contestant.[194]

The third kind of probability differs essentially from the first two because it does not reside in a lack of knowledge in an intelligent agent. Rather it is attributed to matter itself. Matter is presumed to contain the principle of pure random spontaneity. Randomness and spontaneity are said to be part of a material thing's nature. But that means that a thing does things without a cause, which violates the principle of causality in physics—a physical effect must have a physical cause. Or it is its own cause, which violates the scholastic dictum that the cause must be adequate to the effect; it means that matter is able to "lift itself by its own bootstraps." Such probability is not observed at all in the macroscopic world, but the so-called Copenhagen interpretation of quantum mechanics, championed by Niels Bohr and Werner Heisenberg, implies that things in the submicroscopic world of electrons and other elementary particles behave just so. Innate randomness and spontaneity is inferred to be part of their nature because some information about them is indeterminate *in principle*.[195] This view was opposed by the so-called hidden variables interpretation, championed by Albert Einstein and David Bohm, which sees the probabilities of quantum mechanics as caused by an incompleteness of the theory. This incompleteness manifests itself in a lack of information conveyed to intelligent observers of nature. Hidden variables carry the missing information. This interpretation therefore employs the first kind of probability. John Bell provided a theoretical basis on which experiments could be made to test whether quantum mechanics is complete or incomplete. Such experiments seem to demonstrate that quantum mechanics is complete and that there are no hidden variables, unless the information hidden variables carry could be communicated instantly over any distance (nonlocality), which would violate the tenet of special relativity that the speed of light is the ultimate speed in the universe.[196] [ag]

<< Quantum Fluctuations and Creation >>

Physicists have never seriously considered the second kind of probability because it touches on metaphysics and theology, despite the fact that the Copenhagen interpretation has already brought in metaphysics by eliminating the principle of causality. It is Catholic doctrine that God exercises His providence over nature

---

ag. David Bohm formulated a theory employing hidden variables that is equivalent to standard quantum mechanics and retains causality. It is a nonlocal theory, but the nonlocality is not "signal nonlocality," that is, intelligent agents cannot use nonlocality to communicate instantly because they cannot control the phenomenon. See James T. Cushing, *Quantum Mechanics: Historical Contingency and the Copenhagen Hegemony* (Chicago: University of Chicago Press, 1994).

through the medium of the angels. It may very well be that angels are directly responsible for quantum behavior. This may sound to some like medieval theologizing. But medieval theologians knew from their reflections on the data of divine revelation things that scientists are only beginning to learn from their experiments. Furthermore, the wave functions that physicists use to calculate probabilities in quantum theory are not physical entities; they are pure mathematical forms. This strongly suggests that at the quantum mechanical level, the material world is in intimate contact with an immaterial spiritual world. Physicists should, of course, try to make further advances in this area to explain quantum phenomena in terms of material causes. But it may be that physics has reached the end of the line and has indeed come in unavoidable contact with the spiritual realm.[ah]

It should now be clear that the argument that the universe could have come in existence spontaneously according to quantum mechanical principles alone is not tenable. If the universe came into existence by a quantum mechanical fluctuation, it would have been through the agency of an intelligent spiritual being. But it was shown that God created the world immediately, that is, without the use of instrumental causes. The universe came into existence through the direct activity of God Himself. And even if He had used quantum mechanics to do so, He created the natures it describes.

The idea that the universe came into existence spontaneously through a quantum fluctuation was inspired by the phenomenon of virtual particles. Even in empty space, quantum mechanics allows for the possibility that particle-antiparticle pairs can spontaneously spring into a tenuous "virtual" existence for a brief time before reannihilating into nothing. This phenomenon is a sleight of hand of nature that certainly cannot serve as a model for the spontaneous creation of the universe because the duration of existence of the particles is very short, being limited by the Heisenberg uncertainty principle. The uncertainty principle allows the law of conservation of energy to be broken enough to produce the matter-antimatter pairs, but only for a very short time. This is not creation in the true sense of the word but only a fluctuation in an already created world, which has

---

ah. Physicist Eugene Wigner considered the relationship of the human mind to the physical world according to "orthodox" quantum theory. He noted that the quantum mechanical description of physical objects is influenced by knowledge acquired by the mind of the observer. See Wigner's article "Remarks on the Mind-Body Question" in *The Scientist Speculates: An Anthology of Partly-Baked Ideas*, I. J. Good, ed., (New York: Basic Books, 1962), pp. 284–302.

laws governing the production of virtual particles built in. Also, other conservation laws, such as that applying to angular momentum, cannot be violated even for short periods of time.

[1] CCC, no. 290.

[2] Gn 1:21, 27; 2:3,4; 5:1,2; 6:7; Ex 34:10; Nm 16:30; Dt 4:32; Pss 51:10; 89:12; 102:18; 104:30; 148:5; Eccl 12:1; Is 4:5; 40:26,28; 41:20; 42:5; 43:1,7; 45:7,8,12; 45:18; 48:7; 54:16; 57:19; 65:17,18; Jer 31:22; Ez 21:30; 28:13,15; Am 4:13; Mal 2:10. A few uses of *bara* apply to human activity but not in the same sense as its meaning when applied to divine activity. Those instances are: Jos 17:15,18 (to clear ground); 1 Sm 2:29 (to fatten oneself); Ez 21:19 (to choose, put or make); Ez 23:47 (to dispatch).

[3] Kidner, Derek, *Genesis: An Introduction and Commentary* (Downers Grove, IL: Inter-Varsity Press, 1967), 43.

[4] Isaiah 48:12.

[5] Isaiah 46:10.

[6] Revelation 21:1.

[7] 2 Maccabees 7:28.

[8] For example, Books XI-XIII of Augustine's *Confessions* are devoted to the creation account in Genesis.

[9] ACC, p. 2.

[10] Ibid.

[11] Ibid.

[12] JR, Vol. 3, p. 371.

[13] ST, Part I, Q.65, A.3.

[14] See, for example, testimonies of Sts. Athanasius, Epiphanius of Salamis, and St. Augustine in JR, nos. 748, 1101, 1747; also see SCG, Book 2, Chapter 16.

[15] NIV.

[16] Wis 11:17.

[17] ACC, p. 5.

[18] Gilson, Etienne, *The Philosophy of St. Bonaventure*, Illtyd Trethowan and Frank J. Sheed, trans. (Paterson, NJ: St. Anthony Guild Press, 1965), pp. 246–247.

[19] ST, Part I, Q. 66, A. 1, Reply Obj. 3.

[20] St. Thomas Aquinas gives a very clear discussion of this topic in *On the Principles of Nature*.

[21] See ST, Part I, Q. 66, A. 1.

[22] DZ, nos. 1 ff., 19, 21, 54, 86, 343, 421, 461, 706, 994; Pope Paul VI, *The Credo of the People of God,* 1968.

[23] CCC, no. 327; DZ, no. 428.

[24] DZ, nos. 1783, 1805.

[25] JR, nos. 178, 764,764a, 1702, 1711, 1865, 2136, 2356.

[26] DZ, no. 428; also see OTT, p. 86.

[27] CCC, no. 318; also see OTT, p. 86.

[28] ST, Part I, Q. 45, A. 5; OTT, p. 86.

[29] ST, Part I, Q. 45, A. 5

[30] Nehemiah 9:6.

[31] ST, Part I, Q. 61, A. 3.

[32] Ibid. (Named by St. Thomas, who said that the Greek Fathers all held this position.)

[33] Ibid. (Named by St. Thomas as holding this position.)

[34] JR, no. 1316.

[35] CG, Book XI, Chapters 9, 32.

[36] JR, no. 1101.

[37] CCC, no. 327; DZ, no. 428.

[38] DZ, no. 1783.

[39] See Gilson, op. cit., p. 149.

[40] DZ, nos. 235, 1804.

[41] DZ, nos. 29, 243.

[42] ST, Part I, Q. 68, A. 4.

[43] Genesis 1:6–8 (RSV).

[44] Ibid. (DR, NAB).

[45] Ibid. (JB).

[46] Ibid. (NIV, JPS).

[47] See Dillow, Joseph C., *The Waters Above: Earth's Pre-Flood Vapor Canopy*, Revised Edition (Chicago: Moody Press, 1982), ch. 6; and Brown, Walt, *In the Beginning: Compelling Evidence for Creation and the Flood*, 7th ed. (Phoenix, AZ: Center for Scientific Creation, 2001), Parts II, III.

[48] 2 Peter 3:5–6 (NAB).

[49] Heinisch, Paul, *Theology of the Old Testament*, English ed. by William Heidt (Collegeville, MN: The Liturgical Press, 1950), p. 141.

[50] Gn 7:11; 49:25; Ex 20:4; Prv 8:27,29; Pss 24:2; 136:6; Jb 26:7.

[51] Heinisch, loc. cit.

[52] Ibid., p. 142.

[53] *Physics*, Book IV, Chapter 12.

[54] CG, Book XI, Chapter 6.

[55] John 17:5.

[56] CG, Book XI, Chapter 5. St. Augustine also discusses time and its creation in *Confessions*, Book XI.

[57] ST, Part I, Q. 46, A. 3, Reply Obj. 1.

[58] DZ, nos. 428, 1783. Emphasis added.

[59] For a clear succinct description see the article "Emanationism" in *The Catholic Encyclopedia* (1907).

[60] DZ, no. 1804; also see no. 348.

[61] See Doctrine Three, God's Freedom in Creating.

[62] Doctrine Two, The Cosmogony of Genesis.

[63] Doctrine Four, The Whole Shebang Cosmogony.

[64] Wisdom 7:25.

[65] See Bonin, Thérèse, *Creation as Emanation: The Origin of Diversity in Albert the Great's* On the Causes and Procession of the Universe (Notre Dame, IN: University of Notre Dame Press, 2001).

[66] ST, Part I, Q. 45, A. 1.

[67] BV, Part II, Chapter 1.2.

[68] See St. Basil the Great, *Hexaemeron*, Homily 1, Chapter 7.

[69] DZ, nos. 501–503.

[70] According to OTT, p. 85.

[71] JR, no. 154.

[72] JR, no. 322.

[73] JR, no. 1317.

[74] JR, Vol. 3, p. 371.

[75] *Sent.* II, d. 1, p. 1, a. 1, q.2; cited by OTT, p. 85. Also see Gilson, op. cit., p. 24; also see pp. 171–177 for a detailed discussion of Bonaventure's arguments against an eternal world.

[76] ST, Part I, Q. 46, A.1; also see SCG, Book 1, Chapters 31–32.

[77] ST, Part I, Q. 46, A. 2.

[78] *Hexaemeron*, Homily 6, Chapter 1. Unless otherwise indicated, translations of the Fathers are taken from *The Early Church Fathers*, a compact disc by Harmony Media, Inc.

[79] *Address to the Pontifical Academy of Sciences*, November 22, 1951, no. 45. Emphasis added.

[80] ST, Part I, Q. 44, A. 1; also see SCG, Book 2, Chapter 15–16.

[81] According to Heinisch, op. cit., p. 148.

[82] According to Heinisch, ibid.

[83] *Timaeus*, 28c.

[84] Ibid., 32b.

[85] Ibid., 32c.

[86] Ibid., 31a.

[87] Ibid., 34b.

[88] Ibid., 51a.

[89] Ibid., 50c.

[90] Ibid., 58a-b.

[91] Ibid., 53b.

[92] Ibid., 53b.

[93] Ibid., 53b.

[94] Ibid., 55c.

[95] Ibid., 37d.

[96] Ibid., 38c.

[97] Ibid., 41b-c.

[98] Ibid., 41c-d.

[99] Ibid., 69c-d.

[100] Ibid., 29c.

[101] Ibid., 59c-d.

[102] JR, no. 1553.

[103] Ibid.

[104] CG, Book VIII, Chapter 11.

[105] *Physics*, Book VIII, Chapter 1.

[106] *On the Heavens*, Book I, Chapter 9.

[107] *Metaphysics*, Book XII, Chapter 6.

[108] Ibid., Book XII, Chapter 7.

[109] Ibid.

[110] Ibid.

[111] Ibid.

[112] Ibid., Book XII, Chapter 9.

[113] Ibid., Book XII, Chapter 7.

[114] Ibid., Book XII, Chapter 8. Also see Weisheipl, James A., *Nature and Motion in the Middle Ages,* edited by William E. Carroll (Washington: The Catholic University of America Press, 1985), pp. 189–195.

[115] *Treatise on Separate Substances*, Chapter 2.

[116] *Metaphysics*, Book XII, Chapter 10.

[117] Ibid.

[118] *The Way Things Are*, Book I, Line 950.

[119] Ibid., Book II, Line 249.

[120] Ibid., Book II, Lines 220–222.

[121] Ibid., Book II, Lines 290–295.

[122] Ibid., Book I, Lines 462–466.

[123] Ibid., Book II, Lines 647–652.

[124] Ibid., Book II, Lines 1060–1068.

[125] Ibid., Book IV, Lines 856–860.

[126] Ibid., Book V, Lines 425–434.

[127] Ibid., Book VI, Lines 652–655.

[128] ST, Part I, Q. 47, A. 3.

[129] Ibid., Reply Obj. 1.

[130] Weinberg, Steven, *The First Three Minutes: A Modern View of the Origin of the Universe* (New York: Basic Books, 1993), p. 8.

[131] Lerner, Eric J., *The Big Bang Never Happened* (New York: Vintage Books, 1991), p. 153.

[132] See Aczel, Amir D., *God's Equation: Einstein, Relativity, and the Expanding Universe* (New York: Delta, 1999).

[133] Quoted in Pais, Abraham, *'Subtle is the Lord…': The Science and the Life of Albert Einstein* (New York: Oxford University Press, 1982), p. 289.

[134] Gentry, Robert V., "The New Redshift Interpretation Affirmed," arXiv:physics/9810051, 26 Oct 1998.

[135] Ibid.

[136] See DeYoung, Donald B., *Astronomy and the Bible* (Grand Rapids, MI: Baker Books, 2000), p. 97.

[137] Hawking, Stephen, *A Brief History of Time: From the Big Bang to Black Holes* (New York: Bantam Books, 1988), p. 116.

[138] Ibid., pp. 140–141.

[139] Dawkins, Richard, *The Blind Watchmaker: Why the Evidence of Evolution Reveals a Universe Without Design* (New York: W. W. Norton and Co., 1987), pp. 164–165.

[140] Einstein, Albert and Infeld, Leopold, *The Evolution of Physics: from Early Concepts to Relativity and Quanta* (New York: Simon and Schuster, 1938), p. 212.

[141] Weinberg, Steven, op. cit., p. 154.

[142] Bondi, H. and Gold, J., "The Steady State Theory of the Expanding Universe," *Monthly Notices of the Royal Astronomical Society*, vol. 108 (July 1948), pp. 252–270.

[143] Quoted by Mulfinger, George "Theories of the Origin of the Universe," *Why Not Creation?*, Walter E. Lammerts, ed. (Grand Rapids: Baker Book House, 1970), p. 54.

[144] Hoyle, Fred, "The Steady State Cosmology," *Albert Einstein's Theory of General Relativity*, Gerald Tauber, ed. (New York: Crown, 1979), p. 284.

[145] See Lerner, op. cit., pp. 268–278; Gentry, Robert V., "A New Redshift Interpretation," *Mod. Phys. Lett. A* **12** (1997) 2919; arXiv:astro-ph/9806280, 20 Jun

1998; and Doctrine Two, << Eternal Matter and Eternal World Cosmologies: Machian Cosmology >>.

[146] CG, Book XII, Chapter 19.

[147] ST, Part I, Q. 7, A. 2–4.

[148] ST, Part I, Q. 7, A. 2.

[149] SCG, Book I, Chapter 69. St. Thomas' hesitation on this question is also displayed in a quotation from his *Disputed Questions on the Knowledge of God*, Q. 2., A. 10, which can be found on p. 12 of Duhem, Pierre, *Medieval Cosmology: Theories of Infinity, Place, Time, Void, and the Plurality of Worlds*, edited and translated into English by Roger Ariew (Chicago: The University of Chicago Press, 1985).

[150] See Gilson, op. cit., pp. 154–157.

[151] Quoted by Hopkins, Jasper, *A Concise Introduction to the Philosophy of Nicholas of Cusa*, 2nd ed. (Minneapolis: University of Minnesota Press, 1978), p. 32.

[152] For a sober and clear historical account of thought about the infinite see Moore, A.W., *The Infinite* (New York: Routledge, 1990).

[153] For Cantor's philosophical and theological views concerning the infinite and the response of the Church to them see Dauben, Joseph Warren, *Georg Cantor: His Mathematics and Philosophy of the Infinite* (Princeton: Princeton University Press, 1979).

[154] Alfvén, Hannes, "Antimatter and the Development of the Metagalaxy," *Review of Modern Physics*, 37 (1965), p. 652.

[155] See, for example, Mulfinger, George, op. cit., pp. 58–60.

[156] Lerner, Eric, op. cit., p. 14.

[157] Ibid.

[158] Ibid., p. 32.

[159] Lerner, op. cit., p. 39.

[160] Lerner, op. cit., p. 343.

[161] Lerner, op. cit., p. 42.

[162] For a summary of the views of Leibniz and Berkeley see Assis, Andre K. T., *Relational Mechanics* (Montreal: Apeiron, 1999) pp. 97–106.

[163] Mach, Ernst, *The Science of Mechanics A Critical and Historical Account of Its Development*, sixth American ed. (La Salle, IL: Open Court, 1960) p. 280.

[164] Ibid., pp. 283–284.

[165] As quoted by Rindler, Wolfgang, *Essential Relativity: Special, General, and Cosmological*, Revised Second Edition (New York: Springer-Verlag, 1977), p. 10.

[166] See Rindler, op. cit., pp. 11–14 and Assis, op. cit., pp. 236–242.

[167] See Assis, op. cit., pp. 125–159; Rindler, op. cit., pp. 242–244; Pais, op. cit., pp. 284–288; and Jammer, Max, *Concepts of Space: The History of Theories of Space in Physics*, 3rd edition (New York: Dover Publications, 1993), pp. 192–199.

[168] See Assis, op. cit.

[169] Ibid., p. 168.

[170] Ibid., pp. 85–96.

[171] Ibid., p. 178.

[172] Ibid., *p.* 145. For a clear description of Weber's electrodynamics and its relational characteristics see Assis, Andre K. T., *Weber's Electrodynamics* (Boston: Kluwer Academic, 1994); for its application to gravitation see pp. 203 ff. Also see Maxwell, James Clerk, *A Treatise on Electricity and Magnetism*, Vol. 2 (New York: Dover Publications, 1954 reprint of 1891 edition), Part IV, Chapter XXIII. In this chapter Maxwell presents Weber's action-at-a-distance theory of electromagnetism, which is conceptually different from but compatible with his own field theory of electromagnetism.

[173] Assis, *Relational Mechanics*, p. 133.

[174] Ghosh, Amitabha, *Origin of Inertia: Extended Mach's Principle and Cosmological Consequences* (Montreal: Apeiron, 2000).

[175] See Ghosh, op. cit., p. 136. Also see Assis, *Relational Mechanics*, p. 188.

[176] See Assis, *Relational Mechanics*, pp. 189–190 and Ghosh, op. cit., pp. 136–137.

[177] See Assis, *Relational Mechanics*, pp. 133–140.

[178] Ibid., pp. 139–140.

[179] Mach, op. cit., pp. 234–235.

[180] Van Flandern, as quoted by G. Galeczki, "Mach's Principle and the True Continuum," in *Mach's Principle and the Origin of Inertia*, M. Sachs and A. R. Roy, eds. (Montreal: Apeiron, 2003), p. 136.

[181] See Rindler, op. cit., p. 244.

[182] See Jammer, Max, op. cit., pp. 212–213.

[183] See Aczel, Amir D., *Entanglement: The Greatest Mystery in Physics* (New York; Four Walls Eight Windows, 2001).

[184] See Assis, *Relational Mechanics*, p. 190.

[185] Ibid., p. 261.

[186] Humphreys, D. Russell, *Starlight and Time: Solving the Puzzle of Distant Starlight in a Young Universe* (Green Forest, AR: Master Books, 1994).

[187] Humphreys, D. Russell, op. cit., pp. 120–122.

[188] Gentry, Robert V., "A New Redshift Interpretation," *Mod. Phys. Lett. A* **12** (1997) 2919; arXiv:astro-ph/9806280, 20 Jun 1998.

[189] See discussion under Doctrine Two, << Eternal Matter and Eternal World Cosmologies: Big Bang Cosmogony >>.

[190] For details see Novikov, I. D., *Evolution of the Universe* (New York: Cambridge University Press, 1983), pp. 60–62.

[191] Gentry, Robert V., *A Major Cosmic Surprise: New Cosmic Model Predicts Enhanced Brightness of Galaxies, SN, Quasars and GRBs With z > 10* (The Orion Foundation, April 1, 2002).

[192] For a history and explanation of this famous brain twister see Hoffman, Paul, *The Man Who Loved Numbers: The Story of Paul Erdős and the Search for Mathematical Truth* (New York: Hyperion, 1998), pp. 249–255.

[193] Vos Savant, Marilyn, "Ask Marilyn," *Parade Magazine*, September 9, 1990.

[194] Another version of this problem is entitled "The Prisoner's Dilemma." For details see Mosteller, Frederick, *Fifty Challenging Problems in Probability* (New York: Dover Publications, 1965).

[195] For a clear and authoritative description of the Copenhagen interpretation see Heisenberg, Werner, *Physics and Philosophy: The Revolution in Modern Science* (New York; Harper and Row, 1958), pp. 44–58. For an explanation of why the Copenhagen interpretation implies a renunciation of causality see Bohm, David, *Causality and Chance in Modern Physics* (Philadelphia: University of Pennsylvania Press, 1957), pp. 84–89.

[196] For a clear discussion of this see Aczel, Amir D., *Entanglement: The Greatest Mystery in Physics*, op. cit.

Doctrine Three
God created a good world.

The Council of Florence declared that the Three Persons of the Holy Trinity are one principle of creation. Sacred Scriptures and the Fathers proclaim that God in His wisdom created everything for a good purpose. The Council of Florence and Vatican Council I stated that God created out of His goodness. Vatican I also confirmed the Catholic teaching that God created with perfect freedom. The Provincial Council of Cologne declared that God was free to create this or any other world. Lateran IV and the Council of Florence formally affirmed the scriptural teaching that God's creatures are good in nature.

The Triune Creator

The Three Divine Persons are one, single common principle of creation. This is *de fide* teaching.[1] It was attested to frequently by the Fathers,[2] and expressed succinctly by the Council of Florence: "[T]he Father and the Son and the Holy Spirit are not three principles of creation but one principle."[3] The *Catechism of the Catholic Church* affirms it in five articles.[4] It says: "The whole divine economy is the common work of three divine persons."[5] The CCC further states, "[E]ach divine person performs the common work according to his unique personal property."[6] All things are *from* the Father, *through* the Son[7] and *in* the Holy Spirit. The work of creation is attributed to God the Father by *appropriation*, which is "a manner of speaking in which the properties and activities of God, though common to the three divine persons, are attributed to an individual person."[8]

St. Bonaventure pointed out that the Trinity is the single threefold cause of all things:

> [S]ince the principle from which the perfection of the universe proceeds is most perfect, it must act from itself, according to itself, and because of itself

since in none of its actions does it need anything outside itself—it must have, with regard to any creature, the force of a threefold cause, namely efficient, exemplary, and final; it is even necessary that every creature be related to the first cause according to this threefold condition. Every creature is constituted in being by the efficient cause, made to conform to the exemplary cause, and ordained to a purpose. Hence every creature is one, true, and good; limited, well-formed, and well-ordered; measured, distinguished, and weighted [see Wisdom 11:20]. Weight is an ordered inclination. This we say in general about every creature, whether corporeal or incorporeal or composed of both qualities, as in the case with human nature.[9]

God's Wisdom in Creating

The *Catechism of the Catholic Church* teaches that God created "according to his wisdom."[10] "*O Lord how manifold are thy works! In wisdom thou has made them all; the earth is full of thy creatures.*"[11] The world "is not the product of any necessity whatever, nor of blind fate or chance."[12] This statement from the CCC rules out any form of atheistic evolution, and it would seem to rule out any form of theistic evolution that attempts to use random processes to explain the origin of world. The world didn't just happen to be. Things didn't just happen to work out to make creation "a gift addressed to man."[13] Everything was ordained to work together in harmony by the wisdom of God. The CCC teaches: "Because God creates through wisdom, His creation is ordered."[14] "*But thou hast arranged all things by measure and number and weight.*"[15] "*No one can say, 'What is this?' 'Why is that?' For everything has been created for its use.*"[16]

Athenagoras of Athens testifies that God's wisdom is not without purpose:

> God did not create man in a purposeless enterprise; for He is wise, and no work performed by wisdom is without a purpose.[17]

St. Augustine affirms that God created everything for a good purpose, even those things that may be harmful if wrongly used, and even if we cannot always discern the purpose:

> Divine providence thus warns us not to indulge in silly complaints about the state of affairs, but to take pains to inquire what useful purposes are served by things. And when we fail to find the answer, either through deficiency of insight or of staying power, we should believe that the purpose is hidden from us, as it was in many cases where we had great difficulty in discovering it.

There is a useful purpose in the obscurity of purpose; it may serve to exercise our humility or to undermine our pride.[18]

St. Irenaeus had this to say about divine wisdom:

And He has fitted and arranged all things by His Wisdom; and while He comprehends all, He can be comprehended by none. He is Himself the Designer, Himself the Builder, Himself the Inventor, Himself the Maker, Himself the Lord of all.[19]

St. Augustine said that God creates in accord with divine ideas:

Individual creatures, therefore, are created according to fit reasons. But where must it be judged that these reasons reside, except in the mind itself of the Creator? For he did not contemplate something located outside Himself as a model by which He might fashion that which He fashioned; to think that would be sacrilege. But if the reasons for all things created and about to be created are contained in the mind of God, and if in the divine mind there can be nothing that is not eternal and unchangeable—and Plato calls these principal reasons of things ideas—they are not only ideas but they are real, because they are eternal and at the same time they remain unchangeable. It is by participation in these that it comes about that a thing is whatever it is in whatever way it is.[20]

God's Motive for Creating

God was moved by His goodness to create the world.[21] The Fathers testify to this.[22] His fullness of existence and perfect bliss excluded any other motive. St. Augustine said: "God did not create under stress of any compulsion, or because He lacked something for his own needs; His only motive was goodness; He created because his creation was good."[23] St. Gregory Nazianzen said that it was in God's nature to pour out His goodness: "Since a movement to contemplation of Self could not alone satisfy the Goodness that is God, and since it was the part of the Highest Goodness that good must be poured out and go forth as multiplying the objects of its beneficence, He first conceived the angelic and heavenly powers."[24] St. John Damascene made a similar statement with the additional comment that His creatures were to "partake of His goodness."[25] St. Thomas Aquinas said that God is "the most perfectly liberal giver, because He does not act for His own profit, but only for His own goodness."[26] He deals with the question at length in his *Treatise on the Work of the Six Days*.[27] The Council of Florence stated: "God ... out of His goodness created all creatures, spiritual as well as corporeal."[28]

The First Vatican Council declared:

> This one, true God, of his own goodness and "almighty power," not for increasing His own beatitude, nor for attaining His perfection, but in order to manifest this perfection through the benefits which he bestows on creatures, with absolute freedom of counsel "and from the beginning of time, made out of nothing both orders of creatures, the spiritual and the corporeal...."[29]

The world was created to the glory of God.[30] The Fathers taught that God created so that His perfections may be manifested and acknowledged.[31] For example, St. Theophilus of Antioch said: "And God has made all things out of those which were not into those which are, so that by His works His greatness may be known and understood."[32] The CCC teaches:

> Scripture and Tradition never cease to teach and celebrate this fundamental truth: "The world was made for the glory of God." ... God has no other reason for creating than his love and goodness.... The glory of God consists in the realization of this manifestation and communication of his goodness, for which the world was created.... The ultimate purpose of creation is that God "who is the creator of all things may at last become 'all in all' thus simultaneously assuring his own glory and our beatitude."[33]

The primary purpose of creation is the glorification of God that proceeds from the revelation of His perfections. The perfections of creatures are images of the perfections of God, and reflection on the perfections of creatures leads intelligent creatures to the perception and acknowledgment of the perfections of God. Thus God is glorified through the participation of creatures in His goodness.

The glorification of God that is made by creatures is called *external glory*. Of this there are two kinds. First, *objective glory* is the glory given to God by all creatures by virtue of their existence, for in this they mirror the divine perfections. *"Bless the Lord, all works of the Lord, sing praise to him and highly exalt him for ever."*[34] Second, *formal glory* is the glory given to God by intelligent creatures, which can render it to Him with knowledge and free will. *"Praise the Lord, O my soul!"*[35]

The secondary purpose of the creation of the world is the communication of His goodness, the bestowal of good on creatures, especially intelligent creatures. God gave man dominion over the works of creation,[36] but this was not to be the ultimate source of his happiness; that was to be the glorification of God.[37] There-fore, the secondary purpose of creation is intimately united with the primary purpose because giving glory to God is the source of bliss for the intelligent creature.

God's Freedom in Creating

God created the world free from exterior compulsion and inner necessity.[38] *"Whatever the Lord pleases he does, in heaven and on earth, in the seas and all deeps."*[39] St. Augustine (see above) and other Fathers have pointed this out.[40] For example, St. Irenaeus said that God "made all things freely and spontaneously."[41] St. Thomas Aquinas devoted an article in his *Summa Theologica* to the question of whether whatever God wills He wills necessarily.[42] Vatican Council I defined this doctrine stating that God created "with most free volition," and "by a volition free of all necessity."[43] Even though God's goodness moved Him to create, it did not compel Him.[44]

In 1347, Pope Clement VI condemned the error of Nicholas of Autrecourt: "That whatever exists in the universe is better that, than not that."[45] In 1860, the Provincial Council of Cologne declared: "God was free to create this world or any other," and Ludwig Ott classifies that statement as *theologically certain.*[46]

The Council was reacting to the *absolute optimism* of the German philosopher Gottfried Wilhelm Leibniz and others. Leibniz held the doctrine: All is for the best in this best of possible worlds. The French satirist Voltaire (1694–1778) ridiculed this doctrine in his novel *Candide,* to which he gave the subtitle, *or Optimism.*

The Church takes the middle ground between the absolute optimism of Leibniz and the pessimism of the German philosopher Arthur Schopenhauer (1788–1860) and others, who hold that this is the worst world imaginable. The Christian view is one of *relative optimism,* "which holds the present world to be relatively the best, since, being the work of Divine Wisdom, it corresponds to the aim predetermined for it by God, and unites in wonderful harmony in itself the various stages of the perfections of the natural and supernatural orders."[47]

It is a clear conclusion from the Church's dogma concerning God's freedom in creating that God was not obliged to create the best of all possible worlds.[48] God certainly did not owe it to His creatures to create the best possible world for them. And He didn't owe it to Himself because His perfections and happiness cannot be increased by even the best world.

The Catholic position was formulated long before Leibniz by Thomas Aquinas:

The universe, the present creation being supposed, cannot be better, on account of the most beautiful order given to things by God; in which the good of the universe consists. For if any one thing were bettered, the proportion of order would be destroyed; as if one string were stretched more than it ought to be, the melody of the harp would be destroyed. Yet God could make other things, or add something to the present creation; and then there would be another and a better universe.[49]

St. Bonaventure also pondered the question of whether God created the best of all possible worlds. Etienne Gilson, summing up St. Bonaventure's thought on the subject, said: "The world in which we live is certainly not therefore the best possible, but such as it is its perfection lacks nothing."[50] He traced Bonaventure's reasoning as follows:

Just as a number is always fixed in a definite degree although God can increase it, so the degree of the world's perfection, whether we consider it as regards to the quality of its essences or as regards the quantity of its mass, is always fixed in a definite degree although God can increase it. Consequently, if we imagine the infinity of possible worlds, each of them is good, although some are better than others; and if God realizes any one of these, what He does will be good; but it does not therefore follow that He could not have made it better, and we are on the contrary certain *a priori* that, whatever the world chosen by God may be, He could make a better, and so on *ad infinitum*.... If God had made a better world, we could always ask why He had not made one still better, and the question would never be meaningless, for no term of the series of possible worlds contains in itself the necessary and sufficient reason for its realization. The only solution possible to such a question does not reside in creatures but in God, and therefore it escapes us. God has created the actual world because He has willed it and He alone knows the reason of it; we know that what he has given, He has given by pure grace, in an act of goodness which allows of no dissatisfaction; the rest is His secret.... [51]

The Goodness of Creation

"And God saw everything that he had made, and behold it was very good" (1:31). Genesis 1 proclaims the goodness of the things God created a total of seven times.[52] Such an emphasis was probably added to highlight the fact that, despite the fact that evil entered into it with the Fall, the world is intrinsically good because it is God's work. St. Paul said: *"For everything created by God is good...."*[53] St. Basil the Great makes the following observation on the work of Day Two in his *Hexaemeron*:

"And God saw that it was good." God does not judge of the beauty of His work by the charm of the eyes, and He does not form the same idea of beauty that we do. What He esteems beautiful is that which presents in its perfection all the fitness of art, and that which tends to the usefulness of its end. He, then, who proposed to Himself a manifest design in His works, approved each one of them, as fulfilling its end in accordance with His creative purpose. A hand, an eye, or any portion of a statue lying apart from the rest, would look beautiful to no one. But if each be restored to its own place, the beauty of proportion, until now almost unperceived, would strike even the most uncultivated. But the artist, before uniting the parts of his work, distinguishes and recognizes the beauty of each of them, thinking of the object that he has in view. It is thus that Scripture depicts to us the Supreme Artist, praising each one of His works; soon, when His work is complete, He will accord well deserved praise to the whole together.[54]

The Council of Florence declared that God's creatures are "good indeed, since they were made by the highest good."[55]

God did not create evil natures. St. Augustine said: "He does not create evil natures and substances insofar as they are natures and substances."[56] Elsewhere he said: "There is no such entity in nature as 'evil'; 'evil' is merely a name for the privation of good."[57] Lateran Council IV stated that even "the devil and other demons were created by God good in nature, but they themselves through themselves have become wicked."[58] And the Council of Florence asserted that "nature is not evil, since all nature, insofar as it is nature, is good."[59]

< Objections > and << Replies >>

< Objection 1 >

God was not completely free in creating the world. He was subject to the laws of metaphysics, logic and mathematics.

<< Reply to Objection 1 >>

The Church teaches that God "is free from any necessity whatsoever in creating things."[60] But some people speak as if metaphysics, logic and mathematics contain ultimate truths to which even God has to defer. Metaphysics, logic and mathematics are not superior to God; they come from Him.

<< God's Freedom from Metaphysical and Logical Necessity >>

If God cannot contradict Himself, it is not because He is subject to a metaphysical principle of noncontradiction. It is because noncontradiction is a quality identified with His very nature. God is Noncontradiction.

Logic is the science of principles for arriving at the truth. It does not apply to God because He is Truth[61] and knows everything without having to reason. It applies only to men, who are creatures that seek truth through the process of reasoning.

<< God's Freedom from Mathematical Necessity >>

Quantity and mathematics, which is the study of quantity, comes from Him because quantity is abstracted or extrapolated from experience of the world He created. So it should really not be a surprise that the world can be described by mathematics. Even something as esoteric as Euler's relation, $e^{i\pi} = -1$, is rooted in the material world.

In the past, many people thought Euclidean geometry was absolute truth, that it was superior to God. They thought that the ratio of the circumference of a circle to its diameter was necessarily the number 3.1415... and that the sum of angles in a triangle was necessarily 180 degrees. However, the inability of mathematicians to prove Euclid's fifth postulate led to the recognition that other consistent geometries are possible in which the preceding relations do not hold, but are subject to choice. This shows the contingency of mathematics and makes it somewhat clearer why God is not bound by mathematics.

Mathematics describes quantitative relationships in the physical world.[a] It is able to make predictions because of the consistency of the language. In this, nature is a reflection of God. He is Noncontradiction, and His divine plan does not contain contradictions within it. The divine plan is written in mathematics

---

a. Many people think that mathematics is a body of unshakable truths about the physical world and that mathematical reasoning is exact and infallible. The mathematician Morris Kline refutes that idea in *Mathematics: The Loss of Certainty* (New York: Oxford University Press, 1980). He points out that there is not one universally accepted mathematical concept. Rather there are many conflicting ones. Yet mathematics has been very effective in describing the physical world.

but with a manifestation of arbitrariness that reflects the freedom of God. Not every possible consistent mathematical model of a natural phenomenon agrees with the observed facts. And it appears that the most fundamental constants of nature (for example, the speed of light, the gravitational constant, Planck's constant) may not be calculable. If so, that reflects an element of God's freedom in creation. Albert Einstein believed that dimensionless[b] combinations of all the natural constants could possibly be calculated in a mathematical theory. He wondered if God had any choice in making the world. He wanted to know whether those *dimensionless natural constants* could have been given different numerical values without changing the laws of physics or whether there is only one possible choice for each of them. The Catholic answer to his question is that God could have created the world according to a complete mathematical system in which such dimensionless constants could be calculated, but He would have freely chosen such a system. And if specific values for those constants are necessary for a consistent mathematical system, then God bound Himself to those values because He does not contradict Himself. But He could have chosen another mathematical system or none at all. The laws of physics do not bind Him because He created them, but His nature is to be consistent in whatever He does.[62]

If genuine paradoxes, like wave-particle duality, exist in the natural world, it is not because God is inconsistent. It is because genuine paradoxes are rooted in infinity and self-reference. And since the act of creation was an act of infinite power, it should not be a surprise that there are paradoxes in it that can never be resolved by the human mind because of its finiteness. The religious term for such paradoxes is *mystery*.

✳   ✳   ✳   ✳

There are things that God cannot do, but they do not limit His freedom. St. Thomas tells us what God can and cannot do, or, rather, what can and cannot be done:

---

b. A dimensionless number is a pure number; that is, it does not express a physical quantity. Pure numbers may be mathematically calculable. Numbers expressing a physical quantity (dimensioned numbers) are not calculable by purely mathematical means. They rely ultimately on physical measurements.

[E]verything that does not imply a contradiction in terms, is numbered amongst those possible things, in respect of which God is called omnipotent: whereas whatever implies contradiction does not come within the scope of divine omnipotence, because it cannot have the aspect of possibility. Hence it is better to say that such things cannot be done, than that God cannot do them. Nor is this contrary to the word of the angel, saying: *"No word shall be impossible with God"* [Lk 1:37, DR]. For whatever implies a contradiction cannot be a word, because no intellect can possibly conceive such a thing.[63]

For example, St. Thomas said that God cannot make the past not to have been because that implies a contradiction.[64]

St. Bonaventure adds that God cannot make something infinite in act:

Power may be spoken of as ordered in a triple sense: according to act, according to aptitude on the part of the creature, and according to aptitude on the part of the uncreated power alone. What is possible with regard to power in the first way, is not only possible but also actual; what is possible in the second way and not in the first is possible simply, though not actually; what is possible in the third way, but not in the first or second, is possible for God but is impossible for the creature. What is not possible according to any of the ways mentioned above, as is the case with that which is directly repugnant to order as regards the primordial and eternal causes and reasons, is impossible simply, as, for instance, that God should make something infinite in act or that He should cause something to exist and not exist at the same time, that He should make that which has happened not to have happened, and other things such as these, for their possibility is contrary to the order and completeness of the divine power. Thus it is clear what the divine power embraces and also what ought to be said to be possible simply and what impossible simply and that the impossibility of doing certain things is compatible with true omnipotence.[65]

✳   ✳   ✳   ✳

< Objection 2 >

The world is not good because there is so much imperfection and suffering in it.

<< Reply to Objection 2 >>

An adequate reply requires a careful inquiry into the meanings of the terms *imperfection* and *suffering*.

<< Imperfection >>

Perfection is measured in terms of what God intended a creature to achieve, not in terms of our perceptions of perfection. Even a creature that we perceive to have defects in its nature could be perfect in that it achieves the end God intended. Catholic doctrine holds that the goodness of creatures comes from the fact that creation is an outpouring of the goodness of God. The goodness of creatures resides in their relationship to God, that He gave them a participation in existence, and not in their own perfection, completeness or permanence. St. Thomas Aquinas said, "every being is necessarily good from the fact that it has existence,"[66] and "creatures are good only by participation[c] and not by their essence."[67]

<< Human Suffering >>

God is the source of good but not the evil in things, although He does allow evil so that He may bring good, even greater good, out of it. God created a perfect world in the beginning. Everything achieved the end for which He intended, until man sinned. By sin man, through his power of free choice that God gave him so that he could freely return God's love, chose to oppose God's plan of creation. He thereby upset the balance God had created with detrimental effects on himself, his progeny and the world around him. The original integrity, harmony and order that God created were damaged by sin. *We know that the whole creation has been groaning in travail together until now.*[68] Evil is the absence of good. Every sin removes some of the good in creation by putting holes in its uniform fabric of goodness, so to speak.

Human suffering is an evil because it is the deprivation of a good. It is the deprivation of internal peace and harmony that is necessary for the perfection of the human person. That lack of perfection interferes with God's plan for man. It is not what God originally intended. God allows the wicked to suffer as just punishment and to bring them back to Him. He allows the innocent to suffer because somehow this patches the holes that sin has put into the fabric of goodness. How it does is a mystery. *How unsearchable are his judgments and how inscrutable his ways!*[69] But we know that the suffering of the just is not in vain and that it will be more than compensated for. We have the example of Jesus

---

c.   For Aquinas things *participate* in *esse* or be-ing, not in forms or ideas as with Plato.

Christ to prove that. St. Paul consoles the innocent who suffer with the words: *"I consider that the sufferings of this present time are not worth comparing with the glory that is to be revealed in us."*[70]

<< Animal Suffering >>

But how are we to understand animal suffering?[71] They cannot sin, so they do not deserve punishment. And they are not promised the rewards of eternal glory, so anything they suffer is in vain. The answer may be that they do not experience pain the way we do.

Man is between the angels, which have purely spiritual life, and animals, which have purely material life. Our ability to empathize is limited by our own personal experiences. We can surmise the feelings of other human persons only because we share the same nature and same experiences. We can imagine neither the inner experiences of a purely spiritual life nor the inner experiences of a purely material life because they are totally outside our range of experience. So we do not know if animals suffer the way we do. They may simulate fear and suffering, just as they do intelligence. Perhaps God made them to *appear* to suffer to teach man compassion. Even if it could be established that they do not suffer, that would not give man the right to treat them badly. God gave man dominion over animals, but good stewardship excludes ruthless behavior toward them. *"A righteous man has regard for the life of his beast, but the mercy of the wicked is cruel."*[72] Man must not be cruel to animals because any kind of cruelty brutalizes him. But cruelty to animals does not violate the rights of animals because animals have no rights. Only humans have rights because they are persons, who are created in the image and likeness of God with the ability to share in His divine life.

That animals do not suffer in the way we do seems to be supported by St. Thomas Aquinas, who held that the "law of tooth and claw" held even before the Fall. He states:

> In the opinion of some, those animals which now are fierce and kill others, would, in that state, have been tame, not only in regard to man, but also in regard to other animals. But this is quite unreasonable. For the nature of animals was not changed by man's sin, as if those whose nature now it is to devour the flesh of others, would then have lived on herbs, as the lion and falcon. Nor does Bede's gloss on Genesis 1:30, say that trees and herbs were given as food to all animals and birds, but to some. Thus there would have been a natural antipathy between some animals.[73]

Leibniz supposed that the mere sense perception, unaccompanied by reflection, could not cause either pain or pleasure. He compared pain and pleasure in animals to reflex action in man.

[1] See OTT, p. 82.
[2] JR, 235, 1317a, 1564, 1662, 1702, 2264.
[3] CCC, no. 258; DZ, no. 704.
[4] CCC, nos. 258, 290–292, 316.
[5] CCC, no. 258.
[6] CCC, no. 258.
[7] John 1:1–3, Colossians 1:16–17.
[8] Hardon, John A., *Modern Catholic Dictionary* (New York: Doubleday, 1980), p. 38.
[9] BV, Book II, Chapter 1.4.
[10] CCC, no. 295.
[11] Psalms 104:24.
[12] CCC, no. 295.
[13] CCC, no. 299.
[14] CCC, no. 299.
[15] Wisdom 11:20.
[16] Sirach 39:21.
[17] JR, no. 168.
[18] CG, Book XI, Chapter 22.
[19] JR, no. 205.
[20] JR, no. 1553.
[21] See OTT, p. 81.
[22] See JR, nos. 168, 231, 462, 884, 1005, 1751, 2282, 2349.
[23] CG, Book XI, Chapter 24.
[24] JR, no. 1005.
[25] JR, no. 2349.
[26] ST, Part I, Q. 44, A. 4, Reply Obj. 1.
[27] ST, Part I, Q. 65, A. 2.
[28] DZ, no. 706.
[29] CCC, no. 293; DZ no. 1783.
[30] See OTT, p. 81, DZ 1805.
[31] JR, nos. 7, 171, 179, 275, 643, 2307.
[32] JR, no. 171.
[33] CCC, nos. 293, 294.
[34] Daniel 3:35.
[35] Psalms 146:1.
[36] Genesis 1:28, Psalms 8:6.
[37] Revelation 4:11.

[38] See OTT, p. 83.

[39] Psalms 135:6.

[40] JR, nos. 168, 196, 205, 235, 391, 397, 748, 1490, 1751.

[41] JR, no. 235.

[42] ST, Part I, Q. 19, A. 3.

[43] DZ, nos. 1783, 1805; also see no. 1655 and CCC, nos. 295, 317.

[44] See the condemned proposition in DZ, no. 1908.

[45] DZ, no. 569.

[46] OTT, p. 84.

[47] OTT, p. 84.

[48] See the condemned proposition of Peter Abelard in DZ, no. 374.

[49] ST, Part I, Q. 25, A. 6, Reply Obj. 3.

[50] Gilson, Etienne, *The Philosophy of St. Bonaventure*, Illtyd Trethowan and Frank J. Sheed, trans. (Paterson, NJ: St. Anthony Guild Press, 1965), p. 160.

[51] Ibid., pp. 158–159.

[52] Verses 3, 10, 12, 18, 21, 25, 31.

[53] 1 Timothy 4:4.

[54] *Hexaemeron*, Homily 3, Chapter 10.

[55] DZ, no. 706.

[56] JR, no. 1974f.

[57] CG, Book XI, Chapter 22.

[58] DZ, no. 428.

[59] DZ, no. 706.

[60] DZ, no. 1655.

[61] John 14:6.

[62] See Barrow, John W., *The Constants of Nature* (New York: Panthenon, 2002), ch. 3.

[63] ST, Part I, Q. 25, A. 3.

[64] ST, Part I, Q. 25, A. 4.

[65] BV, Part I, Chapter 7.3. Also see Gilson, op. cit., pp. 150 ff.

[66] *On Truth*, q. 21, a. 2.

[67] *On Truth*, q. 21, a.5.

[68] Romans 8:22.

[69] Romans 11:33.

[70] Romans 8:18.

[71] C. S. Lewis considers this question in *The Problem of Pain* (New York: Simon and Schuster, 1996), ch. 9; and "The Pain of Animals" and "Vivisection" in *God in the Dock* (Grand Rapids, MI: Eerdmans, 1997).

72 Proverbs 12:10.
73 ST, Part I, Q.96, A. 1, Reply Obj. 2.

Doctrine Four
God created each thing in the world immediately.

Genesis clearly teaches that God created each thing during Creation Week entirely and instantly, without the intervention of another agent. The Fathers and Doctors of the Church all believed that. There is no good reason for a Catholic to deny it. Natural science cannot speak authoritatively on this issue because it is beyond the competence of its methods.

The Whole Shebang Cosmogony

Each thing that God created during Creation Week, He created instantly in its entirety, with the suddenness of Christ's miracles. "In Genesis God commands, and one object after another leaps into existence."[1] Thus He created the earth, its creatures, the stars, the galaxies and other celestial objects pretty much as we see them today. That does not mean that He created a static world. It is obvious that He created a dynamic world, an ever-changing world. But He created a whole, finished world and set it in operation. This is the teaching of Genesis. It can be interpreted no other way without violating the text. This interpretation is confirmed elsewhere in Sacred Scripture, for example:

For he spoke, and it came to be; he commanded, and it stood forth.[2]

For he commanded and they were created.[3]

This is what the Fathers of the Church unanimously believed. They often repeated that God created immediately and instantly. For example, St. Ephrem the Syrian compared the speed of God's acts of creation on the first day to the length of that day:

> Although both the light and the clouds were created in the twinkling of an eye, still both the day and night of the first day continued for twelve hours each.[4]

He introduces the notion of *apparent age*—the young look old:

> Just as the trees, the vegetation, the animals, the birds and even mankind were old, so also were they young. They were old according to the appearance of their limbs and their substances, yet they were young because of the hour and moment of their creation. Likewise, the moon was both old and young. It was young, for it was but a moment old, but was also old, for it was as full as it is on the fifteenth day.[5]

And concerning the creation of plant life on the third day, he said:

> Although the grasses were only a moment old at their creation, they appeared as if they were months old. Likewise, the trees, although only a day old when they sprouted forth, were nevertheless like trees years old as they were fully grown and fruits were already budding on their branches. The grass that would be required as food for the animals two days later was thus made ready.[6]

St. Basil the Great had this to say on the instantaneous nature of God's creation of creatures on the third day:

> At this saying all the dense woods appeared; all the trees shot up.... Likewise, all the shrubs were immediately thick with leaf and bushy; and the so-called garland plants ... all came into existence in a moment of time, although they were not previously upon the earth.[7]

And St. Ambrose said the following about the creation of water creatures and amphibians on the fifth day:

> At this command the waters immediately poured forth their offspring. The rivers were in labor. The lakes produced their quota of life. The sea itself began to bear all manner of reptiles.... We are unable to record the multiplicity of the names of all those species which by Divine command were brought to life in a moment of time.[8]

The Fathers of the Church rejected the idea of a universe being formed by natural forces over eons from primeval matter. St. Ambrose said that when Moses says so abruptly *"in the beginning God created,"* he meant to emphasize the incredible speed of the work. Alluding to the Greek atomists he said:

> He [Moses] did not look forward to a late and leisurely creation of the world out of a concourse of atoms.[9]

He goes on to say:

> And fittingly [Moses] added: *"He created,"* lest it be thought there was a delay in creation. Furthermore, men would see also how incomparable the Creator was Who completed such a great work in the briefest moment of His creative act, so much so that the effect of His will anticipated the perception of time.[10]

St. Athanasius taught that all things in each of the six days were created instantly and simultaneously:

> As to the separate stars or the great lights, not this appeared first and that second, but in one day and by the same command, they were all called into being. And such was the original formation of the quadrupeds, and of birds, and fishes, and cattle, and plants.... No one creature was made before another, but all things subsisted at once together upon one and the same command.[11]

Knowledge concerning the events of Creation Week is beyond the competence the methods of natural science. This is because the very laws of nature were then being created. St. Basil expresses this in his commentary on the third day of Creation. He even proposed that matter and the laws that govern it are separate creations:

> Someone may, perhaps, ask this: Why does the Scripture reduce to the command of the Creator that tendency to flow downward which belongs naturally to water? ... If water had this tendency by nature, the command ordering the waters to be gathered together in one place would be superfluous.... To this inquiry we say this, that you recognized very well the movements of the water after the command of the Lord, both that it is unsteady and unstable and that it is borne naturally down slopes and hollows; but how it had any power previous to that, before motion was engendered in it from this command, you yourself neither know nor have you heard it from one who knew. Reflect that

the voice of God makes nature, and the command given at that time to creation provided the future course of action for creatures.[12]

St. Thomas Aquinas defines creation to be the *immediate* production of a thing. He expresses it as follows: "[I]t is said: *'In the beginning God created heaven and earth,'* by which are understood corporeal creatures. These, therefore, were produced immediately by God.... Hence it remains that nothing can create except God alone, who is the first cause. Therefore, in order to show that all bodies were created immediately by God, Moses said: *'In the beginning God created heaven and earth.'"*[13] The word *immediately* means has two meanings. It means *directly*, without the intervention of another agent, and *instantly*, without an interval of time. Thus St. Thomas excludes any form of cosmic evolution or organic macroevolution, whether it be evolution through chance events or evolution programmed into nature by God.[a] God said: *"Let there be"* not *Let there evolve*. However, Aquinas does not deny that God could have used creatures as secondary causes during Creation Week to give things their final forms. And neither does St. Bonaventure.[14]

The Witness of the Polonium Halos

The existence throughout the world of an enormous number of polonium halos in the bedrocks of the earth strongly suggests that these rocks were created fully formed within three minutes. Polonium-218 is a short-lived isotope with a half-life of only three minutes. Primordial polonium-218 atoms have left their fingerprints in the foundation rocks of the earth in the form of spherical shells of discoloration caused by the energetic decay products. When the rocks are sliced thin and viewed under a microscope, the discolorations appear in the form of halos. Since these halos could not have formed in a liquid, they must have been imbedded in the solid rock. And since the lifetime of the polonium atoms is so short, they must have been there when the rocks were made. This implies a nearly instantaneous crystallization of the rocks. Dr. Robert V. Gentry has been studying these rocks for years and sees the polonium halos as strong evidence in favor of instantaneous creation.[15]

---

a. Macroevolution is the development of a new systematic species from previous ones over immense periods of time by natural causes. Microevolution is variation of features within a natural species by causes included within the nature of the species. For definitions of *systematic species* and *natural species* see Doctrine Five.

It should be noted that the issue is not fully settled. And even if it were, the polonium halos would at best provide strong evidence in favor of instantaneous creation but would not "prove" that the rocks were instantly created. One could conceive of other possible, albeit improbable, scenarios to explain their production.

Irreducible Complexity

Biochemist Michael J. Behe coined the term *irreducible complexity* in *Darwin's Black Box*. An *irreducibly complex system* is "a single system composed of several well-matched, interacting parts that contribute to the basic function, wherein the removal of any one of the parts causes the system to effectively cease functioning."[16] Many basic biological systems are irreducibly complex, which implies that they were designed and were created as a unit. In *Darwin's Black Box*, Behe demonstrates the irreducible complexity of several biochemical "machines."

< Objections > and << Replies >>

< Objection 1 >

We now know that the universe started with the explosion of a primordial mass, a "big bang," some 10–20 billion years ago and evolved into the universe of today. We must accommodate Genesis to that scientific fact. The big bang theory gives the cosmic aspect of the theory of evolution, by which scientific facts have been related and interpreted in a unified explanation.

<< Reply to Objection 1 >>

First we must distinguish two kinds of evolution. First there is cosmic evolution, the evolution of the stars, galaxies, the planets, and so on. Next there is organic evolution, the evolution of living things. Some hold one or the other; some hold both. The former is treated under this objection. The latter is treated under the next objection.[17]

<< The Transience of Non-Biblical Cosmogonies >>

The objection is based on the reigning cosmogony, namely, big bang cosmogony. Cosmogonies come and go. They are a product of the temper and the science of the times. The only enduring cosmogony is that of Genesis. It has survived since

Adam and Eve and will continue to survive, despite the onslaughts against it, because it is the truth. God has assured us of that through the Fathers of the Church, the *sensus fidelium* throughout the centuries, and the Magisterium of the Church. But it has never and will never be accepted by everybody. There are always those who think they know better. Those who promote cosmogonical principles in opposition to Genesis do a disservice not only to religion but also to genuine science because genuine science is in search of the truth. And any science that rejects true principles will not find truth.

Despite the immense popularity of the big bang theory, its foundation and structure are weak. And we don't need biblical creationists to point that out. Noncreationist scientists do a good job of that on their own. Modern noncreationist cosmogonies are discussed elsewhere in this work.[18] It suffices here to mention that the big bang theory is simply a theoretical construct based on equations applied far beyond the range of experience; and it is wanting of unimpeachable empirical evidence, despite the claims of its adherents. This is not even taking into consideration the fact that the origin of the universe is a historical event, the truth of which can be made known only by the testimony of an eyewitness.

Some claim that the beauty of macroevolution is that it unifies our knowledge of nature. They claim that all scientific facts can be related by it. In the beginning was the "big bang," which sent matter flying through space, matter that the forces of nature evolved into the wonder-filled universe we live in today. All this is false. It is just wishful thinking on the part of science worshippers who want to reduce the origin of everything to two great principles, the big bang and macroevolution. The scheme is just an updated version of Greek atomism and is just as incredible. As was seen in the cosmology summaries under Doctrine Two, the big bang does not fit neatly into the cosmic scenario if one takes facts more seriously than ideas. However, the propaganda for it has been relentless, and its winning over of adherents despite its inadequacy is the only real success that it can lay claim to. As to being a scientific fact, one of its most outstanding proponents admits: "I cannot deny a feeling of unreality in writing about the first three minutes [after the big bang] as if we really know what we are talking about."[19] And it will be seen in later discussions that the notions of biological macroevolution and geological eons fit the facts even worse. Evolution is not the successful unifying scheme that it's touted to be.

*   *   *   *

< Objection 2 >

Living organisms did not come into existence immediately. They are the product of millions of years of evolution. Elements spontaneously came together in the primeval atmosphere to form amino acids, the building blocks of living organisms. This process has been demonstrated in the laboratory. Amino acids then spontaneously combined to form proteins, which spontaneously combined to form a living cell, which evolved into more complex living organisms. This emergence of life from nonliving matter does not violate the second law of thermodynamics as some claim because life is a statistical fluctuation from the norm, and it is the norm that is governed by that law. The emergence of life is a highly improbable fluctuation, but it had plenty of time to occur.

<< Reply to Objection 2 >>

There are two assumptions in the above objection. The first one is that the laboratory production of amino acids shows what could have happened on earth. The second is that a living cell is the possible outcome of a statistical fluctuation. An examination of these assumptions reveals that the creation of life requires the immediate activity of an intelligent power.

<< Artificially Produced Amino Acids >>

Amino acids "spontaneously" produced from nonliving matter in the laboratory are actually produced under contrived conditions that could never be duplicated in a lifeless natural situation because they require the intervention of an intelligent agent. In the laboratory, the experimenter whisks away the amino acid molecules before they can decompose. In a natural environment the same forces that produced the molecules would destroy them long before they had the opportunity of entering into extremely complex combinations with a variety of others to form proteins.[b]

<< The Second Law of Thermodynamics >>

The *second law of thermodynamics* was originally applied to heat engines. It states that thermal energy cannot be totally converted into mechanical energy or other useful forms. Since various forms of energy are continually being converted into thermal (disordered) energy, and thermal energy cannot be completely trans-formed back into ordered (useful) energy, the amount of transformable energy in the universe is continually diminishing.

The second law of thermodynamics is rooted in statistics concerning the loca-tions and the motions of the molecules of a material substance, and it states only the most probable situation. The disordered molecular states open to a substance are essentially indistinguishable from each other and are extremely more numer-ous than those that can be considered ordered. Therefore disorder is favored. But it is possible for a statistical fluctuation to occur that takes a substance into an ordered molecular state, although the probability for doing so is extremely small. And such states are highly unstable. Yet evolutionists grab at this straw and claim that living organisms could come about by statistical fluctuations in the molecu-lar states of matter.[20] However, they are blowing smoke. Living organisms would then be states that *are available* via fluctuations. That is, they would be *probable outcomes*. It is the burden of the evolutionists to prove that they are, since the number of ordered molecular states that are *probable outcomes* is much less than all the *conceivable* ordered states. For example, consider trying to assemble an operating watch by throwing all the parts in the air and allowing them to fall on a table. There are an infinite number of ways that the parts can fall on the table, some of them highly ordered. But is one of those ways a wound-up operating watch? Those who would answer yes to that question have the burden of demon-strating it. They would have to establish that the force of gravity acting down-wards, air resistance, and collisions of parts are adequate to produce all of the forces, torques, twists and turns necessary to produce an operative watch. They would be hard put to present a convincing case. After failing, they would be forced to admit the necessity of an *energy conversion mechanism* (something that can produce the necessary forces and torques, twists and turns) and a *control sys-tem that directs the energy conversion* (something that directs the forces, torques,

---

b. For a critique of the Miller-Urey experiment, which evolutionists claim demonstrated the possibility of spontaneous generation of life on earth, see Philip E. Johnson, *Darwin on Trial* (Downer's Grove, IL: InterVarsity Press, 1993), pp. 104–105.

twists and turns). The former are the hands of the watchmaker, and the latter are his soul and brain. And this example does not even take into account that the parts themselves have to be properly constructed to work together as a watch.

Since a living cell is infinitely more complex than a watch, it would be impossible for anyone to demonstrate that it is a possible outcome of statistical fluctuations.

<< Maxwell's Demon and the Creation of Life >>

The second law of thermodynamics is also known as the *law of increasing entropy*. Entropy is a measure of the amount of thermal energy in a system that is not available to do work. In other words, it is a measure of the amount of disordered energy in a system that cannot be ordered. Entropy, then, is a measure of disorder. The more disordered a system the higher its entropy. A perfectly ordered system has zero entropy. The second law of thermodynamics is expressed in terms of entropy as follows: if an isolated physical system undergoes a process that takes it from one thermodynamic state to another, the entropy of the final state cannot be less than that of the initial state. Most often it is higher. In everyday terms this means that things in the world are continually becoming more disordered. The second law of thermodynamics is to order as the law of gravity is to mass. As the law of gravity causes a ball to roll from states of higher elevation to states of lower elevation, so the second law of thermodynamics causes a physical system to "roll" from states of higher order to states of lower order.

The famous nineteenth-century physicist James Clerk Maxwell showed how the second law of thermodynamics could be violated by the introduction of an intelligent agent into a system. In a famous letter, "On the Decrease of Entropy by Intelligent Beings,"[21] he imagined an intelligent creature or "demon" that was assigned the task of opening and closing a door in a partition that divided a container of gas at uniform temperature into two parts. The demon's job was to allow fast molecules to go from one side of the partition to the other, thus making one side of the container hotter and the other side cooler. The hotter side would have a higher pressure than the cooler side, and because of the pressure difference work could be done by the gas. That means that some of the disordered energy of the gas could be converted into ordered energy, which wasn't possible before the intervention of the demon. More disordered energy available to do work means that the entropy of the gas has decreased in violation of the second law of thermodynamics.

In response to Maxwell's proposal, physicists asked how the demon could acquire knowledge about the speed of the molecules. They said that he would have to measure the speed of the molecules by bouncing photons off them. But by doing so he would introduce energy and disorder into the system. It turns out that the amount of disorder introduced would be enough to increase the entropy and therefore validate the second law.

However, if the demon was able to determine the initial positions and velocities of all the molecules, he might be able to build a supercomputer that would calculate their subsequent histories. He would not have to disturb the system because the computer would tell him the positions and speeds of all the molecules at all times.

But that won't work either. The positions and velocities of the molecules are continuous quantities. That means that they are represented by irrational numbers. An irrational number requires an infinite number of decimal digits to pin it down exactly. But a computer, no matter how powerful, is still a finite machine. It would have to approximate the irrational numbers by numbers containing finite numbers of decimal digits. That is, it would have to truncate the irrational numbers. In doing so it would introduce errors, which would accumulate over time to give an inaccurate history that would be useless to the demon.

A third possibility is that, since the demon is a spiritual being, he simply knows what the positions and velocities are. But, even though the demon is a spiritual being, he is still a creature and he is still finite. So he could not possess the infinite amount of information required to do the job. Only God could play the role of Maxwell's "demon" because only God simply knows infinite things. God is the Infinite that transcends all infinites. Therefore, only God and God alone can violate the second law of thermodynamics; and only God alone can create the order manifested by living organisms.

[1] Heinisch, Paul, *Theology of the Old Testament,* English ed. by William Heidt (Collegeville, MN: The Liturgical Press, 1950), p. 148.

[2] Psalms 33:9.

[3] Psalms 148:5–6.

[4] *Commentary on Genesis 1*, as quoted in Rose, Fr. Seraphim, *Genesis, Creation and Early Man: The Orthodox Christian Vision* (Platina, CA: Saint Herman of Alaska Brotherhood, 2000), p. 101.

[5] ACC, p. 47.

[6] ACC, p. 15.

[7] *Hexaemeron*, Homily 5, Chapter 10, as quoted in Rose, op. cit., p. 101.

[8] *Hexaemeron*, Homily 5, Chapters 1,2, as quoted in Rose, op. cit., p. 133.

[9] *Ibid.*, Homily 2, Chapter 1, as quoted in Rose, op. cit., p. 101.

[10] Ibid., Homily 1, Chapter 5, as quoted in Rose, op. cot., p. 101.

[11] *Four Discourses Against the Arians*, Discourse 2, Chapters 48, 60, as quoted in Rose, op. cit., p. 102.

[12] *Hexaemeron*, Homily 4, Chapter 2, as quoted in Rose, op. cit., p. 99.

[13] ST, Part I, Q. 65, A.3.

[14] See Gilson, Etienne, *The Philosophy of St. Bonaventure*, Illtyd Trethowan and Frank J. Sheed, trans. (Paterson, NJ: St. Anthony Guild Press, 1965), pp. 246–247.

[15] Gentry, Robert V., *Creation's Tiny Mystery* (Knoxville, TN: Earth Science Associates, 1992).

[16] Behe, Michael J., *Darwin's Black Box: The Biochemical Challenge to Evolution* (New York; The Free Press, 1996), p. 39.

[17] Also see Doctrine Five, << Reply to Objection 1 >>, << Reply to Objection 2 >>, << Reply to Objection 3 >>.

[18] Doctrine Two, << Reply to Objection 1 >>, << Reply to Objection 2 >>; Doctrine Seven, << Reply to Objection 2 >>.

[19] Weinberg, Steven, *The First Three Minutes: A Modern View of the Origin of the Universe* (New York: Basic Books, 1993), p. 9.

[20] For example, see Prigogine, Ilya and Stengers, Isabelle, *Order out of Chaos: Man's New Dialogue with Nature* (New York: Bantam Books, 1984).

[21] Maxwell also discusses his "demon" in his *Theory of Heat* (Mineola, NY: Dover Publications, 2001), pp. 328–329.

Doctrine Five
God created each living creature according to its kind.

Genesis repeatedly states that each living creature was created *"according to its kind."* The Fathers of the Church unanimously believed that the progenitor of each living creature was specially created, that is, was created in its finished and enduring nature during Creation Week. The scientific facts strongly support this, despite the claims of scientists that life evolved over immense spans of time from simple to more complex forms. The fact that many Catholics today feel free to deny special creation and give more credence to the shaky paradigm of biological evolution than to divine revelation as interpreted by the Church for two thousand years indicates a definite devolution of the faith in the modern Church. It is possible that the Church may one day define the special creation of species as revealed truth because it is deeply rooted in Sacred Tradition and sound scriptural exegesis. The same cannot be said for the evolution of species because that has no support whatsoever in Scripture or Tradition.

Special Creation

Charles Darwin (1809–1882) concluded *The Origin of Species* with the statement: "There is grandeur in this view of life, with its several powers, having been originally breathed by the Creator into a few forms or into one; and that, whilst this planet has gone cycling on according to the fixed law of gravity, from so simple a beginning endless forms most beautiful and most wonderful have been, and are being evolved."[1] Darwin held that all the living species on earth evolved from one or a few primeval living forms and that contemporary species are slowly transforming into new species. This directly contradicts the Genesis account, which states that all living creatures were created in the beginning *"according to their kind."* Darwin's "Creator" is not the God of Genesis, and Darwin's "grandeur" is not the glory of God but the pride of man.

The first chapter of the Book of Genesis repeatedly states that each living creature was created *"according to its kind."* The repetition of the fact that each living creature was created according to its kind is so frequent and so forceful that the sacred author seems to be anticipating its future denial by Darwin and his disciples. Genesis clearly teaches that the progenitors of all living creatures were created in their finished and enduring natures during Creation Week. This is what is meant by the term *special creation.* Special creation can be understood in two ways. It can mean that something was created completely, matter and form together, from nothing. Or it can mean that a form was created from nothing in matter already created from nothing.

The Fathers of the Church accepted, without question, the fact that each living creature was specially created. St. Ambrose makes the point that many different living creatures were created simultaneously:

> At this command the waters immediately poured forth their offspring. The rivers were in labor. The lakes produced their quota of life. The sea itself began to bear all manner of reptiles.... We are unable to record the multiplicity of the names of all those species which by Divine command were brought to life in a moment of time. At the same instant substantial form and the principle of life were brought into existence.... The whale, as well as the frog, came into existence at the same time by the same creative power.[2]

St. John Chrysostom speaks of the wonders of the fifth day:

> Just as He said of the earth only: *"Let it bring forth,"* and there appeared a great variety of flowers, herbs and seeds, and all occurred by His word alone, so here also He said: *"Let the waters bring forth swarms of living creatures, and let birds fly above the earth across the firmament of the heavens"*—and instantly there were so many kinds of crawling things, such a variety of birds, that one cannot number them in words.[3]

St. Gregory of Nyssa lays to rest the pseudoparadox: What came first, the chicken or the egg?

> In the beginning, we see, it was not an ear rising from a grain but a grain coming from an ear, and after that, the ear grows round the grain.[4]

Created Kinds and Natural Species

St. Basil the Great, in discussing the work of the third day, gives the meaning of *"according to its kind"*:

> There is nothing truer than this, that either each plant has seed or there exists in it some generative power. And this accounts for the expression *"of its own kind."* For the shoot of the reed is not productive of an olive tree, but from the reed comes another reed, and from seeds spring plants related to the seeds sown. Thus what was put forth by earth in its first generation has been preserved until the present time, since the kinds persisted through constant reproduction.[5]

The precise meaning of the Hebrew word *min,* translated "kind," is not clear from Scripture. But it is obviously a natural division of some sort. The most probable interpretation of *"kind"* seems to be that it indicates a distinct nature. So we will use the term *created kind* to indicate a distinct plant or animal nature created by God during Creation Week. God may have created one, one pair or a number of individuals with the same nature.

The nature of an animal or plant is not always easy to define. But we have a strong instinctive sense about their natures that we can't transcribe into words. For example, any child is able to distinguish a dog from a cat, even though there are many varieties of each. The child is able to accurately distinguish "dogness" from "catness" even though he is unable to express the distinction in words. All he could do to distinguish them would be to give accidental features, for example: dogs have wet noses; cats have whiskers.

The great naturalist Carolus Linnaeus (1707–1778) believed in the special creation and permanence of the created kinds, and he tried to distinguish these kinds as best as possible in a system of classification. In his system, the basic unit is the *species.* The next highest order of ranking is the *genus,* in which species are grouped according to structural features. Linnaeus assigned a genus and a species to an organism. His system of classification goes by the name *binomial nomenclature.* Modern naturalists use Linneaeus' system in an expanded form with groupings higher than genus. This system is artificial. It is useful for organizing and identifying living organisms, but it does not give much insight into the natures of the organisms it classifies. Linnaeus himself recognized this.

A *natural species* is a complete collection of individual organisms that share the same specific essence. This definition recognizes the existence of natural divisions within the plant and animal kingdoms. Since man, being a rational animal, is obviously a natural species, it seems fitting that the other animals and the plants also belong to their own natural species. The created kinds are the natures of the natural species. The natural species are natural groups, and the kinds are the specific natures of those groups.

A *systematic species* is an artificial grouping; it is a collection of individual organisms grouped together according to some convenient criteria. Systematic species are fleeting. They can change according to the circumstances of the question under consideration. Evolutionists work only with systematic species because they do not believe in the immutability of species.[6]

A. C. Cotter in *Natural Species* tackles the problem of how to identify the natural species in the plant and animal kingdoms. He first argues that we can know the essences of natural corporeal substances. We can know the essences of natural things because

> [A]ll things of nature express God's thoughts and are imitations of God's essence. They are intelligible at least to God's all-comprehending intellect. Now our intellect is an imitation … of the divine. Fundamentally then all things of nature are also intelligible to us.[7]

Therefore we can come to know the specific essences of plants and animals. A specific essence is "the ultimate intrinsic reason for *all* the properties of a being."[8] He goes on to say: "Determining the specific essence of a thing is a step beyond scientific induction. It demands not only knowledge of the properties themselves, but also insight into their *mutual relation*, or rather insight into the necessity with which the properties flow from the essence as their foundation."[9] Adam may have had knowledge of the specific essences of animals since God brought them to him to name (2:19).

Cotter further points out that God created each natural species to fulfill a purpose in the household of nature. This is obvious a priori because God is an intelligent being and does not do things frivolously. It is also observed a posteriori by naturalists in the field, who in their observations come to see the roles that natural species play in the economy of nature. God did not create the natural species to exist merely for their own sake. He made them to serve man, either directly or indirectly, for He gave man dominion over the creatures of the earth.

Cotter goes on to define natural species in terms of their purpose in the balance of nature. "A biological [natural] species is a group of living organisms created for some *purposive activity* [in the household of nature]."[10] He gives some obvious examples of purposes—that of a cow is to produce milk, of sheep to furnish wool, of bees to make honey. Francisco Suarez (1548–1617) said that the purpose constitutes and completes the essence of a natural being.[11] The purpose determines the physical features of the organism. Cotter quotes St. Thomas Aquinas: "As matter is for the sake of form, so the form is for the sake of its specific action; for action is the purpose of creation."[12] He also cites Suarez: "Aristotle rightly argues that the last reason why things of nature have such characteristics or such organs or such parts etc., is not due to matter, but to their purpose.... They were given for some purpose of form, and the form needs them for self-preservation or some activity."[13] As Suarez pointed out, some of those features are directed toward the preservation of the individual or the species. But this again is linked to its purpose because the organism is preserved to achieve it. The *Catechism of the Catholic Church* confirms that each creature serves a purpose in the intricate web of creation.

> God wills the *interdependence of creatures.* The sun and the moon, the cedar and the little flower, the eagle and the sparrow: the spectacle of their countless diversities and inequalities tells us that no creature is self-sufficient. Creatures exist only in dependence on each other, to complete each other, in the service of each other.[14]

The mutual dependence of creatures on one another strongly suggests that all creatures were created together in a short period of time.

Criteria of Natural Species

Following are some criteria that are useful for identifying natural species:

- *Interfertility/Intrasterility*: This criterion, in one form or another, is the one most widely used by naturalists. It states that if individual plants or animals have the power to breed offspring identical in nature, and if those offspring and their offspring and so on have the same power, those individuals belong to the same species. This criterion further states that if this power is not present, the individuals belong to different species. This criterion implies sexual reproduction and its biological possibility, but not necessarily its actuality. There are different varieties of some species that do not mate with each other when brought together but are still biologically capable of producing fertile offspring. Such varieties probably descended from the same created kind, but in the unfolding of their natures over the centuries developed certain distinct features, one being the refusal, reluctance or even the physical inability to mate with certain other varieties. Some varieties do not mate simply because they live in different habitats.

There are living organisms in nature to which the fertility test cannot be applied. These would include organisms that reproduce by asexual processes such as simple fission, budding and forming spores, and those organisms that reproduce by fertilizing their own eggs. However, it is evident in these processes that the organisms are breeding new individuals of their own kinds. Another limitation of the fertility test is that it cannot be applied to fossils.

Hybridism does not present a serious problem for this method of identifying natural species because hybrids are produced through the interference of man and are nearly always sterile. Hybrids are therefore, in a sense, artificial. Nature abhors hybrids. God arranged living organisms so that their kinds will not cross in their natural state. For example, animals with some biological compatibility are kept separate by being natural enemies, by having different seasons of sexual heat and by physical or social incompatibility.

As will be discussed, the process of variation by mutation is at work on the natural species. This could have produced physiological changes over the centuries in certain varieties of the original created species that destroyed the ability of those varieties to interbreed with other varieties. So today there may be several varieties of an original species that look like separate natural species according to this criterion.

- *Likeness of Visible Characteristics*: Differentiating plants and animals by their visible characteristics is the most obvious procedure to follow, and naturalists have developed it in detail. In this way we immediately differentiate between dogs, cats, horses, cows, and so on. Botanists identify plants by their flowers, seeds, fruit, leaves and other characteristics. However, as the saying goes, looks may be deceiving. Things that look alike may be very different, and things that look different may be alike in their nature. Totally unrelated organisms sometimes have similar visible characteristics and related ones dissimilar characteristics.

- *Life Cycle*. Individuals of different species follow a different rhythm of life. Members of the same species generally have the same gestation period, the same maturation stages and chronology, and the same natural lifetime, all within limits and with some exceptions, of course.

- *Instinct.* Members of the same animal species display the same specific instinctive behavior. Members of the same species court, mate, rear their young, and procure food in the same way. They follow the same migratory patterns and chronology. Individuals in a community may have different chores but they work together for the same end. For example, the queen, the drones and the workers in a colony of bees each contribute in their own way to produce a hive and honey. J. Henri Fabre showed in his experiments with insect behavior that, although insects do amazing things, their instinctive behavior is fixed and limited. He demonstrated that what appeared to some observers as intelligent behavior was the slavish following of instinct.[15]

- *Chromosomes.* Another way to differentiate natural species is by the number, size and shape of chromosomes their cells contain. Every species has a definite number of chromosomes, and the number is generally even. The numbers vary from two in a certain small worm to 16,000 in certain one-celled animals. Man has 46. The setback of this method is that there are different species that have the same number of chromosomes. But their size and shape may be different, and ambiguities can often be resolved by macroscopic properties of the species. Also, DNA analysis has become a powerful identification tool.

Discontinuity of Species

Discontinuity of species is an observed fact. In the world of living organisms and in the fossil world, there are only distinct organisms separated by gaps. Evolutionists are forced by the facts to admit that there are no transitional or intermediate forms in the living world today or in the fossil record. Zoologist Theodosius Dobzhansky states:

> If we assemble as many individuals living at a given time as we can, we notice at once that the observed variation does not form any kind of continuous distribution. Instead, a multitude of separate, discrete distributions are found. The living world is not a single array of individuals in which any two variants are connected by unbroken series of intergrades, but an array of more or less distinctly separate arrays, intermediates between which are absent or at least rare.[16]

Paleontologist George Gaylord Simpson acknowledges noncontinuity in the fossil record:

In spite of these examples, it remains true, as every paleontologist knows, that *most* new species, genera, and families, and nearly all new categories above the level of families, appear in the record suddenly and are not led up to by known, gradual, completely continuous transitional sequences.[17]

This presents a problem for evolutionists because their theory predicts a continuum of organic forms, but that just doesn't exist. Distinct forms with gaps are exactly what one would expect to observe according to the Genesis account.

Permanence of the Created Kinds

Genesis implies the stability of kinds. In Genesis 1 it is said the plants and animals were created according to their kind. In Genesis 6, God tells Noah to take two of each kind of animal into the ark. So the distinct kinds persisted from Adam to Noah, a period of some 1650 years.

The created kinds were permanent natures transmitted without change from generation to generation. Accidental features of individuals may vary within certain limits from generation to generation, but the nature is transmitted immutably.

The Fathers believed in the permanence of the kinds throughout successive generations. St. Basil the Great said of the preservation of kinds:

> *"Let the earth bring forth living creatures according to their kinds: cattle and creeping things and beasts of the earth according to their kinds."* Consider the word of God moving through all creation, having begun at that time, active up to the present and efficacious until the end, even to the consummation of the world. As a ball, when pushed by someone and then meeting with a slope, is borne downward by its own shape and the inclination of the ground and does not stop before some level surface receives it, so too the nature of existing objects, set in motion by one command, passes through creation, without change, by generation and destruction, preserving the succession of kinds through resemblance, until it reaches the very end.[18]

> It [nature] begets a horse as the successor of a horse, a lion of a lion and an eagle of an eagle. It continues to preserve each of the animals by uninterrupted successions until the consummation of the universe. No length of time causes the specific characteristics of the animal to be corrupted or extinct, but, as if established just recently, nature, ever fresh, moves along with time.[19]

St. Ambrose said of the preservation of kinds:

In the pine cone nature seems to express an image of itself. It preserves its peculiar properties which it received from that divine and celestial command, and it repeats in the succession and order of the years its generation until the end of time is fulfilled. [20]

The Word of God permeates every creature in the constitution of the world. Hence, as God had ordained, all kinds of living creatures were quickly produced from the earth. In compliance with a fixed law they all succeed each other from age to age according to their aspect and kind. The lion generates a lion; the tiger, a tiger; the ox, an ox; the swan, a swan; and the eagle, an eagle. What was once enjoined became in nature a habit for all time. Hence the earth has not ceased to offer the homage of its service. The original species of living creatures is reproduced for future ages by successive generations of its kind.[21]

St. Augustine said of God's blessing the living creatures in (1:22):

God wanted the blessing to have the power of fecundity, which is revealed in the succession of offspring. Thus, although the animals were made weak and mortal, they might by that blessing preserve their kind by giving birth.[22]

St. Ambrose said that hybrids are the work of humans, not of God:

What pure and untarnished generations follow without intermingling one after another, so that a thymallus produces a thymallus; a sea-wolf, a sea-wolf. The sea-scorpion, too, preserves unstained its marriage bed.... Fish, therefore, know nothing of union with alien species. They do not have unnatural betrothals such as are designedly brought about between animals of two different species as, for instance, the donkey and the mare, or again the female donkey and the horse, both being examples of unnatural union. Certainly there are cases in which nature suffers more in the nature of defilement rather than that of injury to the individual. Man as an abettor of hybrid barrenness is responsible for this. He considers a mongrel animal more valuable than one of a genuine species. You mix together alien species and you mingle diverse seeds.[23]

The visible characteristics of plants and animals have remained essentially unchanged over the centuries. Aristotle described a number of animals over two thousand years ago, and his descriptions agree with present-day observations.[24]

Variety and Stability within Natural Species

The permanence of created kinds does not exclude variations within natural species. It is obvious that there are varieties within the natural species. For example, Frank Marsh points out that there are over 500 varieties of the sweetly scented sweet pea and over two hundred breeds of dogs.[25] We all know how differently different varieties of dogs look and behave, but they all share the same canine nature. The amount of variation possible within a natural species is not unlimited. A species can vary only within the strict limits set by its nature.

Because of variation within a species, the identity of a natural species is not best represented by just a point on a chart. Rather, it is best represented by a point on a chart circumscribed by a circle. In some cases there may even be overlaps at the circumference of the circle with other natural species. But that does not destroy the specific identity of each natural species. Naturalists may sometimes find it difficult to resolve those identities, but that does not destroy them anymore than an astronomer's inability to resolve stars in a distant galaxy destroys the identities of those stars. It simply means that the tools of observation are not powerful enough to do the job.

Throughout the centuries the natural species have diversified within their natural limits to produce the wonderful varieties that fill the world. The species continually unfold the potentialities of their natures, either through natural means or through man's artifice, and thereby continually reveal new facets of grandeur in God's creation.

The biological unit that determines the characteristics of an organism is the gene, which is a long strand of the chemical deoxyribonucleic acid (DNA). The DNA molecule is a chainlike molecule called a *polymer*. The links of the chain are chemical entities called *nucleotides*. There are four different nucleotides, labeled A, T, C and G. Genetic information is coded in the sequence of nucleotides. Genetic information is used by an organism to construct proteins, which, among other things, perform a major role in the transfer of information inside living organisms. Proteins play a dominant role in cell function and therefore in the whole organism. So the DNA, by directing the production of proteins, helps to define the nature of an organism.

Genes may work singly or in blocks to give an organism its specific and individual features. The genes are lined up in strings called *chromosomes,* the number of which depends on the species. The chromosomes are located in the nucleus of the cell, except for bacteria, which do not have nuclei. The entire DNA in all of the chromosomes of a cell is called the *genome*. The information in the genome of a mammal, if written out in type, would fill two thousand volumes. All the cells in an organism, except the reproductive cells, have the same genome.

The information content in a living organism is not confined to the genes. If that were so, complex organisms would always have more DNA than simple organisms. But that is not always the case. For example, mammal DNA is shorter than amphibian DNA. A frog has more information encoded in its DNA than does a chimpanzee. And DNA information in some species of amoeba is about thirty times as large as that in humans. Much of the activity of the cell is carried out without gene involvement, so much so that the cell appears to have its own "built-in intelligence." Even the cells of the simplest organisms are immensely complex. The cell has been compared to a large city with factories, warehouses, hospitals, police, emergency systems, transportation systems, communication systems, refuse deposal systems and more. But it is much more than that. The capability of a cell to carry out its variety of functions, including the duplication of itself, is far beyond the pale of human ingenuity. And its unity of operation is so complete that it must have been created completely functional. To say otherwise is ludicrous.

Each gene in a natural species can come in more than one version. Each version is known as an *allele*. Alleles are the basis for variety in a natural species. The main cause of variations in offspring produced by sexual reproduction is the mixing of the father's and the mother's alleles. This can lead to offspring with a wide variety of characteristics. Subsets of these individuals that have certain common features are called *varieties, races, breeds or strains*. New natural species are never produced this way because there are strict limits within which variation can take place. Luther Burbank, famous for his breeding and crossing experiments, said:

> I know from experience that I can develop a plum half an inch long or one 2½ inches long, with every possible length in between, but I am willing to admit that it is hopeless to try to get a plum the size of a small pea, or one as big as a grapefruit. I have daisies on my farms little larger than my fingernail and some that measure six inches across, but I have none as big as a sunflower, and never expect to have. I have roses that bloom pretty steadily for six months in the year, but I have none that will bloom twelve, and I will not have. In short, there are limits to the development possible, and these limits follow a law.... Experiments carried on extensively have given us scientific proof of what we have already guessed by observation; namely, that plants and animals all tend to revert, in successive generations, toward a given mean or average. Men grow to be seven feet tall, and over, but never to ten; there are dwarfs no higher than 24 inches, but none that you can carry in your hand ... In short, there is

undoubtedly a pull toward the mean which keeps all living things within some more or less fixed limitations.[26]

He also pointed out that nobody had succeeded in growing black tulips or blue roses because the genetic material was simply not there. Artificially bred varieties, when left to their own devices, usually either die out, because of sterility or weakness, or revert to the norm. Biologists have labeled this resistance to change *genetic homeostasis*. It has been confirmed in numberless experiments.

Lee Spetner in *Not by Chance!* shows that if two human parents differ by only one allele in each chromosome, the number of different offspring they could produce is about 70 trillion, about ten thousand times the current population of the earth.[27] It is mind-boggling to think of the genetic potential Adam and Eve had. They had the potential to produce innumerable races with many different traits, and probably many races and traits were lost forever in the Great Flood. Scripture speaks of a human trait that did survive the Flood, giantism. Giant humans existed before and after the Flood.[28]

Another cause of variations in living organisms is the mutability of genes and chromosomes. Genes are subject to mutations. A *mutation* is any heritable genetic change. First, there are *point mutations* that can occur in a gene. These effect a change in a single unit of information in the gene, either changing it to another unit or destroying it completely. They can be caused by replication errors, natural radiations such as x-rays and ultraviolet light, and by manmade chemicals. Replication errors are extremely rare, from one in a billion to one in a hundred billion units of information. Point mutations are nearly always either detrimental to the organism or neutral. Although they may be useful in some circumstances, even then they degrade the organism in some way. They cannot accumulate to transform a natural species as claimed by evolutionists. They can no more transform the nature of an organism than changing some letters can transform the *Encyclopedia Britannica* into the *Catholic Encyclopedia*. All they can produce, if anything, are varieties, freaks or sports. Numerous experiments have been performed producing mutations in fruit flies. But nothing has ever come out of them but fruit flies. Some were quite freakish, with misplaced organs and limbs, and so on, but they were still fruit flies. The natural species preserve themselves.

It seems that the law of genetic homeostasis applies even to varieties with mutant genes. Francis Hitching in *The Neck of the Giraffe* tells of a fascinating series of experiments. In these experiments mutant genes were paired to create an eyeless fly. When these flies were interbred, the offspring were also eyeless, as expected. This continued for a few generations. But then, lo and behold, the unexpected began to happen. A few flies hatched with eyes. The genetic code had a built-in repair mechanism. The natural order reasserted itself. Hitching concludes: "The main function of the genetic system, quite clearly, is one of renewal, of maintenance of the *status quo*, of establishing limits to change."[29]

In addition to point mutations, there are mutations that can affect more than one gene. One such genetic change is known as *recombination* or *crossing over*. In this change *homologues* (paired chromosomes) exchange alleles during the production of germ cells producing chromosomes with new combinations of alleles. This is a complex process that is controlled by special enzymes. Spetner lists five other kinds of mutations: duplication of a segment of a genome, inversion of a segment, deletion of a segment, insertion of a new segment, and transposition of a segment. These processes are not haphazard events. They are too precise and controlled to happen by chance. Geneticists do not know why they occur but believe they play important roles. They are not genetic mistakes but seem to be programmed acts performed on behalf of the cell or organism. Spetner says:

> Genetic rearrangements seem to be as normal an activity of the cell as cell division, even though they don't happen so often. They are mediated by specific enzymes which, as far as we know, the cell synthesizes just for that purpose. Some biologists may want to call them random only because their timing is not yet understood.[30]

These mutations, like the point mutations, do not have the power to produce new natural species. The most they can do is produce another version of a species.

Adaptability of Natural Species

Scientists have discovered the marvelous ability of natural species to adapt to new situations. Spetner points out that this ability is the effect of beneficial mutations:

> There are some mutations that are known to benefit an organism in special cases. We have already seen how a back mutation [a mutation that reverses the effect of a previous one] can restore a lost function. Such a mutation will benefit the organism. There are other examples of "good", or *adaptive*, mutations. There are those that give bacteria a resistance to streptomycin. There are those that give insects resistance to DDT.[31]

The mutant bacteria and insects are new strains, not new species. Spetner further points out that experiments have shown that bacteria can mutate to produce new functions when needed.[32] Thus it appears that the capacity of an organism to adapt to a variety of environments is built into organisms.

In the evolutionary paradigm variations in an organism are random. Adaptive variations imply design and not chance, and so the idea of adaptive variation smacks of "heresy." Spetner remarks how scientific orthodoxy has ignored the fact that organisms adapt to the environment:

> Observed adaptations induced by the environment have been reported for more than a century, but they have been largely ignored by mainstream biology due to the dominance of Darwinian theory and the NDT [Neo-Darwinian Theory]. They have been swept under the rug because they couldn't be understood within the framework of the theory.[33]

The secret of the adaptability of organisms lies in the fact that some genes lie dormant until awakened by some stimulus in the environment. Enzymes turn genes ON and OFF as they are needed without making any permanent change in the genome. This enables the organism to live through short-term changes in the environment. Also, more permanent heritable changes are also possible. Spetner make the following proposition based on scientific facts:

> Organisms contain within themselves the information that enables them to develop a phenotype adaptive to a variety of environments. The adaptation can occur by a change in the genome through a genetic change triggered by the environment, or it can occur without any genetic change.
>
> This capability is an advantage to the population. It helps it survive by adapting to long-term changes in the environment. Suppose a "biological engineer" is designing living organisms. If he has to design a species to live in a range of environments, he is faced with a design dilemma. On one horn of the dilemma, he could make the species well adapted and highly specific to one of the environments. But then it would be less well adapted to other environments. On the other horn, he could make the species less specific and broadly adapted to the whole range of expected environments. But then it would not be so well adapted to any of them as it could have been to one of them. A good way for him to resolve the dilemma would be to build into the species the ability to switch among several forms, each highly adapted to one of the environments. He would design the switch to be triggered by a cue from the environment. I am suggesting here that living organisms have the capability of switching from one phenotype to another when cued by the environment.[34]

This can account, for example, for the differences between the polar bear and the grizzly bear. They are capable of mating and producing fertile offspring, so they belong to the same natural species (although they are classified in modern taxonomy as separate species). So they both might have descended from the same original created parents who had the potentiality for both varieties in their genes. They each adapted to the environment in which they found themselves.

Spetner further points out that nature has its own built-in methods for regulating animal and plant populations to keep them in balance with the natural resources they consume. And they are not the ways proposed by Malthus.[a] Spetner states:

> [A]nimals generally manage their food resources by controlling their own numbers. Populations are kept in check not by the extrinsic forces of mass starvation or disease, but by intrinsic forces built into the animals themselves. This phenomenon may be surprising and even amazing to most people, but biologists studying animals in the wild have reported this kind of control operating in a variety of populations.
>
> Plants do not proliferate in a field to the point where they become crowded. They do not engage in a "struggle for existence" where natural selection would preserve the strong and destroy the weak. Plants tend to control their population by sensing the density of the planting. When the growth is dense, plants produce less seeds; when the growth is thin, they produce more seeds.[35]

The same can surely be said of the human species. There are and always have been those who create panic by crying "overpopulation!" Those who practice contraception and pat themselves on the back for being good citizens by helping keep the population in check are only fooling themselves. God knows the dynamics of population infinitely better than we do, and He built into nature the balances needed to preserve the human species. By contracepting and aborting,

---

a. In *The Essay on the Principle of Population* (1798) Thomas Robert Malthus, an English clergyman maintained that a population tends to increase exponentially while the means of subsistence increases only linearly. The population therefore tends to overcome the means of subsistence. He maintained that human population could be limited only by vice (birth control), famine, war and disease. The human race, therefore, is destined to always hover on the brink of existence. Malthus' theory strongly influenced Charles Darwin, the inventor of the theory of evolution by variation and natural selection.

people are destroying those balances and inviting physical as well as moral and spiritual disaster.

Recap: Kinds, Species and Varieties

God created the plants and animals each according to a specific nature (*kind*). The kinds are permanent; they have remained constant throughout the centuries since Creation. The complete collection of individuals of a certain kind is a *natural species*. Each natural species has a role or roles in the household of nature. God built into the natural species the ability to produce individuals with a variety of characteristics within fixed limits. This power produces diversity and helps species to adapt to different environmental conditions. These individuals form subgroups within a natural species called *varieties, races, breeds and strains*. The genetic processes of *allele mixing* and *mutation* cause these variations. These processes always preserve the nature of the organism and so do not produce new kinds. Thus God has programmed a great potential for diversity in the world of living organisms that does not destroy the identities of the original kinds. And although individual varieties have become extinct over the centuries, it may be that representatives of all the created kinds are still with us today.

For philosophical considerations pertaining to natural species, see Appendix B.

< Objections > and << Replies >>

< Objection 1 >

The finches on the Galápagos Islands are living proof of the transformation of one species to another by variation and natural selection.

<< Reply to Objection 1 >>

This objection and the next one represent the opinions of evolutionary biologists and paleontologists who claim that there is indisputable scientific evidence for the evolution of biological species. This objection concerns the world of living organisms. The next objection concerns the fossil record. Both objections are attacks against the veracity of Genesis made in the name of science, and both will be shown to be without substance.

<< Darwin's Finches >>

The picture of the thirteen varieties of finches of the Galápagos Islands, all with different beaks, has become an icon of Darwinism. It appears widely in biology textbooks. Evolutionary biologists claim that this bird demonstrates "evolution in real time."[36] Darwinists really believe that they have observed the transformation of species by variation and natural selection in these little birds.

The Galápagos Islands straddle the equator about 600 miles west of the coast of Ecuador. Charles Darwin visited these islands in 1835 on his famous voyage on the H.M.S. *Beagle*. In his diary of that voyage Darwin makes only a passing reference to the finches on those islands, and he does not mention them at all in *The Origin of Species*. So they were not instrumental in the formulation of his theory of evolution, as many biology textbooks claim.

Darwin and later naturalists observed that there were thirteen varieties of finches on the islands. And so it is today. The varieties differ in that each has its own distinctive beak. Some have large beaks useful for cracking seeds, and others have slender beaks suited to catching insects. Some have beaks shaped for probing flowers, and one variety has a straight wood-boring beak. They also differ in their size and plumage, some being as large as a blackbird and others as small as a sparrow. Each is adapted to its habitat. At least half the finch varieties are known to interbreed, although they do so infrequently. There are features that show that they are closely related. For example, they all exhibit the same display and song pattern; they are all obviously finches. And chromosome studies show no differences among the finches.

Evolutionary biologists label these different varieties as different species. They assume that originally a few finches found their way to the islands and since then variations appeared in the birds. The changes in the birds were preserved by natural selection. As a result the birds diversified into the thirteen "species" now found on the islands.

The thirteen varieties of finches remain distinct primarily because of mating behavior. Evidence suggests that the birds choose their mates on the basis of beak morphology and song pattern. The former is inherited, while young birds learn the latter from their parents. Mating habits do not make a reliable criterion for classifying species. In human populations race is inherited and language is learned. Human populations that are separated by race and language are unquestionably the same species, even though such differences make interbreeding uncommon. And morphological features make an unreliable criterion. Pigeons vary more in appearance than Darwin's finches, yet are considered one species. Dogs differ markedly, but are regarded as one species.

What are observed in "Darwin's finches" are variations within a natural species. The observations made by naturalists in the Galápagos Islands were not of transformations of species. They were observations of one natural species adapting to a variety of habitats. In fact, transformation of species has never been observed in nature. Geneticist Thomas Hunt Morgan (1866–1945) stated:

> Within the period of human history, we do not know of a single instance of the transformation of one species into another, if we apply the most rigid and extreme tests to distinguish wild species from each other.[37]

Thus the question reduces to the Darwinists' definition of the word *species*. The *Penguin Dictionary of Biology* under "species" states:

> Zoologists find the criterion of reproductive isolation especially valuable in demarcating species in the wild. As such, the *biological species concept* includes as species groups of populations which are phenotypically similar and reproductively isolated from other such groups, but which are actually or potentially capable of interbreeding among themselves.[38]

This definition was originally formulated by the biologist Ernst Mayr in 1942 and has been used by many biologists since. "Reproductive isolation" is caused by "mechanisms preventing gene flow between parts of an originally interbreeding species population."[39] By employing the notion of reproductive isolation, biologists conveniently exclude the requirement that for two groups to be of different species they must be *biologically unable* to interbreed. Instead they require only that, for some reason, they *don't* interbreed. This means, for example, that if two groups of a fertile population become physically separated, they then become two separate species. Since the different varieties of finches occupy different ecological niches, biologists label them as different species and thus make their claim that they observed the transformation of species.

Evolutionary biology is thoroughly nominalistic. That is why it is unable to come up with an adequate definition of species. The *Penguin Dictionary of Biology* acknowledges this:

> Inability to find a unified species concept is no disgrace.... It is probably no accident that the species concept does not figure prominently in biological theory: species may best be regarded not as NATURAL KINDS (such as elements

in chemistry) but as individuals, each historically unique and irreplaceable once extinct. If species are individuals then species names are proper names, so that the properties of species would describe but not define them.[40]

It is obvious then that evolutionary biology rejects a priori the reality of natural species, and the facts of biology do not a posteriori justify that rejection. It all amounts to a blatant and arbitrary rejection of Genesis.

✳   ✳   ✳   ✳

< Objection 2 >

Paleontology assures us that not all species of plants and animals originated at one and the same time.

<< Reply to Objection 2 >>

If this objection were valid, then several possible conclusions would follow. If one assumes that new natural species came into existence through natural processes, then either simple organisms transformed into more complex ones slowly in a process of evolution, or new organisms came into existence rapidly through massive mutations. Neither conforms to Genesis, and neither one lies on a sound scientific basis. Many reputable authorities have discredited the former explanation,[41] and the latter (*punctuated equilibrium*) is preposterous. If one assumes that new natural species came into existence by supernatural means then they were specially created after Creation Week. This too is inconsistent with Genesis because God completed creation on the sixth day (2:1). The only possible explanation conforming to Genesis would be the actualization of seminal reasons as proposed by St. Augustine.[42] However, the above objection is not valid because paleontologists are not able to assure us all living organisms did not originate at the same time. In fact, the evidence strongly indicates otherwise.

<< The Fossil Record and Its Origin >>

Paleontologists point to the fossil record in support of their claim that all the natural species did not come into existence at the same time. *The Penguin Dictionary of Biology* describes *fossil* as follows:

Remains of an organism, or direct evidence of its presence, preserved in rock, ice, amber, tar, peat or volcanic ash. Animal hard parts (hard skeletons) commonly undergo mineralization, a process which also turns sediment into hard rock. (both regarded as diagenesis).[43]

Of special interest here are those fossils found in sedimentary rocks. These are fossils that are formed by plants and animals being buried in sediment that then hardens to become rock. Such rock is present throughout the earth stacked in layers called *strata*. There are a great number of the fossils in these strata, comprising some one hundred thousand "fossil species."[44] Throughout the eighteenth century and well into the nineteenth it was widely held by theologians and scientists that the great majority of sedimentary fossils in all the strata were produced in one unique tremendous worldwide catastrophe, the Great Flood of Genesis. The first major attack on this view was a new catastrophism, advocated by the French scientist Georges Cuvier (1769–1832), considered today as the father of paleontology. Cuvier held the opinion that the fossil-bearing strata were laid down by a series of great floods beginning long before the creation of man and separated by immense periods of time. The last of these floods was the Flood of Genesis. After each of these catastrophes, the surviving animals multiplied to fill the earth again, only to be destroyed in another great flood. This was, at best, a rewriting of the Genesis account. Cuvier's introduction of many floods separated by immense times was extremely gratuitous. The different strata may have suggested separate formation, but many floods and immense time periods were not required. One massive worldwide flood working on the surface of the earth for five months producing layer after layer of sediment could explain the strata, if there was a mind to hold to the Genesis account.

The English lawyer Charles Lyell (1797–1875) promoted a geological theory that eliminated all catastrophism. In his *Principles of Geology* he argued that the fossiliferous strata were produced by the geological processes of erosion and sedimentation working slowly over immensely long periods of time. He explicitly rejected any explanations that involved a worldwide catastrophe stating: "[A]ll theories are rejected which involve the assumption of sudden and violent catastrophes and revolutions of the whole earth, and its inhabitants."[45] He does not mention the Great Flood, but it is clear that this statement was directed to it. It was a bold-faced and gratuitous rejection of Genesis.

In both Cuvier's theory and Lyell's theory, the fossils in different strata were produced at different times in the earth's history. For Cuvier they were laid down by extraordinary phenomena, for Lyell they were laid down by the usual geological processes. It is an established fact that Lyell's usual geologic processes do not form fossils. Fossil formation requires rapid burial, which, considering the large numbers of fossils found in many deposits, implies catastrophic conditions. There are no known fossil-bearing rocks forming anywhere in the world today. For both Cuvier and Lyell the time periods separating the strata were immense. But there are observed facts that provide strong evidence that the different strata were laid down one after another in quick succession. They certainly were not laid down ages apart. Three of the most glaring facts follow:

- There are no surface irregularities in the interfaces where strata meet. This means that each succeeding stratum in a formation must have been laid shortly after the preceding one because no erosion took place.

- *Polystrate fossils* are single fossils that pass though more than one stratum. Fossilized upright trees have been found that pass through several strata, the tops and bottoms of the trees sometimes differing in age by millions of years according to uniformitarian reckoning.[46]

- Traditional geology assumes that all the strata were laid one on top of the other like a pile of carpets. However, experiments in sedimentology by the French scientist Guy Berthault give a different picture of their formation. They show that when there is a water current present, which is generally the case, strata do not form successively but laterally and vertically at the same time.[47]

The great worldwide flood of Genesis explains the geological record much better than uniformitarian geology. It explains things difficult for established academic geology to explain such as wavy strata, why most rock is sedimentary, and why marine fossils are found on mountains.

The fossil record generally, but with many exceptions, contains invertebrates in the lower strata, fish above them, then amphibians, reptiles and mammals. But instead of being evidence for evolution, it is what one would expect if a great worldwide flood produced the fossil record by pouring successive waves of sediment into the sea. Invertebrates that live on the ocean floor would be buried first, then fish, and so on. The creatures would tend to be buried in the order of the elevation of their habitat and their degree of mobility. The facts about the fossil record are recorded in many places. James Perloff gives an insightful presentation of them with pictures in *Tornado in a Junkyard*[48] as does Richard Milton in *Shattering the Myths of Darwinism*.[49]

The fossil record shows that life forms have remained essentially unchanged during their history. They have no ancestral forms, and forms that are preserved in the fossil record are either extinct or identical to forms currently living.

A great worldwide flood explains the fossil record so well that, if one weren't mentioned in the Bible, geologists would probably postulate one as the best explanation of the facts.

It should now be clear that the fossil record provides no evidence whatsoever that all plant and animal species did not originate at the same time.

<< The Geologic Column >>

The geologic column was originally conceived as a division of the layers of rock on the surface of the earth into "systems" of strata, without any age attached. Evolutionists converted the systems from representations of rock formations into historical "periods" or "eras." They dated the systems according to the fossils they contained, based on how long they believed it took for the fossilized creatures to evolve. Fossils are then dated according to the rocks in which they are found, and the geological column is said to demonstrate the evolution of species over millions of years. Such reasoning is circular. This is admitted by paleobiologist R. R. West:

> Contrary to what most scientists write, the fossil record does not support the Darwinian theory of evolution because it is this theory (there are several) which we use to interpret the fossil record. By doing so we are guilty of circular reasoning if we then say that the fossil record supports this theory.[50]

Other scientists have admitted this as well.[51]

The idea that a geologic column of sedimentary rock uniformly covers the face of the earth is an artificial construct. Textbooks present the geologic column with the strata neatly stacked on one another, progressing from the oldest rocks on the bottom to the youngest rocks on the top. This is not an accurate representation of the face of the earth. Geologist S. A. Austin writes:

> The notion that the earth's crust has an "onion skin" structure with successive layers containing all strata systems distributed on a global scale is not according to the facts. Data from continents and ocean basins show that the ten systems are poorly represented on a global scale: approximately 77% of the earth's surface area on land and under the sea has *seven or more* (70% or more) of the strata systems *missing* beneath; 94% of the earth's surface has *three or*

more systems *missing* beneath; and an estimated 99.6% has *at least one missing* system. Only a few locations on earth (about 0.4% of its area) have been described with the succession of the ten systems beneath (west Nepal, west Bolivia, and central Poland).... The entire geologic column, composed of complete strata systems, exists only in the diagrams drawn by geologists.[52]

A striking contradiction to the standard chronology of the geologic column is the fact that there are many areas of rock strata that contain fossils in inverse evolutionary sequence, that is, with the allegedly younger rocks on the bottom and the older rocks on the top. A well-known instance of this is the Heart Mountain Thrust in Wyoming. There the rocks are inverted over a triangular area thirty miles wide at its base by sixty miles long. Another is the Lewis Overthrust in Montana, which presents evolutionists the problem of explaining why a volume of rock three hundred miles long, twenty five miles wide and two miles thick is "upside down." A third is the famous Matterhorn, which is one of many mountains in the Alps that are out of the standard geological order. To explain how such inversions could have happened after the rock hardened, evolutionists would have to invent local catastrophes so enormously powerful that they would make the Genesis Flood look like a spring shower. And at the same time they would have to be very gentle catastrophes so as not to damage the rock![53]

Another problem with the dating of the rocks in the geologic column is that the rocks do not contain meteorites, which they should if it took millions of years for them to form. This fact has been known for many years. In 1932 W. A. Tarr wrote:

> For many years I have searched for meteorites or meteoric material in sedimentary rocks.... I have interviewed the late Dr. G. P. Merrill of the U.S. National Museum, and Dr. G. T. Prior, of the British Natural History Museum, both well-known students of meteorites, and neither man knew of a single occurrence of a meteorite in sedimentary rocks.[54]

Only a few meteorites have been found below the highest levels of the geologic column, much less than would be expected if they had continually bombarded the earth for millions of years at the rate at which they now do.

✳   ✳   ✳   ✳

This picture shows that each rock stratum sits perfectly on the other. There is no erosion of the interfaces and no soil in between, which indicate that they were laid down in rapid succession, not over millions of years.

This is a picture of a polystrate fossilized tree. It must have been rapidly buried. Polystrate trees are found in many places. This one is in Germany.

These are folded mountains (wavy strata) near Sullivan River in southern British Columbia, Canada. They had to be formed when soft by lateral compression.

This is the 150-feet deep Berlingame Canyon in Washington State. Uniformitarian geologists tell us that canyons like this were formed slowly over millions of years. But it is a documented fact that rainwater carved out this canyon in only two days. It was formed in 1926 when an irrigation ditch overflowed during a major storm. It is a dramatic example of rapid erosion.

This is a one-hundred foot cliff of sedimentary rock formed by mud flows from Mt. St. Helens after its eruption in 1980. The mud flows were caused by rapid melting of the mountain's glacier. Sediment piled up to 600 feet in some places. Notice the different strata that were formed by successive mud flows. The sediments hardened into rock within five years. The man standing at the top gives us a measure for the height of the cliff. Mt. St. Helens is like a geological laboratory. Its eruption has provided much information about rapid geological formation, like that which took place during the Great Flood.

< Objection 3 >

In his address to the Pontifical Academy of Sciences on October 22, 1996, Pope John Paul II said that the theory of evolution is more than a hypothesis. This can only mean that the Church has now officially accepted that the evolution of species as a fact or, at least, that it is not harmful to believe that the evolution of species is a fact.

<< Reply to Objection 3 >>

That is not true. The pope makes it very clear at the beginning of his 1996 address to the Pontifical Academy of Sciences (PAS) that his address is in the form of a dialogue between the Church and science. No doctrinal development is implied. The talk contains some reflections on the issue of evolution, and they are not presented as binding on the faithful. Furthermore, the pope's reflections are colored by the information given to him by members of the Pontifical Academy of Sciences (PAS), who were exclusively evolutionists of one form or another. Here is how the pope introduces his reflections:

> In celebrating the 60th anniversary of the Academy's refoundation, I would like to recall the intentions of my predecessor Pius XI, who wished to surround himself with a select group of scholars, relying on them to inform the Holy See in complete freedom about developments in scientific research, and thereby to assist him in his reflections.
> He asked those whom he called the Church's *Senatus scientificus* to serve the truth. I again extend this same invitation to you today, certain that we will all be able to profit from the fruitfulness of a trustful dialogue between the Church and science.[55]

In that talk the pope did not go so far as to explicitly endorse evolution as a fact, but he did give it more credibility than it deserves.[b] And even if the pope did profess belief in evolution as a fact, that could not be interpreted as a development of dogma because it would not be a statement about faith and morals but one about natural science, which is outside the range of his authority.

Despite the credibility that the pope gave to the theory of evolution, his statement does not mitigate its harmfulness. Its harmfulness resides chiefly in the atheistic spirit in which it was conceived and is promulgated, and in the loss of confidence in Sacred Scripture that it has engendered. The injecting of God into the process by theistic evolutionists does not erase the essentially atheistic spirit of the theory of evolution. Atheistic evolutionists see that as a compromise by theists who have succumbed to their propaganda. Atheists remain completely comfortable with their belief that evolution is a self-consistent godless explanation of the origin of things.

<< Evolution, Tradition and the Magisterium >>

It is conceivable that a pope or an ecumenical council could some day define the special creation of species as revealed truth because it is deeply rooted in Catholic Tradition and sound scriptural exegesis. Of course, this would only take place if,

---

b. Although this address received much publicity, it was not the first time Pope John Paul publicly gave credence to evolution. Following are other instances:
    "[B]elief in evolution and the properly understood teaching of creation do not stand in one another's way. Creation represents itself in the light of evolution as an event extending through time.... Therefore I welcome this symposium..." (Address to symposium entitled "Christian Faith and the Theory of Evolution," April 26, 1985).
    "All the observations concerning the development of life lead to a similar conclusion. The evolution of living beings, of which science seeks to determine the stages and to discern the mechanism, presents an internal finality which arouses admiration. This finality which directs beings in a direction for which they are not responsible or in charge, obliges one to suppose a Mind which is its inventor, its creator" (General Audience, July 10, 1985).
    "This text [the creation account in Genesis 1] has above all a religious and theological importance. There are not to be sought in it significant elements from the point of view of the natural sciences. Research on the origin and development of the individual species in nature does not find in this description any definitive norm nor positive contributions of substantial interest. Indeed, the theory of natural evolution, understood in a sense that does not exclude divine causality, is not in principle opposed to the truth about the creation of the visible world, as presented in the Book of Genesis" (General Audience, January 29, 1986).
    He even went so far as to use the terminology of Teilhard de Chardin:
    "Man goes towards God—and this is his advent—not only as towards an unknown Absolute of being, not only as towards a symbolic point, the "Omega" point of the world's evolution. Man goes towards God, so as to arrive at God himself: the Living God, the Father, the Son and the Holy Spirit. And he arrives when God himself comes to him, and this is the Advent of Christ" (General Audience, December 19, 1981).

somehow, conditions in the Church required it. This could not happen for the evolution of species because it has no roots whatsoever in Scripture or Tradition.

For the same reason no pope could ever incorporate evolution into the ordinary Magisterium, as he could special creation, because evolution has no basis in Tradition. The popes are servants of Tradition. Their duty is to uphold and preserve Tradition, not to introduce novelties into Catholic teaching. For example, when Pope Paul VI issued *Humanae vitae* he did not introduce new doctrine but upheld two thousand years of Catholic Tradition. Pope John Paul II said that he could not authorize the ordination of woman priests because it was opposed to the will of the Lord as expressed in Sacred Tradition. No pope could claim evolution to be a doctrinal development because it does not possess the doctrinal continuity and conformity to the analogy of faith as required for authentic magisterial teaching. Evolution would represent a discontinuity in and not an organic growth of Catholic teaching on origins.

But a pope could make a faulty pastoral judgment by teaching that the theory of evolution is not harmful to the faith. God uses the talents and backgrounds of popes just as he does with those of ordinary Catholics. Popes are certainly given special graces for their office of supreme pastor, but they depend on others with expertise in various fields to provide them with input, just as civil leaders do. And the charism of infallibility does not extend to pastoral judgments. If a pope is given faulty input, he can make faulty pastoral judgments based on it.

<< More Than a Hypothesis? >>

The pope gave his reason for believing that evolution is more than a hypothesis. He stated; "It is indeed remarkable that this theory has been progressively accepted by researchers, following a series of discoveries in various fields of knowledge. This convergence, neither sought nor fabricated, of the results of work that was conducted independently is in itself a significant argument in favor of this theory."[56] This is obviously what he was told by his scientific advisors, since he himself did not have the scientific background to make such a judgment. And for this reason it can be challenged without disrespect to the pope.

Scientists work within strictly regulated scientific paradigms that put boundaries on the way they think and on the way they do things.[57] Paradigms facilitate a science by helping to coordinate data and by giving rules for their interpretation, and they suggest new experiments or observations. They give a science direction at the expense of putting it in a box. Anomalous observations that do not fit the paradigm are ignored or set aside. Paradigms make sciences conservative. Only when anomalies accumulate to the point of crisis will a paradigm be discarded and replaced by another paradigm.

Evolution is one such paradigm. It differs from other scientific paradigms in two ways. First, the only alternative paradigm invokes a Creator who revealed knowledge about the origin of the world and natural species. Such a paradigm is unacceptable to those who insist that everything can be explained in terms of natural causes only. And they are the ones who have wrested control of the thinking of the scientific community. Revealed knowledge is ruled out a priori. It is dismissed as "religion," as if science had the only handle on truth.

Second, it is also a scientific paradigm that is not only an operational framework but is also a pseudophilosophy. It is a pseudophilosophy because it rests on the false premise that evolution is a *necessary* process. Being all-embracing, it is applied to "various fields of knowledge." It is not a philosophy that is "progressively accepted" but one that is *progressively imposed.* Any "series of discoveries" is required to be interpreted within its framework. There are numerous anomalous phenomena that are not amenable to interpretation within its framework. These are set aside and ignored because "convergence" *is* "sought and fabricated." Research may have been "conducted independently," but the interpretation of research is predetermined by a scientific orthodoxy irreversibly committed to the evolution paradigm.

Science concerns itself only with natural causes, which are *contingent.* The material that evolution deals with is beyond the competence of natural science because it involves the First Cause, which is *necessary;* but many scientists, even theistic ones, will not admit that. And the success of natural science in describing many things has awed and seduced many Christians to give evolution more credibility than the Genesis account. If it were any other paradigm it would be considered at a point of crisis because of its inability to give credible explanations for many natural phenomena. In the field of biology, for example, there exists a body of scientific literature published in the past forty or so years that strongly supports the position that the macroevolution of species has not occurred. Macroevolution finds no strong support in the database of facts from the various natural sciences. Evolutionists find themselves in the uncomfortable position of having to invent theories to explain why unimpeachable evidence for evolution does not exist.

But the evolution paradigm will not be rejected by materialistic science because it is the crutch of materialism. And it is rigorously enforced. Any biologist or astronomer who does not work within its constraints cannot expect to advance in academia or win grants. Although it is a failed paradigm, scientists will not let go of it because from their naturalistic point of view they have no alternative. To make it credible they piggyback it on the success of successful paradigms.

It is appropriate here to recall what was said about Teilhard de Chardin in the Introduction to this book:

> His guide to God and the world was not Scripture or Tradition or the Magisterium or even genuine science. It was evolution. Evolution was the mold into which he forced everything, as the following quote reveals: "Is evolution a theory, a system or a hypothesis? It is much more: it is a general condition to which all theories, all hypotheses, all systems must bow and which they must satisfy henceforward if they are to be thinkable and true. Evolution is a light illuminating all facts, a curve that all lines must follow." In other words, evolution defines truth. Teilhard was a dogmatic evolutionist before all else.

Teilhard is an exemplar of evolutionary scientists, both atheistic and theistic, who insist that all reality *must* be explained in terms of evolution.

<< The Notion of Divinely Programmed Evolution >>

In a newspaper article following the pope's speech, Fr. Stanley L. Jaki, a member of the PAS, stated: "But it would have been a most grave fault on the part of this brave Pope if he had failed to recognize the vastly growing set of data in evolutionary biology. They further support a much older philosophical truth: Matter as created by God is capable of producing, without further interventions by Him, all *material* effects, including the human body, a very material thing indeed."[58] What Fr. Jaki states as being a philosophical truth is no more philosophical than the statement: All crows are black. Neither is philosophical because neither is *necessarily* true. They are statements that, if they were true, would be so only *contingently*. Their verifications fall in the realm of natural science and not in the realm of philosophy. That is, their truth can only be confirmed by observation. And there is no convincing evidence from biology or any of the other sciences that Fr. Jaki's "philosophical truth" is a truth of natural science, despite the constant claims by him and other evolutionists. The *vastly growing set of data in nonevolutionary biology* indicates the opposite. Both the fossil and biospheric records show that living species are stable and do not transform one into another, and scientists have not been able to achieve such transformations in the laboratory despite strenuous efforts to do so. Furthermore, evolutionists cannot provide a mechanism for evolution. In the article Fr. Jaki speaks of a "mechanism as yet imperfectly understood," but he gives no hint as to what the nature of such a mechanism might be. Natural selection simply doesn't work and there is no evidence whatsoever for built-in mechanisms. Fr. Jaki, being a Catholic priest and a member of the PAS, undoubtedly had a great influence in the writing of the pope's address. Not a single member of the PAS was a creationist. So it is safe to assume that the pope did not have a balanced input on which to deliberate, which Pope Pius XII called for in *Humani generis*.

[1] Darwin, Charles, *The Origin of Species by Natural Selection or The Preservation of Favoured Races in the Struggle for Life,* 6th edition, 1872 (New York: Collier, 1962), pp. 484–485.

[2] *Hexaemeron,* Homily 5, Chapters 1,2, as quoted in Rose, Fr. Seraphim, *Genesis, Creation, and Early Man: The Orthodox Christian Vision* (Platina, CA: Saint Herman of Alaska Brotherhood, 2000), p. 133.

[3] *Commentary on Genesis,* Book 7, Chapter 3, as quoted in Rose, op. cit., p. 130.

[4] ACC, p. 15.

[5] ACC, p. 22.

[6] For an account of how evolutionists define species to accommodate Darwinism see Milton, Richard, *Shattering the Myths of Darwinism* (Rochester, VT: Park Street Press, 1997), pp. 143–153.

[7] Cotter, A. C., *Natural Species* (Weston, MA: Weston College Press, 1947), pp. 121–122.

[8] Ibid., p. 126.

[9] Ibid., pp. 126–127.

[10] Ibid., p. 168.

[11] Ibid., p. 169.

[12] ST, Part I, Q. 105, A. 5.

[13] Cotter, op. cit., p. 172–173.

[14] CCC, no. 340.

[15] Fabre, J. Henri, *The Wonders of Instinct: Chapters in the Psychology of Insects* (Honolulu: University Press of the Pacific, 2002), reprinted from 1922 edition.

[16] Dobzhansky, Theodosius, *Genetics and the Origin of Species,* 3rd ed. (New York: Columbia University Press, 1951), p. 4.

[17] Simpson, George Gaylord, *The Major Features of Evolution* (New York: Columbia University Press, 1953), p. 360.

[18] ACC, p. 25.

[19] ACC, p. 22.

[20] ACC, p. 22.

[21] ACC, p. 22.

[22] ACC, p. 24.

[23] ACC, pp. 22–23.

[24] See Aristotle, *The History of Animals.*

[25] Marsh, Frank Lewis, "The Genesis Kinds in the Modern World," *Scientific Studies in Special Creation,* Walter E. Lammerts, ed. (Nutley, NJ: Presbyterian and Reformed Publishing Company, 1971), p. 147.

[26] Quoted in Macbeth, Norman, *Darwin Retried* (Boston: Gambit, 1971), p. 36.

[27] Spetner, Lee, *Not by Chance!: Shattering the Modern Theory of Evolution* (Brooklyn, NY: The Judaica Press, 1998), p. 47. Chapter 2 of this work contains a very clear and concise summary of the principles of genetics.

[28] Gn 6:4; Nm 13:28, 33; Dt 2:10–11, 2:20–21, 3:11, 9:2; Jos 11:21–22, 12:4, 13:12, 15:8, 17:15, 18:16.

[29] Hitching, Francis, *The Neck of the Giraffe: Darwin, Evolution and the New Biology* (New York: Mentor, 1982), p. 43.

[30] Spetner, op. cit., pp. 180–181.

[31] Ibid., pp. 133–134.

[32] Ibid., p. 159.

[33] Ibid., pp. 181–182.

[34] Ibid., p. 201.

[35] Spetner, op. cit., pp. 16–17.

[36] Jonathan Weiner as quoted by Richard Milton, op. cit., p. 143.

[37] Morgan, Thomas Hunt, *Evolution and Adaptation* (Quoted by Perloff, James, *Tornado in a Junkyard: The Relentless Myth of Darwinism* (Arlington, MA: Refuge Books, 1999), p. 48.

[38] Thain, M. and Hickman, M., *Penguin Dictionary of Biology*, Tenth Edition (New York: Penguin Books, 2001), p. 597.

[39] Ibid., p. 557.

[40] Ibid., p. 598.

[41] See Select Bibliography.

[42] See Doctrine Six, The Seventh Day, << St. Augustine on Creation >>.

[43] Thain and Hickman, op. cit., p. 250.

[44] See Denton, Michael, *Evolution: A Theory in Crisis* (Chevy Chase, MD: Adler and Adler, 1985), pp. 160–161.

[45] Lyell, Charles, *Principles of Geology*, 11th ed. rev. (New York: Appleton, 1892), I, pp. 317, 318.

[46] For photographs of such fossils see Wysong, R.L., *The Creation-Evolution Controversy* (East Lansing, MI: Inquiry Press, 1976), pp. 367–368 and Brown, Walt, *In the Beginning: Compelling Evidence for Creation and the Flood* (Phoenix, AZ: Center for Scientific Creation, 1995), p. 9.

[47] Berthault, Guy, "Geological Dating Principles Questioned—Paleohydraulics: A New Approach," article first published in French in *Fusion*, n°81, mai-juin 2000, Editions Alcuin (Paris); *Journal of Geodesy and Geodynamics*, Vol. 22, No. 3, Aug. 2002, pp. 19–26. Also, "Analysis of Main Principles of Stratigraphy on the Basis of Experimental Data," *Lithology and Mineral Resources*, Vol. 37, No. 5, Sep.–Oct. 2002, pp. 442–446. His work is discussed by Gerard J. Keane, *Cre-*

ation Rediscovered: Evolution and the Importance of the Origins Debate (Rockford, IL: TAN Books, 1999) pp. 20–21, 102, 142; and Richard Milton, op. cit., pp. 77–78.

[48] Perloff, op. cit., chapter 14.

[49] Milton, op. cit., chapter 7.

[50] West, Ronald R., 'Paleoecology and Uniformitarianism," *Compass* 45 (May 1968), p. 216; as cited by Perloff, op. cit., p. 153.

[51] See Perloff, op. cit., pp. 153–154.

[52] Austin, Stephen A., "Ten Misconceptions about the Geologic Column," *Impact* 137 (November 1984), p. 2; as quoted by Perloff, op. cit., p. 154.

[53] See Whitcomb, John C. and Morris, Henry M., *The Genesis Flood: The Biblical Record and Its Scientific Implications* (Phillipsburg, NJ: P & R Publishing, 1960), pp. 180–200.

[54] Tarr, W. A., "Meteorites in Sedimentary Rocks?" *Science* 75 (1 January 1932), p. 17; as quoted by Perloff, op. cit., p. 133.

[55] Pope John Paul II, *L'Osservatore Romano*, weekly English edition, no. 44, 30 October 1996, p. 3.

[56] Ibid., p. 7.

[57] For the role that paradigms play in science see Kuhn, Thomas S., *The Structure of Scientific Revolutions*, 2nd ed. (Chicago: University of Chicago Press, 1970).

[58] Jaki, Stanley L., "Did the Pope Surrender to Evolutionary Theory?" *The Wanderer*, January 30, 1997.

Doctrine Six
God created the world in six natural days.

Scholars generally agree that the Hebrew word *yom* used in Genesis 1 was intended by the sacred author to mean a literal natural day and not an indefinite period of time. The great majority of the Fathers of the Church believed that God created the world in six natural days. None of them professed belief that God took eons of time to create the world. The Pontifical Biblical Commission in 1909 allowed interpreters of Scripture to argue that *yom* means "the natural day" or that it means "a certain space of time." But it is out-of-bounds to assert that "a certain space of time" means undefined millions of years because this cannot be established as a "necessary" interpretation. Considering 1) that *yom* is never used in Sacred Scripture for a period of time of definite length other than a natural day, 2) the hermeneutical principle of Leo XIII that Scripture must be understood in its "literal and obvious sense" unless reason or necessity forces us to do otherwise, 3) the near unanimous belief of the Fathers and Doctors of the Church, 4) that the creation day is the prototype of the natural day, which sets the rhythm for our lives and life on earth in general, and 5) the fact that the natural sciences are unable to confirm or refute it, there is no justification for a Catholic to deny that God created the world in six natural days.

A Real Six Days of Creation

The *Catechism of the Catholic Church* says: "Scripture presents the work of the Creator symbolically as a succession of six days of divine 'work,' concluded by the 'rest' of the seventh day."[1] [a] But that is not to say that the six days and the works of the six days weren't real.[b] The prophet Ezekiel performed real actions in his

---

a. Both Genesis 1 and Exodus 20:11 declare that God created the world in six days.

personal life that had symbolic meaning for the life of Israel.[2] Likewise, God parceled out His work of creation into six natural days, and that has symbolic meaning for our lives. Among the Fathers of the Church, St. Ephrem the Syrian gives clear witness to the belief in the reality of the works of the six days:

> So let no one think that there is anything allegorical in the works of the six days. No one can rightly say that the things pertaining to these days were symbolic, nor can anyone say that they were meaningless names or that other things were symbolized for us by their names.[3]

The Fathers of the Church do not say much about the duration of the six days. It seems that they took it for granted that each of the six days was a natural day. It was not an issue for debate with them. St. Ephrem the Syrian clearly regards the days of Creation Week as natural days:

> Although both the light and the clouds were created in the twinkling of an eye, still both the day and night of the First Day continued for twelve hours each.[4]

> Although the grasses were only a moment old at their creation, they appeared as if they were months old. Likewise, the trees, although only a day old when they sprouted forth, were nevertheless like trees years old as they were fully grown and fruits were already budding on their branches. The grass that would be required as food for the animals two days later was thus made ready. And the new corn that would be food for Adam and his descendants, who would be thrown out of paradise four days later, was thus prepared.[5]

St. Basil considered the first day as setting the standard for the natural day:

> *"There was evening and morning."* This means the space of a day and a night.... *"And there was evening and morning, one day."* Why did he say *"one"* and not "first"? ... He said *"one"* because he was defining the measure of day and night and combining the time of a night and a day, since the twenty-four hours fill up the interval of one day, if, of course, night is understood with day.[6]

---

b. The Pontifical Biblical Commission, in a response issued in 1909, rejected the idea that the first three chapters of Genesis "contain allegories and symbols destitute of any foundation in objective reality but presented under the garb of history for the purpose of inculcating religious and philosophical truth" (DZ, no. 2122).

As did St. Ambrose:

> In notable fashion has Scripture spoken of a *"day,"* not the "first day." Because a second, then a third, day, and finally the remaining days were to follow, a "first day" could have been mentioned, following in this way the natural order. But Scripture established a law that twenty-four hours, including both day and night, should be given the name of day only, as if one were to say the length of one day is twenty-four hours in extent.[7]

And St. John Chrysostom in his commentary on Genesis clearly regards God's creation as the work of six natural days.[8] St. Gregory of Nyssa, St. Jerome and St. Gregory the Great also believed that God created the world successively in six natural days.[9]

In his *Summa Theologica* St. Thomas Aquinas ascribes the work of creation to six days, but it is not clear whether he means six literal days. He considers the question of whether or not the six days are all one day.[10] He treats this question in response to St. Augustine's suggestion that God created all things at once and that light referred to the angels, as did the word *day*. In this St. Augustine differed from the other Fathers. Augustine's reasoning goes thus:

> The obvious conclusion is that if the angels are among the works of God of those days, they are that light which received the name of "day." And the unity of that day is underlined by its not being called "the first day," but *"one day."* Thus the second day, and the third, and the rest are not different days; the same *"one day"* was repeated to complete the number six or seven, to represent the seven stages of knowledge [in the minds of the angels], the six stages comprehending the created works, and the seventh stage embracing God's rest.
>
> For when God said, *"Let there be light,"* and light was created, then, if we are right in interpreting this as including the creation of the angels, they immediately became partakers of the eternal light, which is the unchanging Wisdom of God, the agent of God's whole creation; and this Wisdom we call the only begotten Son of God. Thus, the angels, illuminated by that light by which they were created, themselves became light and are called "day" by participation in the changeless light and day, which is the Word of God, through whom they themselves and all other things were made.[11] [c]

---

c. Cardinal Ernesto Ruffini notes that Augustine explained many things figuratively that he later thought he should have taken literally. See *The Theory of Evolution Judged by Reason and Faith* (New York: Joseph F. Wagner, Inc., 1959), p. 122, footnote.

Thus in Augustine's view the works of the six days were simultaneous. He held that the plants and animals were produced potentially in the works of the six days, whereas the other Fathers held that they were produced actually[d]. St. Thomas seems to present both views impartially in the *Summa*, but elsewhere he clearly sides with Augustine against the majority of the Fathers.[e]

St. Augustine cited the Book of Sirach as confirmation that everything was created at once:

> It was written elsewhere, certainly without contradiction, of the same Creator, about whom the Scripture narrates that He completed all the works in six days—that *"He created all things together"* (Sirach 18:1). And, therefore, He who made all things together, also made together those six or seven days, or rather one repeated six or seven times. What need was there, then, that six days should be described distinctly and in order? Just because those who cannot understand what was said— *"He created all things together"*—cannot arrive whither the text is leading them, unless the discourse does not proceed more slowly for them.[12][f]

The modern (RSV) translation of Sirach 18:1 is: *"He who lives forever created the whole universe."* The traditional (DR) translation is *"He that liveth forever created all things together"* (Ecclesiasticus 18:1). E. Ruffini maintained that even the traditional translation "does not mean that God created all things *at the same time* but rather that He has created all things *equally*, namely, without any exception. Such is the sense of the Greek term χοινη rendered in Latin in the ambiguous

---

d.   Some rabbinic masters also held that all things were created simultaneously on the first day but made their appearances later at different times. See Abraham Cohen, *Everyman's Talmud: The Major Teachings of the Rabbinic Sages* (New York, Schocken Books, 1975 reprint of 1949 edition), p. 37.

e.   *II Sent. Dist.,* XII, Q. 1, A. 2. The pertinent passage follows: "However, Ambrose and other saints hold that there was an order of time by which things were distinguished. This opinion is indeed more generally held, and seems to accord better with the apparent literal sense (of Scripture). Still, the previous theory (that of Augustine) is the more reasonable, and ensures a better defense of Holy Scripture against the derision of unbelievers. To this, insists Augustine, must the fullest heed be given: 'the Scriptures are so to be explained that they will not incur the ridicule of unbelievers' (*Gen. ad litt.* 1, 19); and his theory is the one that appeals to me" (as quoted by Cardinal Ernesto Ruffini, op. cit., pp. 72–73). Cardinal Ruffini goes on to say that Aquinas gives the same opinion in Disputed Questions (IV: *De Creatione materiae informis*, a. 2). Also see ST, Part I, Q. 69, A. 1.

manner, *simul.*"[g] Augustine's interpretation of Sirach 18:1 was also that of Origen, St. Athanasius and St. Gregory of Nyssa.[14]

The Meaning of *Yom*

In Genesis 1, the Hebrew word *yom* is used in two of the same ways that we use the word *day*. In 1:5a it means the bright part of the natural day; in the other verses it means a full natural day. A computer search of the Hebrew Old Testament for the word *yom* revealed that it is used 1904 times, 57 times in Genesis 1–11. It is always used in the same senses that we use the English word *day*: the bright part of the natural day, the full natural day, a specific calendar day, a period of time of indefinite length as in "in grandfather's day," and age as in "the days of his life." *Day* and *yom* are never used for a definite period of time with a beginning and an end other than the natural day.

Whenever *yom* is used with an ordinal number, it clearly means a natural day. It is used that way some 359 times in the Hebrew Bible.

Some argue that the word *day* can bear the sense of the word *epoch*. They cite Psalms 90:4: *"For a thousand years in thy sight are but yesterday when it is past, or as a watch in the night."* But that is simply a way of saying that God transcends time. It has no bearing on the interpretation of the word *yom* in Genesis. The English word *day* is never used to mean an exceedingly long period of time as denoted by the words *eon*, *epoch* and *era*, and neither is the Hebrew word *yom*.[h]

Also, considering that heaven and earth and the things in them were created instantly,[15] it makes good sense that the work of each day of Creation Week was

---

f.   Number symbolism had strong influence on the psyche of the ancients. A number had the power to evoke ideas and emotions in them in the same way a metaphor, simile, literary allusion, slogan, or the number 13 does in moderns. The Fathers and medieval theologians believed that God planted numbers in Scripture with such a purpose (see Vincent Foster Hopper, *Medieval Number Symbolism: Its Sources, Meaning and Influence on Thought and Expression*, reprint of 1938 edition (Mineola, NY: Dover Publications, 2000)). St. Augustine said that Creation was described as being completed in six days because "six is the number of perfection" (CG, Book XI, Chapter 30). The number six is the first *perfect number*, that is, it is the first number that is equal to the sum of its divisors (1+2+3=6). Augustine also sees the number seven as "perfect" but "for a different reason." Seven "stands for unlimited number." Day Seven of Creation Week is unlimited in that it has no evening (see CG, Book XI, Chapter 31).

accomplished in a natural day, anticipating the human workday. Creation Week is the archetype of the human workweek, and for that reason alone it makes sense that its duration was the same. If Moses wished to convey periods of time measured in millennia, as theistic evolutionists would have us believe, he could have certainly done it much more clearly and effectively in other words. For example, he could have used the Hebrew word *olam,* which means "a long indefinite time."

Some contend that there is a problem reconciling Genesis 1 and Genesis 2 if the sixth day is a natural day. They say that the events in (2:4–24) cannot be reconciled with (1:24–31) if the sixth day is a natural day because too much is going on for one natural day—God creates the land animals and Adam; Adam names the animals; God creates Eve from Adam's side. But a natural day is long enough for those activities. God created the animals and Adam instantaneously. He could have done that early in the morning. The naming of the animals need not take as long as critics suppose. God did not parade every kind of animal before Adam to

---

g. Some maintain that the Latin word *simul* is *not* ambiguous in ecclesiastical Latin. Modern secular Latin dictionaries indicate that *simul* can be translated either as "at the same time, at once" or as "together," which has meanings that do not necessarily imply simultaneity. But *A Latin-English Dictionary of St. Thomas Aquinas* by Roy J. Deferrari (Boston: St. Paul Editions, 1986), which gives translations of Latin words and phrases based on their use by St. Thomas Aquinas, indicates that he used it only to mean "at the same time, simultaneously." This has added significance because St. Thomas' meaning is most likely the meaning that the Fathers of Lateran Council IV would have attached to the word. Lateran IV decreed that God "who by His own omnipotent power at once [*simul*] from the beginning of time created each creature from nothing, spiritual and corporeal, namely, angelic and mundane, and finally the human, constituted as it were, alike of the spirit and the body" (DZ, no. 428). Critics of the ambiguous interpretation argue that modern theologians introduced the ambiguity in their effort to reconcile Lateran IV's declaration on the creation of the world (which was restated verbatim by Vatican Council I) with the immensely long geologic times advanced by nineteenth century scientists. (See *Lateran IV and Evolution Theory: The Importance of "Simul"* by Peter Wilders and Hugh Owen, available from the Kolbe Center for the Study of Creation, 952 Kelly Rd., Mt. Jackson, VA 22842.) However, "at once," does not necessary mean "at the same instant" but can also mean "over the same *short* period of time," namely, Creation Week. This latter interpretation must be applied to the decree of Lateran IV if it is to be interpreted in literal agreement with Genesis. During Creation Week God created His creatures "together" into a functioning unity.

name. He showed him only cattle, the birds of the air, and the beasts of the field. And Adam may have given only generic names to groups of similar kinds of animals. *"The man gave names to all cattle, and to the birds of the air, and to every beast of the field ... "* (2:20). God showed Adam enough animals on Day Six to convince him that he needed a mate like himself. The creation of Eve need not have taken long. The sixth day was Adam and Eve's "wedding day" as well as their "birthday." All these events could fit comfortably into a natural day.

The Pontifical Biblical Commission in its 1909 responses concerning the interpretation of the first three chapters of Genesis allowed free discussion by interpreters on the question of whether the word *yom*, when used to distinguish the six days in Genesis 1, means strictly "the natural day" or less strictly "a certain space of time."[16] But this freedom must be exercised in accordance with the hermeneutical principle of Leo XIII that Scripture must be understood in its "literal and obvious sense" unless reason or necessity forces us to do otherwise.

---

h.   Ernesto Cardinal Ruffini comments on this: "We may pass over the opinion that the term *yom* (day) can, *per se*, be taken also in the sense of period or epoch, although from biblical texts produced to support this interpretation, we get the meaning of a day of uncertain date rather than that of an epoch of uncertain duration. However, we are not persuaded that in our present case day is equal to period. If the author really wished to speak of ordinary days, as we believe, what expressions should he have used that are clearer than those he adopted? Almighty God in verse 5 expressly calls *yom* the light of day, in verses 14–16 He created the luminaries of heaven to divide the *yom* from the night, and entrusted to the sun the office of presiding over the *yom*, and to the moon that of presiding over the night. Therefore, what reason could there be for holding that the word *yom* was used in the same context and, indeed, in the same verse, in two completely distinct senses, namely, that of a common day and that of a period?...It is an evident principle that the best commentator, the most authentic interpreter of a book or a phrase is its author. Now in Exodus the Hexaemeron is taken to be an ordinary week.... Holy Scripture limits the account to the space of a week: for six days the Lord works in creating, on the seventh He rests. This is all. It goes no further; and precisely because it wishes to stop, it does not make the usual evening and morning follow the sabbath. Therefore, the sacred text evidently speaks of civil, ordinary days and not of periods; and the unanimous interpretation of the Fathers bears witness to this. If the periodists, in order not to go against [false] science, are constrained to take *yom*, with its evening and its morning, as a period or epoch, how can it be maintained that the rest of the narration should be taken in the proper literal sense?" (Ruffini, op. cit., pp. 77–79)

Therefore, one cannot argue arbitrarily that *yom* means a "certain space of time" other than a natural day but must establish that it is "necessary" to interpret it that way.

Considering then 1) that *yom* is never used in Sacred Scripture for a period of time of definite length other than a natural day, 2) the hermeneutical principle of Leo XIII, 3) the nearly universal understanding of the Fathers and their successors, 4) that the creation day is the prototype of the natural day, which sets the rhythm for our lives and life on earth in general, and 5) the fact that the natural sciences are unable to confirm or refute it, it is not reasonable to take the word *yom* in Genesis 1 to mean other than a literal natural day.

The Work of the Six Days

This is God's program of activities for the six days of Creation Week:

DAY ONE	Create the heavens and the earth.
	Create light.
	Make day and night.
DAY TWO	Separate the waters into two parts.
	Put an expanse between them.
DAY THREE	Make dry land.
	Gather the water into seas.
	Create plant life.
DAY FOUR	Create the heavenly bodies.
DAY FIVE	Create living water creatures and birds.
DAY SIX	Create living land creatures.
	Create man.

There is a logical structure to this program. When a workman starts a new project, he first provides himself with the raw materials. This is what God did on the first day when He produced a formless and empty earth. The workman next provides for himself a well-lighted workplace. God provided for Himself the lighting on the first day. He produced a workplace on the second day when he

created an expanse bound below and above by water. The workman them separates his raw materials, placing them where he is going to work with them. This is
what God did on the third day when He separated the land from the water. Next
the workman makes his adornments, of every size and shape, of every color and
texture. God did this on the Day Three through Day Six when he created the
heavenly bodies and living creatures of all kinds. Finally, the workman produces
his masterpiece, the product that he most identifies himself with. This God did
on Day Six, when He created man in His image and likeness.

There is symmetry between the first three days and the last three. On the first
day, God created light; on the fourth day He created luminous bodies. On the
second day God formed the sea and the sky; on the fifth day He created the occupants of the sea and sky. On the third day God brought forth dry land; on the
sixth day He created the inhabitants of the dry land.

St. Bonaventure, in summarizing the work of Creation Week, comments that
heaven and earth were made *before* any day:

> We should consider corporeal nature as regards its becoming, as regards its
> being, and as regards its operation. We should especially hold these truths
> about corporeal nature as regards its becoming: that it was brought into exist-
> ence in six days so that in the beginning before any day God created heaven
> and earth. On the first day light was made, on the second the firmament was
> made in the midst of waters, on the third day the waters were separated from
> the land and gathered in one place, on the fourth day the heavens were filled
> with luminous bodies, on the fifth day the air and water were filled with birds
> and fishes, on the sixth day the earth was filled with animals and men, on the
> seventh day God desisted not from toil or work, for He still worked, but from
> the creation of new forms because He had done all things either in likeness, as
> is the case of things which are propagated, or in a seminal reason, as is the case
> with those things which are brought into existence in other ways.[17]

He further explains: "And because creation is from nothing, it was in the
beginning before all days as the foundation of all things and of all times."[18]

Psalms 104 and Job 38–39 sing the glories of Creation Week.

The Creation of the First Day

God created light on the first day. He separated the light from the darkness and
called the light *"Day"* and the darkness *"Night."* It has been a cause of consterna-
tion that day and night were created before the sun and the moon. The latter
weren't created until the fourth day. Some readers of Genesis can't understand

how there was a first day before the sun was created and so dismiss the creation account as myth or allegory.[i] But Genesis says that God created the sun and the moon to *"rule"* the day and the night, not to *determine* them. This means that the periods of day and night ontologically precede the sun and moon. The sun and moon were created to regulate periods of time that had already been determined. St. John Chrysostom expressed it this way: "He created the sun on the fourth day lest you think that it is the cause of the day."[19] Another question that bothers readers concerns the source of the light that God created on the first day. Where did the light come from if the sun and stars were not yet made? A possible source for the light could have been chemical and nuclear reactions in the raw matter of earth itself. But according to modern physics a source really isn't needed. Light is not tethered to a source. Once a photon of light leaves its source it is free and has an existence of its own. So modern physics has no problem with the idea that God created light without a source, and it has no problem with the fact that He set up a standard of time independent of the sun and moon. And neither did St. Thomas Aquinas have a problem with it. He stated:

> I answer, then, with Dionysius (*The Divine Names*, Book IV), that the light was the sun's light, formless as yet, being already the solar substance, and possessing illuminative power in a general way, to which was afterwards added the special and determinative power required to produce determinate effects.[20]

St. Bonaventure was modern in physical thought and literal in his interpretation of (1:2). In opposition to Aristotle, who held that light is an accidental form, Bonaventure held that it is a substantial form.[21] He also did not accept Augustine's identification of the creation of light with the creation of angels because that interpretation strays too far from the literal meaning of Scripture.[22]

The earth being bathed in "free" light in the beginning is another instance of the beginning being pregnant with the end. In the Book of Revelation we read: *"And the city [the New Jerusalem] has no need of sun or moon to shine upon it, for the glory of God is its light, and its lamp is the Lamb."*[23]

---

i.   St. Augustine struggled with this problem, but he did not dismiss the creation account because of it. In CG, Book XI, Chapter 7 he says: "But what kind of light that was, and with what alternating movement the distinction was made, and what was the nature of this evening and this morning; these are questions beyond the scope of our sensible experience. We cannot understand what happened as it is presented to us; and yet we must believe it without hesitation."

*   *   *   *

The early Christians recalled the first day of Creation in their liturgical celebration of the Eucharist. St. Justin Martyr wrote:

> We hold our common assembly on Sunday because it is the first day of the week, the day on which God put chaos and darkness to flight and created the world, and because on that same day our Savior Jesus Christ rose from the dead. For He was crucified on Friday and on Sunday He appeared to His apostles and disciples and taught them the things that we have passed on for your consideration.[24]

It was appropriate that Jesus should have risen from the dead and instructed His disciples on the first day of the week. For by His resurrection He pledged to them a renewal of creation, and with His instruction He filled their souls with the light of truth.

The Corporeal Matter of the First Day

Corporeal matter was created on the first day neither deprived of all form nor clothed with all its forms. What then was the original condition of matter? That question was a subject of intense interest to medieval theologians. E. Gilson compares the teachings of St. Thomas Aquinas and St. Bonaventure on the subject:

> Perhaps we shall gain a better understanding of St. Bonaventure's meaning by comparing it on this point with the teaching of St. Thomas. For the latter, creation resulted at once in a completely defined matter, that of the four elements. Creation was not finished on the first day, because God had not yet divided the waters from the earth and the firmament and because the elements were not yet in their places. Besides, all the mixed bodies which were to be formed eventually by means of these elements were not yet constituted or organized; thus the account of creation given by St. Thomas also allows for the absence of forms which Scripture attributes to the work of the first day. Yet the world of bodies as he conceives it is very different from that which St. Bonaventure describes. For St. Thomas, this world is incomplete, but what God has already created is complete. The elements alone are there, but they are there as elements in their complete form, as the four simple constituents with which the superior forms have only to connect in order to compose them into mixed and organized bodies. For St. Bonaventure, on the other hand, matter is rather like the undifferentiated mass of flesh that constitutes the

embryo; the limbs are not there yet, but they can develop. It is still something less complete than this, for the embryo is already a highly actualized matter and the limbs of the child are in a sense preformed in it; its form is a visible form and, as we shall see, it has already from nature all it needs to develop to its proper perfection. The corporeal matter of the first day is very different; there is nothing in it ordered or preformed, it has no distinguishable figure, it would escape the eye by its very indetermination, it is inert and incapable of developing its further forms without the power and working of God; thus we do not discover in it the definite distinction of the four elementary forms, we can neither understand nor even imagine it, except perhaps as some undifferentiated mass, a little thicker in some places, a little thinner in others, a sort of extended corporeality, inert and in expectation of all the forms. Yet this confused mass is not a mere nothing; it is so manifestly something that it occupies a position and fills space, and we have had to refer already to its corporeal extension in order to fill the emptiness of the empyrean at the beginning of the world; therefore the least defined matter can exist only as such through its form and we must now determine the first formal principle of bodies.[25]

Summarizing with terms used in modern physics: St. Thomas sees the original condition of matter as an undefined mixture of elements waiting to be organized,[j] and St. Bonaventure sees it as pure undifferentiated energy.

The Distinction of Works

St. Thomas discusses the work of the six days in his *Treatise on the Work of the Six Days*.[26] In that treatise he distinguishes three works during Creation Week: 1) the work of creation, 2) works of distinction or separation, and 3) works of adornment.

The work of creation is the work of the first day. *"In the beginning God created the heavens and the earth."*

The works of distinction were done on the first, second and third days. On the first day, *"God separated the light from the darkness."* On the second day, God *"separated the waters which were under the firmament from the waters which were above the firmament."* On the third day, God separated the land from the waters.

The separation of the light from the darkness was discussed in the preceding article. The interpretation of the firmament as an expanse was considered under a

---

j. Modern cosmogony fails to explain how the elements aggregate in the supposed chaotic primordial soup. That is, big bang theory does not tell us how hydrogen atoms migrate to other hydrogen atoms, helium atoms to other helium atoms, and so forth to form quantities of distinct substances.

previous doctrine.[27] St. Thomas introduces his discussion of the firmament with a sound hermeneutical principle for establishing the relationship between scriptural exegesis and natural science:

> In discussing questions of this kind two rules are to be observed, as Augustine teaches (*The Literal Interpretation of Genesis*, Book I, Chapter 18). The first is, to hold the truth of Scripture without wavering. The second is that since Holy Scripture can be explained in a multiplicity of senses, one should adhere to a particular explanation, only in such measure as to be ready to abandon it, if it be proved with certainty to be false; lest Holy Scripture be exposed to the ridicule of unbelievers, and obstacles be placed to their believing.[28]

St. Thomas himself sees two interpretations for *"firmament."* The first is the "starry firmament." "Another possible explanation is to understand by the firmament that was made on the second day, not that in which the stars are set, but the part of the atmosphere where the clouds are collected, and which has received the name 'firmament' from the firmness and density of the air."[29] St. Thomas holds that there are waters above the firmament. He says:

> It is written: *"God ... separated the waters which were under the firmament from the waters which were above the firmament"* (Genesis 1:7).
> I answer with Augustine: "These words of Scripture have more authority than the most exalted human intellect. Hence, whatever these waters are, and whatever their mode of existence, we cannot for a moment doubt that they are there" (*The Literal Interpretation of Genesis*, Book II, Chapter 5). As to the nature of these waters, all are not agreed. Origen says (*Homily 1 on Genesis*) that the waters that are above the firmament are "spiritual substances." Wherefore it is written: *"Praise him, you highest heavens, and you waters above the heavens!"* (Psalms 148:4), and *"Bless the Lord, all waters above the heaven"* (Daniel 3:38). To this Basil answers that these words do not mean that these waters are rational creatures, but that "the thoughtful contemplation of them by those who understand fulfills the glory of the Creator" (*Hexaemeron*, Homily 3). Hence in the same context, fire, hail, and other like creatures, are invoked in the same way, though no one would attribute reason to these.
> We must hold, then, these waters to be material, but their exact nature will be differently defined according as opinions on the firmament differ. For if by the firmament we understand the starry heaven, and as being of the nature of the four elements, for the same reason it may be believed that the waters above the heaven are of the same nature as the elemental waters. But if by the firmament we understand the starry heaven, not, however, as being of the nature of the four elements then the waters above the firmament will not be of the same nature as the elemental waters, but just as, according to Strabus, one heaven is

called empyrean, that is, fiery, solely on account of its splendor: so this other heaven will be called aqueous solely on account of its transparence; and this heaven is above the starry heaven. Again, if the firmament is held to be of other nature than the elements, it may still be said to divide the waters, if we understand by water not the element but formless matter. Augustine, in fact, says that whatever divides bodies from bodies can be said to divide waters from waters (*Genesis Defended Against the Manicheans*, Book I, 5, 7).

If, however, we understand by the firmament that part of the air in which the clouds are collected, then the waters above the firmament must rather be the vapors resolved from the waters which are raised above a part of the atmosphere, and from which the rain falls. But to say, as some writers alluded to by Augustine, that waters resolved into vapor may be lifted above the starry heaven, is a mere absurdity (*The Literal Interpretation of Genesis*, Book II, Chapter 4). The solid nature of the firmament, the intervening region of fire, wherein all vapor must be consumed, the tendency in light and rarefied bodies to drift to one spot beneath the vault of the moon, as well as the fact that vapors are perceived not to rise even to the tops of the higher mountains, all go to show the impossibility of this. Nor is it less absurd to say, in support of this opinion, that bodies may be rarefied infinitely, since natural bodies cannot be infinitely rarefied or divided, but up to a certain point only.[30]

St. Thomas also seems to hold, with Augustine, that the waters above the firmament are held there by natural processes and not miraculously.[31] St. Basil had also held that the forces of nature held up the firmament. He supposed that the waters above the firmament are not fluid but exist outside it in a solid state, as a mass of ice; and that this is the crystalline heaven of some writers.[32] He also believed that the firmament preserved a mild temperature over the whole earth.[33]

Concerning the separation of the waters from the lands, we saw previously how St. Basil interpreted this as the creation of the law of gravity for water and that obedience to the law of gravity is not inherent in the nature of water.[34] Water has an important place in Genesis because it is so important for our lives. The importance of water for life cannot be overstated. Water has so many properties necessary to sustain life that evolutionists are stymied when they try to explain them away by chance. Liquid water accounts for two-thirds of our body weight. To stay healthy, we need to consume about a quart of water a day. Water helps blood to transport oxygen and nutrients and to remove waste products, and it helps the body to regulate its temperature. Water can dissolve more substances than any other liquid, a property very important for supporting life. It is easily purified by distillation or percolation. Water, unlike other substances, expands rather than contracts when it solidifies Thus ice floats on water preventing lakes and oceans from freezing over. Oceans and lakes are able to moderate climates because water has a high heat capacity. The adhesiveness of water enables it to rise by capillary action, a property that plants use to transport water. It easily evaporates to be transported and distributed throughout the earth by clouds and rain. Rivers and streams are natural source of power; and water in the form of steam is used to power machinery. God used the immense power of water to totally reshape the face of the earth during the Great Flood. The properties of water can in no way be construed as accidental. They are part of God's master plan of creation.

On Day Three through Day Six God adorned His work of creation. On the third day, He created plant life, which was to be food for other living creatures He would create.[k] The variety of plant life on earth is immense. And it was probably much more so before the Flood because many species were probably lost forever in the Flood or could not adapt to the new world after the Flood. God gave the plants to us for food, but Genesis 1 does not mention that they were also given for medicine. This is probably because there was no need for medicine before the Fall. Each species of plant was created for a purpose. Even noxious plants may have been created for their chemical value or for their medicinal value in anticipation of the Fall. Saints Basil the Great, John Chrysostom and Ambrose all make a point of the fact that the plants were created before the sun, and therefore do not depend on the sun for their origin.[35] Also, although the plants were created on Day Three, (2:4–10) seems to indicate that some of them may not have germinated until later.[36]

On the fourth day God created the heavenly bodies that would regulate the lives of the plants He created and the other living creatures He would create. St. Cyril of Jerusalem marveled at the well-ordered movements of the heavenly bodies:

> Men ought to have been astonished and amazed not only at the arrangement of the sun and moon but also at the well-ordered movements of the stars and their unfettered courses and the timely rising of each of them; how some are signs of summer, others of winter; how some indicate the time for sowing, others the times of navigation.[37]

---

k. This explains the biochemical unity of all living things. Men, animals and plants are similar biochemically not because they all came from the same ancestor, but because they all came from the same Creator. Since plants were to serve as food for both men and animals, it follows that God would have created them all with common biochemical components.

The cosmos is delicately balanced to serve life on earth. For example, the sun's orbit is inclined to the earth at just the right angle to produce the seasons, and the sun is just the right distance away to keep the earth within a temperature range favorable to life. Small deviations from the assigned arrangement of the earth and sun would be catastrophic for life on earth.

The astronomers continually discover new wonders in the sky that reflect more and more of God's great power and majesty. The text of Genesis gives only the barest outline of His mighty works.

On the fifth day God created the living creatures of the sea and air. Apparently God did not fill the earth with animal life at once. He made either one pair of each kind or a small community of each kind. He then told them to be fruitful and to multiply and to fill the waters and to multiply on the earth. On the sixth day God created the living creatures of the land, culminating with that creature which He created in His own image and likeness and to which He was to give dominion over the other creatures, namely, man. The animals mimic and instruct men in many ways by their behavior. St. Cyril of Jerusalem noted this:

> Different natures of animals sprang forth from the one earth at a single command—the gentle sheep and the carnivorous lion—and the various tendencies of irrational animals that display analogies to various human characteristics. Thus the fox typifies the craftiness of men, the snake the venomous treachery of friends and the neighing horse the wanton young man. There is the busy ant to rouse the indolent and sluggish.... [38]

God created the other creatures for the use and spiritual benefit of man, as pointed out by St. John Chrysostom:

> It wasn't simply for our use that He produced all these things; it was also for our benefit in the sense that we might see the overflowing abundance of His creatures and be overwhelmed at the Creator's power, and be in a position to know that all these things were produced by a certain wisdom and ineffable love out of regard for the human being that was destined to come into being. [39]

The Seventh Day

No new matter or new kinds of living organisms were created after Creation Week. *"Thus the heavens and the earth were finished, and all the host of them. And on the seventh day God finished the work he had done...."* [40] Even Jesus in His miracles did not create ex nihilo. He transformed that which already existed. The only ongoing creation is the creation of human souls. But even that is connected in with the original order of creation. St. Thomas Aquinas explains how nothing new was created after the sixth day:

> Nothing entirely new was afterwards made by God, but all things subsequently made had in a sense been made before in the work of the six days. Some things, indeed, had a previous experience materially, as the rib from the side of Adam out of which God formed Eve; whilst others existed not only in matter but also in their causes, as those individual creatures that are now generated existed in the first of their kind. Species, also, that are new, if any such appear, existed beforehand in various active powers; so that animals, and perhaps even new species of animals, are produced by putrefaction by the power which the stars and elements received at the beginning. Again, animals of new kinds arise occasionally from the connection of individuals belonging to different species, as the mule is the offspring of an ass and a mare; but even these existed previously in their causes, in the works of the Six Days. Some also existed beforehand by way of similitude, as the souls now created. And the work of the Incarnation itself was thus foreshadowed, for as we read, the Son of God *"being born in the likeness of men"* (Philippians 2:7). And again, the glory that is spiritual was anticipated in the angels by way of similitude; and that of the body in the heaven, especially the empyrean. Hence it is written, *"Nothing under the sun is new, for it hath already gone before, in the ages that were before us"* (Ecclesiastes 1:10, DR).[41]

St. Thomas believed in the production of new species after Creation Week because he believed in the spontaneous generation of life in putrefied matter, which we now know does not take place—life comes only from life. But he would never have adhered to the evolution of species a la Darwin because he believed in the instantaneous creation of the original kinds.[42] Thomas' "active powers" applied only for a very limited number of species and involved the instantaneous production of the individuals of those species, not the evolution of the species over time.

God rested on the seventh day in that He ceased creating. But His work continues on in His holding the created world in existence and in His governing it through the natural laws that He created. He also governs it directly by revealing His will to men, and by intervening in the course of nature through miracles, both visible and invisible. His loving care over creation is called *providence*.[1] St. John Chrysostom expresses this as follows:

---

1. The word *providence* is used for the first time in the Book of Wisdom. See Wisdom 14:3; 17:2.

You see, in saying at this point that God rested from His works, Scripture teaches us that He ceased creating and bringing from nonbeing into being on the Seventh Day, whereas Christ, in saying, *My Father is working still, and I am working,"* (John 5:17), reveals His unceasing care for us: He calls "work" the maintenance of created things, bestowal of permanence on them and governance of them through all time. If this wasn't so, after all, how would everything have subsisted, without the guiding hand above directing all visible things and the human race as well?[43]

The seventh day is related to the Day of the Lord, which is often mentioned in Sacred Scripture.[44] The Day of the Lord is that day when the Lord will come to judge the world and save the faithful. Again, this is an instance of the beginning being pregnant with the end. The seventh day is not given an ending like the other days in Genesis, and thus the Fathers of the Church see it as being the archetype of eternal life. St. Augustine said:

Heaven, too, will be the fulfillment of that Sabbath rest foretold in the command: *"Be still, and know that I am God"* (Psalms 46:10). This, indeed, will be that ultimate Sabbath that has no evening and that the Lord foreshadowed in the account of his creation.[45]

And St. Ephrem the Syrian said:

It [the Sabbath] was given to them in order to depict by a temporal rest, which He gave to a temporal people, the mystery of the true rest, which will be given to the eternal people in the eternal world.[46]

Venerable Bede had this to say about the practice of resting on the Sabbath because God rested on the seventh day:

Mystically speaking, we are counseled by all this that those who in life devote themselves to good works for the Lord's sake are in the future led by the Lord to Sabbath, that is, to eternal rest.[47]

St. Thomas Aquinas makes a connection between the seventh day and the consummation of the world at the end of time:

Now the final perfection, which is the end of the whole universe, is the perfect beatitude of the Saints at the consummation of the world; and the first perfection is the completeness of the universe at its first founding, and this is what is ascribed to the seventh day.[48]

St. Thomas says that God "rested in Himself" on the seventh day. And so it is fitting "that the seventh day should have been sanctified, since the special sanctification of every creature consists in resting in God."[49]

The Seven-Day Week Observed

Sacred Scripture does not present time as a continuum with the present separating past from future in a uniform advance. That conception of time we received from Enlightenment thinkers and their mechanical view of nature. Rather, Sacred Scripture marks off the passage of time in terms of events of significance: Creation, The Fall, The Great Flood ... The Passover, and so on. And it perceives time as a hierarchy of rhythms: heartbeat, day, week, month, and year. All but the week are based on natural rhythms. The week is a specially created divine rhythm. The week is like a repeating melody, a series of seven musical notes with the accent put on the Sabbath.[50]

Everywhere at all times people have observed a seven-day week. This presents a problem for those who seek only natural causes for things because there is no natural explanation for it. The day is determined by the rising and setting of the sun, the month by the phases of the moon, and the year by the elevation of the sun. But there is no natural process that defines the seven-day week. Yet it has existed for thousands of years. The only reasonable explanation is that God ordained the seven-day week, as we are told in Genesis.

Atheistic regimes have attempted to erase this testimony to Creation from human memory but have failed. In 1792 the French government introduced a calendar with a ten-day week, but it disappeared after fourteen years because the people of France did not accept it. In 1929 the communist government in Russia, among its efforts to eradicate Judaism and Christianity, eliminated Saturday and Sunday from the week by introducing a ten-day week. That unpopular calendar lasted only a year.

< Objections > and << Replies >>

< Objection 1 >

St. Augustine and St. Gregory of Nyssa both held that inorganic materials were created all at once in the beginning and were given the potency to evolve into other living beings over periods of time. For them the six days are symbolic.

<< Reply to Objection 1 >>

It is incorrect to say that Augustine and Gregory of Nyssa were evolutionists or that they can be held up as examples to show that organic evolution is a respectable position for Catholics to hold.

<< St. Augustine on Creation >>

St. Thomas Aquinas neatly summarizes the position of Augustine on the creation of things:

> Augustine's view is that at first in creation certain things were given existence in their own nature, according to their distinct species, for example, the elements, the heavenly bodies and spiritual substances (angels); but that certain others—such as plants, animals and men—existed only in their germinal principles (*rationes seminales*). Afterwards all of these latter were produced in their distinct types by that operative governance which God, ever since the six days, has continued to exercise upon His original creation. This divine activity is alluded to in John 5: *"My Father works until now, and I work."* Furthermore, when distinguishing among things, we have to take into account not only the order of time, but the order of nature and the order of teaching. First, of nature: for example, the sound is prior to the song in nature, but not in time. Hence, whatever precedes in the order of nature is recorded as having been made first; thus, the land before the animals, the water before the fishes, and so on. Then, the order of teaching, as when geometry is being taught: although the parts of a figure constitute that figure without any succession in time, geometry nonetheless teaches the constitution of the figure by the drawing of one line after another. So, too, Moses, when instructing an unlearned people about the creation of the world, divided up into several steps what was done all at once.[51]

As St. Thomas observed, Augustine believed in the appearance of new species after Creation Week. Augustine explained their appearance this way: "Within corporeal things through all the elements of the world there are certain hidden seminal reasons (*seminariae rationes*) by which temporal and causal opportunity presenting itself, various kinds burst forth, distinguished by their own style and purposes.... God, however, is the one and only Creator who implanted the causes themselves and the seminal reasons in things."[52] Augustine said that angels bring the seminal reasons to fruition just as a farmer causes plants and trees to spring up from seeds.[53] In that way God perfects that which He made imperfect.[m] Scholastic writers give the name *seminal principle* to Augustine's seminal reason. The notion of seminal reason is Augustine's alternative for potency and act in substantial change.[54] Since he holds that it is angels that reduce potency to act and not natural forces, and since he does not advocate the continual transformation of living organisms from one kind into another,[55] Augustine cannot be seen as giving legitimacy to the idea of biological evolution.

<< St. Gregory of Nyssa on Creation >>

St. Gregory of Nyssa also held that God created everything simultaneously; but He created them in a confused state, that is, indistinctly. Then "the work of nature" distinguished them according to an order fixed by God. He gives as an analogy a mixture of oil, water and quicksilver. Mixed together they are indistinguishable. But after a while the quicksilver sinks to the bottom, the water settles on it, and the oil rises to the top. The three liquids are distinct substances, but this becomes apparent only after gravity is allowed to do its work.[56] St. Gregory was not a transformist nor did he hold that the six days were symbolic. For he professed allegiance to the teaching of St. Basil, who strongly upheld the fixity of living species and the literalness of the six days of Creation. Introducing his treatise on the six days, Gregory stated:

> Before commencing, I wish to testify that I am certain I do not contradict anything that has been written by St. Basil concerning the creation of the world.... Let, therefore, his writings be confirmed, and let them hold a place of honor, and let them not yield to other documents but those of the Testament, written under the dictation of the Divine Spirit.[57]

It is clear that Catholic evolutionists cannot show a precedent for their ideas in the writings of Gregory of Nyssa.

---

m. St. Augustine said that it is not unfitting that God should make things imperfect and later perfect them. See ST, Part I, Q. 70, A. 2, Reply Obj. 5.

✳   ✳   ✳   ✳

< Objection 2 >

Genesis 2:4 states, "*in the day that God made the earth and the heavens....*" The six days are contracted into one. Also, verse 2:5 states that the plants and herbs did not yet exist. Thus the second account of Creation, which begins with Genesis 2:4, implies that the six days are symbolic and that everything was created at once, either actually or in potency. God actualized the potencies in matter at various times throughout the history of the world.

<< Reply to Objection 2 >>

This objection is similar to the previous one but appeals directly to Genesis rather than the Fathers. In one form or another, it is made by a number of Catholics who oppose Darwinian evolution but have still been led to believe that the earth is millions of years old and that different life forms have appeared successively on the earth during the course of its history. St. Lawrence of Brindisi's exegesis of Genesis 2:4–5 puts that objection to rest.

<< St. Lawrence of Brindisi on Genesis 2:4–6 >>

St. Lawrence of Brindisi (1559–1619) makes it clear in his *Explanatio in Genesim* that verse 2:4 is not the beginning of another account of Creation with an entirely different outlook, as some exegetes propose; but rather it is a development of what went before. Concerning the use of the singular "*day,*" he states:

> It is very frequent in Sacred Scripture that a singular word is taken in place of a plural, which I think occurred here, such that "*in the day*" was written for "*in the days.*" One could perhaps argue differently that, in primordial creatures that received their being on the first day, by a kind of power, whatever was formed in the course of the following days was produced and created together at the same time and was contained in these primordial creatures. Accordingly, for that reason Scripture says "*in the day* {and not *days*} *that the Lord God made.*" (trans. by C. Toth)

St. Lawrence goes on to explain the puzzling phrase in Genesis 2:5: "*when no plant of the field was yet in the earth and no herb had yet sprung up.*" He says:

How did God produce those things *before they were?* A twofold understanding can be assigned to this manner of speaking. The first explanation is that, although they did not exist, God already made them entirely, and so He made them *before they were,* that is, when they did not exist. The second understanding is that God made every plant and herb by His omnipotence *before they existed,* that is, outside the natural causes that were suitable for every plant and herb to come into existence, and they were brought forth into being before their natural causes from which they naturally had to be produced. For these plants sprout in the common course of nature from the watery moisture that extends over the earth through rain along with the assistance and order of able men's agriculture, diligence, and skill. But at that time when these things were brought forth, there had been no rain nor man to cultivate the earth. This understanding seems to be the better sense of the Scripture, for the next verse excludes the effects of man and rain. (trans. by C. Toth)

But (2:6) states, *"a mist went up from the earth and watered the whole face of the ground."* Did God use that mist to water the plants and herbs rather than rain? St. Lawrence answers:

The Hebrew original has *"And a mist will rise up and water all the surface of the earth."* As a result, it does not refer to the production of plants and fruits that took place on the third day, but to the production that will afterwards take place by the power of Nature. The sense of Moses therefore is that the first production of shrubs and plants was achieved by divine power, but subsequent production will take place through the power of Nature. A mist will ascend and, condensed into water in the clouds of heaven, rain will be made, and it will water the entire surface of the earth. Infusing the earth with watery moisture, the rain will make it fruitful. (trans. by C. Toth)

[1] CCC, no. 337.

[2] See Ezekiel 4; 5; 12; 24.

[3] ACC, p. 9.

[4] *Commentary on Genesis 1*, as quoted in Rose, Fr. Seraphim, *Genesis, Creation and Early Man: The Orthodox Christian Vision* (Platina, CA: Saint Herman of Alaska Brotherhood, 2000), p. 101.

[5] ACC, p. 15.

[6] *Hexaemeron*, Homily 2, Chapter 8, as quoted in Rose, op. cit., p. 401.

[7] *Hexaemeron*, Homily 1, Chapter 37, as quoted in Rose, op. cit., p. 401 (editor's note).

[8] According to Rose, op. cit., p. 401.

[9] According to Ruffini, Cardinal Ernesto, *The Theory of Evolution Judged by Reason and Faith* (New York: Joseph F. Wagner, Inc., 1959), pp. 68–69.

[10] ST, Part I, Q. 74, A. 2.

[11] CG, Book XI, Chapter 9; also see JR, nos. 1689, 1690, 1692, 1695, *Confessions*, Book XI, and CG, Book XI, Chapters 32–34.

[12] *On the Literal Interpretation of Genesis*, 4, 333, 52, as quoted by Ruffini, op. cit., p. 71.

[13] Ruffini, op. cit., p. 71, footnote.

[14] According to Ruffini, op. cit., pp. 71–72, footnote.

[15] See Doctrine Four.

[16] DZ, no. 2128.

[17] BV, Part II, Chapter 2.1.

[18] BV, Part II, Chapter 2.2.

[19] ACC, p. 16.

[20] ST, Part I, Q. 67, A. 4, Reply Obj. 2.

[21] See Gilson, Etienne, *The Philosophy of St. Bonaventure*, Illtyd Trethowan and Frank J. Sheed, trans. (Paterson, NJ: St. Anthony Guild Press, 1965), p. 8.

[22] See BV Part II, Chapter 2.5 and Gilson, op. cit., p. 250.

[23] Revelation 21:23.

[24] *The First Apology in Defense of the Christians*. See the Office of Readings for the Third Sunday of Easter, *The Liturgy of the Hours According to the Roman Rite*, Vol. II, (New York: Catholic Book Publishing Co., 1976), p. 695.

[25] Gilson, op. cit., pp. 248–249.

[26] ST, Part I, Q. 65–74.

[27] Doctrine Two, The Cosmography of Genesis.

[28] ST, Part I, Q. 68, A. 1.

[29] Ibid.

[30] ST, Part I, Q. 68, A. 2.

[31] ST, Part I, Q. 68, A. 2, Reply Obj. 1.

[32] *Hexaemeron*, Homily 3, as interpreted by St. Thomas Aquinas (ST, Part I, Q. 68, A. 2, Reply Obj. 2).

[33] Ibid., Chapter 7.

[34] Doctrine Four, The Whole Shebang Cosmogony.

[35] ACC, p. 15.

[36] See ST, Part I, Q. 69, A.2.

[37] ACC, p. 17.

[38] Ibid., p. 26.

[39] Ibid., p. 25.

[40] Genesis 2:1–2.

[41] ST, Part I, Q. 73, A.1, Reply Obj. 3. Also see ST, Part I, Q. 118, A. 3, Reply Objs. 1,2.

[42] See Doctrine Four, The Whole Shebang Cosmogony.

[43] ACC, p. 46.

[44] See Leon-Dufour, Xavier, *Dictionary of Biblical Theology* (Boston: St. Paul Books and Media, 1988), pp. 110–114.

[45] CG, Book XXII, Chapter 30, as quoted in ACC, p. 47.

[46] ACC, p. 46.

[47] Ibid.

[48] ST, Part I, Q. 73, A. 1.

[49] ST, Part I, Q. 73, A. 3.

[50] For an elaboration on this theme see Bowman, Thorleif, *Hebrew Thought Compared with Greek* (New York: W.W. Norton, 1960), pp. 133–138.

[51] *II Sent. Dist.*, XII, Q. 1, A. 2, as quoted by Ruffini, op. cit., pp. 72–73.

[52] JR, no. 1865.

[53] Ibid.

[54] Wuellner, Bernard, *Dictionary of Scholastic Philosophy* (Milwaukee: Bruce, 1956), pp. 97–98.

[55] For insight into Augustine's position on the matter see *The Literal Meaning of Genesis* IX, 17. The chapter can be found on pp. 394–395 of *On Genesis: A Refutation of the Manichees; Unfinished Literal Commentary on Genesis; The Literal Meaning of Genesis (The Works of St. Augustine: A Translation for the 21st Century, Part I, Volume 13).* (Hyde Park, NY: New City Press, 2002).

[56] For pertinent excerpts from St. Gregory's *Hexaemeron* with commentary see Ruffini, op. cit., pp. 197–202.

[57] Preface to *Hexaemeron*, as quoted by Ruffini, op. cit., p. 201.

Doctrine Seven
God created the world several thousand years ago.

None of the Fathers of the Church believed in an ancient universe. From the writings of the Greek atomists they were familiar with the idea of the universe being formed over eons of time by natural forces, and they rejected it. The Church has not made a formal declaration about the age of the world. However, it is possible that she could someday declare that *yom* in Genesis 1 means a literal day because that interpretation has strong support in scriptural exegesis and in Tradition. That means that it is possible for her to formally teach that the world is only thousands of years old. However, she could never declare that *yom* means millions of years because that has no support at all in scriptural exegesis, Tradition, or magisterial teaching. The natural sciences are unable to say anything with certainty about the age of the world.

Biblical Chronology

The exact age of the world cannot be determined from Scripture, but Scripture assures that the world was created only thousands of years ago and not billions. The Bible gives the exact numbers of years from Creation to the death of Abraham, but unfortunately these numbers vary somewhat in variant texts. From Abraham on, biblical texts can be meshed with secular sources to develop chronologies. Genesis 5 gives the genealogy from Adam to the birth of Noah's sons, from which the numbers of years from Creation to the birth of each antediluvian patriarch can be calculated. Genesis 7:6 gives the age of Noah when the floodwaters came. Totaling these numbers, all of the extant Hebrew Masoretic texts give 1656 years from Creation to the Flood, and the Greek Septuagint variants give from 1307 to 2402 years, the most reliable giving 2262 years.[1] Genesis 11 gives the genealogy from Shem to Abram, from which the number of years from the Flood to the birth of Abram can be calculated. The Masoretic texts give 292 years while the Septuagint variants give from 292 to 1513 years, the most accepted variant giving 942 years.[2] Using archaeological evidence, most scholars agree that Abraham lived about 2000 B.C. These numbers tell us that the world is at least 6000 years old and at most 12,000 years old.[3]

The variant texts do not destroy the credibility of the biblical chronology. The Fathers were aware of such discrepancies but were not greatly disturbed by them. They believed that the patriarchs lived to be hundreds of years old, the discrepancies notwithstanding. St. Augustine explicitly considers the question of "whether we should follow the authority of the Hebrew text rather than that of the Septuagint in the reckoning of the years." His answer is:

> I should certainly not be justified in doubting that when some difference occurs in the two versions, where it is impossible for both to be a true record of historical fact, then greater reliance should be placed on the original language from which a version was made by translators into another tongue.[4]

The Septuagint was a translation of the Hebrew Scriptures into Greek by a team of Jewish scribes in the 2nd–3rd centuries B.C. Augustine attributes the original deviation from the Hebrew text to a simple mistake by the scribe who first translated the text from Hebrew into Greek. He says:

> For even in these days, numbers are carelessly copied and even more carelessly checked when they do not direct the reader's attention to something which can be easily understood, or which is evidently useful to learn.[5]

According to Augustine, this somehow set the precedent for more deviations, even to deliberate tampering with the numbers.

Ussher's Chronology

In 1650 and 1654 James Ussher (1581–1656), Anglican archbishop of Armagh Ireland published his work *The Annals of the World*, which was a 1300-page magnum opus in Latin on a history of the world that covered every major event from Creation to A.D. 70. In the *Annals* he calculated that Creation took place on October 23, 4004 B.C. on the Julian calendar (September 21 on the Gregorian calendar). He was not the only person to calculate the date of Creation from Sacred Scripture. Two famous scientists of his time also did so, getting dates close to that of Ussher. Johannes Kepler (1571–1630) calculated the date of Creation as 3992 B.C. and Isaac Newton calculated 4000 B.C.[6]

Ussher probably used the Hebrew Masoretic Text and the Greek Received Text. He used as a common standard Julian years. He believed that these were most suitable because the years of the ancient Egyptians and Hebrews were the same length as the Julian year. He calculated from the years recorded in the Bible that the end of Nebuchadnezzar's reign was in the 3442nd year of the world (3442 A.M.). Using Chaldean history and astronomical information he connected that date with the Julian calendar to show that 3442 A.M. was equivalent to 4152 J.P. (Julian Period) or 562 B.C. From that he deduced that the creation of the world took place in the year 710 J.P. or 4004 B.C.[7]

Ussher assumed that God created the world in the autumn because the Jews and other ancient peoples started their year in the autumn. He chose the first Sunday after the autumnal equinox as the first day of Creation. Consulting astronomical tables, he determined that this fell on October 23. The detailed calculations took up more than 100 pages in the original work.[8]

Jewish and Orthodox Chronologies

Jewish chronology is based on the *Seder Olam Rabbah* or *The Book of the Order of the World*, which was compiled by Rabbi Yose ben Halafta in the second century A.D. Jewish people count the years from the creation of the world. The year A.D. 2000 was the year 5760 according to Jewish reckoning based on the *Seder Olam*. This places Creation in the year 3760 B.C. Thus, according to traditional Jewish chronology, the world is younger by several hundred years than the Masoretic or Septuagint texts indicate.[9]

Orthodox chronology is based on the Septuagint, as indicated in the following passage from an Orthodox Christian source:

> The earliest extant Christian writings on the age of the world according to the biblical chronology are by Theophilus (A.D. 115–181), the sixth bishop of Antioch from the apostles, in his apologetic work *To Autolycus* ... and by Julius Africanus (A.D. 200–245), in his *Five Books of Chronology*.... Both of these early Christian writers, following the Septuagint version of the Old Testament, determined the age of the world to have been about 5,530 years at the birth of Christ.
>
> The common Byzantine Christian reckoning, also derived from the Septuagint, placed the date of creation at 5,508 B.C. This date, which underwent minor revisions before being finalized in the seventh century A.D., served as the starting point of the Calendar of the Byzantine Empire and the Eastern Orthodox Church, and was known as the Imperial Creation Era of Constantinople. The Eastern Church avoided the use of the Christian Era (B.C.-A.D.)

since the date of Christ's birth was debated in Constantinople as late as the fourteenth century.... When Russia received Orthodox Christianity from Byzantium, she inherited the Orthodox Calendar based on the Creation Era. The creation of the world was used as the starting point of the calendar of the Russian Empire until the Westernizing reforms of Peter I at the beginning of the eighteenth century ... and it still forms the basis of traditional Orthodox calendars up to today.

Fr. Seraphim writes that "even the most mystical Fathers" such as St. Isaac the Syrian accepted without question the common understanding of the Church that the world was created "more or less" in 5,500 B.C.[10]

Natural Indicators of Age

Militant atheistic naturalists, who are well-dubbed "secular fundamentalists" because they dogmatically reject divine revelation, have created an "illusion of longevity" for the cosmos that they have successfully imposed on popular imagination. The thinking of many people has been conditioned by their relentless and pervasive propaganda promoting the illusion of longevity. But many observed facts of the various sciences point to a young cosmos, despite the fact that currently fashionable cosmological theories do not.[11] [a] But convincing people of this is difficult. Overcoming the ancient universe mentality in our modern world is a monumental psychological task. Many Christians have been so fooled by the illusion of longevity that they can't even consider the *possibility* of a young universe.

---

a. Evolutionists suppose the earth to be about 4.5 billion years old. This age is derived mostly from measurement of the parent/daughter ratios of radioactive elements in the rocks of the earth. A critique of that method is given in the reply to Objection 1. Evolutionists believe the universe to be 10–20 billion years old. This is the amount of time they believe it would take for light to travel from the farthest stars to earth. They declare that they are able to measure the distances to stars. However, their distance measuring techniques are based on questionable assumptions. This is discussed in Appendix A. Furthermore; they assume that the speed of light has remained constant throughout the history of the universe and that Euclidean geometry is precisely valid for the trajectory of light over interstellar distances. There is evidence that the speed of light was greater in the past (see Paul D. Ackerman, *It's a Young World After All: Exciting Evidences for Recent Creation* (Grand Rapids, MI: Baker Book House, 1986), pp. 72–77 and Walt Brown, *In the Beginning: Compelling Evidence for Creation and the Flood* 7th ed. (Phoenix, AZ: Center for Scientific Creation, 2001), pp. 232–237).

It seems absurd to them. They can't think outside of the box the evolutionists have made for them.[b]

*   *   *   *

Any estimate of the earth's age involves a projection back in time of current measurable conditions. This projection depends on *assumptions* about the constancy of certain factors over time, and initial and boundary conditions. The credibility of any age estimate depends on the quality of the measurements and the credibility of the assumptions. With that caveat, it can now be said that there are more natural indicators that point to a young earth than an ancient one, and the ones that point to an ancient earth are less reliable in their assumptions. Some of the best indicators of a recently created earth will be given here.[12] The principal one offered for an old earth will be treated in the objections.

There are a number of geochronometers, that is, methods used to estimate the age of the earth. Uniformitarian techniques reject any worldwide catastrophe such as the Great Flood and assume that geological and geophysical processes haven't changed much in their intensity throughout the history of the earth.[13] Some geochronometers may seem to indicate an ancient (millions or billions of years old) earth, but most of them clearly indicate a young (thousands of years old) earth. Some chronological methods that make the earth appear old presume that the earth is old to begin with and thus beg the question.

Some phenomena that point to a young earth by uniformitarian reckoning are[14]

---

b. Fascination with the idea of an ancient universe is not new. Jewish cabalists, who look for secret codes in the Bible and who believe in creation by emanation, have long maintained that only children and the simple-minded should be encouraged to believe in a literal six natural day period of creation. They believe that the "wise" understand the Genesis 1 account to express the deep structure of a mysterious, divinely ordered process. The first-century cabalist Nechunya ben HaKanah claimed that his deciphering of the Torah showed that the universe is 15.3 billion years old. This is simply a Jewish form of gnosticism. If God did imbed coded messages into the Torah, as the cabalists believe and is possible, He would not use them to contradict Himself. See Jeffrey Satinover, *Cracking the Bible Code* (New York: HarperCollins, 1997).

- *Decay and reversals of the earth's magnetic field*: For more than a century and a half scientists have been observing that the magnetic field of the earth is decaying. Also, measurements of the orientation of magnetic particles in rock appear to indicate that the earth's magnetic field has reversed in the past. The only reasonable model for the source of this decaying magnetic field is an electric current circulating in the core of the earth. The decay of the current caused by electrical resistance accounts for the decay in the magnetic field. Extrapolating back in time, the electric current increases, as does the heat it generates. Going back only some twenty thousand years, the heat generated would have been great enough to liquefy the earth. Only catastrophic events, like those that took place during the Flood, can account for apparent reversals of the field. Such a model points to an earth only thousands of years old.

- *Helium content in the atmosphere*: Helium is produced by radioactive decay inside the earth. It rises to the surface and enters the atmosphere. A small amount escapes into space; the rest accumulates in the atmosphere. The rate of introduction of helium into the atmosphere and the concentration of helium in the atmosphere have been measured, and the rate of escape into space has been calculated. The low concentration of helium in the atmosphere indicates that the earth is young. And the fact that helium is still being introduced into the atmosphere also implies that the earth is young.

- *Delta formation*: The Mississippi River pours about 300 million cubic yards of sediment into the Gulf of Mexico each year. At that rate the Mississippi delta would have taken only 4000 years to form.

- *Erosion and sedimentation*: If the earth were billions of years old, current geological processes would have completely eroded it and filled the oceans with sediment. The surface of the earth, however has suffered relatively little erosion, and the thickness of the sediment on the ocean floor indicates a much younger earth.

Techniques that recognize the existence of the Great Flood have a worldwide enormous catastrophe as their initial condition and give a young age when corroborated with biblical chronology. Evidence for such a universal catastrophe abounds, especially in the sedimentary rocks and in the fossil record.[15] Uniformitarians have grossly misinterpreted this evidence to support the claims of an old earth and the evolution of species.[16] Likewise, they have misinterpreted astrophysical data by assuming that the universe is very old.

*   *   *   *

There are a number of astronomical phenomena that suggest that certain features of the universe are much younger than evolutionary science would suppose. For example:

- *Short period comets*: The gradual destruction of many short period comets has been observed and recorded by scientists over the centuries. The average lifespan of those comets is fifteen hundred to ten thousand years. If the solar system were the same age as evolutionists say the earth is (4.5 billion years), the comets would be long gone. But there are still many of them circling the sun; and no source of new comets has been observed. Astronomers have postulated two sources for them: the Kuiper belt, located near the outer planets, and the Oort Cloud, a supposed sphere of about 10^{12} comets encasing the solar system at roughly 50,000 astronomical units from the sun. About 300 large objects have been observed in the Kuiper belt, but their sizes, colors and orbits indicate that they are more like asteroids than comets. The Oord cloud has not been observed. The Hubble telescope and other sensors have failed to detect a comet reservoir.[17]

- *Jupiter's volcanically active moon*: NASA's Voyager mission revealed that Jupiter's moon, Io, is "literally bubbling with volcanoes." It is the most volcanically active body in the solar system. Without an external source of thermal energy, Io should have cooled off a long time ago on the evolutionary time scale. Some heat is generated on Io by tidal friction caused by Jupiter and its other large moons. But the measured infrared heat flux is ten times too large to be accounted for by tidal friction alone. This means that Io radiates large amounts of intrinsic thermal energy, which implies that it has not existed long enough to cool off.[18]

- *Saturn's rings*: Saturn is known for its beautiful band of rings, which is 160,000 miles wide. The band contains hundreds, perhaps thousands, of 20-meter thick individual rings that are composed primarily of icy rocks and ice chunks centimeters to meters in size. Some are kept in place by small "shepherd moons" orbiting between them. Evolutionary astronomers have long associated the rings with the evolution of the planet. Supposedly, the rings were residue after the planet was formed from a swirling dust cloud. But they have to admit that the rings are rapidly breaking up and could have remained stable only for a few thousand years and were therefore recently formed.[19]

- *Lunar craters*. The surface features of the moon indicate that it has been bombarded often with large meteors. If the moon's surface were covered with water, the craters produced would last only a few seconds. If the moon's surface were covered with hot tar, the craters produced would last somewhat longer. The lifetime of a crater depends on the viscosity of the material in which it is formed. Water has a very low viscosity and therefore can maintain a shape only for a very short period of time. Rock has a very high but finite viscosity. Therefore, it holds its shape for a very long time but eventually loses it, as has been observed in tombstones and other rock monuments. Granite is one of the most viscous substances on earth. Even if the lunar surface were made of granite, the craters could not last more than a few million years. If the lunar surface is made of basalt, which is less viscous than granite and which the moon rocks brought back by the Apollo astronauts were made of, then the lunar craters are no more than a few thousand years old.[20]

The point of these examples is this: Catholics must not allow themselves to be intimidated into abandoning biblical chronology and accepting the speculations of modern astronomers concerning the age of the universe. The conclusion that the universe is ancient is not the scientific certainty that many of them assert it to be. They interpret data and construct models with the preconceived notion that the universe is ancient, but there is significant scientific evidence that it is not. The *facts* of modern astronomy do not make it a "necessity" to "depart from the literal and obvious sense" in the interpretation of Genesis' chronology. Rather, the opposite is true. A correct interpretation of astronomical data agrees with the literal rendering of Genesis' chronology.

The examples presented above give a small sample of the great diversity of features in the various planets, moons and other heavenly objects that occupy the solar system. These diversities (in such things as size, temperature, topography, chemical composition, orbital direction, spin direction, and spin axis inclination) give each a uniqueness that points to special creation by God. They strongly indicate that the occupants of the solar system do not have a common natural origin, as demanded by evolution theory. Rather, they point to a common supernatural origin, to a recent creation by a God who produced a wonderful heterogeneity among His celestial creatures as He did among His living creatures.

The Church on the Age of the World

None of the Fathers of the Church expressed belief in an ancient universe.[21] They generally believed that the earth was created in six natural days, an exception being St. Augustine, who believed that everything was created at once, either actually or potentially.[22] [c] From the writings of the Greek atomists, the Fathers were familiar with the idea of a universe being formed by natural forces over eons of time; and they rejected it.[23] The Church has not made an explicit official pronouncement on the age of the world. She has left open for now the meaning of the word *yom* in Genesis 1. Unfortunately, theistic evolutionists have used this as an opening to make the preposterous and unnecessary assertion that *yom* means millions of years.[24] The *Catechism of the Catholic Church* states:

> The question about the origins of the world and of man has been the object of many scientific studies which have splendidly enriched our knowledge of the age and dimensions of the cosmos, the development of life-forms and the appearance of man. These discoveries invite us to even greater admiration for the greatness of the Creator, prompting us to give him thanks for all his works and for the understanding and wisdom he gives to scholars and researchers. With Solomon they can say: *"It is he who gave me an unerring knowledge of what exists, to know the structure of the world and the activity of the elements ... for wisdom, the fashioner of all things, taught me"* (Wis 7:17–22).[25]

To some this may seem as an implied endorsement of the scientific opinion that the world is eons old because that is the opinion of the majority of scientists these days. But it is no such thing. It is a carefully worded statement that makes general remarks; it does not endorse any specific scientific opinion. It lauds genuine scientific knowledge, which can only be comprised of facts. And that the cosmos is billions of years old is not a fact; it is an opinion. There is a growing

---

c.   Because he held that some things were created potentially in the beginning and that *yom* does not mean a literal natural day, Augustine might seem to have been open to long durations of time between creation in potency and actualization. (Be aware that Aristotelian terminology is being used here for the sake of clarity, but Augustine was not an Aristotelian.) But elsewhere in his writings he shows distaste for the idea of a world older than biblical chronology indicates (see CG, Book XII, Chapters 11, 13).

number of reputable scientists who do not agree with that opinion.[26] It was shown above that there is much strong scientific evidence that shows that the world is only thousands of years old, and it will be shown later that the evidence offered for an eons-old universe proves nothing. These facts are coming to light despite the efforts of the scientific establishment to suppress them.[27]

Catholic proponents of an ancient cosmos hold up an address by Pope Pius XII as proof of that the Church endorses belief in a hoary universe. In that address the pontiff gave his credence to the claim that the universe is five billion years old.[28] He used conclusions given to him by his scientific advisors that were based on very unreliable assumptions. Apparently, those conclusions were presented to him as scientific facts, which they certainly are not. His acceptance in that address does not mean that that the Church now officially endorses such a large age for the universe. The most that can be said is that the Church tolerates, at present, that position despite its obvious conflict with the plain meaning of Genesis and the belief of the Fathers.

< Objections > and << Replies >>

< Objection 1 >

Radiometric measurements of rocks assure us that the earth is billions of years old.

<< Reply to Objection 1 >>

This is not true. Radiometric dating methods depend on *belief* in the assumptions employed and on data that is often conflicting. That *belief* is often a great leap of faith motivated by philosophical or theological presuppositions. Often the methods give inconsistent results that are never published. Following is a discussion of one of the radiometric methods used for dating rocks. It will serve as a model. Similar critiques apply for other methods.[29]

<< Uranium-238 Radiometric Dating >>

First of all, this method, like all radiometric rock dating methods, applies only to igneous and metamorphic rocks. Igneous rocks were once extremely hot and molten and have cooled into solid rock. Lava, basalt and deep granites are igneous rocks. Metamorphic rock is rock that was transformed by heat or pressure, such as marble. Radiometric methods do not work on sedimentary rock, which is rock formed from the sediment laid down by water. Limestone, sandstone and shale are sedimentary rocks. Most of the fossils are buried in sedimentary rock.

Proponents of radiometric dating presume that the melting of a rock sets its radiometric clock to zero and that the age provided by the method is the time elapsed between the cooling of the rock and the present.

The first radioactive isotope used to date rocks was uranium-238.[30] Through radioactive decay uranium-238 decays, through a number of intermediate decays, to lead-206, which is stable. The half-life of the process is 4.5 billion years. That means that in 4.5 billion years half of the uranium-238 in a rock will have decayed into lead-206. So from a measurement of the ratio of the amount of lead-206 to the amount of uranium-238 in a rock, the age of the rock can be determined *if* 1) all the lead-206 came from uranium-238, that is, if there was no lead-206 in the rock to begin with, 2) no uranium or lead entered or left the rock after it was formed, and 3) the decay rate, that is, the half-life, remained constant.

The first "if" is an assumption about the initial condition of the rock. Is it justifiable to say that there was no lead-206 when the rock formed? If lead-206 had been present, the method could give an age much older than the true age. Does melting really set the clock to zero, eliminating all the lead-206?[d]

The second "if" is an assumption about the boundary condition. Rocks are not as impermeable as one might suppose. Elements can enter or leave a rock in gaseous form or by leaching. Much care is taken selecting rocks, but even the ages determined for good specimens are often not consistent with the ages determined by other methods:

> The common occurrence of discordant results in isotopic geochronometry presents an intriguing and complicated problem. It has become obvious that many mineral samples used in age determinations have not been closed systems throughout their histories. The interpretation of isotopic ages ultimately

---

d. Another radiometric method uses the decay of potassium-40 into argon-40. This method was used on rocks formed out of the molten lava from the eruption of Mount Saint Helens in 1980. It yielded ages measured in hundreds of thousands of years. This indicates that the molten lava had not entirely degassed, that is, the clock was not set to zero. See discussion of measurements by Steve Austin in Guy Berthault's "Geological Dating Principles Questioned—Paleohydraulics: A New Approach," *Journal of Geodesy and Geodynamics*, Vol. 22, No. 3, Aug. 2002, p. 26.

requires knowledge of the processes which can cause alteration of the isotopic ratios.[31]

The third "if" is an assumption about the constancy of a critical parameter in the measurement, the decay rate of the uranium-238. Did the half-life of the uranium-238 remain constant from the time the rock was formed? It is known that the decay rates of some elements change in the presence of a radiation environment, as for example, strong neutron fluxes.[32] Chemist Frederick B. Jueneman noted:

> The age of our globe is thought to be some 4.5 billion years, based on the radiodecay rates of uranium and thorium. Such "confirmation" may be short-lived, as nature is not to be discovered quite so easily. There has been in recent years the horrible realization that radiodecay rates are not as constant as previously thought, nor are they immune to environmental influences.
> And this could mean that the atomic clocks are reset during some global disaster, and events which brought the Mesozoic to a close may not be 65 million years ago but, rather, within the age and memory of man.[33]

Overlaying all these assumptions is the archassumption that the earth *is* billions of years old. So the data must be in accord with that. If it does not, then it is presumed to be bad and is rejected. Geologist Richard L. Mauger states:

> In general, dates in the "correct ball park" are assumed to be correct and are published, but those in disagreement with other data are seldom published nor are discrepancies fully explained.[34]

Evolutionist William Stansfield admits the unreliability of radiometric measurements:

> It is obvious that radiometric techniques may not be the absolute dating methods that they are claimed to be. Age estimates on a given geological stratum by different radiometric methods are often quite different (sometimes by hundreds of millions of years). There is no absolutely reliable long-term radiological "clock."[35]

<< About Clocks >>

The essence of geo- and astro-chronography can be encapsulated in a few remarks about clocks in general. To measure a period of time with a clock, the initial and final physical states of the clock must be known. No clock is useful without that information. For example, the pointer on a stopwatch is set to zero on starting and the pointer is on another number when it is stopped. Also, uniformity of the physical process used to measure time lapse between states is presumed. That is, the physical process used to measure time is presumed to proceed at a constant rate when compared to a standard process. Such uniformity degrades with time. The longer the time lapse measured the more probable it is that inaccuracies will creep in because of the volatile nature of matter; for example, the parts of a mechanical clock wear out or rust, and radiometric clocks become degraded by nonradiometric diagenetic processes that alter the daughter/parent isotope ratio. Thus a clock becomes less reliable as it ages.

God may have planted natural clocks in the world for the purpose of revealing its age to us. But there is no indication that He gave us any direct knowledge of the initial settings of such clocks. However, He did give us the chronology in Genesis by which we may be able to set them. If we ignore Genesis then we must rely on guesswork, which produces very uncertain results.

✻   ✻   ✻   ✻

< Objection 2 >

"The evidence for these ages [billions of years] comes from at least five distinct and independent areas of research in astrophysics: expansion of the universe, stellar structure, isotope dating, white dwarf cooling, and properties of the cosmic microwave radiation. The concordance of these five methods is impressive because they rely on completely distinct types of observations, and different laws of physics, to arrive at their conclusions.

"It is beyond the bounds of reason to suppose that, if the Universe were actually no older than a few thousand years (as the young-Earth proponents claim), many hundreds of researchers from diverse countries and all religious backgrounds would discover five completely different methods which all yield multi-billion year ages....

"There are other theories in physics that are also based on equally solid evidence. For example, calculations of stellar structure are based on the laws of conservation of momentum and energy. They have been widely tested over the past few centuries and have been found to be accurate descriptions of the physical world. As a result, when calculations of stellar structure indicate that the oldest stars have ages between 10 and 20 billion years, these results are reliable. Other theories that have been used by physicists in arriving at similar estimates for the age of the Universe are also based on thoroughly tested evidence....

"Moreover, why would God trick us by setting up an elaborate system of multiple physical clues that point consistently to a Universe that has an age between 10 and 20 billion years? What would God achieve by deceiving us on such a massive scale? Such an activity seems entirely out of character for Someone who (according to the standard theological definition) can neither deceive nor be deceived. It also seems entirely out of character for Christ, who proclaimed Himself to be "the Truth," to engage in worldwide trickery with scientists who are honestly and earnestly seeking the truth about the world."[e]

<< Reply to Objection 2 >>

The phenomena above that supposedly give evidence for an old universe fall into three categories: *radiometric dating*, *big bang cosmology*, and *stellar maturation*. The reliability of radiometric dating was discussed under Objection 1. The expansion of the universe and the properties of cosmic microwave radiation fall under *big bang cosmology*, and stellar structure and white dwarf cooling fall under *stellar maturation*. These will be discussed below followed by comments on the fourth paragraph of the objection.

<< Incredibility of Big Bang Model >>

The "proof" dangled before our eyes that the universe is 10–20 billion years old is the big bang model of the universe. The apparent expansion of the universe and the presence of cosmic microwave radiation are two phenomena that the big bang conjecture claims to explain in support of its credibility. The big bang model is discussed elsewhere in this book.[36] Its deficiencies as a physical theory were pointed out. They are summarized as follows:

- The cosmological principle, on which big bang theory is based, is a presumption, not an observed fact.

- Einstein's gravitational theory is applied far beyond the range of density for which it has been empirically verified.

---

e. This objection is taken verbatim from an article written by a Catholic professor of astrophysics and published in a conservative Catholic periodical. The opinions of the author are, sadly, representative of many Catholic scientists today.

- The probability that the singularity had the necessary initial conditions for producing our universe is vanishingly small.

- The singularity at the start of the big bang is a serious theoretical flaw. Meaningful science abhors singularities.

- Theorists can offer no reason for the big bang. What is the detonator?

- Expansion red shifts violate conservation of energy.[f]

- Big bang theory is unable to explain the complex structure of the universe. The forces we know of would be unable to do the job.

- Galaxies reckoned to be nearby and those reckoned to be faraway display the same kind of spiral structure. According to big bang theory, the nearby galaxies should not be spirals anymore because they have had plenty of time to wind up. The far-away galaxies, which supposedly give us a picture of the early universe, had not had enough time to form spirals.[37]

- The big bang should have produced equal amounts of matter and anti-matter, which would have annihilated each other.

- Cosmic microwave radiation (CMR) is isotropic and has a perfect black-body spectrum, which means that the universe behaves like an enclosed cavity in perfect thermal equilibrium. According to big bang theory, CMR should exhibit irregularities in intensity and spectrum because of irregularities in the formation of the universe.

- It is touted that George Gamow and Ralph Alpher predicted the existence of CMR and the relative abundances of helium and hydrogen in the universe in their model of the big bang. They got those results because they started off with the *assumption* that the universe began in a highly compressed state of extremely hot radiation.[38] They could have gotten the same results if they assumed a la Aristotle that a cool crystalline sphere enclosed the universe and that hydrogen and helium were abundant in order of their simplicity. (Hydrogen is the simplest element and reckoned by astrophysicists to be the most abundant element in the universe;

---

f. It may be true that the law of conservation of energy applies only locally and not globally; it may be the local limit of a global law. See Mendel Sachs, "The Mach Principle and the Origin of Inertia from General Relativity," in *Mach's Principle and the Origin of Inertia* (Montreal: Apeiron, 2003), p. 5.

helium is the second simplest element and is reckoned to be the second most abundant element in the universe.[39]) The point is this: there are many conceivable models of the universe that would give those results. According to big bang theory, CMR and relative element abundance depend on the initial state immediately after the big bang. It seems that there would be plenty of parameters to tweak to get the answers one is looking for.[40]

- Doppler shift and universe expansion are not the only credible explanations for galactic red shift.[41] Also, there are other explanations for CMR.[42] Big bang theory does not have exclusive claim to those phenomena.

Following are even more deficiencies:

- *The horizon problem*: The perfect blackbody spectrum of CMR means that the universe is in thermal equilibrium. Therefore distant regions of the universe must have exchanged energy to make this possible. But it would take radiation more than the supposed age of the universe to travel from one extreme to the other.

- *The flatness problem*: According to big bang calculations, the density of matter in the early universe must have been at a certain critical value for the universe to be what it is. If the density had been greater than the critical density by just one part in a million, the universe would have stopped expanding and collapsed in on itself. If the density had been less than the critical density by one part in a million the universe would have expanded too rapidly for anything to form. There is no explanation for why the density was just right.

- Cosmologist Alan Guth suggested a way to get around the horizon and flatness problems. He proposed that at the very earliest moments of its existence the universe rapidly "inflated" to about a size of ten meters. Thus the edges of the universe were close enough to come into thermal equilibrium, and it could easily attain critical density. However, no explanation in terms of known causes is given for the proposed "inflation." Rather, the supposed cause of this inflation is an invented entity given the name "dark energy."[43] Theoretical cosmologists like the Guth's hypothesis because it can be made to provide "interesting solutions" to the horizon and flatness problems; they see it to be "pretty." Finally, there is the question of turning off the inflation once it starts, the so-called graceful exit problem.

- The standard model of particle physics is the "demiurge" of the big bang cosmogony. But the "dark matter" that the big bang necessitates for the formation of galaxies and a closed universe cannot be particles of the standard model.[44]

The fact that big bang theory may be able to explain some astrophysical phenomena does not qualify it as a satisfactory representation of reality, despite its popularity. There are examples from the history of science about popular physical theories being tipped off their pedestals. The phlogiston theory was popular and held sway for a century. It was neat and tidy because it had a unifying principle, and it explained many experimental facts. But there were some considerable difficulties with that theory, and in the end it proved inadequate and was replaced by Lavoisier's oxygen theory. Another example: Newtonian physics described many terrestrial and astronomical phenomena very accurately, and it reigned supreme for several centuries. At the end of the nineteenth century astronomers pictured the universe as a big machine running smoothly in accord with the laws of Newtonian physics. But twentieth-century physics toppled that simple vision and showed that the real universe is a more complex thing.

Big bang proponents try to piggyback their theory on the stunning successfulness of quantum mechanics, quantum electrodynamics, the theories of special and general relativity and the standard model of particle physics. These sciences are based on repeatable experiments and testable predictions. Big bang theory, on the other hand, is based on conjecture. No one is able to simulate the big bang in a laboratory. In fact, it has been shown that the supposed evolution of the universe is noncomputable and therefore cannot even be simulated on a computer.[45] Scientists know nothing about the forces that would be applicable at the big bang; and of the forces they do have experience with, they have knowledge only of their effects, not of their nature or origin. Scientists do not know much about the constants of nature like the speed of light, Planck's constant and the gravitational constant. They are unable to derive or explain them or to assure themselves that they have really remained constant over the alleged billions of years of cosmic evolution.[46] They can only project back what they know now, which is quite limited despite the successes. *"Where were you when I laid the foundation of the earth? ... Do you know the ordinances of the heavens? Can you establish their rule on the earth?"*[47]

Some proponents of big bang theory go so far as to call it the big bang "law."[48] They say that the evidence is "overwhelming." But whatever evidence they have is circumstantial because they dismiss the testimony of the only eyewitness, the Author of Genesis 1. It has come to light recently, thanks to new DNA techniques, that many people were wrongly convicted of crimes by "overwhelming" circumstantial evidence. Furthermore, advocates of the big bang claim that it may be superseded by another theory but that it will still remain true as part of the bigger theory, just as Newton's laws are valid within boundaries set inside the larger theories of quantum mechanics and relativity. That is nothing but wishful thinking. In the history of science there are theories that were outright rejected and set outside the theories that replaced them. The phlogiston and caloric theories are prominent examples.

Secular science holds on to the big bang tenaciously because it is the only natural explanation for the origin of the universe. The reigning scientific establishment won't even consider models of the universe that are consistent with both the observed facts and special creation because such models have religious overtones. It is part of the mystery of our human condition that a theory as full of holes as the big bang can be considered by so many as being more credible than revealed truth. The "imp of the perverse"[g] is certainly at play here, fabricating myths and enticing people to believe them. Someone once said, "Every age has its myths and calls them higher truths." The big bang and macroevolution are myths of our age posing as higher truths.

Actually, big bang cosmology is more than an attempt to explain natural phenomena as far as possible in terms of natural causes. It is part of a much broader effort by militant atheists to eliminate God from all facets of life. Militant atheists erect walls of separation between science and theology and between Church and State as the first stage in their effort to eliminate God from human consciousness altogether. Big bang cosmogony is their substitute for creation theology. So rather than being called natural science, it should be called "atheology."

<< Stellar Maturation >>

The branch of astrophysics that deals with stellar structure and so-called stellar evolution *presumes* that all the stars evolved over eons of time from a nonstellar state.[h] All practitioners of that science, no matter where they live or what religion

---

g. The allusion is to a short story of that name by Edgar Allan Poe. See 2 Thes 2:11.

they practice, must conform to that paradigm if they want their papers to be published because that is held by the academic community to be "correct" science. However, the phenomena studied by that science could be explained just as well if one considers the stars as developing from the state in which they were created. (The laws of conservation of momentum and energy and other genuine physical laws are applicable in either case.) It is not hard to believe that stars were created in various stages of maturity, as were for example, trees. On the third day, God created trees. It would seem that, for the sake of variety and completeness, He created them in various stages of growth. Some He created as saplings, others as very mature trees with many rings, and others at various stages in between. And so for the stars; on the fourth day God created red giants, white dwarfs and the whole array of heavenly bodies, each with their own color and brightness and splendor for *"star differs from star in glory."*[49] If Cain, the first botanist, had studied the number of rings on the most mature trees to determine how long ago the earth was created he would have gotten a wrong answer. Similarly, our present day astrophysicists get the wrong answer when they infer old ages for the stars from the study of their maturity.

The models of the various phenomena studied in the "independent" areas of research have enough uncertainties in them to produce a sufficient number of adjustable parameters that can be tweaked to assure that they all give similar ages. Models that can't be tweaked to give an acceptable age are rejected. For example, any model in which the comets have their origin at the same time as the sun is rejected because there would be no comets today according to old-universe reckoning. They would have all disintegrated or left the solar system long ago. So instead, some scientists speculate that the sun has a companion star named Nemesis whose orbit brings it close to the solar system about once every 26 million years. On each trip the star unleashes a fresh supply of comets from the "Oort cloud," a hypothetical cloud of comets forming a vast halo around the outskirts of the solar system. Neither Nemesis nor the Oort cloud has been observed. Outlandish theories like that are given more credence than the Genesis account.

---

h. A number of ancient observers reported the star Sirius B to be red. But modern astronomers observe it to be a white dwarf. According to stellar evolution theory, it should take at least a hundred thousand years for a red giant to turn into a white dwarf. But apparently this has happened in less than two thousand years. This presents a serious problem for stellar evolution theory and casts doubt on its credibility. See Ackerman, op. cit., p. 67.

<< Uncertainty of Astrophysical Chronology >>

The doctrine of an ancient cosmos is asserted and proclaimed as fact so often in scientific presentations, even when the context does not call for it, that it becomes obvious that a "gospel" is being preached. It is the gospel of naturalism, in which true religion has no say; and the continual assertions are professions of faith in that gospel. The antibiblical doctrine of an ancient cosmos is a fundamental tenet of that faith, and it is a doctrine held to be true beyond question. But some astronomers are candid enough to admit that the observational evidence in astronomy is not strong enough to support the naturalists' claim that the universe is older than biblical chronology indicates. For example, astronomer J. A. Eddy stated:

> There is no evidence based solely on solar observations that the Sun is 4.5–5 x 10^9 years old. I suspect that the Sun is 4.5 billion years old. However, given some new and unexpected results to the contrary, and some time for frantic recalculation and theoretical readjustment, I suspect that we could live with Bishop Ussher's value for the age of the Earth and Sun. I don't think we have much in the way of observational evidence in astronomy to conflict with that.[50]

<< God's Undeceiving Word >>

God does not deceive us. We deceive ourselves if we choose to ignore His Word and seek the truth elsewhere. Those who reject the Genesis account and seek information about the origin of the world from natural causes alone follow the example of Eve who would not believe what God told her but instead sought truth from the tree of the knowledge of good and evil.

Determination of the age of the universe is beyond the competence of natural science because the creation of the universe was a unique, inimitable supernatural event at which no human being was present. The best scientists can say is that the universe *appears* to be such and such an age according to their *judgment*. Even if the various sciences did objectively converge on the same age, it would prove nothing about its real age. Every newly created thing has the appearance of age by its very existence. That includes the universe as a whole. If every natural means of revealing an age yielded the same apparent age for the universe, it would show how consistent God was in creating it but not how long ago He created it.

It behooves the Catholic scientist or scholar to examine the observed facts of his discipline in the light of divine revelation if he hopes to make genuine contributions to his field of study.

✳   ✳   ✳   ✳

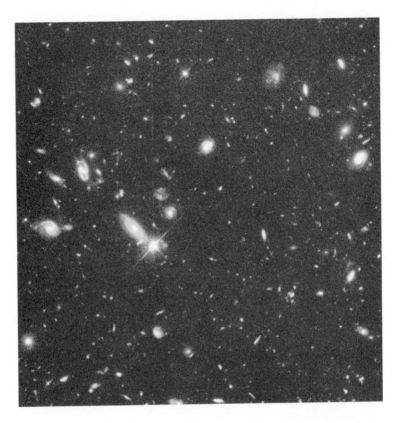

This picture shows a tiny patch of sky called Hubble Deep Field taken by the sensitive space-based Hubble telescope. It is a view from the northern hemisphere taken in late 1995. The telescope was focused for ten days on a patch of sky the size of a dime at 75 feet. Most of the objects in the picture are not individual stars but galaxies, each containing billions of stars. Researchers found at least 1500 galaxies in the observation. These galaxies are mature enough to be distinct. But according to big bang theory, we should be seeing the early universe when the galaxies were just beginning to be formed. This is a confirmation of the biblical truth that the heavenly bodies were specially created by God.

This picture shows the immensity of the material world. It seems that the spiritual world is even more so. Dante Alighieri, the great medieval poet, said that the number of angels is so immense, that "no word or concept can reach that far." Furthermore, each angel is a species in itself that reflects some unique splendor of God, making the spiritual world much richer in variety than the material world.

< Objection 3 >

Science is working toward a mathematical *Theory of Everything* (TOE) that will be able to tell us everything there is to know about the universe and its origin. There is no need for divine revelation.

<< Reply to Objection 3 >>

The Theory of Everything is the goal towards which particle physicists are working. It is the ultimate theory that unifies the four fundamental forces of nature (electromagnetic, weak, strong, gravitational) and all particles. The name *Theory of Everything* is misleading because it is only a theory of subatomic particles. Although it would be useful in studying astrophysical phenomena, it could say nothing about the origin and evolution of the universe without assumptions being made about the initial state of the universe. Applications of the TOE are limited. It would have nothing to say about the phenomenon of life, and one couldn't use it to give better weather predictions. Even if such a theory could tell us certain things about the universe, it could never tell us *why* God created it. That has to be revealed to us.

Furthermore, mathematics can never give a complete description of nature. This is rooted in the nature of mathematics, which can't even say everything about itself, let alone nature. Twentieth-century discoveries in mathematics make vain the pursuit to find a small set of axioms from which all natural phenomena can be logically derived.

<< The Limits of Mathematical Physics >>

In 1930 the Austrian mathematician Kurt Gödel demonstrated that human beings can never formulate a complete description of the set of natural numbers $\{0, 1, 2, 3, \ldots\}$; that is, no system of arithmetic containing a finite number of axioms can predict all the true facts about natural numbers. There will always be statements within the system governed by those axioms that can be neither proved nor disproved on the basis of those axioms. There will always be at least one true proposition whose truth the axioms will not suffice to establish. When a proposition is found to be indemonstrable, it may then be assumed to be true and added to the system as another axiom; and then another proposition will be found to be indemonstrable; then it may be assumed to be true and added as an axiom; and so on forever. Thus, a mathematical system that completely says everything that can be said about natural numbers would require an infinite number of axioms.[51]

Thus mathematics will always remain open-ended and incomplete. There can never be a mathematical system rooted in a finite number of axioms by which all mathematical truths can be derived by deductive reasoning. The British mathematicians Bertrand Russell and Alfred North Whitehead had tried to do just such a thing. From 1910 to 1913 they published their famous *Principia Mathematica,* which was an ambitious attempt to derive all of mathematics from a finite set of axioms. Gödel showed that their efforts were doomed to failure.

A mathematical system is said to be *consistent* if there is no statement in the system that can be both proved and disproved. Gödel showed that it was not possible to establish the internal consistency of a system even the size of ordinary arithmetic. One can only say that one mathematical system is consistent if another is.

The proof of the consistency of a finite set of mathematical axioms can be found only outside that set. Mathematicians can show that Euclidean geometry is consistent if ordinary arithmetic is. No mathematical system can be the "ultimate" system.

In geometry, Euclid's fifth postulate is an example of an indemonstrable proposition. Therefore, alternative propositions can be used in place of the fifth postulate to generate geometries that are not Euclidean. Euclidean geometry cannot say everything that can be said about two-dimensional and three-dimensional spaces.

Since mathematicians cannot fully explore something as simple as number theory, it is safe to presume that physical science will never come to a complete understanding of the material world. Physicists certainly will never expose any "ultimate secret" of the universe. Any system of knowledge about the world is fundamentally incomplete, forever subject to improvement. Moreover, man will never be able to build a machine that can give "all the answers"; this was shown by the mathematician Alan Turing.[52]

Gödel's theorem implies that there are an infinite number of truths. The set of all true statements in mathematics is infinite.

The great French mathematician Blaise Pascal (1623–1662) seems to have anticipated Gödel. In his *Pensees* he makes the following statements:

> Reason's last step is the recognition that there are an infinite number of things which are beyond it. It is merely feeble if it does not go as far as to realize that. If natural things are beyond it, what are we to say about supernatural things?

Strangely enough they wanted to know the principles of things and go on from there to know everything, inspired by a presumption as infinite as their object. For there can be no doubt that such a plan could not be conceived without an infinite presumption or a capacity as infinite as that of nature.

When we know her better, we understand that, since nature has engraved her own image and that of her Author on all things, they almost all share her double infinity. Thus we see that all the sciences are infinite in the range of their researches, for who can doubt that *mathematics, for instance, has an infinity of propositions to expound?* [italics added]. They are infinite also in the multiplicity and subtlety of their principles, for anyone can see that those which are supposed to be ultimate do not stand by themselves, but depend on others, which depend on others again, and thus never allow of any finality.

[A]nd it seems to me that anyone who has understood the ultimate principles of things might also succeed in knowing infinity. One depends on the other, and one leads to the other. These extremes touch and join by going in opposite directions, and they meet in God and God alone.

*   *   *   *

< Objection 4 >

Genesis allows for a long period of time to have elapsed during the era described in (1:1–2). The original creation of the universe and the world is described in (1:1). *"In the beginning God created the heavens and the earth."* Then a period of time followed during which the earth was *"without form and void."* This period may have been of considerable length, from thousands to millions of years.

Further, there are gaps in biblical genealogies. Certain genealogies omit some of the generations. For example, the genealogy in Matthew 1:1–17 omits the kings Ahaziah, Jehoash and Amaziah and indicates that Joram begat Uzziah, who was his great-great-grandson. A compressed genealogy is found in Ezra 7:1–5, where six generations are omitted that are given in a more complete genealogy in 1 Chronicles 6:3–15.[53] Such occurrences indicate that the Scriptures may not give a complete genealogical record but may only draw lines of descent, which may be very long.

<< Reply to Objection 4 >>

These are attempts to accommodate Genesis to the long geological periods invented by nineteenth-century uniformitarian geologists and anthropologists. The first is a version of the so-called gap theory.

<< Gap Theories >>

Gap theories state that there was a very long interval of time between (1:1) and (1:3). Some go as far as to say that an account of primordial creation is related in (1:1), a destruction of that creation in (1:2) and a re-creation in (1:3). In the version given in the objection, the period of chaos is stretched out to accommodate evolution of the universe. Such interpretations are forced. They do not emerge naturally from the narrative. There is no hint at all in (1:2) that the earth and heavens were slowly formed over eons of time. How could there have been matter for eons of time without light? There is an intimate relationship between matter and light, and light was clearly created on the first day. Christ Himself excluded any chronological gap between (1:1) and (1:3). He identified *"In the beginning"* with Creation Week when He said: *"But from the beginning of creation, 'God made them male and female.'"*[54]

<< Genealogical Gaps >>

The existence of gaps in some genealogical records does not necessarily imply gaps in the complete scriptural record. Nor does it imply that the incomplete records are erroneous. One must try to understand what the author of an incomplete record was intending to convey. F. N. Jones takes such an approach for the examples given in the objection.[55] He also treats the "problem of Cainan." Cainan appears between Arphaxad (Arpachshad) and Shelah in the Septuagint translation of Genesis 11 and in Luke's genealogy of Jesus (Lk 3:36), but he does not appear in the Hebrew text.[56] [i] Critics have used this anomaly to discredit biblical chronology.[j] Jones defends it by first giving scriptural cross-references that confirm the genealogy of Genesis 5. He then shows that the omission of Cainan in Genesis 11 does not affect the chronology because that genealogy gives the patriarch's age at the birth of his descendant. He then asks why the sacred author

---

i.   The oldest known manuscript of St. Luke's Gospel, the P75, does not include Cainan in the genealogy. See www.answersingenesis.org/Cainan.

omitted Cainan in Genesis 11. He says that there is no explanation whatsoever for the omission in Sacred Scripture. He then looks at a number or possible reasons, one being that Cainan did not receive the blessing of his father Arphaxad and therefore was passed over or disowned. Jones' arguments show that these genealogical problems do not affect the determination of the age of man and the universe from the biblical text. On the other hand, J. Whitcomb and H. Morris argue that the genealogical problems do create uncertainties in the chronologies. But these uncertainties are only of the order of several thousand years and do not belie the youngness of man and the universe.[57]

---

j.   One notable critic of biblical chronology was St. Jerome. Concerning the chronology of the two kingdoms he said, "Read all the books of the Old or New Testament, and you will meet with great discrepancy of years and confusion of numbers between Judah and Israel; to spend time on such questions is an occupation for those with leisure, but not for scholars" (*Ad. Vit.*, ep. 71,5 as cited by Giuseppe Ricciotti, *The History of Israel*, volumes I and II (Fort Collins, CO: Roman Catholic Books, reprint of 1955 edition), pp. 188–189). It must not be understood that he considered such discrepancies irresolvable; rather, he considered their resolution not worthy of scholarly effort. But defending the inerrancy of Sacred Scripture against skeptics certainly is worth the effort.

[1] Numbers are taken from Morris, John D., *The Young Earth* (Green Forest, AR: Master Books, 1994), p. 38.

[2] Ibid.

[3] Ibid., p. 39.

[4] CG, Book XV, Chapter 13.

[5] Ibid.

[6] According to Sarfati, John, "Archbishop's Achievement: James Ussher's great work *Annals of the World* is now available in English." *Creation*, vol. 26, no. 1 (December 2003–February 2004), pp. 24–27.

[7] See Ussher, James, *The Annals of the World,* trans. by Larry and Marion Pierce (Green Forest, AR: Master Books, 2003), pp. 1, 9.

[8] For an outline of his calculations by the translators see Ussher, op. cit., pp. 891–982.

[9] See Finegan, Jack, *Handbook of Biblical Chronology* (Princeton, NY: Princeton University Press, 1964), pp. 126–131 and Jones, Floyd Nolan, "The *Seder Olam Rabbah*—Why Jewish Dating is Different," Appendix G in Ussher, op. cit., pp. 931–934.

[10] Rose, Fr. Seraphim, *Genesis, Creation and Early Man* (Platina, CA: Saint Herman of Alaska Brotherhood, 2000), p. 236, footnote by editor.

[11] For accounts of 33 phenomena that indicate that the world is young see Wysong, R.L., *The Creation-Evolution Controversy* (East Lansing, MI: Inquiry Press, 1976), pp. 158–179. Also see Brown, Walt, *In the Beginning: Compelling Evidence for Creation and the Flood* 7th ed. (Phoenix, AZ: Center for Scientific Creation, 2001), pp. 1–84; Ackerman, Paul D., *It's a Young World After All: Exciting Evidences for Recent Creation* (Grand Rapids, MI: Baker Book House, 1986); and Johnson, J. W. (Wallace) G., *Evolution?* (Los Angeles: Perpetual Adoration, Inc., 1986), pp. 105–110.

[12] For a clear authoritative discussion about techniques and phenomena used to date the earth see Morris, John D., *The Young Earth* (Green Forest, AR: Master Books, 1994).

[13] See Doctrine Five, << The Fossil Record and Its Origin >>.

[14] See Morris, op. cit., chapter 7 and Wysong, op. cit.

[15] See Morris, op. cit., chapter 8.

[16] See Doctrine Five, << The Fossil Record and Its Origin >>.

[17] See Brown, Walt, op. cit., pp. 189–217; Wysong, op. cit., p. 168; Steidl, Paul M., "Comets and Creation" in *Design and Origins in Astronomy*, vol. 2, Don B. DeYoung and Emmett L. Williams, eds. (St. Joseph, MO: Creation Research Society, 2002), pp. 75–91; and Ackerman, op. cit., pp. 35–40.

[18] See Steidl, Paul M., "The Solar System: An Assessment of Recent Evidence" in *Design and Origins in Astronomy*, George Mulfinger, Jr., ed. (St. Joseph, MO: Creation Research Society, 1983), pp. 89–90; Chaffin, Eugene F., "A Determination of the Speed of Light in the Seventeenth Century" in *Design and Origins in Astronomy*, vol. 2, Don B. DeYoung and Emmett L. Williams, eds. (St. Joseph, MO: Creation Research Society, 2002), p. 116; Ackerman, op. cit., pp. 43–44.

[19] See Steidl, Paul M., ibid., pp. 92–96.

[20] See Morton, Glenn R., Slusher, Harold S., and Mandock, Richard E., "The Age of Lunar Craters," *Creation Research Society Quarterly 20* (September 1983), pp. 105–108, as cited in Ackerman, Paul D., *It's a Young World After All: Exciting Evidences for Recent Creation* (Grand Rapids, MI: Baker Book House, 1986), pp. 52–53.

[21] See Doctrine Six, A Real Six days of Creation, The Meaning of *Yom*.

[22] See Doctrine Six, << St. Augustine on Creation >>.

[23] See Doctrine Four, The Whole Shebang Cosmogony.

[24] See Doctrine Six, The Meaning of *Yom*.

[25] CCC, no. 283.

[26] See Ashton, John, *In Six Days* (Green Forest, AR: Master Books, 2001). This book contains the testimonies of a number of scientists who believe that the scientific evidence shows that the world is young.

[27] For an enlightening account by a noncreationist scientist on how the scientific establishment suppresses information that does not fit into the reigning paradigm see Lerner, Eric J., *The Big Bang Never Happened* (New York: Vintage Books, 1991), pp. 52–57.

[28] Pope Pius XII, Address to the Pontifical Academy of Sciences, November 22, 1951, nos. 35–39.

[29] A very good popular presentation and evaluation of radiometric dating techniques is given in Perloff, James, *Tornado in a Junkyard: The Relentless Myth of Darwinism* (Arlington, MA: Refuge Books, 1999), chapter 13. For a current in-depth scientific study of the issue from a young-earth creationist perspective see Vardiman, Larry; Snelling, Andrew A. and Chaffin, Eugene F., editors, *Radioisotopes and the Age of the Earth* [RATE project], Vol. II (El Cajon, CA and Chino Valley, AZ: Institute for Creation Research and Creation Research Society, 2005). The detailed studies it presents show that radiometric measurements are consistent with the literal-historical interpretation of the Genesis creation and flood accounts. Specifically, the RATE project has shown that the decay rates of radioisotopes have not been constant but have varied by orders of magnitude.

[30] For a clear and more detailed discussion of this method see Morris, op. cit., chapter 5.

[31] Catanzaro, E. J., and J. L. Kulp, "Discordant Zircons from the Little Belt (Montana), Beartooth (Montana) and Santa Catalina (Arizona) Mountains," *Geochimica et Cosmochimica Acta*, vol. 28 (January 1964), pp. 87–124.

[32] See A. E. Wilder-Smith, *The Natural Sciences Know Nothing of Evolution* (Costa Mesa, CA: T.W.F.T. Publishers, 1981), p. 133.

[33] Jueneman, Frederic B., "Secular Catastrophism," *Industrial Research and Development* (June 1982), p. 21.

[34] Mauger, Richard L., "K-Ar Ages of Biotites from Tuffs in Eocene Rocks of the Green River, Washakie, and Uinta Basins, Utah, Wyoming, and Colorado," *Contributions to Geology* (University of Wyoming) 15 (Winter 1997).

[35] Stansfield, William D., *The Science of Evolution* (New York: Macmillan, 1977), p. 84.

[36] Doctrine Two, << Reply to Objection 1 >>, << Reply to Objection 2 >>; Doctrine Four, << Reply to Objection 1 >>.

[37] See McIntosh, Andy and Wieland, Carl, "'Early' Galaxies Don't Fit," Creation, Vol. 25, No. 3, June–August 2003, pp. 28–30.

[38] See Webb, Stephen, *Measuring the Universe: The Cosmological Distance Ladder* (Chichester, UK: Springer-Praxis, 1999), pp. 268–269.

[39] See Weinberg, Steven, *The First Three Minutes: A Modern View of the Origin of the Universe* (New York: Basic Books, 1993), p. 162.

[40] See Weinberg, op. cit., pp. 102 ff.

[41] See Doctrine Two, << Eternal Matter and Eternal World Cosmologies: Machian Cosmology >>; << Cosmologies Constructed to be Consistent with Genesis: New Red Shift Interpretation >>. Also see Webb, op. cit., pp. 272–274 and Johnson, op. cit., pp. 101–102.

[42] See Doctrine Two, << Eternal Matter and Eternal World Cosmologies: Steady State Cosmology, Plasma Cosmology, Machian Cosmology >>; << Cosmologies Constructed to be Consistent with Genesis: New Red Shift Interpretation >>.

[43] See Kane, Gordon, "The Dawn of Physics Beyond the Standard Model," *Scientific American*, vol. 288, no. 6, June 2003, p. 73.

[44] Ibid., p. 74.

[45] See Penrose, Roger, *The Large, the Small and the Human Mind* (New York; Cambridge University Press, 1997), p. 119.

[46] See Barrow, John D., *The Constants of Nature* (New York: Pantheon Books, 2002).

[47] Job 38:4,33.

[48] See, for example, de Grasse Tyson, Neil, *My Favorite Universe*, audiotape/videotape/DVD course, (Chantilly, VA: The Teaching Company, 2003), Lecture 8. The instructor claims that he *knows* the big bang happened. It seems that he protests too loudly.

[49] 1 Corinthians 15:41.

[50] Eddy, John A., *Geotimes*, vol. 23 (September 1978), p. 18, as quoted by Jones, Floyd Nolan, *Chronology of the Old Testament: A Return to the Basics*, 14th ed. (The Woodlands, TX: KingsWord Press, 1999), p. 9.

[51] For a readable explanation of Gödel's Proof for the layman see Nagel. Ernest and Newman, James R., *Gödel's Proof* (New York University Press, 1958).

[52] See Hodges, Andrew, *Alan Turing: The Enigma* (New York: Walker and Company, 2000), pp. 90–110; and Feynman, Richard P., *Feynman Lectures on Computation* (Cambridge, MA: Perseus Publishing, 1996), pp. 52–93.

[53] Instances were taken from Free, Joseph P. and Vos, Howard F., *Archaeology and Bible History* (Grand Rapids, MI: Zondervan, 1992), p. 24.

[54] Mk 10:6. Also see Mt 19:4; Mk 13:19; Lk 11:50.

[55] Jones, Floyd Nolan, *Chronology of the Old Testament: A Return to the Basics*, 14th ed. (The Woodlands, TX: KingsWord Press, 1999), pp. 37–46.

[56] Ibid., pp. 29–37.

[57] Whitcomb, John C. and Morris, Henry M., *The Genesis Flood: The Biblical Record and Its Scientific Implications* (Phillipsburg, NJ: P & R Publishing, 1960), pp. 474–489.

PART II

▼

THE HUMAN SPECIES

The Promise of a Redeemer

Doctrine Eight
God created man in His image and likeness.

The image of God is in man by imitation of the divine nature, which is intellectual and volitional, and also by imitation of divine personhood. This is not so for brute animals, in which there is only a "trace" or "vestige" of the Creator. Therefore, man differs in essence from brute animals, and not only in degree.

The *Catechism of the Catholic Church* frequently refers to Genesis 1:26–27 and the truth that man was created in the image of God. Doctrines connected with that truth are

- Man is able to know and love his Creator. (36, 356)

- Each man enjoys the dignity accorded a person. (225, 357)

- God created everything for man. (299, 358)

- Man is called to a personal relationship with God. (299)

- Man is the summit of the Creator's work and distinguished among creatures. (343)

- Man imitates the creative work of God in his works of art. (2501)

- Man was created crowned with glory and honor. (2809)

Image and Likeness

Genesis 1:26 states that God made man in His image and likeness. In (1:27), (9:6), and again in Sir 17:3, the sacred text states that man was created in God's image but does not use the word *likeness*. The word *man* is used in (1:26–27) with a collective meaning; it means all human persons, not just Adam and Eve. Much has been written about the meaning of the words *image* and *likeness* in these texts and whether the words are synonyms or complements. St. Augustine stated: "Some consider that these two were mentioned not without reason, namely 'image' and 'likeness,' since, if they meant the same, one would have sufficed."[1] St. Thomas Aquinas said that an image of something is both a *likeness* of the thing and a *copy* of it. He distinguished *likeness* from *image* as follows:

> Hence it is clear that likeness is essential to an image; and that an image adds something to likeness—namely, that it is copied from something else. For an image is so called because it is produced as an imitation of something else; wherefore, for instance, an egg, however much like and equal to another egg, is not called an image of the other egg, because it is not copied from it.[2]

Furthermore, not every copy is an image:

> Not every likeness, not even what is copied from something else, is sufficient to make an image; for if the likeness be only generic, or existing by virtue of some common accident, this does not suffice for one thing to be the image of another. For instance, a worm, though from man it may originate, cannot be called man's image, merely because of the generic likeness. Nor, if anything is made white like something else, can we say that it is the image of that thing; for whiteness is an accident belonging to many species. But the nature of an image requires likeness in species; thus the image of the king exists in his son: or, at least, in some specific accident, and chiefly in the shape; thus, we speak of a man's image in copper. Whence Hilary says pointedly, "an image is of the same species."[3]

St. Thomas says that likeness is both prior to image and subsequent to it. Likeness is prior to image because it is more general than image. St. Augustine observed: "Where an image exists, there forthwith is likeness; but where there is likeness, there is not necessarily an image."[4] Likeness is subsequent to image because it signifies a certain perfection of image. "For we say that an image is like or unlike what it represents, according as the representation is perfect or imperfect."[5]

*   *   *   *

The Hebrew word translated into English in (1:26–27) and (9:6) as "image" is *tselem*. It is derived from the root for *shadow* and came to mean a "representative figure." It is also used in Genesis 5:3 where it is again translated as "image": "*When Adam had lived a hundred and thirty years, he became the father of a son in his own likeness, after his image, and named him Seth."* It is used twelve times outside of Genesis, most referring to idols, but also meaning "image" and "vain show."

The Hebrew word translated "likeness" in (1:26) is *demuth,* which means "resemblance." It used in (5:1) where the text repeats that Adam was created *"in the likeness of God"* and also in (5:3) mentioned above. It is used nineteen times outside of Genesis meaning "like" or "likeness."

Tselem designates a complete likeness, of say a statue or picture, to the original that it copies, while *demuth* designates only an approximate likeness. St. Thomas' distinctions are in accord with the Hebrew. This is especially clear where he makes a succinct definition of *image* in terms of *likeness*: "[I]mage means a likeness which in some degree, however small, attains to a representation of the species."[6]

✳   ✳   ✳   ✳

It is a metaphysical principle that every effect bears some likeness to its cause. The artist leaves "traces" of himself in his art.[a] God is reflected in His creatures in the way that an artist is reflected in his art. St. Bonaventure expressed this truth by saying that the Trinity "shines forth" in creatures:

> [T]he creation of the world is a kind of book in which the Trinity shines forth, is represented and found as the fabricator of the universe in three modes of expression, namely, in the modes of vestige, image and similitude, such that the reason for the vestige is found in all creatures, the reason for the image in intelligent creatures or rational spirits alone, and the reason for similitude in the Godlike only. Hence, as if by certain steplike levels, the human intellect is born to ascend by gradations to the supreme principle, which is God.[7]

Every creature resembles its Creator to an extent depending on its perfections. The ontological perfections of being and goodness are common to all creatures. Every creature has a likeness to God in that it exists and is good. Man bears likeness to God in this sense.

St. Thomas compares the "likeness of God" in man to the likeness of a man in a statue:

---

a. St. Thomas points out that an image represents something by likeness in species, whereas a "trace" represents something by way of an effect. He gives animal footprints as an example of a trace. See ST, Part I, Q. 93, A. 6.

Hence the divine likeness is reproduced in man, as the likeness of Hercules is reproduced in stone, in respect of the form represented, but not by community of nature.[8]

Man is an "image of God" because in some way he "copies" Him. St. Thomas says that man is an image of God not in the corporeal part of his nature but in the incorporeal part:

Man is said to be after the image of God, not as regards his body, but as regards that whereby he excels other animals.... Now man excels all animals by his reason and intelligence; hence it is according to his intelligence and reason, which are incorporeal, that man is said to be according to the image of God.[9]

"But God made a spiritual image to Himself in man."[10]

Aquinas further points out that the image of God is in man not only by imitation of the divine nature,[b] which is an intellectual and volitional nature, but also by imitation of divine personhood, which is possessed by each of the Three Persons of the Trinity.[11] So man is an image of God as regards both nature and personhood, which are distinct but closely related. The emphasis here will be placed on the latter because that is the least understood.

Personhood

We get an intuitive grasp of the meaning of *person* through our own experience of 'I'. A man knows that he has a mind and a will, that his nature is that of a rational being. Yet the concept of person seems to be something superadded to that nature. We recognize ourselves to be persons even when the mind and the will are defective or inactive. We have a human nature, which is common with other human beings, and the person that one is acts though his own particular nature. Nature pertains to *what* one is; person pertains to *who* one is.

Some scholars say that the word *person* derives from the Greek word *prosopon*, which means "mask." Other scholars find its origin in the Greek phrase *peri soma*, which means "around the body." Most scholars trace it to the Latin word *person-*

---

b. The image of God is in angels more than in men because in angels "the resemblance of the Divine image is wrought with greater expression," i.e., their "intellectual nature is more perfect." See ST, Part I, Q. 93, A. 3.

are, which means "to sound through." *Persona* of the Roman stage means the same as *prosopon* of the Greek stage. To *sound through* is to speak through the opening in the mouth of a mask.

A person is an individual substance of an intelligent nature.[c] A person is an *individual substance* because he exists in himself and not in anything else, nor is he a part of anything else. Individuality implies that personhood is *incommunicable* because it cannot, like a nature, be shared. According to St. Thomas the very concept of person excludes the idea of it being communicated to something else or of its being assumed by something else. Peter cannot be transformed into Paul, nor can the actions of Peter be the actions of Paul. Personhood cannot be communicated from the whole to the part, for example, the personhood of a man cannot be communicated to his brain alone. Personhood cannot be communicated from the individual to the universal. The species *man* is not a person.

Besides incommunicability, there are other qualifiers that set off personhood. They are the following: *uniqueness* (there is only one Peter), *unrepeatability* (there never was and never could be another Peter), *indivisibility* (there is no half Peter), and *distinctiveness* (Peter is not Paul, is not Mary ...). Other characteristics associated with a person, but which proceed from the intellectual and volitional nature united with a person, are self-knowledge and freedom of choice.

Divine Personhood

In (1:26) God says, *"Let US make man in OUR image, after OUR likeness."* Jewish and some early Christian writers interpreted the use of the personal plural to mean that God was addressing His heavenly court of angels. But the angels could not have helped, even in the fashioning of man's body, because the creation of the whole man from the earth was an act of special creation that could be done only by God.[12] Others say that the plural is used to proclaim the greatness and power of God. But the plural form does not seem to be a plural form of majesty because of the infrequency of its use and because there is no evidence in Scripture

---

c. This is the classic definition of Boethius. It is usually expressed in English as follows: A person is an individual substance of a rational nature. This rendering, however, limits the definition to human persons because only human persons have "rational" natures, that is, only human persons acquire knowledge by reasoning. The term *intelligent nature* is more universal. It includes any being that is capable of knowing and willing. Thus the term applies to God, who simply knows, to angels, who intuit knowledge, and to men.

that the plural form was ever used to denote majesty.[13] The greater part of Catholic Tradition, in the light of the New Testament, sees the plural personal as referring to the Holy Trinity. The Fathers of the Church understood (1:26) to mean that the First Person of the Trinity was addressing the Second Person or the Second and Third Persons.[14]

Revelation of the mysteries of the Trinity and the Incarnation led the Church to make a clear distinction between person and nature. Lateran Council IV clearly defined that God is "indeed three Persons but one essence, substance, or nature entirely simple."[15] The Councils of Ephesus (431) and Chalcedon (451) defined the dogma that Christ is a divine person with both a divine nature and a human nature. Constantinople III (680–81) held that Christ has both a divine will and a human will. Thus it associated the faculty of volition with the nature and not the person. Likewise, the faculty of the intellect is associated with the nature and not the person. The person acts through his nature.

Human Personhood

The Fathers of the Church saw God's image in man in ways other than personhood as such. Tatian the Syrian said that the "heavenly Word" made man "an image of immortality in imitation of the Father who begot Him."[16] A number of the Fathers held that Christ is the true image of God and that man is made to Christ's image. For example, Marius Victorinus wrote, "For Jesus alone is the image of God, but man is 'according to the image,' that is, image of the image."[17] And St. Peter Chrysologus wrote, "The second Adam stamped his image on the first Adam when he created him."[18] Other Fathers held that man was created in the *image* of God but acquires His *likeness* through grace or glory. For example, Origen said that man received the image of God at creation, but "the perfection of God's likeness was reserved for him at the consummation," and that man "should acquire it for himself by his own earnest efforts to imitate God."[19] And St. Gregory of Nyssa said that man is created in the image of God but freely chooses His likeness.[20] Augustine saw the image of God in man's intellect[21] and, because of the use of the personal plural in (1:26), in imitation of the Trinity.[22]

Aquinas makes the possession of intellect a criterion for being created in God's image because only the intellectual creature has a capacity for the highest good: "Therefore things without an intellect are not made to God's image."[23] The intellect is what raises man above the beasts of the field and gives him the capacity for personhood.

St. Thomas identifies three ways in which the human person, through his intellectual nature, can imitate God by knowing and loving Him, who knows and loves Himself. In each of these ways man is an image of God.[24]

1. The image of God is in man inasmuch as he has a natural aptitude for knowing and loving God. This was given to him when he was *created*. It is common to all men.

2. The image of God is in man inasmuch as he actually and habitually knows and loves God, though imperfectly. This image he acquired when he was *re-created* in grace. This image is found only in the just.

3. The image of God is in man inasmuch as he knows and loves God perfectly. This image consists in the *likeness of glory*. It is found only in the blessed.

Being an image of God does not make the human person an equal to God in any way. For St. Thomas says:

> But equality does not belong to the essence of an image; for as Augustine says "Where there is an image there is not necessarily equality," as we see in a person's image reflected in a glass. Yet this is of the essence of a perfect image; for in a perfect image nothing is wanting that is to be found in that of which it is a copy. Now it is manifest that in man there is some likeness to God, copied from God as from an exemplar; yet this likeness is not one of equality, for such an exemplar infinitely excels its copy. Therefore there is in man a likeness to God; not, indeed, a perfect likeness, but imperfect. And Scripture implies the same when it says that man was made to God's likeness; for the preposition *to* signifies a certain approach, as of something at a distance.[25]

The human person is a limited but true image of God. St. Thomas makes the following comparison: "Man is called to the image of God, not that he is essentially an image, but that the image of God is impressed on his mind; as a coin is an image of the king, as having the image of the king."[26] The intellect of man is infinitely weaker than the divine intellect, but man's mind still gives him great stature in creation because it enables him to participate in the life of God. Man is the only corporeal substance that is a person. The following remarks of Pascal dramatize the smallness and the greatness of man:

> Man is but a reed, the most feeble thing in nature, but he is a thinking reed. The entire universe need not arm itself to crush him. A vapor, a drop of water suffices to kill him. But if the universe were to crush him man would still be

more noble than that which killed him, because he knows that he dies, and the advantage which the universe has over him: the universe knows nothing of this.[27]

What is man in nature? A nothing when compared to infinity; a whole when compared to nothing; a middle point between nothing and whole.[28]

Man imitates God in that he is both capable of knowing and knows that he knows. His capacity to know leads him to seek truth. Man is an image of the Trinity in his ability to relate to other persons by knowing them, loving them and freely entering into friendship with them. Man imitates God's creative power in a finite way. He is able to freely fashion matter according to an image in his mind. In his arts man produces images of God's creatures. Aquinas also sees the human person as having a likeness to God in other ways than in his mind. For example, we see likenesses of God in the fact that man proceeds from man as God from God, and in the fact that the soul is in the whole body and in every part, as God is in regard to the whole world. In the former, person proceeds from person, just as life proceeds from life. In the latter, God's exercises His power everywhere in the universe at once; and the soul exercises its power everywhere in the body at once. In these ways, man is more like God than the angels.[29] Angels do not beget angels, and angels can exercise their power at only one place at a time.

Only the whole man, comprised of body and soul, is a person. The body is the principle of a man's individuation, and the soul is the principle of a man's specific nature. The soul maintains the identity of the person through the myriad of changes undergone by the body. The special relationship of the soul to its body remains even after death. St. Thomas says that the soul "is established on the boundary line dividing corporeal from separate [angelic] substances."[30]

Since personhood cannot be communicated from the whole to the part, it cannot be communicated to the disembodied soul. The soul belongs to man as *part* of his nature. It is, therefore, not a person when it exists apart as something separate. The disembodied soul is an *incomplete* substance. Thus, paradoxically, it can be said that after death there is personal survival but not survival of the person.

The *Catechism of the Catholic Church*, under the influence of the personalism of Pope John Paul II, makes the connection between human personhood and the image of God:

Being in the image of God the human individual possesses the dignity of a person, who is not just something, but someone. He is capable of self-knowledge, of self-possession and of freely giving himself and entering into communion with other persons. And he is called by grace to a covenant with his Creator, to offer him a response of faith and love that no other creature can give in his stead.[31]

Man's personhood gives him both rights and responsibilities. Being an image of God accords him a certain dignity that must be respected by other persons, and the liberty he possesses in virtue of having a free will is exercised with accountability both to God and to other human persons. He must act in accord with his dignity as an image of God. Moral law, which is both written on his conscience and taught to him, shows him how to do so.

The *Catechism of the Catholic Church*, quoting *Gaudium et spes*, gives "the fundamental reason" for the dignity of the human person:

Of all visible creatures only man is "able to know and love his creator." He is "the only creature on earth that God has willed for its own sake," and he alone is called to share, by knowledge and love, in God's own life. It was for this end that he was created, and this is the fundamental reason for his dignity.[32]

Finally, Aquinas compares Christ as the perfect Image of God with the human person as an image of God:

The First-Born of creatures is the perfect Image of God, reflecting perfectly that of which He is the Image, and so He is said to be the Image, and never to the image. But man is said to be both image by reason of the likeness; and to the image by reason of the imperfect likeness. And since the perfect likeness to God cannot be except in an identical nature, the Image of God exists in His first-born Son; as the image of the king is in his son, who is of the same nature as himself: whereas it exists in man as in an alien nature, as the image of the king is in a silver coin, as Augustine says.... [33]

The Ontological Person and the Empiriological Person

The *ontological person* is the person as such. The *empiriological person* is the ontological person as he manifests himself through his acts, powers and habits, all of which are accidents. Personality and character express the empiriological person. *Personality* expresses the person through nonmoral acts. *Character* expresses the person through moral acts, that is, acts that have the quality of right or wrong.

Personhood is a gift. Personality and character are largely products of one's own acts. One can cultivate a personality or form a character, but one cannot cultivate or form personhood. Personality is cultivated by the formation of physical, intellectual, and volitional habits. Character is formed by the acquisition of moral virtues. Personalities and characters vary from one individual to another. The phenomenon of multiple personalities affects only the empiriological person. The ontological person remains intact. That is, the same person takes on a number of personalities.

The phenomenon of consciousness (through the introspective analysis of the empiriological person) reveals the existence of the ontological person and the fact that the ontological person is something stable and enduring in the midst of change.

Modern psychology for the most part has abandoned the concept of the ontological person and focuses exclusively on the empiriological person. Influenced by the doctrine of materialistic evolution, psychologists have reduced personhood to little more than states of consciousness, which they claim are epiphenomenona of matter. Therefore they are not getting right answers because they are asking wrong questions, guided by a false paradigm.

[1] As quoted by St. Thomas Aquinas in ST, Part I, Q. 93, A. 9.

[2] ST, Part I, Q. 93, A. 1.

[3] ST, Part I, Q. 93, A. 2.

[4] As quoted by St. Thomas Aquinas in ST, Part I, Q. 93, A. 1.

[5] ST, Part I, Q. 93, A. 9.

[6] ST, Part I, Q. 93, A. 8.

[7] BV, Part II, Chapter 12.1.

[8] SCG, Book 4, Chapter 26.

[9] ST, Part I, Q. 3, A. 1, Reply Obj. 2.

[10] ST, Part I, Q. 93, A. 1, Reply Obj. 1.

[11] ST, Part I, Q. 93, A.5.

[12] See ST, Part I, Q. 91, A. 2.

[13] Taylor, Charles, *The First 100 Words* (Evansville, IN: Jubilee Resources, 1996), pp. 3, 80.

[14] JR, nos. 31, 235, 361.

[15] DZ, no. 428.

[16] JR, no. 156.

[17] ACC, p. 29.

[18] As quoted in CCC, no. 359.

[19] ACC, p. 29.

[20] ACC, p. 31.

[21] JR, no. 1806.

[22] ACC, p. 30.

[23] ST, Part I, Q. 93, A. 2.

[24] ST, Part I, Q. 93, A. 4.

[25] ST, Part I, Q. 93, A. 1.

[26] ST, Part I, Q. 93, A.6, Reply Obj. 1.

[27] *Pensées.*

[28] Ibid.

[29] ST, Part I, Q. 93, A. 3.

[30] *Disputed Questions on the Soul*, a. 1.

[31] CCC, no. 357.

[32] CCC, no. 356.

[33] ST, Part I, Q. 93, A. 1, Reply Obj. 2.

Doctrine Nine
God created the first man immediately from the earth.

The Fathers and Doctors of the Church and all the popes, bishops and faithful for nineteen centuries believed that God created Adam immediately from the dust of the earth. This doctrine was unquestioned by Catholics until the twentieth century and the onslaught of evolutionary thinking. Materialistic human evolution stands condemned by the mere fact that it eliminates the role of God in the origin of man. The Fourth Lateran Council and Vatican Council I both affirmed that God created man. The Provincial Council of Cologne (1860) condemned the notion of natural transformism, which states that natural processes alone prepared the body of a brute to receive a human soul. Pope Pius XII allowed the consideration of special transformism, in which God makes preexistent living matter receptive to a human soul and infuses a human soul in it. But he did not allow it to be held as a fact because it presents serious theological problems. The notion of progressive creation compromises the literal sense of Genesis as a concession to false opinion that the various kinds of animals did not all appear on earth at once. The unearthings of anthropologists, when correctly interpreted, are in harmony with the Genesis account of the creation of man.

Thou art Dust

Adam's body was formed directly from the earth. That is the literal and obvious meaning of (2:7). It is affirmed in (3:19), where Adam is reminded: *"[Y]ou are dust."* The *Catechism of the Catholic Church* says that this is symbolic language, but it is symbolic only in the sense that the word *dust* represents lifeless matter.[1] For this was the belief of the Fathers and Doctors of the Church. God's use of dust suggests the commonality of man with the rest of material creation.

The Hebrew words used in (2:7) are *aphar* and *adamah*, which are translated together as "dust from the ground." The word *aphar* can also be translated "clay," "mud," "slime" or "ashes." The word *adamah* translates into "earth" or "ground." The first man (*adam*) takes his name from this word. The word *adam* is also used for both the first man and the first woman in (1:26–27; 5:2).

Whenever Sacred Scripture speaks of the origin of the human body, it identifies the source as dust or earth.[a] Abraham testifies that he is *"but dust and ashes"* in (18:27). David said: *"[H]e remembers that we are dust."*[2] Sirach asks, *"How can he who is dust and ashes be proud?"*[3] He further proclaims, *"The Lord created man out of earth and turned him back to it again."*[4]

Theodoret of Cyr explains the creation of Adam's body as follows:

> Just like an embryo is planted in the mother's womb and develops from the material which has surrounded it from the beginning, so also God wanted to take the material for the human body from the earth. Thus, clay became flesh and blood, and skin, and nerves, and veins, and arteries, and the brain, and bone marrow and supporting bones, and so on.[5]

The Fathers often refer to God as fashioning Adam with His "hands" to show that God worked with preexistent nonliving matter. St. John Chrysostom expressed it this way:

> Do you see how things were created by a word? But let us see what it says afterwards about the creation of man: *"And God shaped man"* (Gn 2:7). See how, by means of a condescension of terms employed for the sake of our weakness, it teaches at the same time both the manner of creation and its diversity or variety, so that, speaking in human terms, it indicates that man was shaped by the very hands of God, even as another Prophet says: *"Your hands created me and shaped me"* (Jb 10:8).[6]

St. Basil made it clear that God created man directly from the earth to distinguish him from animals:

> Above, the text says that God created; here it says how God created. If the verse had simply said that God created, you could have believed that he created [man] as he did for the beasts, for the wild animals, for the plants, for the grass. This is why, to avoid your placing him in the class of wild animals, the Divine word has made known the particular art which God has used for you: *"God took of the dust of the earth."*[7]

---

a. Genesis does not mention the body of Adam explicitly. It simply says that God formed *"man"* of dust from the ground.

In addition to the above Fathers, St. Irenaeus, St. Cyril of Jerusalem, St. Gregory of Nyssa, St. Cyril of Alexandria, St. John Damascene, St. Ephrem, Tertullian, St. Ambrose, St. Jerome and St. Augustine all expressed the belief that Adam was created from the earth.[8]

St. Thomas Aquinas devotes four articles in the ST to the production of the body of the first man. He argues

1. that the body of the first man was made from the slime of the earth "because earth and water mingled are called slime, and for this reason man is called 'a little world,' because all creatures of the world are in a way to be found in him."[9] "[I]t was fitting that the human body should be made of the four elements, that man might have something in common with the inferior bodies, as being something between spiritual and corporeal substances."[10]

2. that the body of man was made directly by God without the instrumentality of any creature because only God "alone can produce a form in matter, without the aid of any preceding material form. For this reason the angels cannot transform a body except by making use of something in the nature of a seed, as Augustine says.... Therefore as no pre-existing body has been formed whereby another body of the same species could be generated, the first human body was of necessity made immediately by God."[11] "Nevertheless the angels could act as ministers in the formation of the body of the first man, in the same way as they will do at the last resurrection by collecting the dust."[12]

3. that God gave the body of the first man an apt disposition because "God gave to each natural being the best disposition; not absolutely so, but in the view of its proper end.... Now the proximate end of the human body is the rational soul and its operations; since matter is for the sake of the form, and instruments are for the action of the agent. I say, therefore, that God fashioned the human body in that disposition which was best, as most suited to such a form and to such operations."[13]

4. that the production of Adam's body is fittingly described in Scripture. "Yet in describing man's production, Scripture uses a special way of speaking, to show that other things were made for man's sake."[14]

God created the body of Adam in an act of *creatio secunda*. That is, He transformed the accidental and substantial forms of existing matter. This is different from the way that the bodies of his progeny would be formed. They would be formed by the process of *generation*, whereby living bodies give rise to living bodies of the same nature. St. Thomas distinguishes the two modes of production:

> Matter is that from which something is made. Now created nature has a determinate principle; and since it is determined to one thing, it has also a determinate mode of proceeding. Wherefore from determinate matter it produces something in a determinate species. On the other hand, the Divine Power, being infinite, can produce things of the same species out of any matter, such as a man from the slime of the earth, and a woman from out of man.[15]

The Breath of Life

Genesis 2:7 says that God *"breathed"* into the *"nostrils"* of man the *"breath of life,"* and *"man became a living being."* The Hebrew word translated "breath" is *neshamah.* The *"breath of the Almighty"* gave man a spiritual life in imitation of His own.[b] It is the spiritual element in man that makes him what he is and gives him his unique dignity and a special place in the created world.

Genesis 2:7 ends, *"and man became a living being."* The Hebrew words *chay nephesh* are translated in the RSV, NAB, JB and NIV as "living being." They are translated in the DR and KJV as "living soul." *Nephesh* properly means a *breathing* creature. Animals are called *nephesh.*[16] It is also a common term for the human person,[17] and is sometimes used for a dead human body.[18]

Other words are also used in Scripture to designate the spiritual element in man. The Hebrew word *ruach* means "wind" and by resemblance "breath." It is used to mean the spirit of God [19] and for the spiritual principle in man.[20] The heart (*leb, lebab*) is used figuratively as the seat of human life and of affections and passions. It wills, makes decisions and judges between right and wrong. The heart loves, hates, trusts, respects, is joyful, is sad, is sorry, is compassionate and merciful.

The parallelism of Hebrew poetry gives rise to a distinction between soul (*nephesh*) and spirit (*ruach*). They do not denote two different life principles but the lower and higher faculties of the soul.[21] *Soul* is generally used in reference to the more basic functions of life, which we have in common with animals, while *spirit* is used in reference to acts of the mind. In some parallel passages spiritual activities are ascribed to both the soul and the spirit. The Fathers of the Church

---

b. See Jb 32:8; 33:4. In the parallelism of those verses, the *"breath of the Almighty"* is used as a synonym for both *"the spirit in a man"* and *"the spirit of God."*

sometimes speak of man being composed of body, soul and spirit. Augustine makes it clear how that is to be understood:

> And while man consists of these three elements: spirit, soul, and body—which sometimes are reckoned as two, for often the soul is included in the designation of spirit (for it is that certain rational part, which beasts do not have, that is called spirit)—our chief element is the spirit.[22]

St. John Damascene elaborates on the nature of man's soul. His description contains the essentials of scholastic view of the nature of the soul, except for the relationship of the soul to the body:

> The soul, then, is a living being, simple and incorporeal, invisible to the bodily eyes by its very nature, immortal, rational and intelligent, shapeless, making use of an organic body, to which body it imparts life, growth and feeling, and the faculty of generation, mind being its purest part and in no way alien to it; for just as the eye is to the body, so is the mind to the soul. The soul enjoys free choice, having the faculty of willing and of acting; and it is changeable, which is to say, it is subject to change because it was created.[23]

St. Thomas Aquinas wrote extensively on the human soul.[24] His *Treatise on Man* in the ST deals at length with the human soul—its creation, its nature, its powers, its relationship with the body.[25] In commenting on Aristotle's study of the soul, Aquinas formulates the following definition: The soul "is the first principle by which we live, sense, move and understand."[26] St. Thomas, along with the other Schoolmen, teaches that the human soul is spiritual, simple, incorruptible and immortal.

The soul is *spiritual* because it is independent of matter in its existence and, to some extent, in its operations. The soul is not composed of matter. The Fathers and the Scholastics opposed the Greek atomists, who held that the soul is a form of matter, composed of exceedingly fine atoms. The soul uses the brain as an instrument, but this does not mean that the brain and the mind are the same—just as the violinist and the violin are not one and the same. A violinist cannot play very well with a broken violin string. Likewise, the intellectual faculty of the soul cannot function properly with a damaged brain.

The soul is *simple* because there are no quantitative divisions in it. It has powers (faculties), but these are not quantitative parts. One does not think with one part of the soul, desire with another part of the soul and will with yet another part. The soul is an indivisible entity.

The soul is *incorruptible* because it has no quantitative parts to decompose and it has powers that do not depend on matter. So it is incorruptible in itself, and it survives the corruption of the body that it animates.

The soul is *immortal* because the only way that it can be destroyed is by annihilation by God, and God will not do that because it would contradict His justice.

Scholastic philosophy ascribes to the soul two spiritual dimensions: the intellect and free will. Philosopher Dietrich von Hildebrand adds the affections as a third dimension. While scholastic philosophy considers love of a person for a person to be an act of the will, von Hildebrand considers this and other acts of the "heart" to be distinct from those of the intellect and will. He says:

> There arises, however, a problem of freeing ourselves from an old and deep-rooted prejudice. This is the view that what comprises the affective sphere is not really spiritual in nature. The supposition that only intellect and will are part of man's spiritual nature and that the entire realm of emotions, commonly called the "heart," belongs to purely vital and irrational components of man, is a remnant of Greek intellectualism. But this view has never been proved, nor can it claim to be evident.
>
> In various books and articles I have made this point: unbiased analysis of the emotional sphere shows clearly that meaningful responses to value such as joy, mourning, respect, admiration, display all the marks of spiritual activity occurring, for example in knowledge, conviction, presumption and willing. As soon as one understands that full emotional expression is in no way incompatible with spiritual activity and that there are three such spiritual centers in man—intellect, will and heart—as Haecker has already accurately shown, there is no longer any reason for adhering to the interpretation of love which makes it into an act of the will, as frequently but unfortunately happens. Formerly it was thought necessary to turn love into an act of the will to preserve its spirituality. But love is, clearly and beyond doubt, a response of the heart.[27]

Further, von Hildebrand describes the spiritual element in love as a response to value:

> As soon as we analyze such acts as enthusiasm, admiration, and especially love when they are intuitively given we are bound to see what is most characteristic of them—responsiveness to value.[28]

Von Hildebrand says the proper sense of love is that of a person for a person:

Properly understood, and in the most immediate sense, love is only love to the extent that it concerns another person. Whether it is for a child, a parent, or a friend, whether it involves the newly wedded, our love for God, or our love of neighbor—it is always love for someone else. And although love of things which enjoy no personal structure (for example, a nation, one's homeland, a country, a work of art, a house, and so on) is much nearer to love in the proper sense than self-love is, still it is love only in an analogous sense.[29]

The Unity of Man

Plato taught that the soul and the body are distinct independent entities. He held that the soul is to the body as the pilot is to the ship. His concept of the soul accommodated his belief in the transmigration of souls.[c] Aristotle had a holistic outlook and held that the soul is the form of the living body, having a unique inseparable relationship with it. The Fathers of the Church, enlightened by divine revelation, held a position similar to Aristotle, as did the Scholastics, who followed them.

The Fathers expressed this holistic viewpoint in different ways. St. John of Damascus expressed it as the simultaneous creation of the body and the soul:

> From the earth he formed his body and by his own inbreathing gave him a rational and understanding soul, which we say is the divine image.... The body and the soul were formed at the same time—not one before and the other afterward, as the ravings of Origen would have it.[30]

St. Gregory of Nyssa professed the essential unity of man in arguing that the soul was not created for the sake of the body:

> Nor again are we in our doctrine to begin by making up man like a clay figure and to say that the soul came into being for the sake of this, for surely in that case the intellectual nature would be shown to be less precious than the clay figure. But as man is one, the being consisting of soul and body, we are to suppose that the beginning of his existence is one, common to both aspects, so that he should not be found to be antecedent and posterior to himself, as if the bodily element were first in point of time and the other were a later addition.[31]

---

c. The Church has explicitly condemned the notion of preexistence of the soul. See DZ nos. 203, 236 and OTT, p. 99.

St. Justin the Martyr argues the holistic case in terms of God calling the whole man to life and resurrection:

> Indeed, God calls even the body to resurrection and promises it everlasting life. When He promises to save the man, He thereby makes His promise to the flesh: for what is man but a rational living being composed of soul and body? Is the soul by itself a man? No, it is but the *soul of a man*. Can the body be called a man? No, it can but be called the *body of a man*. If, then, neither of these is by itself a man, but that which is composed of the two together is called a man, and God has called man to life and resurrection, He has called not a part, but the whole, which is the soul and the body.[32]

Athenagoras of Athens sees the unity of man in the common end of the body and the soul, which is the end of the person to which they belong, although he does not use the word *person*:

> If every example of human nature is made up jointly of an immortal soul and the body with which it is united at creation; and if God has decreed such an origin, such a life and course of existence, neither for the nature of the soul itself nor for the nature of the body separately, but for men who are composed of the two, so that having passed through life they may arrive at one common end, still composed of the same elements from which they were made and with which they lived, it is absolutely necessary, since one living being is formed of the two, experiencing whatever the soul experiences and whatever the body experiences, doing or performing whatever requires either sensual or rational judgment, that the whole series of these experiences must refer to one and the same end.[33]

The Scholastics taught that the body and soul are substantially united. The soul is the substantial form of the body. This explains man's essential unity while retaining the distinction between the body and the soul. The human soul exists after death but as an incomplete substance. The scholastic picture is called *hylomorphism*. The position of Plato, which was also that of Descartes,[d] is contrary to experience and to the teaching of the Church. It denies genuine unity in the human person. It cannot account for sensations and emotions, which are essentially psychosomatic.

The Council of Vienne (1311–1312), Lateran Council V (1512–1517), and Pope Pius IX (1846–1878) affirmed that the rational soul is the essential form of

---

d. Descartes imagined the soul-body relationship as a soul in a machine.

the body.[34] The CCC devotes a whole section to the unity of the human person.[35]

< Objections > and << Replies >>

< Objection 1 >

"Attentive readers of the Bible can hardly fail to remark a striking discrepancy between the two accounts of the creation of man recorded in the first and second chapters of Genesis. In the first chapter, we read how, on the fifth day of creation, God created the fishes and the birds, all the creatures that live in the water, or in the air; and how on the sixth day he created all the terrestrial animals, and last of all man, whom he fashioned in his own image, both male and female. From this narrative we infer that man was the last to be created of all living beings on earth … that God created the lower animals first and human beings afterwards, and that the human beings consisted of a man and a woman, produced to all appearance simultaneously, and each of them reflecting in equal measure the glory of their divine original. So far we read in the first chapter. But when we proceed to peruse the second chapter, it is somewhat disconcerting to come bolt on a totally different and, indeed, contradictory account of the same momentous transaction. For here we learn with surprise that God created man first, the lower animals next, and woman last of all, fashioning her as a mere afterthought out of a rib which he abstracted from man in his sleep. The order of merit in the two narratives is clearly reversed. In the first narrative the deity begins with fishes and works steadily up to birds and beasts to man and woman. In the second narrative he begins with man and works downward through the animals to woman, who apparently marks the nadir of divine workmanship. And in this second version nothing at all is said about man and woman being made in the image of God.… The flagrant contradiction between the two accounts is explained very simply by the circumstance that they are derived from two different and originally independent documents, which were afterwards combined into a single book by an editor, who pieced the two narratives together without always taking pains to soften or harmonize their discrepancies."[e]

---

e. This objection is taken verbatim from James George Frazer, *Folklore in the Old Testament: Studies in Comparative Religion, Legend, and Law* (New York: Hart, 1975), pp. 1–2. A similar position is taken in the NAB in its commentary on Genesis 2:4b–25.

<< Reply to Objection 1 >>

If one examines the narratives in Genesis 1 and 2 on the creation of man with the eyes of faith, one finds that together they form one consistent account. However, if one reads them with the eyes of skepticism, he will surely find the contradictions he expects to find.

<< Consistency of the Genesis Account of the Creation of Man >>

The narrative on the creation of man in Genesis 2 supplements that in Genesis 1. Genesis 1 relates the creation of creatures in order of time, whereas Genesis 2 relates them in order of significance. Man was the last creature to be created but he is the one for whom all other creatures were created. When it says in (2:19) that God created every beast of the field and every bird of the air and brought them to Adam, it does not mean that they were created *after* Adam but that they had been created *for* him. The Genesis 2 narrative shows that Eve was created not as an "afterthought" but from Adam. It thus makes clear that Adam was the first human and that all human beings, including Eve, proceeded from him. He is the prototype human person. Genesis 1:27 does not say that Adam and Eve were created "simultaneously." In context it only says that they were created on the same day. Genesis 1:28 gives one reason for the creation of two kinds of human persons—so that they may be fruitful and multiply. Genesis 2:18 gives another—so that Adam may have a human mate with complementary characteristics because his nature included a desire for such. The second reason does not contradict the first reason. Rather it complements it by giving the reason why two kinds of human persons rather than one propagate the species. Genesis 2 does not say that Adam and Eve were created in the image of God because it was not necessary for the author to do so. It had already been said. It is a significant omission only for those who have already decided that Genesis 1 and Genesis 2 are two different accounts from two different authors. But the different emphases in the narratives of Genesis 1 and Genesis 2 do not warrant such a conclusion. Both portrayals were obviously rendered by the same eyewitness, God.

✳   ✳   ✳   ✳

< Objection 2 >

Paleontological evidence shows that humans evolved from inferior species.

<< Reply to Objection 2 >>

In the *Descent of Man and Selection in Relation to Sex* (1871) Charles Darwin applied his ideas on evolution by variation and natural selection to the origin of man, contradicting the Genesis account. In that work he wrote, "The main conclusion arrived at in this work, namely, that man is descended from some lowly organized form, will, I regret to think, be highly distasteful to many." His work did arouse a storm of opposition that continues to this day. His ideas inspired the search for the so-called missing link, which was the supposed transitional form between beast and man. The Darwinian viewpoint on the origin of man is encapsulated in the familiar drawing that shows a knuckle-walking ape evolving though a series of hypothetical intermediate forms into an upright human being.[f]

<< Summary of Evolutionary Anthropology >>

In the *Descent of Man* Darwin erased the essential difference between man and animals. He argued, "[T]he difference in mind between man and the higher animals, great as it is, certainly is one of degree and not of kind." He compared similarities between man and beasts, especially the apes, and attempted to determine the origin and probable line of genealogy of the races of mankind. This is the philosophy that underlies modern physical anthropology, except that it no longer views the different human races as different species.

According to the *Encyclopedia Britannica*, the program of evolutionary anthropology "involves the discovery, analysis and description of fossilized human remains. Two key goals are the identification of the differences between human and the human and nonhuman ancestors, and the clarification of the biological emergence of humankind."[36] Collectively modern humans and their "human and

---

f.   This picture has become an icon that enshrines the unfounded claims of evolutionists in regards to the origin of man. See Jonathan Wells, *Icons of Evolution: Science or Myth?* (Washington, DC: Regnery, 2000), ch. 11.

nonhuman ancestors" are called "hominids." According to evolutionary taxonomy, a *hominid* is a creature of the Family *Hominidae* (Order Primates, Suborder
Hominoidea). Following are the major hominid taxons in the supposed evolutionary sequence leading up to and including modern man:[37]

- *Australopithecus* ("southern ape"): According to evolutionary reckoning,
  the oldest known hominid remains (given an age of at least 4 million
  years) are classified as belonging to this genus. The members of this genus
  are portrayed as nonhuman creatures with a humanlike morphology that
  lived in southern and eastern Africa. They are distinguished from apes by
  their upright posture and bipedal gait. The most famous australopithecine
  is "Lucy," found forty percent complete by Donald Johanson in 1974 in
  Ethiopia. An earlier one, *Zinjanthropus* ("East Africa Man"), found in
  1950 by Louis and Mary Leakey in Tanzania, was considered an early
  human. *National Geographic* magazine published an artist's rendition of
  him along with stories about his personal habits. Because of his huge
  molars, "Zinj" was affectionately called Nutcracker Man. He fell from
  glory when anthropologists, including the Leakeys, agreed that he was not
  human after all. He was just another brute.

- *Homo habilis*: ("dexterous man") He is alleged to be the most primitive
  creature in the genus *homo*. He supposedly lived in sub-Saharan Africa
  1.5–2.5 million years ago. He is depicted as having walked on two feet
  and as having been capable of manipulating objects. Crude tools were
  found with fossil remains classified *homo habilis*.

- *Homo erectus*: ("erect man") He is alleged to have lived 250,000 to 1.6
  million years ago in Africa, Asia and parts of Europe. He is described as
  having walked upright and as having been of medium stature with jutting
  brow ridges, a wide nose, palate and jaw, and large teeth. He is touted to
  have been the first to master fire and inhabit caves. The most well known
  of these are Java Man, found by Eugene Dubois in 1891 in Java and
  Peking Man (Zhoukoudian), a number of which were found in a cave in
  China in 1927.

- *Homo sapiens*: ("wise man") This is the supposed genus and species to
  which modern humans belong. *Homo sapiens* is distinguished from earlier
  hominids by his small jaw and teeth, higher brain capacity, and his ability
  to use symbols. He is said to have come onstage 50 or 150 thousand years
  ago, depending on the theory one espouses. The most famous of the text-

book fossils of his type is Cro-Magnon Man, who was first discovered in 1868 in a cave in southern France.

- *Neanderthal (Neandertal) Man*: The name derives from the discovery in 1856 of remains in a cave above Germany's Neander Valley. He is listed separately because anthropologists are not in agreement as how to classify him. Some make him a special species, designating him *Homo neanderthalensis*, and regard him as not being an ancestor of humans but as having the same ancestors as humans. Others regard him as a variety of *Homo sapiens*. He supposedly inhabited much of Europe 35–100 thousand years ago. Neanderthals were short, stout and powerful. Their brain capacity was equal to or exceeded that of humans. There is evidence that they dwelt in caves, hunted animals, used fire and primitive tools and weapons, painted pictures, buried their dead, and practiced a religion.

<< Critique of Evolutionary Anthropology >>

Paleoanthropology, which is the branch of anthropology that deals with fossil hominids, is a field of great uncertainty and hot controversy. Debate among evolutionists concerning the interpretation of the fossils is so intense that the fossils have been dubbed "bones of contention." To one who accepts the Genesis account of the origin of man, such arguments are meaningless and boring. An intelligent inspection of the principles on which the arguments are based reveals that the evolutionist scenario does not have convincing evidence to support it.

For the creationist the "bones of contention" are either the bones of beasts or the bones of descendants of Adam. There are no intermediate species. The species *Homo habilis*, *Homo erectus* and *Homo neanderthalenis* are nonexistent. The fossils put into these categories are fossils of human beings. Marvin Lubenow in *Bones of Contention* has shown this quite ably.[38] Some points Lubenow makes in support of that position are:

- A case study of the famous fossil KNM–ER 1470, a skull found by Richard Leakey in 1967 in Kenya, "reveals that the radiometric dating methods are not independent confirmations of evolution and an old earth, nor are the various dating methods independent of each other. These dating methods are, instead, 'faithful and obedient servants of evolution.'"[39]

- Paleoanthropology is an "inexact kind of science"; its "scientific" statements have little weight. First of all, its method begs the question. It assumes that human evolution took place to begin with, analyses the data on the basis of that assumption, and then turns around and says that the data confirm evolution. He points out a fact that a surprisingly large number of people are blind to: *"Any series of objects created by humans (or God) can be arranged in such a way as to make it look as if they had evolved when in fact they were created independently by an intelligent being.* The fact that objects can be arranged in an 'evolutionary' sequence does not prove that they have a relationship or that any of them evolved from others."[40] And there is no way one can prove conclusively a relationship between fossils from the fossils alone. Historical documentation is needed to do so.

- Piltdown Man is the name given to pieces of an apparently fossilized human skull and ape-like lower jaw found from 1908 to 1913 by Charles Dawson in a gravel pit near Lewes, England. Arthur Smith Woodward of the British Museum reconstructed the fossil fragments and proposed it as a new species of hominid, the missing link needed to complete evolutionary theory. The theory at that time predicted that the ancestor of human beings would have a large brain and an ape-like jaw. Woodward's reconstruction eventually became widely accepted, and it became the paradigm for the interpretation of newly found fossils. This lasted for some forty years, until several fossils were found that didn't fit the paradigm. This led to Piltdown man being exposed as a hoax. In 1953 several scientists proved that the skull belonged to a modern human and the jaw fragment to a modern orangutan. The jaw had been chemically treated to look like a fossil, and its teeth had been filed down to make them look human. This splashed mud on the face of paleoanthropology. Scientists boast that science is self-correcting. It took four decades to discover the fraud because most scientists accepted Woodward's assertion without question. The case showed that science is not unassailable and scientists are not as objective as they make themselves out to be. They can easily be fooled into seeing what they expect to see.

- Science can be genuinely objective only when it is dealing with the present. There is a high degree of subjectivity in scientific reconstructions of the past. Many scientists think that because they are able to make authoritative statements about the present, they can also do so about the past while ignoring the historical record in Genesis. The scientific community fails to realize its subjectivity when it speaks dogmatically about the past. This is the major cause of the so-called warfare of science with theology.

- The australopithecines are simply extinct primates. They lived at the same time as humans and had nothing to do with human origins.

- *Homo habilis* is not a valid taxon. It is constructed from two distinct fossil forms—a large human form and a smaller nonhuman form.

- Humans have wide morphological variation. Anthropologists have only recently come to appreciate this. It is possible that morphological variation in early humans could have exceeded what it is today.

- *Homo erectus* was a human variety that lived at the same time as modern-like humans.

- Neanderthal Man was human, but he had a distinct morphology that distinguishes him from modern humans. He had a cranial capacity larger than modern humans, an elongated skull that was somewhat pointed in the back, large heavy brow ridges, and a low forehead. The evidence indicates that Neanderthals were intelligent, had incredible physical strength, and were probably postdiluvian.[g] The disease rickets may have caused some of their morphological features.

- A clear comprehensive charting of the fossils shows that as far back as the human fossil record goes the human body has remained substantially the same and has not evolved from something else. Evolutionists avoid making such charts.

- The human fossil record, like the general fossil record, is substantial; and it has failed to provide evidence for evolution. This is recognized by evolutionists and is a disappointment to them; so some have come to downplay the importance of the fossil record as a way to escape their dilemma.

Artists and writers have been very skillful at depicting our imagined ancestors and giving them an aura of reality. This has provided evolutionists with a power-

---

g. It is no surprise that early postdiluvian men lived in caves. Noah and his sons and their descendants may have lived in caves until they discovered the natural resources with which to start a new civilization. But they were not without know-how. They inherited knowledge of the various arts and crafts from the antediluvians; they needed only time, material and manpower to build up civilizations. Also, some people who migrated far from the center of culture in Mesopotamia lost knowledge of those arts and regressed into an uncivilized way of life.

ful propaganda tool. The great early-twentieth-century humorist, G. K. Chesterton, commented on the imaginative "science" of the paleoanthropologists, artists and popular science writers of his day:

> The evolutionists seem to know everything about the missing link except the fact that it is missing.[41]

> For instance, I have pointed out the difficulty of keeping a monkey and watch it evolve into a man. Experimental evidence of such an evolution being impossible, the professor is not content to say (as most of us would be ready to say) that such an evolution is likely enough anyhow. He produces his little bone, or a little collection of bones, and deduces the most marvelous things from it. He found in Java a piece of a skull, seeming by its contour to be smaller than the human. Somewhere near it he found an upright thighbone and in the same scattered fashion some teeth that were not human. If they all form part of one creature, which is doubtful, our conception of the creature would almost be equally doubtful. But the effect on popular science was to produce a complete and even complex figure, finished down to the last details of hair and habits. He was given a name as if he were an ordinary historical character. People talked of Pithecanthropus as of Pitt or Fox or Napoleon. Popular histories published portraits of him like the portraits of Charles the First and George the Fourth. A detailed drawing was reproduced, carefully shaded, to show that the very hairs of his head were all numbered. No uninformed person looking at his carefully lined face and wistful eyes would imagine for a moment that this was the portrait of a thigh-bone; or of a few teeth and a fragment of a cranium. In the same way people talked about him as if he were an individual whose influence and character were familiar to us all [42]

Closer to our day, Jonathan Wells writes:

> Just recently, *National Geographic* magazine commissioned four artists to reconstruct a female figure from casts of seven fossil bones thought to be of the same species as skull 1470. One artist drew a creature whose forehead is missing and whose jaws look vaguely like those of a beaked dinosaur. Another artist drew a rather good-looking modern African-American woman with unusually long arms. A third drew a somewhat scrawny female with arms like a gorilla and a face like a Hollywood werewolf. And a fourth drew a figure covered with body hair and climbing a tree, with beady eyes that glare out from under a heavy, gorilla-like brow.
> This remarkable set of drawings shows clearly how a single set of fossil bones can be reconstructed in a variety of ways. Someone looking for an intermediate form to plug into an ape-to-human sequence could pick whatever drawing seems to fit best.[43]

Wells goes on to quote several prominent scientists on the state of paleoanthropology:

> Thus the conventional picture of human evolution is "a completely human invention created after the fact, shaped to accord with human prejudices.... To take a line of fossils and claim that they represent a lineage is not a scientific hypothesis that can be tested, but an assertion that carries the same validity as a bedtime story—amusing, perhaps even instructive, but not scientific."[44]

> "Could it be that, like 'primitive' myths, theories of human evolution reinforce the value-systems of their creators by reflecting historically their image of themselves and of the society in which they live?" "As things stand at the present time, we are in an urgent need of the de-mythologisation of science."[45]

> She concluded that "themes found in recent paleoanthropological writing ... far exceed what can be inferred from the study of fossils alone and in fact place a heavy burden of interpretation on the fossil record—a burden which is relieved by placing fossils into preexisting narrative structures." Paleoanthropologists, in other words, are storytellers.[46]

> Clark suggested "that paleoanthropology has the form but not the substance of a science."[47]

Wells concludes:

> Given the highly subjective nature of paleoanthropology—as acknowledged by its own practitioners—what can the field reliably tell us about human origins?[48]

<< Human Evolution: Materialistic Version >>

Materialistic evolutionism is the philosophy that holds that the whole man evolved into being through natural processes alone. Atheists adhere to it because God does not enter into the picture. Agnostics and Deists espouse it because God can be put so far into the background of the picture that it doesn't matter if He's there or not. It is totally unacceptable to Catholics because it denies man a spiritual soul, thus contradicting Sacred Scripture, Tradition, and defined doctrine. The Fourth Lateran Council and Vatican Council I declared that God created "the human, constituted as it were, alike of the spirit and the body."[49] God created the body of the first man from existing matter and his soul directly from nothing.

When people lose contact with or reject the true account of human origins that is related in Genesis, something else fills in the void. For men have always had a deep-seated need to explain their origins. In the past men produced fanciful myths to fill the vacuum. Modern man has constructed a new metaphysics, an "atheology." It is not a totally godless worldview, however, because it replaces the personal God of Genesis with the impersonal god, Matter/Energy. Matter/Energy is invested with attributes of God—eternity, indestructibility, and the power to create.

The denial of an essential difference between man and beast, which is the hallmark of materialistic evolutionism, has led to an aberrant new phenomenon, animal rights activism.[50] This movement carries evolutionism to its logical conclusion: since there is no essential difference between man and animals, animals have the same rights as men. In fact, they have a priority in rights over man because they were here first. As one animal rights advocate put it: "The baboon doesn't exist for us; the baboon exists for the baboon."[51] The more extreme activists seek to eliminate all uses of animals by men, including their use for food, clothing and pets.

The doctrine of evolution has become the philosophical foundation for all secularist thought. It has been applied beyond the origin of the universe, life and man. For example, evolution is said to be operative today on a societal level. This has given rise to some bizarre notions, such as the whole human species evolving into a single organism. The evolution paradigm has even infected the thought of "Catholic" theologians and has been the cause of much fuzzy thinking in modern "Catholic" theology.[h] The evolutionary fantasies dreamed up by Teilhard de Chardin are seen as profound spiritual insights by far too many Catholics.

Theological modernism is deeply rooted in evolutionary soil. For the modernist, religious and moral doctrines evolve, but curiously from a more ordered state to a less ordered state rather than the other way around as for biological evolution. The modernists confuse evolution of doctrine with the genuine development of doctrine. John Henry Newman describes the latter in *The Development of Doctrine*. The corrupted doctrine of the modernists contradicts that from which it "evolved." Developed doctrine, on the other hand, uncovers what was present but hidden.

---

h. The word *Catholic* is enclosed by quotation marks because the theologians referred to here are Catholic but their theology is not.

<< Human Evolution: First Theistic Version >>

During the twentieth century many Christian intellectuals, including Catholics, came to accept the erroneous opinion that the fossil record demonstrates that life has been here on earth for millions of years and that life has advanced over those years to more and more complex forms. In an attempt to reconcile this view with Genesis Christian thinkers formulated what is now called the *day-age theory*, which states that each of the six days of Creation represents an immense period of time.[i] Some believed that natural processes that were predetermined, guided, or genetically programmed by God brought about this advance in life forms over long ages, but they could not and still cannot offer evidence to support that hypothesis. Others supposed that God intervened intermittently over long ages to specially create new species. The former view is called *theistic evolution*, the latter *progressive creation*. Theistic evolution will be considered now; progressive creation will be taken up below.

Theistic evolutionists, unlike their materialistic counterparts, hold that God created matter and that man has a spiritual soul. Some of them believe that God created the first man by infusing a soul into a body that evolution had prepared for it. One version of theistic human evolution maintains that natural processes *alone* prepared the body of a brute to receive a human soul. This notion is called *natural transformism*.[j]

Cardinal Ruffini points out that in natural transformism an effect is produced that is superior to its cause. This violates a firmly grounded scholastic axiom:

> It is, therefore, repugnant to suppose that the generative action can originate in an organism of an order superior to the generating cause, while it is a most certain postulate that all that is found in the effect must also be found, either *formally* (viz., according to its proper nature), or *eminently* (viz., in a more noble manner) in its efficient cause. And this is precisely the absurdity that the transformists meet when they assert that an animal was able to generate a body fit to be informed by a human soul, namely, with perfections superior to its own constitution and proper to a nature that is specifically diverse: because the human species is composed not only of a soul, but also of a body. In other

---

i. The interpretation of the Hebrew word *yom* in Genesis 1, which is translated into "day" in English, is discussed under Doctrine Six, The Meaning of *Yom*.

j. Sacred Scripture seems to rule out natural transformism in the profession of faith of a courageous Jewish mother: *"[L]ook at the heaven and the earth and see everything that is in them, and recognize that God did not make them out of things that existed. Thus also mankind comes into being"* (2 Maccabees 7:28).

words, they destroy the principle of causality and deny that the nature of the cause is known from its effect.

No one will deny that nature acts always and everywhere in the same way, and never goes beyond the limits of its own order.[52]

He then critically summarizes two would-be modes of natural transformism:

> In short, if we admit the evolutionistic theory of man's body, this dilemma leaps to our intelligence: either God fused the human soul into the fetus conceived in the womb of a beast—most fortunate mother—or into an animal living outside its mother. If the first hypothesis is admitted, we should have the first man a son of two brute beasts. In truth, these fortunate beasts (monkeys of whatsoever species you wish), in virtue of a natural law, even though established by the Creator to regulate the progressive transformation of the species, would have prepared a body naturally fit to be informed with a human soul: which is precisely neither more nor less than what the parents of any man do who produce a body to which is due a rational soul by a law of nature. Now who will be ready to believe that Adam had for his father and mother two brute beasts? Although innocent and holy, he would certainly have been in a much less honorable condition than is ours.
>
> If, then, the second hypothesis is admitted, we fall into the metaphysical absurdity that one and the same organism, without specific change of dispositions, can be informed by two forms substantially different—the bestial and the human; while we know that every substantial form demands a receptive matter specifically adapted to it.[53]

In 1860 the Provincial Council of Cologne, approved by the Holy See, enacted a canon that condemned natural transformism:

> Our first parents were created immediately by God (Gn 2:7). Therefore, we declare as quite contrary to Holy Scripture and the Faith the opinion of those who dare to assert that man, in respect of his body, is derived by spontaneous generation from an imperfect nature, which improved continually until it reached the present human state.[54]

Despite condemnation by the Church, some "Catholic" theologians, holding on to false scientific notions and faulty dating of fossils, still profess natural transformism, which leads to further deviant views. For example:

> Is there clear evidence that we humans evolved from nonhuman primates? Yes. The evidence is abundant, and it is only decided in advance that we humans simply *cannot* be closely linked genetically and historically to other

species of life.... An important question, however, is at what point in the evolution of our species did humans truly appear? Is there any place in the fossil record over the last four million years or so where we can say that we clearly see the arrival of fellow humans?[55]

Reading further, we find this author confuses the boundary between matter and spirit and drifts so far from Catholic moorings that he sounds more like a materialistic evolutionist than a theistic one:

Some would argue that primates became human when the line between mere consciousness on the one hand and *reflective* self-consciousness on the other was crossed. But we will never know when this occurred. Others would cite the invention of language, or laughter, but it is impossible to find hard records of any of these transitions.[56]

And he embraces a "gradual emergence" theory in regards to the human soul:

Once we allow for this broader understanding of soul, we may interpret evolution as the momentous story of soul emergence. Evolution is the adventure of life becoming more conscious, centered, free and capable of love—but also capable of great evil. This understanding allows us to move beyond the artifice of thinking that God abruptly "injects" prefabricated "souls" into our species or into our bodies at certain artificially defined points in evolution or embryogenesis. Instead we must understand the Spirit of God as present in all life, animating each species in a manner proportionate to its characteristic mode of organic or informational capacity.

The emergence of the human soul, then, would not be a glaring exception to the animating process, but instead a most intense exemplification of a general aspect of creation and evolution. This interpretation also leaves open the possibility of analogous developments of life elsewhere in the universe.[57]

<< Human Evolution: Second Theistic Version >>

The second version of theistic human evolution, in which God simultaneously transforms preexistent living matter into a human body and infuses it with a specially created human soul, is called *special transformism*. Pope Pius XII allowed discussion about this kind of evolution in *Humani generis*:

For these reasons the Teaching Authority of the Church does not forbid that, in conformity with the present state of human sciences and sacred theology, research and discussions, on the part of men experienced in both fields, take place with regard to the doctrine of evolution, in as far as it inquires into the origin of the human body as coming from pre-existent and living matter—for the Catholic faith obliges us to hold that souls are immediately created by God. However, this must be done in such a way that the reasons for both opinions, that is, those favorable and those unfavorable to evolution, be weighed and judged with the necessary seriousness, moderation and measure, and provided that all are prepared to submit to the judgment of the Church, to whom Christ has given the mission of interpreting authentically the Sacred Scriptures and of defending the dogmas of faith.[58]

However, the freedom to discuss human evolution is not the freedom to assert it as a fact:

Some however, rashly transgress this liberty of discussion, when they act as if the origin of the human body from pre-existing and living matter were already completely certain and proved by the facts which have been discovered up to now and by reasoning on those facts, and as if there were nothing in the sources of divine revelation which demands the greatest moderation and caution in this question.[59]

In special transformism, God, in a single act, makes living matter receptive to a human soul and creates and infuses a human soul into it. It is not to be thought of as God injecting a prefabricated human soul into a brute that God has separately made receptive to a human soul. Such a notion smacks of dualism, a doctrine that considers a human person as a spiritual reality *in* a body rather than as a unified single reality. Catholic anthropology adopts a holistic view of the human person, in which *this* body is given personhood by *this* soul, which is intimately united with it. The injection of a rational soul into a brute's body cannot be compared with ensoulment at conception. They are two different things. The latter is obviously a holistic event because the material conditions and the soul are brought into existence simultaneously.

A Catholic theistic evolutionist has to demonstrate that the theory of human evolution he advocates is nondualistic. The idea of replacing a brute soul with a human soul treats the soul as an independent complete substance. Such an idea is not in conformity with Catholic teaching on the soul. The relationship of the soul to the body is not that of a soul in a machine a la Descartes. The union is much more intimate. Aristotle expressed the intimacy of this union in this way: "We need not ask if the soul and body are one, as neither do we ask if wax and its shape are one."[60] The *Catechism of the Catholic Church* affirms this intimacy and rejects any kind of dualism. It states, "The unity of soul and body is so profound that one has to consider the soul to be the 'form' of the body: i.e., it is because of its spiritual soul that the body made of matter becomes a living, human body; spirit and matter, in man, are not two natures united, but rather their union forms a single nature."[61] [k]

The only way to avoid the taint of dualism is to admit the simultaneous creation of Adam's body and soul. God created the first man just as a sculptor makes a statue. When a sculptor makes a statue he brings the material element and the shape together at the same time. The creation of Adam would then be exactly parallel to the creation of his descendants, who are brought into being at conception with the simultaneous organization of the material element and the creation of the soul that makes it a living human person. St. Thomas taught that the body and soul of Adam were brought into being at the same time:

> Some have thought that man's body was formed first in priority of time, and that afterwards the soul was infused into the formed body. But it is inconsistent with the perfection of the production of things, that God should have made either the body without the soul, or the soul without the body, since each is a part of human nature. This is especially unfitting as regards the body, for the body depends on the soul, and not the soul on the body. [62]

Furthermore, Scripture only makes sense if God *"breathed"* life into *nonliving* matter. Breathing life into matter already alive is a superfluous action.

The fact that the human soul exists after death provides neither theological nor philosophical evidence that the soul may have been created independently of the body. We have abundant testimony from Scripture, Tradition and magisterial teaching that the human soul survives death.[63] We have no testimony that as much as implies that the soul may have been created independently of the body. An analogy, although quite limited, may be useful here. A mold might be made of a carved statue that perfectly preserves its form. If the statue is destroyed its form still remains in the mold. But the mold could only come into existence with the statue. If the statue didn't exist, neither could the mold.

Cardinal Ruffini summarizes special transformism and shows that it actually excludes evolution and is superfluous:

---

k.   In contrast, the Talmudic sages taught that man has a dual nature. They described the body as "the scabbard of the soul" and taught that that the soul holds the same relationship to the body as God does to the universe. See Abraham Cohen, *Everyman's Talmud: The Major Teachings of the Rabbinic Sages* (New York, Schocken Books, 1975 reprint of 1949 edition), p. 76.

[T]he attempt to maintain that, in the act of infusing the spiritual soul, the Creator transformed the body of an animal in such a way as to render it fit to receive the human soul, is quite sufficient to exclude that evolution which the transformists defend. In fact, to affirm that a particular intervention of God was necessary in order to render the body of a brute fit enough to become the body of the first man is the same as saying that such a privileged body did not and could not reach the stage of development (required for the rational soul) by a law of nature, and this strikes precisely at the basis of all evolutionism.

Now, we ask, if there must be a special divine action, why is an animal assigned as the matter rather than the dust of the earth of which the Bible speaks? It is certainly no more difficult for the Almighty to form Adam's body directly from the clay of the earth than it would be to produce it from the body of an animal![64]

<< Progressive Creation >>

Fr. Patrick O'Connell in *Science of Today and the Problems of Genesis* (1959) makes a valiant effort to uphold the literal meaning of Genesis account of Creation. He is handicapped, however, because he accepts long geological ages as a scientific fact:

> The second direct source of evidence about the origin of the various species comes from the fossils found in the various geological strata. The estimates of the time that has elapsed since the first living things appeared in the world vary from 30 million to 500 million years ago.[65]

He repeats the standard geological dictum that fossils of highly developed and complex animal life appear suddenly in the Cambrian rocks and that fossils of new types of animal life appear suddenly at various times during the geological periods. He rejects evolution as the explanation for this but instead offers the following solution:

> Our first conclusion is that spontaneous generation may be safely dismissed as an explanation of how life first appeared on the earth, and that there is not the remotest possibility that a living cell will ever be produced in the laboratory.
>
> Our next conclusion is that a) as the fossils that appeared in the earliest geological stratum belonged to highly complicated and specialized organisms, b) that as organisms have continued unchanged for hundreds of millions of years, and c) that as fossils of multitudes of new organisms unconnected with that have gone before them have appeared suddenly on the earth just at times when it was in a fit state to receive them, the account given in Genesis best explains these facts that science has discovered.[66]

Fr. O'Connell's interpretation of the fossil record is a form of *progressive creation*, God intervening at certain times in the history of the planet to create new species. Although he is claiming conformity with Genesis, he is forced to make the six days of Creation eons rather than natural days. This *seems* allowable because the Pontifical Biblical Commission ruled in 1909 that the Hebrew word *yom* in Genesis 1 may be interpreted as "a certain space of time."[67] But interpreting "a certain space of time" as millions of years is stretching things quite a bit. Even granting that, one still cannot conform progressive creation to Genesis because the fossil sequence of supposed successive creations does not agree with the Genesis sequence. We don't find only plants (created on Day Three) in the "oldest" layer and only water creatures and birds (created on Day Five) in the next level, and so on. Also, living creatures depend on each other in nature's delicately balanced household. The economy of nature couldn't bear waiting millions of years for new species to come on the scene to do their job.

Fr. O'Connell compromises the literal sense of Genesis as a concession to the false science he had uncritically embraced. His assessment for the age of the human species, however, although high, is in the biblical ballpark, some 12–22 thousand years.

[1] CCC, no. 362.

[2] Ps 103:14.

[3] Sir 10:9.

[4] Sir 17:1. Also see Gn 3:23; Eccl 12:7; Wis 7:1; Sir 33:10.

[5] ACC, pp. 52–53.

[6] JR, no. 1149.

[7] *On the Origin of Man* 2:4, as quoted in Rose, Fr. Seraphim, *Genesis, Creation and Early Man: The Orthodox Christian Vision* (Platina, CA: St. Herman of Alaska Brotherhood, 2000), p. 159.

[8] See Ruffini, Cardinal Ernesto, *The Theory of Evolution Judged by Reason and Faith* (New York: Joseph F. Wagner, Inc., 1959), pp. 124–129.

[9] ST, Part I, Q. 91, A. 1.

[10] Ibid., Reply Obj. 1.

[11] ST, Part I, Q. 91, A. 2.

[12] Ibid., Reply Obj. 1.

[13] ST, Part I, Q. 91, A. 3.

[14] ST, Part I, Q. 91, A. 4, Reply Obj. 1.

[15] ST, Part I, Q. 92, A. 2, Reply Obj. 2.

[16] See Gn 1:21, 24; Lv 24:18.

[17] See Gn 12:5; Ex 1:5; 12:4, 15; Lv 4:2; Jos 10:28.

[18] See Lv 19:28; 21:11; Nm 6:6.

[19] See Gn 6:3; Ps 33:6.

[20] For the many ways that "*ruach*" is used to denote the spiritual in man see Heinisch, Paul, *Theology of the Old Testament,* English ed. by William Heidt (Collegeville, MN: The Liturgical Press, 1950), p. 160.

[21] See CCC, no. 367.

[22] JR, no. 1563. Also see CG, Book XIII, Chapter 24.

[23] JR, no. 2357.

[24] See Brennan, Robert Edward, *Thomistic Psychology* (New York: Macmillan, 1941). This is an excellent work on the philosophy of man of St. Thomas Aquinas. Also see selections from *On the Power of God* in *An Aquinas Reader*, Mary T. Clark, ed. (New York: Fordham University Press, 1972), pp. 302–308.

[25] ST, Part I, Questions 75–102.

[26] *Exposition of Aristotle on the Soul* II, Lecture 2.

[27] von Hildebrand, Dietrich, *Man and Woman* (Chicago: Franciscan Herald Press, 1965), p. 36.

[28] Ibid., p. 37.

[29] Ibid., pp. 37–38.

[30] ACC, p. 53.

[31] ACC, p. 51.

[32] JR, no. 147.

[33] JR, no. 170.

[34] DZ, nos. 481, 738, 1655. Also see CCC, no. 365; OTT, p. 97.

[35] CCC, nos. 362–368.

[36] "Physical Anthropology," *Encyclopedia Britannica*, 2001, CD version.

[37] See "Human Evolution," *Encyclopedia Britannica*, 2001, CD version; Thain, M. and Hickman, M., *The Penguin Dictionary of Biology*, 10th ed. (New York: Penguin Books, 2001), pp. 314–319.

[38] Lubenow, Marvin L., *Bones of Contention: A Creationist Assessment of Human Fossils* (Grand Rapids, MI: Baker Books, 1992).

[39] Ibid., pp. 9, 247 ff.

[40] Ibid., p. 21.

[41] Chesterton, Gilbert Keith, *Evolution*, as cited by Chapin, John, ed., *The Book of Catholic Quotations* (Fort Collins, CO: Catholic Books, 1956 and 1984, reprint), p. 316.

[42] Chesterton, Gilbert Keith, *The Everlasting Man*, Part I, Chapter II.

[43] Wells, Jonathan, op. cit., pp. 219–220.

[44] Henry Gee, Chief Science Writer for *Nature*, as quoted by Wells, Ibid., p. 221.

[45] John Durant, Oxford historian, as quoted by Wells, Ibid., p. 221.

[46] Misia Landau, Yale paleoanthropologist, as quoted by Wells, Ibid., pp. 222–223.

[47] Geoffrey Clark, Curator of the American Museum of Natural History, as quoted by Wells, Ibid., p. 223.

[48] Ibid., p. 223.

[49] DZ, nos. 428, 1783; CCC, no. 327. See OTT, pp. 94–97.

[50] For a Thomistic viewpoint on animal "rights" see Rice, Charles, *50 Questions on the Natural Law: What It Is and Why We Need It* (San Francisco: Ignatius Press, 1993), pp. 63–67.

[51] Tom Regan, philosopher, as quoted by Lubenow, op. cit., p. 187.

[52] Ruffini, op. cit., p. 138.

[53] Ruffini, op. cit., pp. 138–139.

[54] As quoted by Ruffini, op. cit., p. 113.

[55] Haught, John F., *Responses to 101 Questions on God and Evolution* (New York: Paulist Press, 2001), p. 19–20.

[56] Ibid., p. 20.

[57] Ibid., pp. 27–28.

[58] Pope Pius XII, *Humani generis*, no. 36 (DZ, no. 2327).

[59] Ibid.

[60] *On the Soul*, Book II, Chapter 1.

[61] CCC, no. 365.

[62] ST, Part I, Q. 91, A. 4, Reply Obj. 3.

[63] See, for example, CCC, nos. 366, 990, 997, 1005, 1016.

[64] Ruffini, op. cit., pp. 148–149.

[65] O'Connell, Patrick, *Science of Today and the Problems of Genesis* (Rockford, IL: TAN Books, 1993), p. 41.

[66] Ibid., p. 64.

[67] DZ, no. 2128.

Doctrine Ten
God created the first woman immediately from the body of the first man.

The Fathers of the Church believed the Genesis account of the creation of Eve literally, although they sometimes superimposed allegorical interpretations on it. The creation of Eve from the side of Adam is so strongly affirmed in magisterial teaching that it can be considered as having been proposed infallibly by the universal and ordinary Magisterium of the Church. The firmness of the doctrine of the special creation of Eve's body strengthens the case against the evolution of Adam's body. For if Adam's body evolved then Eve would have had a much nobler origin than Adam, God having created her directly and Adam through innumerable secondary causes. There would then have been an unthinkable disparity in dignity between the first man and the first woman.

The Aloneness of Adam

Genesis 2:18–25 tells of the creation of the first woman, Eve. It begins with God saying: *"It is not good that man should be alone. I will make him a helper fit for him."* By saying *"not good"* God meant that His creation was not yet complete. Adam finds himself alone in the garden that God had planted for him to cultivate (2:8–17). God sees that Adam is alone despite the fact that Adam has a personal relationship with God Himself. God made the man a part of creation and put into his condition a need for other creatures and in his nature a desire for communion with other creatures. God first brings animals to Adam to show him that they can be helpers and of service to him,[a] and Adam gives them names "expressive of their respective natures."[1] [b] The animals were created for man. The CCC affirms this:

God entrusted animals to the stewardship of those whom he created in his own image. (Cf. Gn 2:19–20; 9:1–4) Hence it is legitimate to use animals for food and clothing. They may be domesticated to help man in his work and leisure. Medical and scientific experimentation on animals is a morally accept-able practice if it remains within reasonable limits and contributes to caring for or saving human lives.[2]

St. Ephrem the Syrian makes note of the perfect harmony that existed between Adam and the animals:[c]

> Moses said, *"God brought them to Adam."* This happened in order that God might make known the wisdom of Adam and the harmony that existed between the animals and Adam before he transgressed the commandment. The animals came to Adam as to a loving shepherd. Without fear they passed before him in orderly fashion, by kinds and by species. They were neither afraid of him nor were they afraid of each other. A species of predatory ani-mals would pass by with a species of animal that is preyed upon following safely right behind.[3]

Even though the animals lived in perfect harmony with Adam and could be his helpers, they could not be his intimate companions. For Adam had discovered that he was essentially different from the animals and all other creatures.[d] The very fact that he named the animals, something that none of them could do for themselves, set him apart, he *alone* having the very special gift of language. Since he could use his language only to command the animals but not to communicate

---

a. Genesis 2:19 is translated in the RSV: *"So out of the ground God formed every beast of the field and every bird of the air, and brought them to the man to see what he would call them."* This makes it sound like God created the animals after Adam, contradicting the chronology in (1:24–31). But the Hebrew conjunction *waw,* translated "so" can also be translated "also," and the sentence can be put into the past perfect tense because the Hebrew word *yatsar,* which is translated "formed" can also be translated "had formed." So another valid translation of the verse would be: *"Also out of the ground God had formed every beast and every bird of the air, and had brought them to the man to see what he would call them."* This translation is consistent with the understanding that God brought to Adam animals that He had already made earlier in Day Six, before He created Adam. See DR translation.

b. St. Lawrence of Brindisi points out in *Explanatio in Genesim* that (2:19) reveals that Adam had infused knowledge. He also says that Adam probably gave the animals names in the Hebrew language.

himself to them, it became obvious to him that he needed another with the same gift of language. In his loneliness, Adam realized his need for communion with another person.

Pope John Paul II considered the meaning of Adam's original solitude in a series of catechetical talks on Genesis.[4] He says it has two meanings:

> [I]t seems this solitude has two meanings: one derived from man's very nature, that is, from his humanity, and the other derived from the male-female relationship.[5]

The first meaning is based on Adam's awareness of his superiority among creatures;

> [T]he first meaning of man's original solitude is defined on the basis of a specific test or examination which man undergoes before God (and in a certain way also before himself). By means of this test, man becomes aware of his own superiority, that is, that he cannot be considered on the same footing as any other species of living beings on the earth.[6]

In his search for his identity, Adam first finds what he is not:

---

c. Such a harmony may once again exist on earth. Fr. Joseph Iannuzzi, OSJ argues from the writings of the Fathers and Doctors of the Church, from the Magisterium, and from Sacred Scripture that there will be a flowering of Christ's kingdom on earth that will last for a period of time, not necessarily a literal thousand years, during which Christ will reign gloriously on earth, not physically, but in the Eucharist. One of the characteristics of that era will be peace and harmony among men, among animals and among men and animals as depicted by the Prophet Isaiah (Is 11:6–9; 65:17–25). See *The Triumph of God's Kingdom in the Millennium and End Times: A Proper Belief from the Truth in Scripture and Church Teachings* (Havertown, PA: St. John the Evangelist Press, 1999).

d. Genesis 1:26–31 makes clear that the events of (2:18–25) took place on the sixth day of Creation. At first it may seem that this was an impossibly busy day. One may ask how Adam could have inspected and named all the animals in one day. However, Genesis does not say that he named *all* the animals. It says that he named only cattle, the beasts of the field and the birds of the air, not all the species on the earth. And also, he may have given only generic names to some rather than specific names. He could have done the naming in a few hours.

Right from the first moment of his existence, created man finds himself before God as if in search of his own entity. It could be said he is in search of the definition of himself. A contemporary person would say he is in search of his own "identity." The fact that man "is alone" in the midst of the visible world and, in particular, among living beings, has a negative significance in this search, since it expresses what he "is not."[7]

Adam is different because he has self-knowledge:

Self-knowledge develops at the same rate as knowledge of the world, of all the visible creatures, of all the living beings to which man has given a name to affirm his own dissimilarity with regard to them. In this way, consciousness reveals man as the one who possesses a cognitive faculty as regards the visible world. With this knowledge which, in a certain way, brings him out of his own being, man at the same time reveals himself to himself in all the peculiarity of his being. He is not only essentially and subjectively alone. Solitude also signifies man's subjectivity, which is constituted through self-knowledge. Man is alone because he is "different" from the visible world, from the world of living beings.[8]

Adam asserts himself as a person:

Analyzing the text of Genesis we are, in a way, witnesses of how man "distinguishes himself" before God-Yahweh from the whole world of living beings ... with his first act of self consciousness, and of how he reveals himself to himself. At the same time he asserts himself as a "person" in the visible world.[9]

The second meaning of Adam's solitude is contained in his expectation of a communion of persons:

[M]an's solitude is presented to us not only as the first discovery of the characteristic transcendence peculiar to the person. It is also presented as the discovery of an adequate relationship "to" the person, and therefore as an opening and expectation of a "communion of persons."[10]

The Creation of Eve

Genesis 2:21–22 tells of the creation of Eve from the rib of Adam: *"So the Lord caused a deep sleep to fall upon the man, and while he slept took one of his ribs and closed up its place with flesh; and the rib which the LORD God had taken from the man he made into a woman and brought her to the man."* The New Testament affirms the historicity of this account: *"Adam was formed first, then Eve."[11]* *"[M]an was not made from woman, but woman from man."[12]* The Hebrew word *tsela* is translated "rib." It is used forty-one times in the Hebrew Old Testament, and this is the only place that it is translated "rib." It is often translated "side."

The Fathers of the Church generally understood this account of the creation of Eve in a literal sense, but they also read it in an allegorical sense as well.

Augustine took the Genesis account of the creation of Eve in a literal sense. But he saw the putting to sleep of Adam as a kind of mystery because God could have removed the rib from Adam painlessly without putting him to sleep.[13] Augustine found an allegorical meaning in the account that explained why God put Adam to sleep:

> Now in creating woman at the outset of the human race, by taking a rib from the side of the sleeping man, the Creator must have intended, by this act, a prophecy of Christ and his Church. The sleep of that man clearly stood for the death of Christ; and Christ's side, as he hung lifeless on the cross, was pierced by a lance. And from the wound there flowed blood and water, (Jn 19:34) which we recognize as the sacraments by which the Church is built up. This, in fact, is the precise word used in Scripture of woman's creation; it says not that God "formed," or "fashioned" a woman but that *"He built it* (the rib) *up into a woman"* (Gn 2:22). Hence the Apostle also speaks of the *"building up"* of the body of Christ, which is the Church. (Eph 4:12) The woman, then, is the creation of God, just as is the man; but her creation out of man emphasizes the idea of the unity between them; and in the manner of that creation there is, as I have said, a foreshadowing of Christ and his Church.[14]

St. Jerome, also holding to the literal meaning, wrote a similar allegorical interpretation.[15]

St. John Chrysostom said Adam was put to sleep so that the production of Eve would not cause him pain, which might have made him badly disposed towards her:

> Great are these words; they surpass every mind of man: their greatness can be understood in no other way than by beholding them with the eyes of faith.... *"God caused a deep sleep to fall upon Adam, and he slept."* This was not a simple ecstasy and not a usual sleep; but since the most wise and skilled Creator of our nature wished to take from Adam one of his ribs, therefore, so that he might not feel the pain and then be hostilely disposed to the one created from his rib, lest, remembering the pain, he hate the created being, God plunged Adam into a deep sleep and, as it were commanding him to be embraced by a kind of numbness, brought upon him such a sleep that he did not feel in the

least what happened.... Taking a certain small part from an already prepared creation, from this part He made a whole living being. What power does the Highest Artist, God, have to produce from this small part the composition of so many members, to arrange so many organs of sense and form a whole, perfect and complete being which could converse and, because of its oneness of nature, furnish the man great consolation![16]

St. Cyril of Jerusalem connects the creation of Eve and the virgin birth of Christ:

Of whom in the beginning was Eve begotten? What mother conceived her, the motherless? But the Scripture says that she was born out of Adam's side. Is Eve then born out of man's side without a mother, and is a child not to be born without a father, of a virgin's womb? This debt of gratitude was due to men from womankind: for Eve was begotten of Adam and not conceived of a mother, but as it were brought forth of man alone.[17]

St. Thomas Aquinas says that it was befitting the role and dignity of the woman to be made from the rib of the man; also, there was a sacramental significance to it:

It was right for the woman to be made from a rib of man. First, to signify the social union of man and woman, for the woman should neither *"use authority over man,"* and so she was not made from his head; nor was it right for her to be subject to man's contempt as his slave, and so she was not made from his feet. Secondly, for the sacramental signification; for from the side of Christ sleeping on the Cross the Sacraments flowed—namely, blood and water—on which the Church was established.[18]

He goes on to discuss the question about where the rest of the matter came from because the woman contains more matter than a rib:

Some say that the woman's body was formed by a material increase, without anything being added; in the same way as our Lord multiplied the five loaves. But this is quite impossible. For such an increase of matter would either be by a change of the very substance of the matter itself, or by a change of its dimensions. Not by change of the substance of the matter, both because matter, considered in itself, is quite unchangeable, since it has a potential existence, and has nothing but the nature of a subject, and because quantity and size are extraneous to the essence of matter itself. Wherefore multiplication of matter is quite unintelligible, as long as the matter itself remains the same without anything added to it; unless it receives greater dimensions. This implies rarefaction, which is for the same matter to receive greater dimensions, as the Philosopher says.... To say, therefore, that the same matter is enlarged, without being rarefied, is to combine contradictories—viz. the definition with the absence of the thing defined.

Wherefore, as no rarefaction is apparent in such multiplication of matter, we must admit an addition of matter: either by creation or which is more probable, by conversion. Hence Augustine says ... that "Christ filled five thousand men with five loaves, in the same way as from a few seeds He produces the harvest of corn"—that is, by transformation of the nourishment. Nevertheless, we say that the crowds were fed with five loaves, or that woman was made from the rib, because an addition was made to the already existing matter of the loaves and of the rib.[19]

God alone formed the woman:

[T]he natural generation of every species is from some determinate matter. Now the matter whence man is naturally begotten is the human semen of man or woman. Wherefore from any other matter an individual of the human species cannot naturally be generated. Now God alone, the Author of nature, can produce an effect into existence outside the ordinary course of nature. Therefore God alone could produce either a man from the slime of the earth, or a woman from the rib of man.[20]

As Augustine says ... we do not know whether the angels were employed by God in the formation of the woman; but it is certain that, as the body of man was not formed by the angels from the slime of the earth, so neither was the body of the woman formed by them from the man's rib.[21]

The creation of Eve from the side of Adam is well attested to in magisterial teaching. Pope Pelagius I solemnly taught that the first woman was created "from the rib of the man."[22] Pope Leo XIII strongly affirmed it against revilers, saying:

Though revilers of the Christian faith refuse to acknowledge the never-interrupted doctrine of the Church on this subject, and have long striven to destroy the testimony of all nations and of all times, they have nevertheless failed not only to quench the powerful light of truth, but even to lessen it. We record what is to all known, and cannot be doubted by any, that God, on the sixth day of creation, having made man from the slime of the earth, and having breathed into his face the breath of life, gave him a companion, whom He miraculously took from the side of Adam when he was locked in sleep. God thus, in His most far-reaching foresight, decreed that this husband and wife should be the natural beginning of the human race, from whom it might be propagated and preserved by an unfailing fruitfulness throughout all futurity of time.[23]

Fr. Brian Harrison argues that "the formation by God of the first woman, Eve, from the side of the sleeping adult Adam had, by the year 1880, been proposed infallibly by the universal and ordinary *Magisterium* of the Catholic Church as literally and historically true; so that this must forever remain a doctrine to be held definitively (at least) by all the faithful."[24] In 1909 the Pontifical Biblical Commission declared that the literal-historical sense is to be adhered to in regard to "the formation of the first woman from the first man."[25] The CCC upholds the creation of Eve from Adam's rib in its summary of the creation of Eve:

> God created man and woman *together* and willed each *for* the other. The Word of God gives us to understand this through various features of the sacred text. *"It is not good that man should be alone. I will make a fit helper for him"* (Gn 2:18). None of the animals can be man's partner (Gn 2:19–20). The woman God *"fashions"* from the man's rib and brings to him elicits on the man's part a cry of wonder, an exclamation of love and communion: *"This at last is bone of my bones and flesh of my flesh"* (Gn 2:23). Man discovers woman as another "I," sharing the same humanity.[26]

Cardinal Ernesto Ruffini points out that the certainty of Eve's creation from the side of Adam strengthens the case for the creation of Adam immediately from the earth:

> But if it is true, as the transformists are good enough to concede, that the body of woman was formed directly by God and thus does not come by way of evolution, who will be persuaded that man's body, the virile sex, comes from the brute beast? What an absurdity! Therefore, woman would have had a much nobler origin than man; yes, we say, much nobler, as we cannot deny that it is an incomparably greater glory to proceed from God directly than to come from Him through innumerable second causes, among which the most advanced, and, therefore, the nearest, would be bestial. If we wish to stand by Holy Scripture, we must accept it in its entirety; then any repugnant differentiation between man and woman will cease. She gets the name *Virago ('ishah:* woman) because she is taken from the *vir ('ish:* man); likewise the man is called *Adam* (= homo) because, as Genesis says, he is taken from the *adamah* (= humus).[27]

Flesh of My Flesh!

The Genesis account makes it clear that Eve shared not only Adam's nature but also his flesh. This implies that Eve received all of her chromosomes from Adam. She was genetically the same as Adam except for sexual differences. She was the female twin of Adam. Adam had one X and one Y chromosome. God gave Eve two of Adam's X chromosomes but no Y chromosome. A similar event would happen again in the future. The Word Incarnate would become the male twin of His mother because He received all His chromosomes from her. In that case God transformed one of Mary's X chromosomes into a Y chromosome.

All genetic properties of the human race trace back to Adam. Eve did not contribute any new genetic information. Adam possessed all the seed for the entire human species. This does not detract from the dignity of Eve. Rather it makes her one with Adam. This is another way the human species differs from animal species. The animals were created male and female simultaneously, and therefore the genetic information was divided between both sexes.

Scripture does not mention God breathing life into Eve as it does for Adam. It simply says that He made Eve from Adam's rib. St. Ephrem interprets this as meaning that Eve was already inside Adam when God removed his rib:

> Then Moses said, "Male and female he created them," to make known that Eve was already inside Adam, in the rib that was drawn out from him. Although she was not in his mind she was in his body, and she was not only in his body with him but also in soul and spirit with him, for God added nothing to that rib that he took out except the structure and the adornment. If everything that was suitable for Eve, who came to be from the rib, was complete in and from that rib, it is rightly said that *"male and female he created them."* [28]

St. Ambrose said that God created Eve from the body of Adam to assure the unity of the human species, to eliminate the possibility that disparate natures should arise:

> Nor is it a matter of indifference that the woman was not formed of the same clay from which Adam was made, but was made from the rib of Adam himself, so that we might know that the flesh of man and woman is of but one nature, and that there is but one source of the human race. Therefore at the beginning it is not two that are made, man and woman, nor two men, nor two women, but first man is made, and then woman from him. For God willed to settle one nature upon mankind, and starting from the one origin of this creature, He snatched away the possibility of numerous and disparate natures. [29]

Theodoret of Cyr also taught that God made Eve from Adam to assure unity in nature of men and women, lest women think that they have a different nature than men and go contrary to them:

It was very easy for God to give orders for the whole earth and the sea straightway to be filled with inhabitants; but so that no one might suppose there were any difference in the nature of men, He commanded that the myriads of tribes of men come from that one couple. That too is why He did not form the woman in some other way but took the means of her beginning from the man, lest she might think she had a nature other than that of the man and go contrary to men. [30]

St. Thomas Aquinas gave four reasons why it was suitable for the woman to be made from the man:[31]

1. "[T]o give the first man a certain dignity consisting in this, that as God is the principle of the whole universe, so the first man, in likeness to God, was the principle of the whole human race."

2. "[T]hat man might love woman all the more, and cleave to her more closely, knowing her to be fashioned from himself."

3. "[B]ecause ... the human male and female are united, not only for generation, as with other animals, but also for the purpose of domestic life, in which each has his or her particular duty, and in which the man is the head of the woman."[e]

4. "[T]here is a sacramental reason for this. For by this is signified that the Church takes her origin from Christ."

The *Catechism of the Catholic Church* emphasizes the equal dignity of the two sexes:

Man and woman have been *created*, which is to say, *willed* by God: on the one hand, in perfect equality as human persons; on the other, in their respective beings as man and woman. "Being man" or "being woman" is a reality which is good and willed by God: man and woman possess an inalienable dignity which comes to them immediately from God their Creator. (Cf. Gn 2:7, 22) Man and woman are both with one and the same dignity "*in the image of God.*" In their "being-man" and "being-woman," they reflect the Creator's wisdom and goodness.[32]

---

e. Pope Pius XI in *Casti connubii* said that man is the head of the family because "he occupies the chief place in ruling," and the woman is the heart because she occupies the "chief place in love."

One Flesh

The union of the sexes continues God plan of creation through procreation. Man and woman imitate "in the flesh the Creator's generosity and fecundity"[33] by bringing into the world and raising children. "God unites them in such a way that, by forming '*one flesh*' they can transmit human life."[34] The mutual love of spouses "becomes an image of the absolute and unfailing love with which God loves man."[35]

Jesus Christ recalled (1:27–28) and (2:24) when He affirmed the institution and indissolubility of the conjugal union between a man and a woman, which was first established with Adam and Eve: "*Have you not read that he who made them from the beginning made them male and female, and said, 'For this reason a man shall leave his father and mother and be joined to his wife, and the two shall become one?' So they are no longer two but one. What therefore God has joined together, let no man put asunder.*"[36] St. Paul recalls (2:24) in comparing the relationship of husband and wife with that of Christ and the Church.[37] He also refers to (2:24) when condemning sexual immorality.[38]

St. John Chrysostom saw (2:24) as a prophetic utterance by Adam:

> Where, tell me, did these things come from for him to utter? From what source did he gain knowledge of future events and the fact that the race of human beings should grow into a vast number? Whence, after all, did he come to know that there would be intercourse between man and woman? I mean, the consummation of that intercourse occurred after the fall; up to that time they were living like angels in paradise and so were not burning with desire, not assaulted by other passions, not subject to the needs of nature.... Surely it's obvious that before his disobedience he had a share in prophetic grace and saw everything through the eyes of the Spirit.[39]

As John Chrysostom inferred, Scripture does not mention sexual intercourse between Adam and Eve until after the Fall. But it is clear that God intended the human species to multiply because God said to Adam and Eve on the day of their creation: "*Be fruitful and multiply and fill the earth*" (1:28). Some of the Fathers believed that if there were no Fall, human reproduction would have been accomplished by means other than sexual intercourse.[40] Augustine originally held that view but later came to the view that sexual union was part of God's original plan.[41]

St. Thomas said that there would have been generation in the state of innocence for the multiplication of individuals in the human species:

In the state of innocence there would have been generation of offspring for the multiplication of the human race; otherwise man's sin would have been very necessary, for such a great blessing to be its result.... Hence it belongs to man to beget offspring, on the part of the naturally corruptible body. But on the part of the soul, which is incorruptible, it is fitting that the multitude of individuals should be the direct purpose of nature, or rather of the Author of nature, Who alone is the Creator of the human soul. Wherefore, to provide for the multiplication of the human race, He established the begetting of offspring even in the state of innocence.[42]

He points out that even though, in the state of innocence, generation would not be required to preserve the species, it would still be needed for the multiplication of individuals.[43]

And it would have been generation by sexual intercourse because woman is man's *"helper"* in generation:

God made man and woman before sin. But nothing is void in God's works. Therefore, even if man had not sinned, there would have been such intercourse, to which the distinction of sex is ordained. Moreover, we are told that woman was made to be a help to man. But she is not fitted to help man except in generation, because another man would have proved a more effective help in anything else. Therefore there would have been such generation also in the state of innocence.... Some of the earlier doctors, considering the nature of concupiscence as regards generation in our present state, concluded that in the state of innocence generation would not have been effected in the same way. Thus Gregory of Nyssa says ... that in paradise the human race would have been multiplied by some other means, as the angels were multiplied without coition by the operation of the Divine Power. He adds that God made man male and female before sin, because He foreknew the mode of generation which would take place after sin, which He foresaw. But this is unreasonable. For what is natural to man was neither acquired nor forfeited by sin. Now it is clear that generation by coition is natural to man by reason of his animal life, which he possessed even before sin, as above explained (Q. 97, A. 3), just as it is natural to other perfect animals, as the corporeal members make it clear. So we cannot allow that these members would not have had a natural use, as other members had, before sin.

Thus, as regards generation by coition, there are, in the present state of life, two things to be considered. One, which comes from nature, is the union of man and woman; for in every act of generation there is an active and a passive principle. Wherefore, since wherever there is distinction of sex, the active principle is male and the passive is female; the order of nature demands that for the purpose of generation there should be concurrence of male and female. The second thing to be observed is a certain deformity of excessive concupiscence, which in the state of innocence would not have existed, when the lower powers were entirely subject to reason. Wherefore Augustine says ... "We must be far from supposing that offspring could not be begotten without concupiscence. All the bodily members would have been equally moved by the will, without ardent or wanton incentive, with calmness of soul and body."[44]

Dietrich von Hildebrand observed that man and woman are "two different expressions of human nature."[45] Their difference "has a specifically complementary character."[46] Man and woman are "spiritually ordered toward each other," and "a much closer communion and ultimate love is possible between them than between persons of the same sex because of their complementary difference."[47] Von Hildebrand said that it is not possible to overemphasize the fact "that the difference between man and woman is not a merely biological one, but extends to the deep realm of personality."[48] Love between a man and a woman engenders a unique "I-thou communion," an intense longing for union, and blissful enchantment, with the spouse "fully seen *as person.*"[49] Happiness is love's outcome, but never its motive.[50] The happiness of the beloved is of very special importance.[51] Love is so focused on the unique person, "who can never be replaced by another. If it were possible to conceive of someone who perfectly duplicated another person's potential and value in every way—something which is altogether untenable—one of the two would still be the one loved and there would never be a desire to exchange him for the other."[52]

Pope John Paul II makes the point that man is an image of God not only through his intelligence and dominion over nature but also in the communion between the male and female versions of the human person:

> [M]an became the *"image and likeness"* of God not only through his own humanity, but also through the communion of persons which man and woman form right from the beginning. The function of the image is to reflect the one who is the model, to reproduce its own prototype. Man becomes the image of God not so much in the moment of solitude as in the moment of communion. Right "from the beginning" he is not only an image in which the solitude of a person who rules the world is reflected, but also, and essentially, an image of inscrutable divine communion of persons."[53]

A nineteenth-century author expressed the same idea succinctly: "Female and male God made the man, His image in the whole, not half."[54]

< Objections > and << Replies >>

< Objection 1 >

Genetics has shown that the first woman lived in Africa about 200,000 years ago. Science has thus shown that biblical chronology, which gives the first woman an age under 10,000 years, is way off the mark.

<< Reply to Objection 1 >>

This objection is somewhat dated, but it is pertinent because it is a glaring example of how bad science becomes popularized and is used to discredit religion. The genetics referred to in the objection is contained in the so-called mitochondrial Eve theory.

<< Mitochondrial Eve Theory >>

The mitochondrion is a site in a living human cell at which metabolic activities take place that produce energy for the body. It carries its own DNA, labeled mtDNA, which is in addition to the DNA in the nucleus of the cell. Mitochondrial DNA has been called a biological history book of women because it is passed on from generation to generation only by mothers, unlike nuclear DNA, which is passed on by both parents.

In 1987, three California biochemists proposed a new way of tracing human origins using mtDNA.[55] The basic assumption they made is that if it were not for occasional mutations everyone in the world would have identical mtDNA. But mutations do happen, and each mutation establishes a new mitochondrial "family." Those with the same mtDNA descended from the same mother. By tracing all the families back, one could arrive at the original ancestor. The inventors of the method assumed that there was no mixing of families from generation to generation, that all the changes in mtDNA were the result of mutations, and that these mutations occurred at a constant rate. They studied 136 women of various races from around the world. Their analysis led back to a single ancestral mtDNA molecule from a woman living in Africa about 200,000 years ago.

The theory has evolution built into it and is subject to severe criticism on several counts. First, it looks for the family tree with the least number of mutational changes based on the assumption that evolution would have taken the most direct and efficient path—a strange thing for a random process to achieve! A statistical analysis showed that the 136 mtDNA sequences studied could result in more than a billion such family trees.[56] Also, the computer program they used was very sensitive to the order in which the data was fed into it, which affected the place of origin of "Eve." One geneticist suggested that low-level mixing among early human populations may have scrambled the DNA sequences enough to make the method completely ineffective for locating and dating "Eve."[57] One of the original researchers acknowledged that the African Eve has been invalidated.[58]

Marvin Lubenow critiques the theory for its evolutionary assumptions and its claim to be an independent confirmation of evolution. He states:

> The mtDNA study of African Eve, as well as other aspects of molecular genetics, is based on mutations in the DNA nucleotides. Perhaps we could be forgiven for asking the question, When an evolutionist looks at human DNA nucleotides, how does he know which ones are the result of mutations and which ones have remained unchanged? Obviously, to answer that question he must know what the original or ancient sequences were. Since only God is omniscient, how does the evolutionist get the information about those sequences that he believes existed millions of years ago? He uses as his guide the DNA of the chimpanzee. In other words, the studies that seek to prove that human DNA evolved from chimp DNA start with the assumption that chimp DNA represents the original condition (or close to it) from which human DNA diverged. This is circularity with a vengeance.[59]

He continues with an examination of the method by which the "molecular clock" is calibrated. Since there is nothing in the mtDNA molecules that indicates how often they mutate, an outside standard must be used. The standard used is the mutation rate of various species whose divergence or evolution is determined from the dates assigned to fossils. This method made "Eve" 200,000 years old. Lubenow concludes:

> Hence, an evolutionary time scale obtained from an evolutionary interpretation of fossils was superimposed upon the DNA molecules. Once again, the circularity is obvious. The alleged evidence for evolution from the DNA molecules is not an independent confirmation of evolution but is instead based upon an evolutionary interpretation of fossils as its starting point.[60]

[1] ST, Part I, Q. 96, A. 1, Reply Obj. 3.

[2] CCC, no. 2417.

[3] ACC, p. 65.

[4] See John Paul II, Pope, *The Theology of the Body: Human Love in the Divine Plan* (Boston: Pauline Books and Media, 1997), pp. 35–48.

[5] Ibid., p. 35.

[6] Ibid., p. 36.

[7] Ibid., pp. 36–37.

[8] Ibid., p. 37.

[9] Ibid.

[10] Ibid., p. 46.

[11] 1 Tm 2:13.

[12] 1 Cor 11:8.

[13] See JR, no. 1543.

[14] CG, Book XXII, Chapter 17.

[15] See ACC, pp. 70–71.

[16] *Homilies on Genesis*, as quoted in Rose, Fr. Seraphim, *Genesis, Creation and Early Man: The Orthodox Christian Vision* (Platina, CA: Saint Herman of Alaska Brotherhood, 2000), p. 184.

[17] ACC, p. 67.

[18] ST, Part I, Q. 92, A. 3.

[19] Ibid., Reply Obj. 1.

[20] ST, Part I, Q. 92, A. 4.

[21] Ibid., Reply Obj. 2.

[22] DZ, no. 228a.

[23] *Arcanum divinae sapientiae* ("On Christian Marriage," 1880), no. 5.

[24] Harrison, Brian W., "Did Woman Evolve from the Beasts? A Defense of Traditional Catholic Doctrine," *International Catholic Symposium on Creation: October 24–25, 2002, Rome, Italy* (Mt. Jackson, VA: Kolbe Center for the Study of Creation, 2003), p. 142.

[25] DZ, no. 2123.

[26] CCC, no. 371.

[27] Ruffini, Cardinal Ernesto, *The Theory of Evolution Judged by Reason and Faith* (New York: Joseph F. Wagner, Inc., 1959), p. 123.

[28] ACC, p. 36.

[29] JR, no. 1278.

[30] JR, no. 2147.

[31] ST, Part I, Q. 92, A. 2.

[32] CCC, no. 369.

[33] CCC, no. 2335.

[34] CCC, no. 372.

[35] CCC, no. 1604.

[36] Mt 19:4–6. Also see Mk 10:6–9.

[37] Eph 5:31.

[38] 1 Cor 6:16.

[39] ACC, p. 72.

[40] See ACC, pp. 37–41.

[41] Ibid.

[42] ST, Part I, Q. 98, A. 1.

[43] Ibid., Reply Obj. 2.

[44] ST, Part I, Q. 98, A. 2. Also see Q. 92, A. 1.

[45] von Hildebrand, Dietrich, *Man and Woman* (Chicago: Franciscan Herald Press, 1965), p. 14.

[46] Ibid.

[47] Ibid.

[48] Ibid., p. 15.

[49] Ibid., pp. 16–17, 20.

[50] Ibid., p. 39.

[51] Ibid., p. 46.

[52] Ibid., p. 44.

[53] John Paul II, Pope, op. cit., p. 46.

[54] Patmore, Coventry, *The Angel in the House,* as quoted by Chaplin, John, ed., *The Book of Catholic Quotations* (Fort Collins, CO: Roman Catholic Books, reprint of 1956 edition), p. 572.

[55] Cann, Rebecca L.; Stoneking, Mark; and Wilson, Allan C., "Mitochondrial DNA and Human Evolution," *Nature* 325 (1 January 1987), pp. 31–36.

[56] Gee, Henry, "Statistical Cloud over African Eden," *Nature*, 355 (13 February, 1992), p. 583.

[57] See Barinaga, Marcia, "African Eve Backers Beat a Retreat," *Science* 255 (7 February 1992), p. 687.

[58] Hedges, S. Blair; Kumar, Sudhir; Tamora, Koichiro; and Stoneking, Mark, "Human Origins and Analysis of Mitochondrial DNA Sequences," *Science* 255 (7 February 1992), pp. 737–739.

[59] Lubenow, Marvin L., *Bones of Contention: A Creationist Assessment of Human Fossils* (Grand Rapids, MI: Baker Books, 1992), pp. 71–72.

[60] Ibid., p. 72.

Doctrine Eleven
God gave man dominion over all creation.

Sacred Scripture makes it clear that God created everything for man. This was the belief of the Fathers and Doctors of the Church and is affirmed by the *Catechism of the Catholic Church*. Genesis relates that God built the universe around man's home, earth; and modern astrophysical observations indicate that the earth occupies a central position in the universe. The attempt to dethrone man and proclaim his insignificance in the cosmos is not a gesture of humility, but one of infidelity.

The Lord Steward of Creation

The world was created "to the glory of God."[1] But "God created everything for man."[2] [a] "Man is the only creature on earth that God willed for its own sake."[3] He created all other creatures for the good of man, into whose custody He placed them.[4] Man in return was "to serve and love God and to offer all creation back to him."[5] The offering back to God from the gifts of creation is the raison d'etre of ritual sacrifice.

Man's dominion over the world proceeds from his being an image of God. God is the Lord of creation, and He made His image, man, to stand in for Him as the lord steward of creation. God commanded man not to make images of Him[6] not only because man would tend to worship the image rather than God

---

a. Jewish tradition affirms this. The Jewish doctors taught that God made the world to sustain man and to afford him the opportunity of glorifying the Creator. They held that the universe was created as the habitation of man and that everything in it was provided for his benefit. See Abraham Cohen, *Everyman's Talmud: The Major Teachings of the Rabbinic Sages* (New York, Schocken Books, 1975 reprint of 1949 edition), pp. 39–40, 68.

Himself, but also because man is the only authentic image of God in the material world. Idols are not only an affront to God; they are also an affront to man because in a way they usurp a share of his dominion.

Vatican Council II commented on man's work of subduing the earth and perfecting the work of creation:

> By the work of his hands and with the aid of technical means man tills the earth to bring forth fruit and make it a dwelling place fit for all mankind; he also consciously plays his part in the life of social groups; in so doing he is realizing the design, which God revealed at the beginning of time, to subdue the earth (Cf. Gn 1:28) and perfect the work of creation, and at the same time he is improving his own person: he is also observing the command of Christ to devote himself to the service of his fellow men.[7]

That God called man to "perfect the work of creation" does not mean that the world was defective in any way. It just means that God left it unfinished so that man might share in His work. From heaven God sees His image on earth busy completing what He had started.

Pope John Paul II recalls Scripture verses that extol the dominion given to man:

> The biblical text clearly shows the breadth and depth of the lordship which God bestows on man. It is a matter first of all of *dominion over the earth and over every living creature*, as the Book of Wisdom makes clear: *"O God of my fathers and Lord of mercy ... by your wisdom you have formed man, to have dominion over the creatures you have made, and rule the world in holiness and righteousness"* (Wis 9:1, 2–3). The Psalmist too extols the dominion given to man as a sign of glory and honor from his Creator: *"You have given him dominion over the works of your hands; you have put all things under his feet, all sheep and oxen, and also the beasts of the field, the birds of the air, and the fish of the sea, whatever passes along the paths of the sea"* (Ps 8:6–8).[8]

He continues on to say that this dominion is not absolute and calls for responsible stewardship:

> As one called to till and look after the garden of the world (cf. Gn 2:15), man has a specific responsibility toward *the environment in which he lives*, toward the creation which God has put at the service of his personal dignity, of his life, not only for the present but also for future generations. It is the *ecological question*—ranging from the preservation of the natural habitats of the different species of animals and of other forms of life to "human ecology"

properly speaking—which finds in the Bible clear and strong ethical direction, leading to a solution which respects the great good of life, of every life. In fact, "the dominion granted to man by the Creator is not an absolute power, nor can one speak of a freedom to 'use and misuse' or to dispose of things as one pleases...."[9]

He explains that the prohibition *"but of the tree of the knowledge of good and evil you shall not eat"* (2:17) showed that man was subject to moral laws as well as natural laws. It also shows that only God has *absolute* dominion over the world.

Man's Rule Over Man

In the Fourth Eucharistic Prayer of the *Roman Missal*, which summarizes salvation history, God is praised for His wisdom and love in setting man over creation:

> Father, we acknowledge your greatness: all your actions show your wisdom and love. You formed man in your own likeness and set him over the whole world to serve you, his creator, and to rule over all creatures.

Man's rule is fourfold: over himself, over other men, over animals, over inanimate creatures. Man's primary mastery is over himself, as the CCC makes clear:

> The "mastery" over the world that God offered man from the beginning was realized above all within man himself: *mastery of self.* The first man was unimpaired and ordered in his whole being because he was free from the triple concupiscence (Cf. 1 Jn 2:16) that subjugates him to the pleasures of the senses, covetousness for earthly goods, and self-assertion, contrary to the dictates of reason.[10]

Even if there had been no Fall, government would still be needed in order to maintain an orderly society. In the state of innocence all men would have been without defects and equal in dignity but would not have been equal in all ways, as Aquinas indicates:

> We must needs admit that in the primitive state there would have been some inequality, at least as regards sex, because generation depends upon diversity of sex: and likewise as regards age; for some would have been born of others; nor would sexual union have been sterile.

Moreover, as regards the soul, there would have been inequality as to righteousness and knowledge. For man worked not of necessity, but of his own free-will, by virtue of which man can apply himself, more or less, to action, desire, or knowledge; hence some would have made a greater advance in virtue and knowledge than others.

There might also have been bodily disparity. For the human body was not entirely exempt from the laws of nature, so as not to receive from exterior sources more or less advantage and help: since indeed it was dependent on food wherewith to sustain life.

So we may say that, according to the climate, or the movement of the stars, some would have been born more robust in body than others, and also greater, and more beautiful, and all ways better disposed; so that, however, in those who were thus surpassed, there would have been no defect or fault either in soul or body.[11]

And some men would be masters over others, not as slave masters, but as servants serving the common good:

Mastership has a twofold meaning. First, as opposed to slavery, in which sense a master means one to whom another is subject as a slave. In another sense mastership is referred in a general sense to any kind of subject; and in this sense even he who has the office of governing and directing free men, can be called a master. In the state of innocence man could have been a master of men, not in the former but in the latter sense. This distinction is founded on the reason that a slave differs from a free man in that the latter has the disposal of himself, as is stated in the beginning of the *Metaphysics*, whereas a slave is ordered to another. So that one man is master of another as his slave when he refers the one whose master he is, to his own—namely the master's use. And since every man's proper good is desirable to himself, and consequently it is a grievous matter to anyone to yield to another what ought to be one's own, therefore such dominion implies of necessity a pain inflicted on the subject; and consequently in the state of innocence such a mastership could not have existed between man and man.

But a man is the master of a free subject, by directing him either towards his proper welfare, or to the common good. Such a kind of mastership would have existed in the state of innocence between man and man, for two reasons. First, because man is naturally a social being, and so in the state of innocence he would have led a social life. Now a social life cannot exist among a number of people unless under the presidency of one to look after the common good; for many, as such, seek many things, whereas one attends only to one. Wherefore the Philosopher says, in the beginning of the *Politics*, that wherever many things are directed to one, we shall always find one at the head directing them. Secondly, if one man surpassed another in knowledge and virtue, this would not have been fitting unless these gifts conduced to the benefit of others, according to 1 Peter 4:10, *"As every man hath received grace, ministering the same one to another."* Wherefore Augustine says (*The City of God*, Book XIX, Ch. 14): "Just men command not by the love of domineering, but by the service of counsel." and (*The City of God*, Book XIX, Ch. 15): "The natural order of things requires this; and thus did God make man."[12]

Man's Rule Over Animals and Other Creatures

Animals differ essentially from man.[13] He is master over the animals because he is superior to them, not in degree but in nature. The animal nature is between that of machine and man, just as man's nature is between that of animal and angel. Although many characteristics of animals are ordered toward the preservation of the individual or species, it is not for their own sake that they are being preserved; it is for man's sake. Animals have no rights because they are not persons; they were not created in the *"image and likeness"* of God. Some of the obvious signs of this are the following: they do not have a language; they do not invent; they do not have a sense of humor; they show no appreciation for the true, the good, or the beautiful. Animal behavior mimics man's behavior; intelligence, emotions, even expressions of pain may be mimicked. But their behavior is totally instinctive, without reflection. That is why there is no "bad" behavior by animals. They cannot make moral choices. J. Henri Fabre, who was an acute observer of insect behavior, demonstrated that insects always act instinctively.[14] His experiments with them showed that even when at first they appear inventive, closer study shows that they are acting instinctively. Even the use of tools, the ability to adapt behavior, and the ability to communicate with humans are instinctive and not the result of invention and free choices. Animal behavior is not the result of evolution, not the result of natural selection in the struggle for survival. It is the result of instincts God wired into animals so that they may achieve their ends, which are ultimately for the benefit of man.

We have no idea what the inner life of animals is like. Man's nature has something of that of animals, which are purely material, and of that of angels, which are pure spirits. However, since our conscious experience is limited, we are unable to imagine ourselves as wholly animal on one hand or as disembodied spirit on the other. Konrad Lorenz, a renowned expert on animal behavior, has this to say about the subjective experiences of animals:

> It is on principle impossible to make any scientifically legitimate assertion about the subjective experiences of animals. The central nervous system of animals is constructed differently from ours, and the physiological processes in it

are also different from what happens in our brain. These qualitative differences are sufficient to make us conclude that whatever subjective phenomena may correspond to neural processes in animals must be considerably different from what we, ourselves, experience. However, similarities and analogies in the nervous processes of animals and men are sufficiently great to justify the conclusion that higher animals do indeed have subjective experiences which are qualitatively different from but in essence akin to our own. We are convinced that animals do have emotions, though we shall never be able to say exactly what these emotions are. My teacher Heinroth, who was most careful to describe animal behavior as objectively as possible, was often accused by animal lovers of misrepresenting living creatures as being machines, because of his mechanistic interpretations of behavior. To such aspersions he used to answer: "Quite the contrary, I regard animals as very emotional people with very little intelligence!" We cannot know what a gander is feeling when he stands about displaying all the symptoms of human grief on the loss of his mate, or when he rushes at her in an ecstasy of triumph calling on finding her again. But we cannot help feeling that whatever he may experience is closely akin to our own emotions in an analogous situation.[15]

Adam may have had a greater knowledge of the inner life of animals than we do, but if he did it was lost in the Fall. And much of his control over animals was certainly lost. Some saints, like Francis of Assisi, were given the gift of an Adam-like intimacy with animals.[b]

St. Augustine made the point that even though man may have lost some control over animals after the Fall, he remains the master:

> At times the Manichaeans also ask, "In what sense did man receive power over the fish of the sea and the birds of heaven and all the cattle and wild animals? For we see that men are killed by many wild animals and that many birds harm us when we want to avoid them or to capture them, though we often cannot. In what sense then did we receive power over these?" On this point they should first be told that they make a big mistake when they consider man after sin, when he has been condemned to the mortality of this life and has lost that perfection by which he was made in the image of God. But even man's state of condemnation involves such power that he rules many animals. For though he can be killed by many wild animals on account of the fragility of his

---

b. The Orthodox have the concept of a *prepodobny*, which is a saint who effects harmony among animals because he has become like Adam before the Fall. Some Fathers said that Noah was such a saint. See Fr. Seraphim Rose, *Genesis, Creation and Early Man: The Orthodox Christian Vision* (Platina, CA: Saint Herman of Alaska Brotherhood, 2000), p. 253–254.

body, he can be tamed by none, although he tames very many and nearly all of them.[16]

St. Thomas Aquinas believed that when man was in the state of innocence no animal disobeyed him; but because of his disobedience to God, he was punished by the disobedience of animals:

> [F]or his disobedience to God, man was punished by the disobedience of those creatures which should be subject to him. Therefore in the state of inno-cence, before man had disobeyed, nothing disobeyed him that was naturally subject to him. Now all animals are naturally subject to man. This can be proved in three ways. First, from the order observed by nature; for just as in the generation of things we perceive a certain order of procession of the perfect from the imperfect (thus matter is for the sake of form; and the imperfect form, for the sake of the perfect), so also is there order in the use of natural things; thus the imperfect are for the use of the perfect; as the plants make use of the earth for their nourishment, and animals make use of plants, and man makes use of both plants and animals. Therefore it is in keeping with the order of nature, that man should be master over animals. Hence the Philosopher says (*Politics*, Book I, Ch. 5) that the hunting of wild animals is just and natu-ral, because man thereby exercises a natural right. Secondly, this is proved by the order of Divine Providence which always governs inferior things by the superior. Wherefore, as man, being made to the image of God, is above other animals, these are rightly subject to his government. Thirdly, this is proved from a property of man and of other animals. For we see in the latter a certain participated prudence of natural instinct, in regard to certain particular acts; whereas man possesses a universal prudence as regards all practical matters. Now whatever is participated is subject to what is essential and universal. Therefore the subjection of other animals to man is proved to be natural.[17]

Aquinas further argues that the nature of animals did not change with man's sin. There were predators and prey before the Fall, just as there are after. But no animal, including those that were not tame, would have been exempted from the mastership of man. All animals would have obeyed man of their own accord, through their natural instinct, as today some domestic animals obey him.[18]

St. Thomas goes on to say that man was given mastership over all material creatures, even inanimate ones. He is master over inanimate creatures not by commanding them but by using them:

> Man in a certain sense contains all things; and so according as he is master of what is within himself, in the same way he can have mastership over other things. Now we may consider four things in man: his reason, which makes

him like to the angels; his sensitive powers, whereby he is like the animals; his natural forces, which liken him to the plants; and the body itself, wherein he is like to inanimate things. Now in man reason has the position of a master and not of a subject. Wherefore man had no mastership over the angels in the primitive state; so when we read all creatures, we must understand the creatures which are not made to God's image. Over the sensitive powers, as the irascible and concupiscible, which obey reason in some degree, the soul has mastership by commanding. So in the state of innocence man had mastership over the animals by commanding them. But of the natural powers and the body itself man is master not by commanding, but by using them. Thus also in the state of innocence man's mastership over plants and inanimate things consisted not in commanding or in changing them, but in making use of them without hindrance.[19]

Genesis says that man was given dominion over the earth, but it says nothing about dominion over the universe. Man is not able to exercise dominion over the whole universe,[c] but still the whole universe was made for his sake, in ways known to us—to provide light, heat and temporal rhythms, to provide reference points for navigation, to inspire awe and manifest the glory of God—and in ways unknown to us. Scripture confirms this where it says that God created the sun and the moon and the stars *"for signs and for seasons and for days and years"* (1:14) and *"for the service of the nations."*[20]

St. Bonaventure points out that God created the universe for man so that man may use created things to ascend to loving and praising Him:

> Wherefore it is unquestionably true that we are "the end of all things which exist," {Aristotle, *Physics*, Book II, Chapter 2} and all corporeal matter was made for human service so that by these things mankind may ascend to loving and praising the Creator of the universe whose providence disposes of all.[21]

The CCC hails scientific and technological research as an expression of man's dominion over nature, but it adds the caveat that such will not supply the answers to all questions important to man:

---

c. Quantum mechanics seems to indicate that man does have some influence in the universe beyond the macroscopic level of everyday experience; he can produce effects at the submicroscopic level of elementary particles by collapsing wave functions and at the supermacroscopic level through the phenomenon of entanglement. See Amir D. Aczel, *Entanglement: The Greatest Mystery in Physics* (New York: Four Walls Eight Windows, 2001).

Basic scientific research, as well as applied research, is a significant expression of man's dominion over creation. Science and technology are precious resources when placed at the service of man and promote his integral development for the benefit of all. By themselves however they cannot disclose the meaning of existence and of human progress.... [22]

St. Paul said that because of the Fall *"the creation was subjected to futility."*[23] The commentators of the Navarre Bible see this as meaning that man's fallen nature has led him to use nature in a disordered way, which has an effect on nature itself:

> The futility to which creation is subject is not so much corruption and death as the disorder resulting from sin. According to God's plan material things should be resources which enable man to attain the ultimate goal of his existence. By using them in a disordered way, disconnecting them from God, man turns them into instruments of sin, which therefore are subject to the consequences of sin.[24]

The Centrality of Man in the Universe

The Book of Genesis makes it clear that man and his home, earth, are the focus of the universe. Pope John Paul II affirmed this fact in an address to scientists:

> By increasing his knowledge of the universe, and in particular of the human being, who is at its center, man has a veiled perception, as it were, of the presence of God, a presence which he is able to discern in the 'silent manuscript' written by the Creator in creation, the reflection of his glory and grandeur.[25]

Modern popular science writers like to point out that man is midway in order of magnitude of size between the smallest things in the universe and the largest, which gives him the optimal vantage point for observing both.

Medieval scholars expressed man's centrality geometrically in their earth-centered astronomy. Philosopher of science E. A. Burtt nicely summarizes the medieval Christian vision:

> For the Middle Ages man was in every sense the center of the universe. The whole world of nature was believed to be teleologically subordinate to him and his eternal destiny. Toward this conviction the two great movements which became united in the medieval synthesis, Greek philosophy and Judeo-Christian theology, had irresistibly led. The prevailing world-view of the period was

marked by a deep and persistent assurance that man, with his hopes and ideals, was the all-important, even controlling fact in the universe.[26]

"[M]edieval science testified to the presupposition that man, with his means of knowledge and his needs, was the determinative fact in the world."[27] Man "occupied the centre; his good was the controlling end of the natural creation."[28] "The world of nature existed that it might be enjoyed by man. Man in turn existed that he might 'know God and enjoy him forever.'"[29]

The medieval poet Dante put "in sublime form the prevailing conviction of the essentially *human* character of the universe."[30] Dante vividly portrays the glory of God permeating the universe, in some places more, in others less. For Dante, like Aristotle, love moves the heavens; but for Dante the Love that moves is the God of Genesis:

> The glory of the One Who moves all things
> penetrates all the universe, reflecting
> in one part more and in another less.
>
> ...
>
> At this point power failed high fantasy
> but, like a wheel in perfect balance turning,
> I felt my will and my desire impelled
>
> by the Love that moves the sun and the other stars.[31]

The theological confusion caused by Galileo's aggressive advocacy of sun-centered astronomy had the sad effect of clouding the truth of man's centrality and shattering the medieval vision.[32] Cardinal Robert Bellarmine, Consultor of the Holy Office, eloquently upheld that vision in the assault by Galileo. In an authoritative but unofficial statement on the Copernican system he wrote:

> To demonstrate that the appearances are saved by assuming the sun at the center and the earth in the heavens is not the same thing as to demonstrate that *in fact* the sun is in the centre and the earth in the heavens. I believe that the *first demonstration may exist, but I have very grave doubts about the second*; and in case of doubt one may not abandon the Holy Scriptures as expounded by the holy Fathers.... [33]

Bellarmine's judgment was penetrating. It reached the heart of the issue. The sun-centered system did prove very useful in describing the motions of the planets relative to the sun and each other. But it has never been proven, nor can it be proven that the sun is at absolute rest with the earth and other planets in absolute motion around it. In fact, according to Albert Einstein, statements about the absolute motion of the earth and sun are meaningless because it is possible to eliminate the notion of absolute motion from physics.[34] One is free to choose the earth at rest or the sun at rest; it's simply a matter of convenience. Genesis 1 states that God created the earth first and built the rest of the universe around it.[d] Nothing that modern science can demonstrate contradicts that truth, and nothing that modern science can demonstrate gives an account for the origin of motion in the universe.

Burtt contrasts the drab view of man in the universe begun by Galileo and developed by Enlightenment thinkers with the bright picture of the medievals:

> Note, however the tremendous contrast between this view of man and his place in the universe, and that of the medieval tradition. The scholastic scientist looked out upon the world of nature and it appeared to him a quite sociable and human world. It was finite in extent. It was made to serve his needs. It was clearly and fully intelligible, being immediately present to the rational powers of his mind; it was composed fundamentally of, and was intelligible through, those qualities which were most vivid and intense and his own

---

d. There is evidence from modern astronomy that our galaxy is at the center of the universe. It is summarized by Russell Humphreys: "Over the last few decades, new evidence has surfaced that restores man to a central place in God's universe. Astronomers have confirmed that numerical values of galaxy redshifts are 'quantized', tending to fall into distinct groups. According to Hubble's law, redshifts are proportional to the distances of the galaxies from us. Then it would be the distances themselves that fall into groups. That would mean the galaxies tend to be grouped into (conceptual) spherical shells concentric around our home galaxy, the Milky Way. The shells turn out to be on the order of a million light years apart. The groups of redshifts would be distinct from each other only if our viewing location is less than a million light years from the centre. The odds for the Earth having such a unique position in the cosmos by accident are less than one in a trillion. Since big bang theorists presuppose the cosmos has naturalistic origins and cannot have a unique centre, they have sought other explanations, without notable success so far. Thus, redshift quantization is evidence (1) against the big bang theory, and (2) for a galactocentric cosmology, such as one by Robert Gentry or the one in my book, *Starlight and Time*" (Abstract for "Our galaxy is the centre of the universe, 'quantized' redshifts show" (*TJ* 16(2):95–104, 2002)). Also see Doctrine Two, << The Temporality of the World: Big Bang Cosmogony >>.

immediate experience—colour, sound, beauty, joy, heat, cold, fragrance, and its plasticity to purpose and ideal. Now the world is an infinite and monotonous mathematical machine.... It was simply an incalculable change in the viewpoint of the world held by intelligent opinion in Europe.[35]

The modern view, held by many scientists and scholars today, was clearly expressed by Bertrand Russell:

Such, in outline, but even more purposeless, more void of meaning, is the world which Science presents for our belief. Amid such a world, if anywhere, our ideals henceforward must find a home. That man is the product of causes which had no prevision of the end they were achieving; that his origin, his growth, his hopes and fears, his loves and his beliefs, are but the outcome of accidental collocations of atoms; that no fire, no heroism, no intensity of thought and feeling, can preserve an individual life beyond the grave; that all the labours of the ages, all the devotion, all the inspirations, all the noonday brightness of human genius, are destined to extinction in the vast death of the solar system, and that the whole temple of Man's achievement must inevitably be buried beneath the debris of a universe in ruins—all these things, if not quite beyond dispute, are yet so nearly certain, that no philosophy which rejects them can hope to stand. Only within the scaffolding of these truths, only on the firm foundation of unyielding despair, can the soul's habitation henceforth be safely built.[36]

What a dismal philosophy! Yet this is what we are continually being told by scientists, by the communications media, and by other opinion makers. We are told that we are being egocentric when we assert that man is the center of the world; we are told that we humans are just inconsequential specks in the vastness of the universe, that there are probably many species out there more intelligent and virtuous than us. But actually the egocentricity is on the side of those who so sanctimoniously depreciate man.[e] They smugly set aside the truth in the Word of God to worship their own thoughts.

---

e. The devil is fond of turning things upside down; one of his symbols is an upside down cross. He tries to make the bad look good and the good look bad, the false look true and the true look false. This is part of his strategy for ensnaring souls. The prophet Isaiah gave a stern warning to those who would invert the moral and natural orders: *"Woe to those who call evil good and good evil, who put darkness for light and light for darkness, who put bitter for sweet and sweet for bitter!"* (Is 5:20).

In the medieval view nature is subservient to man; in the modern view man is a product of nature. Burtt makes that point clearly:

> [J]ust as it was thoroughly natural for medieval thinkers to view nature as subservient to man's knowledge, purpose, and destiny; so now it has become natural to view her as existing and operating in her own self-contained independence, and so far as man's ultimate relation to her is clear at all, to consider his knowledge and purpose somehow produced by her, and his destiny wholly dependent on her.[37]

Philosophers of science have created a whole new lexicon for modern metaphysics and cosmology that does not contain the terms of the Scholastics. The Schoolmen thought in terms of substance, accident, essence, matter, form, actuality and potentiality. Modern philosophers think only in terms of space, time and energy/matter. The first two had little importance for the medieval philosophers. For them space and time were accidental and not self-subsistent. Instead, they thought of the ongoing passage of potentiality into actuality. Further, modern science looks for efficient causes, the *how* of things. The medieval scientist looked for final causes, the *why* of things—the *why* of material things in terms of their usefulness to men and the *why* of man in terms of his relationship with God.

The time is ripe for a return to the medieval view, not unaltered but enhanced by authentic discoveries of the natural sciences. The restoration will follow a return to the correct understanding of Genesis. Scientific research carried out in the light of the Word of God will deepen and unify our understanding of nature and bring us to its Creator. Pope John Paul implored scientists to recognize this:

> Faith for its part is able to integrate and assimilate every research, for all research, through a deeper understanding of created reality and all its specificity, gives man the possibility of discovering the Creator, source and goal of all things.[38]

Where is Everybody?

Now that the modern worldview has dethroned man from his unique place in creation, men have begun to look elsewhere in the universe for intelligent life. Evolutionists apply themselves to the search with religious fervor. They believe that life evolved here and therefore could also have evolved elsewhere. But despite several decades of intense looking, searchers for extraterrestrial life have not seen any sign of life out there, intelligent or otherwise. The failure to find intelligent life is called the Fermi Paradox after the Italian physicist Enrico Fermi who asked the famous question, "Where is everybody?" This was a response to the belief that, considering the supposed size and age of the universe, extraterrestrial civilizations must exist, and some should have made themselves known to us by now. The believers in extraterrestrial life find themselves in the awkward position of having to contrive reasons to explain why there is no evidence for their belief. The topic has generated a pile of literature.[39] Actually, it is only a "paradox" to those who think that there *must* be other intelligent life in the universe, those who subscribe to the so-called principle of mediocrity, which says that there is nothing special about the earth. Those who don't subscribe to that principle have no problem with the idea that we are alone in the universe, since we are alone here on earth. There are no rational creatures here besides us. There are no fairies, elves or leprechauns. They are creatures of human imagination, not creatures of God. Perhaps the lack of the evidence is saying that the same is true for extraterrestrials.

The modern Christian writer C. S. Lewis liked to toy with the idea of other rational species in the universe. In his science fiction novel *Perelandra*, he tells the story of the "Eve" of a newly created species on the planet Venus, whom the hero of the story adjures to resist the overtures of Satan. The hero, being an earthling, knew the consequences for her species if she submitted. In a short essay entitled "Religion and Rocketry"[40] he brings up the questions: Are there intelligent species on other planets? If so, are any of them fallen? If fallen, have they been redeemed? If redeemed, how? He suggests that even if there are other intelligent species, man may still hold a special place among them because their redemption may work through his: "There is a hint of something like this in St. Paul (Romans 8:19–23) when he says that the whole creation is longing and waiting to be delivered from some kind of slavery, and that this deliverance will occur only when we, we Christians, fully enter upon our sonship to God and exercise our *glorious liberty.*"[41] In the end the questions he asks are moot because he is convinced that intelligent extraterrestrial species will never be discovered:

> "But supposing," you say. "Supposing all these embarrassing suppositions turned out to be true?" I can only record the conviction that they won't; a conviction which has for me become in the course of years irresistible. Christians and their opponents again and again expect that some new discovery will either turn matters of faith into matters of knowledge or else reduce them to patent absurdities. But it has never happened.[42]

Is it reasonable for a Catholic to believe that there are other personal corporeal substances in the universe a la *Star Wars* and *Star Trek*? It seems not because such a notion opens the door to the notion of multiple incarnations. If the Second Person of the Blessed Trinity united His divine nature with a human nature, why couldn't He do so with other intelligent corporeal natures if they existed? The reason He couldn't is because the union between Christ's two natures is so complete that it demands uniqueness if it is not to contradict itself. The very essence of the union excludes any additional unions with other rational corporeal natures, as if the Word were the Hindu god Vishnu with his various avatars. Consider that Jesus Christ is an individual substance and that each such union would also be an individual substance, but all would be the same Person! So the idea that the Word of God would have multiple incarnations is as senseless as the idea of a human being sharing his personhood among a number of human bodies. Or, if there were other rational corporeal natures, and He took on only one of them, why would he have taken on a human nature rather than some other? St. Paul affirmed the uniqueness of Christ. For he wrote that it was Christ whom God sent *"to reconcile to himself **all things, whether on earth or in heaven**, making peace by the blood of his cross."*[43]

Also, consider that Mary holds the titles Queen of the Universe, Queen of Angels. If she is the queen of angels, the highest of creatures, then she is queen of all creatures. If there were other rational corporeal creatures, then she would be their queen too. If other rational species did exist, there would probably be millions of them, considering the immensity of the universe. Then, indeed, we would be members of a highly favored species to have one of us chosen to be the Queen of the Universe!

Man's Preeminence as God's Manifestation of Himself in the World

St. Peter Chrysologus, the "golden-worded," eloquently sums up the eminence of man in creation. He reproves those who devalue man and declares that God created the universe for the sake of man. He points out that God reveals Himself in man as His image and His representative in the world:

Why then, man, are you so worthless in your own eyes and yet so precious to God? Why render yourself such dishonor when you are honored by him? Why do you ask how you were created and do not seek to know why you were made? Was not this entire visible universe made for your dwelling? It was for you that the light dispelled the overshadowing gloom; for your sake was the night regulated and the day measured; and for you were the heavens embellished with the varying brilliance of the sun, the moon and the stars. The earth was adorned with flowers, groves and fruit; and the constant marvelous variety of lovely living things was created in the air, the fields, and the seas for you, lest sad solitude destroy the joy of God's new creation. And the Creator still works to devise new things that can add to your glory. He has made you in his image that you might in your person make the invisible Creator present on earth; he has made you his legate, so that the vast empire of the world might have the Lord's representative.[44]

Chrysologus goes on to say that God did much more than place His image as representative in the world. In Jesus Christ God fully revealed Himself in man, His creature, not merely as an image but in reality:

Then in his mercy God assumed what he made in you; he wanted to be truly manifest in man, just as he had wished to be revealed in man as in an image. Now he would be in reality what he had submitted to be in symbol.
And so Christ is born that by his birth he might restore our nature.[45]

The Creator brought great dignity to the human species by manifesting Himself in the man Jesus Christ. This He did without any loss of His own dignity:

He who made man without generation from pure clay made man again and was born from a pure body. The hand that assumed clay to make our flesh deigned to assume a body for our salvation. That the Creator is in his creature and God is in the flesh brings dignity to man without dishonor to him who made him.[46]

[1] DZ, no. 1805. See Ps 19:1 and Prv 16:4. Also, see Doctrine Three, God's Motive for Creating.

[2] CCC, no. 358.

[3] GS, no. 24, as quoted in CCC, no. 356.

[4] Gn 1:26–29. Ps 8:3–8. Ps 115:16. Is 45:18. CCC, no. 373.

[5] CCC, no. 358.

[6] Ex 20:3 ff; Dt 5:7 ff.

[7] GS, no 57.

[8] *Evangelium vitae*, no. 42.

[9] Ibid. Quotations are from other documents written by John Paul II.

[10] CCC, no. 377.

[11] ST, Part I, Q. 96, A. 3.

[12] ST, Part I, Q. 96, A. 4.

[13] Also see discussions about animals in Doctrine Three, << Animal Suffering >>; Doctrine Nine, << Human Evolution: Materialistic Version >>; and Doctrine Ten, The Aloneness of Adam.

[14] Fabre, J. Henri, *The Wonders of Instinct: Chapters in the Psychology of Insects* (Honolulu: University Press of the Pacific, 2002), reprinted from 1922 edition.

[15] Lorenz, Konrad, *On Aggression* (New York: Harcourt and Brace Co., 1966), p. 210.

[16] ACC, pp. 40–41.

[17] ST, Part I, Q. 96, A. 1.

[18] Ibid., Reply Objs. 3, 4.

[19] ST, Part I, Q. 96, A. 2.

[20] Dt 4:19 (DR).

[21] BV, Part II, Chapter 4.5.

[22] CCC, no. 2293.

[23] Rom 8:20.

[24] NB, commentary on Rom 8:19–21.

[25] Address on Jubilee of Scientists, 25 May 2000. Also see Rom 1:20, which he cites in this talk.

[26] Burtt, Edwin Arthur, *The Metaphysical Foundations of Modern Science* (Garden City, NY: Doubleday, 1954), p. 18.

[27] Ibid., p. 19.

[28] Ibid.

[29] Ibid., p. 20.

[30] Ibid.

[31] *Paradise,* Canto I, 1–3; Canto XXXIII, 142–145, trans. by Mark Musa (New York: Penguin Books, 1986).

[32] For a balanced account of the Galileo controversy see Koestler, Arthur, *The Sleepwalkers: A History of Man's Changing Vision of the Universe* (New York: Penguin Books, 1989 reprint). For another enlightening examination of the issue see Rowland, Wade, *Galileo's Mistake* (New York: Arcade, 2001).

[33] From a letter to Fr. Foscarini, as quoted by Koestler, op. cit., p. 455; italics are Koestler's.

[34] See Einstein, Albert and Infeld, Leopold, *The Evolution of Physics: from Early Concepts to Relativity and Quanta* (New York: Simon and Schuster, 1938), p. 212.

[35] Burtt, op. cit., pp. 123–124.

[36] *A Free Man's Worship (Mysticism and Logic)* New York, 1918, p. 46, as quoted by Burtt, op. cit., p. 23.

[37] Burtt, op. cit., p. 24.

[38] John Paul II, op. cit.

[39] For a detailed discussion of fifty answers to Fermi's question see Webb, Stephen, *Where is Everybody? Fifty Solutions to the Fermi Paradox and the Problem of Extraterrestrial Life* (New York: Copernicus, 2002). The proposed solutions range from "they are already here" to "they do not exist."

[40] Lewis, C. S., "Religion and Rocketry," *The World's Last Night and Other Essays* (New York: Harcourt Brace, 1987).

[41] Ibid., p. 88.

[42] Ibid., p. 92.

[43] Col 1:20. Emphasis added.

[44] From a sermon by St. Peter Chrysologus in the Office of Readings for July 30, *The Liturgy of the Hours According to the Roman Rite,* Vol. III, (New York: Catholic Book Publishing Co., 1976), pp. 1563–1564.

[45] Ibid., p. 1564.

[46] Ibid., p. 1563.

Doctrine Twelve
God created the first man and woman
in a state of happiness and innocence.

According to Scripture and Tradition, God created the first human beings with many unspoiled natural gifts and with the preternatural gifts of freedom from suffering, infused knowledge, absence of concupiscence, and bodily immortality. The Church has many times formally affirmed the original immortality of the first man. Further, the Church formally decreed that God established the first man in holiness and justice. This picture is in sharp contrast with that given us by evolutionists, who depict the first humans as primitive creatures ascending by degrees from bestiality.

The Garden of Eden

Genesis 2:8–14 gives a brief description of the Garden of Eden. The similar sounding Hebrew word *eden* means "delight." So is might be called the "garden of delight." It is also called *Paradise*, which is Greek for "Pleasure Park." The climate of the garden was mild, allowing *"every tree that is pleasant to the sight and good for food"* (2:9) to grow, and there were pleasant variations of temperature in the day (3:8). Adam and Eve had no need for clothing to protect them against the elements (2:25). A river flowed out of Eden to water the garden, and there it divided and became four rivers: the Pishon, the Gihon, the Tigris and the Euphrates.[a] The Pishon river flowed around the whole land of Havilah, where there were gold and semiprecious stones. The Gihon flowed around the whole land of Cush and the Tigris flowed east of Assyria.[b] Since the rivers flowed out of Eden, the land of Eden was elevated.[c] Adam and Eve probably had a spectacular view of the neighboring lowlands from the garden. The description given in Genesis of Eden and its environs is probably Adam's own, considering that the verses 11–14 are written in the present tense. Also, at the time of the writing Adam was probably living west of Eden, where he could see the sun rise out of the garden each morning.[d] The garden was a well-known location to antediluvian people, but its location was completely washed out by the Flood. There is no hint in Scripture or Tradition about where the Garden of Eden was located. It could have been located anywhere on the earth. Fossil evidence seems to indicate that the climate of the whole world was once temperate.[1] In addition to favorable temperatures,[e] there was a tranquil hydrological system before the Flood, which may have employed pressurized underground water. Scripture tells us *a mist went up from the earth and watered the whole face of the ground* (2:6). Rain falling and cold weather are not mentioned before the Flood account; and storms, snow, hail, and lightning are not mentioned at all in Genesis 1–11.

The Orthodox mystic, Gregory the Sinaite, recorded his vision of the Garden of Eden, a place in which there is transformation without decay:

Eden is a place in which there was planted by God every kind of fragrant plant. It is neither completely incorruptible, nor entirely corruptible. Placed

---

a. The latter two must not be confused with the Tigris and Euphrates rivers that flow though modern Iraq. Those are postdiluvian rivers that were named after the original ones. The Euphrates is the largest river in western Asia. The Tigris is important for its irrigation capacity. Both sustained early civilizations after the Flood. Many ancient cities were built on their banks. The rivers are not far from Mount Ararat, where Noah's Ark landed. Noah probably named them himself, and, because of their importance, named them after two of the four great rivers of the antediluvian world. Some of the Fathers, thinking that these rivers still exist, identified the Pishon with the Danube of Europe or the Ganges of India, the Gehon with the Nile of Egypt and the Tigris and Euphrates with the Mesopotamian rivers. See selections from St. Ephrem, St. Ambrose, and St. John of Damascus in ACC, pp. 56–58.

b. The original Cush and Assyria were antediluvian lands. Postdiluvian Cush, the biblical name for Ethiopia, was named after the original Cush. Likewise, the postdiluvian Mesopotamian land of Assyria was named after the original Assyria. Since the Flood completely reshaped the surface of the earth, there is probably no geographical connection between the postdiluvian lands and their antediluvian counterparts.

between corruption and incorruption, it is always both abundant in fruits and blossoming with flowers, both mature and immature. The mature trees and fruits are converted into fragrant earth which does not give off any odor of corruption, as do the trees of this world. This is from the abundance of the grace of sanctification which is constantly poured forth there.[2]

In the garden God planted two special trees: the tree of life and the tree of the knowledge of good and evil. Perhaps each was not an individual tree but a kind of tree. There is no good reason to believe that these trees were not real.[f] The tree of life could very well have provided the nutrients needed for physical immortality, which God made unavailable to man after the Fall. (3:24). Both St. Augustine and St. Thomas Aquinas held that the tree of life was a cause of immortality because its fruit warded off bodily corruption that occurs with aging.[3] A literal interpretation is not excluded by modern medical science, which knows next to nothing about the aging process. The tree of the knowledge of good and evil had tempting fruit (3:6) that God used to test Adam's and Eve's obedience.

Genesis need not be interpreted as saying that God made Adam first and then planted the garden afterwards because that is the sequence in which they are mentioned. St. Augustine points out, "the narrative, without mentioning it, refers to previous events that had been left unmentioned."[4] The wording for the planting of the garden is such than it can be interpreted in either temporal sequence. But it makes more sense to say that the garden was planted before

---

c. Some Fathers mention the garden as being elevated. St. Ephrem said that Paradise was "set on a great height" (ACC, p. 56). St. John Chrysostom said that it was on a "high tableland" (ACC, p. 59). St. Cyprian saw Paradise as representing the Church and the waters flowing from it as representing the grace of baptism (ACC, p. 59).

d. Adam probably lived east of Eden immediately after Fall because God placed cherubim east of the garden to guard entrance to it (3:24). However, he probably migrated to the west of the garden because he refers to the garden as being in the eastern part of the world (2:8). St. Basil the Great said, "We all look toward the East when we pray; but few know that it is because we are looking for our own former country, Paradise, which God planted in Eden in the East" (JR, no. 954a).

e. Some attribute this to a vapor canopy surrounding the earth that acted like the windows of a greenhouse. See, for example, Joseph C. Dillow, *The Waters Above: Earth's Pre-Flood Vapor Canopy* (Chicago: Moody Press, 1982). The author considers the proposed antediluvian vapor canopy from an exegetical and scientific viewpoint.

Adam was created and is mentioned after his creation because it was created for him. It seems that God would have had the world completely prepared for Adam's arrival, just as a mother would have the nursery completely prepared for her baby's arrival. St. Thomas Aquinas argued that man was created outside of Paradise and then placed there by God so that man's incorruptibility "might be attributed to God [as a supernatural gift], and not to human nature."[5]

St. Augustine says that a number of interpreters give a symbolic meaning to the whole of Paradise.[6] He recalls that St. Paul did the same with the stories of Sarah and Hagar[7] and the rock struck by Moses[8] without denying their historical reality. He goes on to give his own allegorical interpretation of Paradise saying, "There is no prohibition against such exegesis, provided we also believe in the truth of the story as a faithful record of historical fact":[9]

> And so no one can stop us from interpreting paradise symbolically as the life of the blessed; its four rivers as the four virtues, prudence, courage, temperance, and justice; its trees as all the beneficial disciplines; the fruit of the trees as the character of the righteous; the tree of life as wisdom, the mother of all good things; and the tree of knowledge of good and evil as the experience of disobedience to a commandment. For it was certainly a good thing, because it was just, that God should have imposed a punishment for sinners; but it is not a good thing for man himself that he experiences it.
>
> We can also interpret the details of paradise with reference to the Church, which gives them a better significance as prophetic indications of things to come in the future. Thus paradise stands for the Church itself, as described in the *Song of Songs*, (4:12 ff.) the four rivers represent the four Gospels; the fruit trees, the saints; and the fruit, their achievements; the tree of life, the Holy of Holies, must be Christ himself; while the tree of knowledge of good and evil symbolizes the personal decision of man's free will.[10]

---

f.   Besides having been real, the trees are types. The tree of life is a type of the Eucharist. As the tree of life nourished and preserved natural life, the Eucharist nourishes and preserves supernatural life. The tree of knowledge is a type of the Cross of Christ. The tree of knowledge tested Adam's obedience and he fell. The Cross tested Christ's obedience and He conquered. (An ancient popular legend relates that Christ's Cross was made from the wood of the tree of the knowledge of good and evil. For details see Dante, *Purgatory*, trans. by Mark Musa (New York: Penguin Books, 1985), Notes on Canto XXXII, 49–51, pp. 350–351.)

The Preternatural Gifts

Besides natural gifts like perfect bodies, an abundant variety of food and drink, and pleasant weather, God gave Adam and Eve certain other gifts. These were the gifts of freedom from suffering, infused knowledge, absence of concupiscence, and bodily immortality. They are called *preternatural gifts* because they are above and beyond the ordinary powers and capacities of human nature. They are also call *gifts of integrity* because they contribute to the uprightness and completeness of the human person. Finally, they are called *relatively supernatural gifts* because they are beyond the nature of man but not beyond created nature in general. For example, infused knowledge is natural for angels, but it is supernatural for human beings.

The Pontifical Biblical Commission in 1909 upheld that Genesis affirms "the original happiness of our first parents in the state of justice, integrity, and immortality."[11]

∗   ∗   ∗   ∗

God gave Adam and Eve a wonderful brand-new earth to live on with many things pleasant to the senses, and He provided for all their bodily and spiritual needs. They lived at first in perfect happiness, free from suffering, as St. Augustine describes:

> Certainly in paradise man lived as he willed to live as long as he willed what God commanded. He lived in the enjoyment of God, from which good he was good. He lived without any want, and had it in his power so to live forever. Food was there, lest he hunger; drink, lest he thirst; the tree of life, lest old age waste him. There was no corruption in his body or from his body to produce anything unpleasant to any of his senses. He feared no disease from within nor any blow from without. In his flesh there was health supreme, and in his soul total tranquility. Just as in paradise there was no excessive heat nor chill, so too in its inhabitants there was no encroachment on good will whether through cupidity or through fear.[12]

St. Bonaventure made the point that the original bodies of Adam and Eve were without pain, even though they were able to suffer. He linked this with the innocence of their souls:

[T]he body was so conformed to the soul that, as the soul was innocent and yet able to fall into sin, so the body was without pain and yet able to fall into suffering.[13]

Adam and Eve had complete peace of mind.[14] There was no fear, no sadness, and perfect love and harmony between man and wife.[15] There was also perfect harmony between the couple and the creatures about them. They were endowed with all the virtues.[16] There was neither boredom nor weariness.

Since poisonous and thorny plants are a threat to the physical integrity of man, St. Augustine said they were created as a result of sin:

> The Manichaeans are accustomed to say, "If God commanded that the edible plants and the fruit trees come forth from the earth, who commanded that there come forth so many thorny or poisonous plants that are useless for food and so many trees that bear no fruit?" ... We should say then that the earth was cursed by reason of the sin of man so that it bears thorns, not that it should suffer punishment since it is without sensation but that it should always set before the eyes of man the judgment upon human sin. Thus men might be admonished by it to turn away from sins and to turn to God's commandments. Poisonous plants were created as a punishment or as a trial for mortals. All this is the result of sin.[17]

But everything that God created is good in itself and created for a good reason. It seems that there were thorns and thistles and poisonous plants before the Fall because they were created for a purpose beneficial to man. Before the Fall these things posed no threat to our first parents' well-being because God provided them with the wherewithal to avoid danger and with His continual protection, as St. Thomas explains:

> Man's body in the state of innocence could be preserved from suffering injury from a hard body; partly by the use of his reason, whereby he could avoid what was harmful; and partly also by Divine Providence, so preserving him, that nothing of a harmful nature could come upon him unawares.[18]

God exercised His providence through their guardian angels.[19]

After the Fall, the thorns and thistles interfered with Adam's farming (3:18). But that is not why God created them.

*   *   *   *

Adam enjoyed excellence in intelligence and knowledge. St. Cyril of Alexandria held that he was created perfected in both:

> Our forefather Adam does not seem to have progressed gradually in wisdom as is the case with us, but immediately and from the very first days of his existence he is found perfected in intelligence, preserving in himself the enlightenment given him by God still unsullied and pure, and having the dignity of his nature still unadulterated.[20]

St. Thomas Aquinas said that Adam had knowledge of all things that he was capable of knowing:

> [A]s the first man was produced in his perfect state, as regards his body, for the work of generation, so also was his soul established in a perfect state to instruct and govern others.
>
> Now no one can instruct others unless he has knowledge, and so the first man was established by God in such a manner as to have knowledge of all those things for which man has a natural aptitude. And such are whatever are virtually contained in the first self-evident principles, that is, whatever truths man is naturally able to know. Moreover, in order to direct his own life and that of others, man needs to know not only those things which can be naturally known, but also things surpassing natural knowledge; because the life of man is directed to a supernatural end: just as it is necessary for us to know the truths of faith in order to direct our own lives. Wherefore the first man was endowed with such a knowledge of these supernatural truths as was necessary for the direction of human life in that state. But those things which cannot be known by merely human effort, and which are not necessary for the direction of human life, were not known by the first man; such as the thoughts of men, future contingent events, and some individual facts, as for instance the number of pebbles in a stream; and the like.[21]

But he still had the joy of learning new things:

> Adam would have advanced in natural knowledge, not in the number of things known, but in the manner of knowing; because what he knew speculatively he would subsequently have known by experience. But as regards supernatural knowledge, he would also have advanced as regards the number of

things known, by further revelation; as the angels advance by further enlightenment.[22]

*   *   *   *

Sacred Scripture suggests that there was perfect harmony in our first parents between reason and sensuality: *"And the man and his wife were both naked, and were not ashamed"* (2:25). God gifted them with free will and tempered all their emotions and appetites so as to be subject, at all times, to the dictates of reason.[23] All the Fathers believed that Adam and Eve were free from concupiscence (irregular desire) in the garden. But they differed as to how this freedom was exercised. Some of the Fathers believed that Adam and Eve lived in the garden like sexless beings. For example, St. John Chrysostom said they "lived like angels, and there was no talk of cohabitation."[24] St. John Damascene wrote that virginity was practiced in Paradise and that if there were no Fall, God may have used means other than sexual intercourse to increase the numbers of the human species:

> But they may ask, What then, does *"male and female"* mean, and *"increase and multiply"*? To which we shall reply that the *"increase and multiply"* does not mean increasing by the marriage union exclusively, because if they had kept the commandment unbroken for ever, God could have increased the race by some other means. But since God, Who knows all things before they come to be, saw by His foreknowledge how they were to fall and be condemned to death, He made provision beforehand by creating them male and female and commanding them to increase and multiply.[25]

St. Thomas cites St. Gregory of Nyssa as holding a similar position and says that it is unreasonable:

> Thus Gregory of Nyssa says … that in paradise the human race would have been multiplied by some other means, as the angels were multiplied without coition by the operation of the Divine Power. He adds that God made man male and female before sin, because He foreknew the mode of generation which would take place after sin, which He foresaw. But this is unreasonable. For what is natural to man was neither acquired nor forfeited by sin.[26]

St. Augustine, however, believed that there would have been sexual union if the Fall had not taken place, but it would have been free of lust:

When mankind was in a state of ease and plenty, blest with such felicity, let us never imagine that it was impossible for the seed of children to be sown without the morbid condition of lust. Instead, the sexual organs would have been brought into activity by the same bidding of the will as controlled the other organs.... the two sexes might have been united by an act of will, instead of by a lustful craving.[27]

St. Thomas cites Augustine as saying that "our first parents did not come together in paradise, because on account of sin they were ejected from paradise shortly after the creation of the woman; or because, having received the general Divine command relative to generation, they awaited the special command relative to time."[28]

Aquinas concurs with Augustine's interpretation:

Beasts are without reason. In this way man becomes, as it were, like them in coition, because he cannot moderate concupiscence. In the state of innocence nothing of this kind would have happened that was not regulated by reason, not because delight of sense was less, as some say (rather indeed would sensible delight have been the greater in proportion to the greater purity of nature and the greater sensibility of the body), but because the force of concupiscence would not have so inordinately thrown itself into such pleasure, being curbed by reason, whose place it is not to lessen sensual pleasure, but to prevent the force of concupiscence from cleaving to it immoderately. By "immoderately" I mean going beyond the bounds of reason, as a sober person does not take less pleasure in food taken in moderation than the glutton, but his concupiscence lingers less in such pleasures. This is what Augustine means by the words quoted, which do not exclude intensity of pleasure from the state of innocence, but ardor of desire and restlessness of the mind. Therefore continence would not have been praiseworthy in the state of innocence, whereas it is praiseworthy in our present state, not because it removes fecundity, but because it excludes inordinate desire. In that state fecundity would have been without lust.[29]

*   *   *   *

St. Theophilus of Antioch said that God created man neither mortal nor immortal by nature. He made man capable of both, and man himself made the choice:

Someone, however, will say to us, "Was man made by nature immortal?" Certainly not. "Was he, then, immortal?" Neither do we say that. But someone will say, "Was he, then, made nothing?" Not so, I reply. By nature, in fact, he was made neither mortal nor immortal. For if God had made him immortal from the beginning, He would have made him God. Again, if He had made him mortal, it would seem as if God were the cause of his death. He made him, then, neither mortal nor immortal, but, as we said above, capable of either. Thus, if he should incline to the ways of immortality, keeping the command of God, he should receive from God the reward of immortality, and become God. If, however, he turn aside to the ways of death, disobeying God, he should become for himself the cause of death. For God made man free and self-determining.[30]

St. Augustine echoed that viewpoint, adding that the tree of life provided immortality:

For Adam, before he sinned, can be said to have had a body that was in one way mortal, but in another way immortal. His body was mortal, because it was able to die; but it was immortal because it was also able not to die. It is one thing not to be able to die, like certain immortal natures God created; but it is another thing to be able not to die, which is the way in which the first man was created immortal. This was provided him by the tree of life, and not by the constitution of his own nature. When he sinned he was separated from that tree, so that he was able to die, who, if he had not sinned, had been able not to die. He was mortal, therefore, by the condition of his living body, but immortal by the kindness of the Creator.[31]

It is impossible to conceive of a world before the Fall in which there were no dangers to man's life and limb. For example, fire still had the nature of fire, and man's body was material so it could be destroyed by fire. Physical immortality does not mean that our first parents' bodies were incapable of destruction, just as Mary's sinlessness does not mean that she was incapable of sin. It means that God preserved Adam and Eve from physical harm and bodily corruption just as He preserved Mary from sin. He preserved them from physical harm by divine providence and from bodily corruption through a special gift He gave to their souls. St. Thomas clearly explains that man was not incorruptible because his body had a disposition to incorruptibility, but because in his soul there was a power preserving the body from corruption:

For man's body was indissoluble not by reason of any intrinsic vigor of immortality, but by reason of a supernatural force given by God to the soul, whereby it was enabled to preserve the body from all corruption so long as it remained itself subject to God. This entirely agrees with reason; for since the rational soul surpasses the capacity of corporeal matter, as above explained (Q. 76, A. 1), it was most properly endowed at the beginning with the power of preserving the body in a manner surpassing the capacity of corporeal matter.[32]

He later states, "The promised reward of the immortality of glory differs from the immortality which was bestowed on man in the state of innocence."[33] In the state of glory, the body, although corruptible by nature, will have "an inherent disposition which preserves it wholly from corruption."[34]

The Church has many times affirmed the original immortality of Adam.[35]

The Supernatural Gifts

The *supernatural* (in an absolute sense) transcends the nature of creatures; no created nature has a claim to it. It is superadded to nature by God, and it presupposes a created nature because it exists in one. Therefore, the supernatural is not a substance but an accident; and it perfects the nature in which it operates because it affects the nature intrinsically by elevating it to the divine order of being and activity.

The greatest gift that God bestowed on our first parents was the supernatural gift of sanctifying grace, which is the gift of supernatural life that made them children of God[36] and heirs to heaven. God created Adam and Eve in a state of innocence and holiness, which made them pleasing to God and full of love for Him. In Paradise Adam and Eve enjoyed an intimacy with God that was greater than any prophet, including Moses, was granted. The Council of Trent (1546) affirmed that Adam was "established" in "holiness" and "justice," but left the question undecided as to *when* he was established in grace.[37] St. Thomas Aquinas and the Dominican school had held that our first parents were established in sanctifying grace at creation.[38] Peter Lombard and the Franciscan school had held that they were first given actual grace to help them prepare themselves for the reception of sanctifying grace.[39]

The Church teaches that the justice of Adam was not a consequence of creation or due to nature itself,[40] that God could have created man without supernatural grace,[41] and that to preserve the original state man needed grace.[42]

Vatican Council I affirmed that God conferred a supernatural destiny on man:

God in His infinite goodness has ordained man for a supernatural end, to participation, namely, in the divine goods which altogether surpass the understanding of the human mind since *"eye hath not seen, nor ear heard, neither
hath it entered into the heart of man, what things God hath prepared for them
that love him"* (1 Cor 2:9).[43]

The natural end of man is to know, love and serve God with his natural powers. His supernatural end is to enjoy eternal life with God in heaven. His nature
transformed by supernatural grace is directed to that ultimate goal. St. Augustine
describes how the transition from natural happiness to eternal glory would have
taken place if our first parents had not sinned:

> How fortunate, then, were the first human beings! They were not distressed
> by any agitations of the mind, nor pained by any disorders of the body. And
> equally fortunate would be the whole united fellowship of mankind if our first
> parents had not committed an evil deed whose effect was to be passed on to
> their posterity, and if none of their descendants had sown in wickedness a crop
> that they were to reap in condemnation. Moreover, this felicity would have
> continued until, thanks to the blessing pronounced in the words, *"Increase and
> multiply,"* (Gn 1:28) the number of the predestined saints was made up; and
> then another and a greater happiness would have been granted, the happiness
> which has been given to the blessed angels. In this state of bliss there would
> have been the serene assurance that no one would sin and no one would die,
> and the life of the saints, without any previous experience of toil, or pain, or
> death, would have been already what it is now destined to become after all
> these experiences, when our bodies are restored to incorruptibility at the resur-
> rection of the dead.[44]

St. John Damascene describes the divinization of man that would then take
place:

> He made him a living being to be governed here according to this present life,
> and then to be removed elsewhere, that is, to the world to come, and so to
> complete the mystery by becoming Divine through reversion to God—this,
> however, not by being transformed into the Divine substance, but by partici-
> pating in the Divine illumination.[45]

Man's life in Paradise, then, was a preparation for eternal life. Our first parents
were able to merit supernatural reward, that is, greater enjoyment of God, by
their acts.[46] The Church teaches that such merit was not merely human and natural.[47]

The *Catechism of the Catholic Church* sums up our first parents' supernatural endowment as follows:

> The Church, interpreting the symbolism of biblical language in an authentic way, in the light of the New Testament and Tradition, teaches that our first parents, Adam and Eve, were constituted in an original "state of holiness and justice." (Cf. Council of Trent, DZ, no. 788) This grace of original holiness was "to share in ... divine life." (Cf. LG, no. 2)[48]

The CCC continues saying that the gift of grace influenced every aspect of the lives of our first parents:

> By the radiance of this grace all dimensions of man's life were confirmed. As long as he remained in the divine intimacy, man would not have to suffer or die. (Cf. Gn 2:17; 3:16, 19) The inner harmony of the human person, the harmony between man and woman, (Cf. Gn 2:25) and finally the harmony between the first couple and all creation, comprised the state called *original justice*.[49]

Man's Work in the Garden

It is obvious from its construction that God designed the human body for work. The capacity for and availability of work is a gift from God. Through his work, man cooperates with God in shaping creation and exercises his dominion over it. Symeon the New Theologian points out that man was created with a nature inclined to work:

> In the beginning man was created with a nature inclined to work, for in paradise Adam was enjoined to till the ground and care for it, and there is in us a natural bent for work, the movement toward the good. Those who yield themselves to idleness and apathy, even though they may be spiritual and holy, hurl themselves into unnatural subjection to passions.[50]

God provided work for the benefit of man; He did not create man for work:

> In work, the person exercises and fulfills in part the potential inscribed in his nature. The primordial value of labor stems from man himself, its author and its beneficiary. Work is for man, not man for work. (Cf. Pope John Paul II, *Laborem exercens*, no. 6)[51]

St. Thomas Aquinas, following Augustine, says God gave man work in Paradise so that He might work in man, to sanctify man, and to give man pleasure:

> As Augustine says ... these words in Genesis [Gn 2:15] may be understood in two ways. First, in the sense that God placed man in paradise that He might Himself work in man and keep him, by sanctifying him (for if this work cease, man at once relapses into darkness, as the air grows dark when the light ceases to shine); and by keeping man from all corruption and evil. Secondly, that man might dress and keep paradise, which dressing would not have involved labor, as it did after sin; but would have been pleasant on account of man's practical knowledge of the powers of nature. Nor would man have kept paradise against a trespasser; but he would have striven to keep paradise for himself lest he should lose it by sin. All of which was for man's good; wherefore paradise was ordered to man's benefit, and not conversely.[52]

The CCC points out that work in Paradise was not a burden but collaboration with God in perfecting visible creation:

> The sign of man's familiarity with God is that God places him in the garden. (Cf. Gn 2:8) There he lives "to till it and keep it." Work is not yet a burden, (Gn 2:15; cf. 3:17–19) but rather the collaboration of man and woman with God in perfecting the visible creation.[53]

By "conscientious work ... man participates in the good of others and of society."[54] The CCC further points out that work is a duty:

> *Human work* proceeds directly from persons created in the image and likeness of God and called to prolong the work of creation by subduing the earth, both with and for one another. (Cf. Gn 1:28; GS, no. 34; Pope John Paul II, *Centesimus annus*, no. 31) Hence work is a duty: *"If anyone will not work, let him not eat."* (2 Thes 3:10; cf. 1 Thes 4:11) Work honors the Creator's gifts and the talents received from him.[55]

> Everyone should be able to draw from work the means of providing for his life and that of his family, and of serving the human community.[56]

The Beginning and the End

Isaiah prophesied: *"I am God, there is no other; I am God, there is none like me. At the beginning I foretell the outcome; in advance, things not yet done. I say that my plan shall stand, I accomplish my every purpose."*[57] This verse shows that God has a master plan for creation that is being fulfilled in its history. The end is already there at the beginning because it is the reason for the beginning. D. Kidner picks up this theme in his commentary on the opening words of Genesis, summarizing it in the words, "The beginning is pregnant with the end":

> The opening expression, *In the beginning*, is more than a bare note of time. The variations on this theme in Isaiah 40 ff. show that the beginning is pregnant with the end, and the whole process present to God who is First and Last (e.g., Is 46:10; 48:12). Proverbs 8:22 f. reveals something of the Godward side of the beginning of creation; John 1:1–3 is more explicit; and the New Testament elsewhere at times reaches back behind it (e.g., Jn 17:5, 24) into eternity.[58]

There are allusions to the end in the beginning and allusions to the beginning in the end. There are striking similarities between the beginning and the end, and there are striking dissimilarities between the beginning and the end.

*　　　*　　　*　　　*

The Old Testament prophets compare life in the messianic era to the peaceful, loving life in Paradise. For example, Hosea tells of the restoration of harmony between man and man and man and beast:

> *And I will make for you a covenant on that day with the beasts of the field, the birds of the air, and the creeping things of the ground; and I will abolish the bow, the sword, and war from the land; and I will make you lie down in safety.*[59]

Isaiah tells of the paradisal tranquility and harmony in the messianic kingdom in this famous passage:

> *The wolf shall dwell with the lamb, and the leopard shall lie down with the kid, and the calf and the lion and the fatling together, and a little child shall lead them. The cow and the bear shall feed; their young shall lie down together; and the lion shall eat straw like the ox. The suckling child shall play over the hole of the asp, and the weaned child shall put his hand on the adder's den. They shall not hurt or destroy in all my holy mountain; for the earth shall be full of the knowledge of the* LORD *as the waters cover the sea.*[60]

The Book of Revelation says that that period of peace will come on earth before the end and last for a thousand years:

Then I saw an angel coming down from heaven, holding in his hand the key of the bottomless pit and a great chain. And he seized the dragon, that ancient serpent, who is the devil and Satan, and bound him for a thousand years, and threw him into the pit, and shut and sealed it over him, that he should deceive the nations no more, till the thousand years were ended. After that he must be loosed for a while.[61]

The Holy Office in 1944 decreed that Chiliasm, which states that Christ will rule visibly on earth before the final judgment, cannot be taught safely.[62] But there is good reason to believe that there will be a great era of peace on earth before the end of time. Fr. Joseph Iannuzzi[63] argues from Sacred Scripture, the writings of the Fathers and Doctors of the Church, and from the teachings of Magisterium that there will be a flowering of Christ's kingdom on earth before the end times that will last for a period of time, not necessarily a literal thousand years, during which Christ will reign gloriously on earth, not visibly, but in the Eucharist. During this period he says:

> The temporal kingdom, therefore, will have at its core, in the hearts and souls of all its faithful, the glorious Person of Christ Jesus who will shine forth above all in the triumph of his Eucharistic Person. The Eucharist will become the summit of all humanity, extending its rays of light to all the nations. The Eucharistic heart of Jesus, dwelling in their midst, will thus cultivate in the faithful a spirit of intense adoration and worship never before seen.[64]

Perhaps this is the era of peace promised by Our Lady of Fatima, and perhaps the spread of perpetual Eucharistic adoration that we are witnessing heralds its approach!

*   *   *   *

St. Gregory of Nyssa wrote that at the resurrection the bodies of the just will be changed into that which was at the beginning:

> We learn from Scripture in the account of the first creation that first the earth brought forth *"the green herb"* (as the narrative says), and then from this plant seed was yielded, from which, when it was shed on the ground, the same form of the original plant sprang up. The [A]postle, it is to be observed, declares that this very same thing happens in the resurrection also. And so we learn from him the fact not only that our humanity will then be changed into something nobler but also that what we have therein to expect is nothing else than that which was at the beginning.[65]

The resurrection promises us nothing else than the restoration of the fallen to their ancient state; for the grace we look for is a certain return to the first life, bringing back again to paradise those who were cast out from it. If then the life of those restored is closely related to that of the angels, it is clear that the life before the transgression was a kind of angelic life, and hence also our return to the ancient condition of life is compared to the angels.[66]

St. Augustine had a different view. He said that the flesh of the risen just will be restored to a better state that that of our first parents before they sinned. He goes so far as to say that their spiritualized bodies will have no need of physical nourishment:

We will be restored, therefore, from the long duration of sin, not to the pristine living body in which Adam was, but to a better, that is, to a spiritual body, when we are made equal to God's angels (Mt 22:30), suited to a heavenly dwelling place, where we will have no need of victuals that perish. We shall be renewed, therefore, in the spirit of our mind (Eph 4:23), in accord with the image of Him who created us, which Adam lost by sinning.[67]

Not only will the body be different from the body as it is now even when in perfect health, it will not even be such as it was in the first human beings, before their sin. For though they would not have been destined to die, if they had not sinned, still, as human beings, they took nourishment, since the bodies they bore were not yet spiritual but animal, still bodies of earth.[68]

The bodies of the righteous, after the resurrection, will not need any tree to preserve them against death from disease or from extreme old age, nor any material nourishment to prevent any kind of distress from hunger or thirst. This is because they will be endowed with the gift of assured and inviolable immortality, and so they will eat only if they wish to eat; eating for them will be a possibility, not a necessity.[69]

The bodies of the risen just "will be spiritual, not by ceasing to be bodies, but by being supported in their existence by a life-giving spirit."[70] "The first man, however, was 'of the earth, earthly', and he was made as a 'living soul', not a 'life-giving spirit'; (cf. 1 Cor 15:47, 45) that condition was reserved for him after he merited it by obedience."[71] "The body will thus be related to the life-giving spirit as it is now to the living soul."[72]

St. Thomas summarizes the difference between the spirituality of our first parents and the spirituality of the elect:

In paradise man would have been like an angel in his spirituality of mind, yet with an animal life in his body. After the resurrection man will be like an angel, spiritualized in soul and body.[73]

He also says that Adam and Eve did not enjoy the Beatific Vision, as do the elect:

Man was happy in paradise, but not with that perfect happiness to which he was destined, which consists in the vision of the Divine Essence.[74]

Neither were they able to see the angels in their essence, as can the elect, because their souls' "connatural object [of knowledge] fell short of the excellence of separate substances."[75]

Traditional Catholic theology holds that the risen bodies of the elect will have four properties that they do not now possess, according to the pattern of the risen body of Christ. First, they will not be subject to death, corruption, pain, disease, hunger, thirst, fatigue or suffering of any kind. (*impassibility*). "*He will wipe away every tear from their eyes, and death shall be no more, neither shall there be mourning nor crying nor pain any more, for the former things have passed away.*"[76] Second, they will be able to move from place to place at the speed of thought (*agility*). Third, there will be no obstacles to their movement from place to place (*subtility* or *spirituality*). Recall how Jesus appeared to His disciples in the upper room while the doors were closed and bolted. Fourth, the beauty of their souls will shine through their bodies with brilliance proportionate to their merits (*radiance* or *brightness* or *clarity*). "*Then the righteous will shine like the sun in the kingdom of their Father.*"[77] A preview of this was given on Mt. Tabor when Jesus' body was transfigured. The bodies of Adam and Eve enjoyed only the first property, and even then it was given through the special providence of God and not through the spiritualized nature of their bodies. Because of the absence of concupiscence, the elect will be able to gaze on each other's bodies with pleasure but without lust, just as Adam and Eve were able to do before the Fall.

*   *   *   *

The present world will be destroyed on the last day. This was predicted in Psalms 102:

Of old thou didst lay the foundations of the earth, and the heavens are the work of thy hands. They will perish, but thou dost endure; they will all wear out like a garment. Thou changest them like raiment, and they pass away; but thou art the same, and thy years have no end.[78]

The prophet Isaiah echoes this:

All the hosts of heaven shall rot away, and the skies roll up like a scroll. All their hosts shall fall, as leaves fall from the vine, like leaves falling from the fig tree.[79]

Lift up your eyes to the heavens, and look to the earth beneath; for the heavens will vanish like smoke, and the earth will wear out like a garment.[80]

Christ confirms it:

Immediately after the tribulation of those days the sun will be darkened, and the moon will not give its light, and the stars will fall from heaven, and the powers of the heavens will be shaken. [81]

St. Paul said, *"the form of this world is passing away."*[82]

And St. Peter foretells the destruction of the world by fire:

But the day of the Lord will come like a thief, and then the heavens will pass away with a loud noise, and the elements will be dissolved with fire, and the earth and the works that are upon it will be burned up.[83]

St. John describes the vision he had of the end of the world:

Then I saw a great white throne and him who sat upon it; from his presence earth and sky fled away, and no place was found for them.[84]

St. Augustine comments on the preceding verse. He points out that the event described happened after the final judgment and that the universe was transformed and not annihilated, citing 1 Cor 7:31: "It is, then, the outward form, not the substance, that passes."[85]

The end of the world will be a supernatural event. Pope Pius II in 1459 condemned the notion that "the world should be naturally destroyed."[86]

*   *   *   *

Scripture also says that the world will be restored on the last day. The prophet Isaiah foretold a new heaven and a new earth:

> *For behold I create new heavens and a new earth; and the former things shall not be remembered or come into mind.*[87]

St. Peter, after he predicts the destruction of the world, foretells new heavens and a new earth:

> *But according to his promise we wait for new heavens and a new earth in which righteousness dwells.*[88]

St. John tells of his vision of a new heaven and a new earth:

> *Then I saw a new heaven and a new earth; for the first heaven and the first earth had passed away, and the sea was no more.*[89]

The center of the new universe is new Jersusalem:

> *And I saw the holy city, new Jerusalem, coming down out of heaven from God, prepared as a bride adorned for her husband.*[90]

John, in describing the New Jerusalem, refers back to Paradise with its river and the tree of life:

> *Then he showed me the river of the water of life, bright as crystal, flowing from the throne of God and the Lamb through the middle of the street of the city; also, on either side of the river, the tree of life with its twelve kinds of fruit, yielding its fruit each month; and the leaves of the tree were for the healing of the nations.*[91]

And there will be no need for the light of the sun or the moon:

> *And night shall be no more; they need no light of lamp or sun, for the Lord God will be their light, and they shall reign forever and ever.*[92]

This recalls the first day of Creation Week during which there was light without the sun.

The *Catechism of the Catholic Church*, quoting St. Irenaeus, says the world will be restored to its original state:

> The visible universe, then, is itself destined to be transformed "so that the world itself, restored to its original state, facing no further obstacles, should be at the service of the just," sharing their glorification in the risen Jesus Christ (St. Irenaeus, *Adv. haeres.* 5, 32, 1).[93]

The CCC also says that the new creation in Christ will surpass the original in glory:

> The first man was not only created good, but was also established in friendship with his Creator and in harmony with himself and with the creation around him, in a state that would be surpassed only by the glory of the new creation in Christ.[94]

¹ See Rehwinkel, Alfred M: *The Flood: In the Light of the Bible, Geology and Archaeology* (St. Louis, MO: Concordia, 1951), ch. 1. and Whitcomb, John C. and Morris, Henry M., *The Genesis Flood: The Biblical Record and Its Scientific Implications* (Phillipsburg, NJ: P & R Publishing, 1960), ch. 6.

² As quoted by Rose, Fr. Seraphim, *Genesis, Creation and Early Man: The Orthodox Christian Vision* (Platina, CA: Saint Herman of Alaska Brotherhood, 2000), p. 166.

³ See CG, Book XIII, Chapter 20 and ST, Part I, Q. 97, A. 4.

⁴ ACC, p. 54.

⁵ ST, Part I, Q. 102, A. 4.

⁶ See, for example, the symbolic interpretations by Saints Ambrose, Cyprian and Chrysostom in ACC, pp. 56–59.

⁷ Gal 4:22 ff.

⁸ 1 Cor 10:4.

⁹ CG, Book XIII, Chapter 21.

¹⁰ Ibid.

¹¹ DZ, no. 2123. Also see Wis 2:23.

¹² CG, Book XIV, Chapter 26, as quoted in JR, no. 1762.

¹³ BV, Part II, Chapter 10.5.

¹⁴ See CG, Book XIV, Chapter 10.

¹⁵ See ST, Part I, Q. 95, A. 2.

¹⁶ See ST, Part I, Q. 95, A. 3.

¹⁷ ACC, p. 15.

¹⁸ ST, Part I, Q. 97, A. 2, Reply Obj. 4.

¹⁹ CCC, no. 336.

²⁰ JR, no. 2104.

²¹ ST, Part I, Q. 94, A. 3.

²² Ibid., Reply Obj. 3.

²³ See CCT, p. 29.

²⁴ *Eight Homilies on Genesis* 8:4, as quoted by Rose, op. cit., p. 151.

²⁵ *On the Orthodox Faith*, 4:24, as quoted by Rose, op. sit., p. 152.

²⁶ ST, Part I, Q. 98, A. 2.

²⁷ CG, Book XIV, Chapter 26.

²⁸ ST, Part I, Q. 98, A. 2, Reply Obj. 2.

²⁹ ST, Part I, Q. 98, A. 2, Reply Obj. 3.

³⁰ JR, no. 184.

³¹ JR, no. 1699.

³² ST, Part I, Q. 97, A. 1. Also see ST, Part I, Q. 102, A. 2.

[33] Ibid., Reply Obj. 4.

[34] ST, Part I, Q. 97, A. 1.

[35] See DZ, nos. 101, 175, 788, 793, 1006, 1078, 1517, 2123, 2212.

[36] See DZ, no. 1024.

[37] DZ, no. 788.

[38] See ST, Part I, Q. 95, A.1

[39] See ST, Part I, Q. 95, A. 1, Obj. 4 and OTT, p. 103.

[40] See DZ, nos. 1008, 1023 ff., 1026, 1385 ff.

[41] See DZ, nos. 1021, 1023 f., 1079, 1516 f., 1055.

[42] See DZ, nos. 192, 1001ff.

[43] DZ, no. 1786.

[44] CG, Book XIV, Chapter 10.

[45] *On the Orthodox Faith*, 2, 11–12, as quoted by Rose, op. cit., p. 172.

[46] See ST, Part I, Q. 95, A. 4.

[47] See DZ, nos. 1001 ff., 1007, 1009, 1384.

[48] CCC, no. 375.

[49] CCC, no. 376.

[50] ACC, pp. 60–61.

[51] CCC, no. 2428.

[52] ST, Part I, Q. 102, A. 3.

[53] CCC, no. 378.

[54] CCC, no. 1914.

[55] CCC, no. 2427.

[56] CCC, no. 2428.

[57] Is 46:9–10 (NAB).

[58] Kidner, Derek, *Genesis: An Introduction and Commentary* (Downers Grove, IL: Inter-Varsity Press, 1967), p. 43.

[59] Hos 2:18.

[60] Is 11:6–9. Also see Is 65:25.

[61] Rv 20:1–3.

[62] See DZ, no. 2296 and OTT, p. 475.

[63] Iannuzzi, Joseph, *The Triumph of God's Kingdom in the Millennium and End Times: A Proper Belief from the Truth in Scripture and Church Teachings* (St. John the Evangelist Press: 222 S. Manoa Rd., Havertown, PA 19083, 1999).

[64] Ibid., p. 127.

[65] ACC, p. 23.

[66] ACC, p. 73.

[67] JR, no. 1698.

[68] CG, Book XIII, Chapter 20.

[69] CG, Book XIII, Chapter 22.

[70] Ibid.

[71] CG, Book XIII, Chapter 23.

[72] Ibid.

[73] ST, Part I, Q. 98, A. 2, Reply Obj. 1.

[74] ST, Part I, Q. 94, A. 1, Reply Obj. 1.

[75] ST, Part I, Q. 94, A. 2, Reply Obj. 2.

[76] Rv 21:4.

[77] Mt 13:43.

[78] Ps 102:25–27.

[79] Is 34:4.

[80] Is 51:6.

[81] Mt 24:29. Also see Mt 24:35; 28:20.

[82] 1 Cor 7:31.

[83] 2 Pt 3:10. Also see 2 Pt 3:7, 11–12.

[84] Rv 20:11.

[85] CG, Book XX, Chapter 14.

[86] DZ, no. 717a.

[87] Is 65:17. Also see Is 66:22.

[88] 2 Pt 3:13.

[89] Rv 21:1.

[90] Rv 21:2.

[91] Rv 22:1–2.

[92] Rv 22:5.

[93] CCC, no. 1047.

[94] CCC, no. 374.

Doctrine Thirteen
The first man and woman sinned and lost the state of original happiness and innocence.

Genesis relates that God commanded Adam and Eve not to eat from the tree of the knowledge of good and evil. Eve, seduced by the devil in the form of a serpent, ate and enticed Adam to do so. In 1909 the Pontifical Biblical Commission, following the Fathers of the Church, ruled that "the divine command laid upon man to prove his obedience," "the transgression of that divine command at the instigation of the devil under the form of a serpent," "the fall of our first parents from their primitive state of innocence," and "the promise of a future Redeemer" are things in Genesis that must be taken in the "literal and historical sense" because they "pertain to the foundations of the Christian religion."

As a consequence of their sin, Adam and Eve lost Paradise with many of its natural gifts, all the preternatural gifts and the gift of grace, for themselves and their progeny. The Council of Trent formally decreed that when Adam transgressed the commandment of God in Paradise he immediately lost his holiness and the justice in which he had been established and that he was transformed in body and soul for the worse.

The Command

God commanded Adam not to eat from the tree of the knowledge of good and evil (2:17) to test his trust, faithfulness and obedience so that he might merit heaven.[a] It was called the tree of the knowledge of good and evil, not because its fruit provided this knowledge, but because the test provided by the tree did. The fruit of the tree of the knowledge of good and evil may have contained a toxic substance that countered the life-giving qualities of the tree of life, making physical death the *natural* consequence of disobedience. Even if that were so, the tree in itself was good because it was created by God to serve His purpose. The Eastern Fathers tended to identify the tree with contemplative knowledge or self-knowledge. St. Gregory Nazianzen, without denying the literal reality of the tree of the knowledge of good and evil, said:

> The tree was, according to my theory, contemplation, which is safe only for those who have reached maturity of habit to enter upon, but which is not good for those who are somewhat simple and greedy, just as neither is solid food good for those who are tender and have need of milk.[1]

St. John Damascene's interpretation is similar:

> The tree of knowledge of good and evil is the power of discernment by multi-dimensional vision. This is the complete knowing of one's own nature. Of itself it manifests the magnificence of the Creator, and it is good for them that are full-grown and have walked in the contemplation of God—for them that have no fear of changing, because in the course of time they have acquired a certain habit of such contemplation. It is not good, however, for such as are still young and are more greedy in their appetites, who, because of the uncertainty of their perseverance in the true good and because of their not yet being solidly established in their application to the only good, are naturally inclined to be drawn away and distracted by their solicitude for their own bodies.[2]

St. John Chrysostom saw the tree of the knowledge of good and evil as being the object of contest and the tree of life as being the reward for victory:[b]

> The tree of life was in the midst of Paradise as a reward; the tree of knowledge as an object of contest and struggle. Having kept the commandment regarding this tree, you will receive a reward. And behold the wondrous thing. Everywhere in Paradise every kind of tree blossoms, everywhere they are abundant in fruit; only in the center are there two trees as an object of battle and exercise.[3]

---

a. The Pontifical Biblical Commission in 1909 decreed that the literal historical sense is not to be doubted regarding the command given by God to Adam to prove his obedience. See DZ, no. 2123.
b. There is probably some symbolic significance to the fact that both trees were in the middle of the garden.

God accompanied His command with a threat, *"you shall die,"* literally, *"dying, you shall die."* St. Augustine points out that the threat of death was threefold—spiritual, bodily and eternal:

> God, referring to the forbidden fruit, said to the first man whom he estab-lished in paradise: *"In the day that you shall eat of it, you shall die the death."* His threat included not only the first part of the first death, that is, the soul's dep-rivation of God; not only the second part of the first death, that is, the body's deprivation of the soul; not only the whole of the first death in which the soul, separated from both God and the body, is punished; but whatever of death is up to and including that absolutely final and so-called second death ... in which the soul, deprived of God but united to the body, suffers eternal pun-ishment.[4]

The CCC gives a figurative interpretation for the tree of the knowledge of good and evil, but there is no good reason for denying its literal reality and the lit-eral nature of God's command:

> God created man in his image and established him in his friendship. A spiri-tual creature, man can live this friendship only in free submission to God. The prohibition against eating *"of the tree of the knowledge of good and evil"* spells this out: *"for in the day that you eat of it you shall die"* (Gn 2:17). The *"tree of the knowledge of good and evil"* (Gn 2:17) symbolically evokes the insurmount-able limits that man, being a creature, must freely recognize and respect with trust. Man is dependent on his Creator and subject to the laws of creation and to the moral norms that govern the use of freedom.[5]

Adam was put in the garden to till and *"to keep"* it (2:15). The Hebrew word translated "to keep" means "to guard." St. Augustine interpreted this to mean that Adam was enjoined to guard what he possessed.[6] Actually, Adam had to guard it from encroachment by the Evil One.

The Temptation

The temptation narrative begins with the appearance of Satan in the form of a serpent.[c][d] *"Now the serpent was more subtle than any other wild creature that the LORD God had made"* (3:1). There is a tendency among exegetes today to inter-

---

c. Genesis does not explicitly identify the serpent with Satan, but that identification is made explicit in Rv 20:1–2.

pret this verse allegorically. However, St. Paul confirmed that the devil actually took the form of a serpent: *"But I am afraid that as the serpent deceived Eve by his cunning, your thoughts will be led astray from a sincere and pure devotion to Christ."*[7] And the interpretation of the Fathers was quite realistic. Following them, the Pontifical Biblical Commission in 1909 stated that the temptation of Eve by the devil "under the guise of a serpent" is one of the things in Genesis that must be taken in "the literal and historical sense" because it "pertain[s] to the foundations of the Christian religion."[8] Any figurative or symbolic meaning in the devil taking the form of serpent must be understood in light of that. For example, Pope John Paul II referred to Satan as "symbolized by the serpent."[9] This does not mean that the serpent was not real; it means that Satan took the form of a serpent to represent himself as one would costume himself to project an identity. We know that demons are able to enter into animal bodies. Recall the story of the demons entering the swine in St. Luke's Gospel.[10] St. Augustine had also said, "The serpent signifies the devil."[11] But it is clear elsewhere in his writings that he believed the serpent to be quite real.[12]

St. Ephrem said that the serpent was more cunning than the other animals, but he was not a rational animal. His cunning was pure animal cunning.[13] The saintly deacon considered the serpent's means of communication:

> As for the serpent's speech, either Adam understood the serpent's own mode of communication, or Satan spoke through it, or the serpent posed the question in his mind and speech was given to it, or Satan sought from God that speech be given to the serpent for a short time.[14]

Severian of Gabala also gives an explanation of how the devil was able to communicate through the serpent:

> Do not think of the snake the way he currently is, since we now run from him and are disgusted by him. It was not this way in the beginning; the snake was friend of humanity, even the closest of servants. What, then, made him our enemy? The declaration of God *"You are more cursed than all the cattle, and*

---

d. This is one of the places in Sacred Scripture where the same figure is used for Satan that is used for Christ. The serpent of the tree of knowledge was Satan, who brought death, and the serpent on Moses' pole represented Christ, who brings life (Nm 21:8; Jn 3:14–15). Another instance is the use of the lion as a figure. Christ is the Lion of Judah (Rv 5:5) and Satan prowls like a roaring lion (1 Pt 5:8).

more than any wild animal. I will place hostility between you and the woman" (Gn 3:14–15). This hostility destroyed the friendship. I say "friendship," but I do not mean an intellectual relationship, it was instead one which mindless creatures are capable of having. The snake used to serve humans in the same way the dog displays friendship—not with word but by body language. Since it was a creature who held such great closeness to humanity, the snake was a convenient tool for the devil....

So the devil spoke through the snake in order to deceive Adam. Please hear me in love and do not receive my words carelessly. My question is not easy to take. Many scoff, "how did the snake speak, with a human voice or with a snake's hiss?" or "how did Eve understand him?" Before the fall, Adam was filled with wisdom, discernment and prophecy.... When the devil noticed the snake's intelligence and Adam's high opinion of it (Adam considered the snake very wise), the devil spoke through the snake so that Adam would think that the snake, being intelligent, was able to imitate even human speech.[15]

St. John Damascene writes in a similar vein but seems to personalize the serpent:

And the serpent was on intimate terms with man, associating with him more than all the rest and conversing agreeably with him. For that reason it was through this relation that the devil, who is the source of evil, made that most evil suggestion to our first parents.[16]

Some Fathers thought that the serpent lived outside Paradise. St. Ephrem wrote: "The serpent could not enter paradise, for neither animal nor bird was permitted to approach the outer region of paradise, and Adam had to go out to meet them."[17] St. Augustine also said that the serpent was not in Paradise: "For paradise signifies the happy life, from which the serpent was absent, since it was already the devil." He continues, "And we must not be confused as to how the serpent could speak to the woman, when she was in paradise and he was not. The serpent entered paradise spiritually and not bodily...."[18]

Some scholars maintain the Hebrew word *nachash,* which is translated "serpent," originally meant "shining upright creature."[19] St. Augustine said that the serpent was created upright.[20] So the serpent may originally have been a beautiful upright creature that could stand eye to eye with Adam and Eve. It may have been related to the dragon, which is found in stories of every ancient culture. St. John identified the red dragon of his vision with the serpent of Genesis: *"And the great dragon was thrown down, the ancient serpent, who is called the Devil and Satan, the deceiver of the whole world...."[21]* There have been encounters with live dragon-like creatures (dinosaurs) in relatively recent times. B. Cooper has found examples in early Anglo-Saxon and other records.[22] One is particularly germane. It concerns a sighting in 1614 of a strange reptile in St. Leonard's Forest in Sussex, England:

> "The serpent (or dragon as some call it) is reputed to be nine feete, or rather more, in length, and shaped almost in the form of an axletree of a cart: a quantitie of thickness in the middest, and somewhat smaller at both endes. The former part, which he shootes forth as a neck, is supposed to be an elle {3 ft., 9 in. or 114 cm} long; with a white ring, as it were, of scales about it. The scales along his back seemed to be blackish, and so much as is discovered under his bellie, appeareth to be red ... it is likewise discovered to have large feete, but the eye may there be deceived, for some suppose that serpents have no feet ... {The dragon} rids away (as we call it) as fast as a man can run. His food {rabbits} is thought to be, for the most part, in a conie-warren, which he much frequents.... There are likewise upon either side of him discovered two great bunches so big as a large foote-ball, and (as some thinke) will in time grow to wings, but God, I hope, will (to defend the poor people in the neighbourhood) that he be destroyed before he grows to fledge."[23]

St. Cyprian of Carthage gives us the motive for Satan's scheming:

> The devil bore impatiently the fact that man was made in the image of God; and that is why he was the first to perish and the first to bring others to perdition.[24]

*   *   *   *

The serpent said to Eve: *"Did God say, 'You shall not eat of any tree of the garden'?"* (3:1). This is Satan's subtle entry. He probably said it with an incredulous tone of voice with the implication, How could He do that! thereby slyly opening the forum at once to questioning God's word. No doubt, he knew that it was only the tree of the knowledge of good and evil that was forbidden. But he couldn't come right out and question that. That would be a frontal attack on God's authority. Rather he questioned something that seemed unreasonable and that both he and Eve knew wasn't true.

The deadly conversation continues:

> *And the woman said to the serpent, "We may eat of the fruit of the trees of the garden; but God said, 'You shall not eat of the fruit of the tree which is in the midst of*

the garden, neither shall you touch it, lest you die.'" But the serpent said to the woman, "You will not die. For God knows that when you eat of it your eyes will be opened, and you will be like God, knowing good and evil." (3:2–5).

The serpent lied when he said that they will not die; but he was telling the truth when he said they would become like God, knowing good and evil (3:5).[e] That's how the devil works, mixing the truth with lies. The truth is the bait; the lie is the hook.

Eve mentions an additional command, not mentioned earlier. That is the command to not even touch the tree. The tree was *"good for food and a delight to the eyes, and … was to be desired to make one wise"* (3:6). Thus the fruit itself was a temptation, even without the instigation of the serpent. That is why God would not even allow Adam and Eve to touch the tree. St. Ephrem explains:

> The words of the tempter would not have caused those two to be tempted to sin if their avarice had not been so helpful to the tempter. Even if the tempter had not come, the tree itself, by its beauty, would have caused them a great struggle due to their avarice. Their avarice then was the reason that they followed the counsel of the serpent. The avarice of Adam and Eve was far more injurious to them than the counsel of the serpent.[25]

St. Ambrose said that Satan approached Eve rather than Adam because she did not receive the command directly from God and was therefore an easier target:

> {The devil} aimed to circumvent Adam by means of the woman. He did not accost the man who had in his presence received the heavenly command. He accosted her who had learned of it from her husband and who had not received from God the command which was to be observed. There is no statement that God spoke to the woman. We know that He spoke to Adam. Hence we must conclude that the command was communicated through Adam to the woman.[26]

St. Bonaventure said that Satan's temptation of Eve was threefold:

---

e. In (3:22) God confirms the devil's declaration *"you will be like God"* (or *"you shall be as gods"*). In contrast, St. John Chrysostom says that declaration is also a lie because he can never have the devil telling the truth (ACC, pp. 100–101). In that case (3:22) would simply be a mocking of Adam by the Trinity, as proposed by St. Ephrem (ACC, p. 100).

[T]he devil enticed woman through a triple desire, namely, by knowledge which corresponds to the rational desire, by excellence in the mode of God which corresponds to the irascible desire, and by sweetness of the tree which corresponds to the concupiscible desire. Thus he tempted all that was temptable in woman and through which she could be led to temptation, and this is the triple desire of the world, namely, *"the concupiscence of the flesh and the concupiscence of the eyes, and the pride of life"* (1 John 2:16). The origin of all temptation lies in these three: the world, the flesh, and the devil.[27]

St. Thomas Aquinas said that in the state of innocence Eve could not have been deceived in the intellect because in that state "it was impossible for the intellect to assent to falsehood as if it were truth."[28] So she understood perfectly what she was being tempted to do. She sinned by interior pride before she was deceived to sin in deed:

Though the woman was deceived before she sinned in deed, still it was not till she had already sinned by interior pride. For Augustine says ... that "the woman could not have believed the words of the serpent, had she not already acquiesced in the love of her own power, and in a presumption of self-conceit."[29]

The Sin

"[S]he took of its fruit and ate; and she also gave some to her husband and he ate" (3:6). Thus the sin was consummated. St. Ephrem sees in Eve's eating first the desire to dominate her husband:

She hastened to eat before her husband that she might become head over her head, that she might become the one to give command to that one by whom she was to be commanded and that she might be older in divinity than that one who was older than she in humanity.[30]

The sin was a sin of disobedience to God by the literal eating of the forbidden fruit. The root of the disobedience was pride: *"you will be like God"* (3:5).[f] The eating of the fruit is not symbolic of sexual sin, as ancient (St. Clement of Alexandria and St. Ambrose)[31] and modern commentators have proposed. Those who look for symbolic meanings in opposition to the literal meaning do injustice to the text. One wonders why they do not accept the narrative as it stands because it gives a credible and consistent account of the first sin.

Adam and Eve, by choosing to eat from the tree, had made themselves like God by deciding for themselves what is good and what is evil (3:22), as Pope John Paul II explains:

> This is the human condition vividly described by the Book of Genesis when it tells us that God placed the human being in the Garden of Eden, in the middle of which there stood *"the tree of knowledge of good and evil"* (2:17). The symbol is clear: man was in no position to discern and decide for himself what was good and what was evil, but was constrained to appeal to a higher source. The blindness of pride deceived our first parents into thinking themselves sovereign and autonomous, and into thinking that they could ignore the knowledge which comes from God.[32]

The *Catechism of the Catholic Church* summarizes the story of man's first sin as follows:

> Man, tempted by the devil, let his trust in his Creator die in his heart and, abusing his freedom, disobeyed God's command. This is what man's first sin consisted of. (Cf. Gn 3:1–11, Rom 5:19)[33]

> In that sin man *preferred* himself to God and by that very act scorned him. He chose himself over and against God, against the requirements of his creaturely status and therefore against his own good. Constituted in a state of holiness,

---

f.   Eve first sinned against the virtue of Faith by doubting God's truthfulness and love. She doubted His truthfulness when she allowed herself to be led into disbelieving God's warning, *"you shall die,"* and she doubted His love when she became suspicious about God's motive for forbidding them to eat from the tree of knowledge. Genesis does not say explicitly that she committed those sins, but it implies so. She may also have put herself into an occasion of sin by lingering around the forbidden tree, being attracted by its desirable fruit.

St. Augustine describes an incident in his youth that parallels the sin of Adam and Eve. He and some friends stole pears from his neighbor's tree. He did not do so out of need or desire for the pears. Rather he "simply wanted to enjoy the theft for its own sake, and the sin" (*Confessions*, Book II). He said that he derived pleasure from the deed simply because it was forbidden. He said, "[T]here was no motive for my malice except malice." Could our first parents' sin have been the similar? Perhaps they took pleasure in the malice of their sin because they were motivated by a desire for complete independence from God that was aggravated by resentment at any restriction on their behavior.

man was destined to be fully "divinized" by God in glory. Seduced by the devil, he wanted to *"be like God"* but "without God, before God, and not in accordance with God" (St. Maximus the Confessor, *Ambigua*: PG 91, 1156C; cf. Gn 3:5).[34]

The Consequences

If Adam and Eve had been faithful to God, they would have passed, without suffering or dying, from Paradise to heaven, where they would see God face to face.

Because of their sin, Adam an Eve lost sanctifying grace and the preternatural gifts. Having lost sanctifying grace, they lost the friendship of God and the right to heaven. God drove them out of Paradise[g] and barred their reentry (3:23–24), removing from them access to the tree of life. They became subject to suffering, toil and death (3:16–19); their minds and wills were weakened; and they acquired an inclination to evil. St. Augustine expressed the consequences in terms of decay and chaos:

> The effect of that sin was to subject human nature to all the process of decay which we see and feel, and consequently to death also. And man was distracted and tossed about by violent and conflicting emotions, a very different being from what he was in paradise before his sin, though even then he lived in an animal body.[35]

He also pointed out that even though Adam lost the freedom associated with innocence, he did not lose his free will:

> Who of us would say that by the sin of the first man free will perished from the human race? Certainly freedom perished through sin, but it was that freedom which was had in paradise, of having full righteousness with immortality; and it is on that account that human nature has need of divine grace.[36]

In its decree on original sin, the Council of Trent vividly describes Adam's fall from grace:

> If anyone does not confess that the first man Adam, when he transgressed the commandment of God in Paradise, immediately lost his holiness and the justice in which he had been established, and that he incurred through the

---

g.   St. Lawrence of Brindisi in *Explanatio in Genesim* said that Adam was sent to the location (outside Paradise) where he was formed.

offense of that prevarication the wrath and indignation of God and hence the death with which God had previously threatened him, and with death captivity under his power, who thenceforth *"had the empire of death"* {Heb 2:14}, that is of the devil, and that through that offense of prevarication the entire Adam was transformed in body and soul for the worse {see no. 174}, let him be anathema.[37]

Augustine comments on why Adam's punishment was so severe:

> Adam, the first man, was of such an excellent nature, because that nature was not yet weakened, that his sin was much greater by far than are the sins of other men. Therefore his punishment too, which was the immediate consequence of his sin, seemed much more severe.[38]

✳   ✳   ✳   ✳

The immediate consequence of the sin of Adam and Eve, which they suffered even before encountering God, was awareness of their nakedness (3:7). Earlier (2:25) the sacred author pointed out that they were both naked and not ashamed. Now they are ashamed at their nakedness, and they fashion fig leaves to cover themselves. Later God will clothe them with garments of skins (3:21).[h] Following their sin, *"the eyes of both were opened"* to a new law operating in them, which St. Paul described: *"[I] see in my members another law at war with the law of my mind and making me captive to the law of sin which dwells in my members."*[39] According to Diadochus of Photice, an inordinate inclination to sensuality was stimulated by the intense sensuality of tasting the fruit.[40] One feels shame in exposing one's weaknesses. Adam and Eve now felt shame because of the terrible weakness they now felt in their sexual appetites, so they felt compelled to hide it by covering themselves.

---

h. St. Ephrem believed that God specially created those skins and did not kill any animal for them (see ACC, p. 98). However, it is not hard to believe that God killed animals for them since death entered the world with Adam. In fact, there may even been animal death before the Fall; there was certainly plant death, the plants being used for food.

St. Lawrence of Brindisi in *Explanatio in Genesim* said that the sacrifice of the animal to remove the shame of our first parents prefigured the Sacrifice of Christ.

St. Ephrem said that Adam and Eve were ashamed because their bodies lost their cloaks of glory:

> They were not ashamed [before the Fall] because of the glory with which they were clothed. It was when this glory was stripped from them after they had transgressed the commandment that they were ashamed because they were naked.[41]

St. John Chrysostom said the same:

> *"The two were naked,"* it says, *"and were not ashamed"* (2:25). For when sin and disobedience had not yet entered upon the scene they were clothed with glory from above, which is why they were not ashamed. But after their transgression of the command shame did enter in, and the knowledge of their nakedness.[42]

And St. Ambrose said that when he fell Adam "lost the image of the heavenly and took on the image of the terrestrial."[43]

St. Dorotheus of Gaza said that with the first sin man fell from a state in accord with his nature to a state contrary to his nature:

> When he disobeyed the command and ate of the tree God commanded him not to eat of, he was thrown out of paradise and fell from a state in accord with his nature to a state contrary to nature, a prey to sin, to ambition, to a love of the pleasures of this life and to other passions; and he was mastered by them and became a slave to them through his transgression.[44]

✳   ✳   ✳   ✳

After they covered themselves, Adam and Eve heard God walking in the garden (3:8). This need not be taken as an anthropomorphism. God took on a human appearance before the Incarnation when he appeared to Abraham by the oaks of Mamre.[45] So it is not hard to believe that He conversed with Adam in human form as they walked together through the garden. God allowed His footsteps to be heard "so that Adam and Eve might be prepared, at that sound, to make supplication before Him who made the sound."[46] The sound frightened them so much that they tried to hide from God.

Then God called out to Adam asking where he was (3:9). Adam replied that the sound of the footsteps frightened him because he was naked (3:10). God then asked him how he knew he was naked and if he had eaten the forbidden fruit (3:11). The question, of course, was a reproof since God knew what had happened. Symeon the New Theologian said that Adam was so deceived "he hoped that God would not know his sin."[47] Adam replied that the woman gave him the fruit (3:12). He tried to put the blame on her. This marked the end of the perfect harmony between man and woman and the beginning of discord between the sexes. Augustine and Dorotheus of Gaza remark that Adam actually accused God for his sin when he said *"the woman you gave to me"* led him to eat.[48] Eve, in turn, blamed it on the serpent (3:13). Neither took responsibility for their sin. According to Augustine, this lack of repentance was worse than the sin itself:

> Even worse, and more deserving of condemnation, is the pride shown in the search for an excuse, even when the sins are clear as daylight. This was shown in the first human beings, when the woman said, *'The serpent led me astray, and I ate'*; and the man said, *'The woman whom you gave me as a companion, she gave me fruit from the tree and I ate.'* There is not a whisper anywhere here of a plea for pardon, nor of any entreaty for healing ... But in the case of so obvious a transgression of the divine command, to talk like this is really to accuse rather than to excuse oneself.[49]

St. Ephrem said that if Adam and Eve had repented they would have escaped God's curses:

> If Adam and Eve had sought to repent after they had transgressed the commandment, even though they would not have regained that which they possessed before their transgression of the commandment, they would have escaped from the curses that were decreed on the earth and upon them.[50]

Symeon the New Theologian said that if Adam had admitted his sin and asked for mercy "he might have stayed in paradise. By this one word [of repentance] he might have spared himself that whole cycle of evils without number that he endured by his expulsion and in spending so many centuries in hell."[51]

*   *   *   *

Next God pronounces His sentences on the serpent, Eve, Adam and the earth (3; 14–19).

God first cursed the serpent. But His wrath was not directed at the animal but at the evil spirit that resided in it. However, His curse applied to both. The evil spirit will suffer spiritually what the animal has to endure physically. Although the serpent, as an animal, was free of guilt, it was cursed on account of Adam's sin, as was all nature.[52] But it was cursed "above *all cattle and* above *all wild animals*" (3:14) as a sign of the curse on Satan. St. John Chrysostom says the curse on the animal is a sign of the dishonor inflicted on it:

> But perhaps someone will say: If the counsel was given by the devil, using the serpent as an instrument, why is the animal subjected to such a punishment? This also was a work of God's unutterable love of mankind. As a loving father, in punishing the murderer of his son, breaks also the knife and sword by which he performed the murder, and breaks them into small pieces—in a similar fashion the All-good God, when this animal, like a kind of sword, served as the instrument of the devil's malice, subjects it to a constant punishment, so that from this physical and visible manifestation we might conclude the dishonor in which it finds itself. And if the one who served as the instrument was subjected to such anger, what punishment must the other be undergoing? ... The unquenchable fire awaits him (Mt 25:41).[53]

The serpent's motive was envy: "[T]hrough the devil's envy, death entered the world."[54] St. Ephrem and St. Augustine pointed out that God cursed the serpent without questioning him because he was incapable of confessing his sin and repenting.[55] The serpent's punishment was to crawl at the feet of those he envied and to have his head crushed by one of them (3:14–15). Ambrose, Augustine and Caesarius of Arles said that his being cursed to eat dust means that the serpent's prey will be those who live close to the ground, those who saturate themselves with earthly pleasures.[56] Since dust represents death (3:19), his prey will be those who are spiritually dead.

Genesis 3:15 is called the Protoevangelium (First Gospel) because it is the first announcement of the good news of the Redeemer.[57] It wasn't presented as a promise to Adam and Eve but as a curse on the devil. He was being told that his days were numbered. The devil and his followers will be put at enmity with the woman, whom the Church has always seen as the mother of the Savior, and her seed, her Son the Messiah and Savior of the World.[58] He is the New Adam who, because He "became obedient unto death, even death on a cross,"[59] atoned for the disobedience of Adam. Satan will strike at the heel of His Mystical Body, the Catholic Church, and bruise it. But He will crush the head of the serpent through the instrumentality of His mother.[i] Mary is the New Eve.[j] Like Eve she was created without sin, but unlike Eve she never sinned. The first Eve was the first to succumb to the influence of the devil. Mary, the New Eve, will destroy his influence forever. St. Irenaeus brings this to light:

> As Eve was seduced by the word of a {fallen} angel to flee from God, having rebelled against his word, so Mary by the word of an angel received the glad tidings that she would bear God by obeying his word. The former was seduced to disobey God {and so fell}, but the latter was persuaded to obey God, so that the Virgin Mary might become the advocate of the virgin Eve. As the human race was subjected to death through the act of a virgin, so it was saved by a virgin, and thus the disobedience of one virgin was precisely balanced by the obedience of another.[60]

Through a woman Satan entered the world, and through a woman he will take leave of it. St. John had a vision of his destruction: *"[A]nd the devil who had deceived them was thrown into the lake of fire and brimstone where the beast and the false prophet were, and they will be tormented day and night for ever and ever."*[61]

So the LORD would punish Adam and Eve for their sin, but He would not abandon them. *"Wisdom protected the first formed father of the world when he alone had been created; she delivered him from his transgression and gave him strength to rule all things."*[62] God started to unfold His plan for sending a Savior to reopen the gates of heaven. But why did He allow our first parents to sin to begin with? The CCC explains that He allowed Adam to sin to bring about an infinitely great good, the Incarnation:

---

i. The DR reads, *"she* [the woman] *shall crush thy head, and thou shalt lie in wait for her heel,"* after St. Jerome's interpretation of the phrase. The Hebrew text is ambiguous. The reference could be either to the woman or her seed in direct contact with the serpent. The Fathers were divided on the question. In either case: "The sense is the same: for it is by her seed, Jesus Christ, that the woman crushes the serpent's head" (footnote on Gn 3:15 of 1899 version of Douay-Rheims Bible).

j. Pope Pius XII wrote in *Munificentissmus Deus*: "But this especially must be remembered, that ever since the second century the Virgin Mary has been presented by the Holy Fathers as the new Eve, very closely connected with the new Adam, although subject to Him in that struggle with the enemy of hell, which, as is presignified in the protoevangelium (Gn 3:15) was to result in a most complete victory over sin and death, which are always joined together in the writings of the Apostle of the Gentiles {Rom 5:6; 1 Cor 15:21–26; 54–57}." See DZ, no. 2331.

But *why did God not prevent the first man from sinning?* St. Leo the Great responds, "Christ's inexpressible grace gave us blessings better than those the demon's envy had taken away" (*Sermons*, 73, 4). And St. Thomas Aquinas wrote, "There is nothing to prevent human nature's being raised up to something greater, even after sin; God permits evil in order to draw forth some greater good. Thus St. Paul says, *'Where sin increased, grace abounded all the more'*; and the Exultet sings, 'O happy fault, which gained for us so great a Redeemer!'" (ST, Part III, Q. 1, A. 3, Reply Obj. 3; cf. Rom 5:20).[63]

* * * *

St. Ephrem said that God punished the serpent first to instill fear in Adam and Eve so that they might repent; and when they didn't, God proceeded to punish them. He punished Eve first because it was through her that sin was passed on to Adam.[64] She was first cursed to bear suffering in childbirth. Natural processes of the body produce pleasurable sensations (when operating properly). So would childbirth have done if there were no Fall. But sin has made childbirth the only painful bodily process. This will be a reminder to Eve that she will pass on to her progeny, which will be the entire human species, the painful effects of her sin. St. John Chrysostom said that each birth would remind her of "the magnitude of this sin of disobedience."[65] The second punishment Eve suffered was subjection to Adam. According to St. John Chrysostom, this was not part of God's original plan:

> In the beginning I created you equal in esteem to your husband, and my intention was that in everything you would share with him as an equal, and as I entrusted control of everything to your husband, so did I to you; but you abused your equality of status. Hence I subject you to your husband.[66]

Although there was equality of status before the Fall, Chrysostom makes it clear elsewhere that Adam was the head of the human race and therefore had a responsibility for guiding and correcting Eve:

> After all, you are head of your wife, and she has been created for your sake; but you have inverted the proper order: not only have you failed to keep her on the straight and narrow but you have been dragged down with her, and whereas the rest of the body should follow the head, the contrary has in fact occurred, the head following the rest of the body, turning things upside down."[67]

Eve's punishment was connected with her mission to be the womb of the human species. Adam's punishment was connected with the mission God gave him to till the soil and make it fruitful (2:15; 3:17, 23). Before his sin Adam always experienced pleasurable sensations when exercising the various faculties God gave him. There was no admixture of drudgery with pleasure as there is in work today. And the earth cooperated perfectly with his efforts. The thorns and thistles that were later to become scourges to him then worked to his benefit.[k] After his sin things would be different. There would be much toil against a resistant earth in making it fruitful so that he and Eve and their children may eat.

The Fall introduced new dimensions into the meaning of work. In addition to being a means of cooperating in God's work of creation, work also became a means of cooperating with His plans of redemption and sanctification:

> It [work] can also be redemptive. By enduring the hardship of work (Cf. Gn 3:14–19) in union with Jesus, the carpenter of Nazareth and the one crucified on Calvary, man collaborates in a certain fashion with the Son of God in his redemptive work. He shows himself to be a disciple of Christ by carrying the cross, daily, in the work he is called to accomplish. (Cf. Pope John Paul II, *Laborem exercens*, no. 27) Work can be a means of sanctification and a way of animating earthly realities with the Spirit of Christ.[68]

God then tells Adam that in the end his body will become one with the earth because he will die. Theodoret of Cyr said that the death sentence was a mixture of love with punishment. It "brings evil works to an end" and "ends the suffering of the body."[69]

St. Ambrose said that Adam himself and not God was the agent of his death:

> Still another problem arises. "From what source did death come to Adam? Was it from the nature of a tree of this sort or actually from God?" ... The solution, unless I am mistaken, lies in the fact that since disobedience was the cause of death, for that very reason not God but man himself was the agent of his own death. If, for example, a physician were to prescribe to a patient what he thought should be avoided, and if the patient felt that these prohibitions were unnecessary, the physician is not responsible for the patient's death.

---

k. St. Ephrem said that the thorns and thistles were specially created after the Fall (see ACC, p. 98). But this does not seem likely, considering that Scripture says that God's work of creation was completed on the sixth day (2:1). Also, would God create something new specifically as a punishment? See ST, Part I, Q. 69, A. 2, Reply Obj. 2.

Surely in that case the patient is guilty of causing his own death. Hence God as a good physician forbade Adam to eat what would be injurious to him.[70]

*   *   *   *

God said to Adam: *"Cursed is the ground because of you"* (3:17). All creation suffers corruptibility as the effect of Adam's sin. St. Paul referred to this in his epistle to the Romans. He said that creation was *"subjected to futility,"* has been *"groaning in travail,"* and is in *"bondage to decay."*[71] The phrase *"bondage to decay"* does not imply that there was no decomposition of matter before Fall. It is the nature of matter to change. *Decomposition* is the breaking down of ordered matter into its constituent parts. It serves a useful purpose if the constituent parts are recomposed into other ordered material structures, as happens with living organisms. The result is that order is maintained. The process of recomposition requires the intervention of an intelligent agent, as in the case of the Designer of living organisms. Decomposition before the Fall was useful and served man. *Decay* or *corruption* is useless decomposition; the constituent parts do not enter into new ordered structures, thus order is lost. After the Fall, the process of decay causes a continual loss of order in the universe, which often counters man's welfare. This is called the *law of morpholysis* (loosening of structure). It has been formulated mathematically in the second law of thermodynamics.[72]

With its renewal at the end of time, the world will be restored to a state of incorruptibility. It *"will be set free from its bondage to decay."*[73] But first it will be destroyed to complete the process of decomposition:

> *"Thou Lord, didst found the earth in the beginning, and the heavens are the work of thy hands; they will perish, but thou remainest; they will all grow old like a garment, like a mantle thou wilt roll them up, and they will be changed...."*[74]

St. John Chrysostom, commenting on Romans 8:19–23, explains that man's sin impacted creation:

> Paul means by this that creation became corruptible. Why and for what reason? Because of you O man! For because you have a body which has become mortal and subject to suffering, the earth too has received a curse and has brought forth thorns and thistles.... The creation suffered badly because of you, and it became corruptible, but it has not been irreparably damaged. For it

will become incorruptible once again for your sake. This is the meaning of *"in hope."*[75]

St. Cyril of Alexandria, commenting on Romans 8:19–23, connects the transformation of creation at the end of time with the glorification of the just:

> But by the secret plan of God, which orders all things for the best, it will come to this end. For when the sons of God, who have lived a righteous life, have been transformed into glory from dishonor and from what is corruptible into what is incorruptible, then will creation too be transformed into something better. (See Rom 8:21; 1 Cor 15:54.)[76]

[1] ACC, p. 62.

[2] ACC, pp. 62–63.

[3] *On the Creation of the World*, 5:7, as quoted by Rose, Fr. Seraphim, *Genesis, Creation and Early Man: The Orthodox Christian Vision* (Platina, CA: Saint Herman of Alaska Brotherhood, 2000), p. 174.

[4] CG, Book XIII, Chapter 12, as quoted in ACC, p. 62.

[5] CCC, no. 396.

[6] See ACC, p. 60.

[7] 2 Cor 11:3.

[8] DZ, no. 2123.

[9] *General audience of September 19, 1979*. See John Paul II, Pope, *The Theology of the Body: Human Love in the Divine Plan* (Boston: Pauline Books and Media, 1997), p. 31.

[10] Lk 8:30–33.

[11] ACC, p. 76.

[12] See, for example, CG, Book XIV, Chapters 7, 9, 11, 13, 14; Book XV, Chapters 7, 23.

[13] See ACC, p. 74.

[14] ACC, p. 75.

[15] ACC, pp. 74–75.

[16] ACC, p. 75.

[17] ACC, p. 75.

[18] ACC, p. 76.

[19] According to Morris, Henry M., *The Genesis Record* (Grand Rapids, MI: Baker Book House, 1976), commentary on Gn 3:1.

[20] ACC, p. 124.

[21] Rv 12:9.

[22] Cooper, Bill, *After the Flood: The Early Post-Flood History of Europe Traced Back to Noah* (Chichester, England: New Wine Press, 1995), ch. 10.

[23] Ibid., p. 134.

[24] JR, no. 567.

[25] ACC, p. 77.

[26] *Paradise*, 12, as quoted by Rose, op. cit., pp. 194, 196.

[27] BV, Part III, Chapter 2.5.

[28] ST, Part I, Q. 94, A. 4.

[29] Ibid., Reply Obj. 1. For more of Augustine on this see CG, Book XIV, Chapter 13.

[30] ACC, p. 78.

[31] According to OTT, p. 107.

[32] *Fides et Ratio*, no. 22.

[33] CCC, no. 397.

[34] CCC, no. 398.

[35] CG, Book XIV, Chapter 12.

[36] JR, no. 1883.

[37] DZ, no. 788.

[38] JR, no. 2013.

[39] Rom 7:23; also see Gal 5:17.

[40] ACC, p. 78.

[41] ACC, p. 72.

[42] JR, no. 1150; also see ACC, p. 72.

[43] JR, no. 1318.

[44] ACC, p. 73.

[45] Gn 18:1ff.

[46] St. Ephrem, ACC, p. 82.

[47] ACC, p. 86.

[48] See ACC, pp. 86–87.

[49] CG, Book XIV, Chapter 14.

[50] ACC, p. 85.

[51] ACC, p. 86.

[52] See (3:17); Rom 8:19–23.

[53] *Homilies on Genesis*, 17:6, as quoted by Rose, op. cit., pp. 202–203.

[54] Wis 2:24.

[55] See ACC, pp. 88–89.

[56] See ACC, pp. 89–90.

[57] See CCC, no. 410.

[58] See CCC, no. 411.

[59] Phil 2:8.

[60] ACC, pp. 78–79.

[61] Rv 20:10.

[62] Wis 10:1–2.

[63] CCC, no. 412; also see no. 420.

[64] See ACC, p. 92.

[65] ACC, p. 93.

[66] ACC, p. 93.

[67] ACC, p. 94.

[68] CCC, no. 2427.

[69] ACC, p. 96.

[70] ACC, p. 96.

[71] See Rom 8:19–23.

[72] See Glossary.

[73] Rom 8:21.

[74] Heb 1:10–12.

[75] *Homilies on Romans* 14, as quoted in Oden, Thomas, general ed., Bray, Gerald, ed., *Ancient Christian Commentary on Sacred Scripture, New Testament, Vol. VI, Romans* (Downers Grove, IL: InterVarsity Press), p. 224.

[76] *Explanation of the Letter to the Romans*, as quoted in Oden, op. cit., p. 223.

Doctrine Fourteen
The whole human species descended from the first man and woman.

Genesis makes it explicitly clear that Adam and Eve were the first human beings from whom the whole human species descended. Pope Pius II in 1459 excluded the existence of pre-Adamites and colonization from outer space by condemning the notions that Adam was not the first man and that God created another world. Pope Pius XII in 1950 explicitly rejected polygenism. The Church formally teaches that God specially creates each human soul at conception, that every descendant of Adam and Eve, with the exception of Jesus and Mary, is conceived with original sin, and that original sin is transmitted by propagation and not by imitation.

Unity of the Human Species

Sacred Scripture explicitly testifies that Adam and Eve were the first human beings from whom the whole human species descended: *"And there was no man to till the ground"* (2:5). *"The man called his wife's name Eve because she was the mother of all living"* (3:20). *"And he made from one every nation of men to live on all the face of the earth...."[1]* Thus there were no "pre-Adamites" and no primordial human community of more than two.[a] St. Ambrose said that the flesh of man and woman is of one nature and that there is only one source for the human race.[2] St. Augustine said: "In that very beginning Adam and Eve were the parents

---

a. This was affirmed by St. Paul where he identifies all human beings as brethren of Christ: *"For he who sanctifies and those who are sanctified have one origin. That is why he is not ashamed to call them brethren..."* (Heb 2:11).

of all peoples…."[3] He refers to the human species being in Adam's loins.[4] He also said: "Now the whole human race took its beginning from one man. This we believe on the authority of the holy Scriptures."[5]

Augustine also said that animal species do not have the same unity as the human species. God commanded many individuals of the various species to come into existence at once.[6] He goes on to give a reason for God giving unity to the human species:

> God's intention was that in this way the unity of human society and the bonds of human sympathy be more emphatically brought home to man, if men were bound together not merely by likeness in nature but also by the feeling of kinship. And to this end, when he created the woman who was to be joined with the man he decided not to create her in the same way as he created man himself. Instead he made her out of the man (Gn 2:22) so that the whole human race should spread out from one original man.[7]

Theodoret of Cyr said that "the myriads of tribes [came] from one couple" so that men may not suppose that there was any difference in their natures.[8] One might say that Theodoret was a fifth-century antiracist anticipating future Enlightenment intellectuals and Darwinists who would classify the different races (tribes) as different species and therefore different in nature. Also, the human species is not a "race." A *race* is a variety within a species; all races within a species have the same nature. The term *human race* is not a proper term because it implies that there are nonhuman races that have the same nature as humans.

Cardinal Ernesto Ruffini emphasized the importance of the doctrine of the unity of the human species:

> It is a truth of Faith that the human species is one, and that all men spring from the same two parents. It could be said that this is one of the most fundamental truths of the Catholic religion. We shall go further: to impugn this basic principle would be to attack the very existence of Christianity.[9]

He goes on to give examples of opposition to this doctrine:

> In the eighteenth century the irreligious philosophy of Voltaire, with the design of catching the Bible in error, held the multiplicity of the human origin: "only a blind man would be allowed to doubt that the whites, the negroes, the Hottentots, the Laplanders, the Chinese, the Americans are of entirely different races (species)."

In the nineteenth century even politics entered into the question. While the Americans were practicing the "slave trade" on a large scale, a minister, Calhoun, wanting to excuse his compatriots, answered in 1844 the remonstrances of the European states by saying that the Negroes were not at all of the same species as Whites.

From the second half of the nineteenth century the question was proposed in a new light. The different colors of the various races, the variations noted in the vertebral column, the capacity of the skull, the facial angle, the linguistic differences, and now especially the fossil men have given even noted authors the urge and the argument to propose and sustain, more or less vehemently, the hypothesis of various human species (*Polygeny*).[10]

Ruffini offers the following facts that refute those claims: 1) the anatomical and physiological resemblances and the interfecundity of the races, 2) psychological resemblances in the races—use of spoken language, religious and moral awareness, artistic and practical creativity. He says that the Church has always upheld the doctrine and modern secular disciplines recognize its truth:

> The Catholic Church, which has always upheld the physical and psychical unity of the human race [species] and has strenuously defended it—chiefly in recent times—against not a few contrary opinions proposed as scientific, is today supported by the majority of representatives of anthropology, linguistics and ethnology.[11]

Although Ruffini struggles with the paleontological evidence, saying that it presents the "greatest difficulties" for the doctrine, in the end he finds it nonthreatening.[12 b]

As Cardinal Ruffini indicated, the Church has spoken on the unity of the human race. It is important to her because it is a prerequisite for dogma concerning original sin and redemption. Pope Pius II in 1459 excluded the existence of pre-Adamites and colonization from outer space by condemning the proposition: "That God created another world than this one, and that in its time many other men and women existed and that consequently Adam was not the first man."[13] The Pontifical Biblical Commission in 1909 decreed that "the oneness of the human race" is a fact that "pertain[s] to the foundation of the Catholic religion."[14] Pope Pius XII in his encyclical letter *Summi Pontificatus* (1939) upheld the natural unity of the human race saying, "The Bible narrates that from the first

---

b. A more recent look at paleontological evidence shows that it strongly supports the doctrine. See Doctrine Nine, << Reply to Objection 2 >>.

marriage of man and woman all other men took their origin...."[15] In *Humani generis* Pius XII definitely ruled out polygenism, which was inferred from an evolutionary interpretation of human fossils:

> When there is question of another conjectural opinion, namely, of polygenism so-called, then the sons of the Church in no way enjoy such freedom [of inquiry]. For the faithful in Christ cannot accept this view, which holds that either after Adam there existed men on this earth, who did not receive their origin by natural generation from him, the first parent of all; or that Adam signifies some kind of multitude of first parents; for it is by no means apparent how such an opinion can be reconciled with what the sources of revealed truth and the acts of the *magisterium* of the Church teaches about original sin, which proceeds from a sin truly committed by one Adam, and which is transmitted to all by generation, and exists in each one as his own.[16]

Pius XII closed discussion on the question of polygenism; and Pope Paul VI affirmed this saying: "It is evident that you will not consider as reconcilable with the authentic Catholic doctrine those explanations of original sin, given by some authors, which start from the presupposition of polygenism which is not proved...."[17] Still some Catholic theologians do not want to admit that the Church has absolutely ruled out polygenism because they are afraid that "science" may someday prove the Church wrong. O, you of little faith! Although the teaching on polygenism is not presented as infallible, it can be considered infallible in light of its intimate and unbreakable connection with infallible teaching on original sin. Pius XII didn't ask theologians to study whether polygenism is reconcilable with Catholic dogma; he told them that it is not. It is temerarious for Catholic theologians to consider that it is still an open question. But many Catholic theologians are temerarious about Catholic doctrine but are timorous about pseudoscientific doctrine.

The CCC states: "Because of its common origin the *human race forms a unity*...."[18]

Special Creation of the Human Soul

The human soul is not propagated by natural generation like the human body. Rather God infuses each human soul in a special act of creation. Eve implied this when she said: *"I have gotten a man with the help of the LORD'"* (4:1). Scripture alludes in several other places to the special creation of the soul: *"In the place where you were created, in the land of your origin, I will judge you."*[19] *"[A]nd the*

spirit returns to God who gave it.[20] *"[H]e failed to know the one who formed him
and inspired him with an active soul and breathed into him a living spirit.*[21]

St. Jerome asks how Cain and Abel got their souls, concluding that God specially created them:

> Whence did Cain and Abel, the first offspring of the first human beings, have
> their souls? And the whole human race afterwards, what do you suppose is the
> origin of their souls? Was it from propagation like the brute animals, in such a
> way that just as body comes from body so too soul is generated from soul? ...
> But certainly ... God is engaged daily in making souls; God, for whom to will
> is to have done and who never ceases to be the Creator.[22]

St. Augustine castigates the notion that human soul is generated through the
semen,[c] saying that the soul would then be corporeal:

> Those who assert that souls are propagated from the one that God gave the
> first man, and say that they derive from parents, if they follow the opinion of
> Tertullian, they certainly maintain that souls are not spirits but bodies, and
> that they take their origins from corporeal seed. What more perverted a notion
> could be expressed?[23]

But he left open the question of soul being generated by soul:

> Without doubt, therefore, the original direction of the happiness of the soul is
> God Himself, who certainly did not beget it from Himself, but created it from
> no other thing, as He created the body from the earth. For what touches on its
> origin and how it comes to be in the body, whether it is from that man who
> was first created, when man was made into a living soul (Gn 2:7; 1 Cor
> 15:45), or whether in a like fashion individual souls are created for individual
> men, I did not know then, nor do I know now.[24]

St. Augustine wavered between *creationism* (the special creation of the soul)
and *spiritual generationism* (the generation of soul by soul). He found it difficult
to reconcile the special creation of the soul by God with the propagation of original sin:

---

c. This opinion is called *traducianism*, after *tradux*, which is the shoot of a vine
prepared for transplanting. See OTT, pp. 99–100 and JR, Volume 3, p. 165,
footnote 2.

A reason must be sought and given why souls, if they are newly created for each one being born, are damned if the infants die without Christ's Sacrament. That they are damned if they so depart the body is the testimony both of Holy Scripture and of Holy Church.[25]

Theodoret of Cyr holds for the special creation of each human soul:

It is easy for God to be an Artisan both with what does not exist and with what does exist. Indeed, He did this both in the past and, quite literally, He does it every day. For He shapes the bodies of living things from existing bodies, and from what does not exist He creates souls, not for all living creatures, but only for man.[26]

St. Thomas Aquinas held that the sensitive souls of animals are seminally generated.[27] But he condemns as heretical the seminal generation of human souls:

Again, since the intellectual soul has an operation independent of the body, it is subsistent, as proved above (Q. 75, A. 2): therefore to be and to be made are proper to it. Moreover, since it is an immaterial substance it cannot be caused through generation, but only through creation by God. Therefore to hold that the intellectual soul is caused by the begetter, is nothing else than to hold the soul to be non-subsistent and consequently to perish with the body. It is therefore heretical to say that the intellectual soul is transmitted with the semen.[28]

St. Thomas also rejected the notion that human souls were created together at the beginning of time because the soul is the substantial form of the body and it is unnatural for it to be without a body.[d] Rather, souls are created at the same time that they are infused into bodies.[29] He also replies to the objection that human souls could not be created every day because Scripture says; *"on the seventh day God finished his work which he had done ..."* (2:2):

God is said to have rested on the seventh day, not from all work, since we read: *"My Father worketh until now"* (Jn 5:17); but from the creation of any

---

d. The Talmud teaches the preexistence of souls. The rabbinic scholars believed that souls not yet united to bodies are stored in the seventh heaven. It was common belief among Jews that the Messianic era would not come until all those unborn souls have had their term of existence on earth. See Abraham Cohen, *Everyman's Talmud: The Major Teachings of the Rabbinic Sages* (New York, Schocken Books, 1975 reprint of 1949 edition), p. 78.

new genera and species, which may not have already existed in the first works. For in this sense, the souls which are created now, existed already, as to the likeness of the species, in the first works, which included the creation of Adam's soul.[30]

Something can be added every day to the perfection of the universe, as to the number of individuals, but not as to the number of species.[31]

Pope St. Anastasius II condemned seminal generation of the human soul in 498.[32] The Symbol of Faith of Pope Leo IX (1053) states: "I also believe and declare that the soul is not a part of God but was created from nothing...."[33] In 1341 Pope Benedict XII declared erroneous the proposition: "that the human soul of the son is propagated from the soul of his father, as the body is from the body."[34] Lateran Council V declared that the soul is infused into the body.[35] Pope Alexander VII in 1661 spoke of the "creation and infusion into her body" of the soul of the Blessed Virgin Mary.[36] The Holy Office under Pope Leo XIII in 1887 condemned the notion that the soul may be multiplied by human generation by proceeding from the imperfect (the sensitive grade) to the perfect (the intellectual grade).[37] Pope Pius XII in *Humani generis* taught: "[T]he Catholic Faith obliges us to hold that souls are immediately created by God."[38] The *Catechism of the Catholic Church* neatly summarizes the Church's teaching on the origin and destiny of the human soul:

The Church teaches that every spiritual soul is created immediately by God— it is not "produced" by the parents—and also that it is immortal: it does not perish when it separates from the body at death, and it will be reunited with the body at the final Resurrection.[39]

Created "immediately" means created at the moment of conception. "From the time that the ovum is fertilized, a life is begun which is neither that of the father nor of the mother; it is rather the life of a new human being with his own growth. It would never be made human if it were not human already."[40]

Damaged Nature of the Human Species

Adam at the suggestion of the devil sinned, and as a consequence of his sin Adam was changed for the worse in body and soul, was made a "mass of perdition," and fell under the power of the devil. Furthermore, his damaged nature was passed on to his whole progeny. His progeny, like him, suffer mortality, pain, weakened intellects and wills, an inclination to evil from which they cannot completely free themselves, and subjection to the power of the devil.[41] *"Therefore as sin came into the world through one man and death through sin, and so death spread to all men because all men sinned."*[42] Sin and death enter together with the murder of Abel by Cain (4:8). Sin spread for some 1600 years until the earth was filled with corruption and violence (6:11–12), to the point where God decided to destroy the earth and its inhabitants and start anew with eight survivors, Noah and his three sons and their wives.[43]

Adam's sin caused him to pass on a damaged nature to his posterity, but not a completely corrupted nature. His descendants, even though their wills were weakened, still retained the freedom to resist their inclination to evil; and even though their intellects were darkened, they still could come to know the existence of God with their natural power of cognition.[44] The former was affirmed when God told Cain: *"If you do well, will you not be accepted? And if you do not do well, sin is couching at your door: its desire is for you, but you must master it"* (4:7). And St. Paul affirms the latter: *"Ever since the creation of the world his invisible nature, namely his eternal power and deity, has been clearly perceived in the things that have been made."*[45]

Original Sin

David the Psalmist sang mournfully: *"Behold I was brought forth in iniquity, and in sin did my mother conceive me."*[46] St. Paul said, *"[O]ne man's trespass led to condemnation for all men ... by one man's disobedience all were made sinners...."*[47] Thus all of Adam's descendants, with the exception of the Blessed Virgin Mary and her Son, are conceived without the gift of supernatural life, that is, sanctifying grace. They are born without the friendship of God and the right to heaven.[48] [e] This state of deprivation is called *original sin.*[49] [f] The Council of Trent called it "the death of the soul."[50]

---

e. An exception is John the Baptist who was cleansed from original sin while in the womb of his mother. That is why the Church celebrates his birthday along with those of Jesus and Mary.

f. The term *original sin* is used in two senses. First, it means the original sin of disobedience committed by Adam; this is sometimes called *originating* original sin. Second, it means the deprivation of grace in the newly created souls of Adam's progeny; this is sometimes called *originated* original sin. Here the term *original sin* will be reserved for originated original sin. Originating original sin will be called *Adam's sin* or *the sin of Adam.*

Bishop L. L. Morrow points out: "God is not unjust in punishing us on account of the sin of Adam, because original sin does not take away from us anything to which we have a strict right as human beings, but only the free gifts which God in his goodness would have bestowed on us if Adam had not sinned." He also points out: "Original sin does not come to us from Eve, but from Adam alone, since God made him representative and head of the whole human race."[51] For St. Paul said, *"sin came into the world through one man."*[52]

St. Augustine said that in Adam we all sinned because we were all one Adam:

> In Adam all sinned when, by that power innate in his nature, by which he was able to beget them, all were as yet the one Adam.[53]

Augustine further said that we imitate Adam when we sin, but original sin is transmitted not by imitation but by propagation:

> Adam, in whom all die, besides being an example for imitation to those who willfully transgress the commandment of the Lord, by the hidden depravity of his own carnal concupiscence, depraved in his own person all those who came from his stock.... *"Through one man,"* the Apostle says, *"sin entered the world, through sin death"* (Rom 5:12). And this refers not to imitation but propagation.[54]

Augustine's mentor, St. Ambrose, had said it this way:

> Adam was brought into being; and we were brought into being in him. Adam perished and in him all perished.[55]

The contraction of original sin is connected with the nature and not the person.[56] It is "called 'sin' only in an analogical sense: it is a sin 'contracted' and not 'committed'—a state and not an act."[57] There is no personal guilt associated with it, except with its originator, Adam. The Church has always insisted that it is passed on by natural generation, by propagation, and not by imitation.[58] The *Catechism of the Catholic Church* summarizes the mystery of the transmission of original sin as follows:

> How did the sin of Adam become the sin of all his descendants? The whole human race is in Adam "as one body of one man" (St. Thomas Aquinas, *De Malo* 4, 1). By this "unity of the human race" all men are implicated in Adam's sin, as all are implicated in Christ's justice. Still, the transmission of

original sin is a mystery that we cannot fully understand. But we do know by Revelation that Adam had received original holiness and justice not for himself alone, but for all human nature.[59]

Genesis itself does not give explicit doctrine on original sin. But it dramatically shows the effects of Adam's sin in his descendants. Furthermore, it never tells whether Adam and Eve reconciled themselves with God, but the accounts of the births of Cain, Abel, and Seth (4:1, 2, 25) seem to imply that they did. Also, Sirach said that Adam was honored *"above every living being in creation."*[60] That would hardly be so if he had remained at enmity with God. The Book of Wisdom affirms that Adam was delivered from his transgression: *"Wisdom protected the first-formed father of the world, when he alone had been created; she delivered him from his transgression, and gave him strength to rule all things."*[61]

The Antediluvians and Their World

The world from the creation of Adam and Eve to the Great Flood was a very different world from ours. It was in the beginning, and the laws of development were different, just as the laws for the development of an embryo differ from those for an adult. St. Augustine said: "These first works of God are, of course, unparalleled just because they are the first. Those who refuse to believe in them ought to refuse credence to any extraordinary phenomena. But in fact these events would not be classed as extraordinary, if they had occurred in the normal course of nature. For no event is to no purpose under the all-embracing government of God's providence, even if the reason for it is hidden from us."[62]

Before proceeding, a few words about biblical chronology are in order. Biblical chronology is a reliable guide for determining the approximate age of the human species, which is that of the earth, despite the variations in the texts and the possibility of omissions in the genealogies.[63] F. N. Jones compiled a list of the dates of Creation as calculated by thirty different scholars. They range from 3836 B.C. to 5426 B.C., the most famous being 4004 B.C., calculated by James Ussher.[64]

St. Augustine reckoned "from the evidence of holy Scriptures that fewer than 6000 years have passed since man's first origin."[65] He argues from historical records available to him to refute "the nonsense of the writings which allege many more thousands of years, and to show how utterly inadequate is their authority on this subject."[66] He said that little credence "should be given to those writings packed with fairy-tales about reputed antiquity, which our opponents may decide to produce in attempts to controvert the authority of our sacred books, whose inspiration is so generally acknowledged. This is the authority which foretold that the whole world would believe in it; and the belief of the whole world has answered to that prophecy. The fulfillment in reality of those prophecies of the future guarantees the truth of the biblical narrative of the past."[67]

St. Augustine could have written that today, so timely is his message. Only in his day he had to refute false history. Today he would have to refute false science. Evolutionary anthropologists "controvert the authority of our sacred books" by telling us that the human species is hundreds of thousands or even millions of years old. But they can't make up their minds exactly how old. This is a reflection of the total unreliability of the dating methods they use, which are discussed elsewhere.[68] Suffice it to say here that we need not worry about being contradicted by the facts of science, as opposed to the speculations of scientists, if we accept the biblical testimony that the human species has been around only a few thousand years.

In the beginning there had to be marriage between sisters and brothers for the human species to grow. This is one of the original laws of development that is no longer applicable. The practice was ended, according to St. Augustine, to multiply relationships so that affections would be more distributed, thereby promoting social harmony.[69] Also, the genetic deterioration that accompanied the growth of sin causes harmful effects in the offspring of consanguineous unions.

The first descendant of Adam and Eve mentioned in Scripture is Cain. But that does not necessarily mean that he was their first offspring.[70] It only means that he was the first child of significance in the history of salvation. He probably wasn't the first because when God exiled him the earth was already populated (4:14).

Cain was the father of the first of two major lines of descent that Genesis focuses in on. His line lived by human standards. The other was the line of Seth, which lived according to God's will.[g] St. Augustine calls the two lines, allegorically, two cities: the city of man and the city of God.[71] These two lines are the succession of leaders of the two cities. The cities are populated by all the descendants of Adam and Eve, not just those of Cain and Seth. Scripture refers to the

---

g. Seth took on the role of Abel as "a fit heir in the order of holiness." Seth is mentioned next after Abel as being born of Adam and Eve. But that does not necessarily mean that he was their first child after Abel. Seth was born when Adam was 130 years old, so he may have fathered many children between Abel and Seth. Seth's birth was the next of significance after Abel in the history of salvation. He was a son in the likeness of Adam, after his image (5:3). See CG, Book XV, Chapter 15.

inhabitants of the city of men as the *"daughters* [and sons] *of men"* and the inhabitants of the city of God as the *"sons* [and daughters] *of God"* (6:2). The cross-breeding of the two resulted in the powerful world leaders of the antediluvian world (6:4), who led it to destruction (6:13).[72] [h]

Genesis 4:17–24 records the genealogy of the princes of the city of man. The individuals listed are not necessarily the first born of their fathers. It is a line of men preoccupied with the things of the world. Cain was a farmer who would not give (or resentfully gave) the best of his crop as an offering to God (4:3–5).[i] He killed his generous shepherd brother Abel in a fit of jealousy. (4:8). Cain built the first city mentioned in the Bible and named it after his son, Enoch (4:17). Lamech was the first polygamist of note, having taken two wives (4:19). He was also a murderer, having slain a young man for wounding him (4:23). Jabal was the father of nomadic herdsmen (4:20) and his brother Jubal was the father of musicians (4:21). Tubal-cain was a metalworker (4:22).[k]

Antediluvian people lived much longer lives than we do. Man had lost the gift of immortality, but he still held the gift of a long life. It wasn't until after the Flood that the human life span decreased to what it is today. The antediluvians' longevity was probably the result of two major factors: diet and genetic conditions. First, a wide variety of fruits, vegetables, cereals, seeds and herbs were available to the antediluvians, and, although they no longer had access to the tree of life, there may have been other food available that contributed to longevity. The

---

h. The Hebrew word translated "sons of God" in (6:2) is *ben elohiym*. It is used in the Hebrew Bible to mean both angels and men of faith. Some, like St. Clement of Alexandria and Nemesius of Emesa, supposed the meaning in (6:2) is angels. Others, like Sts. Augustine, Ephrem, John Chrysostom and Cyril of Alexandria, supposed that they were descendants of Seth. The latter interpretation seems the most reasonable. If angels did somehow mate with human females, they would not have been good angels but devils. They would certainly not be called *"sons of God"* unless that incident was the occasion of their fall. St. Augustine argues that it was not (CG, Book XV, Chapter 23). See ACC, pp. 123–124, NB commentary on Genesis 6:1–4, and Gleason L. Archer, *Encyclopedia of Bible Difficulties* (Grand Rapids, MI: Zondervan Publishing House, 1982), pp. 79–80.

i. Abel offered the *"firstlings of his flock"* while Cain offered only *"fruit of the ground."*

j. Gn 4:3–5 shows that sacrifice is a primordial custom.

k. St. Augustine discusses the question of why Genesis records Cain's line only to the eighth generation, while it records Seth's to the tenth (CG, Book XV, Chapter 20).

Great Flood destroyed forever many species of plants. Perhaps some that helped provide for longevity were among those destroyed; or, if they survived, were soon lost. Second, much genetic information was lost during the Great Flood with the destruction of nearly the whole human species. Some of that information may have played an important role in longevity. Additionally, favorable environmental conditions may have also contributed to longevity.

Following is a list of the ten antediluvian patriarchs, each with the approximate year of their birth and life spans in years (5:1–32; 9:29). These patriarchs, who were the renowned princes of the city of God, are the antediluvian ancestors of Christ[73] and of all who live after the Flood. Again, the patriarchs are not necessarily the first born of their fathers.

Adam	4004 B.C.	930
Seth	3874 B.C.	912
Enosh	3769 B.C.	905
Kenan	3679 B.C.	910
Mahalalel	3609 B.C.	895
Jared	3544 B.C.	962
Enoch	3382 B.C.	365
Methuselah	3317 B.C.	969
Lamech	3130 B.C.	777
Noah	2948 B.C.	950

It is not unreasonable to accept the life spans of the patriarchs as factual. Modern scientists know next to nothing about the aging process and therefore have no grounds whatsoever for criticizing the biblical account. St. Augustine refuted those who tried to whittle down the ages of the patriarchs to agree with contemporary lifetimes.[74]

Scripture says explicitly that each of the patriarchs died, except for Enoch. Concerning the end of life on earth for Enoch it says: *"Enoch walked with God; and he was not, for God took him"* (5:24). Sirach said: *"No one like Enoch has been created on earth, for he was taken up from the earth."*[75] St. Paul said that because of his great faith he did not die: *"By faith Enoch was taken up so that he should not see death; and he was not found, because God had taken him.*[76] St. Jude cites a prophecy uttered by Enoch concerning Judgment Day:

> *It was of these also that Enoch in the seventh generation from Adam prophesied, saying, "Behold, the Lord came with his holy myriads, to execute judgment on all, and to convict the ungodly of their deeds of ungodliness which they have committed in such an ungodly way, and of all the harsh things which ungodly sinners have spoken against him.*[77]

Some of the Fathers identified Enoch and Elijah as the two witnesses in the Book of Revelation who are killed and then rise from the dead.[78] Neither Enoch nor Elijah suffered death.

Methuselah is the longest-lived human being in the Bible. He died in the year the Great Flood began (2348 B.C.).

Besides being long-lived, there is evidence of there being antediluvians of great physical stature. Genesis says *"The Nephilim were on the earth in those days"* (6:4). The Nephilim was a race of giants.[79] St. Augustine said that we know from Scripture and from Hebrew and Christian traditions that in the period before the Flood there were many giants, though not all the antediluvians were giants.[80] He also offers historical evidence for giants living after the Flood.[81] There is also fossil evidence for the existence of giants in the past. R. L. Wysong provides photographs of such evidence along with documentary information. He says: "Human footprints, both normal size and giant size, sometimes side by side with dinosaur prints, have been found in Mexico, New Mexico, Arizona, Texas, Missouri, Kentucky, Illinois and other U.S. locations."[82]

*   *   *   *

The earth on which the antediluvians lived was much different from what it is today. It was much more like God's original creation. The antediluvian world was totally destroyed by the Great Flood. As St. Peter put it: *"[T]he world that then existed was deluged with water and perished.*[83] By the time of the Flood the human species had been in existence more than 1600 years and had probably spread throughout the whole earth.[84] Everyone spoke the same language or dialects of a single language. In addition to the Nephilim, there was probably a large variegated assortment of other races of people with a cultural diversity that far surpassed that of the postdiluvian world. Since much of the water that is now on the surface of the earth was then beneath or above it, there was a much larger

landmass to support the superabundance of life. The geography was totally different than it is today, and the topography was probably gentler because the Great
Flood completely reshaped the surface of the earth and produced the rugged
topography of the earth as it is today. The fossil record shows that there was a
huge abundance and rich variety of plant and animal life, which the Flood transformed into vast coal and oil deposits. Dinosaurs and other gigantic creatures,
including insects, roamed the earth feeding on the lush vegetation. And apparently the climate was moderate worldwide.

One credible explanation for the uniformly warm climate is that a blanket of
water vapor surrounded antediluvian earth. Genesis speaks about water located
above the firmament (1:6–7). St. Thomas Aquinas, following St. Augustine, said
that even if we can't explain that water, we cannot doubt its existence.[85] J. C. Dillow considers the question of *"the water above"* in a full-length book.[86] He examines several models to explain the waters in conformity with natural laws[1] and
concludes that the vapor canopy model is the only feasible one. The canopy he
envisions begins about six miles above the surface of the earth and extends for
many miles. The canopy would produce the following effects:

- *A uniformly moderate climate:*[87] The canopy would act like the glass on a
  greenhouse, which traps infrared radiation inside, keeping the inside
  warm.

- *Greater atmospheric pressure:*[88] The weight of the canopy would double the
  air pressure at the surface of the earth. The increased pressure would significantly affect life on earth. It would facilitate flight for those gigantic
  winged reptiles found in the fossil record. The increased concentration of
  oxygen may have supported the gigantism in animals. The increased concentration of carbon dioxide would have contributed to the lush vegetation.

- *Radiation shielding:*[89] The canopy would have shielded the earth from
  radiation from the sun and from deep space. This probably was beneficial
  to biological organisms and may have contributed to their longevity.

- *Daytime sky appearance:*[90] The sun would appear as a reddish disk, and the
  daytime sky would have had a soft reddish glow because of Rayleigh scattering of the blue light.

---

1. That is, without assuming that the waters were held up by supernatural
   means.

- *Nighttime sky appearance*:[91] The night sky was always clear because there were no clouds, and it was dark because of attenuation of the light from the moon and the stars. For the same reason, fewer stars were visible than are today.

A network of warm ocean currents is another possible explanation for the warm antediluvian climate. The oceans could have been warmed from the top by the sun and from underneath by the infusion of hot water from subterranean springs. Also, the ecliptic may have been inclined differently before the Flood. The redistribution of solid matter and water on and beneath the surface of the earth during the Flood might have changed its moments of inertia enough to significantly affect the length of the day and the obliquity of the ecliptic.[m] That would have affected both the climate of the earth and the diurnal period. Before the Flood, the year may have been exactly 360 days.

Many of the gifts of the antediluvian world were lost. Whenever God punishes people for sin by withdrawing gifts from them, the posterities of those punished also suffer loss of the gifts—as Adam lost many gifts for his offspring. But God is good and merciful. He often replaces lost gifts with other gifts, even better ones.

---

m. There is evidence from ancient astronomical observations that the earth's axis has tilted from its original position. See Paul D. Ackerman, *It's a Young World After All: Exciting Evidences for Recent Creation* (Grand Rapids, MI: Baker Book House, 1986), pp. 88–99. Also, Christian Marchal showed that the uplift of a large mountain mass, such as the Himalayas, would affect the earth's moments of inertia enough to change the obliquity of the ecliptic by several tens of degrees. This information appeared in a 1996 article in the journal of the Muséum National d'Histoire Naturelle entitled "Earth Polar Displacements of Large Amplitude: a Possible Mechanism," with an erratum published in *Geodiversitas* in 1997.

[1] Acts 17:26. Also see Wis 10:1; Heb 2:11.

[2] See JR, no. 1278.

[3] JR, no. 1813.

[4] See JR, 2013.

[5] CG, Book XII, Chapter 9.

[6] See CG, Book XII, Chapter 22.

[7] Ibid.

[8] JR, no. 2147.

[9] Ruffini, Cardinal Ernesto, *The Theory of Evolution Judged by Reason and Faith* (New York: Joseph F. Wagner, Inc., 1959), p. 96.

[10] Ibid., p. 97.

[11] Ibid., p. 98.

[12] Ibid., pp. 98–99, 109–110.

[13] DZ, no. 717c.

[14] DZ, no. 2123.

[15] DZ, no. 2280.

[16] DZ, no. 2328.

[17] "Address to Theologians at the Symposium on Original Sin (1966)", excerpt in TCF, no. 516.

[18] CCC, no. 360.

[19] Ez 21:30; also see Ez 28:13, 15.

[20] Eccl 12:7.

[21] Wis 15:11.

[22] JR, no. 1385.

[23] JR, no. 1448.

[24] JR, no. 1965.

[25] JR, no. 1441. See footnote 31 in JR, Volume 3, pp. 14–15 for comments on infant baptism. Also see OTT, pp. 113–114 and CCC, nos. 1261, 1283.

[26] JR, no. 2146.

[27] ST, Part I, Q. 118, A. 1.

[28] ST, Part I, Q. 118, A. 2. St. Thomas believed in a succession of three distinct souls: the nutritive, the sensitive and the intellectual. See Reply Obj. 2.

[29] See ST, Part I, Q. 118, A. 3.

[30] Ibid., Reply Obj. 1.

[31] Ibid., Reply Obj. 2.

[32] See DZ, no. 170.

[33] DZ, no. 348.

[34] DZ, no. 533.

[35] DZ, no. 738.

[36] DZ, no. 1100.

[37] DZ, no. 1910.

[38] *Humani generis*, no. 36. DZ, no. 2327 cites this passage but omits the statement quoted here.

[39] CCC, no. 366.

[40] *Declaration on Procured Abortion*, Sacred Congregation for the Doctrine of the Faith, 18 November 1974, no. 12. Also see Ruffini, op. cit., pp. 141–146.

[41] See DZ, Systematic Index, pp. 21–21 for a wealth of citations on pertinent Church teaching. Also see OTT, pp. 112–113 and CCC, nos. 404–409, 415–421.

[42] Rom 5:12; also see 1 Cor 15:21–22 and CCC, no. 1008.

[43] See CCC, no. 401.

[44] See OTT, pp. 110–111 and CCC, nos. 405–406, 418.

[45] Rom 1:20.

[46] Ps 51:5.

[47] Rom 5:18–19.

[48] See OTT, pp. 110–111 and CCC, nos. 402–409, 416.

[49] See CCC, no. 417.

[50] DZ, no. 789.

[51] Morrow, Louis LaRavoire, *My Catholic Faith: A Catechism in Pictures* (Kansas City, MO: Sarto House, 2000, reprint of 1954 edition), p. 41.

[52] Rom 5:12.

[53] JR, no. 1728.

[54] JR, no. 1715.

[55] JR, no. 1306a.

[56] See CCC, no. 404, 405.

[57] CCC, no. 404.

[58] See DZ, nos. 109a, 790, 791, 795, 2229; CCC, nos. 404, 419. Also see Paul VI, "Address to Theologians at the Symposium on Original Sin (1966)," excerpt in TCF, no. 516.

[59] CCC, no 404; also see no. 406.

[60] Sir 49:16. Also see the second reading in the Office of Readings for Holy Saturday.

[61] Wis 10:1.

[62] CG, Book XII, Chapter 28.

[63] See Doctrine Seven. Also see Ruffini, op. cit., pp. 150–153.

[64] Jones, Floyd Nolen, *Chronology of the Old Testament: A Return to the Basics*, 14th ed. (The Woodlands, TX: KingsWord Press, 1999), p. 26.

[65] CG, Book XII, Chapter 11.

[66] Ibid.

[67] Ibid.

[68] See Doctrine Seven, << Reply to Objection 1 >>; Doctrine Nine, << Reply to Objection 2 >>.

[69] See CG, Book XV, Chapter 16.

[70] See CG, Book XV, Chapter 8.

[71] See CG, Book XV, Chapter 1.

[72] See CG, Book XV, Chapters 22–23.

[73] See Lk 3:23–38.

[74] See CG, Book XV, Chapter 12–14.

[75] Sir 49:14.

[76] Heb 11:5.

[77] Jude 14–15.

[78] See NB commentary on Rv 11:3–6.

[79] Nm 13:33.

[80] See CG, Book XV, Chapter 23.

[81] See CG, Book XV, Chapter 9.

[82] Wysong, R.L., *The Creation–Evolution Controversy* (East Lansing, MI: Inquiry Press, 1976), p. 373.

[83] 2 Pt 3:6.

[84] Whitcomb, John C. and Morris, Henry M., *The Genesis Flood: The Biblical Record and Its Scientific Implications* (Phillipsburg, NJ: P & R Publishing, 1960), pp. 23–33.

[85] See Doctrine Six, The Distinction of Works.

[86] See Dillow, Joseph C., *The Waters Above: Earth's Pre-Flood Vapor Canopy*, Revised Edition (Chicago: Moody Press, 1982).

[87] Ibid., pp. 139–145.

[88] Ibid., pp. 146–157.

[89] Ibid., pp. 157–182.

[90] Ibid., pp. 304–305.

[91] Ibid., pp. 292–304.

PART III

▼

THE EARTH

A New Earth

Doctrine Fifteen
God destroyed the world that was with a worldwide flood.

Scripture and Tradition clearly proclaim the historical fact that a worldwide flood destroyed the earth in the time of Noah. The Flood blotted out all men and all land-living animals except those on the ark. Signs of the Flood abound in the legends of all peoples and in the geological features of the earth.

The Biblical Account of the Flood

As the population of the antediluvian world grew, sin increased. Even the descendants of Seth became corrupted by sin. The people became so hardened in sin that God saw fit to destroy the whole world along with all the people in it, except for one righteous man named Noah, his wife, and his three sons and their wives. *"The LORD saw that the wickedness of man was great in the earth, and that every imagination of the thoughts of his heart was only evil continually. And the LORD was very sorry that he made man on the earth, and it grieved him to his heart. So the LORD said: 'I will blot out man whom I have created from the face of the ground, man and beast and creeping things and birds of the air, for I am sorry that I have made them.' But Noah found favor in the eyes of the LORD"* (6:5–8).

In (6:5–8) the text attributes human emotion to God. He is said to be sorry and grieved. It seems as if He gets angry and has second thoughts. St. Augustine explains that Scripture attributes human emotions to God for the sake of man:

> Now God's anger is not an agitation of his mind; it is a judgment by which punishment is inflicted on sin. And his consideration and reconsideration are his unchanging plan applied to things subject to change. For God does not repent of any action of his, (cf. Nm 23:19) as man does, and his decision on any matter whatsoever is as fixed as his foreknowledge is sure. But if Scripture

did not employ such words, it would not strike home so closely, as it were, to all mankind. For Scripture is concerned for man, and it uses such language to terrify the proud, to arouse the careless, to exercise the inquirer, and to nourish the intelligent; and it would not have this effect if it did not bend down and, as we may say, descend to the level of those on the ground.[1]

Augustine goes on to explain that the text speaks of the destruction of animals not because they were guilty of sin but to project the magnitude of the coming disaster:

When it goes on to announce the annihilation of all living creatures on earth and in the air, it is proclaiming the magnitude of the coming disaster. It is not threatening the destruction of creatures bereft of reason, as if they too had sinned.[2]

St. Ambrose said that the animals were to be destroyed because they were created for the sake of man:

What transgression could the irrational creatures have ever committed? But since they had been created for the sake of man, after that for whom they had been created was wiped out, it was logical that they were destroyed too, because there was no one who could profit from them. This is also clear in a deeper sense. Man is a mind endowed with reason. Man is defined as a living, mortal and rational being. When he, who is the principal element, disappears, every aspect of sensible life also disappears.[3]

The Fathers taught that God had given the antediluvians 120 years to repent, but they refused to do so. That is how the Fathers interpreted (6:3) which states: *"Then the LORD said: 'My spirit shall not abide in man for ever, for he is flesh, but his days shall be a hundred and twenty years.'"* St. Ephrem said that if they had repented they could have saved themselves from the Flood:

This generation will not live nine hundred years like the previous generations, for it is flesh and its days are filled with the deeds of flesh. Therefore, their days will be one hundred and twenty years. If they repent during this time, they will be saved from the wrath that is about to come upon them. But if they do not repent, by their deeds they will call down wrath upon themselves. Grace granted one hundred and twenty years for repentance to a generation that, according to justice, was not worthy of repentance.[4]

St. Jerome argued that the 120 years mentioned in (6:3) refers to a period of repentance and not to the lifetime of man. He also said that because of the antediluvians' utter recalcitrance, God reduced that period to one hundred years:

> Furthermore, lest {God} may seem to be cruel in that he had not given sinners a place for repentance, he added *"But their days will be 120 years,"* that is, they will have 120 years to do repentance. It is not therefore that human life was contracted to 120 years, as many wrongly assert, but that 120 years were given to that generation for repentance, since indeed we find that after the flood Abraham lived 175 years and others more than 200 and 300 years. Since indeed they despised to do repentance, God was unwilling for his decree to await its time, but cutting off the space of twenty years he brought on the flood in the one hundredth year that had been destined for doing repentance.[5]

Noah pleased God. *"Noah was a righteous man, blameless in his generation; Noah walked with God"* (6:9). God found him *"perfect and righteous."*[6] Since his generation was totally corrupt, Noah's virtue shined even more brightly. St. John Chrysostom said, "Virtue in fact is admirable even for itself. If someone cultivates virtue among those who refuse it, he makes it more worthy of admiration. Therefore the Scriptures, as though in admiration of this just man, point out the contrast: that only one man who was living among those who soon would experience the wrath of God, this Noah, *'found favor in the eyes of the Lord God.'*"[7] Scripture singled out Noah for special praise because he was blameless "at that time when the obstacles to virtue were many."[8] St. Paul held up Noah as an example of a man filled with faith in God.[9]

Apparently Noah and his family were the only just people on earth at the time of the Flood.[a] St. Augustine said, "[T]he entire human race, except for eight persons, deserved to be destroyed by the Flood."[10] He also stated:

> It is a well-founded belief that the Flood happened at a time when there were no longer to be found on earth any beings who did not deserve such a death as served to punish the wicked.[11]

The Genesis account implies that the antediluvians were given time to repent (6:3), but it does not say that Noah preached repentance to the antediluvians. Christian tradition, however, holds that he did. St. Peter called Noah a *"preacher*

---

a. The NAB and JBS translate (7:1) as saying that God found Noah *"alone"* as righteous in that age. Other translations omit the word *"alone."*

of holiness."[12] He was the only one in his time capable of preaching repentance. Christian tradition also teaches that the antediluvians mocked Noah for his preaching and for building the ark.

Those descendants of Seth, other than Noah and his family, who remained loyal to God, like Methuselah for example, died before the Flood. This seems to be the position of St. Augustine.[13]

✱   ✱   ✱   ✱

God told Noah to build an ark in which he and his family were to be rescued from the flood of waters God was going to send upon the earth. God gave Noah detailed instructions about the construction of the ark:

> *Make yourself an ark of gopher wood; make rooms in the ark, and cover it inside and out with pitch. This is how you are to make it; the length of the ark three hundred cubits, its breadth fifty cubits, and its height thirty cubits. Make a roof for the ark, and finish it to a cubit above; and set the door of the ark in its side; make it with lower, second, and third decks* (6:14–16).

The Fathers reckoned that God gave Noah a hundred years to build the ark, probably because Scripture says that Noah's sons were born after he was five hundred years old (5:32), and the Flood began when he was six hundred years old (7:6).[14] Certainly a long time was needed to build the ark, even if Noah employed hired help, because it was of enormous size. It was in the shape of a box about 600 feet long by 100 feet wide by 60 feet high,[b] having a capacity of 3.6 million cubic feet, which is the same as that of about a thousand railroad cattle cars. Its design made it very stable afloat but nonmaneuverable. Its purpose was simply to house the occupants safely on the surface of the water.

God gave Noah further instructions on the loading of the ark:

> *But I will establish my covenant with you; and you shall come into the ark, you, your sons, your wife, and your sons' wives with you. And of every living thing of all flesh, you shall bring two of every sort into the ark, to keep them alive with you; they shall be male and female. Of the birds according to their kinds, and of the animals according to their kinds, of every creeping thing of the ground according to its kind, two of every sort shall come to you to keep them alive. Also take with you*

---

b. Assuming that a cubit equals two feet.

every sort of food that is eaten, and store it up; it shall serve as food for you and for them (6:18–21).

God further instructed Noah to take additional clean animals and birds, seven pairs of each (7:2–3). Some of those will be used for sacrifice after the Flood (9:20).

There was supernatural assistance in the collection of animals. The text makes it clear that God sent the animals to Noah; he did not have to collect them. God informed their instincts at the appropriate times to migrate towards the ark. This need not have happened all at once, but could have taken place over a number of weeks or even months, with Noah holding them as they came in a menagerie. There were no barriers to their migration in the antediluvian world as there are in the postdiluvian world. There may have been only one landmass, or if there were more than one landmass there was probably a complete collection of animals on each, at least on the one where Noah lived. And all the animals need not have been full grown. Of the very large animals, like for example, dinosaurs, very young ones may have been taken aboard to minimize space and feeding problems. Many animals may have entered into natural or supernaturally induced hibernation, thereby minimizing feeding and waste disposal problems. St. Ephrem said that God "established a state of peace between the predatory animals and those who are preyed upon."[15] Also, the number of *"kinds"* of animals taken onto the ark cannot be measured in terms of the number of "species" identified by modern taxonomy. The numbers of kinds on the ark was smaller than the number of modern "species." In some cases many different modern "species" descended from only one kind on the ark. Noah took on only creatures that needed to be put on the ark for survival. Creatures that did not need to be put on the ark to survive, for example, fish, were left to fend for themselves during the Flood. J. Woodmorappe has studied in detail the various problems that Noah and his family would encounter in caring for the animals in the ark during the Flood.[16]

*   *   *   *

St. Augustine insisted that the biblical account of the Flood is *both* historical and allegorical:

> [N]o one, however stubborn, will venture to imagine that this narrative was written without an ulterior purpose; and it could not plausibly be said that the

events, though historical, have no symbolic meaning, or that the account is not factual, but merely symbolical, or that the symbolism has nothing to do with the Church. No; we must believe that the writing of this historical record had a wise purpose, that the events are historical, that they have a symbolic meaning, and that this meaning gives a prophetic picture of the Church.[17]

Augustine saw Noah's ark as a symbol of the Church on pilgrimage in the world. It is a haven made safe by the wood of the ark, which represents the wood of the Cross on which Christ saved us. The ark also symbolizes the Person of Christ. The dimensions of the ark symbolize the human body, in which Christ came, because they are in the same proportions. The door in the side of the ark represents the wound in the side of Christ. The three decks of the ark represent the repopulating of the earth by the three sons of Noah. And the clean and unclean animals represent the wheat and the chaff that will not be separated until the end of time.[18] Augustine also saw Noah and his sons as prefiguring the Church. Noah was a symbol of Christ, and his sons symbolized the nations.[19]

Other Fathers also saw allegorical meanings superimposed on the historical record of the Flood. Jerome saw mystical meaning in the dimensions of the ark. Three hundred represents the crucifixion because the letter T, the cross, is the Roman numeral for 300; fifty symbolizes penance because the fiftieth psalm of David is the prayer of his repentance; thirty represents the age of Jesus when he was baptized; and the one cubit above stands for one faith in God.[20] St. John Damascene said, "It was with water that God washed away the sin of the world in the time of Noah."[21] Thus it was a figure of Baptism.[22] Maximus of Turin wrote that the forty days of rain prefigured Lent and the cleansing of sin by the floodwaters prefigured Baptism.[23] St. Ambrose said that God telling Noah to go into the ark symbolized Him telling the righteous to enter themselves to seek the truth, which will direct them to salvation.[24] He also said that seven pairs of clean animals were taken on the ark because the number seven is "pure and holy"; "it is united to no number and generated by no number. Therefore it is said to be virgin because it generates nothing from itself...." Two of the unclean animals were taken aboard because "the number two ... is not full because it is divided" and "has some void in itself."[25]

The *Catechism of the Catholic Church* recalls an "image dear to the Church Fathers, she [the Church] is prefigured by Noah's ark, which alone saves from the flood."[26] It also recalls 1 Peter 3:21 saying, "[T]he flood and Noah's ark prefigured salvation by Baptism."[27] The *Roman Missal* recalls the floodwaters as a sign of the waters of Baptism in the blessing of the water at the Easter Vigil:

The waters of the great flood you made a sign of the waters of Baptism, that make an end of sin and a new beginning of goodness.[28]

✳   ✳   ✳   ✳

God directed Noah to take the animals and his family on to the ark. Noah did as God commanded. The loading took seven days. The animals entered the ark two-by-two, and when all the occupants were aboard, God closed the ark (7:1–16). Then the rain came; Noah was 600 years old:

> [O]n that day all the fountains of the great deep burst forth and the windows of the heavens were opened. And rain fell upon the earth forty days and forty nights (7:11–12).

The Flood was a supernaturally induced unleashing of natural powers, for God said that He would send the rain upon the earth (7:4). He collapsed the antediluvian vapor blanket (if there was one),[29] released pressurized subterranean waters,[c] and perhaps induced volcanic activity as well.[d] The Flood was worldwide because it covered all the mountains by at least thirty feet (7:19–20).[e] The Flood killed all living creatures that lived on land (7:21–23).[f] Noah, his wife, his three sons and their wives were the only human beings that survived the Flood. Christ confirmed this:

---

c. Walt Brown argues that all the water that flooded the earth came from below because he doesn't think that a vapor canopy is a workable model for the antediluvian atmosphere. According to Brown, the waters shot up from the earth high into the sky and came down as rain. See *In the Beginning: Compelling Evidence for Creation and the Flood* (Phoenix, AZ: Center for Scientific Creation, 1995), pp. 75–105, 174–178.

d. There are signs of much volcanic activity having taken place in the past. So the bursting forth of the *"fountains of the great deep"* probably included volcanic activity. See John C. Whitcomb and Henry M. Morris, *The Genesis Flood: The Biblical Record and Its Scientific Implications* (Phillipsburg, NJ: P & R Publishing, 1960), pp. 126–127; 137–139.

e. The antediluvian mountains were probably much lower than the higher postdiluvian ones, the latter being products of the Flood. See Whitcomb and Morris, op. cit., pp 127–128.

They [the antediluvians] ate, they drank, they married, they were given in marriage, until the day when Noah entered the ark, and the flood came and destroyed them all.[30]

And twice St. Peter affirmed it:

... when God's patience waited in the days of Noah, during the building of the ark, in which a few, that is, eight persons, were saved through water.[31]

... if he did not spare the ancient world, but preserved Noah, a herald of righteousness, with seven other persons, when he brought a flood upon the world of the ungodly.[32]

It would be naive to suppose that the Flood was a tranquil affair, like the filling and draining of a bathtub. Everyone knows that small local floods lasting only hours produce great changes in landscape. So it should not be hard to believe that a furious flood of rain over the whole earth for forty days and forty nights could completely reshape the face of the earth.[33] The Flood piled layer upon layer of sediment to form the mountains. Plants and animals were buried rapidly in the sediments to form fossils. Massive collections of plant and animal debris were compressed under great pressures to form oil and coal deposits. Great tectonic movements caused by the weight of the water sitting for one hundred and fifty days (7:24), and apparently aided by divine intervention (8:1),[g] caused the continents to rise and the sea floors to sink. Thus *"the waters of the earth receded from the earth continually"* (8:3). This process lasted for another one hundred and fifty

---

f. The Flood obviously was not a local one, as some maintain, because if that were the case God could just have told Noah to move to another area rather than go to the trouble of building a gigantic ark. And a local flood would not have killed all the inhabitants of the earth. Further, God's promise in (9:11) that the earth would never again be destroyed by a flood would be meaningless if He was speaking of a local flood. Local floods do not destroy the earth, although they do great damage on it. And if it weren't a meaningless promise, it would have been a broken promise because there have been innumerable local floods since the Genesis Flood.

   St. Lawrence of Brindisi, relating Catholic Tradition in his *Explanatio in Genesim*, affirms that the Flood was geographically universal.

g. St. Ambrose proposed that the wind sent by God in (8:1) was the Holy Spirit. He said that "that deluge was subsided by the invisible power of the Spirit" because "the wind had no power to dry the deluge." See ACC, p. 143.

days (8:3). Psalm 104 recalls the work of the Flood and God's promise not to destroy the world by water again (9:15):

Thou didst cover it [the earth] with the deep as with a garment; the waters stood above the mountains. At thy rebuke they fled; at the sound of thy thunder they took to flight. The mountains rose, the valleys sank down to the place which thou didst appoint for them. Thou didst set a bound which they should not pass, so that they might not again cover the earth.[34]

St. Peter paralleled the devastation caused by water in the Flood to that which will be caused by fire on the Last Day:

First of all you must understand this, that scoffers will come in the last days with scoffing, following their own passions and saying, "Where is the promise of his coming? For ever since the fathers fell asleep, all things have continued as they were from the beginning of creation. They deliberately ignore this fact, that by the word of God heavens existed long ago, and an earth formed out of water and by means of water, through which the world that then existed was deluged with water and perished. But by the same word the heavens and earth that now exist have been stored up for fire, being kept until the day of judgment and destruction of ungodly men.[35] h

Exactly five months after the rain began the ark came to rest on the mountains of Ararat (8:4). Two months and thirteen days later the tops of the mountains could be seen (8:5). These were probably new mountains being raised as the waters drained into permanent basins. The original antediluvian mountains were probably eroded away by the Flood. The waters *"were dried from off the earth"* ten months and thirteen days after the rain began (7:11; 8:13).

Forty days after observing the mountain tops, Noah sent out a raven that *"went to and fro until the waters were dried up from the earth"* (8:6–7). The Fathers explained that the raven did not return to the ark because it fed on carrion floating in the waters. It symbolizes those who were baptized but have fallen away from the Catholic faith to follow the ways of the world.[36] Later Noah sent out a dove, but it returned to the ark because it found no place to set foot because the earth was still covered with water (8:8). Seven days later he again sent out the

---

h. This verse could well be directed against modern uniformitarians who scoff at the scriptural account of the Flood and attempt to explain all the geological features of the earth in terms of currently operative processes acting over periods of millions of years.

dove. The dove returned with a freshly plucked olive branch in its mouth indicating that the water had subsided from the earth (8:10–11). The olive branch thus came to signify everlasting peace.[37] Seven days later he sent out the dove again, and it did not return, indicating that the earth was ready to be occupied (8:12). Maximus of Turin commented on the eschatological symbolism of the ark and the dove:

> For as Noah's ark preserved alive everyone whom it had taken in when the world went under, so also Peter's church will bring back unhurt everyone whom it embraces when the world goes up in flames. And as a dove brought the sign of peace to Noah's ark when the flood was over, so also Christ will bring the joy of peace to Peter's church when the judgment is over, since he himself is dove and peace, as he promised when he said, *"I shall see you again and your heart will rejoice"* (John 16:22).[38]

God then directed Noah to leave the ark along with his family and the animals. Noah obeyed, and one year and ten days after the rain began, the occupants began to leave the ark. (8:14–19). God assured Noah that the animals would be *"fruitful and multiply upon the earth"* (8:17).[i] Noah then built an altar to the LORD and offered burnt offerings of every clean animal (8:20). God was pleased with the offering and in turn promised never to curse the ground again because of man's transgressions, never to destroy every living creature again by water, and to maintain the regularity of the seasons, which had been disturbed during the Flood (8:21–22; 9:15).

The Flood in Folklore

The Genesis account is the only completely true and authoritative account of the Great Flood. It is a sober, detailed and consistent report that was written by eyewitnesses. The postdiluvian patriarchs preserved it faithfully and passed it on to their posterity intact. Eventually it reached Moses, through whom the divine seal was put on it, certifying its accuracy.

Other peoples, not in the line of the patriarchs, drifted away from the true religion. They recalled the story of the Deluge, but because of their lack of devotion to the one true God, they corrupted it, transforming it into fantastic tales. Such tales are found in the traditions of nearly all peoples throughout the

---

i.   According to some of the Fathers, there were no sexual relations among men or beasts on the ark. See ACC, pp. 136, 148.

world—in those of the most advanced civilizations and the most barbarous tribes. Although they may differ in details, the tales generally agree that there was a destruction of all human beings by water and that an ark or boat provided the means for some to survive and repopulate the world. Many also attribute the Flood to the wickedness of man. One compiler of the mythologies said:

> Among all traditions there is none so general, so widespread on earth, and so apt to show what may develop from the same material according to varying spiritual character of a people as the Flood tradition.[39]

J. G. Frazer[40] has collected a number of these legends from around the world, including ones from Australia and North and South America. The most famous of all is the Babylonian *Epic of Gilgamesh*. In that story a friendly god tells one Utnapishtim to tear down his house, abandon his possessions, and build a cube-shaped boat 120 cubits on a side. In it he was to save himself from the deluge that the warlike god Enlil was about to bring. Utnapishtim built the boat with seven stories, each of which he divided into nine sections. He sealed the boat with pitch. He brought his family and relatives on the ship along with his gold and silver. He also brought the animals of the field and craftsmen onboard. The rainstorm lasted six days and six nights. It was so severe that it even frightened the gods. On the seventh day the storm abated. Utnapishtim looked upon the sea and saw that all "was silence." All mankind "had turned to clay." The boat landed on Mount Nisir. Seven days after landing Utnapishtim sent out a dove, which returned to him because there was no resting place. Then he sent out a swallow, and it returned because there was no resting place. Then he sent out a raven, which did not return because the waters had abated. He then sent forth everything "to the four winds" and offered a sacrifice that pleased the gods.

The similarities between this account and the biblical account should not be a surprise because it was derived from the biblical account. The differences, however, show how far men had drifted from worship of the one true God, thereby losing contact with the truth and becoming open to falsehood. The one God is multiplied into many gods. It is not through the justice of God that the Flood is brought about but through the rashness of the god Enlil, who did not want any man to survive the deluge. The seaworthy ark of Noah is transformed into a less stable cubical shape, perhaps because the cube was seen as geometrically more beautiful. The gods "gathered like flies over the sacrificer" as if they were in need of nourishment, having been deprived of sacrifices for six days and six nights. At the end Utnapishtim and his wife are made gods and taken to the realm of the gods. Further, the Babylonian account does not say when the Flood happened. The biblical account is a restrained historical account, whereas the Babylonian account has no historical setting and is filled with imaginary accretions and distortions.

The Greeks also preserved some elements of the Flood story in their mythology. Plato, in his dialogues *Timaeus* and *Critias*,[41] describes the large island of Atlantis, which was located in the Atlantic Ocean just beyond the Pillars of Hercules. It was "larger than Libya and Asia put together."[42] On Atlantis there was a "great and wonderful empire" that ruled the whole island.[43] The island was blessed with many natural gifts—very fertile soil; ample pasture land; the unparalleled beauty of its mountains, plains, lakes, rivers and marshes; a variety and abundance of minerals; forests filled with all kinds of timber; many different flowers, fruits, vegetables, oils and aromatic substances; many wild and domesticated animals. It was a completely self-sufficient island. And its people, who were part god, were good. "They thought scorn of all things save virtue and counted their current prosperity a little thing."[44] But when they drifted away from virtue "by constant crossing with much mortality" they began to take on "the infection of wicked coveting and pride of power." "Zeus, the god of gods, ... was minded to lay a judgment on them, that the discipline might bring them back to tune. So he gathered all the gods...."[45] Plato does not tell what Zeus did, but he does say that the island of Atlantis "disappeared into the depths of the sea."[46]

The Latin poet Ovid preserved the Flood tradition of the Romans in his poem *Metamorphoses*. The poem begins with the story of creation. Man was of heavenly seed, made in the likeness to the gods that govern everything. Man originally lived in a state of happiness and innocence. There was no threatening law and no fear of punishment. Towns were not enclosed with walls. There were no swords. The earth was fertile and yielded produce without tilling. Springtime lasted all year. Milk and wine and honey flowed like streams.

Then came another age, when men were forced to labor. Jupiter put an end to the continual springtime and made the four seasons with their heat and their cold. The land had to be tilled with oxen. And when men began to use iron they grew wicked. Their wickedness grew. Men enraged Jupiter by their arrogance and lawlessness. He called a council of the gods and announced that he would destroy mankind. He decided to do this with water rather than fire and commenced to drown men with incessant showers from heaven. The waters washed away or covered nearly everything and waves lapped at the tops of the highest mountains. A just, devout, righteous, god-fearing couple, Deucalion and his wife Pyrrha, arrived in their little boat at a sacred hill that stood out of the waters. They were the only survivors. Jupiter then called the Flood to an end and ordered for the waters to be abated. Deucalion and Pyrrha were distressed at seeing that they were the only mortals left. They walked to the shrine of the goddess Themis and prayed to her there. She instructed them to scatter stones on the earth as they walked away from her temple. Those dropped by Deucalion turned into men, and those thrown by Pyrrha were turned into women. Thus came into being a new race of men and women.[47]

The first century Jewish historian Flavius Josephus records that there were stories about the Flood and the ark in Gentile nations and that there were even reports that there were remains of the ark:

> Now all the writers of barbarian histories make mention of the flood and this ark; among whom is Berosus the Chaldean; for when he is describing the circumstances of the flood, he goes on thus:—"It is said there is still some part of this ship in Armenia, at the mountain of the Cordyaeans; and that some people carry off pieces of the bitumen, which they take away, and use chiefly as amulets for the averting of mischiefs." Hieronymus the Egyptian, also, who wrote the Phoenician Antiquities, and Mnaseas, and a great many more, make mention of the same. Nay, Nicholaus of Damascus, in his ninety-sixth book, hath a particular relation about them, where he speaks thus:—"There is a great mountain in Armenia, over Minyas, called Baris, upon which it is reported that many who fled at the time of the Deluge were saved; and that one who was carried in an ark came on shore upon the top of it; and that the remains of the timber were a great while preserved. This might be the man about whom Moses, the legislator of the Jews wrote."[48] j

---

j. There have been claims in more recent times of sightings of the remains of the ark high on the snow-covered slopes of Mt. Ararat in the Armenian area of Eastern Turkey. But confirmation is elusive. A number of expeditions to Mt. Ararat in search of the ark have failed. Exploration of Mt. Ararat is quite difficult because of hazardous weather and continually changing topography. In 1955 a French explorer salvaged three pieces of a wooden beam embedded in solid ice at the top of Mount Ararat. The wood seems to be very old and could possibly be a relic of the ark. (Scoffers have already decided that if the wood is part of an ark, it is not Noah's ark but a shrine that was built on the site by people who believed that Noah's ark landed there.) For a more complete albeit skeptical account about Mount Ararat and the ark see Werner Keller, *The Bible as History*, 2nd revised edition (New York: Bantam Books, 1982), pp. 37–40.

Geological Signs of the Flood

God had the Flood leave many signs on the face of the earth to remind men how much He hated iniquity. However, modern uniformitarian geologists attempt to explain the signs in terms of currently operative, relatively mild geological processes acting over millions of years. But many of the geological features of the earth give such strong evidence of catastrophic processes having been at work that uniformitarian geologists are forced to admit the occurrence of catastrophes they cannot explain. Yet they resolutely refuse to explain the features as being caused by a worldwide flood because that reeks of "religion," and "science" must distance itself from religion. However, the father of uniformitarian geology, James Hutton (1726–1797), rejected the biblical Deluge with his own "theological" explanation: "[G]eneral deluges form no part of the theory of the earth; for, the purpose of this earth is evidently to maintain vegetable and animal life, and not to destroy them."[49] But the evidence in favor of the Flood is so strong that if it weren't in the Bible, geologists would probably postulate a worldwide flood as the best explanation of the data. Following are geological phenomena that are certain signs of the Deluge:

- *Ossiferous fissures*: These are found in many places throughout the world. They are rents in the earth, some measuring 140 to 300 feet deep, filled with the incomplete remains of many different animals mixed together. The broken bones show no sign of weathering, and are cemented together by calcite, so they were obviously deposited quickly with water. Streams could not have deposited them because there are no signs of rolling on the bones. The bottom line is that great numbers of animals of every kind were heaped together and rapidly buried by water in many different places on the face of the earth. In the United States such a deposit was found in Agate Springs in northwestern Nebraska. It contains the bones of about nine thousand animals, including rhinoceroses, camels and giant wild boars, thrown together and buried. The only reasonable explanation for this and other such stupendous fossil graveyards is that the Flood produced them.[50]

- *Fossil lakes*: These are large inland bodies of water or the remains of large inland bodies of water that were left by the Flood. They exist all over the world, and there is no explanation for their existence other than that they were caused by a great inundation. Even in the Tibetan plateau, which averages over sixteen thousand feet in height, there are numerous salt lakes that indicate that this high tableland, the "roof of the world," was once submerged beneath the sea. In the United States there are a number of such lakes. The most famous one is the Great Salt Lake, which is a small remnant of Lake Bonneville. Lake Bonneville was nearly the size of Lake Michigan and occupied parts of Utah, Nevada and Idaho.[51]

- *Rivers*: There is evidence everywhere that the rivers of the world were once much larger and carried much greater volumes of water. Raised river terraces indicate this, as do extensive deposits of alluvium along the flood-plains of rivers.[52]

- *Coal beds*: The source of all coal is vegetable matter. Coal was produced by the rapid burial of the lush vegetation of the antediluvian world during the Flood. The coal seams are full of signs of their origin. Well-preserved plants are found in wonderful profusion in the rocks that overlie and underlie the coal beds. They are not present in the coal itself because the processes that produced the coal destroyed their forms. The rocks contain the wood, leaves, flowers and fruits of a large variety of plants in a remarkable state of preservation. Among the plants found preserved are the following: sassafras, laurel, magnolia, cinnamon, sequoia, poplar, willow, maple, birch, chestnut, elder, beech, elm, palms, cypress, oak, rose, plum, tulip, almond, myrtle, and acacia. Coal is found on every continent and on many islands. There is enough coal in the earth to provide mankind with power, light, heat and byproducts for thousands of years.[53] [k]

- *Oil deposits*: Oil is found in fossiliferous strata and is a product of organic matter. It was produced during the Flood when huge quantities of living organisms, which manufactured the oil, were rapidly buried. Their oil was distilled by the heat and pressure; and it collected in sand between impermeable strata, where it remained stored. Great reservoirs of oil exist at many places throughout the world.[54] [l]

- *Fossils*: Fossils are the remains of living organisms. They are usually found petrified by the infiltration of water and the deposition of dissolved min-

---

k. Chemists have succeeded in making artificial coal from natural materials. Artificial coal was produced from a composite of wood combined with clay and heated to about 150 degrees Celsius in the absence of oxygen. The artificial coal took eight months to produce and was indistinguishable from the real thing. See *Nature*, March 28, 1985, p. 316.

erals. The Fathers of the Church knew of them. Fossils of all kinds of living and extinct species of plants and animals have been found throughout the world. Recently, the fossil remains of a sixteen hundred pound rodent dubbed "Ratzilla" were found in Venezuela.[55] Fossils have been found in great numbers everywhere—on mountaintops, in valleys, on plains, in deserts, in caves, in coal mines. At least one has been found as far as six thousand feet under the earth. Fossilized bones or plant parts are found scattered here and there over a wide area or heaped together in countless numbers to form a mountain. Marine fossils are found on mountaintops far inland away from the sea. The number of fossils entombed throughout the world is immense, that of trilobites alone is estimated to be in the trillions. The worldwide fossil record is a three-dimensional snapshot of the destruction of the antediluvian world by water.[56]

- *Mammoth remains*: The mammoth was a kind of elephant with long coarse hair. It was larger than the Indian elephant but smaller than the African elephant, and its tusks and head were larger than those of modern elephants. Mammoths were preserved in great numbers, encased in the frozen tundra of northern Siberia. They were frozen so quickly that their flesh has been preserved intact. Sub-tropical plants were found undigested in their stomachs. Bears, wolves and prisoners of the "Gulag Archipelago" have fed on their defrosted flesh. Many other kinds of animals were buried with them, including horses, buffaloes, rhinoceroses, oxen and sheep. It appears that all of Siberia is one vast graveyard of such beasts. Their quick burial in loam or gravel occurred during the Flood. Their quick freezing was probably caused by a catastrophic change in climatic conditions brought on by the Flood.[57] [m]

---

l.   Researchers at Oregon State University have published reports about present day oil production in the Gulf of California. Oil is being produced under six thousand feet of water by superheated water from the earth acting on organic sediments. The oil produced is indistinguishable from the crude oil obtained from wells.

Some researchers propose that oil may be a natural nonbiological product. Thomas Gold says that oil is a "renewable primordial soup continually manufactured by the earth under ultrahot conditions and tremendous pressures. As this substance migrates toward the surface, it is attacked by bacteria, making it appear to have an organic origin dating back to the dinosaurs" (*Creation* magazine, Vol. 27, No. 3, June–August, 2005, p. 9).

It was dramatically demonstrated in recent history that geologic forces, like those unleashed during the Great Flood, can rapidly change the features of the earth. In 1980, a major volcanic eruption took place at Mount St. Helens in Washington State. The eruption was so violent that it knocked down millions of trees, changed the flow of rivers, and formed rock strata and large canyons—all in just a few days. This presents a direct challenge to the uniformitarian principle that the features on the surface of the earth were produced over millions of years by slowly acting forces.[58]

Postdiluvial Flooding

Some discoveries presented as evidence of the Great Flood are only signs of local early postdiluvian floods. Josephus mentions that the flooding of the plain of Shiner by the Tigris and Euphrates rivers was so severe after the Great Flood that some early postdiluvians were afraid to migrate there.[59] Similar flooding happened throughout the whole world as the surface of the earth settled. Also climatic conditions took some time to settle. That probably accounts for the signs that the Sahara Desert was once a populated fertile land with lakes and rivers.[60] Residual effects of the Flood were great immediately afterwards and still linger with us today in tectonic and volcanic activity.

A discovery once offered as evidence for the Great Flood is the alluvial deposit found by Leonard Woolley in 1929 covering the ancient city of Ur in southern Mesopotamia.[61] Near the base of the tell at the site on which Ur was built and rebuilt a number of times, Woolley found eight to ten feet of clay that covered the original city. Subsequent excavations in Mesopotamia by other archaeologists also yielded alluvial deposits. Woolley concluded that an area 400 miles long by 100 miles wide from the Persian Gulf northwest and centered on the Tigris and Euphrates rivers had once been flooded, and he identified this with the Great Flood of Genesis. Further excavations, however, led to the discovery of new deposits and to the conclusion that the deposits were produced by a number of different local floods. Interpreted biblically, this means that the clay-covered original Ur discovered by Woolley was not an antediluvian city but an early postdilu-

---

m. Another view is that the mammoths were postdiluvian animals and that their freezing occurred during the ice age that followed in the wake of the Flood. See Michael J. Oard, *An Ice Age Caused by the Genesis Flood* (El Cajon, CA; Institute for Creation Research, 1990), pp. 86–91.

vian city. It is unlikely that archaeologists will dig up an antediluvian city because it seems that the Great Flood washed away all signs of antediluvian civilization.

More recently, scientists have identified a flooding of the Black Sea with Noah's Flood. A team of geophysicists and oceanographers discovered evidence that the Black Sea was once a vast freshwater lake lying hundreds of feet below sea level. The geophysicists involved, W. Ryan and W. Pitman, proposed that 7600 years ago rising oceans burst through the Bosporus valley, and the salt water of the Mediterranean poured with immense force into the lake causing the human population to disperse from there to other parts of the world, carrying with them the story of the Flood.[62] But if such a geological event really happened, it probably was one of a number of such events that took place during the Great Flood, or it happened soon after the Flood as the earth settled and the waters receded, long before the arrival of men in the area.

< Objections > and << Replies >>

< Objection 1 >

If there was a worldwide flood that destroyed man and beast together, we should find human fossils mixed with the animal fossils; but we don't.

<< Reply to Objection 1 >>

This is a favorite objection of evolutionists. It is easy to answer.

<< The Flood Scenario >>

In the beginning God created a world filled with animals. But He created only two human beings. As human beings multiplied, so did the animals. By the time of the Flood human beings spread throughout the world. But they still occupied only a very small percentage of the huge habitable landmass of the antediluvian world, while wild animals occupied the rest of the land and the seas as well. The numbers of animals exceeded the numbers of men by orders of magnitude. When the floodwaters came, many highly mobile animals, being able to run much faster and having more physical endurance than men, were able to escape to the highlands. Men who lived in the highlands or managed to flee there were consumed by huge multitudes of ravenous beasts. These creatures that were created for man, God now turned against him. Men trapped in the lowlands were the first creatures to be drowned. Their bodies quickly decayed or were consumed by hungry fish. So it is easy to see why there would not be many human remains available for fossilization.

However, a number of human fossils have been found.[63] And even if one of them is established conclusively to be a contemporary of dinosaurs and other fossil beasts, that is enough to invalidate the theory of evolution.[n] On the other hand, even if no human fossils whatsoever were found, that could not be used to substantiate the theory of evolution. To make use of such a finding, evolutionists would have to first explain why there were no fossils of millions and millions of human beings who have lived in postdiluvian history.

✳   ✳   ✳   ✳

< Objection 2 >

"In the ancient Hebrew legend of a great flood, as it is recorded in the Book of Genesis, Biblical critics are now agreed in detecting the presence of two originally distinct and partially inconsistent narratives, which have been combined so as to present the superficial appearance of a single homogeneous story. Yet the editorial task of uniting them has been performed so clumsily that the repetitions and inconsistencies left standing in them can hardly fail to attract the attention of even a careless reader."[o]

<< Reply to Objection 2 >>

The repetitions in the text are not the result of clumsy patching together of disparate narratives. Rather, they are the result of careful pedagogy designed to impress the story on the minds of its hearers. As for the inconsistencies, they exist

---

n. Fossilized dinosaur and giant human footprints were found together in the bed of the Paluxy River near Glen Rose, TX. However, it is not known whether the footprints are antediluvian or postdiluvian. For an extensive analysis of this evidence see Cecil N. Dougherty, *Valley of the Giants* (Glen Rose, TX: Valley of the Giants Publishers, 1978). Also, see Whitcomb and Morris, op. cit., pp. 173–175.

o. This objection is taken verbatim from James George Frazer, *Folklore in the Old Testament: Studies in Comparative Religion, Legend, and Law* (New York: Hart, 1975), pp. 56–57. A similar position is taken in the NAB in its commentary on Genesis 6:5–8, 22.

only in the minds of those who look superficially at the text with a mind to find contradictions, and not in the text itself.

<< Consistency of the Genesis Flood Account >>

One supposed inconsistency concerns the number of pairs of each animal taken on to ark. In (6:19) God tells Noah, *"And of every living thing of all flesh, you shall bring two of every sort into the ark, to keep them alive with you; they shall be male and female."* In (7:2–3) God gives Noah the additional instruction concerning clean animals: *"Take with you seven pairs of all clean animals, the male and his mate; and a pair of the animals that are not clean, the male and his mate; and seven pairs of the birds of the air also, male and female, to keep their kind alive upon the face of all the earth."* Some critics have suggested that these two passages contradict each other and indicate that some inept redactor put both of them into the account without noticing the difference between them. However, the reason for God ordering seven of each of the clean species is perfectly evident. They were to be used for sacrifices after the Flood was over, as made clear in (8:20): *"Then Noah built an altar to the LORD, and took of every clean animal and of every clean bird, and offered burnt offerings on the altar."*

The other alleged inconsistency trotted out concerns the timetable of the Flood. Critics claim that there are dates built around seven- and forty-day periods, and others around months in a 365-day year. But such would not indicate inconsistencies but only the best ways of expressing facts. Days and months are natural ways of expressing time, based on the motions of astronomical bodies. There is no indication that the number forty has any numerological significance. It is used twice for actual time periods: for the number of days of flooding and for the number of days after landing on Ararat when Noah opened the window of the ark. Other time periods are given that do not fit into a forty-day scheme. They are the following: the water abated after 150 days; the earth was dry on the twenty-seventh day of the second month. In fact, the detailed chronology of the Flood is a sign that the human author of the account was an eyewitness to the event. The chronology can appear to be inconsistent only to those who have already decided in advance that the account is a hodgepodge put together from two or more conflicting sources.

[1] CG, Book XV, Chapter 25.

[2] Ibid.

[3] ACC, p. 128.

[4] ACC, p. 125.

[5] Ibid., Also see CG, Book XV, Chapter 24.

[6] Sirach 44:17.

[7] ACC, p. 129.

[8] Ibid.

[9] Hebrews 11:7.

[10] CG, Book XV, Chapter 20.

[11] CG, Book XV, Chapter 24.

[12] 2 Peter 2:5 (NAB).

[13] CG, Book XV, Chapter 24.

[14] See CG, Book XV, Chapter 27; ACC, p. 125 (St. Jerome); ACC, p. 135 (St. Ephrem).

[15] ACC, p. 135.

[16] Woodmorappe, John, *Noah's Ark: A Feasibility Study* (Santee, CA: Institute for Creation Research, 1996). Also see Rehwinkel, Alfred M: The Flood: *In the Light of the Bible, Geology and Archaeology* (St. Louis, MO: Concordia, 1951), ch. V; Whitcomb, John C. and Morris, Henry M., *The Genesis Flood: The Biblical Record and Its Scientific Implications* (Phillipsburg, NJ: P & R Publishing, 1960), pp. 63–79.

[17] CG, Book XV, Chapter 27.

[18] See CG, Book XV, Chapters 26–27 and ACC, p. 135.

[19] See ACC, p. 136.

[20] See ACC, p. 131.

[21] ACC, p. 132.

[22] See ST, Part III, Q. 66, A. 11, Reply Obj. 3.

[23] See ACC, p. 140.

[24] ACC, p. 134.

[25] ACC, pp. 134–135.

[26] CCC, no. 845.

[27] CCC, no. 1094.

[28] *Roman Missal*, Easter Vigil 42: Blessing of Water; cited in CCC, no. 1219.

[29] See Dillow, Joseph C., *The Waters Above: Earth's Pre-Flood Vapor Canopy*, Revised Edition (Chicago: Moody Press, 1982).

[30] Luke 17:27. Also see Matthew 24:38–39.

[31] 1 Peter 3:20.

[32] 2 Peter 2:5.

[33] For details see Whitcomb and Morris, op. cit., chapters. V–VII.

[34] Psalms 104:6–9.

[35] 2 Peter 3:3–7.

[36] See ACC, pp. 144–145.

[37] See ACC, p. 145.

[38] ACC, p. 148.

[39] Riem, Johannes, as quoted by Rehwinkel, op. cit., p. 129.

[40] Frazer, James George, *Folklore in the Old Testament: Studies in Comparative Religion, Legend, and Law* (New York: Hart, 1975), pp. 46–143. Also see Rehwinkel, op. cit., chapters. IX–X; Dillow, op. cit., ch. 4; and Whitcomb and Morris, op. cit., pp. 37–42.

[41] *Timaeus* 24e–25d; *Critias* 113b–121c.

[42] *Timaeus* 25a.

[43] Ibid.

[44] *Critias* 120e.

[45] Ibid., 121b–c.

[46] *Timaeus* 25d.

[47] *The Metamorphoses*, Book I.

[48] *The Antiquities of the Jews*, Book 1, Chapter 3.6.

[49] Quoted by Albritton, Claude C., *The Abyss of Time: Changing Conceptions of the Earth's Antiquity after the Sixteenth Century*, reprint of 1980 edition (Mineola, NY: Dover Publications, 2002), p. 100.

[50] See Rehwinkel, op. cit., pp. 179–187; Whitcomb and Morris, op. cit., pp. 128–130; 154–169.

[51] See Rehwinkel, op. cit., pp. 188–192; Whitcomb and Morris, op. cit., pp. 313–317.

[52] See Whitcomb and Morris, pp. 318–324.

[53] See Rehwinkel, op. cit., pp. 192–200; Whitcomb and Morris, op. cit., pp. 277–279.

[54] See Rehwinkel, op. cit., pp. 200–209; Whitcomb and Morris, op. cit., pp. 429–437.

[55] See *Science News*, vol. 164, no. 12, Sept. 20, 2003, p. 179.

[56] See Rehwinkel, op. cit., pp. 210–237.

[57] See Rehwinkel, op. cit., pp. 238–254; Whitcomb and Morris, op. cit., pp. 288–291; Dillow, op. cit., pp. 311–426; Brown, Walt, *In the Beginning: Compelling Evidence for Creation and the Flood* (Phoenix, AZ: Center for Scientific Creation, 1995), pp. 106–136.

[58] For vivid video documentation of this event see the VHS videotape *Mount St. Helens: Explosive Evidence for Catastrophe* with geologist Steve Austin (El Cajon, CA: Institute for Creation Research).

[59] *The Antiquities of the Jews*, Book 1, Chapter 4.1.

[60] See O'Connell, Patrick, *Science of Today and the Problems of Genesis* (Rockford, IL: TAN Books, 1993), p. 246.

[61] See O'Connell, op. cit., p. 250–268 and Keller, Werner, 2nd revised edition, *The Bible as History* (New York: Bantam Books, 1982), pp. 22–30.

[62] See Ryan, William and Pitman, Walter, *Noah's Flood: The New Scientific Discoveries About the Event That Changed History* (New York: Simon and Schuster, 1998).

[63] See Lubenow, Marvin L., *Bones of Contention: A Creationist Assessment of Human Fossils* (Grand Rapids, MI: Baker Books, 1992), ch. 3.

Doctrine Sixteen
All the races of men on earth today descended from the three sons of Noah.

Scripture and Tradition clearly teach that all people on earth today are descended from the three sons of Noah and that God multiplied the languages of man in response to the rebellion at Babel, after which men dispersed throughout the world.

God's Covenant with Noah

God made a covenant with Noah, his sons, their descendants and every living creature. He promised to never again send a flood to destroy the earth. The sign of this covenant was the rainbow (9:8–17). The rainbow is a beautiful phenomenon that the people of the antediluvian world had probably not experienced. And it is associated with water. The colors in its concentric bands are formed opposite the sun by refraction and internal reflection of the sun's light rays by raindrops, spray or mist. The new atmospheric conditions of the postdiluvian world were conducive to the phenomenon, but those of the antediluvian world probably were not. Rain may have been unknown in the antediluvian world (2:4–6). If so, there would have been no coarse moisture in the atmosphere to produce rainbows.

God also told Noah that the beasts of the world would dread man, and that they would become food for him (9:2–3). This is also something new. In the antediluvian world there was much greater harmony between man and beast than there is in the postdiluvian world. And antediluvian man did not eat animal flesh because God had not given it to him to eat. Men did not need it then because there was a great variety of plant foods that satisfied all nourishmental needs.

God made two prohibitions: eating meat with blood in it and murder (9:4–6). The first was intended as a sign of respect for the lives of animals, which are gifts from God. Leviticus 17:10–16 reaffirms the prohibition not to eat blood because blood represents the life of an animal. Blood is an apt symbol for the soul because it permeates the whole body just as the soul is completely present everywhere in the body. And it is as necessary for life as is the soul. So the blood can be considered as the material counterpart of the soul. St. John Chrysostom identified the blood of an animal with its soul.[1] St. Augustine compared someone saying that the blood of a beast is its soul to Christ saying, "This is My Body" when He wanted to give a sign of His body.[2] In other words, blood is to the presence of life as the Eucharistic species is to the presence of Christ.

The second prohibition upheld the right to life of all men, who are created in God's image. Murder was to be paid for by the life of the person who committed it. This command was also something new. (God did not demand that Cain give his life in payment for Abel's.) It became the most fundamental statute in the Law of Nations, that common body of laws recognized by the nations descended from Noah's sons.

Origins of the Nations

All the people in the world today descended from three lines—those of Shem, Ham and Japheth, Noah's three sons (9:18). The line of Shem was especially blessed because God chose it to be the one to hold on to the true worship of Him. It is the line in which the Redeemer was born. Noah prophesied that God would enlarge the line of Japheth. His descendants would be numerous, and they would *"dwell in the tents of Shem"* (9:27), that is, they would share in the spiritual blessings of Shem. Noah cursed Ham because of his immodesty and gross disrespect (9:20–23), declaring that his offspring would be the slaves[a] of the offspring of Shem and Japheth (9:26–27).[b] St. Ephrem summarizes the fulfillment of Noah's prophecies:

> Japheth increased and became powerful in his inheritance in the north and in the west. And God dwelt in the tent of Abraham, the descendant of Shem, and Canaan became their slave when in the days of Joshua son of Nun, the Israelites destroyed the dwelling places of Canaan and pressed their leaders into bondage.[3]

---

a. St. Augustine pointed out that this is the first time the word *slave* is used in Scripture. See CG, Book XIX, Chapter 15.

According to some commentators,[4] the three lines distinguished themselves by their pursuits. They each displayed special talents that contributed to the overall advancement of all the nations. The line of Shem was characterized by a strong spiritual and religious sense, that of Ham by practical skills, and that of Japheth by intellectual acumen. The early descendants in each line developed the expertise in their special area from which the others eventually learned. For example, Semites preserved true worship of God in preparation for the coming of Christ. God said to Abraham, a descendant of Shem: *"[I]n your descendants all the nations of the earth shall find blessing."*[5] The children of Shem also founded false monotheistic religions like Zoroastrianism and Islam. Japhethites shared in the blessing of Shem most fully after the coming of Christ. The Semitic disciples of Christ easily converted the descendants of Japheth in Europe and western Asia. The Japhetic peoples, most notably the Greeks of the European branch, were inclined to intellectual pursuits. They were the first to develop philosophy and mathematics as logical disciplines. The Indian branch also showed interest in metaphysical speculation, which is manifested in Hinduism. The descendants of Ham built the first civilizations. The advanced civilizations of Sumer and Egypt were the products of the Hamitic genius for organizing, building and inventing. The Hamitic people developed arithmetic, geometry and astronomy to solve practical problems in commerce, surveying and navigation. They were the original explorers and settled in all parts of the world following the dispersion at Babel. They were able to adapt to the harshest environments and to live in the most primitive conditions. It should be kept in mind that the skills of the early postdiluvians were not built up from nothing. Shem, Ham and Japheth had knowledge they brought with them from the antediluvian civilization.[6] And considering the growth of sin and the cultural and intellectual decline that accompanies it, proba-

---

b. Actually Noah cursed Canaan, Ham's son. The Fathers gave several reasons why Canaan was cursed and not Ham (see ACC, pp. 158–159). The sons themselves were blessed or cursed in their posterity. Probably Noah did not want to direct the curse directly at Ham because he was his son and would be the patriarch of a primordial lineage of people. So Noah directed his curse at Canaan to indicate that the curse on Ham applied to his descendants. It is a mystery why Ham's descendants should suffer for his sin, but then it is also a mystery why Adam's descendants should suffer for his sin. The prophet Jeremiah clearly stated the paradox of a just and loving God visiting the iniquity of the fathers upon their children, but he did not resolve it: *"Nothing is too hard for thee, who showest steadfast love to thousands, but dost requite the guilt of fathers to their children after them"* (Jer 32:17–18).

bly more knowledge was lost than was gained as the descendants of Noah's sons proceeded from generation to generation.

Genesis 10 contains the original table of nations. It is an authoritative account of how the families of Noah's' three sons grew and spread throughout the world. Like the antediluvian genealogy, the men mentioned were not the only sons of their fathers. They are only those sons who became the patriarchs of nations. St. Augustine reckoned seventy-two such nations:[7] twenty-six from Shem, thirty-one from Ham, and fifteen from Japheth.[c]

St. Augustine points out that Scripture does not proclaim the devotion to God of anyone between Noah at the time of the Flood and the time of Abraham, a period of some 426 years according to the chronology of J. Ussher;[8] and so he asks if there was an interruption in the true worship of God during that period. He concludes that it is difficult to answer that question.[9] However, it seems that the patriarchs listed from Shem to Abram through Eber and Peleg did preserve true worship because at the beginning of Genesis 12 Abram is shown as being familiar with and pleasing to God. Scripture suggests that Abraham may have known about God and his will before God revealed Himself to him. This knowledge he would have received from his ancestors.[d]

St. Augustine also discusses why Eber, the fourth in the line of Shem and the father of Peleg, who was the great great grandfather of Abram, is given special mention at the beginning of Shem's lineage (10:21). He said that is because the people of Israel called themselves Hebrews after Eber and that the Hebrew language was their exclusive property.[10] If the multiplication of languages occurred during the lifetime of Peleg, Eber's son, then Eber spoke the original antediluvian language or a derivative of it. This is the language that he would have passed on to Peleg, who, by a special grace of God, would have retained it and passed it on.

---

c. Shem, Ham and Japheth each went their separate ways in accordance with God's command to *"fill the earth"* (9:1). They gave birth to three family groups, but they themselves were not considered as founders of nations. The early descendants of the three families apparently did not crossbreed, and therefore were able to form nations with three distinct lineages.

d. Scripture mentions that the ancestors of Abram, including his father Terah, worshipped idols; but it does not say that they lost all knowledge of the true God (see Joshua 24:2; Judith 5:6 ff.). They may have recognized both, as apparently some of the Israelites did (Joshua 24:14–15) and as some of Judas Maccabeus' soldiers did (2 Maccabees 12:38–46). Also, Abram may have received instruction in genuine tradition not from Terah but directly from Shem, who was still alive in Abram's time.

St. Augustine held that the Hebrew language was Eber's language because it is named after him, and therefore it is the language that was common to all mankind before the confusion of tongues at Babel.[11] Augustine also said that Peleg is the only person in the genealogies of Genesis 10 who was not the patriarch of a nation. He belonged to Eber's nation. His name was mentioned only because the world was divided in his time. Thus Augustine counted seventy-three names in the genealogies of Genesis 10, which, by eliminating Peleg, he reduced to seventy-two nations, each with a different language.[12] He further argued that all the seventy-two nations existed at the time of the building of the tower at Babel.[13] Peleg was the fifth in the line starting with Shem: *"[I]n his days the earth was divided"* (10:25).[e]

Chapter 10 records only three generations for the lines of Ham and Japheth and six generations for the line of Shem. A more extended genealogy for Shem going through Peleg and ending with Abram and his brothers, who were tenth in the line of Shem, is given at the end of chapter 11. In addition, chapter 11 gives the years of birth and the deaths of the patriarchs. Following is a list of them:[14]

Patriarch	Birth*	Death*	Lifetime**
Noah	1056	2006	950
Shem	1558	2158	600
Arpachshad	1658	2096	438
Shelah	1693	2126	433

---

e. The phrase *"In his days the earth was divided"* can be interpreted three ways. First, it may mean that mankind was divided because of the multiplication of languages and dispersion of peoples. Second, it may mean that the earth itself was divided. Residual effects of the Flood may have divided one landmass into separate continents. Land bridges to the western hemisphere and to Australia, which would have allowed human and animal migration to those places, may have existed and been destroyed at that time. Peleg lived for 239 years (11:18); both the dispersion of peoples and the destruction of land bridges could have happened during his lifetime. Third, the phrase might instead mean that the line of Shem was, for some unstated reason, divided at that time. There are two lines of Shem given in Genesis 10–11. In chapter 10 the line of Joktan, Peleg's brother is given. In chapter 11, that of Peleg is given.

Eber	1723	2187	464
Peleg	1757	1996	239
Reu	1787	2026	239
Serug	1819	2049	230
Nahor	1849	1997	148
Terah	1878	2083	205
Abram	2008	2183	175

* Years from Creation   ** Years

Noah died only two years before Abram was born. God changed Abram's name to Abraham when he was 99 years old.[15] Shem lived until Abraham was one hundred and fifty years old, Arpachshad until Abram was 88 years old, Shelah until Abraham was one hundred and eighteen years old, Eber until Abraham would have been one hundred and seventy-nine years old, Rue until Abram was eighteen years old, Serug until Abram was forty-one years old, and Terah until Abram was seventy-five years old. When Abram met Melchizedek he was eighty-four years old.[16] Since Melchizedek was a highly respected personage, he may have been one of the patriarchs. Four would have been alive when Abram met Melchizedek: Shem, Arpachshad, Shelah and Eber. Shem is the best candidate. St. Paul said that Melchizedek was without genealogy.[17] Shem had no genealogy because he was at the head of the line. Also, Abraham paid tithes to Melchizedek and was blessed by him. It would make sense that Abram would pay tithes to Shem and be blessed by him since Shem was the supreme patriarch, and as such would be a great high priest. St. Paul compares Melchizedek with Jesus,[18] whom he called *"a great high priest."*[19] Shem would be superior to Abram as a father is to a son; and a father blessed the son, as Isaac blessed Jacob.[20]

There is a persistent decline in longevity from Noah to Abram, which continues beyond Abraham in biblical history until it levels off at *"threescore and ten, or even by reason of strength fourscore."*[21] It seems that some kind of natural process may have been at work that gradually decreased the lifetime of men. It may have been that the plants supplying the nutrients that prolonged life gradually became extinct or diminished in effectiveness or abundance in the years following the Flood. Or it may have been caused by the loss of genetic information that the

Flood brought about. Much of the genetic pool of the antediluvian world was lost in the Flood, and even more may have been lost during close inbreeding in the first years after the Flood.

The Tower of Babel

Josephus said that that Shem, Ham and Japheth were the first to descend from the mountains onto the plain of Shinar. They fixed their habitations there and persuaded the others to follow. The others were very reluctant to venture to lower ground "on account of the floods."[22] [f] Scripture says that they migrated from the east into the plain of Shinar (11:2). If Josephus is correct, then they probably migrated southeast from Ararat into the highlands of western modern Iran and then west into Shinar. During those years the first settlers, possessors of antediluvian technology, built cities and established civilization using available materials (11:3).

Originally the descendants of Shem, Ham and Japheth all spoke the same language, which was that brought from the antediluvian world (11:1).[g] God had commanded the nations through Noah and his sons to disperse and fill the earth (9:1). Josephus said that God gave this command so "that they might not raise seditions among themselves."[23] But after settling in the land of Shinar (11:2), located in modern day Iraq, they resisted this command saying: *"Come, let us build ourselves a city, and a tower with its top in the heavens, and let us make a name for ourselves, lest we be scattered upon the face of the whole earth"* (11:4). The building of the tower of Babel took place one hundred and five years after the Flood, five years after the birth of Peleg, according to Ussher's chronology.[24] It seems that Nimrod, a grandson of Ham, instigated or at least led the revolt of the people. Josephus said that Nimrod "excited them to such an affront and contempt of God."[25] According to Josephus, Nimrod convinced the people that he was responsible for their happiness and prosperity. He was determined to turn men

---

f. There may have been extensive residual flooding of the Tigris and Euphrates Rivers onto the plain while the earth was settling into geological equilibrium.

g. The antediluvian language spoken by Noah and his sons may or may not have been the language of Adam and Eve. The primeval language of Adam and Eve may have developed into a number of mutually incomprehensible dialects over the 1656 years that the antediluvian world existed, just as Latin developed into the various Romance languages. The only difference in this comparison is that Latin had other distinct languages to interact with, whereas the primeval language did not.

away from the fear of God and bring them into dependence on his power. The multitude was very ready to follow Nimrod for they had already convinced themselves that their prosperity was man's doing and not God's. Furthermore, they were perversely suspicious that God wanted to disperse them so that He could more easily oppress them.

St. Augustine also attributes the rebellion to Nimrod. Scripture says that Nimrod *"was the first on earth to be a mighty man. He was a mighty hunter before the* LORD.... *The beginning of his kingdom was Babel [Babylon], Erech, and Accad, all of them in the land of Shiner. From that land he went into Assyria, and built Nineveh, Rehoboth-Ir, Calah, and Resen between Nineveh and Calah; that is the great city"* (10:8–12). Augustine said that Nimrod was the founder and not just the conqueror of Babylon and that it was the capital of his kingdom. He also said that the proper interpretation of the Scripture passage concerning Nimrod is that he was a hunter "against the Lord," and not "for the Lord" in the sense of being on the Lord's side.[26] The latter was the interpretation of St. Ephrem[27] and St. John Chrysostom, [28]who qualified it by saying that in the end Nimrod became corrupted by his own power. Augustine said:

> It is in [this] sense that we must take it the description of Nimrod; that giant was "a hunter against the Lord." For the word "hunter" can only suggest a deceiver, oppressor and destroyer of earth-born creatures. Thus he, with his subject peoples, began to erect a tower against the Lord, which symbolizes his impious pride.[29]

God foiled their endeavor by multiplying their languages. Each of the seventy-two nations of Genesis 10 was given its own language. These were the seventy-two original languages that transformed throughout the course of history into the six thousand or so languages in use today and many that have become extinct. The loss of a common language caused divisions among the nations that resulted in their dispersal. St. Ephrem said that the confusion of languages led to war breaking out among them and Nimrod scattering them:

> [B]ecause of their new languages, which made them foreigners to each other and incapable of understanding one another, war broke out among them on account of the divisions that the languages brought among them. Thus war broke out among those who had been building that fortified city out of fear of others. And all those who had been keeping themselves away from the city were scattered throughout the entire earth. It was Nimrod who scattered them. It was also he who seized Babel and became its first ruler. If Nimrod

had not scattered them each to his own place, he would not have been able to take that place where they all had lived before.[30]

St. Jerome said that God dispersed the nations for their own welfare, so that they would not have to endure each other:

> Just as when holy men live together, it is a great grace and a blessing; so, like-wise, that congregation is the worst kind when sinners dwell together. The more sinners there are at one time, the worse they are. Indeed, when the tower was being built up against God, those who were building it were disbanded for their own welfare. The conspiracy was evil. The dispersion was of true benefit even to those who were dispersed.[31]

St. Lawrence of Brindisi, in his *Explanatio in Genesim,* adds that those who spoke the same language as Nimrod remained with him in Babel and preserved the city.

Early Post-Babel Communities

All the population of the world dispersed from the plain of Shinar. Those that remained close to Shinar developed high civilizations.[h] Settlements on new frontiers were primitive until natural resources were discovered and exploited. Some tribes that dispersed far from the center of high civilization in Mesopotamia lost antediluvian knowledge and adapted to permanently barbarous ways of living, especially in areas where natural resources were scarce. Inbreeding in small populations produced distinct racial and tribal features.[i] Josephus described the dispersion of peoples:

---

h. The so-called Stone Age, Bronze Age and Iron Age are not true historical periods. Rather, they are inventions of evolutionists who believe that mankind gradually gained skills with these materials. Archaeological evidence indicates that bronze and iron were fashioned in the earliest Sumerian and Egyptian civilizations. Stone implements were used by those who either lost knowledge of those skills or did not have access to the metals. Also, archaeologists have discovered stone products side by side with products of copper or bronze. See T. K. Derry and T. I. Williams, *A Short History of Technology: From the Earliest Times to A. D. 1900* (New York: Dover Publications, 1993), ch. 4 and Giuseppe Ricciotti, *The History of Israel,* vol. I (Fort Collins, CO: Roman Catholic Books, reprint of 1955 edition), p. 58.

After this they were dispersed abroad, on account of their languages, and went out by colonies everywhere; and each colony took possession of that land which they light upon and unto which God led them; so that the whole continent was filled with them, both the inland and the maritime countries. There were some also who passed over the sea in ships, and inhabited the islands.[32]

The first nations mentioned in Genesis 10 are those descended from Japheth (10:2–5). The descendants of Japheth went north and westward into Europe and eastward into Russia. One branch headed southeast into Iran and India. Seven sons of Japheth are mentioned as the founders of nations. Josephus lists the nations they founded, many of which are still familiar to us:

Gomer founded those whom the Greeks now call Galatians {Galls}, but were then called Gomerites. Magog founded those that from him were named Magogites, but who are by the Greeks called Scythians. Now as to Javan and Madai, the sons of Japhet; from Madai came the Madeans, who are called Medes by the Greeks; but from Javan, Ionia and all the Grecians are derived. Thobel [Tubal] founded the Thobelites, who are now called Iberes; and the Mosocheni were founded by Mosoch [Meshech]; now they are Cappadocians.... Thiras [Tiras] also called those he ruled over Thirasians; but the Greeks changed the name into Thracians.[33]

He then goes on to name nations founded by grandsons of Japheth. Two of them are the following: Tarshish, son of Javan, founder of the Tharsians, whose home was later called Cilicia and whose major city was Tarsus; and Kittim, son of Javan, who occupied the island of Cyprus. The coastland peoples sprung from the sons of Javan (10:5). The earliest Europeans recorded their descent from Japheth in meticulously kept records.[34]

Genesis 10 then goes on to list the nations descended from Ham (10:6–20). The Hamites migrated south, east and west from Shinar and eventually spread throughout the whole world. They developed into the nonwhite races. They were founders both of high civilizations in the eastern and western hemispheres and of tribes adapted to barbarous living conditions. The sons of Ham who begot nations were Cush, Egypt (Mizraim), Put and Canaan. According to Josephus, Ethiopia was settled by Cush, Egypt by Mizraim, Libya by Put and Judea by Canaan.[35] Of Ham's grandsons, Casluhim, son of Mizraim, was the progenitor of the Philistines, who occupied Palestine in the time of David. Sidon, the

---

i. Inbreeding was probably less dangerous then than later because there were fewer mutant genes in the populations.

first-born of Canaan, was the progenitor of the Phoenicians. According to Josephus he built the city named after him. Heth, another son of Canaan, was the ancestor of the Hittites, who founded a great civilization centered in modern Turkey. Others sons of Canaan were the forefathers of the Jebusites, Amorites and other nations that occupied the Land of Canaan in the days of Moses and Joshua.

Hamites founded the original civilization on the Plain of Shinar (Sumer). From Sumer some moved to Egypt and founded a civilization there. According to Ussher, Mizraim led his colony into Egypt in 2188 B.C., fifty-four years after the multiplication of tongues at Babel.[36] From Egypt Hamites made their way to Crete to found the Minoan civilization. Hamites also migrated to the Indus River Valley in northwestern India and to Africa and the western hemisphere. Archaeological evidence indicates that the western hemisphere was settled well before 2000 B.C.[37]

Apparently Hamites spread more rapidly than the Japhethites. The first waves of migration were composed of Hamitic peoples, who settled and built civilizations. Later Japhethites conquered them and assimilated their civilizations. This happened, for example, in the Indus River Valley and in Crete.

Finally, Genesis 10 gives the lineage of Shem. Josephus develops it as follows:

> Shem, the third son of Noah, had five sons, who inhabited the land that began at Euphrates, and reached to the Indian Ocean; for Elam left behind him the Elamites, the ancestors of the Persians. Ashur [Asshur] lived at the city Nieve; and named his subjects Assyrians, who became the most fortunate nation, beyond others. Arphaxad [Arpachshad] named the Arphaxadites, who are now called Chaldeans. Aram had the Aramites, which the Greeks call Syrians; as Laud [Lud] founded the Laudites, which are now called Lydians.
>
> Of the four sons of Aram, Uz founded Trachonitis and Damascus; this country lies between Palestine and Celesyria. Ul [Hul] founded Armenia....[38]

The line of Arphashad leads to Abram and to Jesus Christ. The language of Aram, Aramaic, was adopted by many nations and became the lingua franca of the ancient Near East. It was the native tongue of Christ. The Semites did not migrate much. Even today most of the Semitic peoples live in the Near East.

Some mixing of the three primeval lines occurred early on. For example, the descendants of Elam, son of Shem, merged with the Medes, who descended from Madai, son of Japheth, to form the Persian empire. Nimrod, grandson of Ham, conquered the Assyrians, founded by Asshur, son of Shem. The civilization resulting from the fusion of Semitic and Hamitic elements later became the great Assyrian empire that dominated the Near East.

The Multiplication of Languages: A Penalty and a Premium

God's punishments are blessings in disguise. They are not vindictive, but corrective. God punishes out of love and mercy, not anger. When God took away from men a single language, He took away a means of achieving prosperity. Unity of language facilitates commerce, education, travel, and technological innovation, which are all conducive to building up material wealth. But material prosperity becomes a substitute for God. Immersed in prosperity, men tend to praise their own cleverness in achieving it rather than to thank God for providing it. And they look to their material wealth for their well-being rather than to God. Eventually they fall away from devotion to God into idolatry, which is accompanied by social disharmony.

Unity in language is also conducive to the accumulation of military and political power by tyrants. With a single language all of mankind was susceptible to being subjected to dynasty after dynasty of despots. Perhaps God ordered men to disperse throughout the world to prevent them from engaging in continual civil wars on the one hand, or from being enslaved in a one-world tyranny on the other. The first would bring on the second. For "anarchy produces tyranny."[39] History has shown that people accept a tyrannical centralized government as a lesser evil than anarchy.

A centralized government brings prosperity and peace but at a price. God warned the Israelites of the price they would have to pay if they rejected His providence and placed their trust in a worldly king instead:

So Samuel told all the words of the LORD to the people who were asking a king from him. He said, "These will be the ways of the king who will reign over you: he will take your sons and appoint them to chariots and to be his horsemen, and to run before his chariots; and he will appoint for himself commanders of thousands and commanders of fifties, and some to plow his ground and to reap his harvest, and to make his implements of war and the equipment of his chariots. He will take your daughters to be perfumers and cooks and bakers. He will take the best of your fields and vineyards and olive orchards and give them to his servants. He will take the tenth of your grain and of your vineyards and give it to his officers and his servants. He will take your menservants and maidservants, and the best of your cattle and your asses, and put them to his work. He will take the tenth of your flocks, and you shall be his slaves. And in that day you will cry out because of your king, whom you have chosen for yourselves; but the LORD will not answer you in that day."[40]

Domination of the whole world by a single king would have had even worse consequences because it would be more difficult to escape from such an absolute power.

When men did not disperse as God commanded, he forced them to do so by multiplying their languages. This was an act of love. God wanted to foster in each of the nations an identity and an independent spirit that would maintain a balance of power in the world and counter any tendency to domination by a centralized world power. The various languages He gave the nations would insulate them to some extent so that they might develop their own distinct cultures in which they would exercise their own distinctive talents. Thus God prevented a homogenized humanity and, instead, provided for a wonderful variety of peoples, cultures and traditions that would fulfill the potentials of the human species.

Since God does nothing in vain, it is reasonable to suppose that He gave each nation a language with a vocabulary and structure specifically tailored to the needs and aptitudes of its people.

The Early Postdiluvian World

After the Flood, when the earth was ready to be occupied, God told Noah to lead his family out of the ark into the new world. God also instructed Noah: *"Bring forth with you every living thing that is with you of all flesh—birds and animals and every creeping thing that creeps on the earth—that they may breed abundantly on the earth, and be fruitful and multiply on the earth"* (8:17). Noah complied. *"And every beast, every creeping thing, and every bird, everything that moves upon the earth went forth by families out of the ark"* (8:19). The animals went forth from the ark into the world, where they multiplied and migrated, with groups settling in habitats suited to their natures. God built into the kinds of animals the ability to produce varieties that adapt to various environmental conditions.[41] Rapid multiplication, close inbreeding, and rapidly changing environments gave rise to distinct varieties within the different kinds of animals, which modern taxonomists classify as distinct "species." This ability to vary is limited in extent; it cannot produce new kinds of animals. J. Woodmorappe considers questions concerning the recovery of the earth's biosphere and animal repopulation after the Flood.[42]

The animals spread throughout the whole world. Many crossed land bridges that then existed to the western hemisphere and Australia. Others migrated across water on floating debris. Some were not able to adapt permanently to the harsh environments of the new world and became extinct after a number of generations. This was the fate of the dinosaurs.[j]

The world that Noah and his sons now occupied was very different geographically, geologically and meteorologically from the one they had been born in. During and after the Flood, the great forces of nature—water, ice, wind, volcanoes and earthquakes—worked together to reshape the face of the earth. The oceans were much larger than before and the land masses much smaller. And a much smaller fraction of the land mass was habitable. The vegetation was not as lush as before nor did things grow as big as they had before the Flood. Piles of sediment uplifted after the Flood, which hardened into mountains, many higher and more rugged than the antediluvian ones. Residual volcanic and seismic activity took place all over the world for many centuries and continues to some extent in the present. New patterns of air circulation produced sharply contrasting climatic conditions throughout the earth. Huge stores of coal and oil lay hidden in the earth, which would be utilized by man only much later in his history.

Volcanic activity continued after the Flood, causing a shroud of volcanic dust and aerosols to cover the entire earth that kept out much of the sunlight. This reduced the temperature of the atmosphere and landmasses. The fountains of the deep introduced hot water into the oceans that made them very warm.[k] The combination of cool air and land and warm oceans gave rise to the ice age. The warm oceans produced copious moisture in the atmosphere that cooled to produce snow. The summers were not warm enough to melt all the snow at high lat-

---

j. Dinosaurs (dragons) were contemporaries of postdiluvian man. The literature of early civilizations testifies to this, and pictographs and petroglyphs of dinosaurs have been found on walls of caves and canyons. See Ken Ham, *The Great Dinosaur Mystery Solved!* (Green Forest, AR: Master Books, 1998), pp. 82, 161–162. B. Cooper has set out a number of examples in early Anglo-Saxon and other written records in which dinosaurs are mentioned. See *After the Flood: The Early Post-Flood History of Europe Traced Back to Noah* (Chichester, England: New Wine Press, 1995), Chapter 10.

k. The Book of Job tells of the existence of springs on the ocean floor. *"Have you entered into the springs of the sea, or walked in the recesses of the deep?"* (Job 38:16). In 1973 direct observations of suboceanic hot springs were made on the Mid Atlantic Ridge. In 1977, hot springs were discovered on Galapagos Rift in the Pacific and in 1979 on the East Pacific Rise (see Steven A. Austin, "Springs of the Ocean," *Impact*, no. 89, August 1981, Institute for Creation Research, El Cajon, CA).

itudes and high altitudes. Therefore the snow accumulated to produce glaciers. Cooling of the oceans and diminished volcanic activity led to a reduction in snowfall and to warming of the continents, thus ending the ice age. The ice age probably lasted about seven hundred years.[43] The Book of Job alludes to the ice age. The LORD said to Job: *"From whose womb did the ice come forth, and who has given birth to the hoarfrost of heaven? The waters become hard like stone, and the face of the deep is frozen."* [44]

Archaeology and Early Civilizations

The *Miriam Webster Collegiate Dictionary* defines archaeology as "the scientific study of material remains (as fossil relics, artifacts, and monuments) of past human life and activities."

Archaeology bearing on biblical questions mostly involves the excavation of tells in the Middle East. The word *tell* comes from the Arabic word for "hill." A tell is an artificial mound that conceals the debris of ancient cities, one built on another. In many places a city was destroyed by warfare or natural disaster and a new city rebuilt on the remains, this occurring a number of times during the course of centuries. The site supposed to be that of ancient Troy, for example, had nine levels that contained the remains of nine different cities. A layer in which archaeological material (such as artifacts and the remains of houses) is found is called a *stratum*. Tells vary from fifty to one hundred feet in elevation and tend to be flat-topped. Artifacts, such as pottery, cuneiform tablets, jewelry and monuments found in a tell give archaeologists insights about the cultures of the various peoples that lived there.[45]

Archaeologists can date artifacts back to 1000 B.C. with reasonable accuracy and back to 2500 B.C. within a hundred years. But beyond that their dating methods are subject to significant errors.

A reliable dating method used by archaeologists is pottery dating. This is based on the idea that the pottery of every civilization has characteristic features (shape, style, decorations, material, method of production, and so on) that distinguish it from pottery of other civilizations. Sites at different tells at which the same pottery is found are assumed to be the remains of cities that were occupied at the same time and that traded with or influenced each other. This method is called *sequence dating*. It helps archaeologists to establish chronological sequences of sites, but it does not give them absolute dates. Absolute dates of pottery must be determined from other data.

Cuneiform king-lists and chronicles are orderly lists of royal reigns and events. They were used to draw up the accepted chronologies for Assyria, Babylonia, the Hittites and their contemporaries. Historians used fixed points from astronomical observations and events in Greek and Egyptian history to calculate the dates of individual kings backwards into the third millennium B.C. However, some modern historians question the truth of such records because often their authors exaggerated or distorted the facts so as to praise their ruler and denigrate their enemies. The most ancient peoples leaving historical records were inhabitants of Mesopotamia, Egypt and other Near-Eastern areas.

Historical dates are ultimately connected to astronomical observations recorded by ancient astronomers, who kept meticulous astronomical records, usually for religious reasons. They kept records of astronomical events such as solar and lunar eclipses, conjunctions of planets and occultations of stars and planets. In theory at least, astronomers can calculate backwards very accurately because of the regular movement of the heavens.

No credible archaeological dating of an ancient civilization antedates 3000 B.C., and therefore all fall within the framework of biblical chronology. Earlier dates have been assigned to various cultures or civilizations; but they are based on radiocarbon or geological methods rather than written human records, which are much more certain.

The oldest civilizations according to archaeological reckoning are located in the Near East and were quite advanced with some form of written communication. They used fire, built houses, played music and practiced some form of religion. All of this is in accordance with the biblical record. The oldest archaeological find is believed to be Old Sumer, which is located at the southeastern corner of the Fertile Crescent. Many scholars believe that Nimrod founded it.

The facts discovered by archaeologists are in perfect agreement with Sacred Scripture, although their interpretations are not always so. A noted Jewish scholar observed:

> As a matter of fact, however, it may be stated that no archaeological discovery has ever controverted a Biblical reference. Scores of archaeological findings have been made which confirm in clear outline or in exact detail historical statements in the Bible. And, by the same token, proper evaluation of Biblical descriptions has often led to amazing discoveries. They form tesserae in the vast mosaic of the Bible's almost incredibly correct historical memory.[46]

Scripture indicates that as soon as men left the ark they planted vineyards (9:20) and established communities. Also, it is reasonable to suppose that they brought with them from the antediluvian world writing and much technological knowledge. Modern archaeologists are continually making finds that substantiate this and complement the biblical record on ancient civilizations.

But it must not be supposed that it is the role of biblical archaeology to confirm the Bible. The truth of Sacred Scripture is a given for the believer. It does not need to be confirmed. The role of biblical archaeology is to flesh out the biblical record with details, to give deeper insights and to fill in lacunas.

The prominent Dominican priest and biblical scholar Roland de Vaux is quoted as having said: "… if Israel's historical faith does not have its roots in history, then it is wrong and the same is true of our faith."[47] If he said that in defending the historical truth of Sacred Scripture in the same spirit as St. Paul defended the truth of Christ's resurrection when he said: *"If Christ has not been raised, then our preaching is in vain and your faith is in vain"*[48] his outlook is Catholic, as we should expect. Then his statement is a rhetorical way of proclaiming that the veracity of Sacred Scripture is a foundational doctrine of the Catholic faith. However, he was seriously wrong if he meant that Scripture and the Catholic faith are subject to verification by archaeology.

The historical conclusions of archaeologists, when based on archaeological information alone, are often subjective and inconclusive. This has been shown clearly in the theories of archaeologists about the Trojan War. After analyzing diverse opinions on the subject one commentator observed: "There can never be a final word, only a new interpretation by each generation in terms of its own dreams and needs."[49]

So archaeology must look to Sacred Scripture as the basis and guide for the interpretation of its data when it deals with the earliest civilizations. If it doesn't it will quickly lose its way and get lost in false historical conclusions.

< Objections > and << Replies >>

< Objection 1 >

The multiplication of languages of the Tower of Babel is a fascinating tale that attempts to give a reason for the existence of many languages in the world. But scientists know that they did not come about that way. Language is a highly developed form of animal signaling. It probably developed in eastern Africa about a hundred thousand years ago when humans discovered that they were able to produce a range of sounds that could be used to communicate information to other humans.

<< Reply to Objection 1 >>

Linguists admit that they have no direct knowledge of the origins and early development of language, nor can they even imagine how such knowledge could be obtained. They can only speculate.[50] The prominent linguist Noam Chomsky denied any relationship between human language and "animal signaling": "[H]uman language appears to be a unique phenomenon, without significant analogue in the animal world."[51] Animal signals are fixed, limited, and instinctively used. Human communications are variable, unlimited, and freely made.

<< Divine Creation of Original Languages >>

Susanne Langer observed: "Languages are not invented; they grow with our need for expression."[52] Only God can create matter, energy and life from nothing. But He gave man the ability to manipulate and transform them. Likewise, only God can create language from nothing. Man has the instinct to learn language and the ability to transform it, but he is not able to create it. A child can instinctively abstract grammatical rules of a language and apply them creatively,[1] but he must first be exposed to the sounds, words and use of the language. Once a language is learned it can be modified and expanded. This is done when children raised with a pidgin transform it into a full-fledged creole. But no individual or group of individuals has ever created a spoken language out of nothing. They must always start with something.[m] The idea that man, just advancing out of bestiality, could create language is absurd. Although language is not the cause of thought, it is a tool of thought. One needs a language to construct a language, just as a black-

---

1. The abstraction of grammatical rules is a function of what the Scholastics called the *active intellect*, which abstracts universals from particulars. The grammatical universals are apprehended by the *possible intellect*, which is the spiritual power of knowing or understanding. Application of the grammatical rules is a function of the *practical intellect*, which is the possible intellect seeking knowledge for the sake of action.

m. The Mogul Emperor of India, Akbar the Great (1542–1605) believed that children could learn to speak only by listening to others. He put this idea to a test by having infants raised by tongue-tied nurses in a house isolated from contact with other humans. As he expected, the children did not learn to speak. This cruel and immoral experiment confirmed the fact that humans do not create language. See David Crystal, *The Cambridge Encyclopedia of Language*, 2nd ed. (New York: Cambridge University Press, 2002), p. 230.

smith needs a hammer to forge a hammer. For man to create language would be a mental feat comparable to the physical feat of lifting himself up by his own bootstraps. Both are impossible. As life comes only from life, so language comes only from language. God specially created the original languages and infused them into the minds of the first users.

*   *   *   *

< Objection 2 >

Archaeological finds have been dated by radiocarbon dating to be as old as 50,000 years. Thus science has invalidated biblical chronology and the history that goes along with it.

<< Reply to Objection 2 >>

A critical examination of the radiocarbon method and its calibration by tree-ring dating shows that this objection is false.

<< Radiocarbon Dating >>

The method of radiocarbon dating is used to date something that was once a living organism or was once part of a living organism. While the organism was still living it ingested the radioisotope carbon-14, which is produced in the upper atmosphere by cosmic rays, along with the stable isotope carbon-12. While it was living, it remained in equilibrium with the carbon reservoir in the atmosphere and the ratio of the number of carbon-14 atoms to the number of carbon-12 atoms that it contained remained constant. After the organism died, it ingested no new carbon. As time went on the carbon-14 decayed into nitrogen-14 but the carbon-12 remained intact. So the ratio of the number of carbon-14 to carbon-12 atoms decreased. This ratio is measured and is used to calculate how far in the past the organism died.

In this method it is, first of all, assumed that the ratio of carbon-14 to carbon-12 in the atmospheric carbon reservoir is uniform throughout the earth and constant in time. The latter implies that the rate of production of carbon-14 in the atmosphere has remained constant over time. Atmospheric contamination by fossil fuels must be considered because it could have significantly altered the ratio. To correct for this the estimated ratio before the industrial revolution is used as a standard. However, there are indications that the concentration of carbon-14 in the atmosphere varied significantly even before the industrial revolution.[53] To account for variations in the atmospheric reservoir, the method has been calibrated by the technique of tree-ring dating, but the improvement in reliability it gives is quite limited (see below).

Also to be taken into account are other effects that could have altered the carbon ratio in a specimen. There are processes such as ground water leaching and bacterial action that can alter the carbon ratio, so care is taken to choose samples free of contamination.

The method is reliable only for measurements up to a few thousand years. Some scientists and historians do not trust the method for dating items beyond 1000 B.C. The dates it gives often differ from dates derived by historical methods. Anthropologist Robert E. Lee admitted that carbon-14 dating is unreliable:

> The troubles of the radiocarbon dating method are undeniably deep and serious. Despite 35 years of technological refinement and better understanding, the underlying *assumptions* have been strongly challenged and warnings are out that radiocarbon may soon find itself in a crisis situation. Continuing use of the method depends on a "fix-it-as-we-go" approach, allowing for contamination here, fractionation there, and calibration whenever possible. It should be no surprise, then, that fully half of the dates are rejected. The wonder is, surely, that the remaining half come to be *accepted*.
>
> No matter how "useful" it is, though, the radiocarbon method is still not capable of yielding accurate and reliable results. There are gross discrepancies, the chronology is uneven and relative, and the accepted dates are actually selected dates.[54]

One subtle assumption of radiocarbon dating is that life has been on earth long enough for the rate of decay of carbon-14 in dead organisms to equal the rate of production of carbon-14 in the atmosphere. The beginning of production of carbon-14 from nitrogen-14 by the bombardment of neutrons in the atmosphere is like turning on the faucet in a bathtub. Its accumulation in living organisms is like the accumulation of water in the bathtub. Its decay in dead organisms is like there being a leak in the bathtub plug. As the water level rises the leak rate increases because of the increased pressure. After a while, the water will reach a level at which the rate of water pouring into the tub equals the rate of water draining out. Thus equilibrium is reached, and the water level in the tub remains constant. Measurements have shown that equilibrium has not been reached in the case of carbon-14. Even Willard Libby, who invented the method and wrote a monograph on it, recorded a difference in rates of about 20%, which he dismissed as experimental error. Later estimates gave even higher discrepancies. If those discrepancies are taken seriously they imply that the carbon-14 "faucet" was turned on only several thousand years ago, implying either Creation or some catastrophe took place at that time.[55]

Radiocarbon dating proved much less precise for dating ancient Near-Eastern civilizations than historical chronology. Therefore it is used little when historical data is available. Despite this, it is still used to establish dates when historical data is not available. Enthusiastic proponents of this method claim that it is useful for dating to 50,000 years. This, of course, greatly exceeds the range of biblical chronology. In addition, it exceeds the competence of the method, even if the earth were that old. There are no 50,000 year-old historical records or trees that can be used to calibrate it for such extreme measurements. It would not even be capable of dating antediluvian finds, if any archaeological find could be certainly established as such, because the Flood would probably have greatly affected the production and distribution of carbon-14. The fact that there is practically no carbon-14 in coal suggests that there was no carbon-14 in the atmosphere before the Flood.[56] Furthermore, for measurements of 50,000 years old the carbon-14 concentration would be very low (0.2% of maximum) because 50,000 years is close to nine half-lives of carbon-14.[n] Such measurements require very sensitive instruments and very pure samples.[57]

Libby admitted that the radiocarbon dating method lent support to the biblical revelation that human civilizations appeared abruptly on earth only several thousand years ago:

> The first shock Dr. Arnold and I had was that our advisors informed us that history extended back only 5000 years. We had thought initially that we would be able to get samples all along the curve back to 30,000 years, put the points in, and then our work would be finished. You read books and find statements that such and such a society or archaeological site is 20,000 years old. We learned rather abruptly that these numbers, these ancient ages, are not known; in fact, it is at about the time of the first dynasty in Egypt that the last historical date of any real certainty has been established.[58]

<< Dendrochronology >>

The science of *dendrochronology* or *tree-ring dating* is also used in archaeology, both in its own right and to provide calibration for radiometric dating. It is based

---

n.   The half-life of carbon-14 is 5730 years.

on the fact that each year a tree adds a ring to its growth, the size and composition of which depends on that year's weather and environmental conditions. Trees growing in the same area will have matching sequences, so scientists have been able gradually to construct an absolute chronology by overlapping sequences of successively older ring patterns. The ring patterns are those in pieces of wood taken from living trees and in old timbers found at various places. From these overlapping sequences a master chart can be drawn up. The composers of the master chart must take great care in matching the pieces together. They must be skilled at recognizing the distinguishing features of ring patterns so that correct matches are made. Correct matches are not as easy to make as one may suppose. M. Baillie writes:

> It has to be remembered that there is only one correct pattern: each tree has grown only once and ultimately its ring pattern can only fit at one place in time. Simply because two pieces look alike does not necessarily mean that they fit together. An important part of dendrochronology is the formulation of techniques to ensure that the fit between pieces is real. So we have a jig-saw [puzzle] which may not be complete and for which the pieces are not acquired in any particular order. The result of this is that frequently the writer on dendrochronology is forced to distort the order in which things happened (in which samples were acquired and *matched*) to impose a logical sequence of events on a particular study. It is this distortion which leads to the excessively tidy nature of some reports and by extension to the mistaken belief that dendrochronology is easy. It *is* easy in concept, but it can be extremely difficult, time-consuming and frustrating in reality.[59]

A sample from an ancient wooden beam from an archaeological site can be sent to a laboratory to be compared against the chart to establish its age. By studying the rings of many samples of timber from different sites and strata within a particular region, archaeologists build up a historical sequence. This technique is particularly well developed in the American Southwest. It is particularly useful for dating wood up to 2000 years old. In that range the ages it deduces can be compared with historical information.

The oldest known living thing is the bristlecone pine. Microscopic study of the growth rings of some living specimens of bristlecone pines in California and Nevada yielded ages from 4600 to 4900 years. That means that they would have sprouted shortly after the Flood. However, dendrochronologists try to extend the range of the method by looking for matching tree-ring patterns in timbers they think to be even older. In this way sequences derived from the bristlecone pine have been extended to 6700 B.C., which corresponds to nearly twice the age of the oldest living specimens. It is needless to say, in light of the above quotation, that such extrapolation is difficult, subjective and uncertain. Even trees of the same kind living today do not always display the same ring pattern. Factors such as disease, temperature, insect infestation, frost damage, wind, available sunlight, amount of rainfall and ground water, and soil nutrients cause variations in the patterns from tree to tree, especially those removed from each other in place and time. All this makes comparisons very tricky. Scientists have been concerned about this:

> Among the pines, {the bristlecone} is, if anything, even more undependable than the Junipers.... We have many cores from bristlecones growing in the White Mountains of California, east of the Sierra Nevadas, at altitudes of 10,000 feet, where the rainfall is low and erratic. There are also a number of cores from bristlecones growing at high altitudes in south-western Utah and on the San Francisco Peaks at Flagstaff, Arizona. Comparison of charts of measured rings show no similarity whatever.[60]

Also, two or more rings may grow in a single year, but those are usually recognizably different from normal rings.

The tree-ring method is used to calibrate radiocarbon dating. The carbon-14/carbon-12 ratios are measured for individual tree rings. From this data, a "calibration curve" is drawn, which supposedly enables the user to compensate for variations in carbon ratio in the atmospheric carbon reservoir over time. This at best could increase the reliability of the method only to the age of the oldest living trees. Even then there are problems. R. H. Brown writes:

> Attempts to derive historical age from radiocarbon age yield increasingly uncertain conjectures for samples older than 2000 years. Tree-ring chronology has been extended from 59 B.C. to approximately 2400 B.C. using the Bristlecone Pine. The growth characteristics of this tree make it unsatisfactory for the establishment of a precise long-term growth-ring sequence. Attempts to correlate Bristlecone Pine growth-rings with radiocarbon ages indicate that either ring counting has over-estimated the age of the oldest Bristlecone Pine by 500 to 1000 years, or the relative amount of Carbon-14 in the atmosphere around 2000 B.C. was in the order of ten percent greater than in A.D. 1850 [the standard year].[61]

[1] See ACC, p. 152.

[2] JR, no. 1566.

[3] ACC, p. 160.

[4] See, for example, Custance, Arthur, *Noah's Three Sons: Human History in Three Dimensions*, Vol. 1 of Doorway Papers series (Grand Rapids, MI: Zondervan, 1975); Morris, Henry M., *The Genesis Record* (Grand Rapids, MI: Baker Book House, 1976).

[5] Genesis 22:18 (NAB).

[6] For examples of the technological know-how of the builders of ancient civilizations in both hemispheres see Chittick, Donald, *The Puzzle of Ancient Man: Advanced Technology in Past Civilizations?* (Newberg, OR: Creation Compass, 1998).

[7] Others reckon seventy nations. See, for example, H. Morris, *The Genesis Record*.

[8] Ussher, James, *The Annals of the World*, trans. by Larry and Marion Pierce (Green Forest, AR: Master Books, 2003), nos. 40, 72.

[9] CG, Book XVI, Chapter 1.

[10] CG, Book XVI, Chapter 3.

[11] CG, Book XVI, Chapter 11.

[12] Ibid.

[13] Ibid.

[14] See Ussher, op. cit., nos. 24–64, 102.

[15] Ussher, op. cit., no. 82.

[16] Ussher, op. cit., no. 77.

[17] Hebrews 7:3.

[18] Hebrews 7.

[19] Hebrews 4:14.

[20] See Hebrews 7:7.

[21] Psalms 90:10.

[22] *The Antiquities of the Jews*, Book 1, Chapter 4:1.

[23] Ibid.

[24] Ussher, op. cit., no. 49.

[25] *The Antiquities of the Jews*, Book 1, Chapter 4:2.

[26] CG, Book XVI, Chapter 4.

[27] See ACC, p. 164.

[28] ACC, p. 165.

[29] CG, Book XVI, Chapter 4.

[30] ACC, p. 169.

[31] Ibid.

[32] *The Antiquities of the Jews*, Book 1, Chapter 5.

[33] *The Antiquities of the Jews*, Book 1, Chapter 6:1.

[34] See Cooper, Bill, *After the Flood: The Early Post-Flood History of Europe Traced Back to Noah* (Chichester, England: New Wine Press, 1995).

[35] *The Antiquities of the Jews*, Book 1, Chapter 6:2.

[36] Ussher, op. cit., nos. 49, 52.

[37] See Stanton, Mary and Hyma, Albert, *Streams of Civilization, Vol. 1: Earliest Times to the Discovery of the New World* (Arlington Heights, IL: Christian Liberty Press, 2000), pp. 68–69.

[38] *The Antiquities of the Jews*, Book 1, Chapter 6:4.

[39] Johnson, Samuel: From *The Life of Samuel Johnson, LL.D.* by James Boswell.

[40] 1 Samuel 8:10–18.

[41] See Doctrine Five, Adaptability of Natural Species.

[42] Woodmorappe, John, *Noah's Ark: A Feasibility Study* (Santee, CA: Institute for Creation Research, 1996), Parts III and IV.

[43] This picture of the ice age is that given by Oard, Michael J., *An Ice Age Caused by the Genesis Flood* (El Cajon, CA: Institute for Creation Research, 1990). Also see Rehwinkel, Alfred M: *The Flood: In the Light of the Bible, Geology and Archaeology* (St. Louis, MO: Concordia, 1951), pp. 298–341; Whitcomb, John C. and Morris, Henry M., *The Genesis Flood: The Biblical Record and Its Scientific Implications* (Phillipsburg, NJ: P & R Publishing, 1960), pp. 292–311. For a clear brief account see Perloff, James, *Tornado in a Junkyard: The Relentless Myth of Darwinism* (Arlington, MA: Refuge Books, 1999), pp. 190–192.

[44] Job 38:29–30.

[45] For more details about tells and their excavation see Free, J. P. and Vos, H. F., *Archaeology and Bible History* (Grand Rapids, MI: Zondervan, 1962), pp. 16–20.

[46] Glueck, Nelson, *Rivers in the Desert* (New York: Farrar, Straus and Cudahy, 1968), p. 31.

[47] As quoted by Joachim Rehork in Keller, Werner, 2nd revised edition, *The Bible as History* (New York: Bantam Books, 1982), p. 434.

[48] 1 Corinthians 15:14.

[49] From a television documentary entitled "In Search of the Trojan War," as quoted by Climer, Philip, "Archaeology and the Bible" in Ussher, op. cit., p. 937.

[50] See Crystal, David, *The Cambridge Encyclopedia of Language*, 2nd ed. (New York: Cambridge University Press, 2002), p. 290.

[51] Chomsky, Noam, *Language and Mind* (New York, Harcourt, Brace, Jovanovich, 1972), p. 67.

52 Langer, Susanne K., as quoted by Kane, Thomas, S., *The New Oxford Guide to Writing* (New York: Oxford University Press, 1988), p. 283.

53 See Whitcomb and Morris, op. cit., p. 374.

54 Lee, Robert E., "Radiocarbon Ages in Error," *Anthropological Journal of Canada*, Vol. 19, No. 3, 1981, pp. 9, 29; as quoted in Morris, John D., *The Young Earth* (Green Forest, AR: Master Books, 1994), p. 67.

55 See Whitelaw, Robert L., "Radiocarbon Confirms Biblical Creation," *Why Not Creation?* Lammerts, Walter E., ed., (Nutley, NJ: Presbyterian and Reformed Publishing Co., 1970), pp. 90–96 and Cook, Melvin A., "Do Radiological Clocks Need Repair?" in Lammerts, Walter E., *Scientific Studies in Special Creation* (Nutley, NJ: Presbyterian and Reformed Publishing Co., 1971), pp. 79–83.

56 See Armstrong, Harold L. "An Attempt to Correct for the Effects of the Flood in Determining Dates by Radioactive Carbon" in Lammerts, Walter E., *Scientific Studies in Special Creation* (Nutley, NJ: Presbyterian and Reformed Publishing Co., 1971), p. 98. Also see Whitcomb and Morris, op. cit., pp. 374–376.

57 See Cook, Melvin A., op. cit., p. 95.

58 Libby, W. F., "Radiocarbon Dating," *American Scientist*, Vol. 44, January 1956, p. 107, as quoted by Whitcomb and Morris, op. cit., p. 372.

59 Baillie, M. G. L., *Tree-Ring Dating and Archaeology* (Chicago: University of Chicago Press, 1982), pp. 23–24.

60 Gladwin, Harold s., "Dendrochronology, Radiocarbon and Bristlecones," *Anthropological Journal of Canada*, Vol. 14, No. 4, 1976, p. 5, as quoted by Morris, John D., op. cit., p. 66.

61 Brown, R. H., "Radioactive Dating Indicates a Young Earth" in Lammerts, Walter E., ed., *Why Not Creation?* (Nutley, NJ: Presbyterian and Reformed Publishing Co., 1970), p. 85.

Epilogue

The Medieval Catholic Perspective on Creation

The technological powers of observation of medieval Catholic scholars were more limited than ours, but they stuck to the observed facts more closely than we do. They were much less speculative about the nature of the cosmos than modern scientists are. And, of course, they deeply respected revealed truth about the world, which modern scientists consider irrelevant. For these reasons their vision of the cosmos was less distorted and more realistic than ours, despite its limitations. And they were aware of its limitations. They knew that man discovers only what God allows him to discover, that nature reveals only what God permits her to reveal.

In contrast, the science idolaters of our age are presumptuous and sophomoric. They think that they know more about the world than they really do and fail to recognize the blind spots in their powers of observation and reasoning, the kinds of blind spots that magicians and charlatans exploit. There are many things that elude the narrow means of investigation that they praise so highly. One inclined to give the natural sciences more than their due would do well to ponder what Hamlet said to his friend Horatio: "There are more things in heaven and earth, Horatio, than are dreamt of in your philosophy."[1] One must not fail to realize that the world is holistic, while the human mind, in this world being limited to the reasoning process, functions analytically. Consequently, we will never completely comprehend the universe. We will never come to know the world perfectly though we will always discover more and better ways of using the things in it. With every genuine advance in scientific knowledge, creation becomes more awe-filled, wondrous and mysterious; and it becomes more apparent how little we really know about it.

＊　　　＊　　　＊　　　＊

The theology of creation elaborated by the Fathers of the Church was systematized by the Catholic theologians of the thirteenth century. The traditional Catholic perspective on creation that was formulated by them was adorned with Greek cosmology, but it was not tied fast to that cosmology. It could adopt any cosmology that was consistent with the Genesis account.

A seminal work in the medieval systemization of Catholic theology was the *Four Books of Sentences* of Peter Lombard (ca. 1100–1164). Peter Lombard taught theology in Paris and was consecrated archbishop of that city in 1159. His *Four Books of Sentences* (1148–51) is essentially a collection of sayings of the Fathers of the Church. The titles of the four books are "The Godhead," "Creation," "The Incarnation," and "The Sacraments." The *Sentences* was widely read and gained great popularity in theological schools. It came to serve as the standard theological text of the Middle Ages and was the subject of a great many commentaries.

Following are summaries of the medieval Catholic vision of creation as projected by St. Thomas Aquinas (ca. 1225–1274) and St. Bonaventure (1221–1274), who both early in their theological careers wrote a commentary on the *Sentences,* and Dante Alighieri (1265–1321), who enshrined traditional Catholic theology in poetry. All three are notable exponents of medieval Catholic belief.

St. Thomas Aquinas and St. Bonaventure on Creation

St. Thomas Aquinas, the Angelic Doctor, and his mentor, St. Albert the Great (ca. 1206–1280), the Universal Doctor, were the great Dominican masters of the thirteenth century. Aquinas' doctrine on creation is found chiefly the treatises on creation, the distinction of things, the angels, the work of the six days, and man in Part I, Questions 44–102 of his *Summa Theologica* (1266–1268) and in Book 2 of his *Summa contra Gentiles* (1259–1264). He also discusses creation in Question 3 of *Quaestiones Disputatae de Potentia Dei* (1265–1266) and in his *Writings on the "Sentences"* (1252–1256).

St. Thomas believed that natural world has a religious value. In Chapter 2 of the second book of the *Summa contra Gentiles* he argues that the consideration of creatures is useful for building up faith in God. He gives four reasons to support his claim. First, "through meditating on His works we are able somewhat to admire and consider the divine wisdom." He cites Sir 1:10: *"[H]e poured her [wisdom] out upon his works."* Second, "this consideration leads us to admire the sublime power of God, and consequently begets in men's hearts a reverence for God." He cites Wis 13:4–5: *"And if men were amazed at their power and working, let them perceive how much more powerful is he who formed them. For from the greatness and beauty of created things comes a corresponding perception of their Creator."* He also cites Rom 1:20: *"Ever since the creation of the world his invisible nature, namely his eternal power and deity, has been clearly perceived in the things that have been made."* Third, "this consideration inflames the souls of men to the love of the divine goodness." He cites Ps 92:4: *"For thou, O LORD, hast made me glad by thy work; at the works of thy hands I sing for joy."* Fourth, "this consideration bestows on man a certain likeness to the divine perfection" because "to know creatures by the light of divine revelation ... results in man a certain likeness to the divine wisdom." He cites 2 Cor 3:18: *"And we all, with unveiled face, beholding the glory of the Lord, are being changed into his likeness...."* He closes the chapter by citing Sir 42:15: *"I will now call to mind the works of the Lord, and will declare what I have seen."*

In Chapter 3 of the second book of the *Summa contra Gentiles*, St. Thomas argues that consideration of creatures is also necessary for refuting errors about God because "errors about creatures sometimes lead one astray from the truth of the faith, in so far as they disagree with the true knowledge of God." He says that this happens in several ways. First, "because through ignorance of the nature of creatures men are sometimes so far misled as to deem that which can but derive its being from something else to be the first cause and God, for they think nothing exists besides visible creatures." He cites Wis 13:1–2: *"For all men who were ignorant of God were foolish by nature; and they were unable from the good things that are seen to know him who exists, nor did they recognize the craftsman while paying heed to his works; but they supposed that either fire or wind or swift air, or the circle of the stars, or turbulent water, or the luminaries of heaven were the gods that rule the world."* Second, "because they ascribe to certain creatures that which belongs to God alone." "Into this error fell those who ascribe the creation of things, or the knowledge of the future, or the working of miracles to causes other than God." (This is the error of evolutionists, who attribute powers to creatures that properly belong to God.) St. Thomas cites Wis 14:21: *"And this became a hidden trap for mankind, because men, in bondage to misfortune or to royal authority, bestowed on objects of stone or wood the name that ought not be shared."* Third, "because something is withdrawn from the divine power in its working on creatures, through ignorance of the creature's nature." This is evidenced in those who say that there is more than one principle of creation, in those who say that things proceed from God not by the divine will but by necessity, and in those who deny that God can work outside the ordinary course of things. He cites Wis 12:17: *"For thou dost show thy strength when men doubt the completeness of thy power."* Fourth: "Man, who is led by faith to God as his last end, through ignoring the natures of things, and consequently the order of his place in the universe, thinks himself to be beneath certain creatures above whom he is placed." This is the error of those who subject man's will to the stars. He cites Jer 10:2: *"[N]or be dismayed at the signs of the heavens."* He closes the chapter saying that Scripture threatens punishment to those who err about creatures. He cites Ps 28:5: *"Because they do not regard the works of the LORD, or the work of his hands, he will break them down and build them up no more."* He also cites Wis 2:21–23: *"Thus they reasoned, but they were led astray, for their wickedness blinded them, and they did not know the secret purposes of God, nor hope for the wages of holiness, nor discern the prize for blameless souls."*

In Chapter 4 of the second book of the *Summa contra Gentiles*, St. Thomas considers that philosophers and theologians treat of creatures in different ways. The philosopher is interested in the creatures in themselves, that is, in their natures, whereas the theologian is interested in the relation of creatures to God, especially in how they manifest His glory. He cites Ecclus (Sir) 42:16–17: *"The sun giving light hath looked upon all things, and full of the glory of the Lord is his work. Hath not the Lord made the saints to declare all his wonderful works, which the Lord Almighty has firmly settled to be established for his glory?"* (DR). Philosophy is handmaid to theology. For in considering creatures in themselves it leads us from them to the knowledge of God.

James Weisheipl, a noted biographer of Aquinas, nicely summarizes Thomas' philosophic principles pertaining to creation that he professed in the *Writings on the "Sentences"*:

> In this earliest work by Thomas, all of his principal conclusions are established: the real distinction between *esse* and essence in creatures and their real identity in God; rejection of the hylomorphic composition of separated substances, or angels; the pure potentiality of first matter; the unicity of substantial form [one form as opposed to more than one] in corporeal creatures; consideration of the agent and possible intellects in man as powers of the individual soul; insistence that matter designated by quantity is the sole principle of natural individuation; insistence that nature is not the 'efficient cause' but only the active principle in the free fall of natural bodies; and defense of the possibility of natural motion in a void.[2]

Steven E. Baldner and William E. Carroll have translated the six articles that comprise Book 2, Distinction 1, Question 1 of Aquinas' *Writings on the "Sentences."*[3] These articles are essentially a commentary on Genesis 1:1. In the first article St. Thomas argues, in opposition to Manichean dualism, that there is only one principle of creation, namely, God. In the second article, Aquinas defines creation as production from nothing, from nonbeing to being. He says:

> It ought to be known, moreover, that the meaning of creation includes two things. The first is that it presupposes nothing in the thing which is to be created. In this way it differs from other changes, because a generation presupposes matter, which is not generated, but rather which is transformed and brought to completion through generation. In other changes a subject which is a complete being is presupposed.... The causality of the Creator, however, extends to everything that is in the thing....
>
> The second thing is that non-being is prior to being in the thing which is said to be created. This is not a priority of time or of duration, such that what did not exist before does exist later, but a priority of nature, so that, if the created thing is left to itself, it would not exist, because it only has its being from the causality of the higher cause. [4]

He then goes on to distinguish creation from the eternal generation of God the Son from God the Father:

> What a thing has in itself and not from something else is naturally prior in it to that which it has from something else. (In this way creation differs from eternal generation, for it cannot be said that the Son of God, if left to Himself, would not have being, since He receives it from the Father that very same being which the Father has, which is absolute being, not dependent upon anything.)[5]

He says that creation as understood by the above two points (creation *from nothing* and creation *by another*) can be demonstrated by philosophers. He then goes on to add a third point (creation *in time*) to the meaning of creation, which he says cannot be demonstrated:

> If, however, we should add a third point to the meaning of creation, that the creature should have non-being prior to being *in duration*, so that it is said to be "out of nothing" because it is temporally after nothing, in this way creation cannot be demonstrated and it is not granted by philosophers, but is taken on faith.[6]

In the third article Aquinas considers whether agents other than God can create. He argues, "being and non-being are separated by an absolute infinity."[7] Therefore the act of creation requires an infinite power, which belongs to God alone. This power cannot be given to any creature because the creature would then be the primary cause of being, which it is not.

In the fourth article Thomas considers whether agents other than God are able to cause anything. In other words, he treats the question of whether or not secondary causes had a role in the production of things in the world. He sums up his position as follows:

> [I]f God were the immediate cause of all things, one thing would not depend upon another, as effect upon its cause. If such were the case, a thing would not come to be by the agency of one thing rather than by the agency of another. We see, however, from experience that one thing is not made by just anything, but rather man is always generated from the seed of man. The seed of the father, therefore, is the efficient cause of the son.[8]

He holds that God alone is the immediate cause of those things that come into being by creation. This includes angels and human souls because these are pure forms, that is, they are not composites, and, as such, cannot be produced by other creatures. God is also the immediate cause of prime matter. Of those things composed of matter and form, God directly created the elements because other material substances are not capable of producing them. Aquinas also held that the heavenly bodies, such as the sun, were also directly created because, following Aristotle, he believed that they were composed of an incorruptible substance incapable of being produced by other creatures.

Concerning living creatures, Aquinas said that there are some that (by nature) necessarily produce what is similar in species, through the process of generation. Of such creatures "the first members were immediately created by God, such as the first man, the first lion, and so forth. Man, for instance, can only be generated from man."[9] However, since he believed in the spontaneous generation of some living creatures, for example, flies, he allowed for the production of living things that are not generated by an agent similar in species. He said:

> It is, however, otherwise with those things which are not generated by an agent that is similar to them in species. For these, rather, the power of celestial bodies along with appropriate matter is sufficient, as, for example, those things which are generated by putrefaction.[10]

Although Aquinas here is saying that living organisms need not, in principle, be generated by a parent or parents of the same species, it cannot be said that he would be open to the modern doctrine of macroevolution if he were alive today. First of all, he would know that spontaneous generation has never been observed and that it has never been observed that a living organism proceeds from anything other than a living organism of the same kind. And holding to the literal truth of Genesis, as he did, he would still insist that God created a first man, a first lion (or lions) and so forth. He probably would say that macroevolution is theoretically possible; but a Catholic is not free to profess belief in it because it is not evident that macroevolution can be harmonized with Sacred Scripture, and natural science has not demonstrated that it is necessary to seek such harmonization.

In the fifth article Aquinas considers whether the world is eternal. He produces a number of arguments saying that it is and a number of arguments saying that it isn't. He says that there are three positions on the question: 1) that God and all other things are eternal, 2) "that the world and everything other than God began to exist after they had not existed, and that God could not have made an eternal world, not because of a lack of his power, but because the world could not have been made eternally since it was created" and 3) "that everything other than God began to exist, but nevertheless the fact that the world has begun to exist cannot be demonstrated but is rather held and believed to be so by divine revelation." He goes on to say that he himself holds the third position:

> And I agree with this [the third] position, because I do not believe that we are able to formulate a demonstrative argument for this, just as for the Trinity, although it is impossible that the Trinity not exist. In confirmation of this is the weakness of the arguments given as demonstrations, all of which have been taken up and refuted by the philosophers who maintain the eternity of the world. If someone should try to prove the newness of the world by relying on such arguments against the philosophers, his arguments would become rather a mockery of the faith than a confirmation of it.
>
> I say then that there are demonstrations for neither side of the question but probable or sophistical arguments on both sides.[11]

St. Thomas then goes on to gives his reason for saying that neither the eternity nor the newness of the world can be demonstrated:

> The reason this question cannot be demonstrated is that the nature of a thing is quite different in its complete being from what it was when it was in the process of being made by its cause. For example, the nature of a man who is

already born is different from that of a man while he is still in his mother's womb. Hence, if someone should argue on the basis of a full-grown man what must be true of the man in the incomplete state in the womb of his mother, he would be deceived.... [This is the case with] those who, from the way things happen in the world in its complete state, wish to show either the necessity or the impossibility of the beginning of the world. What now begins to be begins through motion; hence what causes motion must always precede in duration and in nature, and there must be contraries; but none of these are necessary in the making of the universe by God.[12]

In one of his replies to the arguments set forth, he sets forth his view that what we call "space" is defined by the objects in it and was created with the world:

[I]t ought to be said that before the creation of the world there was no void, as there is none after, because the void is not a simple negation but a privation. Hence, in order that there be a void, as those who suppose that there is one would say, there must be a place or real dimensions, neither of which did exist before the world.[13]

In another reply he sets forth his view on *real* and *imaginary* time:

[I]t ought to be said that God precedes the world not only in nature, but also in duration, not, however, in a duration of time, but in a duration of eternity. Before the world there was no time in reality, but in imagination only, because we now imagine that God could have added many years earlier to this finite time, and to all of these earlier years God's eternity would have been present.[14]

In yet another reply, he makes the surprising assertion that Aristotle understood the first cause as not only a mover, but also as a giver of being:

It ought to be said that, as the Commentator [Averroes] says in *On the Substance of the World*, ch. 2, Aristotle never intended that God was the cause of only the motion of the heavens, [but] that he was [also] the cause of its substance, giving it being.[15]

He also attributes a doctrine of creation from eternity to Aristotle in *Commentary of Aristotle's Physics*, Book 8, Lectures 3, 21 and in a number of other places.[16] In his *On Separated Substances* 9 Aquinas says that Plato and Aristotle "do not deviate from the position of the Catholic faith because they have supposed these things to be uncreated but because they have supposed them to have always existed."[17]

Again, in another of his replies, St. Thomas affirms his belief in the impossibility of the actually infinite:

[I]t ought to be said that an actual infinity is impossible, but an infinity in succession is not impossible.[18]

He goes on in another reply to say that "one effect cannot have an infinite number of essential causes, but it can have an infinite number of accidental causes."[19] This is because an infinite number of essential causes would be an *actual* infinity but an infinite number of accidental causes would be an infinity *in succession*. He gives as an example the making of a knife. He says "some efficient causes are essentially required, such as a craftsman and a tool, and it is impossible that these be infinite in number, because then there would consequently be an *actual* infinity of things. If, however, the knife is made by an old craftsman who many times replaces his tools, there would be a *successive multitude* of tools; this is accidental. Nothing prevents an infinite number of tools from existing which come before this knife, if the craftsman should be eternal."[20] He concludes from this argument that it is possible for an animal to have had an infinite number of progenitors and for there to have been an infinite number of days before this day "because the substance of the sun is eternal."[21] [a]

In the sixth article, Aquinas examines the meaning of Genesis 1:1: *"In the beginning God created the heavens and the earth."* He discusses the Trinitarian nature of the Creator,[b] saying:

---

a. From this argument can be deduced the possibility for God to have sequentially created a universe of infinite extent, for God could have created a heavenly body each day for an infinite number of days before this day. Thus Thomas' allowance for the possibility of a temporally infinite world also allows for the possibility of a spatially infinite world. Further, if God could create a new heavenly body each day, why not one each second, or each microsecond? Or going to the limit, why couldn't God have created an infinite universe instantly?

b. Walter Lang points out that the very first verse of the Bible suggests the Trinity. He notes that the plural word for God (*Elohim*) is used with a singular verb (*bara*—create). See *Genesis and Science* (Minneapolis, MN: Bible-Science Association, 1982), p. 4.

[I]t ought to be said that the designation of being the efficient cause is appropriated to the Father, whereas the designation of being the exemplar cause for a work of art is appropriated to the Son, who is the Wisdom and Art of the Father.[22]

And the goodness of creation is appropriated to the Holy Spirit. By explaining the Creator Trinity he refutes the error of the Manichees who held there to be more than one creative principle.

He defends the interpretation of *"in the beginning"* as "in the beginning of time" to refute the error of the eternity of the world. And, finally he defends the interpretation of *"in the beginning"* as "before *all* things" to defend against the error of those who hold that the visible things were created by God through the mediation of angels. He says that God created *everything* "in the beginning":

> [I]t ought to be said that by "heavens" is understood also the angelic nature, which is said to dwell in the heavens, and by "earth" is understood all generable and corruptible things.[23]

✳   ✳   ✳   ✳

St. Bonaventure, the Seraphic Doctor and his mentor, Alexander of Hales (?–1245), were the great Franciscan masters of the thirteenth century. Bonaventure's doctrine on creation is found chiefly in his *Commentary on the Sentences* (1248–1255) and in the *Breviloquium* (before 1257). In his philosophy/theology of creation he generally agreed with Aquinas. Like Aquinas, he interpreted Genesis literally unless he felt compelled to do otherwise. In Part II of the *Breviloquium* he deals with the creation of the world. He argues, like St. Thomas, that God created the world out of nothing and not from Himself. He holds to six literal days of creation, saying:

> We should especially hold these truths about corporeal nature as regards its becoming: that it was brought into existence in six days so that in the beginning before any day God created the heaven and earth.[24]

He may seem to be contradicting himself by saying on one hand that corporeal nature was brought into existence in "six days," and on the other hand that God created the heaven and earth "before any day." But he goes on to explain. He seems to say that creation per se, that is, the production ex nihilo, took place at the first instant of time. Once heaven and earth came into existence, so did time:

> And because creation is from nothing, it was in the beginning before all days as the foundation of all things and of all times.[25]

The works of the first six days were works of "distinction" and "embellishment." During the first three days God made distinct four natures, namely, light, water, air and earth. During the next three days God embellished the earth with things according to the above four natures: the heavenly bodies correspond to light, the fish to water, the birds to air, and the beasts and man to earth. Bonaventure goes on to say:

> Though God was able to do all these things instantaneously, He preferred to accomplish them in a series of periods as a distinct and clear representation of power, wisdom and goodness [power corresponding to creation, wisdom to distinction, and goodness to embellishment].... [26]

He does, however, allow for Augustine's belief that creation, distinction and embellishment all took place at once and that the six days represent stages of angelic consideration; but he clearly prefers the interpretation that he himself has given:

> If, however, it should be said in another way that all things were made together,[27] then all these seven days are referred to the angelic consideration. Yet truly the first manner of speaking is wholly consonant with Scripture and with the authority of the saints, both those who have gone before and those who have followed Augustine.[28]

He further elaborates on Ecclus (Sir) 18:1, which led Augustine to interpret the six days in terms of ideas in the minds of the angels:

> We must not understand the passage *"He that liveth forever created all things together"* [DR] to mean that He created all things into a total chaos about which the poets talk, for He made this triple nature [see below]: the highest in the highest, the middle nature in the middle, and the lowest in the lowest; nor on the other hand are we to believe that He created it with complete distinction, since heaven is perfect and the empty earth is a middle nature, as it were holding a middle place, not yet brought to a perfect distinction.[29]

The triple nature that he is speaking about is comprised of three fundamental natures 1) the luminous, which is the nature of light, 2) the transparent, which is the nature of water and air, and 3) the opaque, which is nature of earth. He is saying that these three natures were not created in the beginning in a mixed-up, chaotic state. Rather, they were created somewhat but not perfectly distinct. The distinctions were perfected during the first three days.

Bonaventure agrees with Aquinas that God did not stop working on the seventh day, but He desisted from the creation of new forms:

> [O]n the seventh day God desisted not from toil or work, for He still worked, but from the creation of new forms because He had done all things either in likeness, as in the case with those things which are propagated, or in a seminal reason, as is the case with those things which are brought into existence in other ways.[30]

And like Aquinas he believed that there would have been no Incarnation if there had been no Fall.

There are three major exceptions to Bonaventure's general agreement with Aquinas. First, although he adopted the hylomorphic theory of matter and form, his interpretation of it differed from that of Aquinas. Unlike Aquinas, he held that prime matter was not merely that which is undetermined. Rather, he believed that it contains seminal principles, or potentialities, that were infused by God in the beginning. When God creates, He does not produce new essences. Rather, He actualizes that which is potential. Also, he did not hold to the unicity of substantial form in corporeal creatures, as did St. Thomas. Rather, he subscribed to the doctrine of the plurality of forms. For Bonaventure, a form is the principle of a perfection. Created light, the luminous form, which cannot be separated from prime matter, is the common form of all things. The various corporeal creatures, including the elements, also possess other forms according to their perfections. Further, he did not limit matter to corporeal things, but held that one and the same kind of matter is the substratum of both spiritual and corporeal things.[31]

Another point on which Bonaventure differs from Thomas is on the possibility of an eternal world. St. Thomas held that it cannot be proven by reason alone that the world was not created from eternity. Conversely, St. Bonaventure held that such can be proven by reason alone.[32]

The third point on which Bonaventure differs from Aquinas concerns the perpetuation of being. Both Aquinas and Bonaventure agree that creatures will cease to exist if God ceases to cause their existence. For Aquinas, only a single act of

God is required to bring a creature into existence and maintain it in existence. God gives a creature being, and it exists. However, for Bonaventure, God performs two different acts. First, He gives existence. Then, since the creature is unable to keep itself in existence, He conserves the creature in existence.[33]

In the *Breviloquium*, Bonaventure professes Greek cosmology, which was accepted in one form or another by all of Christendom. He says that heavenly bodies influence "the effective production of things generable and corruptible, namely mineral, vegetative, and sensitive life and human bodies." But "they are not certain signs of future contingencies, nor do they exert influence upon the freedom of choice through the power of the constellation, which some philosophers say is fate."[34] So he, like other medieval theologians, believed that the stars influenced things on earth. But he, like the others, cannot be accused of believing in astrology, as we understand that term today. The influences he spoke of were purely physical causes, not occult influences.

Dante Alighieri on Creation

Dante was a native of Florence of noble ancestry. He is Italy's most famous poet and is esteemed as the one who single-handedly made Italian a literary language. His magnum opus is *The Divine Comedy* (ca. 1310–14), which is an epic poem that paints a profoundly Christian picture of human destiny. In it Dante tells of a pilgrimage made by him the through the afterlife, first through hell, then through purgatory, and finally through heaven until he ultimately acquires a glimpse of the Beatific Vision. Accordingly, it is divided into three parts: *Inferno, Purgatory,* and *Paradise*. His portrayal of medieval belief concerning creation is given in *Paradise*, in which his pilgrimage takes him up through the universe to the abode of God.

Dante constructs the physical universe of his poem on the Ptolemaic system, which is geocentric. The earth is at the center of the universe, and the sun, moon, planets and stars revolve around it. His universe is made up of nine concentric spheres, each composed of ethereal substance. Contained within this substance and carried along within these spheres are the heavenly bodies. They are, in ascending order from the earth: the moon, Mercury, Venus, the sun, Mars, Jupiter, Saturn, and the fixed stars or constellations. The ninth sphere, the Primum Mobile, is the outer boundary of the universe, the edge of space. It is empty and Dante describes it in terms of pure motion. It is the largest of the nine spheres and contains within it the eight heavens below it, to which it communicates its motion. Enclosing the nine spheres is a tenth one that is motionless and of immeasurable size. It is called the empyrean and is the realm of pure spirit. It is the abode of God, the angels, and the souls of the saints.

God moves the Primum Mobile, which in turn moves the spheres below it. Each of the nine spheres is governed by its own angel or hierarchy of angels. The collective influence of the angels on the spheres is what Dante calls "Nature."[35] God transcends the laws of Nature. "[F]or where God rules directly without agents, the laws of Nature in no way apply."[36] The individual nature of each human being is influenced by the heavenly bodies in a way and toward an end ordained by God. God created every thing and every person for a purpose. Dante expresses this truth through the voice of the soul of Charles Martel:

> The Good that moves and satisfies the realm
> that you now climb, endows these mighty orbs
> with all the power of His own providence;
>
> and in that One Mind perfect in Itself
> there is foreseen not only every type
> of nature but the proper goal for each,[37]

As he approached the end of his pilgrimage, Dante encountered the soul of Adam, the first man. Dante had four questions in his mind for Adam: 1) How long ago was he created? 2) How much time did he spend in the Garden of Eden? 3) What did he do to provoke God's wrath? 4) What language did he speak?[38]

Adam answered the first question by telling Dante that the number of years he spent in limbo (the place where Dante met the Roman poet Virgil, his guide through hell) was 4,302 solar years. (This is the number of years from the death of Adam to the death of Christ.) Adam then said he lived 930 years on earth (the biblical number). Adding both numbers gives 5232 years from Creation to the death of Christ.

Adam said that he remained in Eden from sunrise to noonday, a period of six hours. He said that tasting of the tree in itself was not his sin but the "transgression of God's bounds."

Adam said that he "formed" the language that he spoke, but he did not say whether he formed it out of anything. He also said that the language he spoke was long extinct before the multiplication of languages at the tower of Babel. (Here Dante reversed his beliefs for some reason. In an earlier work, *De vulgari eloquentia* (I, vi, 5–7), Dante held that language was a divine creation, unsusceptible to change, and that Adam spoke Hebrew, as did all his descendants until the incident at Babel, and that from that time on only the sons of Eber spoke the language of Adam.) Adam also said God was called *I* (pronounced JAH) first but was later called *El* because men's habits change.

Dante gives his views on creation though the voice of the soul of his beloved Beatrice, who escorted him through most of the latter part of his journey. Beatrice told him that God created "not to increase His good, which cannot be, but rather that His own reflected glory in its resplendence might proclaim *I am* in His eternity, beyond all time, beyond all comprehension, as pleased Him, new loves blossomed from the eternal love. Nor did He lie in idleness before, for neither 'after' nor 'before' preceded the going forth of God upon the waters."[39] She goes on to say that God created "pure form, pure matter, form and matter mixed."[40] Creatures of pure form are the angels. She also refers to the angels as "pure act."[41] They were set at "the summit of the world."[42] "[P]ure potential [prime matter] held the lowest place; and in between, potential-to-act was tied so tight that they can never be untied."[43]

Beatrice saw in the mind of God a question that Dante had about why things decay. She explained that things directly created by God do not decay but things created by means of secondary causes do decay. She said that angels and space are unchanging and entire because God created them directly. The matter of elements was created directly, but the things the elements compose were formed by created powers. Combinations of elements have the potential for life (a la Augustine). The "informing power within the constellations circling them," was directly created.[44] The "stars' rays and their sacred motions" draw out the souls of animals and plants that are virtually in the "potentiated complex" of elements.[45] Animal and plant souls are mortal because they are generated by secondary causes. Human souls, however, are immortal because God directly created them with an everlasting natural desire for Him.

Beatrice answered questions she saw in the mind of God that Dante had about the angels and their creation. She said that the number of angels is immense beyond human comprehension. Their number and diversity is so great that "no word or concept can reach that far."[46] And each angel manifests some splendor of God. "Eternal Goodness … divides Itself into these countless mirrors that reflect Itself, remaining One, as It was always."[47] Each angel possesses a different capacity to love based on its vision of God. "And since the visual act always precedes the act of loving, bliss of love in each burns differently: some glow while others blaze."[48]

Beatrice takes issue with St. Jerome's view that the angels were created centuries before the rest of creation. She said that the angels were created at the same time as other creatures. She goes to Scripture for proof, saying to Dante: "[T]his truth is declared in many texts by writers of the Holy Spirit's word, and you will find it if you look with care."[49] She further appeals to reason pointing out that the angels are the movers of the heavens and to have them idle for so long would not make any sense. Indeed, the angels were created at the same time as the universe and started working almost immediately, just after the rebellion of Lucifer and his followers, which took place less than a minute after their creation.

Beatrice is severely critical of those who attempt to explain away miracles as natural phenomena. She uses as an example the darkness that fell over the land when Christ was crucified (Mt 27:45; Lk 23:44). She condemns preachers who try to explain it as an eclipse of the sun by the moon rather than as a supernatural phenomenon. (What would she have to say about theistic naturalists?)

Back to the Future

Medieval thinking on creation was not perfected before it was overshadowed by Enlightenment ideology and finally came to be ignored by intellectual leaders in the Church, many of them either intimidated or awed by the successes of the new sciences. Thus Christendom gradually lost the faith in the literal truth of Genesis 1–11 that was so strongly held by the Fathers and Doctors of the Church and even became embarrassed by their teachings.[c] But although the new sciences were able to overshadow traditional Catholic theology on creation, they were unable to undermine it because it sits on a rock solid foundation, namely, God's word in Sacred Scripture. Nothing that modern science has discovered or can discover is able to shake that foundation. Scientists and scholars must place their faith in Sacred Scripture and accept its guidance if they are to lead their disciplines in the direction of truth.

Catholic scientists and scholars must get it out of their minds that the Church will lose her credibility if she rejects uniformitarian geology, evolutionary biology and anthropology, and big bang cosmology. The notions that the practitioners of these pseudosciences advance have not contributed a mite to our understanding of the nature of things or to our technological progress. The great advances in science and technology that we enjoy were brought about by careful observations of nature here and now and by technical innovations, not by theories about the past.

---

c. The history of the intimidation of religion by false or partially-digested science, which began with certain assertions by Galileo, could be the subject of a full-length treatise.

Holy Mother Church will increase her credibility many times over if her teachers and preachers once more clearly and confidently profess her traditional theology of creation. And that will help restore moral soundness to Western civilization because much of the immorality prevalent today can be traced to a false conception of the nature of man, which is rooted in false conceptions about origins. We must go "back to the future" to recover that religious, social, and scientific sanity that was enjoyed by medieval Christendom during the Age of Faith.

[1] *Hamlet*, Act 1, Scene 5.

[2] Weisheipl, James, *Friar Thomas d'Aquino: His Life, Thought, and Works* (New York: Doubleday, 1974). With corrigenda and addenda (Washington, D.C., The Catholic University of America Press, 1983), p. 76, as quoted by Baldner, Steven E. and Carroll, William E. in *Aquinas on Creation: Writings on the "Sentences" of Peter Lombard 2.1.1* (Toronto: Pontifical Institute of Mediaeval Studies, 1997), pp. 32–33.

[3] Baldner, Steven E. and Carroll, William E., op. cit.

[4] Ibid., pp. 74–75.

[5] Ibid.

[6] Ibid.

[7] Ibid., p. 79.

[8] Ibid., p. 83.

[9] Ibid., p. 85.

[10] Ibid.

[11] Ibid., pp. 95–96.

[12] Ibid., pp. 96–97.

[13] Ibid., p. 97.

[14] Ibid., p. 98.

[15] Ibid., p. 102.

[16] Ibid., p. 128.

[17] Ibid., p. 129.

[18] Ibid., p. 103.

[19] Ibid., p. 104.

[20] Ibid. Italics added.

[21] Ibid.

[22] Ibid., p. 108.

[23] Ibid., p. 109.

[24] BV, Part II, Chapter 2.1.

[25] BV, Part II, Chapter 2.2.

[26] BV, Part II, Chapter 2.5.

[27] Ecclus (Sir) 18:1 (DR)

[28] BV, Part II, Chapter 2.5.

[29] BV, Part II, Chapter 2.4.

[30] BV, Part II, Chapter 2.1.

[31] See Gilson, Etienne, *The Philosophy of St. Bonaventure*, Illtyd Trethowan and Frank J. Sheed, trans. (Paterson, NJ: St. Anthony Guild Press, 1965), pp. 267ff.; Healy, Emma T. *St. Bonaventure's De Reductione Artium ad Theolgiam* (Disserta-

tion) (St. Bonaventure, NY: St. Bonaventure College, 1939), pp. 70–73; Delio, Ilia, *Simply Bonaventure: An Introduction to His Life, Thought, and Writings* (Hyde Park, NY: New City Press, 2001), pp. 57–58; and the *Catholic Encyclopedia* (1914, "Bonaventure, Saint").

[32] See Baldner, Steven E. and Carroll, op. cit., pp. 43–45, 53–54.

[33] Ibid., pp. 48–49.

[34] BV, Part II, Chapter 4.1.

[35] See, for example, *Paradise*, Canto VIII, 114, 127.

[36] *Paradise*, Canto XXX, 121–123.

[37] *Paradise*, Canto VIII, 97–109.

[38] See *Paradise*, Canto XXVI, 109–142.

[39] *Paradise*, Canto XXIX, 13–21.

[40] *Paradise*, Canto XXIX, 22.

[41] Ibid., 33.

[42] Ibid., 32.

[43] Ibid., 34–36.

[44] *Paradise*, Canto VII, 137–138.

[45] Ibid., 140–141.

[46] Ibid., 132.

[47] Ibid., 143–144.

[48] Ibid., 139–141.

[49] Ibid., 40–42.

▼

The Attempt to Span the Heavens

THE DEFECTIVE RUNGS ON THE "LADDER TO THE STARS"

Astronomers claim to be able to directly measure distances to celestial objects as far as 300 light-years away. The method they use is called *trigonometric parallax*. They measure the angular displacement of a nearby star over a period of six months against the background of the far stars, which do not manifest such a displacement. (This phenomenon of star displacement is called *stellar parallax*.) They then calculate the distance to the star by applying the technique of triangulation, using the angle of displacement with the line between the earth and the sun as a baseline. The distance between the earth and the sun is determined by geometric methods applied to data from optical and radar astronomy. Thousands of stars supposedly fall within the range of this technique.

The trigonometric parallax method is based on two assumptions, which are these: that the earth moves annually around the sun and that the stars remain at rest with respect to the sun. The latter is equivalent to saying that no parallax would be observed from the sun. Both those assumptions are arbitrary. Because of the relativity of motion, other kinematical scenarios are possible in which a star at a given distance would produce a different angle of displacement than that given by the model above. For example, the totally heliocentric model of the astronomers could be modified to a partially heliocentric model by having the stars move annually around the midpoint between the earth and the sun. In that case the same amount of parallax would be observed on both the earth and the sun, and the astronomers' calculations would yield a larger distance than the totally heliocentric model. A Scripture-friendly and physically appealing model would be a geostationary one in which the stars rotate annually around their center of mass.[a] If the center of mass is located outside the orbit of the sun, the astronomers' calculations would yield a smaller distance than the totally heliocentric model. Thus the earthbound method of trigonometric parallax is inconclusive. The proper application of trigonometric parallax would require observations from both the earth and the sun (or some other distant body in the solar system).[b]

Astronomers use additional methods by which they profess to measure even farther distances.[c] Popular science writers refer to them as the rungs on a ladder by which the astronomers ascend into the heavens because each subsequent method supposedly measures farther up into the sky. The methods of *secular parallax* and *statistical parallax* use an arbitrarily chosen *local standard of rest*, which supposedly gives a larger baseline than the alleged orbit of the earth, to measure the distance to selected groups of stars. Distances up to 1600 light-years are inferred. These methods are inconclusive for the basically same reason as trigono-

---

a. Robert Sungenis and Robert Bennett in *Galileo was Wrong*, Vol. 1: The Scientific Evidence (CD book, Catholic International Publishing, 2006) clearly refute the claim that stellar parallax demonstrates that the earth absolutely moves. Geraldus Bouw in *Geocentricity: The Biblical Cosmology* (Cleveland, OH: Association for Biblical Astronomy, 1992) advances a geostationary model that, like the totally heliocentric model, displays stellar parallax on the earth but not on the sun. In his model he has the stars rotate annually around the center of the sun.

b. Parallax measurements by Hipparcos (High Precision Parallax Collecting Satellite) were essentially earthbound measurements because Hipparcos orbited the earth.

c. For a clear exposition at the undergraduate level of methods alleged to measure astronomical distances see Stephen Webb, *Measuring the Universe: The Cosmological Distance Ladder* (Chichester, UK: Springer-Praxis, 1999). Although somewhat mathematical, the essential ideas can be abstracted without wading through the mathematics. For a more popular account see Kitty Ferguson, *Measuring the Universe: Our Historic Quest to Chart the Horizons of Space and Time* (New York: Walker and Co., 1999). This book has a useful glossary. For a Christian perspective see Donald B. DeYoung, *Astronomy and the Bible* (Grand Rapids, MI: Baker Books, 2000).

metric parallax. They are further invalidated by the fact that they employ trigono-metric parallax to determine the local standard of rest.

Another method is the *moving cluster* method, by which astronomers propose to deduce the distance to certain groups of stars that appear to be moving away from the earth as a cluster because the angular width of the cluster is observed to get smaller over time. The radial speed of the cluster relative to earth is determined from the Doppler shift of its spectra. The distance to the cluster is calculated from the angular width of the cluster, the rate of change of the angular width, and the radial speed of the cluster. Distances up to 550 light-years have been reckoned by this method. This method is not conclusive. It assumes that the change in the angular width of the cluster is caused exclusively by the radial motion of the cluster, that is, only if there is no inherent expansion or contraction of the cluster, which cannot be determined from earthbound observations.[d]

Spectrographic parallax and *main sequence fitting* use the spectral characteristics of stars and their relative brightness to infer distances. These methods have their own inherent assumptions. Measurements made with the Hipparcos satellite gave conflicting luminosity calibrations, shedding doubt on the validity of these methods. Their ultimate calibration depends on the moving cluster method.

The *Cepheid variable method* uses brightness to infer the distance to certain kinds of stars, called *Cepheid variables*, whose brightness varies periodically. The brightness of the Cepheid being spanned is compared to that of a standard Cepheid with the same period and from that the distance is inferred. The distances of the standard Cepheids are the calibration distances and are determined by statistical parallax. Distances as far as 60-million light-years have been inferred by this method.

The *Hubble's Law method* is the supposedly longest tape measure in the astronomer's toolbox. The distance to a galaxy is inferred via Hubble' Law from the amount of red shift in the light from the galaxy. In deducing his law, Hubble calculated distances using the Cepheid variables method, which ultimately depends on trigonometric parallax.

Thus the "ladder to the stars" has defective rungs. Earthbound trigonometric parallax and the moving cluster method are inconclusive; they cannot reliably provide distances to stars. And since all the other methods ultimately depend on them for their calibration, those techniques are also inconclusive.

---

d. For a clear and concise explanation of the moving cluster method see Martin Harwit, *Astrophysical Concepts* (New York: John Wiley and Sons, 1973), pp. 54–55.

The prophet Jeremiah implied the futility of attempting to span the heavens. He said, *"Thus says the Lord: 'If the heavens above can be measured, and the foundations of the earth below can be explored, then I will cut off all the descendants of Israel for all that they have done, says the Lord'"* (Jer 31:37).

▼

Philosophical Considerations Pertaining to Natural Species

FUNDAMENTAL NOTIONS

Among the topics considered by scholastic philosophy are the multiplicity and limitation of created beings, their mutability, and their relationship to God. The Schoolmen did this for spiritual creatures (angels), material creatures (living and nonliving) and composite creatures (man, who is both spiritual and material).

All material substances are an inseparable union of prime matter and substantial form. *Prime matter* is the first principle of corporeal existence. It is the principle of permanence because it is that which perseveres when a material substance changes from one thing to another. *Substantial form* informs prime matter to complete a substance and give it its nature. It is the principle of change because it is that which is changed when a material substance changes from one thing to another.

Among material substances there are not only many species but also many individuals of the same species. Such are not individuated by nature (as are spiritual creatures) but by matter itself, prime matter determined by the accident of quantity. Matter so individuated is called *signate matter* or *matter marked by quantity*.

In his exposition of the principles above that account for substantial change, Aristotle employed the notions of *act* and *potency*. *Act* is that which is complete, perfect or fully real. *Potency* is a capacity of something or in a something to be, to act, or to receive. Prime matter is pure potency to material substantial existence because it has the potential to be any material thing. Substantial form actualizes the potency in prime matter. Act and potency are not two beings but two intrinsic principles of being that determine each other (like, for example, husband and wife) but which, while really distinct, do not each have a distinct existence.

Although the notions of potency and act had their origin in the philosophy of nature, they have important applications elsewhere, especially in metaphysics. Metaphysical reasoning leads to the conclusion that God is pure act because He is everything He can be. He has no potency to anything.

All finite creatures are in act in that they exist, but they are not pure act because they exist in potency to other things. That is, all finite things are subject to change. St. Thomas Aquinas points out that things are closer to God the more they are in act than in potency:

> Therefore these [spirits] are distinguished one from another by their degree of potentiality and act, so that the superior spirit closer to the First Being has more act and less potentiality, and so of the others.[1]

Act and potency are the cardinal principles of Thomistic metaphysics. St. Thomas made a more radical and precise analysis of them under the notions of *essence* and *existence*. *Essence* is that by which a thing is what it is and which differentiates a thing from other things. Essence as a source of a thing's specific activities is called *nature*. *Existence* is the ultimate act of a being that causes it *to be*. The problem of essence and existence arises out of the multiplication and limitations of created beings, especially spiritual beings. The individuation of material substances was described above, but angelic substances do not have matter that can be limited to individuate them. So they have to be limited and multiplied some other way. St. Thomas discovered that the limitation and multiplicity of spiritual substances are accounted for by the composition of essence and existence.

St. Thomas made a real distinction between essence and existence, as opposed to a strictly mental distinction. He treated them as two distinct principles of being. But being distinct does not mean they have independent existences. They are not preexistent things that come together to form a third. Like act and potency, they only exist together. Furthermore, the being whose constituent principles are essence and existence is a concrete substance, not merely a possibility; it is real.

Essence and existence complement each other as potency and act respectively. If essence is identified as potency, existence is act. The potency of essence is different from that of prime matter because essence is something determinate whereas prime matter is not. However, in spiritual substances essence is comparable to prime matter because it too is in potency, although not in the same way. The spiritual essence is in potency to existence, but as essence it is all act. St. Thomas describes it as "actual being of a kind, existing in potency."[2]

The essence/potency and existence/act identifications are used with qualifications. Essence does not receive existence in the way that prime matter becomes signate (or sensible) matter through the accident quantity. Existence is not an accident like quantity. Rather, existence is the ultimate perfection. It is "the actuality of all acts, and for this reason it is the perfection of all perfections."[3] Essence limits and determines the existence. Essence limits the infinite possibilities of existence to *this* thing rather than *that* thing. *Be-ing* is an existence determined by an essence.

Material substances, then, have a twofold composition. They are composed of matter and form in their essence, and of essence and existence in their concrete reality. Substantial form actualizes prime matter to give the substance an essence, and the accident quantity individualizes it. The essence of the material substance is further composed with its ultimate actuality, existence.

Angelic substances are said to be *simple* in essence because they are not composed of matter and form. The angelic essence, as essence, is not a composite of act and potency but is pure act or form. It is, however, composed of essence and existence; and the essence is in potency with respect to existence. Since matter does not enter into its composition, the principle of individuation lies in the essence. Since the essence is pure act without any admixture of potency, it is necessarily unique, incapable of multiplication. This is because potency is the principle of limitation, and for that reason it is the principle of multiplication. Therefore, each angel is unique. Each angel has its own specific nature. Each angel is its own species.

St. Thomas distinguishes two kinds of natures. The first is that whose act of existence does not belong to its intelligibility. For example, the nature of a phoenix, a man or even an angel can be known without knowing whether or not it exists. This kind of nature must receive its existence from outside of itself. The other nature is that whose very act of existence is related to its intelligibility. The act of existence itself is its nature. This is the nature of God. He gives existence to the first kind of nature. So essence differs from existence in all things except God alone. His essence is to exist.[4]

THE KNOWABILITY OF ESSENCES

Another question considered by scholastic philosophers is this: Can we know the essences of natural corporeal substances? We know that we can understand the essences of human artifacts, like the automobile and the computer, because man has designed them and built them; and we can know the essences of mathematical entities, like triangles and differential equations, because these are, to some extent, constructions of our own minds. But, considering that they are not the inventions of man, can we understand the essences of natural substances, especially living substances? St. Thomas Aquinas says we can:

> As is clear from what has been said (Q. 17, A. 3), our intellect, which takes cognizance of the essence of a thing as its proper object, gains knowledge from sense, of which the proper objects are external accidents. Hence from external appearances we come to the knowledge of the essence of things.[5]

Although we acquire knowledge of the outside world through our senses, the senses are not competent in themselves to perceive the essence of a thing. It is the human intellect that has the power to abstract an essence from the material supplied by the senses. To have knowledge of the essence of a thing does not necessarily mean one has a complete knowledge of the causes and properties of a thing; it is sufficient to perceive certain likenesses and differences when compared to other things. Thus, for example, we are able to distinguish "dogness" from "catness" without a zoology textbook.

ESSENCES AND EVOLUTION

Scholastic doctrine does not imply that something cannot lose its essence and acquire another. The scholastic doctrine of essences is based on the intelligibility of things. But the intelligibility of things does not depend on the fixity of their essences. If it did, then we could never know anything about the material world because it is in a continuous state of flux. Essences are immutable only when considered in an abstract sense, separated from the objects they define. The essence of a dog could never become the essence of a cat or vice versa. But in that case one is not talking about real material things but about Platonic forms or divine ideas.

St. Thomas argued that only God is immutable. Finite material and spiritual beings are mutable "inasmuch as they are producible from nothing by Him, and are by Him reducible from existence to non-existence."[6] Finite things are also mutable in respect to essences and accidents and through powers within them and external to them. Material substances are mutable with respect to their forms and accidents. Spiritual beings have no mutability with respect to their form or essence but they do have mutability with respect to the exercise of their powers. For example, an angel has mutability with respect to place because an angel is considered to be at the place where it exercises its powers.

Although the Schoolmen did not define substances, even spiritual ones, as permanent beings, they did see permanency as a valuable guide for determining substances and essences.[7]

So the scholastic doctrine of essences cannot be used to make a case against the evolution of natural species because it applies for both fixed and mutable species. Furthermore, philosophical arguments in general cannot be used to make a case against the evolution of species. Philosophy allows for God to have created many different kinds of worlds in many different ways. Sacred Scripture tells us how He actually did create the world, and observation of the world tells us what it is really like. Thus the case for the fixity of natural species can only come from divine revelation and natural science.

¹ *On Being and Essence*, Chapter 4. See Clark, Mary T, ed., *An Aquinas Reader* (New York: Fordham University Press, 1972), p. 43. Also see Gardeil, H. D., *Introduction to the Philosophy of St. Thomas Aquinas, IV. Metaphysics* (St. Louis, MO: B. Herder Book Co., 1967), p. 283.

² *De substantiis separatis*, cap. 5, no. 35. See Gardeil, op. cit., p. 209.

³ St. Thomas Aquinas, *De Potentia*, q.7, a.2, ad 9. See Gardeil, op. cit., p. 208.

⁴ See citation from *Commentary on the Sentences II*, d.3, q.1, a.1 *in* Clark, op. cit., p. 47 and citations from *On Being and Essence*, Chapter 5 and ST, Part I, Q. 3, A. 4 in Gardeil, op. cit., pp. 205–206.

⁵ ST, Part I, Q. 18, A. 2.

⁶ ST, Part I, Q. 9, A. 2.

⁷ See Cotter, A. C., *Natural Species: An Essay in Definition and Classification* (Weston, MA: The Weston College Press, 1947), pp. 130–131.

Glossary

accident: Something that exists in a **subject**, for example, a color, a shape, a texture. Contrast with **substance**.

act: That which already exists is said to be in *act*. God is pure act because He is everything He can be. He has no **potency** to anything. All finite creatures are in act in that they exist, but they are not pure act because they exist in potency to other things. That is, all finite things are subject to change.

age of the world: Any estimate of the universe's (or earth's) age involves a projection back in time of current measurable conditions. This projection depends on *assumptions* about the constancy of certain factors over time, and initial and boundary conditions. The credibility of any age estimate depends on the quality of the measurements and the credibility of the assumptions. See **biblical chronology, radiocarbon dating**, and **radiometric dating**.

allele: Each **gene** in a **natural species** can come in more than one version. Each version is known as an *allele*. Alleles are the basis for variety in a natural species. The main cause of variations in offspring produced by sexual reproduction is the mixing of the father's and the mother's alleles. This can lead to offspring with a wide variety of characteristics.

alteration: Change in the qualities of a thing.

anthropic principle: A statement of the observation that the universe is especially suited for the well-being of mankind. Offers a powerful argument that the universe was designed.

big bang: The cosmological theory that the universe originated with an explosion/expansion 10–20 billion years ago. There are two versions of *big bang* cosmology. In the most popular version the universe is finite, unbounded, three-dimensional, and expanding. The expansion is analogous to that of the unbounded two-dimensional surface of an inflating balloon. In the other version, the universe is infinite in all dimensions and in material content. An infinite universe expands into an infinite vista. The expansion manifests itself as a decreasing in the density and temperature of matter and **energy**.

catastrophism: The view that most of the geological features on the face of the earth were produced by gigantic catastrophes of relatively short duration, the most gigantic being the Great Flood of Genesis. Contrast with **uniformitarianism**.

cause: A **principle** from which something originates with dependence.

cause, efficient: That which unites the **material and formal causes** to produce a thing. Also called the *agent*. The sculptor is the agent in the making of a statue.

cause, final: Also called the *end* or *purpose*. A good for the sake of which something is made. First, there is the end to be achieved by the thing itself. Second, there is the end of the agent for producing the thing. The purpose of a statue may be to honor God, but the purpose of the sculptor may be to earn money.

cause, formal: That which informs matter or a subject and makes a thing what it is. **Substantial forms** and **accidental forms** are *formal causes*. For example, the shape of a statue is its formal cause; it makes it the statue that it is.

cause, instrumental: An instrument or tool used by the agent as a subordinate cause. For example, the hammer and chisel are instrumental causes employed by a sculptor in producing a statue. The instrument must have the *proper effect* to be a subordinate cause. For example, one cannot cut wood with a hammer because cutting wood is not the proper effect of a hammer. No creature can cooperate with God as an *instrumental cause* in creation because no finite thing can produce something from nothing as its proper effect.

cause, material: That from which or in which something is produced. For example, marble is the *material cause* of a statue.

chromosome: See **information, genetic.** The number of chromosomes in the cell is one criterion that can be used to help identify a **natural species.**

chronology, biblical: The exact age of the world cannot be determined from Scripture, but Scripture assures that the world was created only thousands of years ago and not billions. The Bible gives the exact numbers of years from Creation to the death of Abraham, but these numbers vary somewhat in variant texts. From Abraham on, biblical texts can be meshed with secular sources to develop chronologies.

collapse, gravitational: The collapse of a celestial body caused by its own weight. The process releases a great amount of energy and could be a source of the sun's radiant energy. If it were the only source, the sun could burn for only about twenty million years, which is not long enough for evolution to take place according to evolutionary reckoning. Also see **thermonuclear fusion.**

complementarity: The principle that a submicroscopic entity, such as an electron or a photon, can be described either as a particle or as a wave. These two pictures are mutually exclusive, so that a given experiment will demonstrate only one of them but not both. Niels Bohr suggested that living organisms and their physical structures are complementary. A given biological experiment will either give information on life processes at the expense of information on physical structure or vice-versa. To study the anatomy of an organism, one must kill it. To study its physiology, one must keep it alive and be denied access to information about its structure. We cannot completely observe its structure and operations simultaneously.

complexity: See **order and complexity.**

complexity, irreducible: Term coined by Michael J. Behe in *Darwin's Black Box.* An *irreducibly complex* system is "a single system composed of several well-matched, interacting parts that contribute to the basic function, wherein the removal of any one of the parts causes the system to effectively cease functioning." Many basic biological systems are irreducibly complex, which implies that they were designed and were created as units.

contingent: That which can be or not be or be other than it is. Contrast with **necessary.**

cosmological principle: The *cosmological principle* is an assumption that requires everything to look pretty much the same from wherever you stand in the universe. There is no special or preferred place in the universe; it is perfectly "democratic." This rules out, for example, a rotating universe because then there would be a very privileged place, namely, the center of rotation. Physical observations in a rotating universe would not look the same everywhere; they would depend on how far from the center of rotation the observer is located.

creatio prima: Creation in the strict sense. St. Thomas defined it as follows: "Creation is the production of a thing in its entire substance, nothing being presupposed either uncreated or created." No creature can create something out of nothing because that is an act of infinite power, which is possessed by God alone. God's creation of matter and His creation of life in matter were acts of *creatio prima.*

creatio secunda: The act of giving form to matter. This is what God did when He formed the earth. Genesis 1:2 says: *"The earth was formless and empty."* This stage of creation is recalled in Wisdom 11:17, *"For thy all-powerful hand created the world out of formless matter...."*

creation, progressive: The doctrine that God created the world in a number of successive acts of creation separated by millions of years. It has no support in Sacred Scripture or scientific fact. See **day-age theory.**

creation, special: (1) The truth, clearly taught in Genesis, that the heavenly bodies and the progenitors of all living creatures were created in their finished and enduring natures during Creation Week. (2) The creation of the human soul at conception.

criticism, biblical: The discipline that investigates of books of the Bible with regard to their literary characteristics.

Darwinism: After Charles Darwin, who proposed the notion that new "species" of living organisms continually arise while others become extinct by means of the processes of *natural variation of properties* and *natural selection*. A variation in individuals of a "species" that is beneficial in the *struggle for existence* will help those individuals survive, and those individuals will pass the variation on to their progeny. Those that do not have it become extinct. Thus nature "selects" the most apt organisms. This process acting over eons of time, beginning with one or several forms produced by the Creator, accumulated variations producing the diversity of life we witness today. Modern evolutionists have supplanted Darwinism with *neo-Darwinism*, which looks to **mutations** as the cause of heritable changes in organisms rather than natural variations. Also see **macroevolution**. Contrast with **special creation** and **microevolution**.

dating, radiocarbon: A method that is used to date something that was once a living organism or was once part of a living organism. While the organism was still living it ingested the radioisotope carbon-14 along with the stable isotope carbon-12. While it was living the ratio of the number of carbon-14 atoms to the number of carbon-12 atoms that it contained remained constant. After the organism died, it ingested no new carbon. As time went on the carbon-14 decayed into nitrogen-14, but the carbon-12 remained stable. So the ratio of the number of carbon-14 to carbon-12 atoms decreased. This ratio is measured and is used to calculate how far in the past the organism died. Some scientists and historians do not trust the method for dating items beyond 1000 B.C.

dating, radiometric: A technique for determining the age of igneous and metamorphic rocks. The ratio of the number of atoms of a daughter isotope to the number of atoms of its radioactive parent is measured. From that ratio the age of the rock can be determined *if* 1) there were no daughter atoms when the rock was formed or the original daughter/parent ratio is somehow known, 2) no daughter or parent atoms entered or left the rock since it was formed, and 3) the decay rate of the parent remained constant over the history of the rock. These are three big *ifs* that are not easily justified. Radiometric measurements are used to date the earth at billions of years old. But they are generally unreliable. Radiometric dating methods depend on *belief* in the assumptions employed and on data that is often conflicting. That *belief* is often a great leap of faith motivated by philosophical or theological presuppositions. The methods often give inconsistent results that are never published.

dating, sequence: Also called *seriation*. A technique for giving chronological order to a set of archaeological finds by comparing the characteristics of potsherds.

dating, tree-ring: See **dendrochronology**.

day-age theory: Holds that the Hebrew word *yom* in Genesis 1 represents an indefinite period millions of years long. Associated with **theistic evolution** and **progressive creation**.

dendrochronology: A technique for constructing archaeological chronologies from the study of annual tree-ring sequences.

DNA: See **information, genetic**.

DNA, mitochondrial: The mitochondrion is a site in a living human cell at which metabolic activities take place that produce energy for the body. It carries its own DNA, labeled mtDNA, which is in addition to the DNA in the nucleus of the cell. *Mitochondrial DNA* has been called a biological history book of women because it is passed on from generation to generation only by mothers, unlike nuclear DNA, which is passed on by both parents.

emanationism: The doctrine that interprets the origin of the world as a hierarchy of effusions proceeding from the Godhead through intermediate stages to matter.

energy: A measure of the ability to do *work*, that is, the ability to change the physical state of a corporeal body by applying a force to it through a distance. A body contains *energy* with respect to another body by virtue of its position with respect to it (*potential energy*) and/or by virtue of its speed with respect to it (*kinetic energy*). Electromagnetic radiation possesses energy.

energy conservation: The law of *conservation of energy* states that the total energy of an isolated physical system remains constant, no matter what physical changes the system undergoes. **Mass** is reckoned in the accounting because energy may be converted to mass and vice versa. The *first law of thermodynamics* is a restatement of the law of conservation of energy for systems that contain thermal energy.

energy and mass equivalence: **Special relativity** and the law of conservation of momentum together predict that the inertial **mass** of a body increases with its speed. As a consequence of this, the kinetic **energy** of a material body manifests itself as an increase in its inertial mass. This led Einstein to propose that even at rest a material body possesses energy by virtue of its inertial mass. This is expressed in the famous formula $E = mc^2$. However, relativistic dynamics alone cannot verify universal identity of mass and energy (that is, whether they are synonyms for the same underlying physical substratum), nor can it say whether inertial mass can be completely transformed into energy. Those questions were answered in the affirmative only by further investigations in theoretical and experimental physics. Compare this concept with **prime matter.**

essence: What a thing is; the internal **principle** whereby a thing is *what* it is. Also called quiddity, from the Latin word *quid* meaning "what." Both **substances** and **accidents** have essences.

evolution, materialistic: A theory of the origin of the universe that states 1) only matter and energy exist, 2) from a primordial assemblage of matter and energy the universe as we know it today was formed by natural processes alone. Condemned by the Church because of its exclusion of God. Contrast with **theistic evolution.**

evolution, theistic: Evolution with God injected into the process. There are two kinds of *theistic evolution.* The first is *cosmic evolution,* which is the formation of the stars, the galaxies, the planets, and so on from a primordial assemblage of matter and energy by natural processes. God is fit in as Creator of the matter and energy and Programmer/Director of the natural processes. The second is *organic evolution,* which is the evolution of all living things, either from nonliving matter or from one or a few originally created living organisms. Some theistic evolutionists hold one kind or the other; some hold both kinds. Neither kind has the support of divine revelation or a strong foundation in observed facts. Also see **Darwinism** and **macroevolution.** Contrast with **special creation, materialistic evolution,** and **microevolution.**

evolutionism: The ideology that interprets reality as a continuous advance from the simple, disordered or worse to the complex, ordered or better.

existence, accidental: Existence in a qualified sense. A statue, as *shaped* marble, is said to have *accidental existence*. The marble itself is said to have **substantial existence**.

existence, substantial: Existence in an unqualified sense. For example, a man *is* in the unqualified sense.

form, accidental: That which *informs* a **subject** to give something **accidental existence**. For example, a statue, as a statue, is said to have an accidental existence because it is composed of preexistent material and an accidental form that inheres in the material.

form, substantial: That which *informs* **prime matter** to complete a **substance** and gives it its **nature**. It actualizes the potency in prime matter. For material substances it exists separately only in the mind, not in reality. The only exception is the human soul, which is the living form of a human being. It can exist separately from the matter (the body) it informs. Angels, which are spiritual substances, are pure substantial forms.

fossil: The "remains of an organism or direct evidence of its presence, preserved in rock, ice, amber, tar, peat or volcanic ash. Animal hard parts (hard skeletons) commonly undergo mineralization, a process which also turns sediment into hard rock" (*The Penguin Dictionary of Biology*). Of special interest are those fossils found in sedimentary rocks. These are fossils formed by plants and animals being buried in sediment that hardens to become rock. This rock is present throughout the earth stacked in layers, each called a **stratum**. There are a great number of fossils in these strata, comprising some one hundred thousand "fossil species."

Friedmann-Lemaitre expansion: Expanding space-time paradigm for the universe. Named after Alexander Friedmann and Georges Lemaitre, who discovered expanding space-time solutions to Einstein's gravitational field equations of **general relativity**. Einstein abandoned his static model of the universe after he read Friedmann's arguments for a nonstationary universe. Lemaitre is acknowledged as "father of the **big bang**."

fusion, thermonuclear: A process in which thermal motion imparts enough kinetic energy to atomic nuclei to enable them to fuse and release radiant energy. The dominant view of modern scientists is that the sun's radiant energy is produced by the thermonuclear fusion of hydrogen nuclei into helium nuclei. The process is favorable to evolutionists because it would allow the sun to be capable of burning for billions of years. Another possible source of solar energy is **gravitational collapse**.

gap theories: Theories that hold that somewhere between Genesis 1:1 and Genesis 1:3 an immense interval of time elapsed. Such interpretations are forced; they do not emerge naturally from the text.

gene: See **genetic information**.

generation: The origination of a living being from a living being of the same nature.

genome: See **genetic information**.

halos, polonium: These are "photographs" of radioactive decay events of the short-lived radioisotope polonium-218 that are found in the bedrocks of the earth. Since polonium-218 has a half-life of only three minutes and the halos could not have been produced in a liquid, the phenomenon implies nearly instantaneous crystallization of the rocks. Dr. Robert V. Gentry has been studying these rocks for years and finds in them strong evidence in favor of instantaneous creation.

hole, black: An entity consistent with general relativity. It is a region of space bounded by an *event horizon*. Once matter and light cross the event horizon and enter into a *black hole* they are trapped inside it and lose their identity. The event horizon expands as the black hole gobbles up light and matter. An unbounded universe, as envisioned by **big bang** theory, could not have originated in a black hole.

hole, white: The converse of a **black hole**; also consistent with general relativity. It is a region of space bounded by an *event horizon*. Substance within the event horizon expands outward giving birth to light and matter as it crosses the event horizon. The light and matter proceeding from the event horizon cannot reenter the *white hole*. The diameter of the event horizon is proportional to the amount of substance inside it. So the event horizon shrinks as light and matter travel away from the white hole. Eventually the white hole shrinks to nothing. There is then no white hole but only light and matter moving away from a central point. General relativity puts no limit on the rate at which shrinkage of the event horizon can take place. An *unbounded* universe, as envisioned by **big bang** theory, could not have originated in a white hole. D. Russell Humphreys invented a model of a *bounded* expanding universe that has expanded out of a white hole.

hominid: According to evolutionary taxonomy, a *hominid* is a creature of the Family Hominidae (Order Primates, Suborder Hominoidea). Hominids are erect bipedal primate mammals. Humans and their alleged proximate nonhuman ancestors are hominids.

Hubble's law: Astronomers have long observed that the color of the light coming from distant galaxies is shifted toward the red end of the spectrum, a phenomenon called **red shift**. The red shift was originally interpreted exclusively in terms of a Doppler shift caused by a galaxy receding from us. The American astronomer Edwin Hubble noticed that the dimmer galaxies had greater red shifts, which he assumed means that they are moving away with greater speed. Hubble associated the brightness of a galaxy with its red shift and proposed that the speed of recession of a galaxy is proportional to its distance from us. This is known as *Hubble's law*. The constant of proportionality is called the *Hubble constant*. A working estimate of its value is 15 kilometers per second per million light-years.

Humani generis: Encyclical letter issued by Pope Pius XII in 1950. Contains explicit teaching on the theory of evolution. Pius XII does not show himself a friend of evolution in the encyclical, but he does allow restricted discussion for and against the evolution of the human body, as long as it is not held as a fact. He excludes the possibility of polygenism and upholds the historicity of Genesis 1–11.

inflation: A notion in **big bang** theory that the size of the very early universe increased by an immense factor in an extremely short period of time. This was postulated to allow the universe to come into thermal equilibrium and to prevent it from collapsing or from expanding too fast. Theorists have no explanation for its cause. The term *inflation* is also applied to the supposition that the galaxies are receding from us at an increasing rate.

information: Refers to knowledge and its communication. Implies both a sender and a receiver that are intelligent or intelligently designed. *Information* can be coded for transmission into a sequence of ones and zeros (*bits*). Each one and zero can be thought of as the answer to a true-false question. Thus any message can be reduced to a set of answers to a carefully concocted set of true-false questions. The sender of the message is **nature** when a scientist observes her or questions her in an experiment. Any sequence of ones and zeros is not information; only those that have *meaning* qualify as information. The word *meaning* implies the involvement of intelligent agents.

information, genetic: The biological unit that determines the characteristics of an organism is the *gene*, which is a long strand of the chemical *deoxyribonucleic acid* (*DNA*). The DNA molecule is a chainlike molecule called a *polymer.* The links of the chain are chemical entities called *nucleotides*. There are four different nucleotides, labeled A, T, C and G. The *genetic information* is coded in the sequence of nucleotides. Since there are four different nucleotides, each nucleotide in the chain carries two bits of **information**. Genetic information is used by an organism to construct *proteins,* which, among other things, perform a major role in the transfer of information inside living organisms. Proteins play a dominant role in cell function and therefore in the whole organism. So the DNA, by directing the production of proteins, helps to define the **nature** of an organism.

Genes may work singly or in blocks to give an organism its specific and individual features. The genes are lined up in strings called *chromosomes,* the number of which depends on the species. The chromosomes are located in the nucleus of the cell, except for bacteria, which do not have nuclei. The entire DNA in all of the chromosomes of a cell is called the *genome.* The information in the genome of a mammal, if written out in type, would fill two thousand volumes. All the cells in an organism, except the reproductive cells, have the same genome.

The information content in a living organism is not confined to the genes. Much of the activity of the cell is carried out without gene involvement, so much so that the cell appears to have its own "built-in intelligence." Even the cells of the simplest organisms are immensely complex. The cell has been compared to a large city with factories, warehouses, hospitals, police, emergency systems, transportation systems, communication systems, refuse deposal systems and more. But it is much more than that. The capability of a cell to carry out its variety of functions, including the duplication of itself, is far beyond the pale of human ingenuity. And its unity of operation is so complete that it must have been created completely functional.

kind: God created the plants and animals each according to a specific **nature** called a *kind*. The kinds are permanent; they have remained constant throughout the centuries since Creation. See **natural species**.

Lamarckism: Theory proposed by Jean Baptiste de Lamarck that states that "species" evolved by the transmission of biological characteristics acquired in adapting to the environment. Rejected by evolutionists because there are no clear examples of the inheritance of acquired characteristics.

Mach's principle: The idea, proposed by Ernst Mach, that the inertial effects experienced by a material body are caused by its motion *relative* to the rest of the matter in the universe. See **relational mechanics**.

macroevolution: The alleged development of new living "species" from previous ones over immense periods of time by natural causes. Also called vertical variation. Also see **Darwinism** and **theistic evolution**. Contrast with **microevolution**.

mass: A measure of the "quantity" of matter in a corporeal body. It is either a measure of the resistance of a body to a change in its state of motion (*inertial mass*) or a measure of its interaction with other corporeal bodies (*gravitational mass*). The properties of *mass* that make it useful as a measure of the quantity of matter are that it is universal, that is, it applies to all material bodies, and that it is additive; that is, the mass of an aggregate of two bodies in identical physical states is the sum of the masses of the individual bodies. The theory of special relativity predicts that the inertial mass increases with the speed of a body with respect to the observer. This effect was predicted even before the advent of the theory of relativity from electromagnetic considerations. It is significant only at speeds approaching the speed of light and has been experimentally observed. Although mass is a very important fundamental concept in physics, it is not well understood. Max Jammer concludes his *Concepts of Mass* with the acknowledgment: "One has to admit that in spite of the concerted effort of physicists and philosophers, mathematicians and logicians, no final clarification of the concept of mass has been reached. The modern physicist may rightfully be proud of his spectacular achievements in science and technology. However, he should always be aware that the foundations of his imposing edifice, the basic notions of his discipline, such as the concept of mass, are entangled with serious uncertainties and perplexing difficulties that have as yet not been resolved." See **energy and mass equivalence**.

matter, dark: A hypothetical entity that has mass but isn't observed to radiate energy in any part of the electromagnetic spectrum. It is said to be detectable only by its gravitational effects. The nature of *dark matter* is unexplained. It was invented by evolutionists to support the notions of a closed universe and long-term stability of spiral galaxies.

matter, primal or primordial: This is the formless matter of Genesis 1. It has **substantial form** and **accidental forms**. It is called formless or undifferentiated because it has not yet received its final forms. It must not be confused with **prime matter**.

matter, prime: Matter out-of-which something exists. It is that which is in **potency** to substantial existence. It is pure **potency** because it has the potential to be any material thing. Contrast this with God, who is pure **act**. It is the **principle** of permanence because it perseveres through any change. It exists separately in the mind only. It does not exist separately in reality. It has no form in its rational character, yet it is never stripped away from form in reality. St. Thomas Aquinas in *On the Principles of Nature* points out that *prime matter* is "numerically one in all things." That is, it "exists without dispositions making it numerically different." It must not be confused with **primal or primordial matter**.

mechanics, relational: A system of mechanics that employs only relative quantities; that is, it employs only the distances between material bodies and the relative velocities and accelerations between material bodies. The word *relational* is used to distinguish this mechanics from Einstein's relativistic mechanics; but relational mechanics, unlike relativistic mechanics, is completely relativistic because all forces are referred to relative distances, velocities and accelerations of bodies and not to absolute space or inertial frames. It implements **Mach's principle** quantitatively and posits the *principle of dynamic equilibrium,* which states that the sum of all forces of any nature acting on any body is always zero in all frames of reference.

mechanism: The view that living organisms are nothing but highly complex machines governed by the laws of chemistry and physics. See **biological reductionism**. Contrast with **vitalism**.

Michelson-Morley experiment: An experiment performed in 1887 that attempted to measure the velocity of the earth as it moved through the *luminiferous ether* (the supposed medium in which light waves in matter-free space are propagated). The experiment yielded a null result; no such motion was detected.

microevolution: The variation of features within a **natural species** by causes included within the **nature** of the species. Also called horizontal variation. Contrast with **macroevolution**.

Miller-Urey experiment: An experiment performed in the early 1950s in which small amounts of *amino acids* (the "building blocks" of living organisms) were produced in an artificially contrived environment that allegedly simulated the environment of early earth. Evolutionists claimed that the experiment demonstrated the possibility of the spontaneous emergence of life on earth. That conclusion is false because the success of the experiment depended on the intervention of intelligent agents, namely, the scientists who did the experiment.

model, standard: Another name for the **big bang** theory. This should not be confused with the standard model of particle physics, which is a mathematical theory that identifies the basic particles of nature and describes their interactions.

mutability of matter: Modern elementary particle physics has demonstrated the extreme mutability of matter. Elementary particles can be changed into other particles and into radiant energy, the possibilities being restricted by the law of conservation of energy and other conservation laws. So it is not hard to see that God can manipulate and transform matter while working within the framework of the laws He created.

mutation: A cause of variations in **natural species** is the mutability of genes and chromosomes. Genes are subject to mutations. A *mutation* is any heritable genetic change. First, there are *point mutations* that can occur in a gene. These effect a change in a single unit of information in the gene, either changing it to another unit or destroying it completely. They can be caused by replication errors, natural radiations such as x-rays and ultraviolet light, and by manmade chemicals. Replication errors are extremely rare, from one in a billion to one in a hundred billion units of information. Point mutations are nearly always either detrimental to the organism or neutral. Although they may be useful in some circumstances, even then they degrade the organism in some way. They cannot accumulate to transform one natural species into another.

In addition to point mutations, there are mutations that can affect more than one gene. One such genetic change is known as *recombination*. In this change two chromosomes or parts of two chromosomes exchange places. This is a complex process that is controlled by special enzymes. Lee Spetner in *Not by Chance!* lists five other kinds of mutations: duplication of a segment of a genome, inversion of a segment, deletion of a segment, insertion of a new segment, and transposition of a segment. These processes are not haphazard events. They are too precise and controlled to happen by chance. Geneticists do not know why they occur but believe they play important roles. They are not genetic mistakes but seem to be programmed acts performed on behalf of the cell or organism.

nature: (1) The **essence** considered as the intrinsic **principle** of activity. For example, an animal behaves according to its *nature*. The nature of a thing is known through its **accidents**, which include its activity (behavior). (2) The world of material creatures.

naturalism: The credo that holds that the world alone can tell us everything there is to know about it and therefore there is no need for divine revelation about the world.

necessary: That which must be and be as it is. A thing is *absolutely necessary* if the denial of it produces a contradiction. A thing may also be necessary *by supposition*; if it is supposed some thing is, then some other thing is necessary. Contrast with **contingent**.

nominalism: The view that there are no universal **essences** or **natures**. Evolutionary biology is thoroughly nominalistic. That is why it is unable to come up with an adequate definition of *species*. The *Penguin Dictionary of Biology* acknowledges this: "Inability to find a unified species concept is no disgrace.... It is probably no accident that the species concept does not figure prominently in biological theory: species may best be regarded not as NATURAL KINDS (such as elements in chemistry) but as individuals, each historically unique and irreplaceable once extinct. If species are individuals then species names are proper names, so that the properties of species would describe but not define them." See **systematic species**.

Ockham's razor: A principle of economy of thought in philosophic and scientific explanation. As stated by William of Ockham (ca. 1285–1349): "Entities are not to be multiplied beyond necessity." It means that philosophers and scientists should seek to explain a phenomenon using as few concepts as possible and with a minimum of complexity. Also call the *law of parsimony.*

order and complexity: *Order* is inversely related to **information.** The more order a system (something composed of parts) has the less amount of information (number of bits) is required to describe its state (the disposition of its parts). The *most ordered state* of a system is the one that requires the least amount of information to describe.

Information is also a measure of *complexity.* One system is more complex than another if more information in needed to describe its most ordered state.

paleohydraulics: The study of **strata** formation when water currents are present. Traditional geology assumes that all the rock strata were laid one on top of the other like a pile of carpets. However, experiments in sedimentology by Guy Berthault give a different picture of their formation. They show that when there is a water current present, which is generally the case, strata do not form successively but laterally and vertically at the same time. Thus the **fossils** deposited in the higher strata and the lower strata were produced at the same time. This demolishes the evolutionists' argument that the fossils in the strata demonstrate evolution.

parallax: A term used for several different methods purported to measure the distance to celestial objects. The calibration of most methods ultimately depends on trigonometric parallax, which assumes that the earth moves annually around the sun and that the stars are at rest with respect to the sun.

parsimony, law of: See **Ockham's razor**

person: A *person* is an individual substance of an intelligent nature. A person is an *individual substance* because he exists in himself and not in anything else, nor is he a part of anything else. Individuality implies that personhood is *incommunicable* because it cannot, like a nature, be shared. The very concept of person excludes the idea of it being communicated to something else or of its being assumed by something else. Peter cannot be transformed into Paul, nor can the actions of Peter be the actions of Paul. Personhood cannot be communicated from the whole to the part, for example, the personhood of a man cannot be communicated to his brain alone. Personhood cannot be communicated from the individual to the universal. The species *man* is not a person. Besides incommunicability, there are other qualifiers that set off personhood. They are the following: *uniqueness* (there is only one Peter), *unrepeatability* (there never was and never could be another Peter), *indivisibility* (there is no half Peter), and *distinctiveness* (Peter is not Paul, is not Mary ...). Other characteristics associated with a person, but which proceed from the intellectual and volitional nature united with a person, are self-knowledge and freedom of choice.

plasma: A hot electrically conducting gas. A gas becomes a *plasma* when its temperature becomes so high that the electrons are stripped from their atoms and allowed to flow freely.

Pontifical Biblical Commission (PBC): Established by Pope Leo XIII in 1902 to promote and direct biblical studies. Pope St. Pius X in 1907 determined the authority of its decisions: "We do now declare and expressly order, that all are bound by the duty of conscience to submit to the decisions of the Pontifical Biblical Commission, both those which thus far have been published and those which will hereafter be proclaimed ... and that all who impugn such decisions as these by word or in writing cannot avoid the charge of disobedience, or on this account be free of grave sin; and this besides the scandal by which they offend, and the other matters for which they can be responsible before God, especially because of other pronouncements in these matters made rashly and erroneously" (DZ, no. 2113). In 1906 the PBC rendered decisions upholding Mosaic authorship of the Pentateuch. In 1909 it rendered decisions upholding the historicity of Genesis 1–3 and allowing the Hebrew word *yom* in Genesis 1 to be interpreted as either a "natural day" or a "certain space of time." Many contemporary Scripture scholars, without just cause, ignore these decisions. The Church has never revoked them. The first Pontifical Biblical Commission as an independent commission came to an end through an apostolic letter issued by Pope Paul VI in 1971. He demoted it to a merely consultative body. Roman scuttlebutt had it that Paul VI did this because the commission had a document ready to demythologize parts of the New Testament. Apparently modernism had seeped all the way into the PBC. The PBC in its new form is not an organ of the teaching office of the Church.

positivism: The view that only those things that can be perceived by the senses are real and only experienced sensible facts can be known with certainty. This is *positive* knowledge because it can be directly affirmed. Theology and metaphysics are considered imperfect modes of knowledge.

potency: Capacity of something or in something to be, to act, or to receive. That which can-be is said to exist in *potency*. Something may be in potency to **accidental existence** or to **substantial existence**. Contrast with **act**.

principle: That from which something proceeds in any manner whatsoever. The concept of *principle* has a wider application than the concept of **cause**. The former is unqualified but the latter implies dependence. Every cause is a principle but not every principle is a cause. For example, a point is the principle of a line but not the cause. God is the first principle of everything because He is the first being, and He is the first cause of everything because He is the source of all being. St. Thomas Aquinas said, "[T]hat whence a motion starts is the principle of the motion but not the cause." He held that **nature** is a principle of the free fall of a body but not the cause.

privation: The absence of something from where it ought to be. For example, the lack of the power of sight is a *privation* in a human person or a dog because the power of sight belongs to the nature of those creatures. But lack of the power of sight in a tree is a *negation* and not a privation because the power of sight does not belong to the nature of a tree. Evil is the privation of good. St. Thomas Aquinas said that the void is a privation and not a negation. He said that before the creation of the world there was no void because there were no "real dimensions" and no "place."

Providentissimus Deus: Encyclical letter on the study of Holy Scripture issued by Pope Leo XIII in 1893. It contains the hermeneutical principle that states that in the interpretation of Sacred Scripture one is "not to depart from the literal and obvious sense, except only where reason makes it untenable or necessity requires."

radiation, blackbody: The thermal radiation emitted by a blackbody (a body that absorbs all the radiation incident upon it). The spectrum of this radiation has a distinct shape that depends on the temperature of the blackbody. The radiation spectrum inside an enclosed cavity is that of a blackbody at the temperature of the enclosure.

radiation, cosmic microwave: The earth is immersed in a bath of microwave radiation corresponding to that found inside a box kept at a temperature of 2.7 Kelvin. This radiation, called *cosmic microwave radiation* (CMR), is very isotropic, having intensity variations with direction no greater than one part in one hundred thousand. But observations show that the CMR wavelength spectrum is shifted down in one direction of the sky and shifted up by the same amount in the opposite direction. This phenomenon is called *dipole anisotropy*. It is attributed to the Doppler effect caused by a speed of about 260 kilometers per second of the earth relative to the radiation.

reductionism, biological: The doctrine that holds that all biological processes can be explained by physical and chemical laws alone. See **mechanism** and **vitalism**.

reductionism, general: The attempt to explain anything by reducing it to its elementary parts.

relativity, general: In his theory of general relativity, Albert Einstein proceeded to formulate the laws of physics so that they look the same in all coordinate systems moving relative to each other, both uniformly and nonuniformly. To do this the notions of absolute motion in space and absolute rest in space had to be eliminated. This was made possible by the equivalence of inertial and gravitational mass, which allowed for gravity to eliminate absolute motion. Motion of massive bodies could then be looked at as being determined by the geometry of space-time that was shaped by gravitating masses. The first law to be formulated for all possible coordinate systems had to be that of gravity itself because of its central importance. The result was a set of ten differential equations for the metric of space-time, Einstein's famous gravitational field equations. These are the equations modern cosmologists use to model the universe. See **big bang** and **Friedmann-Lemaitre expansion**.

relativity, special: A kinematical theory proposed in 1905 by Albert Einstein that is based on two postulates: 1) that the fundamental laws of nature have the same mathematical form for all observers moving uniformly (with constant speed and direction) with respect to each other, and 2) that the speed of light is the same for all such observers, no matter what the relative speed of the source of the light. These postulates assure that no observer can detect uniform motion in absolute space. No observer can claim to be absolutely still while the others are absolutely moving. One consequence of these postulates is that different observers do not always measure the same distances between events they observe; another is that the different observers do not always measure the same time intervals between events.

revelation, primeval: Truths revealed by God to Adam and passed down from generation to generation.

Scholasticism: The system of philosophy and theology developed by the Schoolmen of medieval Europe. It was based on the teachings of the Fathers of the Church, used the insights of Aristotle and Plato, and conformed to Catholic orthodoxy. St. Thomas Aquinas, following a course set by St. Albert the Great and others, synthesized it into a coherent system that is still in use.

scientism: The epistemological viewpoint that places exaggerated trust in efficacy of the methods of natural science, applying them to other fields of knowledge with an air of superiority.

seminal principle: A notion proposed by St. Augustine. A seed or **principle** hidden in the elements, implanted by God during Creation and awaiting favorable opportunity for development. In Aristotelian terms, it is a **potency** created during Creation Week waiting for favorable conditions to be reduced to **act**. In Augustine's words: "Within corporeal things through all the elements of the world there are certain hidden seminal reasons (*seminariae rationes*) by which temporal and causal opportunity presenting itself, various kinds burst forth, distinguished by their own style and purposes.... God, however, is the one and only Creator who implanted the causes themselves and the seminal reasons in things." Augustine said that angels bring the seminal reasons to fruition just as a farmer causes plants and trees to spring up from seeds. In that way God perfects that which He made imperfect.

seriation: See **sequence dating**.

shift, red: The loss of energy by a photon of light. Manifested by a shift of wavelength to the red end of the spectrum. A *Doppler red shift* occurs when the emitter of the photon and its receiver are receding from each other. According to **special relativity**, a *transverse Doppler red shift* occurs when the emitter is moving perpendicularly to the receiver; this effect is due entirely to time dilation. A *gravitational red shift* occurs when a photon travels from a region with a stronger gravitational field to one with a weaker gravitational field. **Big bang** theorists believe that the expansion of the universe after the big bang causes a so-called *expansion red shift*. The notion of light losing **energy** and reddening as it transverses the cosmos is called *tired light*. *Cosmic drag* and other mechanisms are proposed as causes of tired light. See **Hubble's law**.

soul: The **principle** of life in a living organism. The **substantial form** of a living organism. The human (rational) *soul* is an incomplete spiritual **substance** that is the seat of the intellect and free will along with the vegetative and sensitive powers. Unlike plant and animal souls, the human soul can exist apart from the body, but it is naturally ordained to the body. It is not a complete **nature** in itself. St. Thomas Aquinas said of the rational soul: "The soul of man is on the boundary line between corporeal and incorporeal being. It dwells, as it were, on the fringes of time and eternity. It approaches the highest by receding from the lowest. When, then, it shall have been separated from the body, it will be perfectly assimilated to the higher [angelic] substances that exist apart, and will receive of their influence abundantly. And so, though the mode of intellection which we presently employ, according to the conditions of our earthly life, is destroyed with the destruction of the body, it will be replaced by another and more perfect mode of understanding" (SCG, Book 2, Chapter 81). See **vitalism**.

species: (1) A class of individuals having the same unique **nature**, for example, the human *species*. (2) A likeness or representation of an object, for example, the image of Caesar on a coin or the image of an object in the mind. (3) **Accidents** or appearances, for example, the Eucharistic *species* of bread and wine.

species, natural: The complete collection of individuals of a certain **kind**. Each *natural species* has a role or roles in the household of **nature**. God built into the natural species the ability to produce a variety of characteristics within fixed limits. This power produces diversity and helps natural species to adapt to different environmental conditions. These individuals form subgroups called *varieties, races, breeds* and *strains*. The genetic processes of **allele** mixing and **mutation** cause these variations. These processes always preserve the **nature** of the organism and do not produce new kinds. Thus God has programmed a great potential for diversity in the world of living organisms that does not destroy the identities of the original kinds.

species, systematic: An artificial grouping of living organisms. It is a collection of individual organisms grouped together according to some convenient criteria. Systematic species are fleeting. They can change according to the circumstances of the question under consideration. Evolutionists work only with systematic species because they do not believe in **natural species**. See **nominalism**.

stratum: (1) A sheetlike layer of sedimentary rock. (2) A layer in an archaeological excavation in which significant materials (such as artifacts and the remains of houses) are found.

subject: Matter in-which something exists. It is that which is in **potency** to accidental existence. For example, the marble that is shaped into a pieta is the *subject* of the pieta. The subject has existence in itself and gives existence to an **accident**. The distinction between subject and accident exists in the mind only. They do not have separate existences in reality. For example, the shape of the statue and its marble are inseparable in reality. Only in the miracle of the Eucharist do accidents (the physical and chemical properties of bread and wine) exist without a subject.

substance: Something that exists in itself. An elephant, an oak tree and a table are examples of material *substance*. An angel is a spiritual or separated substance, one that is completely independent of matter. The human or rational **soul** is an incomplete spiritual substance. It can exist by itself, but it is naturally ordained toward a body. It is not a complete **nature** in itself.

tell: From the Arabic word for "hill." An artificial mound that conceals the debris of ancient cities, one built on another. *Tells* vary from fifty to one hundred feet in elevation and tend to be flat-topped.

thermodynamics, the first law of: See **energy conservation**.

thermodynamics, the second law of: A law originally applied to heat engines. It states that thermal **energy** cannot be totally converted into mechanical energy or other useful forms. Since various forms of energy are continually being converted into thermal (disordered) energy, and thermal energy cannot be completely transformed back into ordered energy, the amount of transformable energy in the universe is continually diminishing.

transformism, natural: A theistic theory of human evolution that holds that natural processes alone prepared the body of a brute to receive a human soul. The Provincial Council of Cologne, approved by the Holy See, enacted a canon that condemned the theory.

transformism, special: A theistic theory of evolution that holds that a brute body was specially prepared by God to receive a human soul. Pope Pius XII allowed restricted discussion of this notion in *Humani generis*.

uniformitarianism: A geological theory based on the assumption that the geological features of the earth can be explained in terms of current geological processes working over immense periods of time. It is summed up in the doctrine: The present is the key to the past. According to this theory, the same erosion and sedimentation processes at work today laid down the fossil-bearing **strata** over millions of years. Contrast with **catastrophism**.

vitalism: A doctrine that holds that biological processes are not explicable by the laws of chemistry and physics alone and that there is a distinct vital **principle** that transcends matter and directs the processes of a living organism. In its Platonic form, the vital principle, or **soul**, is an independent entity. Plato held that the soul is to the body as the pilot is to the ship. His concept of the soul accommodated his belief in the transmigration of souls. Aristotle had a holistic outlook and held that the soul is the form of a living organism, having a unique inseparable relationship with it. Scholastic philosophy, following Aristotle and enlightened by divine revelation, holds that plant and brute souls cease to exist after the death of the organism, whereas the rational human soul does exist after death but as an incomplete substance. Contrast with **mechanism** and **biological reductionism**.

Select Bibliography

Bibles

Douay-Rheims Bible (Fitzwilliam, NH: Loreto Publications, 2004). First published by the English College at Douay in 1582 (NT) and 1609 (OT). Translated from the Latin Vulgate and carefully compared with other editions in various languages. Notes by Bishop Challoner.

JPS Hebrew-English TANAKH (Philadelphia, PA: The Jewish Publications Society, 2000). Contains Hebrew text alongside modern English translation.

The Navarre Pentateuch (Princeton, NJ: Scepter Publishers, 1999). Contains Latin Vulgate along with Revised Standard Version, Catholic Edition and commentary by the members of the Faculty of Theology of the University of Navarre.

New American Bible (New York: Benzinger, 1970). An English translation from the original languages, with notes, by the members of the Catholic Biblical Association of America.

New International Version, electronic version (Mount Holly, NJ: Franklin Electronic Publishers, 1989–1994). Includes complete concordance.

Revised Standard Version, Catholic Edition, 1966 (San Francisco: Ignatious Press). An English translation from the original languages, with notes, prepared by the Catholic Biblical Association of Great Britain.

History, Language and Literature

Crystal, David, *The Cambridge Encyclopedia of Language*, 2nd ed. (New York: Cambridge University Press, 2002). Provides a good introduction to all aspects of language.

Frazer, James George, *Folklore in the Old Testament: Studies in Comparative Religion, Legend, and Law* (New York: Hart, 1975). This volume contains material excerpted from the author's much larger work, *The Golden Bough*. Frazer does not give due respect to Sacred Scripture, but his collection of universal flood stories is comprehensive.

McIver, Tom, *Anti-Evolution: A Reader's Guide to Writings before and after Darwin* (Baltimore: The Johns Hopkins University Press, 1992). An annotated bibliography of books and other literature opposing macroevolution.

Ovid, *The Metamorphoses*, Horace Gregory, trans. (New York; Mentor Books, 1960). This work is an attempt to link all the Greek myths, before and after Homer, in a cohesive whole, to Roman myths. Of special interest are its creation and flood accounts.

Philosophy

Aquinas, Thomas, *Treatise on the Principles of Nature*. This treatise sets forth in a clear and simple style, mainly in definitions, Aristotelian-Thomistic philosophy of nature. It is a summary of established doctrine rather than a methodical inquiry. The complete treatise is published under the heading "Principles, Causes and Natural Generation" in *The Pocket Aquinas* (New York: Washington Square Press, 1960), pp. 61–77. It is also published in *An Aquinas Reader*, Mary T. Clark, ed., (New York: Fordham University Press, 1972), pp. 163–177.

Brennan, Robert Edward, *Thomistic Psychology* (New York: Macmillan, 1941). An excellent work on the philosophy of man of St. Thomas Aquinas.

Burtt, Edwin Arthur, *The Metaphysical Foundations of Modern Science* (Garden City, NY: Doubleday, 1954). Analyzes the shift from the medieval view to the modern view of man's place in the universe.

Carus, Titus Lucretius, *The Way Things Are* (Bloomington, IN: Indiana University Press, 1968). Didactic poem in which author sets out to tell "the way things are" according to Greek atomistic philosophy.

Cotter, A. C., *Natural Species: An Essay in Definition and Classification* (Weston, MA: The Weston College Press, 1947). A neoscholastic study of the problems involved in the concept of *species.*

Dauben, Joseph Warren, *Georg Cantor: His Mathematics and Philosophy of the Infinite* (Princeton: Princeton University Press, 1979). Presents Cantor's philosophy and theology of the infinite and its relationship to Catholic teaching.

Dawkins, Richard, *The Blind Watchmaker: Why the Evidence of Evolution Reveals a Universe Without Design* (New York: W. W. Norton and Co., 1987). Atheistic evolutionism pushed to the limit.

Duhem, Pierre, *Medieval Cosmology: Theories of Infinity, Place, Time, Void, and the Plurality of Worlds*, edited and translated into English by Roger Ariew (Chicago: The University of Chicago Press, 1985). This book contains selections from *Le système du monde*, a classic ten-volume history of cosmological doctrines from Plato to Copernicus. These selections illustrate the depth and sophistication of medieval cosmology.

Gardeil, H. D., *Introduction to the Philosophy of St. Thomas Aquinas, IV. Metaphysics* (St. Louis, MO: B. Herder Book Co., 1967). Provides a readable introduction to Aristotelian-Thomistic metaphysics. Has an extensive glossary of technical terms.

Hamilton, Edith and Cairns, Huntington, eds., *The Collected Dialogues of Plato* (Princeton, NJ: Princeton University Press, 1973). All the writings of Plato generally considered to be authentic are collected together in this volume.

Heisenberg, Werner, *Physics and Philosophy* (New York; Harper and Row, 1958). An authoritative source for the Copenhagen interpretation of quantum theory.

Kuhn, Thomas S., *The Structure of Scientific Revolutions*, 2nd ed. (Chicago: University of Chicago Press, 1970). A classic essay on the role of scientific paradigms in the history of science.

McKeon, Richard, ed., *The Basic Works of Aristotle* (New York, Random House, 1941). A one-volume collection of the major works of Aristotle. Each work is preceded by a detailed outline.

Moore, A.W., *The Infinite* (New York: Routledge, 1990). An excellent introduction to the mathematics and philosophy of the infinite.

Pelikan, Jaroslav, *What Has Athens to Do with Jerusalem?* Timaeus *and* Genesis *in Counterpoint* (Ann Arbor: The University of Michigan Press, 1997). This book contains a printed version of series of lectures given by the author on the history of the interpretation of the creation narrative given by Moses (Jerusalem) in Genesis in relation to that given by Plato (Athens) in *Timaeus*.

Philo of Alexandria (Philo Judaeus), *The Works of Philo: Complete and Unabridged: New Updated Version*, C. D. Yonge, trans. (Hendrickson Publishers, 1993). Contains much commentary on Genesis by a first-century Hellenistic Jewish philosopher who was widely read by the Fathers of the Church.

Rowland, Wade, *Galileo's Mistake* (New York: Arcade, 2001). "Galileo's mistake" was "that there is a single and unique explanation to natural phenomena, which may be understood through observation and reason, and which makes all other explanations wrong." He insisted that natural science, and only natural science, provides the truth about physical reality.

Schilpp, Paul Arthur, ed., *Albert Einstein: Philosopher-Scientist; The Library of Living Philosophers, Vol. 7* (La Salle, IL: Open Court, 1949). Contains Einstein's intellectual autobiography, essays on his work and philosophy by prominent scientists and philosophers, and Einstein's replies to those essays.

Suarez, Francisco, *On Creation, Conservation, and Concurrence: Metaphysical Disputations 20–22*, Alfred J. Freddoso, trans. (South Bend, IN: St. Augustine's Press, 2002). Metaphysical considerations concerning the act of creation and the acts of created beings by an eminent sixteenth-century scholastic philosopher-theologian. Especially interesting is his discussion about Aristotle and creation on pp. 18–21.

Von Hildebrand, Dietrich, *Man and Woman* (Chicago: Franciscan Herald Press, 1965). A penetrating philosophic analysis of human love, especially conjugal love, from a Catholic perspective.

Weisheipl, James A., *Nature and Motion in the Middle Ages*, edited by William E. Carroll (Washington: The Catholic University of America Press, 1985). In this collection of essays the author corrects modern misconceptions about the scholastic understanding of the concepts of nature and motion. Fr. Weisheipl further corrects the false notion that modern science has replaced natural philosophy. He argues that natural philosophy offers another way of understanding the world, different from that of the physicomathematical sciences. He says, "Nature cannot be exhausted by any one type of knowledge. The totality of nature cannot be boxed in an equation." Scholastic concepts, such as being, substance, potency, act, principle and cause, remain valuable tools in the quest to understand physical reality.

Wuellner, Bernard, *Dictionary of Scholastic Philosophy* (Milwaukee: Bruce, 1956). A good resource for definitions of scholastic terms.

Sacred Scripture

Archer, Gleason L., *Encyclopedia of Bible Difficulties* (Grand Rapids, MI: Zondervan Publishing House, 1982). Gives answers to vexing biblical questions from an Evangelical Protestant viewpoint.

Augustine, Saint, *On Genesis: A Refutation of the Manichees; Unfinished Literal Commentary on Genesis; The Literal Meaning of Genesis* (*The Works of St. Augustine: A Translation for the 21ˢᵗ Century*, Part I, Volume 13). (Hyde Park, NY: New City Press, 2002). In these early works of his, St. Augustine considers in great detail questions raised by the creation and fall accounts in Genesis 1–3.

Beechick, Ruth, *Genesis: Finding Our Roots* (Pollock Pines, CA: Arrow Press, 1997). A course on Genesis 1–11 ordered according to the six patriarchal books. Contains many enlightening little facts.

Bermant, Chaim and Weitzman, Michael, *Ebla: A Revelation in Archaeology* (New York: Times Books, 1979). The finds at Ebla highlight historical precision of the Bible.

Bowman, Thorleif, *Hebrew Thought Compared with Greek* (New York: W. W. Norton, 1960). A classic study of the differences between Hebrew and Greek thought.

Breen, A. E., *A General Introduction to Holy Scripture*, 2nd ed. (Fort Collins, CO: Roman Catholic Books), reprint of 1908 edition. A good Catholic source of general information on the Bible.

Cooper, Bill, *After the Flood: The Early Post-Flood History of Europe Traced Back to Noah* (Chichester, England: New Wine Press, 1995). The author lays out astonishing evidence showing how the early Europeans recorded their descent from Noah through Japheth in meticulously kept records, knew all about the Creation and the Flood, and had encounters with creatures we would call dinosaurs.

Custance, Arthur, *Noah's Three Sons: Human History in Three Dimensions*, Vol. 1 of Doorway Papers series (Grand Rapids, MI: Zondervan, 1975). Discusses the lineages of Shem, Ham and Japheth and the special contributions they each made to human culture. This is a very informative and eye-opening work.

Farmer, William R., ed., *The International Bible Commentary: A Catholic and Ecumenical Commentary for the Twenty-First Century* (Collegeville, MN: The Liturgical Press, 1998). A good resource for the opinions of modern biblical scholars.

Finegan, Jack, *Handbook of Biblical Chronology* (Princeton, NY: Princeton University Press, 1964). A standard reference work.

Heinisch, Paul, *Theology of the Old Testament*, English ed. by William Heidt (Collegeville, MN: The Liturgical Press, 1950). A comprehensive and informative Catholic treatise. Nicely organized according to theological topics.

John Paul II, Pope, *The Theology of the Body: Human Love in the Divine Plan* (Boston: Pauline Books and Media, 1997). This is a series of 129 catechetical talks given at Wednesday audiences between 1979 and 1984 on the bodily dimension of human personhood, sexuality, and marriage in the light of biblical revelation.

Josephus, Flavius, *The Complete Works*, trans. by William Whiston (Nashville, TN: Thomas Nelson, 1998). A comprehensive account of Jewish history from Creation to the Roman occupation by a first-century Jewish historian.

Kidner, Derek, *Genesis: An Introduction and Commentary* (Downers Grove, IL: Inter-Varsity Press, 1967). A sometimes helpful non-Catholic commentary.

Knecht, Frederick Justus, *A Practical Commentary on Holy Scripture* (Rockford, Il: TAN Books, 2003), reprint of 1923 edition. Written by a Catholic bishop. Contains a good brief survey of traditional Catholic doctrine on origins but with a trace of influence of uniformitarian geology.

Lawrence of Brindisi, Saint, *Explanatio in Genesim*, vol. III of *Opera Omnia*, (Venice, Italy: Venetian Capuchin Province, 1935). A commentary on Genesis 1–11 by a 16–17th century Doctor of the Church. Pope John XXIII said of this work: "Especially pleasing to us is the book *Explanation of Genesis*, in which Lawrence, employing the doctrine of the Jewish masters, the Fathers of the Church, and that of the schoolmen, examines the divine truth, and as a most severe judge, passes judgment on various opinions and controversies."

Leon-Dufour, Xavier, *Dictionary of Biblical Theology* (Boston: St. Paul Books and Media, 1988). A handy Catholic reference work.

Morris, Henry M., *The Genesis Record* (Grand Rapids, MI: Baker Book House, 1976). Commentary on Genesis by a Bible Christian from a creationist viewpoint.

Most, William G., *Free From All Error: Authorship, Inerrancy, Historicity of Scripture, Church Teaching, and Modern Scripture Scholars* (Libertyville, IL: Franciscan Marytown Press, 1985). A Catholic defense of the inerrancy and historicity of Sacred Scripture.

Neuhaus, Richard John, ed., *Biblical Interpretation in Crisis: The Ratzinger Conference on Bible and Church* (Grand Rapids, MI: William B. Eerdmans Publishing Co., 1989). Contains Cardinal Ratzinger's critique of the historical-critical method of scriptural exegesis, his "criticism of criticism."

Oden, Thomas C., general ed., *Ancient Christian Commentary on Sacred Scripture*, multivolume set (Downers Grove, IL: InterVarsity Press), being compiled. Selections from the Fathers of the Church and other early Christian writers on Scripture. Organized according to book, chapter and verse of the Bible.

Radday, Yehuda T. and Shore, Haim, *Genesis: An Authorship Study in Computer-Assisted Statistical Linguistics* (Rome: Biblical Institute Press, 1985). A statistical study of the language of Genesis that defangs the documentary hypothesis.

Ratzinger, Cardinal Joseph, *'In the Beginning...': A Catholic Understanding of the Story of Creation and the Fall* (Huntington, IN: Our Sunday Visitor, Inc., 1990). A series of four Lenten homilies given in 1981 in the cathedral of Munich.

Ricciotti, Giuseppe, *The History of Israel*, volumes I and II (Fort Collins, CO: Roman Catholic Books, reprint of 1955 edition). A readable and informative work on many aspects of Bible history.

Rose, Fr. Seraphim, *Genesis, Creation and Early Man: The Orthodox Christian Vision* (Platina, CA: Saint Herman of Alaska Brotherhood, 2000). Compiled from lectures and letters of an Orthodox priest and monk on the patristic understanding of Genesis 1–11.

Satinover, Jeffrey, *Cracking the Bible Code* (New York: Harper Collins, 1997). Contains information about cabalists and their belief in an ancient earth.

Stanton, Mary and Hyma, Albert, *Streams of Civilization, Vol. 1: Earliest Times to the Discovery of the New World* (Arlington Heights, IL: Christian Liberty Press, 2000). This is a history textbook that upholds the biblical account of early civilization.

Steinmueller, John E., *A Companion to Scripture Studies: Volume I. General Introduction; Volume II. Special Introduction to the Old Testament*, revised edition (New York: Joseph F. Wagner, Inc., 1969). A sound Catholic reference work on the Bible.

————, *The Sword of the Spirit: Which is the Word of God* (Fort Worth, TX: Stella Maris Books, 1977). Has information not found elsewhere about the Pontifical Biblical Commission and its decrees.

Taylor, Charles, *The First 100 Words* (Evansville, IN: Jubilee Resources, 1996). A collection of commentaries on one hundred Hebrew words from Genesis 1:1–2:4 by an Evangelical Protestant.

Ussher, James, *The Annals of the World*, trans. by Larry and Marion Pierce (Green Forest, AR: Master Books, 2003). A translation into modern English of the classic work of the much maligned Anglican Archbishop of Armagh. This is a history of the world from Creation to A.D. 70 derived from numerous ancient sources, some no longer existing or not available. The events are chronicled with dates being calculated from biblical and secular sources.

Science and Mathematics

Ackerman, Paul D., *It's a Young World After All: Exciting Evidences for Recent Creation* (Grand Rapids, MI: Baker Book House, 1986). A clear popular account of the major scientific evidence for a recent creation.

Aczel, Amir D., *God's Equation: Einstein, Relativity and the Expanding Universe* (New York: Delta, 1999). Gives an account of Einstein's cosmological constant and recent observations that seem to indicate that the universe is expanding at an increasing rate.

————, *Entanglement: The Greatest Mystery in Physics* (New York: Four Walls Eight Windows, 2001). A clear presentation of the quantum mechanical phenomenon of entanglement.

Albritton, Claude C., *The Abyss of Time: Changing Conceptions of the Earth's Antiquity after the Sixteenth Century*, reprint of 1980 edition (Mineola, NY: Dover Publications, 2002). A popular history of secular science's rejection of Genesis 1–11 by an anticreationist author.

Ashton, John F., ed., *In Six Days* (Green Forest, AR: Master Books, 2001). Contains the testimonies of fifty men and women holding doctorates in a wide range of scientific disciplines who have been convinced by the evidence to believe that God created the world in six natural days.

Assis, Andre K. T., *Relational Mechanics* (Montreal: Apeiron, 1999). Presents a new mechanics that implements Mach's principle and replaces Einstein's theories of relativity. It offers a promising new basis for modeling the cosmos in conformity with Genesis.

Barrow, John D., *The Constants of Nature: From Alpha to Omega—The Numbers that Encode the Deepest Secrets of Nature* (New York: Panthenon, 2002). Discusses scientists' views on God's freedom in creating.

Behe, Michael J., *Darwin's Black Box: The Biochemical Challenge to Evolution* (New York: The Free Press, 1996). Shows that certain biochemical "machines" are so constructed that the removal of just one part will cause them to cease functioning. Such biological systems are examples of "irreducible complexity" and imply "intelligent design."

Bell, J.S., *Speakable and Unspeakable in Quantum Mechanics* (New York: Cambridge University Press, 1987). Contains authoritative material on locality and nonlocality in quantum mechanics. The author includes a chapter on special relativity in which he compares the relativistic theories of Einstein and Lorentz. His conclusion is well worth quoting at length because of its bearing on the biblically-based notion that God defined the earth to be at rest in the universe:

> The approach of Einstein differs from that of Lorentz in two major ways. There is a difference of philosophy, and a difference of style.
> The difference of philosophy is this. Since it is experimentally impossible to say which of two uniformly moving systems is *really* at rest, Einstein declares the notions 'really resting' and 'really moving' as meaningless. For him only the *relative* motion of two or more uniformly moving objects is real. Lorentz, on the other hand, preferred the view that that there is indeed a state of *real* rest, defined by the 'aether', even though the laws of physics conspire to prevent us from identifying it experimentally. The facts of physics do not oblige us to accept one philosophy rather than the other. And we need not accept Lorentz's philosophy to accept a Lorentzian pedagogy. Its special merit is to drive home the lesson that the laws of physics in any *one* reference frame account for all physical phenomena, including the observations of moving observers. And it is often simpler to work in a single frame, rather than to hurry after each moving object in turn.
> The difference in style is that instead of inferring the experience of moving observers from known and conjectured laws of physics. Einstein starts from the *hypothesis* that the laws will look the same to all observers in uniform motion. This permits a very concise and elegant formulation of the theory, as often happens when one big assumption can be made to cover several less big ones.

Berthault, Guy, "Geological Dating Principles Questioned—Paleohydraulics: A New Approach," article first published in French in *Fusion*, n°81, mai–juin 2000, Editions Alcuin (Paris); *Journal of Geodesy and Geodynamics*, Vol. 22, No. 3, Aug. 2002, pp. 19–26. Also, "Analysis of Main Principles of Stratigraphy on the Basis of Experimental Data," *Lithology and Mineral Resources*, Vol. 37, No. 5, Sep.– Oct. 2002, pp. 442–446. These papers discuss experiments that show that rock strata form laterally and vertically at the same time when a water current is present.

Bray, Warwick and Trump, David, *The Penguin Dictionary of Archaeology* (New York: Penguin Books, 1972). A good resource for general archaeological information.

Brown, Walt, *In the Beginning: Compelling Evidence for Creation and the Flood* 7th ed. (Phoenix, AZ: Center for Scientific Creation, 2001). A highly-regarded compilation of creationist arguments.

Cushing, James T., *Quantum Mechanics: Historical Contingency and the Copenhagen Hegemony* (Chicago: University of Chicago Press, 1994). Author argues that the Copenhagen interpretation of quantum mechanics prevailed not because it is a better explanation of subatomic phenomena than the hidden variables interpretation but because it happened to appear first.

Daintith, John and Nelson, R. D., eds., *The Penguin Dictionary of Mathematics* (New York, Penguin Books, 1989). A good resource for clear and concise explanations of mathematical concepts.

Darwin, Charles, *The Origin of Species by Means of Natural Selection or the Preservation of Favoured Races in the Struggle for Life*, 6th ed., 1872 (New York: Collier Books, 1962). The bible of evolutionary biology.

Denton, Michael, *Evolution: A Theory in Crisis* (Chevy Chase, MD: Adler and Adler, 1985). A critique of Darwinism by a molecular biologist.

DeYoung, Donald B., *Astronomy and the Bible* (Grand Rapids, MI: Baker Books, 2000). Answers to 100 questions on modern astronomy and cosmology by an Evangelical Christian scientist.

Dillow, Joseph C., *The Waters Above: Earth's Pre-Flood Vapor Canopy*, Revised Edition (Chicago: Moody Press, 1982). Considers the proposed antediluvian vapor canopy from an exegetical and scientific viewpoint.

Dobzhansky, Theodosius, *Genetics and the Origin of Species*, 3rd ed. (New York: Columbia University Press, 1951). A classic for evolutionists.

Einstein, Albert and Infeld, Leopold, *The Evolution of Physics: From Early Concepts to Relativity and Quanta* (New York: Simon and Schuster, 1938). A clear popular account of the history of physical concepts.

Fabre, J. Henri, *The Wonders of Instinct: Chapters in the Psychology of Insects* (Honolulu: University Press of the Pacific, 2002), reprinted from 1922 edition. Shows that instincts of insects are fixed and limited.

Ferguson, Kitty, *Measuring the Universe: Our Historic Quest to Chart the Horizons of Space and Time* (New York: Walker and Co., 1999). A popular account of techniques currently used for measuring distances to astronomical objects. Has a useful glossary.

Feynman, Richard P., *Six Not-So-Easy Pieces: Einstein's Relativity, Symmetry, and Space-Time* (Cambridge, MA: Perseus Books, 1997). Has section on relativity and philosophy that gives insight about the contingent nature of physics. Addressed to level of beginning science students.

Frank-Kamenetskii, Maxim D., *Unraveling DNA: The Most Important Molecule of Life*, updated ed. (Reading, MA: Perseus Books, 1997). A clear account of the "new biology."

Gentry, Robert V., *Creation's Tiny Mystery* (Knoxville, TN: Earth Science Associates, 1992). Presents remarkable evidence for instantaneous creation in the radiohalos of short-lived radioactive polonium.

———, "A New Redshift Interpretation," *Modern Physics Letters A*, Vol. 12, No. 37, pp. 2919–2925 (1997). This and the following two papers are concerned with a model of the universe that conforms to the Genesis account.

————, "The New Redshift Interpretation Affirmed," arXiv:physics/9810051, 26 Oct 1998.

————, *A Major Cosmic Surprise: New Cosmic Model Predicts Enhanced Brightness of Galaxies, SN, Quasars and GRBs With z > 10* (The Orion Foundation, April 1, 2002).

Gish, Duane T., *Evolution: The Fossils Say No!* (San Diego, CA: Creation Life Publishers, 1973). Shows that the fossil record gives evidence for special creation, not evolution.

Greenstein, George and Zajonc, Arthur G., *The Quantum Challenge: Modern Research on the Foundations of Quantum Mechanics* (Boston: Jones and Bartlett Publishers, 1997). Gives a remarkably clear presentation of the mysteries of quantum mechanics with a minimum of mathematics.

Hawking, Stephen, *A Brief History of Time; From the Big Bang to Black Holes* (New York: Bantam Books, 1988). A layman's introduction to modern cosmological thinking by a practicing cosmologist.

Hitching, Francis, *The Neck of the Giraffe: Darwin, Evolution, and the New Biology* (New York: Mentor, 1982). A critique of Darwinian evolution by a noncreationist.

Humphreys, D. Russell, *Starlight and Time: Solving the Puzzle of Distant Starlight in a Young Universe* (Green Forest, AR: Master Books, 1994). Introduces "white hole cosmology" as a response to the frequently asked question: If the universe is only several thousand years old, how can we see light from galaxies millions of light-years away?

Illingsworth, Valerie, ed., *The Penguin Dictionary of Physics*, 2nd ed. (New York: Penguin Books, 1991). A good resource for clear and concise descriptions of physical phenomena, concepts, and instruments.

Jammer, Max, *Concepts of Mass in Classical and Modern Physics* (Mineola, NY: Dover Publications, 1997). Reprint of a classic historical study of the notion of mass by a noted historian of science.

————, *Concepts of Space: The History of Theories of Space in Physics*, 3rd edition (New York: Dover Publications, 1993). In the foreword Albert Einstein clearly and succinctly presents the conflicting notions of space as "positional quality of the world of material objects" and as "container of all material objects."

Jastrow, Robert, *God and the Astronomers*, 2nd edition (New York: W.W. Norton, 1992). A concise presentation of big bang theory by a believer in it. He gives clear brief explanations of the horizon problem, the flatness problem, and inflation.

Johnson, J. W. (Wallace) G., *Evolution?* (Los Angeles: Perpetual Adoration, Inc., 1986). Shows why evolution is an issue of importance to Catholics and clearly summarizes scientific evidence against evolution. This is the premier Catholic work in the modern creationist movement. Retypeset and published in 2000 by TAN Books and Publishers, Inc., Rockford, IL, under the title *The Death of Evolution*.

Johnson, Philip E., *Darwin on Trial* (Downer's Grove, IL: InterVarsity Press, 1993). Critique of Darwinism by a professor of law who specializes in the logic of arguments.

Keane, Gerard J., *Creation Rediscovered: Evolution and the Importance of the Origins Debate* (Rockford, IL: TAN Books, 1999). Clearly presents scientific evidence against evolution and shows why evolution is an important issue for Catholics. A seminal work for authentic Catholic teaching on origins.

Kline, Morris, *Mathematics: The Loss of Certainty* (New York: Oxford University Press, 1980). The author shows that mathematics is not exact and infallible. He makes the point that even though mathematics has been very successful in describing the physical world, it is not a body of unshakable truths about it.

Koestler, Arthur, *The Sleepwalkers: A History of Man's Changing Vision of the Universe* (New York: Penguin Books, 1989 reprint). Gives a balanced account of the Galileo controversy.

Lammerts, Walter E., ed., *Why Not Creation?* (Nutley, NJ: Presbyterian and Reformed Publishing Co., 1970). A selection of papers from the *Creation Research Society Quarterly*.

———, ed., *Scientific Studies in Special Creation* (Nutley, NJ: Presbyterian and Reformed Publishing Co., 1971). A selection of papers from the *Creation Research Society Quarterly*.

Lang, Walter, *Genesis and Science* (Minneapolis, MN: Bible-Science Association, 1982). A little storehouse of information and observations.

Lerner, Eric J., *The Big Bang Never Happened* (New York: Vintage, 1991). A refutation of big bang theory by a plasma physicist.

Lubenow, Marvin L., *Bones of Contention: A Creationist Assessment of Human Fossils* (Grand Rapids, MI: Baker Books, 1992). A complete and accurate presentation about human fossils that shows they are best explained in accordance with the Genesis account of the origin of man.

Macbeth, Norman: *Darwin Retried: An Appeal to Reason* (Boston: The Harvard Common Press, 1971). A critique of Darwinism by a Harvard-trained lawyer.

McCann, Lester, *Blowing the Whistle on Darwinism* (Lake Mills, IA: Graphic Publishing, 1986). A critique of Darwinism by a biology professor.

Milne, E.A., *Modern Cosmology and the Christian Idea of God: Being the Edward Cadbury Lectures in the University of Birmingham for 1950* (Oxford, UK: Oxford University Press, 1952). In these lectures the author sorts out the notions of scientific fact, scientific dogma, scientific theory, and law of nature in the light of his Anglican faith. He further sums up his theories on the structure of the physical universe. In the third lecture Milne clearly shows that the Lorentz transformation formulas of special relativity express kinematical observational effects connected with the finite speed of light and do not reveal any deep secrets about the nature of space and time. They concern the communication of information about physical events by means of light to intelligent observers.

Milton, Richard, *Shattering the Myths of Darwinism* (Rochester, VT: Park Street Press, 1997). Shows that the theory of evolution is a profession of faith rather than functional science.

Moore, Patrick, general editor, *Philip's Astronomy Encyclopedia* (London: Philips, an imprint of Octopus Publishing Group, 2002). This is a comprehensive and authoritative compendium of evolutionary astronomy. Contains candid admissions of interest to the creationist.

Morris, Henry M., *Science and the Bible* (Chicago: Moody Press, 1986). Reconciliation of Scripture and Science by a Bible Christian.

———, ed., *That Their Words May Be Used Against Them* (Green Forest, AR: Master Books, 1997). Quotes from evolutionists useful for upholding creationism.

Morris, John D., *The Geology Book* (Green Forest, AR: Master Books, 2000). A clear, concise introduction to the science of geology from a creationist viewpoint. Many colorful pictures and illustrations accompany the text.

———, *The Young Earth* (Green Forest, AR: Master Books, 1994). A clear exposition of the evidence for a young earth by a geological engineer.

Novikov, I. D., *Evolution of the Universe* (New York: Cambridge University Press, 1983). A clear popular account of the observations and theories of modern cosmology by a Russian astrophysicist.

Oard, Michael J., *An Ice Age Caused by the Genesis Flood* (El Cajon, CA: Institute for Creation Research, 1990). Argues that there was only one ice age and that the Great Flood of Genesis caused it.

O'Connell, Patrick, *Science of Today and the Problems of Genesis* (Rockford, IL: TAN Books, 1993). A valiant effort by a Catholic priest to uphold the literal meaning of the Genesis accounts of Creation and the Flood that is handicapped by the author's acceptance of uniformitarian geology.

Pais, Abraham, *'Subtle is the Lord ...': The Science and Life of Albert Einstein* (New York: Oxford University Press, 1982). Contains useful information about Einstein's theory of general relativity and its relationship to big bang theory.

Penrose, Roger, *The Large, the Small and the Human Mind* (New York: Cambridge University Press, 1997). Written by a prominent mathematician. Contains useful information about big bang theory.

Perloff, James, *Tornado in a Junkyard: The Relentless Myth of Darwinism* (Arlington, MA: Refuge Books, 1999). A unique presentation of the scientific case against Darwinism, informally written for laymen.

Rehwinkel, Alfred M: *The Flood: In the Light of the Bible, Geology and Archaeology* (St. Louis, MO: Concordia, 1951). Contains a fascinating description of the antediluvian world. Discusses the Great Flood and its effects using both the scriptural account and scientific data. Gives marvelous detailed accounts of historical, geological and paleontological evidence for the Flood.

Simpson, George Gaylord, *The Major Features of Evolution* (New York: Columbia University Press, 1953). A book on evolution by a well-known archevolutionist.

Spetner, Lee, *Not by Chance: Shattering the Modern Theory of Evolution* (New York: The Judaica Press, 1998). Critique of macroevolution from a Jewish perspective by a physicist. Gives clear and concise explanations of concepts in modern genetics.

Stewart, Ian and Golubitsky, Martin, *Fearful Symmetry: Is God a Geometer?* (New York: Penguin Books, 1992). A presentation of the role of symmetry-breaking in mathematics and science. Contains information pertinent to creationism.

Tauber, Gerald, ed., *Albert Einstein's Theory of General Relativity* (New York: Crown Publishers Inc., 1979). Contains useful information on modern cosmology.

Taylor, Ian T., *In the Minds of Men: Darwin and the New World Order* (Minneapolis: TFE Publishing, 1984). Exposes the fuzzy reasoning underlying Darwinist textbook explanations on origins. Shows the social consequences of such explanations and presents counterevidence.

Thain, M. and Hickman, M., *The Penguin Dictionary of Biology*, 10th ed. (New York: Penguin Books, 2001). A useful resource for concise information about evolutionary biology.

Vail, Tom, *Grand Canyon: A Different Perspective* (Green Forest, AR: Master Books, 2003). A collection of short essays and colorful photographs that communicate the creationist way of thinking about the formation of the Grand Canyon.

Webb, Stephen, *Measuring the Universe: The Cosmological Distance Ladder* (Chichester, UK: Springer-Praxis, 1999). Introductory textbook about techniques currently used for measuring distances to astronomical objects.

————, *Where is Everybody? Fifty Solutions to the Fermi Paradox and the Problem of Extraterrestrial Life* (New York: Copernicus Books, 2002). Discusses the lack of evidence for extraterrestrial life.

Weinberg, Steven, *The First Three Minutes: A Modern View of the Origin of the Universe* (New York: Basic Books, 1993). An account of big bang theory by a Nobel-Prize-winning physicist.

Wells, Jonathan, *Icons of Evolution: Science or Myth* (Washington, DC: Regnery, 2000). Shows that the textbook examples Darwinists choose as pillars of their theory are false or misleading.

Whitcomb, John C. and Morris, Henry M., *The Genesis Flood: The Biblical Record and Its Scientific Implications* (Phillipsburg, NJ: P & R Publishing, 1960). The book that inspired the modern creationist movement.

Whitcomb, John C., *The World that Perished: An Introduction to Biblical Catastrophism*, Revised Edition (Grand Rapids, MI: Baker Books, 1988). A sequel to the *The Genesis Flood* that restates in more popular form and updates the evidence and arguments for biblical catastrophism presented in *The Genesis Flood*.

Whitten, D. G. A. with Brooks, J. R. V., *The Penguin Dictionary of Geology* (New York: Penguin Books, 1972). A useful resource for concise information about uniformitarian geology.

Woodmorappe, John, *Noah's Ark: A Feasibility Study* (Santee, CA: Institute for Creation Research, 1996). A study of practical questions concerning Noah and the ark. Also considers questions concerning the restoration of the biosphere and animal repopulation after the Flood.

Wysong, R.L., *The Creation-Evolution Controversy* (East Lansing, MI: Inquiry Press, 1976). A comprehensive view of modern creationism.

Theology

Agius, George, *Tradition and the Church* (Rockford, IL: TAN Books, 2005). A reprint with minor revisions of a 1928 work. Explains what Catholic Tradition is, how it came about, and how it has been passed on intact. Thoroughly discusses the authority of the Fathers of the Church as preservers of Tradition. Shows that the truths deposited in Sacred Tradition were passed on without error with the help of the Holy Spirit. Puts to rest the false notion that orthodoxy in the early Church was just the winner among a number of competing Christianities, as espoused, for example, by Walter Bauer in *Orthodoxy and Heresy in Early Christianity* (1934).

Alighieri, Dante, *The Divine Comedy Vol. III: Paradise*, trans. by Mark Musa (New York: Penguin Books, 1986). Contains Dante's poetic exposition of medieval theology on creation. A clear, readable translation with helpful commentary and notes.

Aquinas, St. Thomas, *Summa contra Gentiles*, English Dominican Fathers translation (London: Burns, Oates and Washbourne Ltd., 1923). A defense of the Roman Catholic faith against criticism from outsiders.

————, *Summa Theologica*, English Dominican Fathers translation (Benzinger Bros., 1947). The principal doctrinal synthesis in Catholic theology.

Augustine, Saint, *City of God* (New York: Penguin Books, 1984). Contains extensive commentary on Genesis 1–11 written by St. Augustine in his mature years.

Baldner, Steven E. and Carroll, William E. in *Aquinas on Creation: Writings on the "Sentences" of Peter Lombard 2.1.1* (Toronto: Pontifical Institute of Mediaeval Studies, 1997). A translation and analysis of St. Thomas Aquinas' *Writings on the "Sentences" of Peter Lombard*, Book 2, Distinction 1, Question 1. St. Thomas' discussion of this question is essentially a commentary on Genesis 1:1.

Bonaventure, Saint, *Breviloquium*, Erwin Esser Nemmers, trans. (St. Louis, MO: Herder, 1946). A concise and readable compendium of Catholic theology/philosophy.

Carlton, Clark, *The Faith: Understanding Orthodox Christianity* (Salisbury, MA: Regina Orthodoxy Press, 1997). This is an Orthodox Christian catechism edited by a committee of four Orthodox bishops. It contains a section that discusses creation and evolution, concluding "[macro]evolution is incompatible with the Orthodox worldview."

Catechism of the Catholic Church (Washington: USCC, 1997). A post-Vatican II exposition of the Catholic faith.

Catechism of the Council of Trent (Rockford, IL: TAN Books, 1982). A Counter Reformation exposition of the Catholic faith.

Catholic Encyclopedia, The, the classic 1914 edition, CD and internet version by New Advent, www.NewAdvent.org. A wonderful resource for things Catholic.

Cohen, Abraham, *Everyman's Talmud: The Major Teachings of the Rabbinic Sages* (New York, Schocken Books, 1975 reprint of 1949 edition). Long regarded as the classic introduction to the teachings of the Talmud. It has sections that nicely summarize the cosmology and anthropology of the Jewish sages.

Delio, Ilia, *Simply Bonaventure: An Introduction to His Life, Thought, and Writings* (Hyde Park, NY: New City Press, 2001). Contains a clearly written chapter about St. Bonaventure's views on creation.

Denzinger, Henry, *Enchiridion Symbolorum (The Sources of Catholic Dogma)*, 30th ed. (Fitzwilliam, NH: Loretto Publications, reprint of 1954 ed.). A handbook of excerpts from official Church documents. Well indexed.

Flannery, Austin, *Vatican Council II: The Conciliar and Post Conciliar Documents*, 2 vols., revised ed. (Collegeville, MN: The Liturgical Press, 1992). Contains English translations of Vatican II documents that are more accurate than earlier translations.

Gilson, Etienne, *The Philosophy of St. Bonaventure*, Illtyd Trethowan and Frank J. Sheed, trans. (Paterson, NJ: St. Anthony Guild Press, 1965). Classic work on the theology/philosophy of St. Bonaventure. St. Bonaventure did not separate philosophy from theology.

Guimarães, Atila Sinhe, *The Murky Waters of Vatican II* (Rockford, IL: TAN Books, 1999). Shows how the notion of "uniform evolution" influenced the composition of Vatican Council II documents.

Haffner, Paul, *Mystery of Creation* (Herefordshire, England: Fowler Wright Books, 1995). A general introduction to the Catholic theology of creation. The author concentrates more on the created world as it exists than on its origin. He is soft on macroevolution, holding that theistic evolution does not necessarily contradict the truth that Genesis presents.

Hardon, John A., *Modern Catholic Dictionary* (New York: Doubleday, 1980). A good resource for definitions of Catholic theological terms.

Iannuzzi, Joseph, *The Triumph of God's Kingdom in the Millennium and End Times: A Proper Belief from the Truth in Scripture and Church Teachings* (St. John the Evangelist Press: 222 S. Manoa Rd., Havertown, PA 19083, 1999). A Catholic priest argues from Sacred Scripture, the writings of the Fathers and Doctors of the Church, and from the Magisterium, that there will be a flowering of Christ's kingdom on earth before the end times.

Jurgens, William A., *The Faith of the Early Fathers*, 3 vols. (Collegeville, MN: The Liturgical Press, 1970). A large selection of excerpts from the writings of the Fathers. Well indexed.

Neuner, J. and Dupuis, J., eds., *The Christian Faith in the Doctrinal Documents of the Catholic Church*, revised edition (New York: Alba House, 1982). A useful supplement to Denzinger's and Ott's works. Contains excerpts from more recent documents.

Ott, Ludwig, *Fundamentals of Catholic Dogma*, 4th ed. (Rockford, IL: TAN Books, 1974), reprint of 1960 edition. A very useful source. Clearly presents dogma along with historical commentary.

Ruffini, Cardinal Ernesto, *The Theory of Evolution Judged by Reason and Faith* (New York: Joseph F. Wagner, Inc., 1959). A clear, comprehensive work on evolution by a member of the Pontifical Biblical Commission.

Sheehan, Most Rev. M., *Apologetics and Catholic Doctrine: A Course of Religious Instruction for Schools and Colleges* (Dublin: M. H. Gill and Son, 1960). By a Roman Catholic bishop. Contains excellent material on evolution from a Catholic viewpoint but tolerant of uniformitarianism and theistic evolution.

About the Author

Father Warkulwiz's varied experience has helped prepare him for a work such as this. It has given him professional expertise in physics and theology and an "educational acquaintance" with philosophy, history and various scientific disciplines. His first technical experience was in electronics. He studied radio and television technology in high school. His first job out of high school was with Remington Rand Univac, where he worked as an electrical draftsman on the first transistorized computer. He went on to become an electronic designer and also worked as an electronic technician at Univac. He continued his study of electronics in the U.S. Naval Air Reserve, specializing in antisubmarine warfare technology. He worked at General Electric Corporation as a mathematics technician doing vibrations studies of reentry vehicles. He received a B.S. in electronic physics from La Salle College. After graduation from college, he worked as an electromagnetics physicist for General Electric Corporation, where he studied the effects of electromagnetic pulse radiation on semiconductor diodes.

Mr. Warkulwiz's interest in electronics led him to physics. He received a Ph.D. in physics from Temple University. At Temple he did experimental work in holography, theoretical work in statistical mechanics, and operated a planetarium. He did his dissertation research at the National Bureau of Standards research reactor, where he gained experience in the fields of precision thermodynamic measurements, cryogenics, vacuum technology, critical phenomena in fluids, neutron diffraction and nuclear instrumentation.

After receiving his Ph.D., Dr. Warkulwiz went to work for the Central Intelligence Agency as a physical scientist/intelligence officer, where he specialized in ballistic missile systems. From there he went on to Magdalen College to teach science and mathematics in a "great books" program. At Magdalen he conducted seminar courses in classical mathematics, natural philosophy, astronomy, atomic chemistry and physics, logic, and philosophical biology. He lectured on ancient and medieval history, the history and nature of communism, and creationism vs. the theory of evolution.

Dr. Warkulwiz then went to work for aerospace consultant firms. He worked at Quest Research Corporation, where he did a study of techniques for producing moving infrared images, and at Analytic Services Corporation, where he specialized in space technology. While at Analytic Services, Dr. Warkulwiz heard the call to the priesthood.

In preparing for the priesthood, Fr. Victor received an M.Div. from Mount St. Mary's Seminary and an M.A. in theology from Holy Apostles Seminary. He taught courses in literature, mathematics and physics in the college seminary at Holy Apostles and courses in philosophy and religion at the Franciscan Friars of Mary Immaculate scholasticate. He also conducted Bible and catechism classes in a summer program for youth.

Fr. Victor was ordained a Roman Catholic priest in 1991. He is a member of the Missionary Priests of the Blessed Sacrament and has helped hundreds of parishes in the U.S. and elsewhere to start or maintain perpetual Eucharistic adoration. He was named national director of the Apostolate for Perpetual Eucharist Adoration in October 1998 and theological reviewer for the Kolbe Center for the Study of Creation in 2001. He is profiled in the 2003 and 2004 editions of *Who's Who in America*.

Index